A History of Preaching

A History *of* Preaching

O. C. Edwards Jr.

ABINGDON PRESS / Nashville

A HISTORY OF PREACHING:
VOLUME 2

This book is printed on acid-free paper.

Volume 1 ISBN 9781501833779
Volume 2 ISBN 9781501833786

Excerpts from "It Is Not True! It Is Not True!" reprinted from *Proclaiming the Acceptable Year,* Edited by Justo L. Gonzalez, copyright © 1982 by Judson Press. Used by permission of Judson Press, 800-4-JUDSON, www.judsonpress.com.

Excerpts in chapter 21 are taken from *Sisters of the Spirit,* edited by William Andrews, copyright 1986 by Indiana University Press. Used by permission.

"Sermon XIII," by Ralph Waldo Emerson is used by permission of the Ralph Waldo Emerson Memorial Association and of Houghton Library, Harvard University *(bMS Am 1280.215 [13]).*

John Calvin, *Sermons from Job,* trans. Leroy Nixon, © 1952 Wm. B. Eerdmans Publishing Company, Grand Rapids, MI. Used by permission.

Excerpts in chapter 29 are taken from *The Gospel in Solentiname, Vol. II* by Ernesto Cardenal, copyright 1976–1982 is used by permission of Orbis Books.

Material in chapter 1 is taken from William Richard Stegner, "The Ancient Jewish Synagogue Homily," published in *Greco-Roman Literature and the New Testament,* edited by David E. Aune, © 1988. Used by permission of The Society of Biblical Literature.

Excerpts in chapter 6 are taken from Fathers of the Church Vol. #47: *St. Caesarius of Arles, Sermons.* Used by permission of The Catholic University of America Press.

"What Is the Matter with Preaching?" by Harry Emerson Fosdick. Copyright ©1928 by *Harper's Magazine.* All rights reserved. Reproduced from the July issue by special permission.

Letter from Henry Smith to Benjamin Lakin in *The Frontier Camp Meeting* by Charles A. Johnson, published by Southern Methodist University Press in 1955, reprinted 1985, is used by permission of Southern Methodist University Press.

Bernard of Clairvaux, "Sermon Six on Conversion," in *Sermons on Conversion: On Conversion, A Sermon to Clerics* and *Lenten Sermons on the Psalm "He Who Dwells,"* trans. Marie-Bernard Said, O.S.B. (Kalamazoo: Cistercian Publications, 1981). All rights reserved by Cistercian Publications.

Gregory the Great, "Homily 37," in *Gregory the Great, Forty Gospel Homilies,* trans. Dom David Hurst (Kalamazoo: Cistercian Publications, 1990). All rights reserved by Cistercian Publications.

"Inviting Others to Our Table," reproduced from *Preaching Biblically* by Don Wardlaw. Used by permission of Westminster John Knox Press.

Excerpts from "Dives in Dallas," reprinted by permission from IMAGERY FOR PREACHING by Patricia Wilson-Kastner, copyright © 1989 Augsburg Fortress.

Excerpts from "Homily on the Passover" are reprinted from CHRISTOLOGICAL CONTROVERSY edited by Richard A. Norris, copyright © 1980 Fortress Press. Used by permission of Augsburg Fortress.

Excerpts from *The Journals and Letters of Francis Asbury Vol. 1* ed. by Clark, Potts and Payton © 1958 by Abingdon Press.

Excerpts from *Imagining a Sermon* by Tom Troger © 1990 by Abingdon Press. Used by permission.

Excerpts from *Charles Albert Tindley: Prince of Preachers* by Ralph Jones © 1982 by Abingdon Press. Used by permission.

"Jacob's Ladder," pp. 281-301, in *Eighteen Sermons Preached by the Late Rev. George Whitefield, A.M. Taken in Verbatim Short-hand and Faithfully Transcribed by Joseph Gurney.* Used by permission of the University of Missouri-Kansas City Libraries, Special Collections Department.

"Likeness to Christ" from *Lucretia Mott: Her Complete Speeches and Sermons,* ed. Dana Greene. Used by permission of The Edwin Mellen Press.

Material from Manfred Hoffman's *Rhetoric and Theology: The Hermeneutic of Erasmus* is used by permission of the University of Toronto Press.

Material from *A Lamp Unto Our Feet* by Norman H. Snaith, pp. 58-59, *The Expository Times,* 63, 1951-52 issued by permission of T&T Clark International.

Excerpts from *Preaching the Story* by Edmund Steimle, Morris Niedenthal and Charles Rice Copyright © 1980 Fortress Press. Used by permission of Augsburg Fortress.

Reprinted by arrangement with the Estate of Martin Luther King Jr., c/o Writers House as agent for the proprietor New York, NY. *Copyright 1969 Martin Luther King Jr., copyright renewed 1991 Coretta Scott King.*

Excerpts from "A Critical Translation of Philip Melanchton's *Elementorum Rhetorices Libri Duo,*" Ph.d. dissertation, University of Michigan, 1968, by Sister Mary Joan LaFontaine, are used by permission of the Grand Rapids Dominicans.

Material from "Hildegard of Bingen: Homilies on the Gospels" is taken from a translation by Beverly Mayne Kienzle and Fay Martineau, from a forthcoming book from Cistercian Publications. Used by permission of the authors and Cistercian Publications.

Excerpts in chapter 8 from "The Way a Sermon Ought to Be Given" by Guibert of Nogent, translated by Joseph M. Miller, from *Readings in Medieval Rhetoric,* edited by Joseph Miller, Michael Prosser, and Thomas W. Benson, 1973, Indiana University Press.

Excerpts from "Alan of Lille: On the Day of Pentecost" in chapter 8 are taken from a forthcoming book of sermons from Cistercian Publications, translated by Gillian R. Evans. Used by permission of the author and Cistercian Publications.

Excerpts from Origen, *On First Principles,* translated by G. W. Butterworth, used by permission of SPCK.

Excerpts from *English Pulpit Oratory from Andrewes to Tillotson: A Study of Its Literary Aspects,* by W. Fraser Mitchell, published in 1932 by SPCK, is used by permission of SPCK.

Excerpt is reprinted from *Home by Another Way* by Barbara Brown Taylor; published by Cowley Publications, 907 Massachusetts Avenue, Cambridge, MA 02139. *www.cowley.org* (800-225-1534)

Excerpts from *Fasciculus Morum* are used by permission of Siegfried Wenzel.

"The Sixth Sermon before Edward VI" from pages 90-113 of *Selected Sermons by Hugh Latimer.* Edited by Allan G. Chester. Used by permission of the Folger Shakespeare Library.

Excerpts from *Dinner with Jesus and Other Left-handed Story-sermons,* used by permission of Zondervan and Donald F. Chatfield.

"Praying through Clenched Teeth," originally published by Abingdon Press in *Twentieth Century Pulpit,* vol. II, ed. James W. Cox, is used by permission of Fred B. Craddock.

The summary of the *Forma praedicandi* (1322) of Robert of Basevorn from *Rhetoric in the Middle Ages,* published originally by the University of California Press in 1974, is used by permision of James J. Murphy.

"Nobody Stands Alone, Part 1," by Bill Hybels, © 1999 Willow Creek Association. Used with permission.

16 17 18 19 20 21 22 23 24 25—10 9 8 7 6 5 4 3 2 1

MANUFACTURED IN THE UNITED STATES OF AMERICA

CONTENTS

PREFACE TO VOLUME 2

This history of preaching has two components, each of which makes up one volume. The first (the book *A History of Preaching,* Vol. 1; also referred to as the survey volume) is a historical survey that reconstructs the way Christian proclamation developed, and the second (the CD-ROM *A History of Preaching,* Vol. 2; also referred to as the sources volume) is a collection of sources that document this development. In the first, therefore, are all the efforts to account for the change of preaching over time; in it is all the discussion of periods, movements, innovations, and practitioners. The second volume consists of specimen sermons and passages from theoretical literature about preaching from each of the periods. These are examples of the data the first volume interprets.

This volume of sources was created to serve at least two purposes. The first is to make it possible for readers of the first volume to see the entire text of some of the documents discussed there, to allow them not only to gain more in-depth understanding of what was said about the documents but also to make independent judgments about them. The second is simply to provide, in one place, convenient access to these documents that are so significant to the history of preaching. Each document was chosen for inclusion, at least in part, because it is intrinsically interesting and requires no external reference to justify being read.

Because many of the documents included in this volume are analyzed in the survey, only short introductions are provided for them here.

To facilitate usage of the two volumes, there are cross-references in the text between the discussion of a document in the survey volume and the text of the document in the sources volume. These cross-references are printed in bold type and take a form like **"See Vol. 1, pp. ___,** for discussion" or **"See Vol. 2, pp. ____,** for the text of this sermon."

Many anthologies of source material comprise a large number of squibs from original works, each chosen for what it has to say about a particular subject. Such an approach would be disastrous for sermons, because it would leave distorted impressions of the original transaction between a preacher and the congregation present. Even the full text of the words delivered is a poor substitute for the living voice, but at least this method allows the entire sermon to have a unified impact on the reader, so that its scope can be experienced. Likewise with the passages from theoretical literature, every argument is more than its bare bones or purple patches. Thus, while complete works cannot always be included, at least there can be complete sections of those works.

Finally, rather than distract readers by citing scripture translations, in Volume 2 I kept the wording of the original sources. Unlike Volume 1, which primarily used the NRSV, scripture translations in Volume 2 may or may not be from the NRSV, and in some cases they even may be paraphrased.

PART I

HOMILETICAL ORIGINS

CHAPTER 1

THE EARLIEST CHRISTIAN PREACHING

A SYNAGOGUE SERMON

This sermon represents a type of rabbinic preaching more like early Christian preaching than any other form of synagogue sermon. It is not known, however, whether this particular sermon was ever preached, since it is preserved in a collection of sermons edited to answer questions about the correct observance of Jewish law. The collection, not edited until after the sixth century of the Common Era, is called Tanchuma, *the Hebrew text of which has been edited by Martin Buber. This sermon appears in the section called* parasha Noah, *chapter 13. It is translated in William Richard Stegner, "The Ancient Jewish Synagogue Homily," in* Greco-Roman Literature and the New Testament, *ed. David E. Aune, SBL Sources for Biblical Study, no. 21 (Atlanta, Ga.: Scholars Press, 1988), 60-62.* ***See Vol. 1, pp. 8-11,** for discussion.*

"And Noah began (to be) a man of the soil." (Gen. 9:20) As soon as he busied himself with the soil he became profane (as opposed to sacred). Said rabbi Yehudah son of rabbi Shalom, "In the beginning (Noah was)

a man righteous and pure, but now (he is) *a man of the soil." "He planted a vineyard"* (Gen 9:20b). After he planted a vineyard, he was called *"a man of the soil."*

Three men busied themselves with the soil and became profane. These were Cain, Noah, Uzziah. Concerning Cain, Scripture says (Gen 4; 2) "... and Cain (was) a tiller of the soil." What else does Scripture say? "... you shall be a fugitive and a wanderer on the earth."

Concerning Noah, scripture says, *"And Noah began (to be) a man of the soil." "He planted a vineyard,"* and he exposed himself. *"And he drank of the vine. . . ."* (Gen 9:21a).

The sages said, "On that day he planted, on that day it produced fruit, on that day he cut (grapes), on that day he treaded (grapes), on that day he drank, on that day he became drunk, on that day his disgrace was exposed."

Our rabbis of blessed memory said, "When Noah came to plant a vineyard, Satan came and stood before him. Satan said to him, 'What are you planting?' He said to him, 'A vineyard.' Satan said to him, 'What kind of vineyard?' Noah replied, 'Its fruits are sweet, neither too green nor too ripe, and they make from them wine which gladdens hearts, as Scripture says (Ps 104:15) 'and wine to gladden the heart of man.' Satan said to him, 'Come and let the two of us join together in this vineyard.' Noah replied, 'To life!' What did Satan do? He brought a sheep and killed it under the vine. After that he brought a lion and killed it there. Then he brought a pig and killed it and after that he brought an ape and killed it under the vineyard. Their blood dripped into that vineyard which absorbed their blood. Thus Satan hinted that before a man drinks wine, he is as pure as this lamb that knows nothing and as a sheep before her shearers is dumb. When he drinks a normal amount, he is a strong man like a lion and says that there is none like him in the world. After he has drunk too much he becomes like a pig soiled in his own urine and in something else. When he is drunk, he becomes like an ape, standing and dancing and laughing and bringing forth obscenities before everyone and he doesn't know what he is doing. And all this happened to Noah the righteous man. What? (Did all this happen to) Noah the righteous one whose praise the Holy One Blessed Be He proclaimed? What then of the rest of humanity? How much the more (might happen to them)!"

There is more, for Noah cursed his offspring and said, *"Cursed be Canaan:* etc." (Gen 9:25) And Ham, because he saw with his eyes the nakedness of his father, his eyes became red. And because he *told* (about it) with his mouth, his lips became curled. And because he turned his face, the hair on his head and his beard was singed. And because he did not cover the *nakedness,* he walked naked and his foreskin grew back over his circumcision. According to all the measure of the Holy One Blessed Be He (he received) measure for measure.

Nevertheless, the Holy One Blessed Be He turned and had mercy on him, for his mercy is upon all his creation. The Holy One Blessed Be He said, "Since he sold himself into slavery, let him go out by the eye which saw and by the mouth which told." It is right that he shall go out to freedom by tooth and by eye for Scripture says (Exod 21:26), "When a man strikes the eye of his slave, male or female, and destroys it, he shall let the slave go free for the eye's sake." And further (Exod 21:27), "If he knocks out the tooth of his slave, male or female, he shall let the slave go free for the tooth's sake."

And is it not a matter of light and heavy (that is, as with human affairs, so with God's)?

If (in terms of human affairs) a man's slave, his property and wealth, because he blinded his eye and knocked out his tooth, will go out from slavery to freedom (in this life), then (in terms of God's dealings), those blessed by God, who are His plantation to be glorified, when they die, is it not so much more proper that they will go to freedom from sins, as Scripture says, "in death, he is free"; indeed, they will go out with all 248 parts of the body (in the Resurrection they became whole). The Holy One Blessed Be He said, "In this world through the evil inclination they multiply sins, but in the world to come 'I will take out of your flesh the heart of stone. . . .'" (Ezek 36:26c). Again Scripture says, "And it shall never again be the reliance of the house of Israel, recalling their iniquity, when they turn to them for aid. Then they will know that I am the Lord God." (Ezek 29:16) And Scripture says, "In those days and in that time, says the Lord, iniquity shall be sought in Israel, and there shall be none." (Jer 50:20)

Concerning Uzziah, scripture says, "for he loved the *soil.*" (II Chron 26:10). For he was king, and he busied himself with the *soil* and he did not busy himself with Torah. One day he entered the house of study and said to the rabbis, "With what are you preoccupied?" They said to him, (Num 1:51) "And if anyone else (that is, a lay person) comes near, he shall be put to death." Uzziah said to them, "The Holy One Blessed Be He is a King and I am a king, it is proper for a king to serve a King and to offer incense in his presence." Then, he "entered the temple of the Lord to burn incense on the altar of incense." (II Chron 26:16) But Azariah the priest went in after him, with eighty priests of the Lord who were men of valor." (II Chron 26:17) And all of them were young priests. "And (they) said to him, 'It is not for you, Uzziah, to burn incense to the Lord, but for the priests the sons of Aaron, who are consecrated to burn incense. Go out of the sanctuary; for you have done wrong....'" (II Chron 26:18) And for this he became angry. "Then Uzziah was angry. Now he had a censer in his hand to burn incense, and when he became angry with the priests leprosy broke out on his forehead...." (26:19) And at the same time the hall was split open this way and the other way twelve upon twelve mil (more than half a mile). "And they thrust him out quickly, and he himself hastened to go out, because the Lord had smitten him." (II Chron 26:20b) Who caused this to happen to him? He neglected the Torah and busied himself with the *soil*!

MELITO OF SARDIS: *HOMILY ON THE PASSOVER*

This sermon comes from around C.E. *165 and is the second oldest Christian sermon we have, an interpretation of Exodus 12 as a type of the death and resurrection of Christ. It was preached at an all-night vigil on the Jewish Passover in a city that had a much larger Jewish than Christian population. Its style is the Asianic rhetoric of the Second Sophistic, which employed Gorgian figures. In style it was a precursor of much in Christian homilies and liturgy. Richard A. Norris Jr.'s translation appears in the volume he edited and translated,* The Christological Controversy, *Sources of Early Christian Thought (Philadelphia: Fortress, 1980), 33-47.* ***See Vol. 1, pp. 17-21,*** *for discussion.*

The passage dealing with the Hebrew Exodus has been read out and the words of the mystery have been explained: how the sheep is sacrificed and how the people is saved. So then, my beloved friends, open your minds to understand. Here is the way in which the mystery of the Passover is new and old, eternal and involved in time, corruptible and incorruptible, mortal and immortal.

It is old according to the Law, but new according to the Word. By being figure it is involved in time, but by being grace it is eternal. As the slaughter of a sheep it is corruptible; as the life of the Lord it is incorruptible. Because of the burial in the ground it is mortal, but because of the resurrection from the dead it is immortal. The Law is old but the Word is new. The figure belongs to a particular time, but the grace is eternal. The sheep is corruptible, but the Lord is incorruptible. As lamb he is slaughtered, but as God he is risen. For though "like a sheep he was carried away to slaughter" [Isa. 53:7], yet he was no sheep; and though like a lamb he was "dumb," yet he was no lamb. For the one, the figure, was there, but the other, the reality, was uncovered.

For in place of the lamb, God appeared, and in place of the sheep a human being, and within the human being, the Christ, who contains all things.

So the slaughter of the sheep and the solemnity of the Passover and the scripture of the Law have arrived at Christ, for whose sake everything came to pass in the old Law, as it does all the more in the new Word. For the Law became Word and the old, new—issuing together out of Zion and Jerusalem. And the commandment became grace, and the figure became reality, and the lamb became the Son, and the human being became God. For as Son he was born, as lamb he was carried off, as sheep he was slaughtered, as human being he was buried. He rose from the dead as God, being by nature both God and a human being.

He is everything: Law inasmuch as he judges, Logos inasmuch as he teaches, grace inasmuch as he saves, Father inasmuch as he begets, Son inasmuch as he is begotten, sheep inasmuch as he suffers, human inasmuch as he is buried, God inasmuch as he rises. This is Jesus the Christ, "to whom be glory to all the ages. Amen."

Such is the mystery of the Passover, as it is written in the Law and as it was read just a moment ago. I will now review in detail what the text says: how God gave a command to Moses in Egypt when he wanted to bind Pharaoh by a plague while freeing Israel from the plague by Moses' hand.

"For behold," he says, "you shall take a faultless and unblemished lamb, and, as evening comes, you together with the sons of Israel shall slaughter it, and at night you shall consume it in haste and you shall break none of its bones" [Ex. 12:lff.]. "This is what you shall do," he says. "You shall eat it in one night gathered in families and in tribes. Your loins will be girded and your staves shall be in your hands. For this is the Lord's Passover, an eternal remembrance for the sons of Israel. Then take the blood of the sheep and smear the porches of your homes, placing the sign of blood on the uprights of the entrance to deter the angel. For behold, I smite Egypt; and in the space of one night, she will be deprived of offspring, from beast to human being." Then when Moses had slaughtered the sheep and carried out the mystery at night together with the sons of Israel, he sealed the doors of their homes as a safeguard for the people and a deterrent to the angel.

So as the lamb is slaughtered and the Passover eaten and the mystery accomplished and the people is glad and Israel sealed, then the angel arrived to smite Egypt—Egypt uninitiated into the mystery, having no part in the Passover, unsealed with the blood, unprotected by the Spirit—this enemy, this unbelieving Egypt he smote and in one night deprived her of offspring. For when the angel had passed about Israel and seen that the people were sealed with the blood of the sheep, it came upon Egypt and tamed the stiff-necked Pharaoh with sorrow, having put about him not a garment of mourning or a mantle torn in shreds but the whole of Egypt torn to pieces, sorrowing for her firstborn. For the whole of Egypt, in hardship and calamity, in tears and lamentations, came all in mourning to Pharaoh—mourning not only in aspect, but also in her soul, torn not only in outward vesture but also on her delicate breasts. There was a new spectacle to see: on the one hand, people striking (themselves), on the other, people wailing; and in their midst a mourning Pharaoh, seated in sackcloth and ashes, surrounded by a tangible darkness like funeral garb—girded by all of Egypt, itself a cloak of mourning.

For Egypt lay around Pharaoh like a vesture of mourning. Such was the cloak which was woven for the tyrant's body. This is the kind of garment in which the angel of justice dressed the harsh Pharaoh: bitter mourning and tangible darkness and childlessness. And the angel went on in its campaign against Egypt's firstborn, for the death of the firstborn was rapid and tireless. One could see a new trophy raised up over those who had fallen dead in one attack. And the ruin of those who lay about gave death something to feed on. And if you pay attention, you will discover a new and unheard-of misfortune to marvel at. For look what enveloped the Egyptians: a long night and tangible darkness, and death groping its way about, and an angel oppressing, and Hades devouring their firstborn.

But there is something yet stranger and more awesome for you to hear. In this tangible darkness, death was hiding untouchable, and the unfortunate Egyptians probed the darkness; but death, searching them out, touched the firstborn of the Egyptians at the angel's order. So if anyone probed the darkness he was led away by death.

If a firstborn child grasps a shadowy body with his hand, he cries out pitiably and fearfully with fright in his soul, "Whom is my hand holding? Whom is my soul afraid of? What darkness is it that encompasses my whole body? If you be my father, help me! If my mother, share my pain! If my brother, address me! If my friend, be well-disposed! If my enemy, depart! For I am a firstborn." But before the firstborn had fallen silent, the great silence seized him as it said, "You belong to me, firstborn. I, the silence of death, am your fate." Another of the firstborn, observing that the firstborn were being taken, denied who he was, lest he die bitterly. "I am not a firstborn. I was born the third fruit of my mother's womb." But [the angel] could not be deceived. He seized the firstborn, who fell face down in silence. In one fell swoop the firstborn of the Egyptians perished. The first conceived, the firstborn, the desired one, the pampered one, was beaten to the ground—the firstborn not only of human beings but also of the irrational animals.

On the fertile plains of the land there was heard a murmuring of beasts lamenting their nurslings, for the cow with a calf and the mare with a colt and the other beasts who were giving birth and swollen with milk were lamenting their firstborn offspring bitterly and pitiably. There went up a wailing and a lamentation because of the destruction of the human [children], the dead firstborn. For the whole of Egypt stank because of the unburied corpses. That was a fearsome sight to see: the mothers of the Egyptians with their hair in disarray, the fathers distracted, all wailing aloud terribly in their own speech, "In one fell swoop we unfortunates have been deprived of our children, even our firstborn offspring." And they beat their breasts, striking instruments with their hands as they did the dance of the dead.

Such was the disaster which seized Egypt and rendered her childless in an instant. Israel, though, was protected by the sacrifice of the sheep and enlightened by the outpoured blood, and the death of the sheep was found to set a rampart around the people.

O strange, unspeakable mystery! The sacrifice of the sheep was found to be Israel's salvation, and the death of the sheep became the life of the people, and the blood deterred the angel!

Tell me, angel, what deterred you? Was it the sacrifice of the sheep or the life of the Lord? The death of the sheep or the prefiguration of the Lord? The blood of the sheep or the Spirit of the Lord? It is clear that you were deterred because you saw the mystery of the Lord coming to pass in the sheep, the life of the Lord in the sacrifice of the sheep, the prefiguration of the Lord in the death of the sheep. That is why you did not strike Israel, depriving only Egypt of children. What is this unheard of mystery? Egypt was stricken for destruction, Israel was guarded for salvation.

Listen, and hear the power of the mystery. The words [read], beloved, and the events which happen are unimportant apart from their character as parables and as preliminary sketches. Everything that happens and everything that is said has the quality of a parable. What is said has the quality of a parable, while what happens has that of an anticipation, in order that just as what happens is revealed by its anticipation, so also what is said is illuminated by the parable. Except in the presence of a model, no work is accomplished. Or is not the coming reality perceived by means of the image which prefigures it? That is why the preliminary sketch of what is coming is made out of wax or clay or wood—so that the future accomplishment may be seen to be more exalted in height, and stronger in power, and beautiful in appearance and rich in its furnishing, by means of the littleness and corruptibility of the preliminary sketch. When the thing to which the prefiguration points arrives, that which once bore the impress of what was coming is destroyed because it is no longer useful. The image has yielded to the truth it signified. What once was honorable becomes dishonorable, because that which is honorable by nature has appeared. Each thing has its own moment. There is a time which belongs properly to the prefiguration, a time which belongs properly to the material. You construct the prefiguration of the truth. You desire it because in it you contemplate the image of what is coming. You bring up the materials before the prefiguration. You want this because of what will come to be by its means. You complete the work. You desire this alone, this alone you espouse, for in this alone you contemplate at once the prefiguration, the material, and the truth.

As it is with the corruptible models, so it is with the incorruptible things. Just as it is with terrestrial things, so also it is with heavenly things. For in the people is prefigured the Lord's salvation and truth, and the principles of the gospel are proclaimed beforehand by the Law. Therefore the people became a prefiguration in a preliminary sketch, and the Law, the writing down of a figure. But the gospel is the Law's explanation and fullness, and the church is the receptacle of the truth. So the type was honorable prior to the truth's coming, and the figure was astonishing prior to its interpretation. That is, the people was honorable before the church arose, and the Law was astonishing before the gospel was brought to light. But when the church arose and the gospel stood forward, the type became an empty thing because it had handed its power over to the truth, and the Law was fulfilled because it had handed its power over to the gospel. Just as the prefiguration becomes an empty thing when it has handed its image over to the true reality so the parable becomes an empty thing when it has been illumined by its interpretation. In the same way too the Law was fulfilled when the gospel had been brought to light, and the people was made an empty thing when the church had been raised up, and the prefiguration was destroyed when the Lord had been manifested. And today, what once was valued has become without value, now that things which are valuable in themselves have been revealed.

For at one time the sacrifice of the sheep was a valuable thing, but now, because of the Lord's salvation, it is without value. The death of the sheep was valuable; but now, because of the Lord's salvation, it is without value. The blood of the sheep was valuable, but now, because of the

Lord's Spirit, it is without value. The lamb which was dumb was valuable, but now, because of the spotless Son, it is without value. The temple here below was valuable, but now because of the Christ on high it is without value. The Jerusalem here below was valuable, but now because of the Jerusalem on high it is without value. The narrow inheritance was once valuable, but now because of the broad grace it is without value. For the glory of God does not settle in one spot or within a narrow allotment of land. Rather, his grace is poured out to the limits of the inhabited world, and that is where the all-ruling God has tabernacled, through Jesus Christ, to whom be glory to the ages. Amen.

You have heard, then, the explanation of the prefiguration and of what corresponds to it. Hear also the shape of the mystery.

What is the Passover [Greek: *pascha*]? The name is taken from what in fact came to pass: "to keep Passover" [*paschein*] comes from the word "to have suffered" [*pathein*].

Learn, then, who it is who suffers and who shares his suffering, and why the Lord is present on the earth—in order that, having garbed himself in the sufferer, he may carry him away into the heights of the heavens.

When "God in the beginning had made the heaven and the earth" [Gen. 1:1] and everything in them by the Logos, he molded the human being out of earth and shared breath with the form [he had made]. Then he set him in paradise, toward the East, in Eden, to live there contentedly. By a commandment he laid down this law: "Eat of every tree in paradise for nourishment, but do not eat of the tree of the knowledge of good and evil. On the day that you eat of it you shall die" [Gen. 2:16-17].

But the human being, being naturally receptive to both good and evil, just as a parcel of soil is receptive to seed from either direction, took evil and gluttonous counsel; he touched the tree, he transgressed the commandment, and he disobeyed God. Therefore he was thrown out into this world as into a prison camp for the condemned. When he had become prolific and very aged and had returned to the earth on account of his eating from the tree, he left an inheritance for his children. He left his children, as an inheritance, not chastity but adultery, not incorruption but corruption, not honor but dishonor, not liberty but slavery, not kingly rule but tyranny, not life but death, not salvation but perdition.

The perdition of human beings on the earth was an unheard-of and frightening thing. Look what befell them: They were carried off by sin, their oppressor, and led into the world of lusts, where they were drowned by insatiable pleasures—adultery, fornication, impudence, lust, love of money, murders, blood-sheddings, the tyranny of evil, the tyranny of lawlessness. For father drew sword against son; and son lifted hand against father and, irreverent, struck his mother's breasts; and brother slew brother; and the host wronged his guest, and the friend murdered friend; and human being slit the throat of his fellow with tyrannical hand. So all the people on earth became murderers or fratricides or patricides or slayers of children. But something yet stranger and more fearful happened. A certain mother laid hands on the flesh to which she had given birth; she laid hands on those who had fed at her breast. She buried in her belly the fruit of her womb, and the ill-starred mother became a fearsome tomb, having devoured the child which she had borne. I will say no more, but many other strange things, more fearsome and more wanton, came to pass among humans. A father lay with his daughter, and a son with his mother, and a brother with his sister, and a male with male, and everyone lusted after his neighbor's wife.

At this, sin was happy. Co-worker with death that she is, sin made her way first into people's souls and got the bodies of the dead ready for death to feed on. Sin left her mark in every soul, and those in whom she left it were those who had to come to an end. So all flesh fell under sin, and every body fell under death, and every soul was removed from its fleshly home, and what had been taken from earth was resolved into earth, and what had been given by God was closed up into Hades, and the happy union was dissolved, and the beautiful body was broken up into parts. Humanity was being cut in parts by death, for a new kind of misfortune and captivity held it. It was carried away captive under the shadow of death. The image of the Father was left desolate. This, then, is the reason why the mystery of the Passover has been completed in the body of the Lord. The Lord, however, laid out the order of his own sufferings ahead of time in the persons of the patriarchs and the prophets and the people as a whole, and set his seal to it through the Law and the Prophets. For since the future will be both unprecedented and grand, it was arranged ahead of time from afar, so that when it came to pass it would encounter faith because it had been foreseen. In this way the mystery of the Lord, prefigured from afar and made visible today, encounters faith now that it is accomplished, even though people judge it to be something novel. The mystery of the Lord is both new and old, old inasfar as it is prefiguration, new inasfar as it is grace. But if you gaze steadily upon this prefiguration, you will see the reality by way of its fulfillment.

So if you want to see the mystery of the Lord, gaze upon Abel who was similarly murdered, Isaac who was similarly bound, Joseph who was similarly sold for slavery, Moses who was similarly exposed, David who was similarly persecuted, the prophets who similarly suffered on account of the Christ. Gaze also upon the sheep sacrificed in the land of Egypt and the one who smote Egypt and saved Israel by means of blood.

Furthermore, the mystery of the Lord is proclaimed by the prophetic voice. For Moses says to the people, "And you will see your life hanging before your eyes by night and by day, and you will not believe in your life" [Deut. 28:66]. David, for his part, said, "Why were the nations troubled, and why did the peoples concern themselves with empty things? The kings of the earth stood there and the rulers were gathered together against the Lord and against his Christ" [Ps. 2:1-2]. Then Jeremiah said, "I am like an innocent lamb led to slaughter. They contrive evil against me, saying, 'Come, let us cast wood into his bread and throw him out of the land of the living, and his name will never be remembered'" [Jer. 11:19]. Then Isaiah said, "Like a sheep he was led to slaughter and like a speechless lamb before his shearer he does not open his mouth. Who can recount his generation?" [Isa. 53:7-8]. Many other things too were proclaimed by many prophets with reference to the mystery of the Passover, which is Christ, "to whom be glory to the ages. Amen."

He arrived on earth from the heavens for the sake of the one who suffered. He clothed himself in the sufferer by means of a virgin's womb and came forth as a human being. He took to himself the sufferings of the sufferer by means of a body capable of suffering, and he destroyed the sufferings of the flesh. By a Spirit incapable of death he killed off death, the homicide.

This is the one who like a lamb was carried off and like a sheep was sacrificed. He redeemed us from slavery to the cosmos as from the land of Egypt and loosed us from slavery to the devil as from the hand of Pharaoh. And he sealed our souls with his own Spirit and the limbs of our body with his own blood. This is the one who covered death with shame and made a mourner of the devil, just as Moses did Pharaoh. This is the one who struck lawlessness a blow and made injustice childless, as Moses did Egypt. This is the one who rescued us from slavery into liberty, from darkness into light, from death into life, from a tyranny into an eternal kingdom (and made us a new priesthood and a peculiar, eternal people).

He is the Passover of our salvation. He is the one who in many folk bore many things. He is the one who was murdered in the person of Abel, bound in the person of Isaac, exiled in the person of Jacob, sold in the person of Joseph, exposed in the person of Moses, sacrificed in the person of the lamb, persecuted in the person of David, dishonored in the person of the prophets. This is the one who was made flesh in a virgin, hanged upon the wood, entombed in the earth, raised from the dead, lifted up to the heights of the heavens. He is the speechless lamb. He is the lamb who was slaughtered. He is the one born of Mary the beautiful ewe. He is the one who was taken from the flock and dragged to slaughter and killed at evening and buried at night, who was not crushed on the cross, was not dissolved into the earth, who rose from the dead and raised humanity from the grave below.

This man was killed. And where was he killed? In the middle of Jerusalem. And why? Because he cured their lame and cleansed their lepers and led their blind to sight and raised up their dead. That is why he suffered. Somewhere it is written in the Law and the Prophets: "They have rendered me evil for good and repaid my soul with childlessness. They reckoned evil against me and said, 'Let us bind the just man, for he is of no use to us'" [Ps. 34:14 LXX].

Why, O Israel, did you do this new misdeed? You dishonored the one who honored you. You have held in low esteem the one who esteemed you. You have denied the one who confessed you. You have renounced the one who publicly called out your name. You have done to death the one who gave you life. What have you done, O Israel? Has it not been written for your sake, "You shall not shed innocent blood, lest you die miserably" [Jer. 22:6]?

"I," says Israel, "slew the Lord. Why? Because he was bound to suffer." You have gone astray, Israel, in using such sophistry to deal with the Lord's sacrifice. He had to suffer, but not because of you. He had to be dishonored, but not by you. He had to be judged, but not by you. He had to be hanged, but not by your hand. These, O Israel, are the words with which you ought to have called to God: "O Master, if indeed your Son must suffer and this is your will, let him suffer, but not because of me; let him suffer at the hands of other nations. Let him be judged by the uncircumcised. Let him be crucified by the hand of a tyrant, but not by mine."

This, however, is not what you called out to God, O Israel. Nor did you make atonement before the Lord. You have not been put to shame by the sight of his works. The withered hand restored for the sake of its body's well-being did not shame you, nor did the eyes of infirm folk opened by his hand, nor did paralyzed bodies restored by his voice. Neither did the most novel of all shame you—when a dead person was raised from the tomb after four days. You, in fact, passed these things by. On the eve of the Lord's sacrifice you prepared sharp nails and false witnesses and bonds and scourges and sour wine and gall and a sword and calamity, as though for a murderous robber. When you had laid scourges to his body and thorns on his head, you bound his good hands, which had formed you out of earth, and fed with gall that good mouth which had fed you with life, and you did your Lord to death on the great feast. And you dined cheerfully while he went hungry. You drank wine and ate bread while he had vinegar and gall. You ate with beaming face while he was of melancholy countenance. You were rejoicing, but he suffered affliction. You sang songs, but he was condemned. You were beating time, but he was being nailed up. You were dancing, but he was being buried. You stretched out on a soft couch, but he was in a grave and in a coffin.

O wicked Israel, why did you carry out this fresh deed of injustice, bringing new sufferings upon your Lord—your master, your creator, your maker, the one who honored you, who called you Israel? But you were discovered not to be Israel, for you have not seen God or acknowledged the Lord. You did not know, O Israel, that this one is God's firstborn, who was generated before the morning star, who made light to come up, who made the daylight gleam, who set the darkness to one side, who established the first limit, who suspended the earth, who dried up the abyss, who stretched out the firmament, who set the cosmos in order, who arranged the stars in heaven, who made the lights gleam, who created the angels in heaven, who fixed the thrones there, who molded humanity upon the earth.

It was this one who called you and guided you, from Adam to Noah, from Noah to Abraham, from Abraham to Isaac and Jacob and the twelve patriarchs. It was this one who led you into Egypt and protected you and there nourished and nursed you. It was this one who gave you light by means of a pillar of fire and sheltered you by means of a cloud, who cut open the Red Sea and led you through and scattered your enemies abroad. It was this one who rained manna on you from heaven, who gave you drink from a rock, who gave you the Law on Horeb, who gave you an inheritance on earth, who sent you the prophets, who raised up your kings. This is the one who came to you, who cured those of you who were suffering and raised up your dead. This is the one whom you treated impiously. This is the one whom you treated unjustly. This is the one whom you put to death. This is the one on whom you set a price in money, after demanding from him didrachmas for his head.

Come, ungrateful Israel, be judged before my face for your ingratitude.

What value have you set on his guiding you? What value have you set on his election of your fathers? What value have you set on the descent into Egypt and your being nourished there by that good man Joseph? What value have you set on the ten plagues? What value have you set on the pillar by night and the cloud by day and the crossing of the Red Sea? What value have you set on the gift of manna from heaven and the possession of water from the rock and the giving of the Law on Horeb and the earthly inheritance and the gifts you received there? What value have you set on the sufferers whom he cured when he was with you? Set me a value on the withered hand which he restored to its body. Set me a value on those blind from birth to whom he brought light by his voice. Set me a value on the dead ones whom he raised from the tomb after three or four days.

His gifts to you cannot be measured. You, however, without honoring him, have repaid him with ingratitude. You have repaid him evil for good and affliction for joy and death for life—to him on whose account you ought to have died.

For if the king of a nation is seized by its enemies, for his sake war is begun, for his sake a wall is breached, for his sake a city is taken, for his sake ransoms are sent, for his sake ambassadors are dispatched, so that he may be taken—either in order that he may be restored to his life or in order that, being dead, he may be buried.

You, on the contrary, voted against your Lord. The nations worshiped him. The uncircumcised marveled at him. The outlanders glorified him. Even Pilate washed his hands in this case. This one you did to death on the great feast.

So for you the Feast of Unleavened Bread is bitter, as it is written, "You will eat unleavened bread with bitter herbs." Bitter for you the nails which you sharpened. Bitter for you the tongue which you sharpened. Bitter for you the false witnesses which you set up. Bitter for you the bonds which you prepared. Bitter for you the whips which you plaited. Bitter for you Judas whom you rewarded. Bitter for you Herod whom you obeyed. Bitter for you Caiaphas in whom you trusted. Bitter for you the gall which you furnished. Bitter for you the vinegar which you produced. Bitter for you the thorns which you gathered. Bitter for you the hands which you stained with blood.

You did your Lord to death in the midst of Jerusalem.

Listen and see, all families of the nations! An unprecedented murder has come to pass in the midst of Jerusalem, in the city of the Law, in the Hebrew city, in the prophets' city, in the city adjudged righteous. And who has been killed? Who is the killer? I am ashamed to say and compelled to speak. If the murder took place by night, or if he was slaughtered in a desert place, to be silent were an easy matter. But it was in the midst of street and city, in the midst of a city of onlookers, that the unjust murder of a just man took place. And so he was lifted up upon a tree and an inscription was provided too, to indicate who was being killed. Who was it? It is a heavy thing to say, and a most fearful thing to refrain from saying. But listen, as you tremble in the face of him on whose account the earth trembled. He who hung the earth in place is hanged. He who fixed the heavens in place is fixed in place. He who made all things fast is made fast on the tree. The Master is insulted. God is murdered. The King of Israel is destroyed by an Israelite hand.

O unheard of murder, O unheard of injustice! The Master, his body naked, has had his appearance altered, and he is not even deemed worthy of a garment to keep him from being seen. That is why the stars turned aside in their courses and the daylight was obscured, so as to conceal him who was stripped naked on the Tree—not obscuring the Lord's body, but the eyes of these people. Though the people did not tremble, the earth trembled. Though the people were not afraid, the heavens were afraid. Though the people did not rend their garments, the angel did. Though the people did not wail and lament, "The Lord thundered from heaven and the Most High gave forth his voice" [Ps. 18:13].

That is why, Israel, you did not tremble before the Lord, you did not fear before the Lord, you did not lament over the Lord, you gave vent to grief over your own firstborn. When the Lord was hanged, you did not rend your garments, but for your own when they had been murdered you rent your garments. You deserted the Lord, you were not found by him. You cast the Lord down, you were cast down to earth. And you—you lie dead, while he rose from the dead and went up to the heights of heaven.

The Lord, when he had put on the human being and suffered for the sake of him who suffered and was bound for the sake of him who was imprisoned and was judged for the sake of the condemned and was buried for the sake of the buried, rose from the dead and cried aloud, "Who will enter into judgment against me? Let him stand up and face me. I have set the condemned free. I have given the dead life. I have raised up the one who was entombed. Who will speak against me? I," he says, "the Christ, I have dissolved death, I have triumphed over the enemy and trodden down Hades and bound the strong man and carried off humanity into the height of the heavens—I," he says, "the Christ.

"So come, all families of human beings who are defiled by sins, and receive remission of sins. For I am your remission, I am the Passover of salvation. I am the Lamb sacrificed for your sake. I am your ransom. I am your life. I am your resurrection. I am your light. I am your salvation. I am your King. I lead you toward the heights of heaven. I will show you the eternal Father. I will raise you up with my right hand."

This is he who made the heavens and the earth, and formed humanity in the beginning, who is announced by the Law and the Prophets, who was enfleshed in a Virgin, who was hanged on the Tree, who was buried in the earth, who was raised from the dead and went up into the heights of heaven, who is sitting on the right hand of the Father, who has the authority to judge and save all things, through whom the Father made the things which exist, from the beginning to all the ages. This one is "the Alpha and the Omega," this one is "the beginning and the end"—the beginning which cannot be explained and the end which cannot be grasped. This one is the Christ. This one is the King. This one is Jesus. This one is the Leader. This one is the Lord. This one is he who has risen from the dead. This one is he who sits on the right hand of the Father. He bears the Father and is borne by the Father. "To him be the glory and the power to the ends of the ages. Amen."

Peace to him who wrote and to him who reads and to those who love the Lord in simplicity of heart.

CHAPTER 2

THE HOMILY TAKES SHAPE

ORIGEN: *ON FIRST PRINCIPLES* (VOL. 4, CHAPS. 2–3)

Since Origen's method of interpreting the Bible allegorically was determinative for most Christian preaching until the Reformation and after, it seems more important to provide this section on the theoretical basis for such interpretation than an example of one of his homilies. This is especially true since many modern readers have only heard this hermeneutical method discussed with horror. This extensive passage, the only source for this chapter, shows Origen to have been a close reader of the biblical text who ran into precisely the same anomalies that caused historical-critical interpreters to bring their method to bear. Not having their presuppositions available, Origen used those of his time and did so with remarkable intelligence and integrity. Even though few would resort to his method today, no one can read his presentation without enormous respect for the brilliance of his accomplishment. ***See Vol. 1, pp. 40-46,*** *for a discussion of the way his hermeneutical theory was employed in his preaching. The edition used is Origen,* On First Principles: Being Koetschau's Text of the *De Principiis, trans., with intro. and notes, G. W.*

Butterworth (London: SPCK, 1936; reprint, New York: Harper & Row, 1966), 4:269-312. While Butterworth translated both parts of the Greek text that are preserved in the Philokalia *and the Latin translations, only the translation of the Greek is provided here, except for passages that seem genuine and have survived only in the Latin.*

Chapter 2: How Divine Scripture Should Be Read and Interpreted

1. Now that we have spoken cursorily about the inspiration of the divine scriptures it is necessary to discuss the manner in which they are to be read and understood, since many mistakes have been made in consequence of the method by which the holy documents ought to be interpreted not having been discovered by the multitude. For the hard-hearted and ignorant members of the circumcision have refused to believe in our Savior because they think that they are keeping closely to the language of the prophecies that relate to him, and they see that he did not literally "proclaim release to captives" or build what they consider to be a real "city of God" or "cut off the chariots from Ephraim and the horse from Jerusalem" or "eat butter and honey, and choose the good before he knew or preferred the evil."

Further, they think that it is the wolf, the four-footed animal, which is said in prophecy to be going to "feed with the lamb, and the leopard to lie down with the kid, and the calf and bull and lion to feed together, led by a little child, and the ox and the bear to pasture together, and their young ones growing up with each other, and the lion to eat straw like the ox"; and having seen none of these events literally happening during the advent of him whom we believe to be Christ they did not accept our Lord Jesus, but crucified him on the ground that he had wrongly called himself Christ.

And the members of the heretical sects, reading the passage, "A fire has been kindled in mine anger"; and "I am a jealous God, visiting the sins of the fathers upon the children to the third and fourth generation"; and "It repenteth me that I have anointed Saul to be king"; and "I, God, make peace and create evil"; and elsewhere, "There is no evil in a city, which the Lord did not do"; and further, "Evils came down from the Lord upon the gates of Jerusalem"; and "An evil spirit from God troubled Saul"; and ten thousand other passages like these, have not dared to disbelieve that they are the writings of God, but believe them to belong to the Creator, whom the Jews worship. Consequently they think that since the Creator is imperfect and not good, the Savior came here to proclaim a more perfect God who they say is not the Creator, and about whom they entertain diverse opinions. Then having once fallen away from the Creator, who is the sole unbegotten God, they have given themselves up to fictions, fashioning mythical hypotheses according to which they suppose that there are some things that are seen and others that are not seen, all of which are the fancies of their own minds.

Moreover, even the simpler of those who claim to belong to the Church, while believing indeed that there is none greater than the Creator, in which they are right, yet believe such things about him as would not be believed of the most savage and unjust of men.

2. Now the reason why all those we have mentioned hold false opinions and make impious or ignorant assertions about God appears to be nothing else but this, that scripture is not understood in its spiritual sense, but is interpreted according to the bare letter. On this account we must explain to those who believe that the sacred books are not the works of men, but that they were composed and have come down to us as a result of the inspiration of the Holy Spirit by the will of the Father of the universe through Jesus Christ, what are the methods of interpretation that appear right to us who keep to the rule of the heavenly Church of Jesus Christ through the succession from the Apostles.

That there are certain mystical revelations made known through the divine scriptures is believed by all, even by the simplest of those who are adherents of the word; but what these revelations are, fair-minded humble men confess that they do not know. If, for instance, an inquirer were to be in a difficulty, about the intercourse of Lot with his daughters, or the two wives of Abraham, or the two sisters married to Jacob, or the two hand-maids who bore children by him, they can say nothing except that these things are mysteries not understood by us.

But when the passage about equipment of the tabernacle is read, believing that the things described therein are types, they seek for ideas which they can attach to each detail that is mentioned in connection with the tabernacle. Now so far as concerns their belief that the tabernacle is a type of something they are not wrong; but in rightly attaching the word of the scripture to the particular idea of which the tabernacle is a type, here they sometimes fall into error. And they declare that all narratives that are supposed to speak about marriage or the begetting of children or wars or any other stories ever that may be accepted among the multitude are types; but when we ask, of what, then sometimes owing to the lack of thorough training, sometimes owing to rashness, and occasionally, even when one is well trained and of sound judgment, owing to man's exceedingly great difficulty in discovering these things, the interpretation of every detail is not altogether clear.

3. And what must we say about the prophecies, which we all know are filled with riddles and dark sayings? Or if we come to the gospels, the accurate interpretation even of these, since it is an interpretation of the mind of Christ, demands that grace that was given to him who said, "We have the mind of Christ, that we may know the things that were freely given to us by God. Which things also we speak, not in words which man's wisdom teacheth, but which the Spirit teacheth." And who, on reading the revelations made to John, could fail to be amazed at the deep obscurity of the unspeakable mysteries contained therein, which are evident even to him who does not understand what is written? And as for the apostolic epistles, what man who is skilled in literary interpretation would think them to be plain and easily understood, when even in them there are thousands of passages that provide, as if through a window, a narrow opening leading to multitudes of the deepest thoughts?

Seeing, therefore, that these things are so, and that thousands of men make mistakes, it is dangerous for us when we read to declare lightly that we understand things for which the "key of knowledge" is necessary, which the Savior says is with "the lawyers." And as for those who are unwilling to admit that these men held the truth before the coming of Christ, let them explain to us how it is that our Lord Jesus Christ says that the "key of knowledge" was with them, that is, with men who as these objectors say, had no books containing the secrets of knowledge and the all-perfect mysteries. For the passage runs as follows: "Woe unto you lawyers, for ye have taken away the key of knowledge. Ye entered not in yourselves, and them that were entering in ye hindered."

4. The right way, therefore, as it appears to us, of approaching the scriptures and gathering their meaning, is the following, which is extracted from the writings themselves. We find some such rule as this laid down by Solomon in the Proverbs concerning the divine doctrines written therein: "Do thou portray them threefold in counsel and knowledge, that thou mayest answer words of truth to those who question thee."

One must therefore portray the meaning of the sacred writings in a threefold way upon one's own soul, so that the simple man may be edified by what we may call the flesh of the scripture, this name being given to the obvious interpretation; while the man who has made some progress may be edified by its soul, as it were; and the man who is perfect and like those mentioned by the apostle: "We speak wisdom among the perfect; yet a wisdom not of this world, nor of the rulers of this world, which are coming to naught; but we speak God's wisdom in a mystery, even the wisdom that hath been hidden, which God foreordained before the worlds unto our glory"—this man may be edified by the spiritual law, which has "a shadow of the good things to come." For just as man consists of body, soul and spirit, so in the same way does the scripture, which has been prepared by God to be given for man's salvation.

We therefore read in this light the passage in *The Shepherd,* a book which is despised by some, where Hermas is bidden to "write two books," and after this to "announce to the presbyters of the church" what he has learned from the Spirit. This is the wording: "Thou shalt write two books, and shalt give one to Clement and one to Grapte. And Grapte shall admonish the widows and the orphans. But Clement shall send to the cities that are without, and thou shalt announce to the presbyters of the church."

Now Grapte, who admonishes the widows and orphans, is the bare letter, which admonishes those child souls that are not yet able to enroll God as their Father and are on this account called orphans, and which also admonishes those who while no longer associating with the unlawful bridegroom are in widowhood because they have not yet become worthy of the true one. But Clement, who has already gone beyond the letter, is to send the sayings "to the cities without," as if to say, to souls that are outside all bodily and lower thoughts; while the disciple of the Spirit is bidden to announce the message in person, no longer through letters but through living words, to presbyters or elders of the whole Church of God, to men who have grown gray through wisdom.

5. But since there are certain passages of scripture which, as we shall show in what follows, have no bodily sense at all, there are occasions when we must seek only for the soul and the spirit, as it were, of the passage. And possibly this is reason why the waterpots which, as we read in the gospel according to John, are said to be set there "for the purifying of the Jews," contain two or three firkins apiece. The language alludes to those who are said by the apostle to be Jews "inwardly" and it means that these are purified through the word of the scriptures, which contain in some cases "two firkins," that is, so to speak, the soul meaning and the spiritual meaning, and in other cases three, since some passages possess, in addition to those before-mentioned, a bodily sense as well, which is capable of edifying the hearers. And six waterpots may reasonably allude to those who are being purified in the world, which was made in six days, a perfect number.

6. That it is possible to derive benefit from the first, and to this extent helpful meaning, is witnessed by the multitudes of sincere and simple believers. But of the kind of explanation which penetrates as it were to the soul an illustration is found in Paul's first epistle to the Corinthians. "For," he says, "it is written; thou shalt not muzzle the ox that treadeth out the corn." Then in explanation of this law he adds, "Is it for oxen that God careth? Or saith he it altogether for our sake? Yea, for our sake it was written, because he that ploweth ought to plow in hope, and he that thresheth, to thresh in hope of partaking." And most of the interpretations adapted to the multitude which are in circulation and which edify those who cannot understand the higher meanings have something of the same character.

But it is a spiritual explanation when one is able to show of what kind of "heavenly things" the Jews "after the flesh" served a copy and a shadow, and of what "good things to come" the law has a "shadow." And, speaking generally, we have, in accordance with the apostolic promise, to seek after "the wisdom in a mystery, even the wisdom that hath been hidden, which God foreordained before the worlds unto the glory" of the righteous, "which none of the rulers of this world knew." The same apostle also says somewhere, after mentioning certain narratives from Exodus and Numbers, that "these things happened unto them figuratively, and they were written for our sake, upon whom the ends of the ages are come." He also gives hints to show what these things were figures of, when he says: "For they drank of that spiritual rock that followed them, and that rock was Christ."

In another epistle, when outlining the arrangements of the tabernacle he quotes the words: "Thou shalt make all things according to the figure that was shown thee in the mount." Further, in the epistle to the Galatians, speaking in terms of reproach to those who believe that they are reading the law and yet do not understand it, and laying it down that they who do not believe that there are allegories in the writings do not understand the law, he says: "Tell me, ye that desire to be under the law, do ye not hear the law? For it is written that Abraham had two sons, one by the handmaid and one by the free woman. Howbeit the son by the handmaid is born after the flesh; but the son by the free woman is born through promise. Which things contain an allegory; for these women are two covenants," and what follows. Now we must carefully mark each of the words spoken by him. He says, "Ye that desire to be under the law" (not, "ye that are under the law") "do ye not hear the law?" hearing being taken to mean understanding and knowing.

And in the epistle to the Colossians, briefly epitomizing the meaning of the entire system of the law, he says: "Let no man therefore judge you in meat or in drink or in respect of a feast day or a new moon or a sabbath, which are a shadow of the things to come." Further, in the epistle to the Hebrews, when discoursing about those who are of the circumcision, he writes: "They who serve that which is a copy and shadow of the heavenly things." Now it is probable that those who have once admitted that the apostle is a divinely inspired man will feel no difficulty in regard to the five books ascribed to Moses; but in regard to the rest of the history they desire to learn whether those events also "happened figuratively." We must note the quotation in the epistle to the Romans: "I have left for myself seven thousand men, who have not bowed the knee to Baal," found in the third book of the Kings. Here Paul has taken it to stand for those who are Israelites "according to election," for not only are the gentiles benefited by the coming of Christ, but also some who belong to the divine race.

7. This being so, we must outline what seems to us to be the marks of a true understanding of the scriptures. And in the first place we must point out that the aim of the Spirit who, by the providence of God through the Word who was "in the beginning with God," enlightened the servants of the truth, that is, the prophets and apostles, was pre-eminently concerned with the affairs of men—and by men I mean at the present moment souls that make use of bodies—his purpose being that the man who is capable of being taught might by "searching out" and devoting himself to the "deep things" revealed in the spiritual meaning of the words become partaker of all the doctrines of the Spirit's counsel

And when we speak of the needs of souls, who cannot otherwise reach perfection except through the rich and wise truth about God, we attach of necessity pre-eminent importance to the doctrines concerning God and His only-begotten Son; of what nature the Son is, and in what manner he can be the Son of God, and what are the causes of his descending to the level of human flesh and completely assuming humanity; and what, also, is the nature of his activity, and towards whom and at what times it is exercised. It was necessary, too, that the doctrines concerning beings akin to man and the rest of the rational creatures, both those that are nearer the divine and those that have fallen from blessedness, and the causes of the fall of these latter, should be included in the accounts of the divine teaching; and the question of the differences between souls and how these differences arose, and what the world is and why it exists, and further, how it comes about that evil is so widespread and so terrible on earth, and whether it is not only to be found on earth but also in other places—all this it was necessary that we should learn.

8. Now while these and similar subjects were in the mind of the Spirit who enlightened the souls of the holy servants of the truth, there was a second aim, pursued for the sake of those who were unable to endure the burden of investigating matters of such importance. This was to conceal the doctrine relating to the before-mentioned subjects in words forming a narrative that contained a record dealing with the visible creation, the formation of man and the successive descendants of the first human beings until the time when they became many; and also in other stories that recorded the acts of righteous men and the sins that these same men occasionally committed, seeing they were but human, and the deeds of wickedness, licentiousness and greed done by lawless and impious men.

But the most wonderful thing is, that by means of stories of wars and the conquerors and the conquered certain secret of the truths are revealed to those who are capable of examining these narratives; and, even more marvelous, through a written system of law the laws of truth are prophetically indicated, all these having been recorded in a series with a power which is truly appropriate to the wisdom of God. For the intention was to make even the outer covering of the spiritual truths, I mean the bodily part of the scriptures, in many respects not unprofitable but capable of improving the multitude in so far as they receive it.

But if the usefulness of the law and the sequence and ease of the narrative were at first sight clearly discernible throughout, we should be unaware that there was anything beyond the obvious meaning for us to understand in the scriptures. Consequently the Word of God has arranged for certain stumbling-blocks, as it were, and hindrances and impossibilities to be inserted in the midst of the law and the history, in order that we may not be completely drawn away by the sheer attractiveness of the language, and so either reject the true doctrines absolutely, on the ground that we learn from the scriptures nothing worthy of God, or else by never moving away from the letter fail to learn anything of the more divine element.

And we must also know this, that because the principal aim was to announce the connection that exists among spiritual events, those that have already happened and those that are yet to come to pass, whenever the Word found that things which had happened in history could be harmonized with these mystical events he used them, concealing from the multitude their deeper meaning. But wherever in the narrative the accomplishment of some particular deeds, which had been previously recorded for the sake of their more mystical meanings, did not correspond with the sequence of the intellectual truths, the scripture wove into the story something which did not happen and occasionally something which might have happened but in fact did not. Sometimes a few words are inserted which in the bodily sense are not true, and at other times a greater number.

A similar method can be discerned also in the law, where it is often possible to find a precept that is useful for its own sake, and suitable to the time the law was given. Sometimes, however, the precept does not appear to be useful. At other times even impossibilities are recorded in the law for the sake of the more skillful and inquiring readers, in order that these, by giving themselves to the toil of examining what is written, may gain a sound conviction of the necessity of seeking in such instances a meaning worthy of God.

And not only did the Spirit supervise the writings which were previous to the coming of Christ, but because he is the same Spirit and proceeds from the one God he has dealt in like manner with the gospels and the writings of the apostles. For the history even of these is not everywhere pure, events being woven together in the bodily sense without having actually happened; nor do the law and the commandments contained therein entirely declare what is reasonable.

Chapter 3: The Principle Underlying the Obsurities in Divine Scripture and Its Impossible or Unreasonable Character in Places, If Taken Literally

1. Now what man of intelligence will believe that the first and the second and the third day, and the evening and the morning existed without the sun and moon and stars? And that the first day, if we may so call it, was even without a heaven? And who is so silly as to believe that God, after the manner of a farmer, "planted a paradise eastward in Eden," and set in it a visible and palpable "tree of life," of such a sort that anyone who tasted its fruit with his bodily teeth would gain life; and again that one could partake of "good and evil" by masticating the fruit taken from the tree of that name? And when God is said to "walk in the paradise in the cool of the day" and Adam to hide himself behind a tree, I do not think anyone will doubt that these are figurative expressions which indicate certain mysteries through a semblance of history and not through actual events.

Further, when Cain "goes out from the face of God" it seems clear to thoughtful men that this statement impels the reader to inquire what the "face of God" is and how anyone can "go out" from it. And what more need I say, when those who are not altogether blind can collect thousands of such instances, recorded as actual events, but which did not happen literally?

Even the gospels are full of passages of this kind, as when the devil takes Jesus up into a "high mountain" in order to show him from thence "the kingdoms of the whole world and the glory of them." For what man who does not read such passages carelessly would fail to condemn those who believe that with the eye of the flesh, which requires a great height to enable us to perceive what is below and at our feet, the kingdoms of the Persians, Scythians, Indians and Parthians were seen, and the manner in which their rulers are glorified by men? And the careful reader will detect thousands of other passages like this in the gospels, which will convince him that events which did not take place at all are woven into the records of what literally did happen.

2. And to come to the Mosaic legislation, many of the laws, so far as their literal observance is concerned, are clearly irrational, while others are impossible. An example of irrationality is the prohibition to eat vultures, seeing that nobody even in the worst famine was ever driven by want to the extremity of eating these creatures. And in regard to the command that children of eight days old who are uncircumcised "shall be destroyed from among their people," if the law relating to these children were really meant to be carried out according to the letter, the proper course would be to order the death of their fathers or those by whom they were being brought up. But as it is the Scripture says: "Every male that is uncircumcised, who shall not be circumcised on the eighth day, shall be destroyed from among his people."

And if you would like to see some impossibilities that are enacted in the law, let us observe that the goat-stag, which Moses commands us to offer in sacrifice as a clean animal, is a creature that cannot possibly exist; while as to the griffin, which the lawgiver forbids to be eaten, there is no record that it has ever fallen into the hands of man. Moreover in regard to the celebrated sabbath, a careful reader will see that the command, "Ye shall sit each one in your dwellings; let none of you go out from his place on the Sabbath day," is an impossible one to observe literally, for no living creature could sit for a whole day and not move from his seat.

Consequently the members of the circumcision and all those who maintain that nothing more than the actual wording is signified make no inquiry whatever into some matters, such as the goat-stag, the griffin and the vulture, while on others they babble copiously, bringing forward lifeless traditions, as for instance when they say, in reference to the Sabbath, that each man's "place" is two thousand cubits. Others, however, among whom is Dositheus the Samaritan, condemn such an interpretation, and believe that in whatever position a man is found on the Sabbath day he should remain there until evening.

Further, the command "not to carry a burden on the sabbath day" is impossible; and on this account the teachers of the Jews have indulged in endless chatter, asserting that one kind of shoe is a burden, but another is not, and that a sandal with nails is a burden, but one without nails is not, and that what is carried on one shoulder is a burden, but not what is carried on both.

3. If now we approach the gospel in search of similar instances, what can be more irrational than the command: "Salute no man by the way," which simple people believe that the Savior enjoined upon the apostles? Again, to speak of the right cheek being struck is most incredible, for every striker, unless he suffers from some unnatural defect, strikes the left cheek with his right hand. And it is impossible to accept the precept from the gospel about the "right eye that offends"; for granting the possibility of a person being "offended" through his sense of sight, how can the blame be attributed to the right eye, when there are two eyes that see? And what man, even supposing he accuses himself of "looking on a woman to lust after her" and attributes the blame to his right eye alone, would act rationally if he were to cast this eye away?

Further, the apostle lays down this precept: "Was any called being circumcised? Let him not become uncircumcised." Now in the first place anyone who wishes can see that these words have no relation to the subject in hand: and how can we help thinking that they have been inserted at random, when we remember that the apostle is here laying down precepts about marriage and purity? In the second place who will maintain that it is wrong for a man to put himself into a condition of uncircumcision, if that were possible, in view of the disgrace which is felt by most people to attach to circumcision?

4. We have mentioned all these instances with the object of showing that the aim of the divine power which bestowed on us the holy scriptures is not that we should accept only what is found in the letter; for occasionally the records taken in a literal sense are not true, but actually absurd and impossible, and even with the history that actually happened and the legislation that is in its literal sense useful there are other matters interwoven.

But someone may suppose that the former statement refers to all the scriptures, and may suspect us of saying that because some of the history did not happen, therefore none of it happened; and because a certain law is irrational or impossible when taken literally, therefore no laws ought to be kept to the letter; or that the records of the Savior's life are not true in a physical sense; or that no law or commandment of his ought to be obeyed. We must assert, therefore, that in regard to some things we are clearly aware that the historical fact is true; as that Abraham was buried in the double cave at Hebron, together with Isaac and Jacob and one wife of each of them; and that Shechem was given as a portion to Joseph; and that Jerusalem is the chief city of Judea, in which a temple of God was built by Solomon; and thousands of other facts. For the passages which are historically true are far more numerous than those which are composed with purely spiritual meanings.

And again, who would deny that the command which says: "Honor thy father and thy mother, that it may be well with thee," is useful quite apart from any spiritual interpretation, and that it ought certainly to be observed, especially when we remember that the apostle Paul has quoted it in the self-same words? And what are we to say of the following: "Thou shalt not kill; thou shalt not commit adultery; thou shalt not steal; thou shalt not bear false witness"?

Once again, in the gospel there are commandments written which need no inquiry whether they are to be kept literally or not, as that which says, "I say unto you, whosoever is angry with his brother," and what follows; and, "I say unto you, swear not at all." Here, too, is an injunction of the apostle of which the literal meaning must be retained: "Admonish the disorderly, encourage the faint-hearted, support the weak, be longsuffering toward all"; though in the case of the more earnest readers it is possible to preserve each of the meanings, that is, while not setting aside the commandment in its literal sense, to preserve the "depths of the wisdom of God."

5. Nevertheless the exact reader will hesitate in regard to some passages, finding himself unable to decide without considerable investigation whether a particular incident, believed to be history, actually happened or not, and whether the literal meaning of a particular law is to be observed or not. Accordingly he who reads in an exact manner must, in obedience to the Savior's precept which says, "Search the scriptures," carefully investigate how far the literal meaning is true and how far it is impossible, and to the utmost of his power must trace out from the use of similar expressions the meaning scattered everywhere through the scriptures of that which when taken literally is impossible.

When therefore, as will be clear to those who read, the passage as a connected whole is literally impossible, whereas the outstanding part of it is not impossible but even true, the reader must endeavor to grasp the entire meaning, connecting by an intellectual process the account of what is literally impossible with the parts that are not impossible but are historically true, these being interpreted allegorically in common with the parts which, so far as the letter goes, did not happen at all. For our contention with regard to the whole of divine scripture is, that it all has a spiritual meaning, but not all a bodily meaning; for the bodily meaning is often proved to be an impossibility. Consequently the man who reads the divine books reverently, believing them to be divine writings, must exercise great care. And the method of understanding them appears to us to be as follows.

6. The accounts tell us that God chose out a certain nation on the earth, and they call this nation by many names. For the nation as a whole is called Israel, and it is also spoken of as Jacob. But when it was divided in the days of Jeroboam the son of Nebat, the ten tribes said to have been subject to him were named Israel, and the other two together with the tribe of Levi, which were ruled over by other men of the seed of David, were called Judah. The entire country which was inhabited by men of this race and which had been given them by God, is Judea, the metropolis of which is Jerusalem, this being the mother city of a number of others whose names lie scattered about in many different places of scripture but are gathered together into one list in the book of Joshua the son of Nun.

This being so, the apostle, raising our spiritual apprehension to a high level, says somewhere: "Behold Israel after flesh," inferring that there is an Israel after the spirit. He says also in another place: "For it is not the children of the flesh that are children of God," nor are "all they Israel, who are of Israel."

And again: "Neither is he a Jew, who is one outwardly, nor is that circumcision, which is outward in the flesh; but he is a Jew, who is one inwardly, and circumcision is of the heart, in the spirit, not in the letter." For if we take the phrase "a Jew inwardly" as a test, we shall realize that as there is a race of bodily Jews, so, too, there is a race of those who are "Jews inwardly," the soul having acquired this nobility of race in virtue of certain unspeakable words. Moreover there are many prophecies spoken of Israel and Judah, which relate what is going to happen to them. And when we think of the extraordinary promises recorded about these people, promises that so far as literary style goes are poor and distinguished by no elevation or character that is worthy of a promise of God, is it not clear that they demand a mystical interpretation? Well, then, if the promises are of a spiritual kind though announced through material imagery, the people to whom the promises belong are not the bodily Israelites.

7. But we must not spend time discussing who is a "Jew inwardly" and who an Israelite "in the inner man," since the above remarks are sufficient for all who are not dull-witted. We will return to the subject before us and say that Jacob was the father of the twelve patriarchs, and they of the rulers of the people, and they in their turn of the Israelites who came after. Is it not the case, then, that the bodily Israelites carry back their descent to the rulers of the people, the rulers of the people to the patriarchs, and the patriarchs to Jacob and those still more ancient; whereas are not the spiritual Israelites, of whom the bodily ones were a type, descended from the clans, and the clans from the tribes, and the tribes from one whose birth was not bodily, like that of the others, but of a higher kind; and was not he born of Isaac, and Isaac descended from Abraham, while all go back to Adam, who the apostle says is Christ? For the origin of all families that are in touch with the God of the whole world began lower down with Christ, who comes next after the God and Father of the whole world and is thus the father of every soul, as Adam is the father of all men. And if Eve is interpreted by Paul as referring to the church, it is not surprising (seeing that Cain was born of Eve and all that come after him carry back their descent to Eve) that these two should be figures of the church; for in the higher sense all men take their beginning from the church.

8. Now if what we have stated about Israel, its tribes and its clans, is convincing, then when the Savior says, "I was not sent but unto the lost sheep of the house of Israel," we do not take these words in the same sense as the poor-minded Ebionites do (men whose very name comes from the poverty of their mind, for in Hebrew *ebion* is the word for poor), so as to suppose that Christ came especially to the Israelites after the flesh. For "it is not the children of the flesh that are children of God."

Again, the apostle gives us the following instances of teaching about Jerusalem: "The Jerusalem which is above is free, which is our mother"; and in another epistle: "But ye are come to Mount Zion and to the city of the living God, the heavenly Jerusalem, and to an innumerable company of angels, to the general assembly and church of the firstborn who are written in heaven."

If therefore Israel consists of souls, and Jerusalem is a city in heaven, it follows that the cities of Israel have for their mother city the Jerusalem in the heavens; and so consequently does Judea as a whole. [A sentence appears to be missing from the Greek at this point.]

In all prophecies concerning Jerusalem, therefore, and in all statements made about it, we must understand, if we listen to Paul's words as the words of God and the utterances of wisdom, that the scriptures are telling us about the heavenly city and the whole region which contains the cities of the holy land. Perhaps it is to these cities that the Savior lifts our attention when he gives to those who have deserved praise for the good use of their talents authority over ten or over five cities.

9. If therefore the prophecies relating to Judea, to Jerusalem, and to Israel, Judah and Jacob suggest to us, because we do not interpret them in a fleshly sense, mysteries such as these, it will follow also that the prophecies which relate to Egypt and the Egyptians, to Babylon and the Babylonians, to Tyre and the Tyrians, to Sidon and the Sidonians, or to any of the other nations, are not spoken solely of the bodily Egyptians, Babylonians, Tyrians and Sidonians. If the Israelites are spiritual, it follows that the Egyptians and Babylonians are also spiritual. For the statements made in Ezekiel about Pharaoh king of Egypt entirely fail to apply to any particular man who was or will be ruler of Egypt, as will be clear to those who study the passage carefully.

Similarly the statements concerning the ruler of Tyre cannot be understood of any particular man who is to rule over Tyre. And as for the numerous statements made about Nebuchadnezzar, especially in Isaiah, how is it possible to interpret them of that particular man? For the man Nebuchadnezzar neither "fell from heaven," nor was he the "morning star," nor did he "rise in the morning" over the earth.

Nor indeed will any man of intelligence interpret the statements made in Ezekiel concerning Egypt, that it shall be "laid waste forty years" so that "no foot of man" shall be found there, and that it shall be so overwhelmed with war, that throughout the whole land there shall be blood up to the knees, as referring to the Egypt which lies next to the Ethiopians whose bodies are blackened by the sun.

[From the Latin translation of Rufinus: Let us see, however whether the above passages may not be more worthily interpreted as follows. Just as there is a heavenly Jerusalem and Judea, and no doubt a people dwelling therein who are called Israel, so it is possible that near to these there exist certain other places, which apparently are called Egypt, or Babylon, or Tyre or Sydon; and the princes of these places and the souls, if there be any, who dwell in them, may be called Egyptians, Babylonians, Tyrians, and Sidonians. From among these souls, in accordance with the manner of life which they lead there, a kind of captivity would seem to have taken place, as a result of which they are said to have gone down from higher and better places into Egypt, or to have been scattered among other nations.]

10. And perhaps, just as people on earth, when they die the common death of all, are in consequence of the deeds done here so distributed as to obtain different positions according to the proportion of their sins, if they are judged to be worthy of the place called Hades; so the people there, when they die, if I may so speak, descend into this Hades, and are judged worthy of different habitations, better or worse, in the whole of this region of earth.

[Latin: For the other lower world, to which are conveyed the souls of those who die on earth, is called by scripture, I believe on account of this distinction, "the lower Hades," as it says in the Psalms, "And thou hast delivered my soul from the lower Hades." Each of those, therefore, who descend into the earth, is destined in accordance with his merits] and of being born of such or such parents, so that an Israelite will occasionally fall among Scythians and an Egyptian descend into Judea. Nevertheless the Savior came to gather together the "lost sheep of the house of Israel," and since many from Israel have not submitted to his teaching, those from the Gentiles are also called.

[Latin: It would appear to follow from this that the prophecies which are uttered concerning the various nations ought rather to be referred to souls and the different heavenly dwelling-places occupied by them. Moreover in regard to the records of events that are said to have happened to the nation of Israel, or to Jerusalem or Judea, when they were assailed by this people or that, there is need of careful inquiry and examination, seeing that in very many cases the events did not happen in a physical sense, to discover in what way these events are more suitably ascribed to those nations of souls who once dwelt in that heaven which is said to "pass away" or who may be supposed to dwell there even now.]

[From the Latin of Jerome, *Ep. ad Avitum,* 11: And since we have compared the souls who travel from this world to the lower regions to those souls who by a kind of death come from the height of heaven to our dwelling-places, we must thoughtfully inquire whether we may make this latter assertion in regard to the birth of every single soul. For in that case souls that are born on this earth of ours would either come from the lower world again to a higher place and assume a human body, in consequence of their desire for better things, or else would descend to us from better places. And so, too, those places which are above in the firmament may be occupied by some souls who have advanced from our seats to better things, and by others who have fallen from the heavenly places to the firmament and yet have not sinned deeply enough to be thrust into the lower places in which we dwell.]

[Latin: 11. If, however, anyone should demand of us clear and manifest declarations on these matters out of the holy scriptures, we must reply that it was the method of the Holy Spirit rather to conceal these truths and to hide them deeply underneath narratives which appear to be records of actual events, narratives in which people are said to go down into Egypt or to be led captive to Babylon, where some were greatly humiliated and put under bondage to masters, while others in the very places of their captivity were regarded as famous and illustrious, so that they held positions of power and leadership and were set to rule over nations.]

But these truths, as we think, have been concealed in the narratives. For "the kingdom of heaven is like unto a treasure hid in a field, which when a man findeth he hideth it, and for joy thereof goeth and selleth all that he hath, and buyeth that field." Now let us consider whether the outward aspect of scripture and its obvious and surface meaning does not here correspond to the field as a whole, full of all kinds of plants, whereas the truths that are stored away in it and not seen by all, but lie as if buried beneath the visible plants, are the hidden "treasures of wisdom and knowledge," which the Spirit speaking through Isaiah calls "dark and unseen and concealed."

These treasures require for their discovery the help of God, who alone is able to "break in pieces the gates of brass" that conceal them and to burst the iron bars that are upon gates, and so to make known all the truths taught in Genesis concerning the various legitimate races and as it were seeds of souls, whether closely akin to Israel or far apart from him, and the descent of the "seventy souls" into Egypt, in order that they may there become "as the stars of the heaven in multitude." But since not all who are sprung from these are a "light of the world," for "they are not all Israel, who are of Israel" there come from the seventy a people "even as the sand which is by the sea shore innumerable."

[Latin: 12. This descent of the holy fathers into Egypt, that is, into this world, will be seen to have been granted by the providence of God for the enlightenment of the rest of men and for the instruction of the human race, that through them all other souls might be enlightened and succored. "For to them first were entrusted the oracles of God," it being this people alone which is said to "see God"; for the name Israel when translated has this meaning. It follows at once that we must adapt and interpret in the light of these principles the statement that Egypt was scourged with ten plagues to allow God's people to depart, or the account of what happened to the people in the desert, or of the construction of the tabernacle by means of contributions from all the people, or of the weaving of the priestly garments, or the description of the vessels of the ministry; because, as it is written, these things truly contain within them a "shadow" and form of the "heavenly things." For Paul clearly says of them that they "serve a shadow and pattern of the heavenly things." In the same law there is also contained an account of the particular laws and institutions under which men are to live in the Holy Land. Threats, too, are held over those who shall transgress the law; and for those who stood in need of purification various kinds of purifications are given, adapted to men who were liable to frequent pollution; the object being that by means of these they should arrive at last at that one purification, after which they must not be polluted any more.

Moreover a reckoning is made of the number of this people, though not of all. For the childlike souls have not yet lived long enough to be numbered in accordance with the divine command; while those souls which cannot become the head of some other but are themselves subject to others as to a head, souls which the scripture terms "women," these, too, are not reckoned in that numbering which is ordered by God. Only those called men are numbered, in order to show that the former souls could not be numbered apart by themselves but that they are included in the number of those called men.

Especially, however, there come to the holy number they who are ready to go forth to the wars of Israel, they who can fight against those enemies and adversaries whom the Father puts in subjection to the Son who sits on his right hand, in order that he may destroy every principality and power. By these numbers of his soldiers, who because they are fighting for God do not entangle themselves in the affairs of this world, he intends to overthrow the kingdoms of the adversary. By these "the shields of faith" are borne and the "darts" of wisdom are hurled; on them gleams the helmet which is the hope of salvation, and the breastplate of charity guards their heart that is filled with God. Such are the soldiers who appear to me to be indicated in scripture, and such is the kind of warfare for which they are prepared who are ordered in the divine books to be numbered by God's command.

But far more renowned and perfect than these are they, the very hairs of whose head are said to be numbered. Those, however, who were punished for their sins, whose carcasses "fell in the wilderness," appear to me to bear a resemblance to those who, though they have made not a little progress, have yet been for various reasons quite unable to reach the goal of perfection; because they are said either to have murmured, or to have worshiped idols, or to have committed fornication, or to have planned some wickedness such as it is wrong for the mind even to think of.

Nor is the following fact, I believe, devoid of some mystical meaning, that certain of the people, who possess large flocks and much cattle, go and seize beforehand a region suitable for pasturing their flocks, which was the first of all the places that the right hand of the Israelites secured by war. This region they beg Moses to grant them, and consequently they are placed apart beyond the streams of Jordan and cut off from the occupation of the Holy Land. Now this Jordan would appear, when taken as a figure of the heavenly things, to water and flood the thirsty souls and minds that lie close beside it.

And here this other fact will not appear to be without significance, that it is Moses who hears from God all that is written down in the law of Leviticus, whereas in Deuteronomy it is the people who are represented as listening to Moses and learning from him what they could not hear from God. This indeed is why it is called Deuteronomy, meaning the second law; a fact which some will think points to this, that when the first law given through Moses came to an end, a second legislation was apparently composed, and this was specially delivered by Moses to his successor Joshua; and Joshua is certainly believed to be a figure of our Savior, by whose second law, that is, by the precepts of the Gospels, all things are brought to perfection.

13. We must also see, however, whether the scriptures may not perhaps indicate this further truth, that just as the legislation is presented with greater clearness and distinctness in Deuteronomy than in those books which were written at the first, so also we may gather from that coming of the Savior which he fulfilled in humility, when he "took upon him the form of a servant," an indication of the "more splendid and glorious second coming in the glory of his Father," at which coming when in the kingdom of heaven all the saints shall live by the laws of the "eternal gospel," the figure of Deuteronomy will be fulfilled; and just as by his present coming he has fulfilled that law which has a "shadow of the good things to come," so also by that glorious coming the shadow of his first coming will be fulfilled and brought to perfection. For the prophet has spoken of it thus: "The breath of our countenance is Christ the Lord, of whom we said that under his shadow we shall live among the

nations," that is, at the time when he shall duly transfer all the saints from the temporal to the eternal gospel, to use a phrase employed by John in the Apocalypse, where he speaks of the "eternal gospel."]

But if we continue our inquiries as far as the passion, to seek for this in the heavenly places will seem a bold thing to do. Yet if there are "spiritual hosts of wickedness" in the heavenly places, consider whether, just as we are not ashamed to confess that he was crucified here in order to destroy those whom he destroyed through his suffering, so we should not fear to allow that a similar event also happens there and will happen in the ages to come until the end of the whole world.

[Latin: 14. But in all these matters let it suffice us to conform our mind to the rule of piety and to think of the Holy Spirit's words not as a composition depending upon feeble human eloquence but in accordance with the sayings of scripture, "All the king's glory is within," and, "a treasure" of divine meanings lies hidden within the "frail vessel" of the poor letter. If, however, a reader is more curious and persists in asking for an explanation of every detail, let him come and hear along with us how the apostle Paul, scanning by the aid of the Holy Spirit, who "searches even the depths of God," the "depth of the divine wisdom and knowledge," and yet not being able to reach the end and to attain, if I may say so, an innermost knowledge, in his despair and amazement at the task cries out and says, "O the depth of the riches of the wisdom and knowledge of God!" And in what despair of reaching a perfect understanding he uttered this cry, hear him tell us himself: "How unsearchable are his judgments and his ways past finding out!" He did not say that God's judgments were hard to search out, but that they could not be searched out at all; not that his ways were hard to find out, but that they were impossible to find out. For however far one may advance in the search and make progress through an increasingly earnest study, even when aided and enlightened in mind by God's grace, he will never be able to reach the final goal of his inquiries.

For no created mind can by any means possess the capacity to understand all; but as soon as it has discovered a small fragment of what it is seeking, it again sees other things that must be sought for; and if in turn it comes to know these, it will again see arising out of them many more things that demand investigation. This is why Solomon, wisest of men, whose wisdom gave him a clear view of the nature of things, says: "I said, I will become wise; and wisdom herself was taken far from me, farther than she was before; and who shall find out her profound depth?" Moreover Isaiah, knowing that the beginnings of things could not be discovered by mortal nature, no, and not even by those natures which, though diviner than man's nature, are yet themselves made and created, knowing, I say, that none of these could discover either the beginning or the end says, "Tell ye the former things, what they were, and we shall know that ye are gods; or declare the last things, what they are, and then shall we see that ye are gods."

My Hebrew teacher also used to teach as follows, that since the beginning or the end of all things could not be comprehended by any except our Lord Jesus Christ and the Holy Spirit, this was the reason why Isaiah spoke of there being in the vision that appeared to him two seraphim only, who with two wings cover the face of God, with two cover his feet, and with two fly, crying one to another and saying, "Holy, holy, holy, is the Lord of hosts; the whole earth is full of thy glory." For because the two seraphim alone have their wings over the face of God and over his feet, we may venture to declare that neither the armies of the holy angels, nor the holy thrones, nor the dominions, nor principalities, nor powers can wholly know the beginnings of all things and the ends of the universe. We must understand, however, that those holy spirits and powers who are here enumerated are nearest to the very beginnings of things and reach a point which the rest of creation cannot attain to. Nevertheless whatever it is that these powers may have learned through the revelation of the Son of God and of the Holy Spirit—and they will certainly be able to acquire a great deal of knowledge, and the higher ones much more than the lower—still it is impossible for them to comprehend everything; for it is written, "The more part of God's works are secret."

It is therefore to be desired that each one according to his capacity will ever "reach out to the things which are before, forgetting those things which are behind," that is, will reach out both to better works and also to a clearer understanding and knowledge, through Jesus Christ our Savior, to whom is the glory for ever.

15. Let everyone, then, who cares for truth, care little about names and words, for different kinds of speech are customary in different nations. Let him be more anxious about the fact signified than about the words by which it is signified, and particularly in questions of such difficulty and importance as these. For example, we may inquire whether there exists any substance in which we can discern neither color nor shape nor possibility of touch nor size, a substance perceptible to the mind alone, which anyone can call whatever he pleases. The Greeks speak of this substance as *asomaton,* or incorporeal; but the divine scriptures call it "invisible"; for the apostle declares that God is invisible,

when he says that Christ is the "image of the invisible God." On the other hand he says that "all things, visible and invisible, were created through Christ." Here it is asserted that there exist even among created things certain existences which are in their own nature invisible. These, however, while not in themselves corporeal, yet make use of bodies, though they themselves are superior to bodily substance. But the substance of the Trinity, which is the beginning and cause of all things, "of which are all things and through which are all things and in which are all things," must not be believed either to be a body or to exist in a body, but to be wholly incorporeal.

Let it suffice, however, for us to have spoken briefly on these matters, in a digression indeed, but one which has been forced upon us by the necessities of the subject. Our aim has been to show that there are certain things, the meaning of which it is impossible adequately to explain by any human language, but which are made clear rather through simple apprehension than through any power of words. This rule must control our interpretation even of the divine writings, in order that what is said therein may be estimated in accordance not with the meanness of the language but with the divine power of the Holy Spirit who inspired their composition.

CHAPTER 3

ELOQUENCE IN CAPPADOCIA

GREGORY NAZIANZEN: PANEGYRIC ON HIS BROTHER CAESARIUS

(Oration 7)

*The preaching of Gregory offers an opportunity to see forms of early Christian proclamation other than the homily, especially the genre of epideictic, the genre of praise and blame. He employed this genre especially for his funerary sermons, the most famous of which is that for Basil of Caesarea (**See Vol. 1, pp. 62-63,** for discussion). A more convenient place to study that form, however, is Gregory's sermon on his brother Caesarius, which, while only a third as long as that on Basil, still follows all the rules of the rhetorical manuals for an encomium.*[1] *The translation below is taken from* NPNF[2], *7:229-38.*

[Proem]

1. It may be, my friends, my brethren, my fathers (ye who are dear to me in reality as well as in name) that you think that I, who am about to pay the sad tribute of lamentation to him who has departed, am eager to

undertake the task, and shall, as most men delight to do, speak at great length and in eloquent style. And so some of you, who have had like sorrows to bear, are prepared to join in my mourning and lamentation, in order to bewail your own griefs in mine, and learn to feel pain at the afflictions of a friend, while others are looking to feast their ears in the enjoyment of my words. For they suppose that I must needs make my misfortune an occasion for display—as was once my wont, when possessed of a superabundance of earthly things, and ambitious, above all, of oratorical renown—before I looked up to Him Who is the true and highest Word, and gave all up to God, from Whom all things come, and took God for all in all. Now pray do not think this of me, if you wish to think of me aright. For I am neither going to lament for him who is gone more than is good—as I should not approve of such conduct even in others—nor am I going to praise him beyond due measure. Albeit that language is a dear and especially proper tribute to one gifted with it, and eulogy to one who was exceedingly fond of my words—aye, not only a tribute, but a debt, the most just of all debts. But even in my tears and admiration I must respect the law which regards such matters: nor is this alien to our philosophy; for [it] says The memory of the just is accompanied with eulogies, [Prov. 10:7, LXX] and also, Let tears fall down over the dead, and begin to lament, as if thou hadst suffered great harm thyself" [Ecclus. 38:16]: removing us equally from insensibility and immoderation. I shall proceed then, not only to exhibit the weakness of human nature, but also to put you in mind of the dignity of the soul, and, giving such consolation as is due to those who are in sorrow, transfer our grief, from that which concerns the flesh and temporal things, to those things which are spiritual and eternal.

[Parents]

2. The parents of Caesarius, to take first the point which best becomes me, are known to you all. Their excellence you are eager to notice, and hear of with admiration, and share in the task of setting it forth to any, if there be such, who know it not: for no single man is able to do so entirely, and the task is one beyond the powers of a single tongue, however laborious, however zealous. Among the many and great points for which they are to be celebrated (I trust I may not seem extravagant in praising my own family) the greatest of all, which more than any other stamps their character, is piety. By their hoar hairs they lay claim to reverence, but they are no less venerable for their virtue than for their age; for while their bodies are bent beneath the burden of their years, their souls renew their youth in God.

3. His father was well grafted out of the wild olive tree into the good one, and so far partook of its fatness as to be entrusted with the engrafting of others, and charged with the culture of souls, presiding in a manner becoming his high office over this people, like a second Aaron or Moses, bidden himself to draw near to God, and to convey the Divine Voice to the others who stand afar off; gentle, meek, calm in mien, fervent in spirit, a fine man in external appearance, but richer still in that which is out of sight. But why should I describe him whom you know? For I could not even by speaking at great length say as much as he deserves, or as much as each of you knows and expects to be said of him. It is then better to leave your own fancy to picture him, than mutilate by my words the object of your admiration.

4. His mother was consecrated to God by virtue of her descent from a saintly family, and was possessed of piety as a necessary inheritance, not only for herself, but also for her children—being indeed a holy lump from a holy firstfruits. And this she so far increased and amplified that some, (bold though the statement be, I will utter it,) have both believed and said that even her husband's perfection has been the work of none other than herself; and, oh how wonderful! she herself, as the reward of her piety, has received a greater and more perfect piety. Lovers of their children and of Christ as they both were, what is most extraordinary, they were far greater lovers of Christ than of their children: yea, even their one enjoyment of their children was that they should be acknowledged and named by Christ, and their one measure of their blessedness in their children was their virtue and close association with the Chief Good. Compassionate, sympathetic, snatching many a treasure from moths and robbers, and from the prince of this world, to transfer it from their sojourn here to the [true] habitation, laying up in store for their children the heavenly splendour as their greatest inheritance. Thus have they reached a fair old age, equally reverend both for virtue and for years, and full of days, alike of those which abide and those which pass away; each one failing to secure the first prize here below only so far as equalled by the other; yea, they have fulfilled the measure of every happiness with the exception of this last trial, or discipline, whichever anyone may think we ought to call it: I mean their having to send before them the child who was, owing to his age, in greater danger of falling, and so to close their life in safety, and be translated with all their family to the realms above.

5. I have entered into these details, not from a desire to eulogize them, for this, I know well, it would be difficult worthily to do, if I made their praise the subject of my whole oration, but to set forth the excellence

inherited from his parents by Caesarius and so prevent you from being surprised or incredulous that one sprung from such progenitors should have deserved such praises himself; nay, strange indeed would it have been, had he looked to others and disregarded the examples of his kinsfolk at home. His early life was such as becomes those really well born and destined for a good life. I say little of his qualities evident to all, his beauty, his stature, his manifold gracefulness, and harmonious disposition, as shown in the tones of his voice—for it is not my office to laud qualities of this kind, however important they may seem to others—and proceed with what I have to say of the points which, even if I wished, I could with difficulty pass by.

[Education]

6. Bred and reared under such influences, we were fully trained in the education afforded here, in which none could say how far he excelled most of us from the quickness and extent of his abilities—and how can I recall those days without my tears showing that, contrary to my promises, my feelings have overcome my philosophic restraint? The time came when it was decided that we should leave home, and then for the first time we were separated, for I studied rhetoric in the then flourishing schools of Palestine; he went to Alexandria, esteemed both then and now the home of every branch of learning. Which of his qualities shall I place first and foremost, or which can I omit with least injury to my description? Who was more faithful to his teacher than he? Who more kindly to his classmates? Who more carefully avoided the society and companionship of the depraved? Who attached himself more closely to that of the most excellent, and among others, of the most esteemed and illustrious of his countrymen? For he knew that we are strongly influenced to virtue or vice by our companions. And in consequence of all this, who was more honored by the authorities than he, and whom did the whole city (though all individuals are concealed in it, because of its size), esteem more highly for his discretion, or deem more illustrious for his intelligence?

7. What branch of learning did he not master, or rather, in what branch of study did he not surpass those who had made it their sole study? Whom did he allow even to approach him, not only of his own time and age, but even of his elders, who had devoted many more years to study? All subjects he studied as one, and each as thoroughly as if he knew no other. The brilliant in intellect, he surpassed in industry, the devoted students in quickness of perception; nay, rather he outstripped in rapidity those who were rapid, in application those who were laborious,

and in both respects those who were distinguished in both. From geometry and astronomy, that science so dangerous to anyone else, he gathered all that was helpful (I mean that he was led by the harmony and order of the heavenly bodies to reverence their Maker), and avoided what is injurious; not attributing all things that are or happen to the influence of the stars, like those who raise their own fellow-servant, the creation, in rebellion against the Creator, but referring, as is reasonable, the motion of these bodies, and all other things besides, to God. In arithmetic and mathematics, and in the wonderful art of medicine, in so far as it treats of physiology and temperament, and the causes of disease, in order to remove the roots and so destroy their offspring with them who is there so ignorant or contentious as to think him inferior to himself, and not to be glad to be reckoned next to him, and carry off the second prize? This indeed is no unsupported assertion, but East and West alike, and every place which he afterward visited, are as pillars inscribed with the record of his learning.

[Career]

8. But when, after gathering into his single soul every kind of excellence and knowledge, as a mighty merchantman gathers every sort of ware, he was voyaging to his own city, in order to communicate to others the fair cargo of his culture, there befell a wondrous thing, which I must, as its mention is most cheering to me and may delight you, briefly set forth. Our mother, in her motherly love for her children, had offered up a prayer that, as she had sent us forth together, she might see us together return home. For we seemed, to our mother at least, if not to others, to form a pair worthy of her prayers and glances, if seen together, though now, alas, our connection has been severed. And God, Who hears a righteous prayer, and honours the love of parents for well-disposed children, so ordered that, without any design or agreement on our part, the one from Alexandria, the other from Greece, the one by sea, the other by land, we arrived at the same city at the same time. This city was Byzantium, which now presides over Europe, in which Caesarius, after the lapse of a short time, gained such a repute, that public honours, an alliance with an illustrious family, and a seat in the council of state were offered him; and a mission was despatched to the Emperor by public decision, to beg that the first of cities be adorned and honoured by the first of scholars (if he cared at all for its being indeed the first, and worthy of its name); and that to all its other titles to distinction this further one be added, that it was embellished by having Caesarius as its

physician and its inhabitant, although its brilliancy was already assured by its throngs of great men both in philosophy and other branches of learning. But enough of this. At this time there happened what seemed to others a chance without reason or cause, such as frequently occurs of its own accord in our day, but was more than sufficiently manifest to devout minds as the result of the prayers to god-fearing parents, which were answered by the united arrival of their sons by land and sea.

9. Well, among the noble traits of Caesarius' character, we must not fail to note one, which perhaps is in others' eyes slight and unworthy of mention, but seemed to me, both at the time and since, of the highest import, if indeed brotherly love be a praiseworthy quality; nor shall I ever cease to place it in the first rank, in relating the story of his life. Although the metropolis strove to retain him by the honours I have mentioned, and declared that it would under no circumstances let him go, my influence, which he valued most highly on all occasions, prevailed upon him to listen to the prayer of his parents, to supply his country's need, and to grant me my own desire. And when he thus returned home in my company, he preferred me not only to cities and peoples, not only to honours and revenues, which had in part already flowed to him in abundance from many sources and in part were within his reach, but even to the Emperor himself and his imperial commands. From this time, then, having shaken off all ambition, as a hard master and a painful disorder, I resolved to practice philosophy and adapt myself to the higher life; or rather the desire was earlier born, the life came later. But my brother, who had dedicated to his country the firstfruits of his learning, and gained an admiration worthy of his efforts, was afterwards led by the desire of fame, and, as he persuaded me, of being the guardian of the city, to betake himself to court, not indeed according to my own wishes or judgment; for I will confess to you that I think it a better and grander thing to be in the lowest rank with God than to win the first place with an earthly king. Nevertheless I cannot blame him, for inasmuch as philosophy is the greatest, so it is the most difficult, of professions, which can be taken in hand by but few, and only by those who have been called forth by the Divine magnanimity, which gives its hand to those who are honoured by its preference. Yet it is no small thing if one, who has chosen the lower form of life, follows after goodness, and sets greater store on God and his own salvation than on earthly lustre; using it as a stage, or a manifold ephemeral mask while playing in the drama of this world, but himself living unto God with that image which he knows that he has received from Him and must render to Him Who gave it. That this was certainly the purpose of Caesarius, we know full well.

10. Among the physicians he gained the foremost place with no great trouble, by merely exhibiting his capacity, or rather some slight specimen of his capacity, and was forthwith numbered among the friends of the Emperor, and enjoyed the highest honours. But he placed the humane functions of his art at the disposal of the authorities free of cost, knowing that nothing leads to further advancement than virtue and renown for honourable deeds; so that he far surpassed in fame those to whom he was inferior in rank. By his modesty he so won the love of all that they entrusted their precious charges to his care, without requiring him to be sworn by Hippocrates since the simplicity of Crates was nothing to his own: winning in general a respect beyond his rank; for besides the present repute he was ever thought to have justly won, a still greater one was anticipated for him, both by the Emperors themselves and by all who occupied the nearest positions to them. But, most important, neither by his fame, nor by the luxury which surrounded him, was his nobility of soul corrupted; for amidst his many claims to honour, he himself cared most for being, and being known to be, a Christian, and, compared with this, all other things were to him but trifling toys. For they belong to the part we play before others on a stage which is very quickly set up and taken down again—perhaps indeed more quickly destroyed than put together, as we may see from the manifold changes of life, and fluctuations of prosperity; while the only real and securely abiding good thing is godliness.

[Struggle with Julian the Apostate]

11. Such was the philosophy of Caesarius, even at court: these were the ideas amidst which he lived and died, discovering and presenting to God, in the hidden man, a still deeper godliness than was publicly visible. And if I must pass by all else, his protection of his kinsmen in distress, his contempt for arrogance, his freedom from assumption towards friends, his boldness towards men in power, the numerous contests and arguments in which he engaged with many on behalf of the truth, not merely for the sake of argument, but with deep piety and fervour, I must speak of one point at least as especially worthy of note. The Emperor of unhappy memory was raging against us, whose madness in rejecting Christ, after making himself its first victim, had now rendered him intolerable to others; though he did not, like other fighters against Christ, grandly enlist himself on the side of impiety, but veiled his persecution under the form of equity; and, ruled by the crooked serpent which possessed his soul, dragged down into his own pit his wretched victims by

manifold devices. His first artifice and contrivance was, to deprive us of the honour of our conflicts (for, noble man as he was, he grudged this to Christians), by causing us, who suffered for being Christians, to be punished as evil doers: the second was, to call this process persuasion, and not tyranny, so that the disgrace of those who chose to side with impiety might be greater than their danger. Some he won over by money, some by dignities, some by promises, some by various honours, which he bestowed, not royally but in right servile style, in the sight of all, while everyone was influenced by the witchery of his words, and his own example. At last he assailed Caesarius. How utter was the derangement and folly which could hope to take for his prey a man like Caesarius, my brother, the son of parents like ours!

12. However, that I may dwell awhile upon this point, and luxuriate in my story as men do who are eyewitnesses in some marvelous event, that noble man, fortified with the sign of Christ, and defending himself with His Mighty Word, entered the lists against an adversary experienced in arms and strong in his skill in argument. In no wise abashed at the sight, nor shrinking at all from his high purpose through flattery, he was an athlete ready, both in word and deed, to meet a rival of equal power. Such then was the arena, and so equipped the champion of godliness. The judge on one side was Christ, arming the athlete with His own sufferings: and on the other a dreadful tyrant, persuasive by his skill in argument, and overawing him by the weight of his authority; and as spectators, on either hand, both those who were still left on the side of godliness and those who had been snatched away by him, watching whether victory inclined to their own side or to the other, and more anxious as to which would gain the day than the combatants themselves.

13. Didst thou not fear for Caesarius, lest aught unworthy of his zeal should befall him? Nay, be ye of good courage. For the victory is with Christ, Who overcame the world. Now for my part, be well assured, I should be highly interested in setting forth the details of the arguments and allegations used on that occasion, for indeed the discussion contains certain feats and elegances, which I dwell on with no slight pleasure; but this would be quite foreign to an occasion and discourse like the present.

And when, after having torn to shreds all his opponent's sophistries, and thrust aside as mere child's play every assault, veiled or open, Caesarius in a loud clear voice declared that he was and remained a Christian—not even thus was he finally dismissed. For indeed, the Emperor was possessed by an eager desire to enjoy and be distinguished by his culture, and then uttered in the hearing of all his famous saying—O happy father, O unhappy sons! thus deigning to honour me, whose culture and godliness he had known at Athens, with a share in the dishonour of Caesarius, who was remanded for a further trial (since Justice was fitly arming the Emperor against the Persians), and welcomed by us after his happy escape and bloodless victory, as more illustrious for his dishonour than for his celebrity.

14. This victory I esteem far more sublime and honourable than the Emperor's mighty power and splendid purple and costly diadem. I am more elated in describing it than if he had won from him the half of his empire. During the evil days he lived in retirement, obedient herein to our Christian law, which bids us, when occasion offers, to make ventures on behalf of the truth, and not be traitors to our religion from cowardice; yet refrain, as long as may be, from rushing into danger, either in fear for our own souls, or to spare those who bring the danger upon us. But when the gloom had been dispersed, and the righteous sentence had been pronounced in a foreign land, and the glittering sword had struck down the ungodly, and power had returned to the hands of Christians, what boots it to say with what glory and honour, with how many and great testimonies, as if bestowing rather than receiving a favour, he was welcomed again at the Court; his new honour succeeding to that of former days; while time changed its Emperors, the repute and commanding influence of Caesarius with them was undisturbed; nay, they vied with each other in striving to attach him most closely to themselves, and be known as his special friends and acquaintances. Such was the godliness of Caesarius, such its results. Let all men, young and old, give ear, and press on through the same virtue to the same distinction, for glorious is the fruit of good labours if they suppose this to be worth striving after, and a part of true happiness.

[Death]

15. Again another wonder concerning him is a strong argument for his parents' piety and his own. He was living in Bithynia, holding an office of no small importance from the Emperor, viz., the stewardship of his revenue, and care of the exchequer: for this had been assigned to him by the Emperor as a prelude to the highest offices. And when, a short time ago, the earthquake in Nicaea occurred, which is said to have been the most serious within the memory of man, overwhelming in a common destruction almost all the inhabitants and the beauty of the city, he alone, or with very few of the men of rank, survived the danger, being shielded by the very falling ruins in his incredible escape, and bearing slight traces of the peril; yet he allowed fear to lead him to a more important

salvation, for he dedicated himself entirely to the Supreme Providence; he renounced the service of transitory things, and attached himself to another court. This he both purposed himself, and made the object of the united earnest prayers to which he invited me by letter, when I seized this opportunity to give him warning, as I never ceased to do when pained that his great nature should be occupied in affairs beneath it, and that a soul so fitted for philosophy should, like the sun behind a cloud, be obscured amid the whirl of public life. Unscathed though he had been by the earthquake, he was not proof against disease, since he was but human. His escape was peculiar to himself; his death common to all mankind; the one the token of his piety, the other the result of his nature. The former, for our consolation, preceded his fate, so that, though shaken by his death, we might exult in the extraordinary character of his preservation. And now our illustrious Caesarius has been restored to us, when his honoured dust and celebrated corse, after being escorted home amidst a succession of hymns and public orations, has been honoured by the holy hands of his parents; while his mother, substituting the festal garments of religion for the trappings of woe, has overcome her tears by her philosophy, and lulled to sleep lamentations by psalmody, as her son enjoys honours worthy of his newly regenerate soul, which has been, through water, transformed by the Spirit.

[Lamentation]

16. This, Caesarius, is my funeral offering to thee, this the firstfruits of my words, which thou hast often blamed me for withholding, yet wouldst have stripped off, had they been bestowed on thee; with this ornament I adorn thee, an ornament, I know well, far dearer to thee than all others, though it be not of the soft flowing tissues of silk, in which while living with virtue for thy sole adorning, thou didst not, like the many, rejoice; nor texture of transparent linen, nor outpouring of costly unguents, which thou hadst long resigned to the boudoirs of the fair; with their sweet savours lasting but a single day; nor any other small thing valued by small minds, which would have all been hidden today with thy fair form by this bitter stone. Far hence be games and stories of the Greeks, the honors of ill-fated youths, with their petty prizes for petty contests; and all the libations and firstfruits or garlands and newly plucked flowers, wherewith men honor the departed, in obedience to ancient custom and unreasoning grief, rather than reason. My gift is an oration, which perhaps succeeding time will receive at my hand and ever keep in motion, that it may not suffer him who has left us to be utterly

lost to earth, but may ever keep him whom we honour in men's ears and minds, as it sets before them, more clearly than a portrait, the image of him for whom we mourn.

17. Such is my offering; if it be slight and inferior to his merit, God loveth that which is according to our power. Part of our gift is now complete, the remainder we will now pay by offering (those of us who still survive) every year our honours and memorials. And now for thee, sacred and holy soul, we pray for an entrance into heaven; mayest thou enjoy such repose as the bosom of Abraham affords, mayest thou behold the choir of Angels, and the glories and splendours of sainted men; aye, mayest thou be united to that choir and share in their joy, looking down from on high on all things here, on what men call wealth, and despicable dignities, and deceitful honours, and the errors of our senses, and the tangle of this life, and its confusion and ignorance, as if we were fighting in the dark; whilst thou art in attendance upon the Great King and filled with the light which streams forth from Him: and may it be ours hereafter, receiving therefrom no such slender rivulet, as is the object of our fancy in this day of mirrors and enigmas, to attain to the fount of good itself, gazing with pure mind upon the truth in its purity, finding a reward for our eager toil here below on behalf of the good, in our more perfect possession and vision of the good on high: the end to which our sacred books and teachers foretell that our course of divine mysteries shall lead us.

[Consolation]

18. What now remains? To bring the healing of the Word to those in sorrow. And a powerful remedy for mourners is sympathy, for sufferers are best consoled by those who have to bear a like suffering. To such, then, I specially address myself, of whom I should be ashamed, if, with all other virtues, they do not show the elements of patience. For even if they surpass all others in love of their children, let them equally surpass them in love of wisdom and love of Christ, and in the special practice of meditation on our departure hence, impressing it likewise on their children, making even their whole life a preparation for death. But if your misfortune still clouds your reason and, like the moisture which dims our eyes, hides from you the clear view of your duty, come, ye elders, receive the consolation of a young man, ye fathers, that of a child, who ought to be admonished by men as old as you, who have admonished many and gathered experience from your many years. Yet wonder not, if in my youth I admonish the aged; and if in aught I can see better than the hoary,

I offer it to you. How much longer have we to live, ye men of honoured [age],[2] so near to God? How long are we to suffer here? Not even man's whole life is long, compared with the eternity of the Divine Nature, still less the remains of life, and what I may call the parting of our human breath, the close of our frail existence. How much has Caesarius outstripped us? How long shall we be left to mourn his departure? Are we not hastening to the same abode? Shall we not soon be covered by the same stone? Shall we not shortly be reduced to the same dust? And what in these short days will be our gain, save that after it has been ours to see, or suffer, or perchance even to do, more ill, we must discharge the common and inexorable tribute to the law of nature, by following some, preceding others, to the tomb, mourning these, being lamented by those, and receiving from some that [recompense][3] of tears which we ourselves had paid to others?

19. Such, my brethren, is our existence, who live this transient life, such our pastime upon earth: we come into existence out of non-existence, and after existing are dissolved. We are unsubstantial dreams, impalpable visions, like the flight of a passing bird, like a ship leaving no track upon the sea, a speck of dust, a vapour, an early dew, a flower that quickly blooms, and quickly fades. As for man his days are as grass, as a flower of the field, so he flourisheth. Well hath inspired David discoursed of our frailty, and again in these words, "Let me know the shortness of my days;" and he defines the days of man as "of a span long." And what wouldst thou say to Jeremiah, who complains of his mother in sorrow for his birth, and that on account of others' faults? I have seen all things, says the preacher, I have reviewed in thought all human things, wealth, pleasure, power, unstable glory, wisdom which evades us rather than is won; then pleasure again, wisdom again, often revolving the same objects, the pleasures of appetite, orchards, numbers of slaves, store of wealth, serving men and serving maids, singing men and singing women, arms, spearmen, subject nations, collected tributes, the pride of kings, all the necessaries and superfluities of life, in which I surpassed all the kings that were before me. And what does he say after all these things? Vanity of vanities, all is vanity and vexation of spirit, possibly meaning some unreasoning longing of the soul, and distraction of man condemned to this from the original fall: but hear, he says, the conclusion of the whole matter, Fear God. This is his stay in his perplexity, and this is thy only gain from life here below, to be guided through the disorder of the things which are seen and shaken, to the things which stand firm and are not moved.

20. Let us not then mourn Caesarius but ourselves, knowing what

evils he has escaped to which we are left behind, and what treasure we shall lay up, unless, earnestly cleaving unto God and outstripping transitory things, we press towards the life above, deserting the earth while we are still upon the earth, and earnestly following the spirit which bears us upward. Painful as this is to the fainthearted, it is as nothing to men of brave mind. And let us consider it thus. Caesarius will not reign, but rather will he be reigned over by others. He will strike terror into no one, but he will be free from fear of any harsh master, often himself unworthy even of a subject's position. He will not amass wealth, but neither will he be liable to envy, or be pained at lack of success, or be ever seeking to add to his gains as much again. For such is the disease of wealth, which knows no limit to its desire of more, and continues to make drinking the medicine for thirst. He will make no display of his power of speaking, yet for his speaking will he be admired. He will not discourse upon the dicta of Hippocrates and Galen, and their adversaries, but neither will he be troubled by diseases, and suffer pain at the misfortunes of others. He will not set forth the principles of Eucleides, Ptolemaeus, and Heron, but neither will he be pained by the tumid vaunts of uncultured men. He will make no display of the doctrines of Plato, and Aristotle, and Pyrrho, and the names of any Democritus, and Heracleitus, Anaxagoras, Cleanthes and Epicurus, and all the members of the venerable Porch and Academy: but neither will he trouble himself with the solution of their cunning syllogisms. What need of further details? Yet here are some which all men honour or desire. Nor wife nor child will he have beside him, but he will escape mourning for, or being mourned by them, or leaving them to others, or being left behind himself as a memorial of misfortune. He will inherit no property: but he will have such heirs as are of the greatest service, such as he himself wished, so that he departed hence a rich man, bearing with him all that was his. What an ambition! What a new consolation! What magnanimity in his executors! A proclamation has been heard, worthy of the ears of all, and a mother's grief has been made void by a fair and holy promise, to give entirely to her son his wealth as a funeral offering on his behalf, leaving nothing to those who expected it.

21. Is this inadequate for our consolation? I will add a more potent remedy. I believe the words of the wise, that every fair and God-beloved soul, when, set free from the bonds of the body, it departs hence, at once enjoys a sense and perception of the blessings which await it, inasmuch as that which darkened it has been purged away, or laid aside—I know not how else to term it—and feels a wondrous pleasure and exultation, and goes rejoicing to meet its Lord, having escaped as it were from the

grievous poison of life here, and shaken off the fetters which bound it and held down the wings of the mind, and so enters on the enjoyment of the bliss laid up for it, of which it has even now some conception. Then, a little later, it receives its kindred flesh, which once shared in its pursuits of things above, from the earth which both gave and had been entrusted with it, and in some way known to God, who knit them together and dissolved them, enters with it upon the inheritance of the glory there. And, as it shared, through their close union, in its hardships, so also it bestows upon it a portion of its joys, gathering it up entirely into itself, and becoming with it one in spirit and in mind and in God, the mortal and mutable being swallowed up of life. Hear at least how the inspired Ezekiel discourses of the knitting together of bones and sinews, how after him Saint Paul speaks of the earthly tabernacle, and the house not made with hands, the one to be dissolved, the other laid up in heaven, alleging absence from the body to be presence with the Lord, and bewailing his life in it as an exile, and therefore longing for and hastening to his release. Why am I faint-hearted in my hopes? Why behave like a mere creature of a day? I await the voice of the Archangel, the last trumpet, the transformation of the heavens, the transfiguration of the earth, the liberation of the elements, the renovation of the universe. Then shall I see Caesarius himself, no longer in exile, no longer laid upon a bier, no longer the object of mourning and pity, but brilliant, glorious, heavenly, such as in my dreams I have often beheld thee, dearest and most loving of brothers, pictured thus by my desire, if not by the very truth.

22. But now, laying aside lamentation, I will look at myself, and examine my feelings, that I may not unconsciously have in myself anything to be lamented. O ye sons of men, for the words apply to you, how long will ye be hard-hearted and gross in mind? Why do ye love vanity and seek after leasing, supposing life here to be a great thing and these few days many, and shrinking from this separation, welcome and pleasant as it is, as if it were really grievous and awful? Are we not to know ourselves? Are we not to cast away visible things? Are we not to look to the things unseen? Are we not, even if we are somewhat grieved, to be on the contrary distressed at our lengthened sojourn, like holy David, who calls things here the tents of darkness, and the place of affliction, and the deep mire, and the shadow of death; because we linger in the tombs we bear about with us, because, though we are gods, we die like men the death of sin? This is my fear, this day and night accompanies me, and will not let me breathe, on one side the glory, on the other the place of correction: the former I long for till I can say, "My soul fainteth for thy salvation;" from the latter I shrink back shuddering; yet I am not afraid that this body of

mine should utterly perish in dissolution and corruption, but that the glorious creature of God (for glorious it is if upright, just as it is dishonourable if sinful) in which is reason, morality, and hope, should be condemned to the same dishonour as the brutes, and be no better after death; a fate to be desired for the wicked, who are worthy of the fire yonder.

23. Would that I might mortify my members that are upon the earth, would that I might spend my all upon the spirit, walking in the way that is narrow and trodden by few, not that which is broad and easy. For glorious and great are its consequences, and our hope is greater than our desert. What is man, that Thou art mindful of him? What is this new mystery which concerns me? I am small and great, lowly and exalted, mortal and immortal, earthly and heavenly. I share one condition with the lower world, the other with God; one with the flesh, the other with the spirit. I must be buried with Christ, arise with Christ, be joint heir with Christ, become the son of God, yea, God himself. See whither our argument has carried us in its progress. I almost own myself indebted to the disaster which has inspired me with such thoughts, and made me more enamoured of my departure hence. This is the purpose of the great mystery for us. This is the purpose for us of God, Who for us was made man and became poor, to raise our flesh, and recover His image, and remodel man, that we might all be made one in Christ, who was perfectly made in all of us all that He Himself is, that we might no longer be male and female, barbarian, Scythian, bond or free (which are badges of the flesh), but might bear in ourselves only the stamp of God, by Whom and for Whom we were made, and have so far received our form and model from Him, that we are recognized by it alone.

24. Yea, would that what we hope for might be, according to the great kindness of our bountiful God, Who asks for little and bestows great things, both in the present and in the future, upon those who truly love Him; bearing all things, enduring all things for their love and hope of Him, giving thanks for all things favourable and unfavourable alike: I mean pleasant and painful, for reason knows that even these are often instruments of salvation; commending to Him our own souls and the souls of those fellow wayfarers who, being more ready, have gained their rest before us.

And, now that we have done this, let us cease from our discourse, and you too from your tears, hastening, as you now are, to your tomb, which as a sad abiding gift you have given to Caesarius, seasonably prepared as it was for his parents in their old age, and now unexpectedly bestowed on their son in his youth, though not without reason in His eyes Who disposes our affairs.

[Prayer]

O Lord and Maker of all things, and specially of this our frame! O God and Father and Pilot of men who are thine! O Lord of life and death! O Judge and Benefactor of our souls! O Maker and Transformer in due time of all things by Thy designing Word, according to the knowledge of the depth of Thy wisdom and providence! do Thou now receive Caesarius, the firstfruits of our pilgrimage; and if he who was last is first, we bow before Thy Word, by which the universe is ruled; yet do Thou receive us also afterwards, in a time when Thou mayest be found, having ordered us in the flesh as long as is for our profit; yea, receive us, prepared and not troubled by Thy fear, not departing from Thee in our last day, nor violently borne away from things here, like souls fond of the world and the flesh, but filled with eagerness for that blessed and enduring life which is in Christ Jesus, our Lord, to whom be glory, world without end. Amen.

Notes

1. For a rhetorical analysis of this oration, see Rosemary Radford Ruether, *Gregory of Nazianzus, Rhetor and Philosopher* (Oxford: Clarendon, 1969), 117-20.
2. *NPNF*[2], "eld."
3. *NPNF*[2], "meed."

CHAPTER 4

HOMILETICS AND CATECHETICS

JOHN CHRYSOSTOM: SERMONS ON THE STATUES, HOMILY 12

*The homily from this famous series discussed in the text (***See Vol. 1, pp. 81-84***) was the first, which has an unparalleled reputation for eloquence. What it does not have, however, is the quality for which the series is named, one of Chrysostom's bulletins bringing the congregation up to date on the crisis precipitated by mob action against statues of the Emperor and his family. It is appropriate that the selection presented here should reflect that feature, and thus Homily 12 was chosen. This sermon lacks the verse-by-verse exegesis for which Chrysostom was so famous. Instead, the body of the homily is taken up with a theme that was stated initially in Homily 7, the reasons the Bible was not available from the beginning of human history. In this homily, he argues that God wished to be revealed first in the purposefulness of creation and in the human conscience. At the end, he returns to the theme he has emphasized throughout the Lent in which the crisis occurred, the elimination of swearing from Antioch. The translation used is not independent, but is rather an attempt to modernize the spelling, punctuation, and usage of that found in* NPNF[1], *9:418-25.*

Report on the Statue Crisis

Yesterday I said "Blessed be God!" and today again I say the very same thing. For although the evils we dreaded have passed away, we should not suffer the memory of them to disappear—not indeed that we may grieve, but that we may give thanks. For if the memory of these terrors abide with us, we shall never be overtaken by the actual experience of such terrors. For what need have we of the experience while our memory acts the part of a monitor? Seeing then that God has not permitted us to be overwhelmed in the flood of those troubles when they were upon us, let us not permit ourselves to become careless when they are passed away. When we were sad, he consoled us; let us, then, give thanks to him now that we are joyful. In our agony he comforted us and did not forsake us; therefore let us not betray ourselves in prosperity by declining into sloth. "Forget not," one says, "the time of famine in the day of plenty." Therefore let us be mindful of the time of temptation in the day of relief.

And with respect to our sins let us also act in the same manner. If you have sinned, and God has pardoned your sin, receive your pardon and give thanks, but be not forgetful of the sin. Not that you should fret yourself with the thought of it, but that you may school your soul not to grow wanton and relapse again into the same snares.

That is what Paul did. For having said, "He counted me faithful, putting me into the ministry," he goes on to add, "who before was a blasphemer, a persecutor, and injurious." "Let the life of the servant," he says, "be openly exposed, so that the lovingkindness of the Master may be apparent. For although I have received the remission of sins, I do not reject the memory of those sins." And this not only manifested the lovingkindness of the Lord, but made Paul himself the more illustrious. For when you have learned who he was before, then you will be the more astonished at him, and when you see out of what he came to be what he was, then you will commend him the more. And if you have greatly sinned, yet upon being changed you will conceive favorable hopes from this instance. For in addition to what has been said, such an example comforts those who are in despair and causes them again to stand erect. The same thing also will happen with regard to our city, for all the events that have happened serve to show your virtue who by means of repentance have prevailed to ward off such wrath while at the same time they proclaim the lovingkindness of God who has removed the cloud that was so threatening in consequence of a small change of conduct, and so raises up again all those who are sunk in despair when they learn from our case that the one who looks upward for divine help is not to be overwhelmed though innumerable waves should encompass that one on all sides.

For who has seen, who has ever heard of sufferings such as ours were? We were every day in expectation that our city would be overturned from its foundations together with its inhabitants. But when the devil was hoping to sink the vessel, then God produced a perfect calm. Let us not then be unmindful of the greatness of these terrors, in order that we may remember the magnitude of the benefits received from God. The one who does not who know the nature of the disease will not understand the physician's art. Let us tell these things also to our children and transmit them to the remotest generations that all may learn how the devil had endeavored to destroy the very foundation of the city and how God was able visibly to raise it up again when it was fallen and prostrate and did not permit even the least injury to befall it, but took away the fear and dispelled with much speed the peril it had been placed in.

For through the past week we were all expecting that our substance would be confiscated, and that soldiers would have been let loose upon us, and we were dreaming of a thousand other horrors. But, lo, all these things have passed away, even like a cloud or a flitting shadow, and we have been punished only in the expectation of what is dreadful. Or rather, we have not been punished, but we have been disciplined and have become better, God having softened the heart of the Emperor.

Let us then always and every day say, "Blessed be God!" and with greater zeal let us give heed to our assembling and let us hasten to the church from which we have reaped this benefit. For you know where you fled at the first, where you flocked together, and from what quarter our safety came. Let us then hold fast by this sacred anchor and, as in the season of danger it did not betray us, so now let us not leave it in the season of relief, but let us await with exact attention the stated assemblies and prayers and let us every day give a hearing to the divine oracles. And the leisure which we spent in busily running about after those who came from the court while we were laboring under anxiety over the evils that threatened us, this let us consume wholly in hearing the divine laws instead of unseasonable and senseless pastimes lest we should again reduce ourselves to the necessity of that sort of occupation.

Continuation of the Explanation of Why the Bible Was Written So Late

That God Might Be Revealed in the Purposefulness of Creation

On the three foregoing days, then, we have investigated one method of acquiring the knowledge of God and have brought it to a conclusion, explaining how "the heavens declare the glory of God," and the meaning of Paul's saying "that the invisible things of him from the creation of the world are clearly seen, being understood by the things that are made." And we showed how from the creation of the world, and how by heaven, and earth, the sea, the Creator is glorified.

But today, after briefly philosophizing on that same subject, we will proceed to another topic. For God not only made it, but also provided that when it was made it should carry on its operations, neither permitting it to be all immovable nor commanding it to be all in a state of motion. The heaven, for instance, has remained immovable just as the prophet says: "He placed the heaven as a vault, and stretched it out as a tent over the earth." But, on the other hand, the sun, with the rest of the stars, runs on its course through every day. And again, the earth is fixed, but the waters are continually in motion—and not the waters only, but the clouds, and the frequent and successive showers, which return at their proper season.

The clouds have one nature, but the things that are produced out of them are different. For the rain, indeed, becomes wine in the grape, but oil in the olive, and is changed in other plants into their juices. And the womb of the earth is one and yet bears different fruits. The heat, too, of the sunbeams is one, but it ripens all things differently, bringing some to maturity more slowly and others more quickly. Who then but must feel astonishment and admiration at these things?

No, this is not the only wonder, that he has formed it with this great variety and diversity, but farther, that he has spread it before all in common: the rich and the poor, sinners as well as the righteous. Even as Christ also declared: "He makes his sun to rise upon the evil and the good and sends his rain upon the just and unjust."

Moreover, when he stocked the world with various animals, and implanted diverse dispositions in the creatures, he commanded us to imitate some of these and to avoid others. For example, the ant is industrious and performs a laborious task. By giving heed then, you will receive the strongest admonition from this animal not to indulge in sloth nor to shun labor and toil. Therefore also the Scripture has sent the sluggard to the ant, saying, "Go to the ant, you sluggard, emulate his ways and be wiser than he." Are you unwilling, this means, to learn from the scriptures that it is good to labor, and that the one who will not work ought not to eat either? Learn it from the irrational creatures! This also we do in our families. When those who are older and who are considered superior have done amiss, we bid them to attend to thoughtful children. We say, "Look at this one who is younger than you, how earnest and watchful that one is."

In the same way you should also receive from this animal the best exhortation to industry, and marvel at your Lord, not only for making heaven and the sun, but also for making the ant. For although the animal be small, it affords much proof of the greatness of God's wisdom. Consider then how prudent the ant is and consider how God has implanted in so small a body such an unceasing desire to work!

But while from this animal you learn industry, take from the bee at once a lesson of neatness, industry, and social concord! For it is not more for herself than for us that the bee labors and toils every day—which is indeed a thing especially proper for Christians, not to seek their own things but the things of others. As then she traverses all the meadows that she may prepare a banquet for another, so also, O mortal, do you likewise. And if you have accumulated wealth, expend it upon others. If you have the faculty of teaching, do not bury the talent but bring it out publicly for the sake of those who need it! Or if you have any other advantage, become useful to those who require the benefit of your labors! Do you not see that for this reason especially the bee is more honored than the other animals: not because she labors, but because she labors for others? For the spider also labors and toils and spreads out his fine textures over the walls, surpassing the utmost skill of woman, but the creature is without estimation since his work is in no way profitable to us. Such are they that labor and toil, but for themselves!

Imitate too the simplicity of the dove! Imitate the ass in his love for his master, and the ox also! Imitate the birds in their freedom from anxiety! For great, great indeed is the advantage that may be gained from irrational creatures for the correction of manners. From these animals Christ also instructs us, when he says, "Be you wise as serpents, and harmless as doves." And again: "Behold the fowls of the air, for they sow not, neither do they reap, nor gather into barns, yet your heavenly Father feeds them." The prophet also, to shame the ungrateful Jews, thus speaks: "The ox knows his owner and the ass his master's crib, but Israel does not know me." And again: "The turtle and the swallow and the crane observe the time of their coming, but my people know not the judgment of the Lord their God."

From these animals and such as these learn to achieve virtue, and be instructed to avoid wickedness by the contrary ones. For as the bee follows good, so the asp is destructive. Therefore shun wickedness lest you hear it said, "The poison of asps is under their lips." Again, the dog is devoid of shame. Hate, therefore, this kind of wickedness. The fox also is crafty and fraudulent. Do not emulate this vice! But, as the bee in flying over the meadows does not choose every sort of flower but selects the one that is useful and leaves the rest, so you should also do: while surveying the whole race of irrational animals, accept any thing profitable that may be drawn from them.

The advantages they have naturally, make it your business to practice of your own free choice. For in this respect also you have been honored by God, that what they have as natural advantages he has permitted you to achieve of your own free choice, in order that you may also receive a reward. For good works with them do not spring from free will and reason, but from nature only. In other words, the bee makes honey, not because it has learned this by reason and reflection, but because it is instructed by nature. Because, if the work had not been natural and allotted to the race, some of them assuredly would have been unskilled in their art. But from the time that the world was first made even to the present day no one has observed bees resting from labor and not making honey. For such natural characteristics are common to the whole race. But those things that depend on our free choice are not common, for labor is necessary that they may be accomplished.

Take then all the best things and clothe yourself with them, for you are indeed king of the irrational creatures. But kings, if there is anything excellent possessed by their subjects—whether gold or silver or precious stones or sumptuous vestments—usually possess the same in greater abundance. From the creation also learn to admire your Lord! And if any of the things you see exceed your comprehension and you are not able to find the reason for them, yet for this glorify the Creator: that the wisdom of these works surpasses your understanding.

Do not say: why does this exist or for what purpose? For everything is useful, even if we do not know the reason for it. Just as, if you go into a surgery and see many instruments lying before you, you wonder at the variety of the implements though ignorant of their use, so also act with respect to the creation. Although you see many of the animals and of the herbs and plants and other things of which you know not the use, admire their variety. And feel astonishment for this reason at the perfect workmanship of God: that God has neither made all things manifest to you, nor permitted all things to be unknown. For God has not permitted all things to be unknown lest you should say that the things that exist are not of providence. Neither has God permitted all things to be known to you lest the greatness of your knowledge should excite you to pride. Thus at least it was that the evil demon precipitated the first human headlong and by means of the hope of greater knowledge deprived him of what he already possessed.

Therefore also, a certain wise person exhorts, saying, "Do not seek out the things that are too hard for you, neither search the things that are too deep for you. But what is commanded you, think upon it with reverence, for the greater part of God's works are done in secret." And again, "More things are showed unto you than people understand." But this he speaks for the purpose of consoling the person who is sad and vexed over not knowing all things. For even those things you observe that you are permitted to know greatly surpass your understanding, for you could not have found them by yourself if you had not been taught them by God. Therefore be content with the wealth given you and do not seek more, but for what you have received give thanks and do not be angry on account of those things that you have not received. And, for what you know, give glory and do not stumble at those things of which you are ignorant. For God has made both alike profitably, and has revealed some things but hidden others, providing for your safety.

One mode of knowing God, then, is by creation, which I have spoken of and which might occupy many days. For in order that we might go over the formation of human beings only with exactness (and I speak of such exactness as is possible to us—not of real exactness, since, as many as are the reasons we have already given for the works of creation, there are many more ineffable ones that God who made them knows—for of course we do not know them all). In order then, I say, that we might take an exact survey of the whole modeling of human beings; and that we might discover the skill there is in every member; and examine the distribution and situation of the sinews, the veins, and the arteries, and the molding of every other part; not even a whole year would suffice for such a disquisition.

That God Might Be Revealed Through the Human Conscience

For this reason, here dismissing this subject, and having given to the laborious and studious an opportunity by what has been said of going over likewise the other parts of Creation, we shall now direct our discourse to another point which is itself also demonstrative of God's providence. What then is this second point? It is that, when God formed human beings, he implanted within them from the beginning a natural law. And what then was this natural law? God gave utterance to conscience within us and made the knowledge of good things and of those which are the contrary to be self-taught.

For we have no need to learn that fornication is an evil thing, and that chastity is a good thing, but we know this from the first. And that you may learn that we know this from the first, the Lawgiver, who afterwards gave laws and said, "You shall not kill," did not add, "since murder is an evil thing," but simply said, "You shall not kill." For God merely prohibited the sin without teaching. How was it then when God said, "You shall not kill," that God did not add, "because murder is a wicked thing." The reason was that conscience had taught this beforehand and God speaks thus as to those who know and understand the point.

Therefore, when God speaks to us of another commandment not known to us by the dictate of consciences, God not only prohibits but adds the reason. When, for instance, God gave commandment respecting the Sabbath, "On the seventh day you shall do no work," God also subjoined the reason for this cessation. What was this? "Because on the seventh day God rested from all the works that God had begun to make." And again, "Because you were a servant in the land of Egypt." For what purpose then, I ask, did God add a reason respecting the Sabbath, but did no such thing in regard to murder? Because this commandment was not one of the leading ones. It was not one of those that were accurately defined of our conscience, but a kind of partial and temporary one. And for this reason it was abolished afterwards. But those that are necessary and uphold our life are the following: "you shall not kill, you shall not commit adultery, you shall not steal." On this account then God adds no reason in this case, nor enters into any instruction on the matter, but is content with the bare prohibition.

And not only from this, but from another consideration also, I will endeavor to show you how humanity was self-taught with respect to the knowledge of virtue. Adam sinned the first sin and after the sin immediately hid himself. But if he had not known he had been doing something wrong, why did he hide himself? For then there were neither letters, nor law, nor Moses. How then does he recognize the sin and hide himself? Yet not only does he so hide himself, but, when called to account, he endeavors to lay the blame on another, saying, "The woman you gave me, she gave me of the tree and I ate." And that woman again transfers the accusation to another, namely, the serpent.

Observe also the wisdom of God. For when Adam said, "I heard your voice and I was afraid, for I was naked, and I hid myself," God does not at once convict him of what he had done, nor say, "*Why* have you eaten of the tree?" But *how*? "Who told you," he asks, "that you were naked, unless you have eaten from the only tree I commanded you not to eat from?" God did not keep silence, nor openly convict Adam. God did not keep silence in order to call him forth to the confession of his crime. God did not convict him openly, lest the whole might come from the divine being and human beings should thus be deprived of the pardon that is granted us from confession. Therefore God did not declare openly the cause from which this knowledge sprang, but carried on the discourse in the form of interrogation, leaving the man himself to come to the confession.

Again, in the case of Cain and Abel, the same proceeding is observable. For, in the first place, they set apart the fruits of their own labors to God. For we would show not only from their sin but also from their virtue that human beings were capable of knowing both these things. That human beings knew sin to be an evil thing, Adam manifested, and that they knew that virtue was a good thing, Abel again made evident. For without having learned it from anyone, without having heard any law promulgated respecting the first fruits, but having been taught from within and from his conscience, he presented that sacrifice. On this account I do not carry the argument down to a later period, but I bring it to bear upon the time of these earlier people when there were as yet no letters, as yet no law, nor as yet prophets and judges, but Adam alone existed with his children, in order that you may learn that the knowledge of good and evil had been previously implanted in their natures.

For from where did Abel learn that to offer sacrifice was a good thing, that it was good to honor God and in all things to give thanks? "Why then?" someone replies, "did not Cain bring his offering?" This man also offered sacrifice, but not in the same way. And from there again the knowledge of conscience is apparent. For when, envying the one who had been honored, he deliberated upon murder, he conceals his crafty determination. And what does he say? "Come, let us go forth into the field." The outward guise was one thing: the pretense of love. The thought another: the purpose of fratricide. But if he had not known the design to be a wicked one, why did he conceal it? And again, after the murder had been perpetrated, being asked of God, "Where is Abel your brother?" he answers, "I do not know. Am I my brother's keeper?" Why does he deny the crime? Is it not evidently because he condemns himself exceedingly? For, as his father had hid himself, so also this man denies his guilt and, after his conviction, again says, "My crime is too great to obtain pardon."

But it may be objected that the Gentile allows nothing of this sort. Come then, let us discuss this point, and as we have done with respect to the creation. Having carried on the warfare against these objectors not only by the help of the scriptures but of reason as well, so also let us now do with respect to conscience. For Paul, too, when he was engaged in controversy with such people, dealt with this issue. What then is it that they urge? They say that there is no self-evident law seated in our consciences and that God has not implanted this in our nature. But if so, why is it, I ask, that legislators have written those laws which are among them concerning marriages, concerning murders, concerning wills, concerning trusts, concerning abstinence from encroachments on one another, and a thousand other things? For those now living may perhaps have learned them from their elders, and they from those who were before them, and these again from those beyond. But from where did those learn who were the originators and first enactors of laws among them? Is it not evident that it was from conscience? For they cannot say that they held communication with Moses or that they heard the prophets. How could it be so when they were Gentiles? But it is evident that laws were laid down and arts and all other things discovered from the very law God placed in human beings when God formed them from the beginning. For the arts too were thus established, their originators having come to the knowledge of them in a self-taught manner.

So also there came to be courts of justice, and so were penalties defined, as Paul accordingly observes. For since many of the Gentiles were ready to controvert this and to say, "How will God judge humankind who lived before Moses? God did not send a lawgiver, God did not introduce a law, God commissioned no prophet, nor apostle, nor evangelist. How then can God call these to account?" Since Paul therefore wished to prove that they possessed a self-taught law and that they knew clearly what they ought to do, hear how he speaks! "For when the Gentiles, who do not have the law, do by nature the things contained in the law, they, though not having the law, are a law unto themselves; they show the work of the law written in their hearts." But how without letters? "Their conscience also bearing witness, and their thoughts the meanwhile accusing or else excusing one another in the day when God shall judge the secrets of men by Jesus Christ according to my gospel." And again: "As many as have sinned without law shall perish without law, and as many as have sinned in the law shall be judged by the law." What is the meaning of: "They shall perish without law"? It is not the law that accuses them, but their thoughts and their conscience. For if they did not have a law of conscience, it would not necessary that they should perish through having done wrong. For how should it be so if they sinned without a law? But when he says, "without a law," he does not assert that they had no law, but that they had no written law, though they had the law of nature. And again; "But glory, honor, and peace to everyone who does good, to the Jew first, and also to the Gentile."

But these things Paul said in reference to the early times, before the coming of Christ. And the Gentile he names here is not an idolater, but one who worshiped God alone, unfettered by the necessity of Jewish observances (I mean Sabbaths, and circumcision, and different purifications), yet exhibiting all kinds of wisdom and piety. And again, discussing such a worshiper, he observes, "Wrath and indignation, tribulation and anguish upon every human soul who does evil, the Jew first, and also the Gentile." Here again he calls by the name of Greek someone who was free from the observance of Jewish customs.

If, then, the Gentile had not heard the law nor conversed with the Jews, how could there be wrath, indignation and tribulation against that one for doing evil? The reason is that this person possessed a conscience inwardly admonishing and teaching and instructing that one in all things. Where is this manifest? From the way that Gentiles punished others when they did wrong, from the way in which they laid down laws, from the way they set up the tribunals of justice.

With the view of making this plainer, Paul spoke of those who were living in wickedness: "those who, knowing the ordinance of God that those which commit such things are worthy of death, not only do the same things, but also consent with those that practice them." "But from where," someone says, "did they know that it is the will of God that those who live in iniquity should be punished with death?" From where? Why, from the way in which they judged others who sinned.

For if you do not consider murder to be a wicked thing, when you have a murderer at your bar, you should not punish that person. So if you do not consider it an evil thing to commit adultery, when the adulterer has fallen into your hands, release that person from punishment! But if you record laws and prescribe punishments and are a severe judge of the sins of others, what defense can you make in matters in which you yourself do wrong by saying that you art ignorant of what ought to be done? For suppose that you and another person have alike been guilty of adultery. On what account do you punish the other person and consider yourself worthy of forgiveness? Since if you did not know adultery to be wicked, it would not be right to punish it in another. But if you punish and expect to escape the punishment yourself, how is it reasonable that the same offenses should not pay the same penalty?

This indeed is the very thing that Paul rebukes when he says, "And do you think, O mortal who judges those who do such things while doing them yourself, that you shall escape the judgment of God?" It is not, it cannot be possible! For Paul means that from the very sentence you pronounce upon another, from this sentence God will then judge you. For surely you are not just and God unjust! But if you do not overlook another suffering wrong, how shall God overlook? And if you correct the sins of others, how will not God correct you?

And though God may not bring the punishment upon you instantly, do not be confident on that account, but fear the more. For Paul told you the same thing, saying, "Do you despise the riches of God's goodness and forbearance and longsuffering, not knowing that the goodness of God leads you to repentance?" For, Paul says, God bears with you, not that you may become worse, but that you may repent. But if you will not, this longsuffering becomes a cause of your greater punishment, remaining impenitent, as you do. This, however, is the very thing he means when he says, "But by your hardness and impenitent heart you are treasuring up wrath for yourself on the day of wrath when the righteous judgment of God will be revealed to every one according to their deeds."

Since, therefore, God renders to everyone according to their works, God both implanted within us a natural law and afterwards gave us a written one in order to be able to demand an account of sins and to crown those who act rightly. Let us then order our conduct with the utmost care like those who soon have to encounter a fearful tribunal, knowing that we shall enjoy no pardon if, after a natural as well as a written law and so much teaching and continual admonition, we neglect our own salvation.

Swearing

I desire then to address you again on the subject of oaths, but I feel ashamed. For to me, indeed, it is not wearisome to repeat the same things to you by day and by night. But I am afraid lest, having followed you up so many days, I should seem to condemn you of great listlessness, that you should require continual admonition respecting so easy a matter. And I am not only ashamed but also in fear for you! For frequent instruction to those who give heed is salutary and profitable, but to those who are listless it is injurious and exceedingly perilous. For the oftener anyone hears, the greater punishment does one draw upon oneself, if one does not practice what one has been told.

With this accordingly God reproached the Jews, saying this: "I have sent my prophets, rising up early and sending them, and even then you did not listen." We therefore do this out of our great care for you. But we fear lest on that tremendous day this admonition and counsel should rise up against you all. For when the point to be attained is easy, and the one whose office it is continually to admonish desists not from this task, what defense shall we have to offer? Or what argument will save us from punishment? Tell me, if a sum of money happens to be due you, do you not always, when you meet the debtor, remind that person of the loan? Act the same way and let all of you imagine that your neighbor owes you something, namely, keeping this precept. And upon meeting that neighbor, remind that person of the payment, knowing that no small danger lies at our door while we are unmindful of our brethren. For this reason I too do not cease to mention these things. For I fear lest by any means I should hear it said on that day, "O wicked and slothful servant, you ought to have invested my money with the bankers." But see, however, that I have paid it down, not once or twice but often. It is up to you then to pay the interest on it. Now the usury paid on hearing is acting on what was heard, for the money deposited belongs to the Lord. Therefore let us not receive negligently what we are entrusted with, but let us keep it with diligence that we may restore it with much interest on that day. For unless you bring others to the performance of the same good works, you shall hear that voice which the one who buried the talent heard. But God forbid that this should happen! But may you hear that different voice Christ uttered to the one who had made profit, "Well done, good and faithful servant. You have been faithful over a few things, I will make you ruler over many."

And this voice we shall hear if we show the same earnestness that he did. And we shall show this earnestness if we do what I am saying. When you depart—while what you have heard is yet warm within you—exhort one another! And as you greet one another at parting, let every one go from here with an admonition and say to a neighbor, "Observe and remember that you keep the commandment," and thus shall we assuredly get the mastery. For when friends also dismiss one with such counsel and, on one's return home, one's wife again admonishes one to the same effect, and our word keeps its hold on you when alone, we shall soon shake off this evil habit. I know, indeed, that you wonder why I am so earnest about this precept. But discharge the duty enjoined and then I will tell you. Meanwhile, I say this, that this precept is a divine law and it is not safe to transgress it. But if I see it rightly performed, I will speak of another reason that is not less than this, that you may learn that it is with justice I make so much ado about this law.

Closing Prayer

But it is now time to conclude this address in a prayer. Therefore, let us all say together: "O God, who does not will the death of sinners but rather that they should be converted and live, grant that we, having discharged this and every other precept, may be found worthy so to stand at the tribunal of your Christ that, having enjoyed great boldness, we may attain the kingdom to your glory. For glory belongs to you together with your only begotten Son and the Holy Spirit, now and ever and world without end. Amen."

CHAPTER 5

AUGUSTINE, THE SIGN READER

AUGUSTINE: *DE DOCTRINA CHRISTIANA*, BOOK 4

Although important things are said about how preaching should be done in Gregory Nazianzen's Second Oration *and Chrysostom's* On the Priesthood, *the first textbook of Christian preaching is Augustine's treatise,* On Christian Doctrine, *or, more accurately translated,* Teaching Christianity. *The first three books of the treatise are devoted to biblical interpretation, while the fourth, which was written later, concerns the use of classical rhetoric in preaching. Determinative as it was of so much to follow, this is one of the most important documents in the whole history of preaching. (***See Vol. 1, pp. 106-10,** *for a discussion of the work.) The two sets of numerals for the divisions of this work cause a little confusion because the paragraphs are numbered consecutively through the whole book instead of starting with one in each new chapter. Yet since the use of both is standard, altering the system could cause even more confusion. Because Book 4 is so long, two sections in which Augustine analyzes the use of rhetorical principles in passages of Christian writing have been omitted, but enough similar sections remain* *to demonstrate the acuity of his analysis. The edition used is that of the NPNF*[1]*, First Series, vol. 3, trans. with intro. J. F. Shaw (New York: Christian Literature Foundation, 1887).*

Book Four

Chap. 1. This Work Not Intended as a Treatise on Rhetoric

1. This work of mine, which is entitled *On Christian Doctrine,* was at the commencement divided into two parts. For, after a preface, in which I answered by anticipation those who were likely to take exception to the work, I said, "There are two things on which all interpretation of scripture depends: the mode of ascertaining the proper meaning, and the mode of making known the meaning when it is ascertained. I shall treat first of the mode of ascertaining, next of the mode of making known, the meaning." As, then, I have already said a great deal about the mode of ascertaining the meaning, and have given three books to this one part of the subject, I shall only say a few things about the mode of making known the meaning, in order if possible to bring them all within the compass of one book, and so finish the whole work in four books.

2. In the first place, then, I wish by this preamble to put a stop to the expectations of readers who may think that I am about to lay down rules of rhetoric such as I have learnt, and taught too, in the secular schools, and to warn them that they need not look for any such from me. Not that I think such rules of no use, but that whatever use they have is to be learnt elsewhere; and if any good man should happen to have leisure for learning them, he is not to ask me to teach them either in this work or any other.

Chap. 2. It Is Lawful for a Christian Teacher to Use the Art of Rhetoric

3. Now, the art of rhetoric being available for the enforcing either of truth or falsehood, who will dare to say that truth in the person of its defenders is to take its stand unarmed against falsehood? For example, that those who are trying to persuade men of what is false are to know how to introduce their subject, so as to put the hearer into a friendly, or attentive, or teachable frame of mind, while the defenders of the truth shall be ignorant of that art? That the former are to tell their falsehoods briefly, clearly, and plausibly, while the latter shall tell the truth in such a way that it is tedious to listen to, hard to understand, and, in fine, not easy to believe it? That the former are to oppose the truth and

defend falsehood with sophistical arguments, while the latter shall be unable either to defend what is true, or to refute what is false? That the former, while imbuing the minds of their hearers with erroneous opinions, are by their power of speech to awe, to melt, to enliven, and to rouse them, while the latter shall in defense of the truth be sluggish, and frigid, and somnolent? Who is such fool as to think this wisdom? Since, then, the faculty of eloquence is available for both sides, and is of very great service in the enforcing either of wrong or right, why do not good men study to engage it on the side of truth, when bad men use it to obtain the triumph of wicked and worthless causes, and to further injustice and error?

Chap. 3. The Proper Age and the Proper Means for Acquiring Rhetorical Skill

4. But the theories and rules on this subject (to which, when you add a tongue thoroughly skilled by exercise and habit in the use of many words and many ornaments of speech, you have what is called *eloquence* or *oratory*) may be learnt apart from these writings, of mine, if a suitable space of time be set aside for the purpose at a fit and proper age. But only by those who can learn them quickly, for the masters of Roman eloquence do not shrink from saying that any one who cannot learn this art quickly can never thoroughly learn it at all. Whether this be true or not, why need we inquire? For even if this art can occasionally be in the end mastered by men of slower intellect, I do not think it of so much importance as to wish men who have arrived at mature age to spend time in learning it. It is enough that boys should give attention to it; and even of these, not all who are to be fitted for usefulness in the church, but only those who are not yet engaged in any occupation of more urgent necessity, or which ought evidently to take precedence of it. For men of quick intellect and glowing temperament find it easier to become eloquent by reading and listening to eloquent speakers than by following rules for eloquence. And even outside the canon, which to our great advantage is fixed in a place of secure authority, there is no want of ecclesiastical writings, in reading which a man of ability will acquire a tinge of the eloquence with which they are written, even though he does not aim at this, but is solely intent on the matters treated of; especially, of course, if in addition he practice himself in writing, or dictating, and at last also in speaking, the opinions he has formed on grounds of piety and faith. If, however, such ability be wanting, the rules of rhetoric are either not understood, or if, after great labor has been spent in enforcing them, they

come to be in some small measure understood, they prove of no service. For even those who have learnt them, and who speak with fluency and elegance, cannot always think of them when they are speaking so as to speak in accordance with them, unless they are discussing the rules themselves. Indeed, I think there are scarcely any who can do both things—that is, speak well, and, in order to do this, think of the rules of speaking while they are speaking. For we must be careful that what we have got to say does not escape us whilst we are thinking about saying it according to the rules of art. Nevertheless, in the speeches of eloquent men, we find rules of eloquence carried out which the speakers did not think of as aids to eloquence at the time when they were speaking, whether they had ever learnt them, or whether they had never even met with them. For it is because they are eloquent that they exemplify these rules; it is not that they use them in order to be eloquent.

5. And, therefore, as infants cannot learn to speak except by learning words and phrases from those who do speak, why should not men become eloquent without being taught any art of speech, simply by reading and learning the speeches of eloquent men, and by imitating them as far as they can? And what do we find from the examples themselves to be the case in this respect? We know numbers who, without acquaintance with rhetorical rules, are more eloquent than many who have learnt these; but we know no one who is eloquent without having read and listened to the speeches and debates of eloquent men. For even the art of grammar, which teaches correctness of speech, need not be learnt by boys, if they have the advantage of growing up and living among men who speak correctly. For without knowing the names of any of the faults, they will, from being accustomed to correct speech, lay hold upon whatever is faulty in the speech of any one they listen to, and avoid it just as city-bred men, even when illiterate, seize upon the faults of rustics.

Chap. 4. The Duty of the Christian Teacher

6. It is the duty, then, of the interpreter and teacher of holy scripture, the defender of the true faith and the opponent of error, both to teach what is right and to refute what is wrong, and in the performance of this task to conciliate the hostile, to rouse the careless, and to tell the ignorant both what is occurring at present and what is probable in the future. But once that his hearers are friendly, attentive, and ready to learn, whether he has found them so, or has himself made them so, the remaining objects are to be carried out in whatever way the case requires. If the hearers need teaching, the matter treated of must be made fully known

by means of narrative. On the other hand, to clear up points that are doubtful requires reasoning and the exhibition of proofs. If, however, the hearers require to be roused rather than instructed, in order that they may be diligent to do what they already know, and to bring their feelings into harmony with the truths they admit, greater vigor of speech is needed. Here entreaties and reproaches, exhortations and upbraidings, and all the other means of rousing the emotions, are necessary.

7. And all the methods I have mentioned are constantly used by nearly every one in cases where speech is the agency employed.

Chap. 5. Wisdom of More Importance than Eloquence to the Christian Teacher

But as some men employ these coarsely, inelegantly, and frigidly, while others use them with acuteness, elegance, and spirit, the work that I am speaking of ought to be undertaken by one who can argue and with wisdom, if not with eloquence, and with profit to his hearers, even though he profit them less than he would if he could speak with eloquence too. But we must beware of the man who abounds in eloquent nonsense and so much the more if the hearer is pleased with what is not worth listening to, and thinks that because the speaker is eloquent what he says must be true. And this opinion is held even by those who think that the art of rhetoric should be taught: for they confess that "though wisdom without eloquence is of little service to states, yet eloquence without wisdom is frequently a positive injury, and is of service never." If, then, the men who teach the principles of eloquence have been forced by truth to confess this in the very books which treat of eloquence, though they were ignorant of the true, that is, the heavenly wisdom which comes down from the Father of Lights, how much more ought we to feel it who are the sons and the ministers of this higher wisdom! Now a man speaks with more or less wisdom just as he has made more or less progress in the knowledge of scripture; I do not mean by reading them much and committing them to memory, but by understanding them aright and carefully searching into their meaning. For there are who read and yet neglect them; they read to remember the words, but are careless about knowing the meaning. It is plain we must set far above these the men who are not so retentive of the words, but see with the eyes of the heart into the heart of scripture. Better than either of these, however, is the man who, when he wishes, can repeat the words, and at the same time correctly apprehends their meaning.

8. Now it is especially necessary for the man who is bound to speak wisely, even though he cannot speak eloquently, to retain in memory the words of scripture. For the more he discerns the poverty of his own speech, the more he ought to draw on the riches of scripture, so that what he says in his own words he may prove by the words of scripture; and he himself, though small and weak in his own words, may gain strength and power from the confirming testimony of great men. For his proof gives pleasure, when he cannot please by his mode of speech. But if a man desire to speak not only with wisdom, but with eloquence also (and assuredly he will prove of greater service if he can do both), I would rather send him to read, and to listen to, and exercise himself in imitating eloquent men, than advise him to spend time with the teachers of rhetoric; especially if the men he reads and listens to are justly praised as having spoken, or as being accustomed to speak, not only with eloquence, but with wisdom also. For eloquent speakers are heard with pleasure; wise speakers with profit. And, therefore, scripture does not say that the multitude of the eloquent, but "the multitude of the wise is the welfare of the world." And as we must often swallow wholesome bitters, so we always avoid unwholesome sweets. But what is better than wholesome sweetness or sweet wholesomeness. For the sweeter we try to make such things, the easier it is to make their wholesomeness serviceable. And so there are writers of the church who have expounded the scriptures, not only with wisdom, but with eloquence as well; and there is not more time for the reading of these than is sufficient for those who are studious and at leisure to exhaust them.

Chap. 6. The Sacred Writers Unite Eloquence with Wisdom

9. Here, perhaps, someone inquires whether the authors whose divinely-inspired writings constitute the canon, which carries with it a most wholesome authority, are to be considered wise only, or eloquent as well. A question which to me, and to those who think with me, is very easily settled. For where I understand these writers, it seems to me not only that nothing can be wiser, but also that nothing can be more eloquent. And I venture to affirm that all who truly understand what these writers say, perceive at the same time that it could not have been properly said any other way. For as there is a kind of eloquence that is more becoming in youth, and a kind that is more becoming in old age, and nothing can be called eloquence if it be not suitable to the person of the speaker, so there is a kind of eloquence that is becoming to men who justly claim the highest authority, and who are evidently inspired of God.

With this eloquence they spoke; no other would have been suitable for them; and this itself would be unsuitable in any other, for it is in keeping with their character, while it mounts as far above that of others (not from empty inflation, but from solid merit) as it seems to fall below them. Where, however, I do not understand these writers, though their eloquence is then less apparent, I have no doubt but that it is of the same kind as that I do understand. The very obscurity, too, of these divine and wholesome words was a necessary element in eloquence of a kind that was designed to profit our understandings, not only by the discovery of truth, but also by the exercise of their powers.

10. I could, however, if I had time, show those men who cry up their own form of language as superior to that of our authors (not because of its majesty, but because of its inflation), that all those powers and beauties of eloquence which they make their boast, are to be found in the sacred writings which God in his goodness has provided to mold our characters, and to guide us from this world of wickedness to the blessed world above. But it is not the qualities which these writers have in common with the heathen orators and poets that give me such unspeakable delight in their eloquence; I am more struck with admiration at the way in which, by an eloquence peculiarly their own, they so use this eloquence of ours that it is not conspicuous either by its presence or its absence; for it did not become them either to condemn it or to make an ostentatious display of it; and if they had shunned it, they would have done the former; if they had made it prominent, they might have appeared to be doing the latter. And in those passages where the learned do note its presence, the matters spoken of are such, that the words in which they are put seem not so much to be sought out by the speaker as spontaneously to suggest themselves; as if wisdom were walking out of its own house,—that is, the breast of the wise man, and eloquence, like an inseparable attendant, followed it without being called for.

(Chapter 7 [11-20], in which Augustine analyzes biblical passages to show their use of rhetorical ornaments, is omitted.)

21. And a number of other points bearing upon the laws of eloquence could be found in this passage which I have chosen as an example. But an intelligent reader will not be so much instructed by carefully analyzing it as kindled by reciting it with spirit. Nor was it composed by man's art and care, but it flowed forth in wisdom and eloquence from the divine mind; wisdom not aiming at eloquence, yet eloquence not shrinking from wisdom. For if, as certain very eloquent and acute men have perceived and

said, the rules which are laid down in the art of oratory could not have been observed, and noted, and reduced to system, if they had not first had their birth in the genius of orators, is it wonderful that they should be found in the messengers of him who is the author of all genius? There let us acknowledge that the canonical writers are not only wise but eloquent also, with an eloquence suited to a character and position like theirs.

Chap. 8. The Obscurity of the Sacred Writers, Though Compatible with Eloquence, Not to Be Imitated by Christian Teachers

22. But although I take some examples of eloquence from those writings of theirs which there is no difficulty in understanding, we are not by any means to suppose that it is our duty to imitate them in those passages where, with a view to exercise and train the minds of their readers, and to break in upon the satiety and stimulate the zeal of those who are willing to learn, and with a view also to throw a veil over the minds of the godless either that they may be converted to piety or shut out from a knowledge of the mysteries, from one or other of these reasons they have expressed themselves with a useful and wholesome obscurity. They have indeed expressed themselves in such a way that those who in after ages understood and explained them aright have in the Church of God obtained an esteem, not indeed equal to that with which they are themselves regarded, but coming next to it. The expositors of these writers, then, ought not to express themselves in the same way, as if putting forward their expositions as of the same authority; but they ought in all their deliverances to make it their first and chief aim to be understood, using as far as possible such clearness of speech that either he will be very dull who does not understand them, or that if what they say should not be very easily or quickly understood, the reason will lie not, in their manner of expression, but in the difficulty and subtlety of the matter they are trying to explain.

Chap. 9. How, and with Whom, Difficult Passages Are to Be Discussed

23. For there are some passages which are not understood in their proper force, or are understood with great difficulty, at whatever length, however clearly, or with whatever eloquence the speaker may expound them; and these should never be brought before the people at all, or only on rare occasions when there is some urgent reason. In books, however, which are written in such a style that, if understood, they, so to speak, draw their own readers, and if not understood, give no trouble to those who do not care to read them, and in private conversations, we must not

shrink from the duty of bringing the truth which we ourselves have reached within the comprehension of others, however difficult it may be to understand it, and whatever labor in the way of argument it may cost us. Only two conditions are to be insisted upon, that our hearer, or companion should have an earnest desire to learn the truth, and should have capacity of mind to receive it in whatever form it may be communicated, the teacher not being so anxious about the eloquence as about the clearness of his teaching.

Chap. 10. The Necessity for Perspicuity of Style

24. Now a strong desire for clearness sometimes leads to neglect of the more polished forms of speech, and indifference about what sounds well, compared with what clearly expresses and conveys the meaning intended. Whence a certain author, when dealing with speech of this kind, says that there is in it "a kind of careful negligence." Yet while taking away ornament, it does not bring in vulgarity of speech; though good teachers have, or ought to have, so great an anxiety about teaching that they will employ a word which cannot be made pure Latin without becoming obscure or ambiguous, but which when used according to the vulgar idiom is neither ambiguous nor obscure, not in the way the learned, but rather in the way the unlearned employ it. For if our translators did not shrink from saying, "*Non congregabo conventicula eorum de sanguinibius,*" because they felt that it was important for the sense to put a word here in the plural which in Latin is only used in the singular, why should a teacher of godliness who is addressing an unlearned audience shrink from using *ossum* instead of *os,* if he fear that the latter might be taken not as the singular of *ossa,* but as the singular of *ora,* seeing that African ears have no quick perception of the shortness or length of vowels? And what advantage is there in purity of speech which does not lead to understanding in the hearer, seeing that there is no use at all in speaking, if they do not understand us for whose sake we speak? He, therefore, who teaches will avoid all words that do not teach; and if instead of them he can find words which are at once pure and intelligible, he will take these by preference; if, however, he cannot, either because there are no such words, or because they do not at the time occur to him, he will use words that are not quite pure, if only the substance of his thought be conveyed and apprehended in its integrity.

25. And this must be insisted on as necessary to our being understood, not only in conversations, whether with one person or with several, but much more in the case of a speech delivered in public: for in conversation

any one has the power of asking a question; but when all are silent that one may be heard, and all faces are turned attentively upon him, it is neither customary nor decorous for a person to ask a question about what he does not understand; and on this account the speaker ought to be especially careful to give assistance to those who cannot ask it. Now a crowd anxious for instruction generally shows by its movements if it understands what is said; and until some indication of this sort be given, the subject discussed, ought to be turned over and over, and put in every shape and form and variety of expression, a thing which cannot be done, by men who are repeating words prepared beforehand and committed to memory. As soon, however, as the speaker has ascertained that what he says is understood, he ought either to bring his address to a close, or pass on to another point. For if a man gives pleasure when he throws light upon points on which people wish for instruction, he becomes wearisome when he dwells at length upon things that are already well known, especially when men's expectation was fixed on having the difficulties of the passage removed. For even things that are very well known are told for the sake of the pleasure they give, if the attention be directed not to the things themselves, but to the way in which they are told. Nay, even when the style itself is already well known, if it be pleasing to the hearers, it is almost a matter of indifference whether he who speaks be a speaker or a reader. For things that are gracefully written are often not only read with delight by those who are making their first acquaintance with them, but re-read with delight by those who have already made acquaintance with them, and have not yet forgotten them; nay, both these classes will derive pleasure even from hearing another man repeat them. And if a man has forgotten anything, when he is reminded of it he is taught. But I am not now treating of the mode of giving pleasure. I am speaking of the mode in which men who desire to learn ought to be taught. And the best mode is that which secures that he who hears shall hear the truth, and that what he hears he shall understand. And when this point has been reached, no further labor need be spent on the truth itself, as if it required further explanation; but perhaps some trouble may be taken to enforce it so as to bring it home to the heart. If it appear right to do this, it ought to be done so moderately as not to lead to weariness and impatience.

Chap. 11. The Christian Teacher Must Speak Clearly, But Not Inelegantly

26. For teaching, of course, true eloquence consists, not in making people like what they disliked, nor in making them do what they shrank from,

but in making clear what was obscure; yet if this be done without grace of style, the benefit does not extend beyond the few eager students who are anxious to know whatever is to be learnt, however rude and unpolished the form in which it is put; and who, when they have succeeded in their object, find the plain truth pleasant, food enough. And it is one of the distinctive features of good intellects not to love words, but the truth in words. For of what service is a golden key, if it cannot open what we want it to open? Or what objection is there to a wooden one if it can, seeing that to open what is shut is all we want? But as there is a certain analogy between learning and eating, the very food without which it is impossible to live must be flavored to meet the tastes of the majority.

Chap. 12. The Aim of the Orator, According to Cicero, Is to Teach, to Delight, and to Move. Of These, Teaching Is the Most Essential

27. Accordingly a great orator has truly said that "an eloquent man must speak so as to teach, to delight, and to persuade." Then he adds: "To teach is a necessity, to delight is a beauty, to persuade is a triumph." Now of these three, the one first mentioned, the teaching, which is a matter of necessity, depends on what we say; the other two on the way we say it. He, then, who speaks with the purpose of teaching should not suppose that he has said what he has to say as long as he is not understood; for although what he has said be intelligible to himself, it is not said at all to the man who does not understand it. If, however, he is understood, he has said his say, whatever may have been his manner of saying it. But if he wishes to delight or persuade his hearer as well, he will not accomplish that end by putting his thought in any shape no matter what, but for that purpose the style of speaking is a matter of importance. And as the hearer must be pleased in order to secure his attention, so he must be persuaded in order to move him to action. And as he is pleased if you speak with sweetness and elegance, so he is persuaded if he be drawn by your promises, and awed by your threats; if he reject what you condemn, and embrace what you commend; if he grieve when you heap up objects for grief, and rejoice when you point out an object for joy; if he pity those whom you present to him as objects of pity, and shrink from those whom you set before him as men to be feared and shunned. I need not go over all the other things that can be done by powerful eloquence to move the minds of the hearers, not telling them what they ought to do, but urging them to do what they already know ought to be done.

28. If, however, they do not yet know this, they must of course be instructed before they can be moved. And perhaps the mere knowledge

of their duty will have such an effect that there will be no need to move them with greater strength of eloquence. Yet when this is needful, it ought to be done. And it is needful when people, knowing what they ought to do, do it not. Therefore, to teach is a necessity. For what men know, it is in their own hands either to do or not to do. But who would say that it is their duty to do what they do not know? On the same principle, to persuade is not a necessity for it is not always called for; as, for example, when the hearer yields his assent to one who simply teaches or gives pleasure. For this reason also to persuade is a triumph, because it is possible that a man may be taught and delighted, and yet not give his consent. And what will be the use of gaining the first two ends if we fail in the third? Neither is it a necessity to give pleasure; for when, in the course of an address, the truth is clearly pointed out (and this is the true function of teaching), it is not the fact, nor is it the intention, that the style of speech should make the truth pleasing, or that the style should of itself give pleasure; but the truth itself, when exhibited in its naked simplicity, gives pleasure, because it is the truth. And hence even falsities are frequently a source of pleasure when they are brought to light and exposed. It is not, of course, their falsity that gives pleasure; but as it is true that they are false, the speech which shows this to be true gives pleasure.

Chap. 13. The Hearer Must Be Moved as Well as Instructed

29. But for the sake of those who are so fastidious that they do not care for truth unless it is put in the form of a pleasing discourse, no small place has been assigned in eloquence to the art of pleasing. And yet even this is not enough for those stubborn-minded men who both understand and are pleased with the teacher's discourse, without deriving any profit from it. For what does it profit a man that he both confesses the truth and praises the eloquence, if he does not yield his consent, when it is only for the sake of securing his consent that the speaker in urging the truth gives careful attention to what he says? If the truths taught are such that to believe or to know them is enough, to give one's assent implies nothing more than to confess that they are true. When, however, the truth taught is one that must be carried into practice, and that is taught for the very purpose of being practiced, it is useless to be persuaded of the truth of what is said, it is useless to be pleased with the manner in which it is said, if it be not so learnt as to be practiced. The eloquent divine, then, when he is urging a practical truth, must not only teach so as to give instruction, and please so as to keep up the attention, but he must also

sway the mind so as to subdue the will. For if a man be not moved by the force of truth, though it is demonstrated to his own confession, and clothed in beauty of style, nothing remains but to subdue him by the power of eloquence.

Chap. 14. Beauty of Diction to Be in Keeping with the Matter

30. And so much labor has been spent by men on the beauty of expression here spoken of, that not only is it not our duty to do, but it is our duty to shun and abhor, many and heinous deeds of wickedness and baseness which wicked and base men have with great eloquence recommended, not with a view to gaining assent, but merely for the sake of being read with pleasure. But may God avert from his church what the prophet Jeremiah says of the synagogue of the Jews: "A wonderful and horrible thing is committed in the land: the prophets prophesy falsely, and the priests applaud them with their hands; I and my people love to have it so: and what will ye do in the end thereof?" O eloquence, which is the more terrible from its purity, and the more crushing from its solidity! Assuredly it is "a hammer that breaketh the rock in pieces." For to this God himself has by the same prophet compared his own word spoken through his holy prophets. God forbid, then, God forbid that with us the priest should applaud the false prophet, and that God's people should love to have it so. God forbid, I say, that with us there should be such terrible madness! For what shall we do in the end thereof? And assuredly it is preferable, even though what is said should be less intelligible, less pleasing, and less persuasive, that truth be spoken, and that what is just, not what is iniquitous, be listened to with pleasure. But this, of course, cannot be, unless what is true and just be expressed with elegance.

31. In a serious assembly, moreover, such as is spoken of when it is said, "I will praise thee among much people," no pleasure is derived from that species of eloquence which indeed says nothing that is false, but which buries small and unimportant truths under a frothy mass of ornamental words, such as would not be graceful or dignified even if used to adorn great and fundamental truths. And something of this sort occurs in a letter of the blessed Cyprian, which, I think, came there by accident, or else was inserted designedly with this view, that posterity might see how the wholesome discipline of Christian teaching had cured him of that redundancy of language, and confined him to a more dignified and modest form of eloquence, such as we find in his subsequent letters, a style which is admired without effort, is sought after with

eagerness, but is not attained without great difficulty. He says, then, in one place, "Let us seek this abode: the neighboring solitudes afford a retreat where, whilst the spreading shoots of the vine trees, pendulous and intertwined, creep amongst the supporting reeds, the leafy covering has made a portico of vine." There is wonderful fluency and exuberance of language here; but it is too florid to be pleasing to serious minds. But people who are fond of this style are apt to think that men who do not use it, but employ a more chastened style do so because they cannot attain the former, not because their judgment teaches them to avoid it. Wherefore this holy man shows both that he can speak in that style, for he has done so once, and that he does not choose, for he never uses it again.

Chap. 15. The Christian Teacher Should Pray Before Preaching

32. And so our Christian orator, while he says what is just, and holy, and good (and he ought never to say anything else), does all he can to be heard with intelligence, with pleasure, and with obedience; and he need not doubt that if he succeed in this object, and so far as he succeeds, he will succeed more by piety in prayer than by gifts of oratory; and so he ought to pray for himself, and for those he is about to address, before he attempts to speak. And when the hour is come that he must speak, he ought, before he opens his mouth, to lift up his thirsty soul to God, to drink in what he is about to pour forth, and to be himself filled with what he is about to distribute. For, as in regard to every matter of faith and love there are many things that may be said, and many ways of saying them, who knows what it is expedient at a given moment for us to say, or to be heard saying, except God who knows the hearts of all? And who can make us say what we ought, and in the way we ought, except him in whose hand both we and our speeches are? Accordingly, he who is anxious both to know and to teach should learn all that is to be taught, and acquire such a faculty of speech as is suitable for a divine. But when the hour for speech arrives, let him reflect upon that saying of our Lord's, as better suited to the wants of a pious mind: "Take no thought how or what ye shall speak; for it shall be given you in that same hour what ye shall speak. For it is not ye that speak, but the Spirit of your Father which speaketh in you." The Holy Spirit, then, speaks thus in those who for Christ's sake are delivered to the persecutors; why not also in those who deliver Christ's message to those who are willing to learn?

Chap. 16. Human Directions Not to Be Despised, Though God Makes the True Teacher

33. Now if anyone says that we need not direct men how or what they should teach, since the Holy Spirit makes them teachers, he may as well say that we need not pray, since our Lord says, "Your Father knoweth what things ye have need of before ye ask him"; or that the Apostle Paul should not have given directions to Timothy and Titus as to how or what they should teach others. And these three apostolic epistles ought to be constantly before the eyes of every one who has obtained the position of a teacher in the church. In the First Epistle to Timothy do we not read: "These things command and teach"? What these things are, has been told previously. Do we not read there: "Rebuke not an elder, but entreat him as a father"? Is it not said in the Second Epistle: "Hold fast the form of sound words, which thou hast heard of me"? And is he not there told: "Study to show thyself approved unto God, a workman that needeth not to be ashamed, rightly dividing the word of truth"? And in the same place: "Preach the word; be instant in season, out of season; reprove, rebuke, exhort, with all long-suffering and doctrine." And so in the Epistle to Titus, does he not say that a bishop ought to "hold fast the faithful word as he hath been taught, that he may be able by sound doctrine both to exhort and to convince the gainsayers"? There, too, he says: "But speak thou the things which become sound doctrine: that the aged men be sober," and so on. And there, too: "These things speak, and exhort, and rebuke with all authority. Let no man despise thee. Put them in mind to be subject to principalities and powers," and so on. What then are we to think?

Does the apostle in anyway contradict himself, when, though he says that men are made teachers by the operation of the Holy Spirit, he yet himself gives them directions how and what they should teach? Or are we to understand, that though the duty of men to teach even the teachers does not cease when the Holy Spirit is given, yet, that neither is he who planteth anything, nor he who watereth, but God who giveth the increase? Wherefore though holy men be our helpers, or even holy angels assist us, no one learns aright the things that pertain to life with God, until God makes him ready to learn from himself, that God who is thus addressed in the psalm: "Teach me to do thy will; for thou art my God." And so the same apostle says to Timothy himself, speaking, of course, as teacher to disciple: "But continue thou in the things which thou hast learned, and hast been assured of, knowing of whom thou hast learned them."

For as the medicines which men apply to the bodies of their fellow-men are of no avail except God gives them virtue (who can heal without their aid, though they cannot without his), and yet they are applied; and if it be done from a sense of duty, it is esteemed a work of mercy or benevolence; so the aids of teaching, applied through the instrumentality of man, are of advantage to the soul only when God works to make them of advantage, who could give the gospel to man even without the help or agency of men.

Chap. 17. Threefold Division of the Various Styles of Speech

34. He then who, in speaking, aims at enforcing what is good, should not despise any of those three objects, either to teach, or to give pleasure, or to move, and should pray and strive, as we have said above, to be heard with intelligence, with pleasure, and with ready compliance. And when he does this with elegance and propriety, he may justly be called eloquent, even though he does not carry with him the assent of his hearer. For it is these three ends, viz., teaching, giving pleasure, and moving, that the great master of Roman eloquence himself seems to have intended that the following three directions should subserve: "He, then, shall be eloquent, who can say little things in a subdued style, moderate things in a temperate style, and great things in a majestic style": as if he had taken in also the three ends mentioned above, and had embraced the whole in one sentence thus: "He, then, shall be eloquent, who can say little things in a subdued style, in order to give instruction, moderate things in a temperate style, in order to give pleasure, and great things in a majestic style, in order to sway the mind."

Chap. 18. The Christian Orator Is Constantly Dealing with Great Matters

35. Now the author I have quoted could have exemplified these three directions, as laid down by himself, in regard to legal questions: he could not, however, have done so in regard to ecclesiastical questions, the only ones that an address such as I wish to give shape to is concerned with. For of legal questions those are called small which have reference to pecuniary transactions; those great where a matter relating to man's life or liberty comes up. Cases, again, which have to do with neither of these, and where the intention is not to get the hearer to do, or to pronounce judgment upon anything, but only to give him pleasure, occupy as it were a middle place between the former two, and are on that account called middling, or moderate. For moderate things get their name from *modus*

(a measure); and it is an abuse, not a proper use of the word *moderate,* to put it for *little.*

In questions like ours, however, where all things and especially those addressed to the people from the place of authority, ought to have reference to men's salvation, and that not their temporal but their eternal salvation, and where also the thing to be guarded against is eternal ruin, everything that we say is important; so much so, that even what the preacher says about pecuniary matters, whether it have reference to loss or gain, whether the amount be great or small, should not seem unimportant. For justice is never unimportant, and justice ought assuredly to be observed, even in small affairs of money, as our Lord says: "He that is faithful in that which is least, is faithful also in much." That which is least, then, is very little; but to be faithful in that which is least is great. For as the nature of the circle, viz., that all lines drawn from the center to the circumference are equal, is the same in a great disk that it is in the smallest coin; so the greatness of justice is in no degree lessened, though the matters to which justice is applied be small.

36. And when the apostle spoke about trials in regard to secular affairs (and what were these but matters of money?), he says: ""Dare any of you, having a matter against another, go to law before the unjust and not before the saints? Do ye not know that the saints shall judge the world? And if the world shall be judged by you, are ye unworthy to judge the smallest matters? Know ye not that we shall judge angels? How much more things that pertain to this life? If, then, ye have judgments of things pertaining to this life, set them to judge who are least esteemed in the Church. I speak to your shame. Is it so, that there is not a wise man among you, no, not one that shall be able to judge between his brethren? But brother goeth to law with brother, and that before the unbelievers. Now therefore there is utterly a fault among you, because ye go to law one with another: why do ye not rather take wrong? Why do ye not rather suffer yourselves to be defrauded? Nay, ye do wrong, and defraud, and that your brethren. Know ye not that the unrighteous shall not inherit the kingdom of God?"

Why is it that the apostle is so indignant, and that he thus accuses, and upbraids, and chides, and threatens? Why is it that the changes in his tone, so frequent and so abrupt, testify to the depth of his emotion? Why is it, in fine, that he speaks in a tone so exalted about matters so very trifling? Did secular matters deserve so much at his hands? God forbid. No, but all this is done for the sake of justice, charity, and piety, which in the judgment of every sober mind are great, even when applied to matters the very least.

37. Of course, if we were giving men advice as to how they ought to conduct secular cases, either for themselves or for their connections, before the church courts, we would rightly advise them to conduct them quietly as matters of little moment. But we are treating of the manner of speech of the man who is to be a teacher of the truths which deliver us from eternal misery and bring us to eternal happiness; and wherever these truths are spoken of, whether in public or private, whether to one or many, whether to friends or enemies, whether in a continuous discourse or in conversation, whether in tracts, or in books, or in letters long or short, they are of great importance. Unless indeed we are prepared to say that, because a cup of cold water is a very trifling and common thing, the saying of our Lord that he who gives a cup of cold water to one of His disciples shall in nowise lose his reward, is very trivial and unimportant. Or that when a preacher takes this saying as his text, he should think his subject very unimportant, and therefore speak without either eloquence or power, but in a subdued and humble style. Is it not the case that when we happen to speak on this subject to the people, and the presence of God is with us, so that what we say is not altogether unworthy of the subject, a tongue of fire springs up out of that cold water which inflames even the cold hearts of men with a zeal for doing works of mercy in hope of an eternal reward?

Chap. 19. The Christian Teacher Must Use Different Styles on Different Occasions

38. And yet, while our teacher ought to speak of great matters, he ought not always to be speaking of them in a majestic tone, but in a subdued tone when he is teaching, temperately when he is giving praise or blame. When, however, something is to be done, and we are speaking to those who ought, but are not willing, to do it, then great matters must be spoken of with power, and in a manner calculated to sway the mind. And sometimes the same important matter is treated in all these ways at different times, quietly when it is being taught, temperately when its importance is being urged, and powerfully when we are forcing a mind that is averse to the truth to turn and embrace it. For is there anything greater than God himself? Is nothing, then, to be learnt about him? Or ought he who is teaching the Trinity in unity to speak of it otherwise than in the method of calm discussion, so that in regard to a subject which it is not easy to comprehend, we may understand as much as it is given us to understand? Are we in this case to seek out ornaments instead of proofs? Or is the hearer to be moved to do something instead of being

instructed so that he may learn something? But when we come to praise God, either in himself, or in his works, what a field for beauty and splendor of language opens up before man, who can task his powers to the utmost in praising him whom no one can adequately praise, though there is no one who does not praise him in some measure! But if he be not worshiped, or if idols, whether they be demons or any created being whatever, be worshiped with him or in preference to him, then we ought to speak out with power and impressiveness, show how great a wickedness this is, and urge men to flee from it.

Chap. 20. Examples of the Various Styles Drawn from Scripture

39. But now to come to something more definite. We have an example of the calm, subdued style in the Apostle Paul, where he says: "Tell me, ye that desire to be under the law, do ye not hear the law? For it is written, that Abraham had two sons; the one by a bondmaid, the other by a free woman. But he who was of the bondwoman was born after the flesh; but he of the free woman was by promise. Which things are an allegory: for these are the two covenants; the one from the Mount Sinai, which gendereth to bondage, which is Hagar. For this Hagar is Mount Sinai in Arabia, and answereth to Jerusalem which now is, and is in bondage with her children. But Jerusalem which is above is free, which is the mother of us all," and so on.

And in the same way where he reasons thus: "Brethren, I speak after the manner of men: Though it be but a man's covenant, yet if it be confirmed, no man disannulleth, or addeth thereto. Now to Abraham and his seed were the promises made. He saith not, And to seeds, as of many; but as of one, and to thy seed, which is Christ. And this I say, that the covenant, that was confirmed before of God in Christ, the law, which was four hundred and thirty years after, cannot disannul, that it should make the promise of none effect. For if the inheritance be of the law, it is no more of promise: but God gave it to Abraham by promise." And because it might possibly occur to the hearer to ask, If there is no inheritance by the law, why then was the law given, he himself anticipates this objection and asks, "Wherefore then serveth the law?" And the answer is given: "It was added because of transgressions, till the seed should come to whom the promise was made; and it was ordained by angels in the hand of a mediator. Now a mediator is not a mediator of one; but God is one." And here an objection occurs which he himself has stated: "Is the law then against the promises of God?" He answers: "God forbid." And he also states the reason in these words: "For if there had been a law given which could have given life, verily righteousness should have been by the law. But the Scripture hath concluded all under sin, that the promise by faith of Jesus Christ might be given to them that believe." It is part, then, of the duty of the teacher not only to interpret what is obscure, and to unravel the difficulties of questions, but also, while doing this, to meet other questions which may chance to suggest themselves, lest these should cast doubt or discredit on what we say. If, however, the solution of these questions suggest itself as soon as the questions themselves arise, it is useless to disturb what we cannot remove. And besides, when out of one question other questions arise, and out of these again still others; if these be all discussed and solved, the reasoning is extended to such a length, that unless the memory be exceedingly powerful and active, the reasoner finds it impossible to return to the original question from which he set out. It is, however, exceedingly desirable that whatever occurs to the mind as an objection that might be urged should be stated and refuted, lest it turn up at a time when no one will be present to answer it, or lest, if it should occur to a man who is present but says nothing about it, it might never be thoroughly removed.

40. In the following words of the apostle we have the temperate style: "Rebuke not an elder, but entreat him as a father; and the younger men as brethren; the elder women as mothers, the younger as sisters." And also in these: "I beseech you, therefore, brethren, by the mercies of God, that ye present your bodies a living sacrifice, holy, acceptable unto God, which is your reasonable service."

And almost the whole of this hortatory passage is in the temperate style of eloquence; and those parts of it are the most beautiful in which, as if paying what was due, things that belong to each other are gracefully brought together. For example: "Having then gifts, differing according to the grace that is given to us, whether prophecy, let us prophesy according to the proportion of faith; or ministry, let us wait on our ministering; or he that teacheth, on teaching; or he that exhorteth, on exhortation: he that giveth, let him do it with simplicity; he that ruleth, with diligence; he that showeth mercy, with cheerfulness. Let love be without dissimulation. Abhor that which is evil, cleave to that which is good. Be kindly affectioned one to another with brotherly love; in honor preferring one another; not slothful in business; fervent in spirit; serving the Lord; rejoicing in hope; patient in tribulation; continuing instant in prayer; distributing to the necessity of saints; given to hospitality. Bless them which persecute you: bless, and curse not. Rejoice with them that do rejoice, and weep with them that weep. Be of the same mind one toward another." And how gracefully all this is brought to a close in a period of two members: "Mind not high things, but condescend to men of low estate!" And a little afterwards: "Render therefore to all their dues: tribute to whom tribute is due; custom to whom custom; fear to whom fear; honor to whom honor."

And these also, though expressed in single clauses, are terminated by a period of two members: "Owe no man anything, but to love one another." And a little farther on: "The night is far spent, the day is at hand: let us therefore cast off the works of darkness, and let us put on the armor of light. Let us walk honestly, as in the day; not in rioting and drunkenness, not in chambering and wantonness, not in strife and envying: but put ye on the Lord Jesus Christ, and make not provision for the flesh, to fulfill the lusts thereof."

Now if the passage were translated thus, "*et carnis providentiam ne in concupiscentiis feceritis,*" the ear would no doubt be gratified with a more harmonious ending; but our translator, with more strictness, preferred to retain even the order of the words. And how this sounds in the Greek language in which the apostle spoke, those who are better skilled in that tongue may determine. My opinion, however, is, that what has been translated to us in the same order of words does not run very harmoniously even in the original tongue.

41. And, indeed, I must confess that our authors are very defective in that grace of speech which consists in harmonious endings. Whether this be the fault of the translators, or whether, as I am more inclined to believe, the authors designedly avoided such ornaments, I dare not affirm; for I confess I do not know. This I know, however, that if any one who is skilled in this species of harmony would take the closing sentences of these writers and arrange them according to the law of harmony (which he could very easily do by changing some words for words of equivalent meaning, or by retaining the words he finds and altering their arrangement), he will learn that these divinely-inspired men are not defective in any of those points which he has been taught in the schools of the grammarians and rhetoricians to consider of importance; and he will find in them many kinds of speech of great beauty, beautiful even in our language, but especially beautiful in the original—none of which can be found in those writings of which they boast so much.

But care must be taken that, while adding harmony, we take away none of the weight from these divine and authoritative utterances. Now our prophets were so far from being deficient in the musical training from which this harmony we speak of is most fully learnt, that Jerome, a very learned man, describes even the meters employed by some of them, in the Hebrew language at least; though, in order to give an accurate rendering of the words, he has not preserved these in his translation. I, however (to speak of my own feeling, which is better known to me than it is to others, and than that of others is to me), while I do not in my own speech, however modestly I think it done, neglect these harmonious endings, am just as well pleased to find them in the sacred authors very rarely.

42. The majestic style of speech differs from the temperate style just spoken of, chiefly in that it is not so much decked out with verbal ornaments as exalted into vehemence by mental emotion. It uses, indeed, nearly all the ornaments that the other does; but if they do not happen to be at hand, it does not seek for them. For it is borne on by its own vehemence; and the force of the thought, not the desire for ornament, makes it seize upon any beauty of expression that comes in its way. It is enough for its object that warmth of feeling should suggest the fitting words; they need not be selected by careful elaboration of speech. If a brave man be armed with weapons adorned with gold and jewels, he works feats of valor with those arms in the heat of battle, not because they are costly, but because they are arms; and yet the same man does great execution, even when anger furnishes him with a weapon that he digs out of the ground.

The apostle in the following passage is urging that, for the sake of the ministry of the gospel, and, sustained by the consolations of God's grace, we should bear with patience all the evils of this life. It is a great subject, and is treated with power, and the ornaments of speech are not wanting. "Behold," he says, "now is the accepted time; behold, now is the day of salvation. Giving no offense in anything, that the ministry be not blamed: but in all things approving ourselves as the ministers of God, in much patience, in afflictions, in necessities, in distresses, in strifes, in imprisonments, in tumults, in labors, in watchings, in fastings; by pureness, by knowledge, by long-suffering, by kindness, by the Holy Ghost, by love unfeigned, by the word of truth, by the power of God, by the armor of righteousness on the right hand and on the left, by honor and dishonor, by evil report and good report: as deceivers, and yet true; as unknown, and yet well known; as dying, and, behold, we live; as chastened, and not killed; as sorrowful, yet always rejoicing; as poor, yet making many rich; as having nothing, and yet possessing all things." See him still burning: "O ye Corinthians, our mouth is opened unto you, our heart is enlarged," and so on; it would be tedious to go through it all.

43. And in the same way, writing to the Romans, he urges that the persecutions of this world should be overcome by charity, in assured reliance on the help of God. And he treats this subject with both power and beauty: "We know," he says, "that all things work together for good to them that love God, to them who are the called according to his purpose. For whom he did foreknow, he also did predestinate to be conformed to the image of his Son, that he might be the first-born among many brethren. Moreover, whom he did predestinate, them he also called; and whom he called, them he also justified; and whom he justified, them he also glorified. What shall we then say to these things? If God be for us, who can be against us? He that spared not his own Son, but delivered him up for us all, how shall he not with him also freely give us all things? Who shall lay anything to the charge of God's elect? It is God that justifieth; who is he that condemneth? It is Christ that died, yea, rather, that is risen again, who is even at the right hand of God who also maketh intercession for us. Who shall separate us from the love of Christ? Shall tribulation, or distress, or persecution, or famine, or nakedness, or peril, or sword? (As it is written, For Thy sake we are killed all the day long; we are accounted as sheep for the laughter.) Nay, in all these things we are more than conquerors, through him that loved us. For I am persuaded, that neither death, nor life, nor angels, nor principalities, nor powers, nor things present, nor things to come, nor height, nor depth, nor any other creature, shall be able to separate us from the love of God, which is in Christ Jesus our Lord."

44. Again, in writing to the Galatians, although the whole epistle is written in the subdued style, except at the end, where it rises into a temperate eloquence, yet he interposes one passage of so much feeling that, notwithstanding the absence of any ornaments such as appear in the passages just quoted, it cannot be called anything but powerful: "Ye observe days, and months, and times, and years. I am afraid of you, lest I have bestowed upon you labor in vain. Brethren, I beseech you, be as I am; for I am as ye are: ye have not injured me at all. Ye know how, through infirmity of the flesh, I preached the gospel unto you at the first. And my temptation which was in my flesh ye despised not, nor rejected; but received me as an angel of God, even as Christ Jesus. Where is then the blessedness ye spake of? For I bear you record that, if it had been possible, ye would have plucked out your own eyes and have given them to me. Am I therefore become your enemy, because I tell you the truth? They zealously affect you, but not well; yea, they would exclude you, that ye might affect them. But it is good to be zealously affected always

in a good thing, and not only when I am present with you. My little children, of whom I travail in birth again until Christ be formed in you, I desire to be present with you now, and to change my voice; for I stand in doubt of you." Is there anything here of contrasted words arranged antithetically, or of words rising gradually to a climax, or of sonorous clauses, and sections, and periods? Yet, not withstanding, there is a glow of strong emotion that makes us feel the fervor of eloquence.

(Chapter 21 [45-50], which presents examples of the three levels of style in the writings of the Fathers, is omitted.)

Chap. 22. The Necessity of Variety in Style

51. But we are not to suppose that it is against rule to mingle these various styles: on the contrary, every variety of style should be introduced so far as is consistent with good taste. For when we keep monotonously to one style, we fail to retain the hearer's attention; but when we pass from one style to another, the discourse goes off more gracefully, even though it extend to greater length. Each separate style, again, has varieties of its own which prevent the hearer's attention from cooling or becoming languid. We can bear the subdued style, however, longer without variety than the majestic style. For the mental emotion which it is necessary to stir up in order to carry the hearer's feelings with us, when once it has been sufficiently excited, the higher the pitch to which it is raised, can be maintained the shorter time. And therefore we must be on our guard, lest, in striving to carry to a higher point the emotion we have excited, we rather lose what we have already gained. But after the interposition of matter that we have to treat in a quieter style, we can return with good effect to that which must be treated forcibly, thus making the tide of eloquence to ebb and flow like the sea. It follows from this, that the majestic style, if it is to be long continued, ought not to be unvaried, but should alternate at intervals with the other styles; the speech or writing as a whole, however, being referred to that style which is the prevailing one.

Chap. 23. How the Various Styles Should Be Mingled

52. Now it is a matter of importance to determine what style should be alternated with what other, and the places where it is necessary that any particular style should be used. In the majestic style, for instance, it is always, or almost always, desirable that the introduction should be temperate. And the speaker has it in his discretion to use the subdued style even where the majestic would be allowable, in order that the

majestic when it is used may be the more majestic by comparison, and may as it were shine out with greater brilliance from the dark background. Again, whatever may be the style of the speech or writing, when knotty questions turn up for solution, accuracy of distinction is required, and this naturally demands the subdued style. And accordingly this style must be used in alternation with the other two styles whenever questions of that sort turn up; just as we must use the temperate style, no matter what may be the general tone of the discourse, whenever praise or blame is to be given without any ulterior reference to the condemnation or acquittal of anyone, or to obtaining the concurrence of anyone in a course of action. In the majestic style, then, and in the quiet likewise, both the other two styles occasionally find place. The temperate style, on the other hand, not indeed always, but occasionally, needs the quiet style; for example, when, as I have said, a knotty question comes up to be settled, or when some points that are susceptible of ornament are left unadorned and expressed in the quiet style, in order to give greater effect to certain exuberances (as they may be called) of ornament. But the temperate style never needs the aid of the majestic; for its object is to gratify, never to excite, the mind.

Chap. 24. The Effects Produced by the Majestic Style

53. If frequent and vehement applause follows a speaker, we are not to suppose on that account that he is speaking in the majestic style; for this effect is often produced both by the accurate distinctions of the quiet style, and by the beauties of the temperate. The majestic style, on the other hand, frequently silences the audience by its impressiveness, but calls forth their tears. For example, when at Caesarea in Mauritania I was dissuading the people from that civil, or worse than civil, war which they called *Caterva* (for it was not fellow-citizens merely, but neighbors, brothers, fathers and sons even, who, divided into two factions and armed with stones, fought annually at a certain season of the year for several days continuously, everyone killing whomsoever he could), I strove with all the vehemence of speech that I could command to root out and drive from their hearts and lives an evil so cruel and inveterate; it was not, however, when I heard their applause, but when I saw their tears, that I thought I had produced an effect. For the applause showed that they were instructed and delighted, but the tears that they were subdued. And when I saw their tears, I was confident, even before the event proved it, that this horrible and barbarous custom (which had been handed down to them from their father and their ancestors of generations

long gone by and which like an enemy besieging their hearts, or rather had complete possession of them) was overthrown; and immediately my sermons was finished. I called upon them with heart and voice to give praise and thanks to God. And, lo, with the blessing of Christ, it is now eight years or more since anything of the sort was attempted there. In many other cases besides I have observed that men show the effect made on them by the powerful eloquence of a wise man, not by clamorous applause so much as by groans, sometimes even by tears, finally by change of life.

54. The quiet style, too, has made a change in many; but it was to teach them what they were ignorant of, or to persuade them of what they thought incredible, not to make them do what they knew they ought to do but were unwilling to do. To break down the hardness of this sort, speech needs to be vehement. Praise and censure, too, when they are eloquently expressed, even in the temperate style, produce such an effect on some, that they are not only pleased with the eloquence of the encomiums and censures, but are led to live so as themselves to deserve praise, and to avoid living so as to incur blame. But not one would say that all who are thus delighted change their habits in consequence, whereas all who are moved by the majestic style act accordingly, and all who are taught by the quiet style know or believe a truth which they were previously ignorant of.

Chap. 25. How the Temperate Style Is to Be Used

From all this we may conclude that the end arrived at by the two styles last mentioned is the one which it is most essential for those who aspire to speak with wisdom and eloquence to secure. On the other hand, what the temperate style properly aims at, viz., to please by beauty of expression, is not in itself an adequate end; but when what we have to say is good and useful, and when the hearers are both acquainted with it and favorably disposed towards it, so that it is not necessary either to instruct or persuade them, beauty of style may have its influence in securing their prompter compliance, or in making them adhere to it more tenaciously. For as the function of all eloquence, whichever of these three forms it may assume, is to speak persuasively, and its object is to persuade, an eloquent man will speak persuasively, whatever style he may adopt; but unless he succeeds in persuading, his eloquence has not secured its object. Now in the subdued style, he persuades his hearers that what he says is true; in the majestic style, he persuades them to do what they are aware they ought to do, but do not; in the temperate style he persuades them that his speech is elegant and ornate. But what use is there in attaining such an object as this last? They may desire it who are vain of their eloquence and make a boast of panegyrics, and such-like performances, where the object is not to instruct the hearer, or to persuade him to any course of action, but merely to give him pleasure. We, however, ought to make that end subordinate to another, viz., the effecting by this style of eloquence what we aim at effecting when we use the majestic style. For we may by the use of this style persuade men to cultivate good habits and give up evil ones, if they are not so hardened as to need the vehement style; or if they have already begun a good course, we may induce them to pursue it more zealously, and to persevere in it with constancy. Accordingly, even in the temperate style we must use beauty of expression not for ostentation, but for wise ends; not contenting ourselves merely with pleasing the hearer, but rather seeking to aid him in the pursuit of the good end which we hold out before him.

Chap. 26. In Every Style the Orator Should Aim at Perspicuity, Beauty, and Persuasiveness

56. Now in regard to the three conditions I laid down a little while ago as necessary to be fulfilled by anyone who wishes to speak with wisdom and eloquence, viz. perspicuity, beauty of style, and persuasive power, we are not to understand that these three qualities attach themselves respectively to the three several styles of speech, one to each so that perspicuity is a merit peculiar to the subdued style, beauty to the temperate, and persuasive power to the majestic. On the contrary, all speech, whatever its style, ought constantly to aim at, and as far as possible to display, all these three merits.

For we do not like even what we say in the subdued style to pall upon the hearer; and therefore we would be listened to, not with intelligence merely, but with pleasure as well. Again, why do we enforce what we teach by divine testimony, except that we wish to carry the hearer with us, that is, to compel his assent by calling in the assistance of him of whom it is said, "Thy testimonies are very sure"? And when any one narrates a story, even in the subdued style, what does he wish but to be believed? But who will listen to him if he do not arrest attention by some beauty of style? And if he be not intelligible, is it not plain that he can neither give pleasure nor enforce conviction?

The subdued style, again, in its own naked simplicity, when it unravels questions of very great difficulty, and throws an unexpected light upon them; when it worms out and brings to light some very acute observations from a quarter whence nothing was expected; when it seizes upon and exposes the falsity of an opposing opinion, which seemed at its first statement to be unassailable; especially when all this is accompanied by a natural, unsought grace of expression, and by a rhythm and balance of style which is not ostentatiously obtruded, but seems rather to be called forth by the nature of the subject: this style, so used, frequently calls forth applause so great that one can hardly believe it to be the subdued style. For the fact that it comes forth without either ornament or defense, and offers battle in its own naked simplicity, does not hinder it from crushing its adversary by weight of nerve and muscle, and overwhelming and destroying the falsehood that opposes it by the mere strength of its own right arm. How explain the frequent and vehement applause that waits upon men who speak thus, except by the pleasure that truth so irresistibly established, and so victoriously defended, naturally affords? Wherefore the Christian teacher and speaker ought, when he uses the subdued style, to endeavor not only to be clear and intelligible, but to give pleasure and to bring home conviction to the hearer.

57. Eloquence of the temperate style, also, must, in the case of the Christian orator, be neither altogether without ornament, nor unsuitably adorned, nor is it to make the giving of pleasure its sole aim, which is all it professes to accomplish in the hands of others; but in its encomiums and censures it should aim at inducing the hearer to strive after or hold more firmly by what it praises, and to avoid or renounce what it condemns. On the other hand, without perspicuity this style cannot give pleasure. And so the three qualities, perspicuity, beauty, and persuasiveness, are to be sought in this style also; beauty, of course, being its primary object.

58. Again, when it becomes necessary to stir and sway the hearer's mind by the majestic style (and this is always necessary when he admits that what you say is both true and agreeable, and yet is unwilling to act accordingly), you must, of course, speak in the majestic style. But who can be moved if he does not understand what is said? And who will stay to listen if he receives no pleasure? Wherefore, in this style, too, when an obdurate heart is to be persuaded to obedience, you must speak so as to be both intelligible and pleasing, if you would be heard with a submissive mind.

Chap. 27. The Man Whose Life Is in Harmony with His Teaching Will Teach with Greater Effect

59. But whatever may be the majesty of the style, the life of the speaker will count for more in securing the hearer's compliance. The man who speaks wisely and eloquently but lives wickedly, may, it is true, instruct many who are anxious to learn; though, as it is written, he "is unprofitable to himself." Wherefore, also, the apostle says, "Whether in pretence or in truth Christ is preached." Now Christ is the truth; yet we see that the truth can be preached, though not in truth,—that is, what is right and true in itself may be preached by a man of perverse and deceitful mind. And thus it is that Jesus Christ is preached by those that seek their own, and not the things that are Jesus Christ's. But since true believers obey the voice, not of any man, but of the Lord himself, who says, "All therefore whatsoever they bid you observe, that observe and do: but do not ye after their works; for they say and do not"; therefore it is that men who themselves lead unprofitable lives are heard with profit by others. For though they seek their own objects, they do not dare to teach their own doctrines, sitting as they do in the high places of ecclesiastical authority, which is established on sound doctrine. Wherefore our Lord himself, before saying what I have just quoted about men of this stamp, made this observation: "The scribes and the Pharisees sit in Moses' seat." The seat they occupied, then, which was not theirs but Moses', compelled them to say what was good, though they did what was evil. And so they followed their own course in their lives, but were prevented by the seat they occupied, which belonged to another, from preaching their own doctrines.

60. Now these men do good to many by preaching what they themselves do not perform; but they would do good to very many more if they lived as they preach. For there are numbers who seek an excuse for their own evil lives in comparing the teaching with the conduct of their instructors, and who say in their hearts, or even go a little further, and say with their lips: Why do you not do yourself what you bid me do? And thus they cease to listen with submission to a man who does not listen to himself, and in despising the preacher they learn to despise the word that is preached. Wherefore the apostle, writing to Timothy, after telling him, "Let no man despise thy youth," adds immediately the course by which he would avoid contempt: "but be thou an example of the believers, in word, in conversation, in charity, in spirit, in faith, in purity."

Chap. 28. Truth Is More Important Than Expression. What Is Meant by Strife about Words.

61. Such a teacher as is here described may, to secure compliance, speak not only quietly and temperately, but even vehemently, without any breach of modesty, because his life protects him against contempt. For while he pursues an upright life, he takes care to maintain a good reputation as well, providing things honest in the sight of God and men, fearing God, and caring for men. In his very speech even he prefers to please by matter rather than by words; thinks that a thing is well said in proportion as it is true in fact, and that a teacher should govern his words, not let the words govern him. This is what the apostle says: "Not with wisdom of words, lest the cross of Christ should be made of none effect." To the same effect also is what he says to Timothy: "Charging them before the Lord that they strive not about words to no profit, but to the subverting of the hearers."

Now this does not mean that, when adversaries oppose the truth, we are to say nothing in defense of the truth. For where, then, would be what he says when he is describing the sort of man a bishop ought to be: "that he may be able by sound doctrine both to exhort and convince the gainsayers"? To strive about words is not to be careful about the way to overcome error by truth, but to be anxious that your mode of expression should be preferred to that of another. The man who does not strive about words, whether he speak quietly, temperately, or vehemently, uses words, with no other purpose than to make the truth plain, pleasing, and effective; for not even love itself, which is the end of the commandment and the fulfilling of the law, can be rightly exercised unless the objects of love are true and not false. For as a man with a comely body but an ill-conditioned mind is a more painful object than if his body too were deformed, so men who teach lies are the more pitiable if they happen to be eloquent in speech. To speak eloquently, then, and wisely as well, is just to express truths which it is expedient to teach in fit and proper words,—words which in the subdued style are adequate, in the temperate, elegant, and in the majestic, forcible. But the man who cannot speak both eloquently and wisely should speak wisely without eloquence, rather than eloquently without wisdom.

Chap. 29. It Is Permissible for a Preacher to Deliver to the People What Has Been Written by a More Eloquent Man Than Himself

62. If, however, he cannot do even this, let his life be such as shall not only secure a reward for himself, but afford an example to others, and let his manner of living be an eloquent sermon in itself.

63. There are, indeed, some men who have a good delivery, but cannot compose anything to deliver. Now, if such men take what has been written with wisdom and eloquence by others, and commit it to memory, and deliver it to the people, they cannot be blamed, supposing them to do it without deception. For in this way many become preachers of the truth (which is certainly desirable), and yet not many teachers; for all deliver the discourse which one real teacher has composed, and there are no divisions among them. Nor are such men to be alarmed by the words of Jeremiah the prophet, through whom God denounces those who steal his words every one from his neighbor. For those who steal take what does not belong to them, but the word of God belongs to all who obey it; and it is the man who speaks well, but lives badly, who really takes the words that belong to another. For the good things he says seem to be the result of his own thought, and yet they have nothing in common with his manner of life. And so God has said that they steal his words who would appear good by speaking God's words, but are in fact bad, as they follow their own ways. And if you look closely into the matter, it is not really themselves who say the good things they say. For how can they say in words what they deny in deeds? It is not for nothing that the apostle says of such men: "They profess that they know God, but in works they deny him." In one sense, then, they do say the things, and in another sense they do not say them; for both these statements must be true, both being made by him who is the Truth. Speaking of such men, in one place he says, "Whatsoever they bid you observe, that observe and do; but do not ye after their works"; —that is to say, "what ye hear from their lips, that do; what ye see in their lives, that do ye not;—for they say and do not." And so, though they do not, yet they say. But in another place, upbraiding such men, He says, ""O generation of vipers, how can ye, being evil, speak good things?" And from this it would appear that even what they say, when they say what is good, it is not themselves who say, for in will and in deed they deny what they say. Hence it happens that a wicked man who is eloquent may compose a discourse in which the truth is set forth to be delivered by a good man who is not eloquent; and when this takes place, the former draws from himself what does not belong to him, and the latter receives from another what really belongs to himself. But when true believers render this service to true believers, both parties speak what is their own, for God is theirs, to whom belongs all that they say; and even those who could not compose what they say make it their own by composing their lives in harmony with it.

Chap. 30. The Preacher Should Commence His Discourse with Prayer to God

63. But whether a man is going to address the people or to dictate what others will deliver or read to the people, he ought to pray God to put into his mouth a suitable discourse. For if Queen Esther prayed, when she was about to speak to the king touching the temporal welfare of her race, that God would put fit words into her mouth, how much more ought he to pray for the same blessing who labors in word and doctrine for the eternal welfare of men? Those, again, who are to deliver what others compose for them ought, before they receive their discourse, to pray for those who are preparing it; and when they have received it, they ought to pray both that they themselves may deliver it well, and that those to whom they address it may give ear; and when the discourse has a happy issue, they ought to render thanks to him from whom they know such blessings come, so that all the praise may be "his in whose hand are both we and our words."

Chap. 31. Apology for the Length of the Work

64. This book has extended to a greater length than I expected or desired. But the reader or hearer who finds pleasure in it will not think it long. He who thinks it long, but is anxious to know its contents, may read it in parts. He who does not care to be acquainted with it need not complain of its length. I, however, give thanks to God that with what little ability I possess I have in these four books striven to depict, not the sort of man I am myself (for my defects are very many), but the sort of man he ought to be who desires to labor in sound, that is, in Christian doctrine, not for his own instruction only, but for that of others also.

SERMON ON PSALM 31 [32]

*The way that Augustine put his own theory into practice may be seen in the following sermon. This is not the sermon discussed in the text (***see Vol. 1, pp. 113-16***), but the one following it. The sermon discussed there was chosen for the way it shows Augustine as a Sign Reader, while the sermon below was chosen because of its treatment of justification by faith, a theme of Augustine that was to be very influential in later church history, especially the Reformation. Both sermons are seen in the lively translation of Edmund Hill, who is able to capture the charm with which Augustine related to his congregation. Taken from* Nine Sermons of Saint

Augustine on the Psalms, *trans. and intro. Edmund Hill (London: Longmans, Green & Co., 1958), 147-72.*

Sermon on Psalm 31 (32)[1]

Psalm 31(32): A Translation from the Latin Text Used by Augustine

Blessed are those whose iniquities are forgiven,
  And whose sins are covered.
Blessed is the man to whom the Lord has not attributed sin,
  And in his mouth there is no guile.
Because I kept silence, my bones grew old,
  From my shouting all day long;
Because day and night your hand was heavy upon me,
  I turned in my anguish while the thorn was stuck in.
I came to know my sin,
  And my injustice I did not cover.
I said: "I shall utter my injustice to the Lord against myself."
  And you have forgiven the ungodliness of my mind.
For this shall everyone that is holy
  Pray to you at the proper time.
And yet in the flood of many waters
  They shall not come near him.
You are a refuge for me from the violence which surrounds me;
  My joy, redeem me from those who surround me.
"I will give you understanding, and set you in this way you must go by;
  I will fix my eyes upon you.
Do not be like the horse and mule which have no understanding."
  Gag their jaws with bit and bridle who do not come near you.
Many are the whippings of the sinner,
But he that hopes in the Lord shall be compassed about with mercy.
Be glad in the Lord, and rejoice, you just,
  And be boastful, all you straight of mind.

Sermon on Psalm 31 (32)

This psalm is about the grace of God and of how he justifies us without our doing anything to deserve it first, the mercy of the Lord our

God getting in ahead of us every time. It is of special interest to us because St. Paul quotes it, as you will have gathered from the epistle which was read just before we sang the psalm. To the best of my ability I must now run through it with you, and so first of all I would ask you to help me with your prayers "that speech will be given to me in the opening of my mouth" (Eph. 6:19), as the Apostle puts it—speech which it will be profitable to your salvation to hear, without being dangerous to mine to utter. Human nature, you see, is such an unreliable thing; it swings lightly from a confession of weakness to a mood of rash self-confidence, dashing from one extreme to the other, and coming a cropper, as likely as not, at both.

Thus supposing it gives in to its weakness all along the line, and is tempted to say that the infinite mercy of God is ready to receive all sinners, however much they persist in sinning, provided they believe that God delivers them, God forgives them, so that none of the faithful, however wicked, will perish in the end; nobody, that is to say, will perish who says to himself, "Whatever I do, no matter what frightful sins I commit, God is there to save me in his mercy because I have believed in him." Well, anyone who talks like that has fallen into the bad mistake of thinking that you can get away with sin unpunished, and God, the just God to whom we "sing mercy and judgment" (Ps. 100:1)—not only mercy, mind you, but judgment as well—God cannot help but condemn someone who so abuses and presumes on his mercy to his own destruction. That is one frame of mind then which brings a man to ruin.

But now suppose somebody else, who is on his guard against that danger, and gets a grip on himself with altogether too much self-assurance, and relying only on his own justice and strength of character makes up his mind to fulfill all justice, to keep every commandment of the Law without breaking a single one, to manage his life so well that he never slips up, is never caught napping, never at a loss; and suppose he thinks he can do all this on his own resources, his own strength of will—then even if he seems to succeed in the eyes of men and there is nothing in his conduct which men can find fault with, yet God will and must condemn his overweening presumption and pride. So what happens if a man tries to justify himself, and presumes on his own justice and his own goodness? He falls. And if, being aware of his own weakness, he presumes on the mercy of God without troubling to mend his ways and tackle his sins, but plunges into every sink of iniquity—why, he falls too.

So let us listen to God when he says to us, "Turn not aside to the right hand or to the left" (Prov. 4:27). Don't presume on your own justice to get you into the kingdom—that is turning aside to the right. Don't presume on the mercy of God to let you get away with sin—that is slipping off to the left. If you try and scramble up that steep bank to the right, you will tumble down, and if you slip down the slope to the left, you will be sunk. I shall say it again, so that you can get it fixed in your minds. Don't presume on your own justice to get you into the kingdom, don't presume on God's mercy to let you get away with sin unpunished. "What am I to do then?" you ask. This psalm gives us our instructions. When we have been through it, I think we shall see, with the help of God's mercy, the road we ought to follow or which perhaps we are marching along already. Let us try to take it in, each as best as we can, and let each as his conscience tells him be sorry at having to be put right or glad at being approved of. If you find that you have gone wrong, come back and carry on along the right road. If you find that you are still on the right road, keep on marching till you reach the end. Don't be obstinate if you are off the road, don't be lazy if you are on it.

We have St. Paul's word for that this psalm is about the grace which makes Christians of us. That is why I wanted this particular epistle read to you. This is what he says when he is upholding the justice which comes from faith against those who boast of the justice which comes from works, or achievements: "What shall we say that Abraham found, our father in the flesh? For if Abraham was justified by works, he has something to boast about, but not before God" (Rom. 4:1). God save us from such boasting! May it rather be for us a case of "He that boasts, let him boast in the Lord" (1 Cor. 1:31). There are many who boast about their works, and in fact you will find that that is why many pagans don't want to become Christians, because they are quite satisfied with the good life they lead as it is. "It's an achievement, isn't it, to lead a good life," says he. "What has Christ got to tell me—to lead a good life? But I already do. What use is Christ to me? I don't murder or steal or do violence, I don't covet other people's property. I am not smirched with adultery. Find something to object to in my life, and then make me a Christian." He has got something to boast about, this man, but not before God. Not so, however, our father Abraham. This passage of Scripture means us to be quite clear on that point. What the Apostle is saying is, "We know for certain, it is quite plain to our faith, that Abraham has something to boast about before God. But if Abraham is justified by works, he can boast all right, but not before God; yet it is before God that he has something to boast about. Therefore it is not by works that he is justified." If not by works then, what was he justified by? He goes on to tell us: "For what does the Scripture say? But Abraham believed God, and it was counted to him for justice" (Rom. 4:3; Gen. 15:6). So it is by faith then that Abraham was justified.

But now, when you hear "not by works but by faith," be careful of that first bog I warned you about. "There you are, you see, Abraham was justified by faith not by works. So I shall do just as I please, and even though I have no achievements to show for it, provided only I believe in God, it will be counted to me for justice." If you say that and really mean it, you have already fallen in and sunk deep. If you are still hesitating and wondering if there isn't perhaps some truth in it, you are in danger. But the Scripture of God and a true understanding of it can not only rescue you from danger, but also pull you out of the depths if you have already fallen in and sunk. So I shall take up the Apostle at this point, as though I disagreed with him, and say something about Abraham which you will find mentioned by another apostle, who wants to correct the people who had got this apostle all wrong. James in his epistle, which he wrote against those who relied on faith alone and couldn't be bothered with doing good, James held up for us the works of Abraham, whose faith was upheld by Paul—and the apostles don't contradict each other. He mentions then a work of Abraham's which everybody knows about, his offering up his son in sacrifice to God (Jas. 2:21; Gen. 22). A great deed surely—but a deed of faith. I admire the architecture of the deed, but I don't forget the foundation of faith. I admire the fruit of a good deed, but I recognize that it has its roots in faith. But if Abraham had done this quite apart from right faith it would have profited him nothing, however great an achievement it might have been. Again, if Abraham had treated his faith in such a way that when God told him to sacrifice his son, he had said to himself, "I'm not going to do any such thing, yet I believe all the same that God will save me, although I ignore his commands," well his faith without deeds would have been dead, it would have remained a dry barren root without fruit.

What is the situation then? Well, we oughtn't to count any achievements of ours before faith. That is, nobody can really be said to have done any good work before he had faith. Because achievements done before faith, however praiseworthy men think they are, are just wasted. As I see it, they are like a terrific sprint from a runner who is disqualified from running—it doesn't get him anywhere. So nobody should count the good works he achieved before he had faith. Where there was no faith, nothing good was done, because it is the *intention* that makes actions good and it is faith which aims and guides the intention. Don't pay too much attention to what a man does, it is what he has in mind when he does it that matters, where he is heading for with all his stout work at the helm. Suppose a man who is first class at steering a boat, but has lost his bearings. What's the good of his superb handling of the sheet, his putting the bow into the waves and never taking them beam on, his having such skill that he can twist and turn the boat to go where he likes and avoid what he likes—and you say to him "Where are you going?" and he says "I don't know"; or he doesn't say "I don't know," but "To Port So-and-so," and all the while he is not heading for port but for the rocks. Surely the cleverer he thinks he is at managing the boat, the more dangerous his control of it is, as he speeds it onwards to break on the rocks. Wouldn't it be better, surely, wouldn't you prefer him to be a rather less stalwart helmsman, to have some difficulty even in managing the helm, and yet to keep on the right course? And it is the same with the runner; he would do better to run with a little less dash and style and stay in the race all the same, than to run like the wind in the wrong direction. So the best man is the one who both keeps to the right course and keeps up a good pace. But there is still plenty of hope for the man who limps, maybe, but not so as to lose the way or get stuck, and keeps on moving bit by bit. There is still hope that he will get there in the end.

And so, brothers, it was by faith that Abraham was justified. But even though no achievements preceded faith, they followed it nevertheless. And surely you are not going to let your faith be barren, are you? If you are not barren, neither is your faith. But do something wicked, and with the fire of your wickedness you have scorched the roots of your faith. So hold on to faith with the intention of doing something with it. "But St. Paul the apostle doesn't say that," you tell me. Oh yes, but St. Paul the apostle does say that. "Faith which works through love" (Gal. 5:6), he says in one place, and, in another, "All the Law is summed up in this one sentence in which it is written 'You shall love your neighbor as yourself'" (ibid. 14). Just see whether he wants you to work at doing good or not: "You shall not commit adultery, You shall not commit murder, You shall not covet, and any other commandment there is, is summed up in this sentence, You shall love your neighbor as yourself. Love of neighbor does not work evil, but the fullness of the Law is charity" (Rom. 13:9). Does charity allow you to do any evil to the one you love? Perhaps you don't do him any evil, and no good either. And does charity then allow you not to do what good you can to the one you love? It is charity, isn't it, which prays even for enemies, and can you leave your friend in the lurch while you are wishing well to your enemies? And so you see, faith will be without works, without achievements, if it is without love. But to save yourself worrying about what faith ought to be doing, just add to it hope and love, and don't worry about what work to accomplish. That love cannot be idle. What is it in any man that works anything, even wickedness, if it isn't love? Just show me love being idle and doing nothing. Shameful deeds or violent deeds, adulteries, murders, lusts of all sorts, isn't it love that commits them all? Clean your love, then; turn the water which runs into the sewer on to the garden. Let the current which flows towards the world flow instead towards the maker of the world. Do you imagine you are being told not to love anything? But of course you are not. It is dead you would be, stagnant, loathsome, if you didn't love anything. Carry on loving, only mind what you love. Love of God, love of neighbor, is called charity; love of the world, love of this life, is called greed. Let greed be chained up, and charity exercised. Because the charity of a man who does good gives him the hope enjoyed by a good conscience. A good conscience brings hope, just as a bad conscience brings desperation. So you have these three which the Apostle speaks of, faith, hope and charity (1 Cor. 13:13); and in another place you get the same three, except that for hope he puts a good conscience. "For the end of the commandment," he says—what does the end of the commandment mean? The end which puts a fine finish on it, not the end which finishes it off. It is one thing to say "The food's finished," and another, "The shirt I was having made is finished." So here he means the end of the commandment in the sense of completing it, like the shirt. "The end of the commandment," he says, "is charity from a pure heart, and from a good conscience, and from an unfeigned faith" (1 Tim. 1:5). He puts a good conscience for hope. To hope for the kingdom you must have a good conscience, and to have a good conscience you must believe and do good. It is the business of faith to believe, and of charity to do good, to work. In one place St. Paul begins with faith, faith, hope and charity, and in the other which I have just quoted he begins with charity. I myself have begun in the middle with hope. To hope, I repeat, you need a good conscience, and to have that you must believe and do good. Starting in the middle, you can work backwards to the beginning, which is faith's job of believing, and forwards to good works, the business of charity which is the end.

But then how can the Apostle say that a man is justified by faith without works, when elsewhere he talks about faith working through love? It isn't James, it seems, we must quote against Paul, it's Paul himself. Let's tackle him on the point. —At one moment you seem to allow us to sin with impunity, when you say "We account a man justified by faith without works" (Rom. 3:28), and at another you are talking about faith working through love (Gal. 5:6). How can the two fit? In the first instance I am made to feel safe, even though I have done no good work at all. In the second I cannot have proper faith unless I work through love. It is yourself I am listening to, my dear Apostle. Here you are, urging faith on me without works. But love is a work of faith. Love cannot be idle, as we have seen. "Decline from evil and do good" (Ps. 33:15), that is what love does. So here you are, apparently commending faith without works, and yet elsewhere you say, "Even though I have faith to move mountains, but have not charity, it profits me nothing" (1 Cor. 13:2). So if faith is no use without charity, and if charity, wherever it is found, cannot help being busy, it follows that faith itself (if it is to be of any use) works through love. And how then will a man be justified through faith without works?

The Apostle answers, "The reason I told you this, my good man, was in case you should think you could rely on your own works, and that by your own works you had deserved to receive the grace of faith. So don't presume at all on the works you did before you had faith. Realize that faith found you a sinner; the faith that was given you made a just man of you out of an ungodly sinner." "To the man," St. Paul goes on, "that believes in him who justifies the ungodly, his faith is counted for justice" (Rom. 4:5). If it is an ungodly man who is justified, it means that a just man is made out of an ungodly one; and if that is so, what good works can the ungodly have before being justified? Let the ungodly man boast of his works if he likes. Let him say, "I give to the poor, I don't do anyone out of anything, I don't covet another man's wife, or kill people, or cheat, or break my word." —Let him say all that. What I want to know is, Is he godly or ungodly? "How can I be ungodly if I behave as decently as that?" In just the same way as those of whom it is said, "They served the creature rather than the Creator, who is blessed forever" (Rom. 1:25). How can you be ungodly? Well, what if by doing all this you hope indeed for what you ought to hope, but not *from whom* you ought to hope for it? Or you hope for something you ought not to hope for, from him whom you ought to hope for everlasting life from? You hope to get some worldly advantage out of these good works of yours, then you are ungodly. That's not what the price of faith is. Faith is something very dear, you have let it go cheap. So you are ungodly, and these good works of yours are worthless. However nimble and sturdy you may appear in handling your boat, you are heading for the rocks. Supposing you hope, though, for the right thing, life everlasting, but not from God through Jesus Christ, through whom alone it is given? Suppose you hope to get it through the host of heaven, the sun, the moon, the powers of air and sea and earth? You are ungodly. Hope in him who justifies the ungodly, so that your good works really may be good works. So long as they don't spring from a good root, I wouldn't call them good at all. Correct your faith then, take to the right road; and if you have got a good pair of legs, you can stride on without any worry at all, you can run as fast as you like. You are on the right road, the better you run the sooner you will get there. But perhaps you are a little flat-footed. It doesn't matter, you will get there, too, though rather more slowly. But whatever you do, keep on the road, don't stop, don't turn back, don't wander off.

Well, well, then who are the lucky ones? Not those in whom God hasn't found sin, because there aren't any. "All have sinned and need the glory of God" (Rom. 3:23). So the lucky ones can only be those whose sins are forgiven. This is the point which St. Paul has been urging on us. "Abraham believed God and it was reckoned to him for justice. Now to the man who works, his hire is not reckoned as a grace—that is, as a favor—but as a debt" (Rom. 4:3). But our hire, he is saying, our reward *is* called grace, that is, it is given us by God as a pure favor. If it is given as a favor, it goes on being a favor as long as you have it. Thus you have done nothing good, and you are given forgiveness of sins. As far as your works go, they are all found bad; if God gave what was owing to them, he would of course condemn you—"the wages of sin is death" (Rom. 6:23). Damnation is what is owed for bad works, the kingdom of heaven for good works. Here you are, found mixed up in bad works, and what happens? God doesn't pay you the punishment he owes you, he grants you the favor of grace which he doesn't owe you. And now, by his kindness and indulgence, you begin to have faith. Now faith, picking up hope and love, begins to do good, real good now. But don't start boasting yet. Remember what a mess you were fetched from to be set on the road. Remember that with a perfectly sound pair of legs you had got lost. Or remember that you may have been on the road, but were found lying on it half-dead, and were put on a donkey and brought to the inn (Lk. 10:30). "But to the man who works, his hire is not reckoned as a favor, but as a debt." If you want to be a stranger to God's favor, start boasting of your deserts. He can see right through you, and he knows what he owes and to whom. "But to the man who does not work"—what? Take an ungodly sinner, he doesn't work—"but believes in him who justifies the ungodly, his faith is reckoned for justice." As David says, "The luck of the man to whose account God credits justice without works" (Rom. 4:5). But what sort of justice? The justice of faith which was not preceded by good works, but is certainly followed by good works.

Look to it then all of you! Otherwise by getting the thing all wrong, you will fall into that awful bog of thinking that you can sin with impunity, and I won't be to blame, just as the Apostle wasn't to blame for all who misunderstood him. In fact, they wanted to misunderstand, so that they wouldn't have to bother about good works. Don't be like that, my dears. It says in one of the psalms about that sort, "He would not understand to do good" (Ps. 35:41). It doesn't say he could not, but would not understand. So you must want to understand to do good. What has to be understood is quite simple, quite clear. Nobody must boast of any good works he did before he had faith, no one must be slack about doing good works after receiving faith. So God shows indulgence to all the ungodly, and justifies them by faith.

"Blessed are those whose iniquities are forgiven, and whose sins are covered. Blessed is the man to whom the Lord has not attributed sin, and in his mouth there is no guile." Here is the psalm beginning at last, and understanding has begun too—true understanding being, remember, that you should know not to boast of your merits, nor think you can get away scot-free with sin. The title of the psalm is, in fact, "Understanding for this man David." It is a psalm of understanding. Well, the first thing that you have got to understand is that you are a sinner. And the second thing to understand is that when you begin to do good out of faith through love, this is not to be put down to your own ability, but to God's grace and favor. In this way there will be no guile in your mind, which we can call the inner mouth of your soul. You won't be saying one thing and thinking another. You won't be one of those Pharisees who were told that they were like whitewashed tombs. Outwardly indeed they seemed to be just, but inwardly they were full of guile and iniquity (Mt. 23:27). Nathaniel wasn't like that: "Behold an Israelite indeed, in whom there is no guile" (Jn. 1:47). That is what our Lord said of him. Why was there no guile in Nathaniel? "When you were under the fig-tree I saw you." He was under the fig tree, under the flesh. That is what the fig-tree stands for, and another psalm tells us what it means to be under the flesh: "For behold in iniquity was I conceived" (Ps. 50:7), under the shadow of original sin, of inherited ungodliness. But he was seen under the fig-tree by him who came bringing grace. To be seen by him means to be pitied by him. So in commending the guilelessness of Nathaniel, our Lord was really commending his own grace active in him. After all, what is the point of saying "I saw you under the fig tree," what's so terrific about that, unless you understand "I saw you" in a special way? What's remarkable about seeing a man under a fig tree, why should Nathaniel have been so staggered by it? Well, if Christ hadn't seen the human race under this fig-tree, we would either have withered up altogether, or else like the Pharisees, in whom there was any amount of guile, we would have produced a lot of leaves—namely words and pious phrases—and no fruit, no good works. And when Christ saw a fig tree of that sort, he cursed it, and it withered away (Mt. 21:19). "I see only leaves on it," he said, "only words and no fruit of good works. Let it wither away then, and not even have leaves." That is what the Jews were like; that tree was the Pharisees, who had plenty of words but no deeds, and our Lord condemned them to wither away. May he see *us* under the fig tree, like Nathaniel, and may he see some fruit, some good work in us, when he sees us under the flesh, so that we won't be shriveled up by his curse. And because whatever good there is in us can all be put down to his grace, not to our own qualities, "Blessed are those whose sins are covered," not those in whom no sins are found. The sins are covered, they are smothered, they are wiped out. If God covers sins, it means he doesn't want to notice them; if he doesn't want to notice them, he doesn't want to punish them; if he doesn't want to punish them, he prefers to forgive them. Don't misunderstand this about sins being covered, as though they lived on under cover, still there to burden the conscience. He uses this phrase about sins being covered, to indicate that they are no longer seen. And God's seeing or not seeing sins is only a way of putting his punishing or not punishing them. So it says in another psalm, "Turn away your face from my sins" (Ps. 50:11). May he not see your sins, but see you instead—as he saw Nathaniel under the fig tree. The shade of the fig tree wasn't too thick for the eyes of God's mercy to see through.

"Nor is there guile in his mouth." But now then, those who won't confess their sins waste a lot of effort in excusing their sins. And the more they try to defend their sins by boosting their fine qualities, the more their real strength and courage is drained away. The really stouthearted man gets his courage from God, not from himself. "Three times I asked the Lord to take it from me and he said to me, 'My grace is enough for you. For strength is made perfect in weakness'" (2 Cor. 12:8). That is St. Paul, and he goes on to say, "When I am being weakened, then am I strong." So whoever wants to be strong on his own, and boasts of his own good qualities, will be like that Pharisee who preened himself on what he admitted he had received from God. "I thank you," he said—just notice, brothers, what sort of pride God would draw our attention to, the sort that can so easily entangle a just man and worm its way into a good conscience. "I thank you," he was saying, which is to admit, isn't it, that he had received whatever good he had. What's wrong with that? After all, what have you got that you haven't received (1 Cor. 4:7)? "I thank you that I am not like other men, extortioners, unjust, adulterers, like this publican here" (Lk. 18:11). Where is his pride then? Not in his thanking God, but in his putting himself above another man because of what God had given him.

Now notice carefully: the gospel tells us what had started our Lord off on this parable. He had just said, "Think you the Son of Man on coming will find faith on the earth?" (Lk. 18:8). And in case any heretics should pick on this and think the whole world had fallen away except themselves—all heretics, you will find, are very select and parochial—and should boast that faith had vanished from the whole earth and only survived among themselves, St. Luke adds straight away, "But he also said to some who thought themselves just and despised others, this parable: 'A Pharisee and a publican went into the temple to pray.'" We have just seen what the Pharisee said, and how he despised the man who kept at a distance, and whom God came close up to, as he made his confession. "But the publican," it goes on, "stood at a distance"—God, though, didn't stand at a distance from him, "for the Lord is near to those who have bruised their hearts" (Ps. 33:19), as you shall see for yourselves when you hear how this publican bruised his heart. "The publican stood at a distance, and would not even lift up his eyes to heaven, but beat his breast"—bruising his heart, you see—"beat his breast and said, 'God be gracious to me, the sinner that I am.'" And what was our Lord's judgment on the two of them? "Amen I tell you that that publican went down from the temple made a juster man, more justified than that Pharisee." Why? What are the grounds for this judgment of God? Please, Lord, explain to us how your justice works, how this law of yours can be called fair. And God does explain the rule his law goes by. Do you want to hear it? "For everyone who exalts himself shall be humbled, and everyone who humbles himself shall he exalted."

So now then please follow carefully. Here was this publican who didn't even dare lift up his eyes to heaven. Why wouldn't he look up to heaven? Because he was looking down, deep down into himself. He was looking at himself, and he didn't like himself very much, and so God liked him. But *you* think highly of yourself, you go about with your nose in the air. God says to the proud man, "Don't you want to look at yourself? I shall look at you then. Would you rather I didn't look at you? Then look at yourself." Like this publican who had a thorough look at himself, and condemned himself, so that God could stick up for him. He punished himself and so God could let him off, he accused himself and so God was able to make excuses for him. In fact he made such a good case for him that judgment went in his favor and he went down justified, he left the court an honest man with right on his side. And so that Pharisee was the sinner after all. Just because he said "I am not like other men," just because he fasted twice a week, just because he gave tithes, he wasn't any the less a sinner for all that, for pride itself is a high crime and misdemeanor, a felony, and yet there he was, boasting for all he was worth. Yet who is without sin? Who can boast that his mind is chaste, or that he is clean of sin (Prov. 20:9)? He had his sins all right, but he was like a stupid man standing in a doctor's surgery, and showing him his good arm while covering up the wounded one. Let God cover your wounds, don't you do it. If you cover them for shame, the doctor won't treat them. Let him cover them and cure them; he covers them with a dressing. Covered by the doctor's dressing the wound will heal, but if the wounded man tries to cover it up himself, it just festers. Who are you hiding it from anyhow? From him who knows everything.

And just see what is said about this in the psalm here. "Because I kept silence, my bones grew old from my shouting all day long." An odd sort of silence if you were shouting all day long. Well, there was something he kept quiet about and something he did not keep quiet about. He said nothing where it would have done him some good, and he said a lot where it did no good at all. "I kept silent," he said, "I didn't confess"—that is where he ought to have spoken; he ought to have hushed up his good points and made a fuss about his sins, but he got it back to front and hushed up his sins and made a song about his good qualities. And what was the result? His bones grew old. If he had made a song about his sins, mark you, and hushed up his good qualities, his bones would have grown young, which means that his virtues would have taken on new life. He would have been strong and sturdy in the Lord, because weak in himself. But as it is, by wanting to be strong on his own, he has weakened himself and his bones have grown old. He has remained stuck in old age, dated, because he hadn't been prepared to confess and thereby make love to youth and become young again. You know of course, don't you, who are the ones who succeed in becoming young again? "Blessed are those whose iniquities are forgiven, and whose sins are covered." But this man wasn't going to have his iniquities forgiven, not he! He piled them on, stood up for them, boasted about what a fine fellow he was. So because he kept quiet about what he ought to have confessed, his bones grew old. And yet, give him his due, he does come to recognize himself. In a moment there will be a glimmer of understanding. He will take one good look at himself, and won't be at all pleased with what he sees, because he will recognize himself for what he is. You shall hear about it in a moment, so you will know how to cure yourselves.

"Because day and night your hand was heavy upon me." What can that mean, do you suppose? Something very important, brothers, very deep. Recall that true judgment he gave between the Pharisee and the publican; the Pharisee is humbled because he exalted himself, the publican is exalted because he humbled himself. And how does God humble the man who exalts himself? By squashing him—putting a heavy hand on him. He wouldn't humble himself by confessing his wickedness, so he is humbled by the weight of God's hand. But then after he had felt the weight of it squashing him down, how light was the touch of it which raised him up again! A strong hand it is on both occasions, strong to press him down, strong to pick him up.

And so, "because day and night your hand was heavy upon me, I turned in my anguish while the thorn was stuck in."[2] The heavy pressure of the hand made me feel wretched, a thorn was stuck into me, my conscience was pricked. What happened, then, when the thorn was stuck into him? Well it hurt, of course, it made him sore, it made him aware of his own weakness. Just see what he did, this man who had kept quiet about confessing his sins, and made a lot of noise in defending them, until his bones, his strength, his virtues had grown old—see what he did when a thorn was stuck into him. "I came to know my sin." He has looked at it squarely at last. Now that *he* has looked at his sin, God will overlook it. He goes on to say so himself, in fact, "I came to know my sin, and my injustice I did not cover." It's what I have just been telling you: don't you cover it up and then God will. "Blessed are those whose sins are covered." But if you cover them yourself, you will be exposed. This man exposed them himself, so that he would be covered. A moment ago he was hushing them up, but now, "I said." Well, what did you say? Something to make up for keeping quiet before? "I said, 'I shall utter my injustice to the Lord against myself,' and you have forgiven the ungodliness of my mind." "I *shall* utter"—he isn't doing so yet, just promising that he will—and God has already forgiven him. Notice this, brothers, it is important. He said "I *shall* utter." Not "I have uttered and you have forgiven," but "I *shall* utter, and you have forgiven." In saying "I shall utter," he shows that although his mouth hasn't yet spoken, his mind has, and therefore the ungodliness of his mind has been forgiven. I hadn't yet spoken a word out loud, but God had his ear to my mind and heard my voice whispering there.

But it wasn't enough to utter his injustice to the Lord. He said "I shall utter it against myself." Oh, it makes a difference, you know. A lot of people utter their iniquity, not against themselves, but against God. When they are caught up in sin, they say God wanted it so. When a man says "I didn't do it," or "It isn't a sin anyhow," he isn't uttering it against himself or against God either. But if he says "Certainly I did it, and I admit it's a sin, but that's how God wanted it, so what could I do?"—then he is uttering it against God. You may think nobody says things like that, nobody talks about sin as if God wanted it. But I assure you many people do. Anyhow, what else does it amount to when they say, "Fate made me do it, my stars made me do it"? It is just a roundabout way of blaming God, because they don't want to come the short, straight way of making their peace with God. So they say, "Fate made me do it, my stars made me do it." And who made the stars? God. Who ordered their courses and conjunctions, in other words who arranged what is usually called fate? God. So you see that what you were saying in fact is "God made me sin." So he is unjust, while you are just, eh? Because you wouldn't have done it unless he had made you, would you now?—No, no, forget all such excuses for your sins. Remember the words of another psalm, "Do not bend my mind down to malicious words, to make excuse on excuse for my sins, with men who work iniquity" (Ps. 140:4). The same psalm goes on, "And I will have nothing to do with the choicest of them." They may be very select, very prominent men, the pick of the bunch in the eyes of the world, you may think them very shrewd, very learned, these stargazers, with their signs of the Zodiac and their calculations of the seasons, with the destinies of men at their finger-tips, and their forecasts of human behavior by the stars. But for all that, God made me with free will; if I have sinned, then it is *I* who have sinned. So I must not merely utter my iniquity to the Lord, I must utter it against myself and not against him.

"For this shall everyone that is holy pray to you at the proper time." When is that? And what is the "this" that he will pray for?—For ungodliness.—For *what*?—For the forgiveness of it, of course. And the reason why every holy person will pray to you is that you have forgiven him his sins. If God didn't forgive sins, there wouldn't be any holy people to pray to him. "At the proper time." When the New Testament, the new covenant is published, when the grace of Christ is published, that will be the proper time. "When the fullness of time had come, God sent his Son, made of a woman,[3] made under the Law, to redeem those who were under the Law" (Gal. 4:4). To redeem them, buy them back—who from? From the devil, and damnation, and their own sins which they had sold themselves to. "To redeem those who were under the Law," under the Law, being squashed by the weight of it. The covenant, the agreement they had made with God was crushing them by convicting them of their guilt without saving them from it. It forbade them to do evil all right, but it didn't help them not to, and since they didn't have it in them to shun evil and make themselves just all on their own, they had to cry to God for help, just as the man who was led away prisoner under the law of sin had to cry, "Wretched man that I am, who will deliver me from the body of this death?" (Rom. 7:23). All men in fact, not only the Jews, were under the Law, though they weren't within the Law. They were outlaws, you might say, and the Law was crushing them, finding them guilty, showing up sin. The Law stuck in the thorn, it had the heart pricked. It was there to make every man recognize his guilt and cry to God for pardon. "For this shall every one that is holy cry to you at the proper time." So you see why I said that the proper time was the fullness of time when God sent his Son. In another place St. Paul quotes Isaiah: "In an acceptable and favorable time I have heard you, and in the day of salvation I have helped you" (Isa. 49:8); and because this prophecy was sent for all Christians at all times, he adds. "Behold now is the acceptable time, now is the day of salvation" (2 Cor. 6:2). "For this shall everyone that is holy pray to you at the proper time."

"But yet in the flood of many waters they shall not come near him." Near whom? Near God. This sudden change of person, from "you" to "him" and back again without warning is quite usual in the psalms. For instance, "Salvation is the Lord's, and your blessing is upon your people" (Ps. 3:9). He begins by talking about the Lord, and ends by talking to him. Here it is the other way round. "For this shall everyone that is holy pray to *you* at the proper time. But yet in the flood of many waters they shall not come near *him*." People who swim about in the flood of many waters shall not come near God. This flood of waters, I think we can say, stands for all the many varieties and changes in doctrine there are. Listen carefully, brothers. The many waters are varieties of doctrine. There is only one true doctrine of God, not many waters but only one true water, one sacrament of baptism, one doctrine of salvation. It says of this water, which the Holy Ghost waters us with, "Drink water from your jars, and from the fountains of your wells" (Prov. 5:15); fountains which the ungodly do not approach, but only those who believe in him who justifies the ungodly. After they have been justified, they come to the fountains. But these other many waters, these many doctrines, defile men's souls; doctrines like the ones I have been telling you about. "Fate is responsible," that is one such doctrine. "My luck is to blame, it is the fault of chance," that is another one, which implies that there is no such thing as providence in control of anything. And another says, "It is the people of darkness who have rebelled against God that make men sin." In such a flood of many waters they shall not come near God. But what is the one water, the true water which flows from the deep clean wells of truth? What can it be, except the doctrine which instructs us that it is good to confess to the Lord? It is the water of the confession of sins, the water of the humbling of the heart, the water of the way of salvation, of self-abasement, of not being over-confident in oneself, or proudly taking all the credit. You won't find that this water can be drawn from the books of any outsiders, whether Epicureans or Stoics or Manichees or Platonists. You will find many excellent things in them about virtue and good morals, but nothing about humility. This way of humility springs from another source; it comes from Christ, who being the highest of the high, came to us in lowliness. What other lesson but this had he to teach in humbling himself, in becoming obedient to the death, even to the death of the cross (Phil. 2:8)? Paying a debt he didn't owe, to free us from our debts, baptized without ever having sinned, crucified though guilty of no crime, what else was he teaching us except this humility? Not without reason did he say, "I am the way and the truth and the life" (Jn. 14:6). In this one water of humility, then, you can come near to God, because the Lord is near to them that have bruised their hearts (Ps. 33:19). But in the flood of many waters which rear themselves up against God and teach proud impieties, they shall not come near to God.

But what about you, who have been justified by God all right, and yet are in the middle of these waters all the same? On all sides, you know, even when we confess our sins, these floodwaters swirl around us. We are not in the flood, but we are surrounded by it. The waters batter us, but they don't swamp us, they soak us with spray, but they don't drown us. Still, what are you going to do, marooned in this flood, living in this world? There is no doubt you will hear people talking such false doctrines, every day you will find your thoughts troubled by their words. So what does this man say, justified by God and full of confidence in him, though surrounded and cut off by this flood? "You are a refuge for me from the violence which surrounds me. My joy, redeem me"—but if you feel joy, why do you still want to be redeemed? I hear the voice of gladness when he says "My joy," and when he says "redeem me," the voice of sadness. You are glad and sad at the same time. "Quite so," he says, "hope of things to come makes me glad, the present state of things makes me sad." "Rejoicing in hope" (Rom. 12:12), says St. Paul, so it is quite right to say "*My joy,* redeem me." But why *"redeem me"*? Because the Apostle goes on, "Rejoicing in hope, patient in trouble." That's why. The Apostle surely was already justified and yet he says, "We, too, who have the firstfruits of the Spirit, we too groan within ourselves." Why "redeem me"? Because "we too groan within ourselves waiting for the adoption, the redemption of our bodies" (Rom. 8:23). So that is why "redeem me": because we are waiting for the redemption of our bodies. And once more, why "My joy"? Because as he goes on to say in the same place, "For by hope we are saved; but hope which is seen is not hope. For why should a man hope for what he can see already? But if we hope for what we do not see, then we wait for it in patience." If you are hoping, you have something to be glad about. But if you are waiting in patience, there is still something to be sad about. There is no need of patience where you have nothing unpleasant to put up with. What we call endurance, what we call patience, and forbearance, and long-suffering, can only have place in adversity, in evil times, when you are feeling the pinch. So if we are waiting in patience, we can still say, "Redeem me from the violence which surrounds me." But because by hope we have been saved, we say at the same time, "My joy, redeem me."

God answers, "I will give you understanding." It is a psalm of understanding, you remember. "I will give you understanding and set you in this way you must go by." I will set you in it, not to get stuck in it, but so that you don't wander off it. I shall give you understanding so that you can always see yourself as you are and always rejoice in hope towards God. Until you come home to that mother country where it will no more be a matter of hoping but a matter of having. "I will fix my eyes upon you," and you must fix yours upon me. Now that you are justified, and your sins forgiven, lift up your eyes to God. Lift up your heart too, which was going moldy on the ground. Don't let that *sursum corda* you hear so often be said for nothing, else your heart will just go on moldering on the ground. Keep your eyes then on God the whole time, so that he may fix his eyes on you. But you are afraid, I suppose, that if you keep your eyes on God, you won't see where you are going, and may trip, or put your foot in a trap. Don't worry about that. His eyes are watching out for that sort of thing; that is why he fixes them on you. Our Lord says, "Don't worry, don't be anxious" (Mt. 6:31), and St. Peter says, "Cast all your anxiety on him, because he takes care of you" (1 Pet. 5:7). So come on then, lift up your eyes to him, and don't be afraid of walking into a trap. Listen to another psalm: "My eyes are always on the Lord" (Ps. 24:15). And as though he were asked, "What do you do about your feet, then, since you are not looking where you are going?" he answers, "For he will pluck my feet from the snare."

After promising this man understanding and his protection, God addresses himself to the proud people who make light of their sins and, in so doing, he shows what understanding is. "Don't be like horse and mule, who have no understanding." Horses and mules are stiff-necked animals, not like the ox which knows his owner, and the donkey his master's manger (Isa. 1:3). But what will happen to you if you are like the horse and mule? "Gag their jaws with bit and bridle who do not come near you." So if you insist on being a horse or mule, and bucking off your rider, your mouth will be gagged with bit and bridle, that mouth of yours which boasts about your deserts, and keeps quiet about your sins. "Many are the whippings of the sinner." It is the obvious thing for the whip to follow the bridle. He wants to stay a wild animal, and untamed, so he is broken in with bridle and whip. If only he can be broken in thoroughly! The danger is that if he jibs too much, he will be left untamed, left to follow his own roving lusts—like people whose sins go unpunished for the time being. May he learn the lesson of the whip then, and let himself be broken in. That is how the psalmist says he was tamed, only he mentioned spurs instead of whips earlier on. "I turned in my anguish, while the thorn—or spur—was stuck in." Whether it is whips or spurs, God tames the beast he is riding on because it is good for the beast to be ridden. It is not because God is tired of walking on foot that he rides on a beast. But if you aren't under this rider, it is you who will fall, not he. Or why do you suppose a donkey was brought to our Lord to ride on into Jerusalem? It is very significant, that, full of hidden meaning. The donkey is the tamed and gentle people of God, who carry the Lord faithfully and are making for Jerusalem. "He will guide the gentle in judgment," says another psalm, "and will teach the meek his ways" (Ps. 24:9). And who are the meek? Those who don't stiffen their necks against the tamer, who put up patiently with the whips and the bridle, so that afterwards when they have been tamed, they can jog along without any whip, and keep to the right road without bit or bridle. "Many are the whippings of the sinner, but he that hopes in the Lord will be compassed about with mercy." First he was encompassed with violence, afterwards with mercy, because "he will give mercy who has given the Law" (Ps. 83:8): the Law in whips, mercy in pattings and pettings and lumps of sugar.

And so what is the conclusion of it all? "Be glad in the Lord and rejoice, you just." Come now, you people who are glad in yourselves, you ungodly men and proud who are so delighted with yourselves, come and believe in him who justifies the ungodly, and let your faith be counted as justice, and then "be glad in the Lord and rejoice, you just." "And rejoice"—still in the Lord, of course! Why rejoice? Because now you are just. And how have you become just? By his grace, not by your own deserts. You are just, because you have been made just, because you have been justified. "And be boastful, all you straight of mind." Straight of mind, not resisting God. Listen carefully, please, and try to understand while I show you shortly what a straight mind is. Thank the Lord that these words, being the last of the psalm, may stick in your minds. Well now, this is the difference between a straight mind and a crooked one. If a man attributes whatever, willy-nilly, he has to suffer—sickness, sorrow, misfortune, humiliation—if he puts it down to the just will of God, and doesn't find fault with him as though he did not know what he was doing, punishing one man and letting off another—then that man is straight of mind. But the crooked-minded, and the bent and the twisted are the ones who say that their suffering whatever they have to suffer is unfair, and so saying blame him who lets them suffer for unfairness. Or, if they dare not call him unfair, they say he has no control over such things. So the crooked-minded, the man with a warped mind, will usually air one of three opinions. Either he will say, as the fool has said in his mind, "There is no God" (Ps. 13:1); or he will say, "God is unjust and likes treating me in a way I don't deserve"; or lastly he will say that God has no control of or interest in human affairs. And why do these three irreligious opinions belong especially to the crooked mind? Because God is straight, the very measure of straightness, and so not to acquiesce in his will is the sign of a warped, bent mind. If you put a bent rod on a level surface, it will not fit, it won't lie flat, it will wobble all the time, not because the surface is uneven, but because the rod is warped. In the same way, while your mind remains warped and twisted, it cannot be squared with the straightness of God, and it cannot be bedded in him so as to stick to him and become one spirit with him (1 Cor. 6:17).

"So boast then, all you straight of mind." Listen to the sort of thing they boast about. "We also boast," says St. Paul, "about our troubles" (Rom. 5:3). There is nothing very special in boasting about happiness and good fortune. The straight of mind boasts about his troubles, and not in vain either. "Knowing," he goes on, "that trouble makes for patience, and patience for testing, and testing for hope, and hope does not let us down, because the charity of God is poured forth in our minds through the Holy Ghost who is given to us."

So that is what a straight mind is like, brothers. When anything nasty happens to you, say, "The Lord has given, the Lord has taken away" (Job 1:21). There was a straight mind for you. "As it has pleased the Lord, so has it happened. May the Lord's name be blessed." Notice, please, he didn't say "The Lord has given and the devil has taken away," in case you are tempted to say "The devil has done this to me." You must put your whippings entirely down to God, because not even the devil can touch you unless God lets him, whether for punishment's sake or correction's. Punishment for an ungodly man, correction for a son. "He whips every son whom he receives" (Heb. 12:6). So don't hope to get along without a whipping, unless of course you are thinking of having yourself disinherited. He whips every son whom he receives. "Absolutely *every* one?" Where do you think you can hide yourself? Yes, every son, without exception. Not one who won't have a taste of the rod. "No, but really, *every* single one?" Do you want to see just how really? Even God's only Son, who was without sin, was not without the rod. And he did not enjoy it any more than you do. He carried your weakness, he the head took on himself the part and character of us his members, and when he came to his passion he was sad and sorrowful so that you could be comforted and joyful. St. Paul was triumphantly cheerful when he was approaching death. "I have fought the good fight, I have finished the race, I have kept faith, and for the rest there remains for me the crown of justice, which God the just judge will give me in that day" (2 Tim. 4:7). He is eager for his crown, and glad to die, while his master, who was going to give it to him, had been sad to die. But he had to share the weakness of all those who lack Paul's great spirit, who are scared stiff of suffering and death. Yet just see how he instructs them in straightness of mind. You want to live, not die, but God wants it otherwise, so there are two wills at odds. Straighten your will to God's, don't try to twist his to yours. Yours is bent, his is the straight rule, and must stay unaltered, so that what is out of true can be adjusted to it and corrected by it. Now see how our Lord Jesus Christ teaches us this lesson. "My soul is sad even to the death. Father, if it be possible let this cup pass from me" (Mt. 26:38). He shows us how, being human, he did not want to die any more than you do. But now see how straight his mind is. "But not what I will, but what you will, Father."

Learn then how to rejoice, whatever happens to you, and, when your last day comes, rejoice. Or if your will is warped a little by some human frailty, be quick to straighten it out towards God, so that you may be counted among those to whom it is said, "Be boastful, all you straight of mind."

Notes

1. The Vulgate combines Psalms 1 and 2, so most of the numbers it gives to later psalms are one number below that given them in the Hebrew Psalter. As will be seen below, in Augustine's Latin text, the title of this psalm was "Understanding for this man David." The NRSV translates that as "Of David. A Maskil." "Maskil" is a term

that appears in the heading of thirteen psalms. Its meaning is uncertain, but its root means "understand" or "ponder." The term probably relates to something about the genre of the psalm or the way it was performed.

2. The NRSV renders the second half of this verse "my strength was dried up as by the heat of summer," but admits in a footnote that the meaning of the Hebrew is uncertain.

3. Here St. Augustine pauses to explain that though in current Latin the word *mulier*, "woman," excluded the idea of virginity, this was not so with the ancients. Since it is not so with the English either, the translator left out the sentence.

Part II

The Middle Ages

CHAPTER 6

THE TREK TO THE MIDDLE AGES

CAESARIUS OF ARLES: SERMON 100, "ST. AUGUSTINE ON THE TEN WORDS OF THE LAW AND THE TEN PLAGUES"

*Caesarius, who served as archbishop of Arles and primate of Gaul at the beginning of the sixth century, had a passionate desire to see the Word of God proclaimed there on the frontier of the Roman Empire (***See Vol. 1, pp. 131-36,*** for discussion). He saw this as the work not just of bishops, but of all clergy, including deacons. And for those who could not write sermons of their own to preach, he prepared a collection of more than two hundred that they could use. Some are entirely his own work, some involve minor rewriting of sermons of earlier church fathers, and some are even compositions of his own that he attributes to a Father in hope of getting it preached more often. In this activity, Caesarius anticipated in some ways the medieval homiliaries that passed on patristic sermons because no one living trusted his own exegetical powers enough to write an original sermon. This sermon is an example of a sermon written by Caesarius and attributed to an earlier Father. It is taken from* St. Caesarius of Arles, Sermons, *trans. Mary*

Magdeleine Mueller, Fathers of the Church, vol. 47 (Washington, D.C.: Catholic University of America Press, 1964), 2:85-92.

St. Augustine on the Ten Words of the Law and the Ten Plagues

(1) Beloved brethren, our Lord and Savior like a spiritual physician has provided remedies for our souls by revealing the truths which lie hidden under the covering of words, in order that we may understand what we should love and what guard against. Therefore, consider, dearly beloved, that the number of the precepts of God's law seems to be equalled by the number of plagues whereby Egypt was struck. Just as there are ten precepts of the law by which the people are admonished to worship God, so we read of ten plagues which afflicted the pride of the Egyptians. For this reason, let us consider why ten commandments are mentioned there and ten plagues here. Doubtless, it is because there are remedies in the former for the wounds in the latter; it was necessary for the healing of the ten commandments to remedy the dangerous wounds of the ten plagues. Therefore, I exhort you, brethren, do not receive this with indifference; if, with Christ's help, you diligently pay attention, you can realize that those ten precepts are respectively opposed in order to the ten plagues. Indeed, the first plague is struck by the first command, the second by the second, the third by the third, and so on to the number ten.

(2) The first command of the law concerns one God: "You shall not have other gods besides me." In the first plague of the Egyptians, water was turned into blood. Compare the first precept with the first plague: consider the one God who is the source of all things, like the water out of which everything was created. Now to what does the blood refer but to mortal flesh? What does the changing of water into blood mean except that for people who refuse to believe in God, as the Apostle said: "Their senseless minds have been darkened; while professing to be wise, they have become fools." So the water was changed into blood because the feelings of the Egyptians became dark and gloomy. By the just judgment of God it happened that they drank blood from that river in which they had been wont to kill the sons of the Hebrews.

(3) The second commandment is: "You shall not take the name of the Lord, your God, in vain. For he who takes the name of the Lord his God in vain shall not be cleansed." The name of our Lord Jesus Christ is truth, for He said, "I am the truth" [Jn. 14:6]. Since the truth purifies while untruth defiles a man, let us see the plague that is opposed to this second command. What is that second plague? An abundance of frogs.

In the frogs we understand heretics and philosophers; you have the superficiality of philosophers and heretics fittingly signified if you consider the loquacity of frogs. Indeed, philosophers and heretics who say that everything in Christ is false are frogs shouting in a muddy swamp; by their pride and vain contentions they may have the sound of a voice, but they are unable to instill the teaching of wisdom. All who contradict the truth of Christ and deceive others while they are deceived in their own vanity are frogs bringing disgust to ears but no food to minds.

(4) The third precept is: "Remember to keep holy the Sabbath day." In this third commandment is suggested a certain idea of freedom, a repose of the heart or tranquility of the mind which a good conscience effects. Indeed, sanctification is there because the Spirit of God dwells there. Now look at the freedom or repose; our Lord says: "Upon whom shall I rest but upon the man who is humble and peaceable, and who trembles at my words?" [Isa. 66:2]. Therefore, restless souls turn away from the Holy Ghost. Lovers of strife, authors of calumnies, devotees of quarrels rather than of charity, by their uneasiness they do not admit to themselves the repose of a spiritual sabbath. Men do not observe a spiritual sabbath unless they devote themselves to earthly occupations so moderately that they still engage in reading and prayer, at least frequently, if not always. As that Apostle says: "Be diligent in reading and in teaching" [1 Tim. 4:13]; and again: "Pray without ceasing" [1 Thess. 5:17]. Men of this kind honor the sabbath in a spiritual manner. However, restless souls are continually involved in earthly activity, and of them it is written: "The burdens of the world have made them miserable."[1] They are unable to have a sabbath, that is, repose. In reply to their restlessness, it is said that they should have, as it were, a sabbath in their heart and the sanctification of the Spirit of God: "Be swift to hear," it says, "but slow to answer" [Ecclus. 5:13]. Cease your uneasiness, let there not be a tumult in your heart because of phantoms flying about to corrupt you, disturbing and pricking you like flies. You are to realize that God is saying to you: "Desist! And confess I am God" [Ps. 45:11]. By your restlessness you do not want to be still; blinded by the corruption of your contentions you demand to see what you cannot. Notice the opposite third plague which is contrary to this commandment. Sciniphs[2] sprang up out of the mud in the land of Egypt, very tiny flies, exceedingly restless, flying around in confusion, rushing into one's eyes, not allowing a man to rest, coming back while they are being driven away, returning again even when expelled. Restless men are like these little flies, when they refuse to observe the sabbath in a spiritual manner, that is, to be zealous for good works and to engage in reading or prayer. Doubtless, such are the

phantoms of quarrelsome hearts; just as the human body is tormented by those flies, so their hearts are disturbed and pricked by opposing thoughts. Keep the commandment, but guard against the plague.

(5) The fourth precept follows: "Honor your father and your mother." Opposed to this command is the fourth plague of the Egyptians: a fly that is a dog-fly, for it is a Greek word. If a person refuses to honor his parents, a dog-fly, that is, the wickedness of the devil, spiritually afflicts and torments him. Indeed, it is doglike not to recognize one's parents, and nothing is so spiteful as lack of recognition of those who have begotten a man.

(6) Fifth, we find: "You shall not commit adultery." The fifth plague is death among the cattle. If a man is intimate with his own wife without any limits or except with a desire for children; if he definitely waits for the wife or daughter of another, his own maid or that of another (which is a very serious sin), he is overcome by bestial passion and becomes like cattle, as though losing his manliness. Such a person is not changed into the nature of cattle but in the form of man bears a likeness to the cattle, for he is unwilling to hear the Lord say: "Be not senseless like horses or mules." Moreover: "Man, for all his splendor, does not abide; he resembles the beasts that perish." If you are not afraid to be cattle, at least fear to die like them.

(7) The sixth commandment is: "You shall not kill"; the six[th] plague, boils on the body, swollen blisters causing burning wounds from the ashes of the furnace. Such are murderous men; they burn with anger because through wrath the fraternal spirit of a murderer perishes. Men burn with indignation but also with grace, for both the man who wishes to kill and the one who desires to help his neighbor glows with passion. The former is inflamed with disease, the latter by precept; the one with poisonous ulcers, the other with good works. O if we could see the souls of murders, doubtless we would bewail them more than the decaying bodies of the ulcerated.

(8) Then follows the seventh commandment: "You shall not steal"; the seventh plague is hail on the fruits of the earth. Whatever you take by theft contrary to God's precept you destroy out of heaven, for no one has an unjust gain without a just loss. For example, the man who steals acquires clothing but destroys faith in the judgment of heaven. There is a loss where there is gain, visibly a gain but invisibly a loss; a gain as the result of his blindness, but a loss of the Lord's countenance. Therefore, all who by evil desires steal outwardly are inwardly hailed upon by God's

just judgment. O if thieves and robbers could behold the field of their heart, surely they would grieve and mourn when they do not find there what they put into the mouth of their soul, even though in their theft they did find something to swallow in the desire of their gluttony. Greater is the hunger of the soul than that of the body; greater the hunger, more dangerous the plague, and more serious the death. What is worse, many men walk around dead because of this soul-hunger, and though alive carry about their own death. Indeed, some men seem to live physically but by their evil deeds are proven to be dead in heart. Moreover, many who suffer hunger in their soul boast about vain riches. Finally, Scripture says that a good Christian is inwardly rich: "The inner life of the heart, which is of great price in the sight of God," it says [1 Pet. 3:4]; he is not rich before men, but before God, in His sight. Therefore, what does it profit you to steal where man does not see, and to be hailed upon by a just judgment where God sees you?

(9) The eighth commandment is: "You shall not bear false witness"; the eighth plague is locusts, creatures harmful with their bite. What does a false witness desire, except to do harm by biting and to destroy by lying? For this reason the Apostle warns us not to attack each other with false charges: "If you bite and devour one another," he says, "take heed or you will be consumed by one another" [Gal. 5:15].

(10) The ninth commandment: "You shall not covet your neighbor's wife"; the ninth plague, dense darkness. If it is a sin to know one's wife except for the sake of children, what kind of an offense do you think it is, not only to sin with one's own wife, but even to desire the wife of another? Truly, the darkness is dense; indeed, nothing causes such pain in the heart of one who suffers it as when his wife is attacked. If a man does this to another, there is nothing that he should not be willing to suffer. Other evils men are wont to accept with patience, but I do not know whether anyone can be found who will bear this calmly. O what dense darkness men suffer when they do and desire such things! Truly, they are blinded with horrible fury, for it is unbridled madness to wish to pollute and defile the wife of another.

(11) The tenth commandment is: "You shall not covet anything of your neighbor's: neither his sheep, nor his ox, nor anything at all that belongs to him." Opposed to this precept is the tenth plague, the death of the firstborn. All the possessions which men have they keep for their heirs, and among heirs no one is more dear than the firstborn. When men wish to possess the goods of another as though justly, they seek to

become heirs of the dying; indeed, what seems so just as to possess something that has been left to a person? Someone says: It was left to me, I read the will. Nothing seems more just than this word. You praise a man who has possessions, as it were, rightly; God condemns him if he desires them unjustly. See what kind of a man you are if you want to become the heir of another; do you not want him to have his own heirs, among whom no one is dearer than the firstborn? You will be punished in the same manner in your firstborn, if, while desiring the possessions of others, that is, what does not rightly belong to you, you acquire them as though under the semblance of justice. For this reason you kill your firstborn. Surely, it is easy, brethren, physically to kill the firstborn; they are mortal men who are certain to die, whether before or after their parents. This is really difficult, not to kill the firstborn of your heart by this secret and unjust concupiscence. Faith is the firstborn of our heart, for no one does good works unless faith precedes it. All your good works are spiritual sons of yours, but among them faith is the firstborn. Whoever secretly desires the possessions of another destroys interior faith. Doubtless at first he will be an obedient imitator through deceit and not by charity, as if loving him whose heir he wants to become. He says he loves the man he wishes to die, and in order that he may see himself in reality the owner of his goods, he hopes that man will not leave his own heir.

(12) This comparison and sort of opposition of the ten commandments and the ten plagues, brethren, should make us cautious so that we may with assurance keep our possessions in accord with God's precepts; I mean our interior possessions which are stored away in the treasury of our conscience. These are our treasures which no thief or robber or wicked neighbor can ever take away, where no moth or rust need be feared. Indeed, these are true riches, namely, a good conscience, justice, mercy, chastity, and sobriety; anyone who is full of such things is rich, even if he dies naked as the result of shipwreck. If you diligently heed these truths and, with the Lord's help, are willing to avoid evil and do good, you will be God's people. Then you will be freed from the unjust persecution of the Egyptians, that is, of spiritual injustice, and will happily reach the land of promise: with the help of our same Lord, to whom is honor and glory world without end. Amen.

GREGORY THE GREAT: HOMILY 37

When Gregory became pope about nine decades after Caesarius began his episcopate, conditions in the Holy City were already representative of a transitional state between the patristic period and the Middle Ages. ***(See Vol. 1, pp. 139-41,** for a discussion.)* *While Gregory continued to use the form of the patristic homily, doing verse-by-verse exegesis of the gospel, his sermons show traits that will be more characteristic of the later period. One of these is the use of narrative illustrations for the points he is making in his sermons. Today it is such a familiar feature of sermons that it is hard to believe it has not been present all along, but Gregory seems to have been the first to employ the device. It did not become common until the preaching of the friars in the High Middle Ages, who became famous for their exempla. The translation used here is from* Gregory the Great, Forty Gospel Homilies, *trans. Dom David Hurst, Cistercian Studies Series, no. 123 (Kalamazoo, Mich.: Cistercian Publications, 1990), 327-37.*

Homily 37

(Luke 14:16-33)

If we reflect on what is promised to us in heaven and how great these things are, dearly beloved, everything we have upon earth comes to appear worthless. When we compare our earthly possessions with the happiness of heaven, they seem a burden and not a help. When we compare our life in time with eternal life, we must call it death rather than life. What is our daily decline into decay but a kind of extension of death? What tongue can describe, what mind can grasp the greatness of the joys of the heavenly city—taking part in the choirs of angels, sharing with the blessed spirits in our Creator's glory, seeing the face of God before us, beholding infinite light, feeling no fear of death, rejoicing in the gift of imperishableness?

We take fire even when we hear of these things! Already we long to be there where we hope to rejoice without end. But we attain great rewards only through great labors. Hence Paul preaches that *A person is not crowned unless he competes according to the rules.* The greatness of the rewards delights us; but let us not be discouraged by the laborious struggle. Hence Truth says to those coming to him: *If anyone comes to me and does not hate his father and mother and wife and children and brothers and sisters, and even his own life, he cannot be my disciple.*

We must carefully inquire how we are commanded to hate our parents and blood relations, when we are ordered to love even our enemies. Truth says of wives, *What God has joined together, let no one separate;* and Paul, *Husbands, love your wives, as Christ loved the Church.* The disciple preaches that we must love our wives even though his Master says that a person who *does not hate his wife cannot be my disciple.* Does a judge announce one thing and the herald proclaim another? Or are we able to hate and to love at the same time?

If we weigh the force of the precept, we find that we are capable of doing both, if we make a distinction. We love those who are united to us by physical relationship because we know them as "neighbors"; and we must not know them, but hate them and flee from them, because we experience them as opponents on our way to God. A person who is unspiritually wise is loved through hatred, so to speak, when we do not listen to the bad things he suggests. The Lord, to show us that this hatred directed toward our neighbors rises not from lack of feeling but from love, added immediately, *and hates even his own life.* We are instructed to hate our neighbors, and to hate our own lives as well. A person then who hates his neighbor as himself must hate him by loving him. We hate our own life in the right way when we do not give in to its bodily desires, when we restrain its appetites, when we resist its pleasures. When we despise our own life and bring it to a better state, we are, as it were, loving it by hating it. We must undoubtedly make a distinction in hating our neighbors, loving in them what they are, and hating in them what causes them to hinder us in our journey toward God.

When Paul was proceeding toward Jerusalem, the prophet Agabus took his belt and bound his own feet with it, saying: *So will they bind at Jerusalem the man whose belt this is.* What did the man say, who perfectly hated his own life? *I am ready not only to be bound but even to die at Jerusalem for the name of the Lord Jesus Christ; I do not account my life as precious to myself.* See how he hated his life by loving it! In hating it he was loving what he longed to deliver up to death for Jesus, so that he might raise it from the death of sin to life.

Let us draw from this distinction the kind of hatred we are to feel toward our neighbor. Let us love anyone at all opposed to us, but, let us not love one who is an obstacle along our road to God, even one related to us. Anyone longing eagerly for the things of eternity ought in the cause of God which he is undertaking to move beyond father, mother, wife, children, relatives, beyond himself, that he may get to know God all the more truly the less he acknowledges anyone else in his cause. It is an important thing that unspiritual feelings divide the heart's attention and obscure its vision; but they do not harm us if we hold them in check. We are, then, to love our neighbors; we are to extend charity to all, relatives and strangers alike, without being turned aside from the love of God for its sake.

We know that when the ark of the Lord was returned from the land of the Philistines to the land of the Israelites, it was placed on a cart. They yoked cows that had recently borne young to the cart, and shut up their calves at home. *And the cows went straight on over the way that leads to Bethshemesh, keeping to the one road, lowing as they went; they turned neither to the right nor to the left.* What do these cows represent but the faithful in the Church? When they ponder the sacred precepts it is as if they are carrying the ark of the Lord placed upon them. We should also notice that they are described as having recently borne young. Many who are inwardly set on the way toward God are externally bound by their unspiritual feelings, but they do not turn aside from the right road because they are carrying the ark of God in their hearts.

The cows were going to Bethshemesh, a name meaning "house of the sun." The prophet says: *For you who fear the Lord, the sun of righteousness shall rise.* If we are moving on toward the dwelling place of the everlasting Sun, we do right not to turn aside from the route toward God on account of our unspiritual feelings. We must consider with all our energy that the cows yoked to God's cart moan as they go, lowing from their depths, but do not turn aside from their road. So surely must God's preachers, so must all believers within holy Church, do. They must be compassionate toward their neighbors through their love, while not deviating from God's way through their compassion.

Truth shows how we should manifest hatred of life when he says: *Anyone who does not bear his cross and come after me cannot be my disciple.* We bear the Lord's cross in two ways, when we afflict our bodies by abstinence, or reckon our neighbor's need to be our own by compassion. A person who manifests his sorrow at another's need is carrying a cross in his heart. But we must be aware that some people display physical abstinence not for God but for the sake of empty glory; and that many offer compassion toward a neighbor, not spiritually but unspiritually, to dispose him not toward virtue but toward sin, as if by taking pity on him. And so they have the appearance of bearing the cross, but they are not following the Lord. Hence Truth rightly says: *Anyone who does not bear his cross and come after me cannot be my disciple.* To carry one's cross and go after the Lord is to manifest either physical abstinence or compassion toward a neighbor with a zeal prompted by eternal motives. Whoever manifests them for temporal motives does indeed carry his cross, but he refuses to go after the Lord.

Since lofty precepts have been given, the Lord immediately adds a comparison with the building of something lofty. *For which of you, desiring to build a tower, does not first sit down and estimate the cost of what is necessary, whether he has enough to complete it? Otherwise, when he has laid a foundation and is not able to finish, all who see it begin to mock him, saying that this fellow began to build, and was not able to finish.* We ought to prepare for everything we do by attention and reflection. According to the voice of Truth, one who builds a tower first provides the cost of the building. If we are eager to construct a tower of humility, we must first ready ourselves against the adversities of this age.

There is this difference between an earthly and a heavenly building. We construct an earthly building by collecting money to defray the expenses, but we construct a heavenly building by distributing it. We make up the cost of the former if we collect what we do not have; we make up the cost of the latter if we leave behind even what we have. The rich man, with many possessions, who inquired of the Master, *Good Master, what shall I do to possess eternal life?* was unable to pay that cost. When he heard the precept to leave behind all things, he withdrew sadly. His inner distress arose from his extensive outer possessions. He loved the cost of his eminence in this life, and was unwilling to pay the cost of humility in his striving for his eternal home.

We must consider the words, *All who see it begin to mock him,* since according to the words of Paul, *We have become a spectacle to the world, to angels and to men.* In everything we do we must consider our hidden adversaries. They are always concerned with our works, and are always rejoicing over our failures. When he saw them, the prophet said: *My God, I trust in you: let me not be put to shame, nor let my enemies deride me.* When we are attentive to good works, unless we guard ourselves carefully against wicked spirits, we suffer derision from those who persuade us to do evil.

After giving us a comparison with the construction of a building, he moves on from a lesser to a greater likeness, so that we may consider an important subject in the light of an unimportant one. *Or what king, going to join battle against another king, does not first sit down and take counsel whether he is able with ten thousand to meet him who comes against him with twenty thousand? And if not, when the other is still some distance away, he sends a delegation and asks for terms of peace.* A king comes to do battle against another king the equal of himself. But if he considers carefully that he is unable to hold out, he sends a delegation and begs for terms of peace.

With what tears should we hope for pardon, who in the dreadful inspection do not come to judgment with our king as an equal! Our status, our weakness, our cause reveal us as inferiors. Perhaps we have already cut away the sins of our wicked deeds, already made an outward change from everything wrong. Are we able to offer an explanation of our thoughts? One is said to be coming with twenty thousand, and another coming with ten thousand cannot hold out against him. Twenty thousand is double ten thousand. If we are making great progress, still we hardly preserve our external works from error. Even if we cut away all outward dissipation, we have still not entirely removed it from our hearts. But the one who will come as judge judges outer and inner matters alike; he weighs deeds and thoughts equally. And so the one who examines us, we who are scarcely ready in works alone, on our works and thoughts alike, comes with an army twice the size of ours.

What must we do, my friends, when we perceive that we are unable to hold out with an army half his size, except send a delegation and ask for terms of peace when he is still some distance away? He is said to be some distance away because we do not yet see him present for judgment. Let us send him our tears as a delegation, let us send him works of mercy. Let us slaughter propitiatory victims on his altar. Let us acknowledge that we cannot contend with him at the judgment; let us consider the power of his strength, and ask for terms of peace. This is our delegation, that reconciles the king who is coming.

Consider, my friends, how fortunate it is that the one who can vanquish us at his arrival is slow in coming. Let us send our delegation to him, as I have said, by weeping, by bestowing alms, and by offering holy sacrifices. The sacrifice of the altar,[3] offered with tears and generosity of heart, pleads in a unique way for our forgiveness, because the one who, *himself rising from the dead, will never die again* is even now suffering for us anew through this sacrifice in his own mysterious way. As often as we offer him the sacrifice of his passion, we renew his passion for our forgiveness.

It is the case, or so I think, dearly beloved, that many of you know the story that I want to recall to your memories. It is related how not long ago a certain man was captured by the enemy and transported far away. He was held for a long time in chains, and when he did not return from captivity his wife considered that he had died. She took care to offer the sacrifice for him every week, as for one already dead, and as often as she offered the sacrifice his chains were unshackled in his captivity. When after a long time he returned, he revealed to his wife, since he wondered greatly at it, how on certain days in each week his chains were unshackled. Considering which days and hours these were, she realized that his chains were loosened whenever she remembered him in the sacrifice offered for him. Think carefully of this, dearly beloved, and draw from it a realization of the power the holy sacrifice has to loose the bonds of our hearts, if when one person offered it for another it was able to loose the chains on his body.

Many of you, dearly beloved, know Cassius, bishop of the city of Narni. It was his practice to offer the sacrifice to God every day, so that scarcely a day of his life passed without his offering God the propitiatory victim. And his life corresponded to the sacrifice: after giving away all that he had in alms, when he came to the time to offer the sacrifice, entirely dissolved in tears he offered himself with great compunction of heart.

I learned of his life and death from a deacon of venerable life whom Cassius had trained. He said that on a certain night the Lord stood by his priest in a vision and said: "Go and tell your bishop: Continue to act as you are acting; do what you are doing. Don't let your foot or your hand stop working. On the Apostles' day[4] you will come to me, and I will pay you your wages." The priest arose; but because the day of the Apostles was near, he feared to report to the bishop that the day of his death was so close. The Lord returned on another night, strongly rebuked his disobedience, and repeated his command in the same words. The priest rose intending to go ahead, but again his heart weakened and prevented him from declaring the revelation. He refused to yield to the command, which had already been repeated once, and failed to make known what he had seen.

Because when grace is rejected great anger follows upon former kindness, the Lord appeared for a third time in a vision of punishment. He now added blows to his words, and gave him such a severe beating that the wounds to his body vanquished his stubbornness of heart. He therefore arose, taught by the blows, and proceeded to the bishop whom he found waiting, as was his custom, to offer the eucharistic sacrifice beside the tomb of the blessed martyr Juvenal. He asked to see him apart from those standing around, and prostrated himself at his feet. When the bishop had with difficulty raised the weeping man, he was eager to learn the reason for his tears. The priest, to reveal the course of the vision, first removed the clothing from his shoulders to disclose the blows his body had received. He showed as what I might call witnesses to the truth and to his sin how severely the blows he had received had cut into his body, and the weals they had caused. When the bishop saw them, he was horrified, and inquired with astonishment who had ventured to do such things to him. The priest answered that he had endured them for him. The bishop's amazement and his alarm grew stronger. Without further delay the priest disclosed to him the secret revelation, and told him the words of the Lord's command which he had heard: "Continue to act as you are acting; do what you are doing. Don't let your hand or your foot stop working. On the Apostles' day you will come to me, and I will pay you your wages." On hearing this the bishop fell prostrate in prayer, with great compunction of heart; he who had come to offer the eucharistic sacrifice at the third hour postponed it until the ninth, owing to the length of his protracted prayer.

From that day the riches of his devotion increased; he became as steadfast in his work as he was certain of his recompense, and he who had been under obligation to the Lord now began to have the Lord under obligation to him, because of his promise. It had been his practice to go to Rome every year on the Apostles' day. Now, apprehensive because of the revelation, he decided not to go according to habit. He was watchful at the same time during the second year too, and the third, in expectation of his death, and felt the same uncertainty during the fourth, fifth and sixth years. He could almost have lost hope in the truth of the revelation if the blows had not given credit to the words.

In the seventh year he had reached the eve of the awaited feast of the Apostles unharmed, but a slight fever beset him then. His flock was expecting him to carry out the solemn mass on the Apostles' day, but he refused, saying that he could not. But because they were equally apprehensive of his departure from this life, they came to him in a body, binding themselves in a unanimous agreement that they would not take part in the celebration of the solemn mass on that day unless their bishop would be their mediator in the presence of God. Then he, constrained to do so, celebrated mass in the bishop's oratory, and distributed with his own hand the Lord's body, and gave the kiss of peace to all.

When the sacrificial offering had been completed, the bishop returned to his bed. As he lay there, and saw his priests and ministers standing round, he gave them a kind of last farewell. He counseled them concerning the preservation of the bond of love, and commended the great harmony that ought to unite them. In the midst of these words of exhortation he suddenly cried out in a terrible voice, "It is the hour," and immediately gave with his own hands to those standing by him the linen cloth which according to custom is placed over the face of the dying. When it was in place he sent forth his spirit, and so the holy soul, reaching eternal joys, was freed from the corruption of the body.

Whom, dearly beloved, did that man imitate in his death if not the one he had contemplated during his lifetime? When he said, "It is the hour," he went forth from his body. Jesus too, when everything had been completed and he had said, *"It is finished," bowed his head and gave up his spirit.* What the Lord did because of his power, his servant did because of his call.

See what great peace and grace the delegation made up of the daily sacrifice, sent with almsgiving and tears, brought about with the king who was on his way! Let one who can do so abandon everything, but let one who cannot do this send a delegation of his tears and his almsgiving while the king is still some distance away, and let him offer the gift of the sacrifice. The one who knows that we cannot bear his wrath wants to be appeased by our prayers. The delay in his coming shows that he is awaiting a delegation of peace. He would have come already if he had wanted to, and would have slaughtered all his adversaries. He reveals how fearful he will be when he comes, and yet that he is slow to come, since he does not want to find any to punish.

So therefore, everyone of you who does not renounce all that he possesses cannot be my disciple. And yet he bestows the remedy of the salvation we are to hope for. He whom we cannot endure because of his anger desires to be appeased by the delegation of peace he has begged for. And so you must wash away the stains of your sins with your tears, dearly beloved, you must wipe them away with your almsgiving, and atone for them with the holy sacrifice. You must not possess by desiring them the things you have not yet abandoned because you need to use them. Put your hope in your Redeemer alone. Pass in your heart to your eternal homeland. If you possess nothing in this world by your love for it, even though you have possessions you have abandoned everything. May he who has bestowed upon us the remedies for eternal peace grant us longed-for joys, Jesus Christ our Lord, who lives and reigns with the Father in the unity of the Holy Spirit, God for ever and ever. Amen.

Notes

1. The source of this quotation is unknown.
2. Stinging or biting insects.
3. The Eucharist.
4. Presumably June 29, the Feast of Peter and Paul, the apostolic founders of the church at Rome. In ancient Roman religion, this was the Feast of Romulus and Remus, the mythical founders of the city.

CHAPTER 7

THE EARLY MEDIEVAL PERIOD

CHARLEMAGNE: CAPITULARY (CHAPTER 82)

*This section of the Capitulary is a sample of Charlemagne's extraordinarily detailed provision for the life of the church, and for preaching in particular (**see Vol. 1, pp. 161-63**). Here it is ordered that sermons be preached on topics that will instruct recently pagan people in Christian belief and behavior. Other chapters of the Capitulary and the General Admonition of* C.E. *789 attend to other aspects of preaching with the same thoroughness. This translation is my own as amended by Professor Sophie Mills.*

82. To all (bishops). But it also ought to be seen to by you, most beloved and venerable shepherds, and rulers of the churches of God, that the presbyters, whom you send through your dioceses to rule and preach in churches serving the people of God, preach rightly and properly, and that you not allow them to teach or preach to the people anything new or uncanonical in its meaning and not in accordance with the holy scriptures. And you yourselves preach things that are useful, proper, and right, and those that lead to eternal life, and instruct others that they should preach the same things.

First of all, it ought to be preached to all generally that they believe the Father, Son, and Holy Spirit to be one God, omnipotent, eternal, invisible, who created the heaven and earth, the sea and all that is in them, and that there is one deity in substance and majesty in the three persons of the Father, Son, and Holy Spirit.

Also it ought to be preached how the Son of God became incarnate by the Holy Spirit and of Mary ever virgin for the salvation and healing of the human race; he suffered, was buried, rose on the third day, and ascended into heaven. And how he will come again in divine majesty to judge all people according to their own merits. And how the impious, on account of their sins, will be sent into eternal fire with the devil, and the righteous with Christ and his angels will be sent into eternal life.

Also there ought to be diligent preaching about the resurrection of the dead so they may know and believe they will receive the reward of their merits in the same bodies.

Again, there ought to be preached with diligence to all for what crimes they will be condemned to eternal punishment with the devil. For we read what was said by the apostle, "Now the works of the flesh are manifest, which are immorality, uncleanness, licentiousness, idolatry, witchcrafts, enmities, contentions, jealousies, anger, quarrels, factions, parties, envies, murders, drunkenness, carousings, and suchlike. And concerning these I warn you, as I have warned you, that they who do such things will not attain[1] the Kingdom of God" (Gal. 5:19-21 Douay-Rheims). On that account, these very things, which a great preacher of the church of God named individually, prohibit with all zeal, knowing that what he said will happen: "Who does these things will not obtain[2] the Kingdom of God."

But with all perseverance admonish them about the love of God and neighbor, about faith and hope in God, about humility and patience, chastity and self-restraint, kindness and mercy, almsgiving and the confession of their sins, and that they forgive their debtors as, according to the Lord's Prayer, their debts [are forgiven], knowing surely that whoever does such things will inherit the Kingdom of God.

And this, therefore, we enjoin of your love, because we know that in the last days false teachers will come, as Our Lord himself predicted in the gospel and the Apostle Paul testified in his letter to Timothy. Therefore, beloved, with our whole heart let us prepare ourselves in the knowledge of the truth that we may be able to resist those who contradict the truth, and that by divinely given grace the Word of God may increase, advance, and multiply in a truly holy church of God, in the salvation of our souls, and to the praise and glory of the name of Our Lord

Jesus Christ. Peace to those who preach, grace to those who obey, and glory to Our Lord Jesus Christ. Amen.

HRABANUS MAURUS: SERMON INTRODUCTION

*The need of Christians in Charlemagne's empire for the most basic instruction in their faith is illustrated in this opening passage from a sermon of Hrabanus (**see Vol. 1, pp. 163-66**). It is taken from J. M. Neale,* Medieval Preachers and Medieval Preaching: A Series of Extracts, Translated from the Sermons of the Middle Ages, Chronologically Arranged with Notes and an Introduction *(London: J. & C. Mozley and J. Masters & Co., 1856), 36-38. This is the only portion of the sermon translated by Neale.*

Against Those Who Raise an Outcry During an Eclipse of the Moon

It is a great joy to me, beloved brethren, that I see you love the name of Christians, frequent the churches, seek the baptism of Christ for your sons and daughters, and study the worship of the true God, but it grieves me exceedingly that I see many of you implicated in certain follies, going astray, and mixing among the truths of the Christian religion certain false things, which in no wise should be done. For it is written, "a little leaven leaveneth the whole lump."

When, some days since, I was sitting quietly at home, and thinking how I might assist your progress in the Lord, suddenly, about evening, and at nightfall, there was such a vociferation of the people, that the irreligious sound penetrated even to heaven. I asked what the noise meant. They told me that there was an eclipse of the moon, and that your shouts and endeavors were intended to assist it in its distress. I laughed, and wondered at your folly that, like devoted Christians, you were offering your assistance to God, as if, forsooth, he were weak and helpless unless he were assisted by your cries, and could not defend the lights which he himself created.

Next morning I inquired from those who came to visit me if they had ever seen any thing similar. They replied that they had not only known the like, but worse things in the places where they lived. One said that he had heard the blowing of horns, as if encouraging to the battle; another, the grunting of pigs; some told me that they had seen men casting javelins and arrows against the moon; that others scattered flakes of fire towards the sky, and affirmed that some terrible monster was destroying that orb and but for this help would entirely devour it; that some, in order to satisfy the illusion of the demons, cut down their hedges and broke all the vessels they had in their houses, as if that would assist the moon in her eclipse.

What madness is this, brethren! What insanity! Are ye stronger than God that ye endeavor to fight for him? Are your swine more powerful than his angels that their grunting is needed? How can ye bring help to the heaven and the stars who are not able to protect yourselves on the earth? "Why are dust and ashes proud?" For it is written,

> No man hath power over his own life: the breath of man goeth forth and he is turned again to his dust. What shall I say, brethren? Shall I praise you in this? I praise you not,

since, being deceived by the devil, ye are devoted in no small degree to pagan errors. And whence is this, except from the pagans whose company ye love and whose customs ye imitate? I have often forbidden you to consort with them or to take part in their abominable feasts; but avarice hinders you from obeying me. Ye love money, and are not afraid of hell. Ye seek the delights of the body, and neglect the eternal salvation of the soul; therefore, ye can neither have health of soul nor body, because, as saith the Apostle Paul, "for this cause many are weak and sickly among you, and many sleep."

AELFRIC: SERMON FOR THE WEDNESDAY IN ROGATIONTIDE

Catechetical sermons have been discussed before, but this is the first example of one to be given. The four basic topics of catechetical instruction are the Creed, the Lord's Prayer, the Sacraments, and Christian behavior (sometimes discussed using the Ten Commandments as an outline). In this sermon, Aelfric discusses the Creed, not so much article by article as in terms of its basic affirmations. These include not only the three persons of the Trinity but the final judgment as well. At times his treatment is almost as complex as that of the Qunicunque vult, *the so-called "Athanasian Creed."* ***See Vol. 1, pp. 166-69,*** *for his preaching in general. This translation is taken from* The Homilies of the Anglo-Saxon Church: The First Part, Containing the *Sermones Catholici, or Homilies* of Aelfric in the Original Anglo-Saxon, with an English Version, *ed. and trans. Benjamin Thorpe (London: Aelfric Society, 1844; reprint, New*

York: Johnson Reprint, 1971), 275-95 (where the Old English is given on facing pages).

Of the Catholic Faith

Every Christian man should by right know both his *Pater noster* and his Creed. With the *Pater noster* he should pray, with the Creed he should confirm his faith. We have spoken concerning the *Pater noster*, we will now declare to you the faith which stands in the Creed, according to the wise Augustine's exposition of the Holy Trinity.

There is one Creator of all things, visible and invisible, and we should all believe in him, for he is true and God alone Almighty, who never either began or had beginning, but he is himself beginning, and he to all creatures gave beginning and origin that they might be and that they might have their own nature, so as it seemed good to the divine dispensation. Angels he created, which are spirits and have no body. Men he created with spirit and with body. Cattle and other beasts, fishes and birds he created in flesh without soul. To men he gave an upright gait, the cattle he let go bending downwards. To men he gave bread for sustenance, and to the cattle grass.

Now, brethren, ye may understand, if ye will, that there are two things: one is the Creator, the other is the creature. He is the Creator who created and made all things of naught. That is a creature which the true Creator created. These are, first, heaven and the angels which dwell in heaven, and then this earth with all those which inhabit it, and sea with all those that swim in it. Now all these things are named by one name, creature. They were not always existing, but God created them. The creatures are many. The Creator who created them all is one, who alone is Almighty God. He was ever, and ever he will continue in himself and through himself. If he had begun and had origin, without doubt he could not be Almighty God, for the creature that began and is created, has no divinity. Therefore every substance that is not God is a creature and that which is not a creature is God.

God exists in Trinity indivisible, and in unity of one Godhead, for the Father is one, the Son is one, the Holy Ghost is one—and yet of these three there is one Godhead and like glory and coeternal majesty. The Father is Almighty God, the Son is Almighty God, the Holy Ghost is Almighty God, but yet there are not three Almighty Gods, but one Almighty God. They are three in persons and in name and one in Godhead. Three, because the Father will be ever Father and the Son will be ever Son and the Holy Ghost will be ever Holy Ghost, and neither of them will ever change from what he is. Ye have now heard concerning the Holy Trinity. Ye shall also hear concerning the true Unity.

Verily the Father and the Son and the Holy Ghost have one Godhead and one nature and one work. The Father created nothing nor creates without the Son or without the Holy Ghost. Nor does one of them anything without the others, but they have all one work and one counsel and one will. The Father was ever, and the Son was ever, and the Holy Ghost was ever One Almighty God. He is the Father who was neither born of nor created by any other. He is called Father because he has a Son whom he begot of himself without any mother. The Father is God [out] of no God. The Son is God [out] of God the Father. The Holy Ghost is God proceeding from the Father and from the Son. These words are shortly said and it is needful for you that we more plainly expound them.

What is the Father? The Almighty Creator, not created nor born, but he himself begot a Child coeternal with himself. What is the Son? He is the Wisdom of the Father and his Word and his Might, through whom the Father created and disposed all things. The Son is neither made nor created, but he is begotten. He is begotten and yet he is coeval and coeternal with his Father. It is not with his birth as it is with our birth. When a man begets a son and his child is born, the father is greater and the son less. Why so? Because when the son waxes the father grows old. Thou findest not among men father and son alike.

But I will give thee an example, whereby thou mayest the better understand the birth of God. Fire begets brightness of itself, and the brightness is coeval with the fire. The fire is not of the brightness, but the brightness is of the fire. The fire begets the brightness, and it is never without the brightness. Now thou hearest that the brightness is as old as the fire of which it comes. Allow therefore that God might beget a Child as old and as eternal as he himself is.

Let him who can understand that our Savior Christ is, in the Godhead, as old as his Father, thank God therefore and rejoice. He who cannot understand it shall believe it, that he may understand it. For the word of the prophet may not be rendered void who thus spake, "Unless ye believe it ye cannot understand it." Ye have now heard that the Son is of the Father without any beginning, for he is the Wisdom of the Father and he was ever with the Father and ever will be.

Let us now hear concerning the Holy Ghost, what he is. He is the Will and the true Love of the Father and of the Son, through whom all things are quickened and preserved, concerning whom it is thus said, "The Spirit of God filleth all the circumference of earth, and he holdeth all things, and he hath knowledge of every speech." He is not made nor created nor begotten, but he is proceeding (that is, going from) the Father and from the Son, with whom he is equal and coeternal. The Holy Ghost is not a son, for he is not begotten, but he proceeds from the Father and from the Son for he is the Will and Love of them both.

Christ spake of him thus in his gospel, "The Spirit of comfort whom I will send unto you, the Spirit of truth, which proceedeth from my Father, will bear testimony concerning me." That is, he is my witness that I am the Son of God. And the right faith also teaches us that we should believe in the Holy Ghost: he is the quickening God who proceeds from the Father and from the Son. How proceeds he from him? The Son is the Wisdom of the Father, ever of the Father, and the Holy Ghost is the Will of them both, ever of them both. There is therefore one Father who is ever Father, and one Son who is ever Son, and one Holy Ghost who is ever Holy Ghost.

Ever was the Father, without beginning, and ever was the Son with the Father, for he is the Wisdom of the Father. Ever was the Holy Ghost, who is the Will and Love of them both. The Father is of no other, for he was ever. The Son is begotten of the Father, for he was ever in the bosom of the Father, for he is his Wisdom, and he is of the Father all that he is. Ever was the Holy Ghost, for he is, as we before said, the Will and true Love of the Father and of the Son. For will and love betoken one thing: that which thou wilt, thou lovest, and that which thou wilt not, thou lovest not.

The sun which shines over us is a bodily creature and has, nevertheless, three properties in itself: one is the bodily substance that is the sun's orb, the second is the beam or brightness ever of the sun which illumines all the earth, the third is the heat which with the beam comes to us. The beam is ever of the sun and ever with it, and the Son of Almighty God is ever of the Father begotten and ever with him existing, of whom the apostle said, that he was the brightness of his Father's glory. The heat of the sun proceeds from it and from its beam, and the Holy Ghost proceeds ever from the Father and from the Son equally, of whom it is thus written, "There is no one who may hide himself from his heat."

Father and Son and Holy Ghost may not be named together, but yet they are nowhere separated. The Almighty God is not threefold, but is Trinity. The Father is God and the Son is God and the Holy Ghost is God: not three Gods, but they all three one Almighty God. The Father is also Wisdom [out] of no other wisdom. The Son is Wisdom [out] of the wise Father. The Holy Ghost is Wisdom. But yet they are all together one Wisdom. Again, the Father is true Love and the Son is true Love and the Holy Ghost is true Love, and they all together one God and one true

Love. In like manner, the Father is ghost and holy, and the Son is ghost and holy undoubtedly. Nevertheless the Holy Ghost is specially called Holy Ghost, that which they all three are in Common.

There is so great likeness in this Holy Trinity that the Father is no greater than the Son in the Godhead, nor is the Son greater than the Holy Ghost, nor is one of them less than the whole Trinity. Wheresoever one of them is, there they are all three, ever one God indivisible. No one of them is greater than other, nor one less than other, nor one before other, nor one after other. For whatsoever is less than God, that is not God. That which is later has beginning, but God has no beginning. The Father alone is not Trinity, nor is the Son Trinity, nor the Holy Ghost Trinity, but these three persons are one God in one Godhead. When thou hearest the Father named, then thou wilt understand that he has a Son. Again, when thou sayest Son, thou knowest, without doubt that he has a Father. Again, we believe that the Holy Ghost is the Spirit both of the Father and of the Son.

Let no man deceive himself so as to say or to believe that there are three Gods or that any person in the Holy Trinity is less mighty than other. Each of the three is God yet they are all one God, for they all have one nature and one Godhead and one substance and one counsel and one work and one majesty and like glory and coeternal rule. But the Son alone was incarnate and born to man of the holy maiden Mary. The Father was not invested with human nature, but yet he sent his Son for our redemption and was ever with him, both in life and in passion and at his resurrection and at his ascension. Also all the church of God confesses according to true faith that Christ was born of the pure maiden Mary, and of the Holy Ghost. Yet is not the Holy Ghost the Father of Christ (never shall any Christian man believe that!), but the Holy Ghost is the Will of the Father and of the Son. Therefore is it very rightly written in our belief that Christ's humanity was accomplished by the Holy Ghost.

Behold the sun with attention, in which there is, as we before said, heat and brightness—but the heat dries and the brightness gives light. The heat does one thing and the brightness another, and, though they cannot be separated, the heating, nevertheless, belongs to the heat and the giving light to the brightness. In like manner Christ alone assumed human nature and not the Father nor the Holy Ghost: they were, nevertheless, ever with him in all his works and in all his course.

We speak of God, mortals of the Immortal, feeble of the Almighty, miserable beings of the Merciful, but who may worthily speak of that which is unspeakable? He is without measure, because he is everywhere. He is without number, for he is ever. He is without weight, for he holds all creatures without toil and he disposed them all in three things, that is, in measure and in number and in weight.

But know ye that no man can speak fully concerning God when we cannot even investigate or reckon the creatures which he has created. Who by words can tell the ornaments of heaven? Or who the fruitfulness of earth? Or who shall adequately praise the circuit of all the seasons? Or who all other things, when we cannot even fully comprehend with our sight the bodily things on which we look? Behold thou seest the man before thee, but at the time thou seest his face, thou seest not his back. So also if thou lookest at a cloth, thou canst not see it all together, but turnest it about that thou mayest see it all. What wonder is it, if the Almighty God is unspeakable and incomprehensible, who is everywhere all and nowhere divided?

Now some shallow-thinking man will inquire how God can be everywhere at once and nowhere divided. Behold this sun, how high he ascends and how he sends his beams over all the world and how he enlightens all this earth which mankind inhabit. As soon as he rises up at early morn, he shines on Jerusalem and on Rome and on this country and on all countries at once, and yet he is a creature and goes by God's direction. How much ampler, then, is God's presence and his might and his visitation everywhere! Him nothing withstands, neither stone wall nor broad barrier, as they withstand the sun. To him nothing is hidden or unknown. Thou seest a man's face, but God seeth his heart. The spirit of God tries the hearts of all men and those who believe in him and love him, he purifies and gladdens with his visitation, and the hearts of unbelieving men he passes by and shuns.

Let everyone also know that every man has three things in himself indivisible and working together, as God said when he first created man. He said, "Let us make man in our own likeness." And he then made Adam in his own likeness. In which part has man the likeness of God in him? In the soul, not in the body. The soul of man has in its nature a likeness to the Holy Trinity, for it has in it three things; these are memory and understanding and will. By the memory a man thinks on the things which he has heard or seen or learned. By the understanding he comprehends all the things which he hears or sees. Of the will come thoughts and words and works, both evil and good.

There is one soul and one life and one substance which has these three things in it working together inseparably; for where memory is, there is understanding and will, and they are ever together. Yet is none of these three the soul, but the soul through the memory reminds, through the understanding comprehends, through the will it wills whatsoever it likes, and it is, nevertheless, one soul and one life. It has therefore God's likeness in itself, because it has three things in it inseparably working. Yet is the man one man and not a trinity, but God—Father and Son and Holy Ghost—exists in a trinity of persons and in the unity of one Godhead. Man exists not in trinity as God, but he has, nevertheless, the likeness of God in his soul by reason of the three things of which we have before spoken.

There was a heretic called Arius who disputed with a bishop who was named Alexander, a wise and orthodox man. The heretic said that Christ the Son of God could not be equal to his Father nor so mighty as he, and said that the Father was before the Son and took example from men, how every son is younger than his father in this life. Then said the holy bishop Alexander in opposition to him, "God was ever, and ever was his Wisdom of him begotten, and the Wisdom is his Son, as mighty as his Father." Then the heretic got the emperor's support to his heresy, and proclaimed a synod against the bishop, and would bend all the people to his heresies. Then the bishop watched one night in God's church, and cried to his Lord and thus said, "Thou Almighty God, judge right judgment between me and Arius." On the morrow they came to the synod. The heretic then said to his companions that he would go forth for his need. When he came to the place and sat, all his entrails came out while he was sitting and he sat there dead. Thus God manifested that he was as void in his inside as he had before been in his belief. He would make Christ less than he is and diminish the dignity of his Godhead when a death was given him as ignominious as he was well worthy of.

There was another heretic who was called Sabellius. He said that the Father was, whenever he would, Father, and again, when he would, he was Son, and again, when he would, was Holy Ghost, and was therefore one God. Then this heretic also perished with his heresy.

Now again, the Jewish people who slew Christ, as he himself would and permitted, say that they will believe in the Father and not in the Son whom their forefathers slew. Their belief is naught and they will therefore perish. For redemption Christ permitted them to slay him. All mankind could not have done it if he himself had not willed it, but the Holy Father created and made mankind through his Son and he would afterwards through the same redeem us from hell-torment when we were undone. Without any passion he might have had us, but that seemed to him unjust. But the devil undid himself when he instigated the Jewish people to the slaying of Jesus, and we were redeemed by his innocent death from the eternal death.

We have the belief that Christ himself taught to his apostles and they to all mankind, and that belief God has confirmed and established by many miracles. First Christ by himself healed dumb and deaf, halt and blind, mad and leprous, and raised the dead to life. After, by his apostles and other holy men he wrought the same miracles. Now also in our time, everywhere where holy men rest, at their dead bones God works many miracles because he will with those miracles confirm people's faith. God works not these miracles at any Jewish man's sepulcher, nor at any other heretic's, but at the sepulchers of orthodox men who believed in the Holy Trinity and in the true Unity of one Godhead.

Let everyone know also that no man may be twice baptized, but, if a man err after his baptism, we believe that he may be saved if with weeping he repent of his sins and, according to the teaching of his instructors, atone for them. We are to believe that the soul of every man is created by God, but yet it is not of God's own nature. The matter of a man's body is from the father and from the mother, but God creates the body from the matter and sends a soul into the body. The soul is nowhere existing previously, but God creates it forthwith, and sets it in the body, and lets it have its own election—whether it shall sin, whether it shall eschew sins. Nevertheless it ever needs God's support that it may eschew sins and again come to its Creator through good deserts. For no man doeth anything good without God.

We are also to believe that every body which has received a soul shall arise at doomsday with the same body that he now has and shall receive the reward of all his deeds. Then will the good have eternal life with God and he will give a meed[3] to everyone according to his deserts. Let us therefore merit eternal life with God through this faith, and through good deserts, who existeth in Trinity One Almighty God ever to eternity. Amen.

Notes

1. *Consequentur.*
2. *Possidebunt.*
3. Reward.

CHAPTER 8

THE RENAISSANCE OF THE ELEVENTH AND TWELFTH CENTURIES

GUIBERT OF NOGENT: "THE WAY A SERMON OUGHT TO BE GIVEN"

This treatise by Guibert, written near the beginning of the twelfth century, is the second oldest surviving textbook in homiletics, the first in the seven centuries since Augustine wrote his De doctrina christiana. *(**See Vol. 1, pp. 175-77,** for discussion.) As such, it is an amazingly confident and competent guide to the preaching office. Guibert gives good advice, much of it relevant today, on the virtue of brevity in preaching, the value of existential knowledge of the struggle against sin, the necessity for experience in biblical interpretation, the usefulness of familiarity with the properties of natural objects the Scriptures use as metaphors, the strategic importance of understanding the psychology of temptation, and the danger of preaching in order to enhance one's reputation. This work was a preface to a commentary Guibert wrote on*

Genesis, thus probably making it the first biblical commentary to acknowledge its future use to help clergy prepare sermons, a sort of medieval Pulpit Commentary. *The translation by Joseph M. Miller is taken from* Readings in Medieval Rhetoric, *ed. Joseph M. Miller, Michael H. Prosser, and Thomas W. Benson (Bloomington and London: Indiana University Press, 1973), 168-81.*

A Book About the Way a Sermon Ought to Be Given

After a discussion of why many who should preach do not, Guibert continues:

Let us then be members of the holy Church, not dead, but performing properly our functions in the body of the Lord, so that, as we celebrate the external rites of the holy mysteries in the manner of the just, we may also be like them inwardly, in the devotion and expression of all piety. Let the book from which flows the text of our speaking be a pure conscience; in that way, while our tongue announces joy to others, the memory of our own sins will not destroy us within and dissipate, with hidden guilt, the force of our speaking. Let a prayer always precede the sermon, so that the soul may burn fervently with divine love; then let it proclaim what it has learned from God so as to inflame the hearts of all hearers with the same interior fire which consumes it. For a tepid sermon, delivered half-heartedly, cannot please even the preacher; wonder of wonders, then, if it should please anyone else. And how can a mangled or stammered phrase serve to inspire others, when we know perfectly well that speech of that kind does not usually soothe the minds of listeners, but rather oppresses them with boredom and seriously irritates and angers them. For this reason, when we recognize that our intellectual acumen is not at its best and that what we ought to be saying simply does not come and that the workings of the mind are under a heavy cloud, then, as I see it, we know that no real usefulness can result from a sermon drawn out to great length in these circumstances.

After all, if a sermon ought not to be given at excessive length even when the words come easily and the fluency is pleasing to the heart, how much less when the memory fails, the delivery is halting, and the mind is sluggish. As St. Ambrose said, a tedious sermon arouses anger; and when the same things are repeated over and over, or when unrelated topics are dragged in during the sermon, it usually happens that the hearers lose everything from the sermon equally, because of their boredom, the beginning, the conclusion, and everything in between. Where a few ideas might have been presented effectively, a plethora of ideas presented at too great length leads to apathy and even, I fear, to hostility.

We know that when food is taken in moderation it serves to nourish the body, but when taken in excess it works to the detriment of the body and even provokes vomiting. Or, again, a man who uses his seed properly and chastely in the marital act generates offspring, while he who masturbates accomplishes nothing good and only befouls his body. So a preacher who abuses words interferes with what is already planted in the hearts of his hearers, what he should be helping to grow. For this reason, if the preacher has great fervor of spirit and has mastered all his material, then he can add the possibility of eloquence and style to the essentials, his own virtues. Let him think of those who must listen in silence to pompous inanities, and he will realize that it is much better for them to hear a few things well-presented than a great many things from which they will retain almost nothing. Then he will not delay making an end to one sermon so that, when he preaches another his audience will be eager rather than resentful.

There is something else he should consider, too. Though he preaches simple and uncomplicated matter to the unlettered, at the same time he should try to reach a higher plane with the educated; let him offer to them what they are capable of understanding. When he expounds such things by explaining them in detail, he will make clear and lucid for the peasants and common people ideas which at first seem difficult and confusing even to the very learned. For just as a diet of milk is familiar and even necessary to small children, so much so that infants cannot live without it, and not to children only, but also to men of mature age, who dip their crusts of bread in it, so also the preacher who offers simple doctrine to the people and at the same time adds something more substantial whereon the more educated can exercise their intellects, by so doing is able both to feed with his words the dull and sluggish of mind and also to inject weightier ideas as well by adding something more solid to the porridge, thus delighting the educated audience as well. For example, the authors of the Gospels, in their narratives, frequently add certain phrases from the Old Testament, using them to make their hearers more attentive thus, when they announced some new doctrine, they reassured their hearers by relating it to the familiar phrasing their ears were accustomed to. Those who wish to explain Scripture now should seize upon this and always seek to imitate it. We learn simple stories to please some, and we bring into the sermon the histories of old and we embellish our words like a painter using many different colors on the same canvas.

Let us also note what treatment is especially suitable to the preacher.

There are four ways of interpreting Scripture; on them, as though on so many scrolls, each sacred page is rolled. The first is history, which speaks of actual events as they occurred; the second is allegory, in which one thing stands for something else; the third is tropology, or moral instruction, which treats of the ordering and arranging of one's life; and the last is ascetics, or spiritual enlightenment, through which we who are about to treat of lofty and heavenly topics are led to a higher way of life. For example, the word Jerusalem: historically, it represents a specific city; in allegory it represents the holy Church; tropologically, or morally, it is the soul of every faithful man who longs for the vision of eternal peace; and anagogically it refers to the life of the heavenly citizens, who already see the God of Gods, revealed in all His glory in Zion. Granted that all four of these methods of interpretation are valid and can be used, either together or singly, yet the most appropriate and prudent for use in matters referring to the lives of men seems to be the moral approach.

Although it is true that the allegorical method of interpretation is widely used in prophetic and apostolic works, still it seems to do little more than strengthen our faith. Even though we read the various revelations of God as he spoke in many ways through the prophets, we already know that in the Christian dispensation we have the sacraments which were only prefigured there. By the grace of God, faith already dwells in the hearts of men; even if it is proper for us to teach prophecy, therefore, and to repeat it often to our hearers, it is no less fitting—indeed, it is more so—for us to say those things which they can apply in their daily lives. We speak more easily and confidently about the nature of virtue than about the mysteries of faith, concerning some of which, we must admit, mild disputations are still taking place. Among the less intelligent, error can result from preaching which is too esoteric; but in moral instruction, we can especially learn the utility of discretion.

Therefore, although the allegorical interpretation can be very agreeable to many when it is brought into the sermon now and then; and although it will strengthen our faith and our understanding of the Sacred Scriptures when it is used as it should be used, with moderation, yet all our efforts and all our words ought to deal first with the interior life of men, that is, with the thoughts which are common to all. In such a case, treatment of this type of subject matter will be absolutely clear to everyone, especially since each will retain within himself, as if written in a book, something which he has drawn from the tongue of the preacher to help in temptation.

The admonition of the preacher should deal as much with the control and avoiding of vice as with the development and protection of virtue.

As a teacher let him show earnestly and clearly which sins are "natural" and which are "contrary to nature," which sins are the consequences of others, and how pernicious they all are in themselves and in what they bring about. Let him show the fruit of sin in every glaring detail. When the secrets of the Scriptures are interpreted for the unlettered and uneducated, they quickly forget; they are accustomed to dealing with physical objects, so it is of no great wonder that they do not possess the same power of understanding the spiritual, which they cannot see, as they possess for the material substances which they can see and touch. Some of them are almost animals and scarcely comprehend anything, unless it is material and evident even to beasts; they are completely ignorant of the vices of their bodies and souls, unless someone explains this to them. Once that is done, however, they will always, we pray, understand and recollect what they have heard.

I have said clearly and I have said often that sometimes as much is accomplished with a discussion of the nature of the vices as with a discussion of the nature of the virtues. For if I do not recognize what a vice is, how can I love the purity of a virtue? And how can I avoid sin unless I am seeking an object which is good, healthy, and untainted, one which I can pursue and enjoy in the very act of fleeing evil? There are nutritious green herbs and there is hemlock; the herbs are of much value, the hemlock is poisonous. If someone likes to eat green vegetables, but knows not the difference between the herbs and the hemlock and believes that hemlock is as edible as other herbs, of what use to him will all his eating of healthful herbs prove to have been on that day when, through his own ignorance, he eats hemlock, falls into a coma, and finally dies?

The roots, therefore, of every sin ought to be carefully examined, so when the nature of sin is clearly recognized, its opposite, the nature of virtue, will be known with equal clarity, as grain is clearly distinguished from chaff. And the more zealously the life which is virtue is pursued, the more carefully the death which is sin will be avoided. It seems to me that no preaching is more efficacious than that which would help man to know himself, that which brings out into the open all that is deep within him, in his innermost heart, that which will shame him, finally, by forcing him to stand clearly revealed before his own gaze.

But perhaps someone may ask how he can be sure of what to treat regarding the interior life of men. I answer that he should master the *Moralia* of St. Gregory and the book called *De institutis et collationibus Patrum* by the famous Cassianus, who is also called John; both of these works will prove extremely fruitful to sincere readers, as will the writings of the other holy authors who have treated this subject. But I think that the most valuable help to the knowledge and understanding of vice for those who know themselves and are unceasingly battling their own weaknesses will be that they are anxiously guarding themselves against their own instability and lack of purpose regarding both acts and thoughts. If they strive faithfully in this, there is no better source from which they can hope to learn about the conditions in which man lives. One who tries to gain mastery of this subject from reading alone, no matter how many volumes he studies, only forgets the more quickly; he never relates what he has read or heard to his own experience. Moreover, nothing is more useful to the human mind than experience: the spirit is always aware of its own struggles and sometimes rejoices in the triumph of its own victory. Also, when the posture of the spirit undergoes a change, when it grows weak in its opposition to the temptations both of the mind and of the flesh, when a man who formerly rejoiced that his soul was adamant against evil suddenly finds himself drained of resistance and willing to tolerate sin, when one's soul vacillates and wavers between hope and fear, then he arises joyfully when God gives him the opportunity and he returns from the treacherous swamp where he has wandered blindly, or even drunkenly, and reaches the solid ground of rational behavior. Thus he has gone full circle.

When we have been thus trapped either in the mire of temptation or in the quicksand of weariness, God gives us the opportunity of rising again from the struggle in one of two ways. Either he suggests a spirit of penance to our reason and makes us aware of the wretchedness our own willfulness has brought us to, or he offers us the grace of hearing someone else praise him, or he forces us to offer consoling words of exhortation to another. On these occasions we must look at ourselves, where we have fallen, and so we are brought to true sorrow. Certainly when we are aroused from languor of soul by the eloquence of another's words or by reading a spiritual book or by any of the other completely distinct forces, we are recalled to a life of virtue.

It must, therefore, be our confession to the Lord, especially those who are "all at sea," that is, who are beaten down by the storm of temptation, but are still protected in their ships, that is, who still follow the compass of devout intentions, that even if we veer off our course we will not sink while "doing business on the great waters" (Ps. 107:23-30), that is, among the shipwrecks and storms which result from the battle between our bodily and our spiritual parts. In this situation men accomplish good work, because they neither abandon their zeal on account of distaste nor fall into a pit of despair because they are weighted down by too many difficulties. Rather, under the guidance of reason, they cast themselves upon God, who is all-powerful; "they see the works of the Lord, his wondrous works in the deep": in other words, despite the dejection of their spirit, despite the confusion of their wanderings, despite their fear of sinning, they become aware of God's power. Those who are greatly tempted and more greatly rescued owe the greatest thanks to him.

So, when men who have escaped such dangers contemplate within themselves the state of virtue in which they are placed, the certainty they felt that they could preserve unspotted faith without great fear and trembling, the foolishness with which they congratulated themselves on their own virtue and ability to persevere therein, and their ultimate fall into either temptation or sloth and indifference, they can learn much. First they gave into their passions, then they overcame them; that is, they avoided the furnace of their own desires. The man who experiences this can profit much from the conflicts within him which effectively instruct the intelligent soul without benefit of books or studying.

Through these points and others of like nature, anyone having the office of teacher can, if he wishes, be prepared in every detail, first by knowing himself, and, second, through the lessons his experience of interior struggles has taught him; this training will be far richer than anything I could express. In this way the events of his life, both good and bad, are indelibly imprinted on his memory; because of them he is able to act wisely for his own salvation and that of others. Any man, even one without experience, one who has never been part of a battle, can talk at great length about war, just because he has seen warriors or heard stories of war; but what a difference there is between this and the man who can reminisce about war, who has fought or been besieged, who has gone to war and suffered!

It is the same in spiritual matters when we hear people speak with overpowering eloquence about what they have read in books or heard from others; how greatly they differ from the man who speaks with real authority of his own spiritual struggles, whose experience is like a mark to underline what he says, whose personal knowledge is the witness to the truth of what his mouth speaks. Certainly it will benefit educated listeners much more also if the speaker uses his eloquence in dealing with matters they themselves have experienced; but if the treatment is inaccurate, they will allow themselves to become bored or even contemptuous. That is why, when we deliver an admonition to the educated and uneducated seated side by side, we must offer to each group something that is not overly familiar, but is, nonetheless, easily understood; this is how we are able to avoid the tedium of saying only what they already know quite well. So it follows that in expounding the lessons of the holy Gospel we must do something more than mouth traditional platitudes; we bring in the moral application, bringing in new stones, as it were, for the reconstruction of an old wall.

Of course there are certain chapters of the gospels, treated only in the allegorical manner by the fathers of the church, which were designed for the instruction of both Jews and Gentiles. Nevertheless, if an alert and serious student of the scriptures wishes to examine them according to the other methods of interpretation, such approaches will never, or hardly ever, be out of the question. On the contrary, when the spirit and the will of the reader would follow a new road, then the chariot, which is the Holy Scripture, will carry him there. Nevertheless, though this kind of approach is quite proper for those who have a strong foundation in Holy Writ, it should not be undertaken by anyone who has not mastered to the full by long usage the proper way to collate the different meanings of allegories which use one and the same subject to express many different ideas.

It should not, I repeat, be undertaken by anyone who is not thoroughly grounded in scholarship and completely instructed in how to recognize many different ideas represented by the same symbols or words. For instance, words like "rock," "foundation," "water," "sky," "plant," "tree," "sun," and "moon," as well as innumerable others, represent many different ideas in the Bible; therefore this must be carefully noted by one who wishes to delve into the hidden meanings, since any of these words may occur in any of the accepted scriptural uses. Thus, "gold" could signify divinity, "gold" could signify wisdom, "gold" could signify nobility of life; the speaker, then, should be sure to use whichever meaning seems applicable in the text he is treating. Then, as his confidence grows little by little each day, he first begins to see how easy it is for him to recognize the various kinds of symbolism in the Holy Scripture; next he proceeds to the more difficult tasks which he would never have dared to attempt on his own, moved by the prodding of his desire for better things, and he is greatly comforted in his effort to penetrate these secrets by the sudden appearance of a mass of evidence from the sacred writings. All this can be done in one of two ways: either by example or by the use of reason. As I have already shown, he can show examples from other scriptural texts; and if no such examples are available, he uses his reason: through consideration of the nature of whatever symbol he is treating he can find the appropriate allegorical or moral meaning. For example, if the text speaks of precious stones, of birds, of beasts, or of anything to be taken figuratively, there is always a connection to be drawn based on the natural qualities; and even if this is not clearly stated anywhere in the Scriptures, still an examination of the nature of the thing will certainly reveal it.

Gregory of Nazianzen, an amazingly learned man, testifies in one of his books that it was his habit to improve his mind by studying carefully everything he saw, for the purpose of finding an allegorical application. So if anyone at all wants to cultivate the habit of sharpening his intellect in this way, not only regarding the divine books, but even regarding everything that comes to his attention, he will find enough metaphorical material to furnish him an ample supply of examples and useful symbolism; there is an extremely rich vein of such material even in subjects which frequent use has caused us to dismiss as commonplace. These are considered all the more useful in the benefits they bring to people and all the more pleasant as well, to the extent that they are not treated in ways already overly familiar to the hearers.

A great deal more might be said about the use of common sense in dealing with this kind of interpretation; but I fear that if I begin to go into detail, I may exceed the space allotted me, and I doubt that even then could I explain it as lucidly as I should like.

My next point is that a preacher is especially likely to help his listeners if he speaks from the heart and without any desire for praise. It will be clear in such a case that he is seeking only the instruction and edification of those who listen to spiritual matters, and that he is not calling their attention to his overwhelming eloquence for the sake of his own fame nor using beautiful figures merely for the sake of novelty. For the listener will consider nothing more offensive than that a preacher leave the impression that he is disputing with his audience either for the sake of gain or in order to display his own talent.

A preacher who is recognized as doing this angers his hearers, he does not edify them; the more he attempts to bedeck his thoughts in outlandish style, the more, alas, he arouses the hearts of his audience to contempt even for the things he may say wisely, and the more he makes people despise him. The very things which he proclaims with arrogance ought to be offered humbly, as divine precepts for the soul.

I have spoken, to the best of my ability, about how you ought to preach, most dear friend; now let me try to suggest a little something about where you can, with God's assistance, find material to speak about.

To every man who is enveloped in a mass of vices it is most useful to describe the pains of hell—how horrible they are and how their unending terrors are beyond description. Make clear that just as no happiness is lacking to those who are established in the kingdom of heaven, so, on the other hand, nothing that could intensify the tortures is lacking to the man condemned to everlasting torment. Let them know when they are suffering with no relief, or with only brief respite, that the thing which will punish their souls beyond comprehension is this: the fact that they will have no hope of escaping their tortures, not even after a million years, but will suffer unceasing death for all time. For hope, even though it is false, sometimes refreshes the spirits of those suffering adversity, but in hell there will be no hope, either true or false, by which they can be consoled. But for the bestial man, for the man who lives like an animal, for the man whose senses are concerned only with what he can see with his bodily eyes, blinded as he is to the things of God by his desire for sensual pleasure, since nothing you can say about the next life will avail to change him, and even if he could be brought to a brief halt, he would still not understand what you are saying, dismiss this approach from your mind.

What you must say to him is to stress the torments he suffers now in the way of anxiety and fear between the time when he sins and the time when he is punished for sin; then remind him of the fact that he can expect nothing except toil and unspeakable pain. For instance, if someone is a confirmed thief, driven by greed for some kind of valuable goods, I do not think that he will give up stealing out of fear of the dark, which I should certainly tremble at, and not even because he fears the loss of his limbs or the hanging which he knows he must endure if he is caught; but he will be afraid, he will tremble from head to foot, if he is threatened with the loss of what he has stolen. Convinced that this will follow, he will be converted.

I would like to speak of unchastity now, but I can best make my point with the words of the noble Boethius: "What is there left to say concerning those pleasures whose desire is filled with shame, and whose gratification is its own punishment?" One beset with this outrageous lust is torn apart: he burns with the knowledge that his vile desire will lead to a viler result; and while he fears that his acts may become known, he is consumed with horrible and intolerable anguish. While his impatient ardor strives to express itself, he assents, he refuses, he seeks eagerly for a solution to the conflict within himself. He calls himself the most wretched of men, so that he despises himself and loathes his own life, and when he has satiated his lust, what tortures, what miseries, what belated repentance overwhelms this pitiful man!

Regarding this, I may say without hesitation that if the sinner would have as much true sorrow and genuine remorse after committing the sin as he has after he experiences the result of lust or any other sin, then before he indulges in the act, while he is in the act of planning it, he would recall the whole course of his agony. He would think, even as he schemed about how to gratify his desire, of the lasting grief which will blanket him from the moment of satisfaction until the time when the habitual desire begins again; he would think of the disgust he will feel for himself, and would offer his contribution to God, completely and wholeheartedly, as the proper fruit of his act. But truly is it written that "the children of this world are wiser in their own generation than are the children of light," and they are more alert also. It was said to the apostles, "Do you not see Judas, that he does not sleep?"[1] This does not mean that the wakefulness of Judas is more virtuous than the sleep of the Apostles, but that his alertness in evil ought also to characterize the devotion of the apostles to good. And Paul, "speaking in human terms because of the weakness of the flesh," urges, "Just as you yielded your members to impurity and greater and greater iniquity, so now yield your members to righteousness for sanctification."

He knew that the drive and cleverness in a human being determined to do evil would, if directed with similar intensity to virtue, be worthy of the highest praise. Therefore we ought to bring up again the terrible tortures and punishments which render these pleasures so wretched; we ought to recall to mind the foul reputation which by itself contaminates the virtue of the unhappy victim with open or secret accusations. Then, if our listeners do not feel moved to fear the future punishments which are not immediately visible or at hand, they will at least fear being so violently hated as the result of so small a pleasure. They will realize that they can gain nothing for themselves but a ruined and destroyed reputation for virtue. I return to the already mentioned Boethius, who says that this pleasure will be very much like that of a bee; it will be like honey in the mouth, that is in the first suggestion of delight, but will carry a sting in its tail, since, after the first taste of foul pleasure, it dies in the savagery of its attack.

St. Gregory has said that nothing is a greater blessing than an unperturbed spirit. Someone else, on the other hand, has said that a heart burdened with sin is continually agitated because of its own urging, since it is consumed unceasingly by internal fires, both in the act of doing evil and in the resultant fear of the evil already done. If, therefore, a man is fearful of eternal damnation, let him be wary of shamelessness in the present; let him take counsel in his heart so as to learn to resist his vile leanings; let him inquire anxiously to discover the difference between the flesh and the spirit (or, more accurately, what the flesh is and what the spirit is). For it is useless to train a soldier in the use of weapons unless he has a strong desire to drive back the enemy. And what is the use of knowing the virtues opposed to the lusts of the flesh, if a lethargic and apathetic spirit refuses to gird itself for battle?

Let us, therefore, take our examples from the events of true history; while we study its deepest meaning, we can at the same time, avail ourselves of new tools for effective teaching. And no one should think that we are suggesting any new methods in this matter; remember what the poet said: "It is proper and will always be proper to imprint our own identity upon whatever comes to hand." Therefore it is much more proper for one who is well versed in the inspired writings, provided that he respects matters of faith and observes the traditional interpretation, to seek out further riches through the various senses of the Sacred Scriptures. Therefore, let us preach.

Here Ends the Prefatory Essay.

ALAN OF LILLE: SERMON FOR THE DAY OF PENTECOST

Alan, who died in 1203, was described in his epitaph as knowing "the two Testaments, the seven liberal arts, everything knowable." He taught at Paris and Montpelier and entered the Cistercian order shortly before death. A prolific writer in all the theological disciplines, he left both a treatise on The Art of Preaching *(which contains the first recorded definition of preaching), and a* Book of Sermons. *(**See Vol. 1, pp. 177-82,** for discussion.) His preaching represents an important transitional stage between patristic homilies and the thematic sermons of the next century. He preached from a text or "theme" as the later preachers would do, but he did not divide it as they did. Instead, he investigated its content by using allegorical interpretation. His sermons, translated by Gillian R. Evans, have not yet been published. The one here appears with her permission and that of Cistercian Publications.*

On the Day of Pentecost

Text: Acts 2:1-3

Just as the Three Persons are distinct, but share one common Essence, so three solemn feasts are celebrated in the year, in honor of the three Persons individually: Christmas, Easter, and Pentecost. There is one feast common to all three, which is called the Feast of the Trinity, and this is celebrated a week after Pentecost. Although the Feast of the Nativity may be called the Feast of the Son, yet it can properly be said to be the Father's Feast, for in that Feast we celebrate the Father's begetting of him from eternity, whence it is said: "The Lord said to me, 'You are My Son, today I have begotten You'" (Ps. 2:7). The Feast of Easter is properly that of the Son, in which we celebrate his Resurrection. The Feast of Pentecost is properly that of the Holy Spirit; that which is celebrated a week later, is that of the whole Trinity. It is a part of the mystery that "when the day of Pentecost was fully come" (Acts 2:1), the Holy Spirit descended upon the disciples. For in the fact that it was after seven weeks that the Holy Spirit was given to the disciples, it is signified that after the passing of a spiritual seven weeks the minds of the faithful will be wholly filled with the Holy Spirit.

The first seven (or "week") is the purging of the seven cardinal vices; this comes first in the justification of everyman. The second is the seven means of remitting sin: by baptism, by penance, by martyrdom, by charity, by almsgiving, by the calming of anger against one's neighbor, by the conversion of one's brother to the faith. The third seven is the seven petitions of the Lord's Prayer; the fourth, the seven gifts which are mentioned in Isaiah, where it is said, "The Spirit of wisdom," etc. (Isa. 11:2).[2] The fifth is the acquiring of the seven virtues, faith, hope, charity and four cardinal virtues. The sixth, the adding together of the seven beatitudes which are listed in Matthew's Gospel, where it is said: "Blessed are the poor," etc. (Mt. 5:3-12). The seventh seven are the seven steps of the ascent from virtue to virtue, which are described in the Psalm; "Lord, who shall dwell in your Tabernacle?" etc. (Ps. 14:1[15:1]).

After he has been confirmed in all these, the Holy Spirit possesses a man wholly. It is a part of the mystery that the feast continues for seven days, for those seven days signify the seven gifts of the Spirit, which were fully bestowed on the Apostles at that time. And therefore it is said: "When the Day of Pentecost was fully come, they were all with one accord in one place." The unity of place signifies the threefold unity of the mind: the unity of faith, the unity of hope, and the unity of charity. These three make up that threefold cord of which it is said: "The threefold cord is hard to break" (Eccl. 4:12). This is the pitch with which the ark of Noah was lined, inside and outside. These are the three unities which make the Church as it were a threefold creation, where Faith is like the Father, from which Hope is born, like the Son, and where Love proceeds from Faith and Hope, like the Holy Spirit. He who sins in faith, then, sins against the Father; he who sins against hope, sins against the

Son, and he who sins against love, sins against the Holy Spirit. He who sins against the Father will be forgiven, however often he sins; He who sins against faith sins through ignorance. He who sins against the Son will be forgiven (that is he who sins against hope), although he will not be forgiven easily. He who sins against the Holy Spirit, that is against love, will not be forgiven, for with terrible difficulty is that sin wiped out.

"When therefore, they were all in one place, there was a sudden sound from above." By the sudden sound which was heard, when the Holy Spirit descended upon the Apostles, is signified the twofold "sound" which was in future to be in the mouths of the Apostles: the sound of preaching, whence: "Their sound went out into all the world" (Rom. 10:18); the sound of repentance and confession, whence, "I have cried unto you with my whole heart" (Ps. 118:145[119:145]); and the sound of rejoicing, whence, "Praise him upon the cymbals with a good sound" (Ps. 150:5). The Apostles preached, filled with the Holy Spirit; they invited others to repentance and confession and praised the Lord, speaking against sin. "Suddenly there was a sound." Through the suddenness of the sound is meant the sudden descent of the Holy Spirit, for he so visits the mind that no one knows whence he comes or where he goes, or how he illuminates the mind of the sinner, justifies the penitent, and heaps Grace upon him who is justified.

That sound comes from Heaven and not from earth. For there is a sound born of the earth, from the collision of solid bodies, there is a sound born of the waters, from the meeting of waves; there is a sound which comes down from the skies, when clouds come together. By the first sound we are to understand that conflict which is born in man from the love of earthly things; by the second, the conflict arising from carnal pleasures; by the third, preaching from "clouds," that is, preaching which is the work of those preachers who are to be compared with clouds, for they rain down doctrines, they sparkle with miracles, they thunder with warnings. That sound was made "as though at the coming of a mighty wind" (Acts 2:2). The Spirit is twofold. There is a Spirit of fear and a Spirit of pride, a Spirit of heaven and a Spirit of earth. The devil is the spirit of pride; he puffs man up with the swellings of pride. The Spirit of Fear is the Holy Spirit, who inspires man with fear and love. The spirit of the earth is the Devil, who invites a man to earthly loves; the spirit of heaven is the Holy Spirit, through whom we desire the heavenly and avoid earthly things.

The Holy Spirit sometimes goes before us; sometimes he comes upon us, sometimes he comes to our aid. He goes before us in the pouring out of Grace; he comes upon us in the multiplying of virtues; he comes to our aid in fortifying us against tribulation. In going before, he is a doctor who heals us from sin; in coming upon us, he is the Lord, who enriches his servant. In coming to our aid he is our protector, fortifying us in battle.

Whence it is appropriately said, that he is "mighty," as if to say that he is fierce and brings woe. For he brings a fourfold woe, that is a fourfold punishment: for there is a testing punishment, as in Job, a cleansing punishment, as in Paul, a punishment which frees, as in the sinner who is ensnared in his sin, an afflicting punishment, as in hell. Or it is said that he is "rushing," as if to say, "carrying outside the mind," for he carries man outside his fleshly mind into the things of the spirit. "And he filled all the house where they were sitting." By the outward sound which filled the house it is signified that the Holy Spirit inspired the inner temple of the mind. Outwardly the sound touched the ear. Inwardly the Holy Spirit soothed the mind.

It is a part of the mystery that the Apostles were sitting. For some lie prostrate, some sit, others stand erect. Those who indulge in earthly things lie prostrate; those who look in their minds up to heaven, but sometimes look down to earth, these sit. Such were the Apostles while they were not yet confirmed by the Holy Spirit. Those who contemplate heavenly things, after they have been confirmed by the Holy Spirit, stand erect.

"And there appeared to them tongues of fire." We are not to believe that actual tongues of fire appeared above the heads of the Apostles, but rather flames of fire like tongues. Nor is it unreasonable that the Holy Spirit should appear in the form of tongues of fire, since fire has two properties. It glows softly, whence, by grace, it calms the mind. It burns when it purges sin. It softens, while it pours forth the light of grace; it destroys, when it consumes sin. The fire also took the form of a tongue. The tongue is the instrument of speech, of discerning taste; it speaks for the other members while it suffers with them. For when the members of the body are injured, the tongue says, "You injure me." Properly, therefore, the Holy Spirit appeared in tongues of fire. He gave the Apostles the power to speak in tongues. He also bestowed on them the power to distinguish between good and evil. He united the members of the Church in one body, so that they may say, suffering with each other, "Who is sick and I am not sick?" (2 Cor. 11:29).

Let us therefore, dearly-beloved brothers, come together in a threefold unity of faith, hope and charity, that we may so deserve to receive the coming of the Holy Spirit that the Holy Spirit may deign to visit the house of our mind, in which there should be three things: a bed, a throne and a dining couch. The dining couch of God is love, upon which the spirit feasts. The bed is divine contemplation, in which the spirit rejoices with its spouse. The throne is discretion, where good and evil are separated by the judgment.

Let us therefore pray to the Holy Spirit that the dining couch of charity may cleanse our senses, the bed of divine contemplation adorn us with virtues, the throne of discretion invest us with the gold of prudence.

This may our Lord Jesus Christ grant, who lives and reigns world without end, Amen.

BERNARD OF CLAIRVAUX: SERMON 6 ON "HE WHO DWELLS" (PSALM 91)

*Bernard, the greatest of the twelfth-century masters of monastic spirituality, was one of the most influential men in Europe in his time, especially in the monastic movement. He preached constantly and then labored to make his insights available to a wider audience by revising his sermon series into treatises. (**See Vol. 1, pp. 187-97,** for discussion.) This sermon is from a series on Psalm 91 that circulated independently as well as serving as the Lenten section of his* Sermons for the Seasons and Principal Festivals of the Year. *Here he gives an allegorical interpretation to each of the phrases of his text, but he does so in a less mechanical and more artistic way than did Alan. Part of the explanation for that is his greater ability, but the rest of it lies in the revision of the text as a treatise in the form of homilies. While only exact quotations from the Bible are identified in this sermon, the careful reader will discern biblical allusions behind almost every line. This translation is taken from* Bernard of Clairvaux, Sermons on Conversion: On Conversion, a Sermon to Clerics, and Lenten Sermons on the Psalm "He Who Dwells," *trans. with intro. Marie-Bernard Saïd, Cistercian Fathers Series, no. 25 (Kalamazoo, Mich.: Cistercian Publications, 1981), 143-50.*

Sermon Six

On the Second Part of This[3] Verse, and on the Sixth: "You will not fear the terror of the night; nor the arrow that flies by day, nor the bogy that prowls in the darkness, nor assault, nor the noonday devil."

1. In Holy Scripture adversity is usually betokened by night, and we know that against those who turn to God the first struggle is generally against vexations of the body. The flesh, never hitherto subdued, will never with good will put up with being chastised and brought into servitude. But remembering still the liberty only recently lost, it will lust

bitterly against the spirit, especially amid those pains by which you die every day, or rather by which you are being killed all day long, for they are not only above your strength and beyond nature, but also contrary to what you are accustomed. Is it astonishing that they cause you trouble, particularly those among you who are not yet used to them and do not have recourse to prayer quickly enough, and do not take refuge in holy meditations in order to lighten the burden of the day and the scorching heat? The shield of the Lord is plainly necessary to us at the beginning of our conversion so that we do not fear the terror of the night. Furthermore, it is exact to say the terror of the night, and not night itself, because this affliction is not so much temptation itself as the fear arising from it. We all struggle, but this does not mean we are all being tempted, and those who are tempted suffer more from the fear of pain to come than from present grief.

2. Because fear itself constitutes the temptation, it is appropriate to say that anyone who is surrounded by the Lord's shield will perhaps be attacked, will perhaps be tempted, will perhaps be afraid of the night, but this fear can do him no harm. Moreover, if it does not dominate him, then he will be blameless and cleansed, as it is written, "the terrified will be made pure" [Job 41:16, Vulg.]. This fear is a furnace, but truth brings it about that it does not sear but refines. This fear is surely dark and nocturnal, but the ray of truth easily overcomes it. This allows the eyes of the heart to see the sins we have committed in such a way that, as the prophet said of himself, we are even ready to be whipped, declaring our iniquity and thinking upon our sin [Ps. 37:19, Vulg.]. Sometimes we think about the eternal punishment which we have deserved until, by comparison with what we have escaped, we consider delightful everything we are now undergoing. Sometimes, too,—frequently—we think about the heavenly reward towards which we are straining, for the sufferings of this present time are not worth comparing with the glory that is to be revealed to us. Sometimes, again, we think about the things Christ bore for us, in order that, frequently meditating upon all that his majesty endured for his worthless servants, we may blush at not being able to suffer even a little on our own behalf.

3. But perhaps truth has prevailed, already surrounding us in so many ways and on so many sides that it enables us not only to push this fear away, but even to cast it out altogether. The night is now far gone, but still, as a child of light now walking honestly as in the day, fear the arrow. It flies lightly and pricks lightly. Yet I tell you, it inflicts no slight wound; it kills fast. This arrow is none other than vain glory, which is why it does

not attack the wavering and the careless. It is those who appear more fervent who must look out for themselves; they must be afraid on this score, and be extremely cautious never to leave the invincible shield of truth. For what could be more opposed to vanity [than truth]? We are not required to protect ourselves from this arrow with the hidden and intimate secrets of truth. The soul should know itself and be conscious of the truth about itself. For, unless I am mistaken, a man cannot easily be misled by someone who praises him during his lifetime, and thus become toplofty, if he carefully examines himself within in the light of truth. Surely if he thinks about his own condition, he will say to himself, "How can you, who are but dust and ashes, be proud?" [Sir. 10:9]. Surely, if he considers his own corruption, he must necessarily admit that there is no good in him. Or, if he does perhaps seem to find some good, he will not, I think, be able to argue against the apostle when he says, "What do you have that you have not received?" [1 Cor. 4:7] and elsewhere, "Let him who stands look out lest he fall" [1 Cor. 10:12]. Finally, if he reckons faithfully, he will have no difficulty in acknowledging that he cannot go out with ten thousand men to meet someone coming against him with twenty thousand, and that all his righteous deeds are to be thought of as filthy rags.

4. Furthermore, truth must be opposed to the temptations which ensue. Our ancient enemy is not going to cease for all that: he will have recourse to craftier arguments. He has verified that the tower is firm on every side: he cannot get at it either on the left by the indecision arising from fear, or on the right by battering it with human praise, but is frustrated in both attempts. So he says, "Well, if I cannot overthrow it by force, then perhaps I shall be able to deceive it by the traitor's ruse." Who do you think will be this traitor? Obviously the love of money, the root of all evils; ambition, a subtle evil, a secret virus, a hidden pest, the craftsman of deceit; the mother of hypocrisy, the begetter of spite, the source of vices, the tinder of crimes, the rust of virtue, the moth of holiness, the blinker of hearts, producing sickness from remedies, and begetting illness from medicine. "He has spurned vain glory because it is vain. Maybe he will conceive a fondness for more solid food: honors, perhaps, or maybe riches." That is what he says. How many people have been thrust into outer darkness by this bogy prowling in the darkness, stripping them of the marriage garment and emptying the exercises of virtue of any fruit of piety? So many have been wickedly deceived by this pest and shamefully overthrown that others for whom he lies in ambush should tremble at the thought of sudden ruin. But what fosters this worm, if not estrangement from reason and obliviousness to truth? And what else but truth will

disclose this looming enemy and show it up as a bogy of darkness? Surely that was meant by the words: "What will it profit a man if he gain the whole world and loses or forfeits himself?" [Mt. 16:26//Lk. 9:25]. And again, "Mighty men will be tempted mightily" [Wis. 6:7, Vulg.]. It is by such unremitting suggestions that [truth] reminds us how silly is the consolation of ambition, how serious its condemnation, how short-lived its utility, and how uncertain its end.

5. These were the Lord's temptations; the enemy did not dare bring up the fourth. For that springs from ignorance, and he knew only too well that a person who gave answers so measured that he could not trip him up by anything he asked must be extremely wise. By the first temptation [the enemy] tried to persuade a hungry man to change stones into loaves of bread; but He, without either denying or affirming that He could do so, held out another bread saying, "Not in bread alone" and so forth [Mt. 4:4]. In the second temptation the devil coaxed him to throw himself down, promising that if he were the Son of God, he would come to no harm and the whole city would praise and honor him; here again, He neither denied nor affirmed who He was. The third [temptation] was one of ambition, when [the devil] promised all the kingdoms of this world, if he would fall down and worship him. Do you see now how ambition leads to worship of the devil, for he promises the honor and glory of this world to those who will worship him? He withheld the fourth temptation from our Lord, as I have said, because he saw from the prudence of his answers that he was a man of experience.

6. But what does he do against others, those who love righteousness and hate wickedness? What else but dress vice up as virtue? For when he recognizes perfect lovers of good he attempts to persuade them to do evil under the appearances of good; not just ordinary good, but something perfect, so that someone who really loves to do good may consent more easily, and in this way he easily trips up the runner. This devil is not just the day devil, but the noonday devil. Was not he the one Mary was afraid of when she took fright at the angel's unusual greeting? Was not he the one the apostle was alluding to when he said, "We are not ignorant of their designs? For this angel of Satan disguises himself as an angel of light" [2 Cor. 2:11, 11:14]. Lastly, was not he the one the disciples feared when they saw the Lord walking upon the sea and cried out thinking he was a ghost? And notice how fitting it is that the disciples were enjoined during the fourth watch to watch against the fourth temptation. Nor do I think it necessary for me to say much about this, which is only the simple truth that discloses veiled fraud.

7. No one who considers them carefully will have difficulty in discovering these four temptations in the general state of the Church. Did not the terror of the night keep the young plant of the Church busy in those days when all who killed the servants of God thought they were offering God service? Then, when persecution ceased and day had returned, the flying arrow troubled her more and afflicted her more grievously; then some people left the Church, puffed up by the spirit of the flesh, hankering after vain and fleeting honor and wanting to make a name for themselves; they magnified their tongues and forged perverse doctrines. And nowadays, there is peace from pagans, peace from heretics, yet there is no peace from her false sons. You have multiplied the people Lord Jesus, but you have not multiplied its joy, for many are called but few are chosen. All are christians, and almost all look after their own interests and not those of Jesus Christ. For they even pursue their nefarious quest and the business of darkness in running after positions of ecclesiastical dignity, and in this they are seeking not the salvation of souls, but the extravagance of riches. This is why they get themselves tonsured, this is why they go to church all the time, celebrate masses, and sing psalms. Today people scrap shamelessly to get archbishoprics and archdeaconries in order to dissipate church revenues in wanton waste and vain pursuits. Now it remains for us to disclose the man of sin, the son of perdition, who is no longer simply the day devil, but the noonday devil disguised as an angel of light and exalting himself above all that is called God or that is worshiped. How cruelly he waits in ambush at the heel of Mother Church, grieving at having had his head bruised. This is clearly going to be a very serious assault! Yet from this too, Truth will free the Church of the elect, shortening the day for them and destroying the midday devil by the light of His coming.

Enough said about these temptations. Now I remember having dealt with them in one of my sermons on the Song of Songs [33:8-16], where mention was made of the noonday devil in connection with the noonday rest of the bridegroom after which the bride was inquiring.

HILDEGARD OF BINGEN: HOMILIES ON THE GOSPELS (24.1-4)

These four sermons by Hildegard on the same gospel represent the range of her visionary preaching. The first is close to the literal/historical sense, although it has a cosmological dimension. The second represents her preaching against the Cathars, and the third reflects her objection to the antipope at the time, who was supported by the emperor, Frederick Barbarossa. The fourth is a psychodrama of the individual soul. The translation is a preliminary stage of a version being prepared by Beverly Mayne Kienzle and Fay Martineau for publication by Cistercian Publications. The notes are theirs. I am grateful to Beverly Mayne Kienzle and Faye Martineau and Cistercian Publications for sharing this as-yet unpublished manuscript. (For a discussion of the preaching of Hildegard, ***see Vol. 1, 197-202.***)

24.1-4: First Sunday of Advent

There will be signs in the sun and the moon and the stars, and upon the earth distress of nations from perplexity at the sound of the sea and of the waves, humans fainting from fear and foreboding of the things that are coming upon the entire world. For the powers of heaven will be shaken. And then they will see the Son of Man coming in a cloud with great power and majesty. When these things begin to take place, look up and lift up your heads, because your redemption is drawing near. And he told them a parable: "Look at the fig tree and all the trees. When they produce their fruit, you know that summer is near. So too, when you see these things happening, know that the Kingdom of God is near. Amen, I say to you, this generation will not pass away until all [these] things have taken place. Heaven and earth will pass away, but my words will not pass away." (Luke 21:25-33)

24.1[4]

"There will be signs in the sun and the moon and the stars;" that is, many portents will give unusual signs, different from those familiar to humankind and from the way in which they were appointed. "And upon the earth distress of nations": what is higher will be transformed, as also will be what is lower. The happiness of humans will be changed into anguish, and increase into loss "from perplexity at the sound of the sea and of the waves." By water indeed greenness[5] and the life of creatures are sustained, because [water] is above the earth and beneath the earth. For the "spirit of the Lord was borne over the water,"[6] and brought the water to life, as it were. Therefore, when human beings perform evil deeds, the air and the water are affected and the water extends ["evil deeds"] to the sun, the moon, and the stars, since these reflect from the water. And so those heavenly bodies shake humans violently with unaccustomed terrors, in accordance with their deeds, "from perplexity at the sound of the sea and of the waves," because the waters have been poured out by the Holy Spirit [and the sea and the waves] emit this sound, wailing on account of the perverse deeds of humankind. "Humans fainting" because human happiness will be changed into aridity and into sadness "from fear and foreboding;" [humans fear] those portents, since they believe greater things are to come: "the things that are coming upon the entire world." Clearly, [they come upon] all the world, because humankind will then lack faith, hope and consolation. "For the powers of heaven will be shaken;" namely the angels ["will be shaken"] towards judgment and into wrath, since humans already will have cast the Lord behind. Therefore, the angels will become angry with them, just as they did before the incarnation of the Lord.

"And then they will see the Son of Man coming in a cloud," that is, Christ ["coming"] in judgment, splendid and terrifying "with great power" of humanity "and majesty" of divinity. "When these things begin to take place," clearly when the signs that were predicted emerge at that time, "look up" to God and "lift up your heads," without shame, fearing nothing, "because your redemption is drawing near," due to the hardships you are suffering.

"And he told them a parable" by way of comparison: 'Look at the fig tree,' because fig trees abound on earth, 'and all the trees.' 'When they produce their fruit,' namely when first they send forth flowers, 'you know' from what is usual 'that summer is near' by the change in the air. 'So too, when you see these things happening,' clearly the signs and the portents that were predicted, 'know that the Kingdom of God is near' for the reward of the righteous. 'Amen, I say to you,' to all humankind, 'This generation' of people 'will not pass away,' that is, be consumed. Evidently, human beings will not be lacking over the earth 'until all [these] things have taken place,' that is, are fulfilled. 'Heaven,' clouds and highest things that humans see, 'and earth,' on which humanity dwells 'will pass away.' [They will be] transformed from instability into a better and more stable condition. 'But my words,' the things I said to you among all these, 'will not pass away.'" They will be transformed into a state other than that in which they have been said, because all things will be fulfilled for certain.

24.2[7]

"There will be signs in the sun and the moon and the stars," that is, portents in Christ, so that some in error will challenge the humanity of the Savior; in the Church, when heretics will attempt to attack the church; among priests, teachers and the spiritual people, when they will turn away from the truth towards falsehood. "And upon the earth," namely among worldly people, [there will be] "distress of nations," clearly of different nations, so that the errors of one people and province will contaminate another people and province and will turn [them] to faithlessness. "From perplexity at the sound" that the resounding "sea" will emit shamelessly, namely the Antichrist, who will summon many storms of errors, "and" [the sound] of the waves," clearly Antichrist's own heretical ministers, who will traverse the entire world with their falsehoods and deceptions. "Humans fainting" in sorrow and doubt "from fear and foreboding," when they doubt and fear which faith will save them," when doubting they await the command and judgment of God. [These] "are coming upon the entire world," that is, pressing down upon all creation. "For the powers of heaven," namely the bishops and the leaders in the Church, who like columns should uphold strongly all the institutions and mysteries of the Church that belong to heaven, "will be shaken" in fear and doubt, so that they will withdraw, not daring openly to defend or to speak about righteousness and the things that regard God.

"And then they will see the Son of Man coming in a cloud;" clearly, in all these things ["they will see"] Christ with both sight and understanding ["coming"] in the minds of the faithful, who will endure in martyrdom much suffering and tribulation for the sake of Christ and of the truth. [He will come] "with great power" of the holy incarnation "and majesty" of divinity, so that the faithful will deny the Antichrist [and] will know [Christ] as true God and true human. "When these things," namely sufferings, "begin to take place, look up and lift up your heads, because your redemption is drawing near. And he told them a parable" by way of comparison. "Look at the fig tree," clearly the prelates who should both gently reproach and mildly rebuke those in their charge,[8] in the same manner as the fig tree produces fruit both sweet and bitter, "and the other trees," namely other persons. "When they produce their fruit" of righteousness, "you know that summer is near;" clearly ["summer" designates] heat from the ardor and gifts of the Holy Spirit. "So too, when you see these things happening," plainly the martyrdom and the tribulations of the saints and the fruit of good works, "know that the Kingdom of God is near." Clearly the reward of eternal blessedness ["is near"]. "Amen, I say to you" with certainty, "this generation" of humans "will not pass away until all [these] things have taken place." ["These things" are] the portents and the signs and the sufferings of the saints. "Heaven," clearly what is hidden, "and earth," namely what is evident in all these aforesaid cases, which humankind can know and see temporally, "will pass away," so that they may be led to the end. "But my words," clearly all the things that I say to you for [the benefit of] your salvation, "will not pass away," so that they may be led to the end, as if they have not existed but will remain forever, leading faithful humanity to eternal glory.

24.3

"There will be signs," that is, portents "in the sun," which are those human beings who by their virtues demonstrate that there is nothing before or after or beyond God. They are so godlike that they surpass human measure, and they are so enkindled by the love of God that they, like Samson,[9] are more excellent in [love of God] than other human beings. [The "portents" in] "the moon" are the virgins and the chaste, who demonstrate that the humanity of the Savior is sinless and spotless; "and the stars" are the good lay people, who demonstrate what the heavenly grace of God is. Through that grace they are engaged in almsgiving and the most holy deed[s]. "And upon the earth distress": namely in the human senses that bend to what is fallen and worldly [there are] error and madness which neither know God nor hold the world upright. "Of nations" [means] of different peoples; "from perplexity at the sound of the sea and of the waves" [refers to] contradiction of the most evil rumor of the princes of this world and the lesser ones: the weak and the poor. "Humans fainting from fear," because they have neither virtues nor the joy of life, such that they also not know death, "and foreboding" of deceitful valuations "of the things that are coming upon the entire world" unexpectedly. [Clearly, "the entire world" means] the human beings living in the world, so that some will allot life to themselves and others death, in accordance with the valuation of their own mockeries. "For the powers of heaven," namely faith, justice, and salvation, because they always point towards what is heavenly, "will be shaken" in sorrow, because then they will find no place nor repose with humankind.

"And then they will see the Son of Man coming in a cloud;" namely through prophecy and miracles ["they will see"] Christ ["coming"] into the world through report, that is, in the minds of humans and in the foreshadowing[10] of prophesy, "with great power" of miracles and mysteries "and majesty" of one marked by divinity.

"When these things begin to take place," namely in the evils that will exist among the faithless through schisms and false beliefs[11] and also in the signs of God's miracles that will happen then among the faithful, "look up" by knowing and "lift up" by fortitude "your heads," namely your faith towards God. "Because your redemption is drawing near" in salvation, such that you will see the sun of righteousness, when in your martyrdom you resist your evil and thus reach [the sun].

"And he told them a parable" by way of comparison: 'Look at the fig tree'—that is, with keen attention ["look at"] the bitterness of martyrdom and of difficulties, because these things will later console the suffering, just as the fig tree produces fruit that is displeasing at first and later sweet—"and all the trees," namely the other virtues that follow with signs and portents. "When they produce their fruit," that is, [when] they reveal martyrdom and then signs, "you know" in your hearts "that summer is near." Clearly the heat of the Holy Spirit and fullness of sanctity in soul and body [are "near"]. "So too, when you see" by sure revelation "these things happening," these bitter things oppose the virtues, and the virtues [oppose them], with the result nonetheless that the virtues attain the victory, as it is written in another Gospel: "The kingdom of heaven endures force.'[12] 'Know that the Kingdom of God is near,' because schisms and other evils will no longer endure for a long time, but at that time will be finished quickly, because the ones who persevere in the good will attain it. 'Amen, I say to you,' to you all, 'This generation,' namely humankind, 'will not pass away' from darkness to light, from the fallen to the eternal, 'until all [these] things have taken place.' [Evidently "these things" designate] those battles among virtues and vices that he foretold; and [humankind "will not pass away"] until all the vices have been so sifted out and scrutinized by the virtues that they will no longer be able to raise themselves up, and even the Devil will be so overcome by the virtues that he will no longer be able to rage. 'Heaven,' namely those longings that reach only towards heaven, so that humankind on account of God abandons earthly things, 'and earth,' clearly earthly desires when humankind trespasses in worldly matters, "will pass away," because those longings and these desires will cease to have a temporal existence on that very last day, because eternal things will be present then. 'But my words,' namely human beings who were created by the word of the Father, 'will not pass away,'" because they will exist forever, such that rewards will be owed to the good and punishments to the evil.

24.4

"There will be signs in the sun and the moon and the stars;" clearly ["there will be"] miracles in faith and human knowledge and human understanding. "And upon the earth," clearly in earthly circumstances, ["there will be] distress of nations from perplexity at the sound of the sea and of the waves," that is, overthrow of carnal desires from the taste of the flesh for the inordinate desires of worldly pleasure and licentiousness. "Humans fainting" in doubt "from fear and foreboding," that is, dread such that they know how to discern neither God nor the Devil [and] investigation "of the things that are coming upon the entire world," namely falling over the sphere of the soul and of the body, where all sensuality is contained. "For the powers of heaven"—namely rationality, faith, hope, charity and the soul's other strengths, because they are heavenly—"will be shaken" before the tempests that are in the sphere of the body, coming and going, like the wheels that Ezekiel saw.[13]

"And then they will see" with a true sign "the Son of Man," namely the virtues already born in the human being, "coming in a cloud," clearly in the pupil of the eye of knowledge, "with great power" overcoming all the darkness "and majesty," when the good conquers evil. "When these things," licit and illicit, good and evil, "begin to take place," such that they complete their course, "look up" gazing "and lift up" with joy "your heads," that is, celestial harmony, "because your redemption is drawing near," in proximity so that you may flee from evil doings.

"And he told them a parable" by way of comparison: 'Look at the fig tree and all the trees.' By [the fig tree] you know good through evil, because when you have been scandalized by evil, you turn towards the good; ["all the trees" represent] all licentiousness, which sows itself in different places. 'When they produce their fruit'—namely when first they were soiled, they reveal their consciences with groaning and weeping sounds of repentance because they were evil—'you know' by sensing 'that summer is near.' Clearly the heat of the Holy Spirit produces the flowers of the virtues. 'So too, when you see these things happening'—that is, when you who wish to understand me, ["you see"] with certainty, so that you hold these things in your understanding—'know that the Kingdom of God is near,' namely [that] the reward of heaven touches you. 'Amen, I say to you,' to believers, 'this generation,' clearly of virtues and vices, 'will not pass away until all [these] things have taken place.' Clearly it will not cease to exist, until [the virtues and vices] complete all their battles, such that the virtues vanquish and the vices succumb. 'Heaven,' namely the heavenly causes that are sluggish in human beings, 'and earth,' clearly earthly cures,[14] which are indeed foolish, 'will pass away.' Evidently, they will be lacking in the erring minds of human beings, who are so impeded that they accomplish neither effectively. 'But my words will not pass away.' Clearly the completed battles that vanquish evil will not be ridiculed by vanity, but they will have a heavenly reward, as it is written: "The righteous will shine like the sun."[15]

Notes

1. While it is obvious that the incident in the garden of Gethsemane is referred to, these words appear in none of the Gospels.

2. In medieval sermon manuscripts, biblical quotations often were not completed, on the assumption that the reader would know what followed and with the intention of saving time from hand lettering the entire passage.

3. The Fifth.

4. The marginal note, Wiesbaden Hs 2, f. 459va, reads: *Littera.*

5. *Viriditas,* a key Hildegardian term discussed by Peter Dronke in "Tradition and Innovation in Medieval Western Color-Imagery," *Eranos Jahrbuch* 41 (1972): 82, 84.

6. Genesis 1:2.

7. Here the marginal note, Wiesbaden Hs 2, f. 459vb, reads: *Allegoria.*

8. Cf. RB 2:23-40; 64:12.

9. Samson in Judges 13:24–16:31.

10. *Umbra* is an exegetical term here.

11. *Incredulitates* can and probably does refer to the erroneous beliefs of heretics.

12. Matthew 11:12.

13. Ezekiel 10:9, a reference to Ezekiel's vision.

14. *Caelestes causae and terrenae curae.* Cf. Hildegard's work *Causae et curae.*

15. Matthew 13:43.

CHAPTER 9

THE EXPLOSION OF PREACHING IN THE THIRTEENTH AND FOURTEENTH CENTURIES

AN ABSTRACT OF AN *ARS PRAEDICANDI*

Most Christian sermons before the High Middle Ages were in the form of patristic homilies. Verse-by-verse comment on the biblical passage being exposited caused these sermons to be essentially shapeless, taking up whatever subjects the passage presented as they appeared. The thematic sermons of the itinerant preachers, therefore, by imposing a rigid shape on a sermon, were an innovation in the history of preaching. The rules for composing such sermons were intricate, and were spelled out in detail in the artes praedicandi, *the numerous textbooks on the composition of such sermons.* **(See Vol. 1, pp. 220-23.)** *The sense of what such textbooks were like can be gained from this summary of one made by James J. Murphy in* Rhetoric in the Middle Ages: A History of Rhetorical Theory from Saint Augustine to the Renaissance *(Berkeley and Los Angeles: University of California Press, 1974), 344-55. This* ars, *which Murphy calls "the most typical" of the genre (p. 342), is by an author who is otherwise unknown. He* *demonstrates the intricacy of the genre acrostically by arranging for the initial letters of his fifty chapters to spell out his name.*

An Abstract of the *Forma Praedicandi* (1322) of Robert of Basevorn[1]

Notwithstanding, the Lord stood with me, and strengthened me, that by me the preaching should be fully known (2 Tim. 4:17).

Prologue. Just as some men attempt to reason without knowing logic, so some men attempt to preach without knowing the form of preaching, which is the system and method of preaching on every subject, as logic is the system of syllogizing in every field of knowledge. Since teaching and preaching are necessary to the Church, that science presents the form of preaching artistically. The four causes of this work are as follows: the final cause is designated when it is said: *The Lord stood with me and strengthened me,* for he is my end; the efficient cause is designated when we say: *by me;* although he who is also the end may be the efficient cause affecting the whole, the material cause is designated when it is said: *preaching,* because the form of preaching is here considered as well as the matter; fourthly, the formal cause is designated implicitly when it is said: *should be fully known,* for a thing is formally transmitted and taught when a continuation carries through in an orderly way what the beginning of the work promises or proffers for investigation, and what the end brings to a conclusion: thus one should have an organized method of procedure. This work includes fifty chapters.

1. Preaching is the persuasion of the multitude, within a moderate length of time, to worthy conduct. For when some determine questions,[2] such determination is not preaching, because it is not persuasion by intent, but rather an investigation of the truth. Nor is a political orator a preacher, for worthy conduct is not his primary aim, but the aid of the state. In like manner, if someone with one small reason persuades many of something which pertains to the merits of eternal life, that is not properly preaching, for I could then write on this paper forty sermons, a thing that is hardly possible. Therefore preaching requires time neither too short nor too long. It is difficult to say how long, but it is commonly held now that preaching should last no more than the space of a Solemn Mass with music, nor less than a Low Mass without music.

2. Who can preach. The Pope, bishops, cardinals, and preachers by office. Religious, constituted preachers by privileges given them, are preachers by commission.

3. Preachers by ordinary institution are held to preach by necessity of salvation, through themselves or through others if that is fitting; if they do not do this they are guilty of a mortal sin. Preachers by commission can preach if they wish, but do not commit a mortal sin if they neglect to do so. And this is why the Church has ordained that stipends be given to ordinary preachers, through tithes and the like, because of necessity they are burdened with sowing spiritual thoughts in their subjects. From pure debt, temporal rewards are due them.

4. The two kinds of preachers may overlap. Three things are necessary for one exercising the act of preaching: the first is purity of life, the second is competent knowledge (at least explicit knowledge of the articles of Faith, the Ten Commandments, and the distinction between sin and non-sin), and the third is authority given by the Church. No lay person or religious, unless permitted by the Bishop or Pope, and no woman, no matter how learned or saintly, ought to preach. Thus parish priests cannot preach without permission, nor is it enough that they be licensed by the rectors.

5. The preacher should see to it above all that he have a good purpose for his sermon, such as the praise of God, or his saints, or the edification of his neighbor, or some object deserving eternal life. He should not seek fame unless by that fame he shows himself learned or wise so that people will listen to him preach the word of God. Seekers after gain should not be preachers: (1) because they frequently have wives or concubines, and do like things, which are opposed to the purity demanded of the preacher; (2) because they are generally uneducated, which is opposed to the knowledge required of the preacher; and (3) because they are not accepted but universally rejected; and finally (4) because they do not have the proper end in view. Whoever permits them to preach sins mortally.

6. We must now come closer to our task, which is to show the required form of preaching. There are as many different kinds of preaching as there are capable preachers; since we cannot present all of them, we shall present a commonly used modern method. God preached many times through others—Moses, the Prophets, etc.—so that those men are proud and vainglorious who disdain to preach using themes of other men; if novelty is to be sought, then everyone's books should be burnt at his death lest things well said in them should be said again. This is absurd. It would be quite praiseworthy to try and imitate the methods of any of the five great preachers: Christ, Paul, Augustine, Gregory, and Bernard.

7. Among the modern methods those more commonly used are the French and the English, emanating from the two famous universities. They have their origin in the aforementioned doctors, and yet follow no particular one. They use in part the method of one or the other and in part their own and also many devices which, as it seems to me, appertain more to curiosity than to edification—for example, vowel concordances. But this practice is characteristic more of the English method. They say that a preacher should please his hearers so that they will listen. Indeed, so great is man's vanity, especially that of the English, that they only consider the elegant and do not commend anything else. When they preach to lay people, these preachers sometimes give their theme in Latin, because it is difficult for the ignorant to do this. Because I can be deceived in my judgment, and in order to satisfy the requests of others, I will explain each of the five approved and honored methods.

8. It is not easy to understand all the methods which Christ used in preaching, for he included all praiseworthy methods in his own as the origin of good. Sometimes he preached clearly; other times he preached profoundly and obscurely. His methods were many: (1) by means of promises, as in the Sermon on the Mount; (2) by threats, a method suitable for the stubborn; (3) by example, a method now used extensively in Paris and in many other places; (4) by reason; (5) obscurely, for it is frequently said of his hearers that they did not understand the Word; and (6) clearly.

9. Paul used reason together with authority. Moving themes may be found readily in Paul's epistles and sayings, because in a sense he includes the entire Gospel, the Law, and the Prophets.

10. Augustine more than the other Fathers read Paul. It is sometimes his custom to explain one whole gospel[3] or some great passage from scripture, and do so diffusely; sometimes it is his habit to take one theme and follow it up extensively. But often he rests his case on reasons. This is why he says that where authority is lacking, we must rest on reason, without which even authority is not authority. The first method should be good for those with poor memories, for the thread of some great gospel is more easily followed than that of a subtle argument. The second method is of greater use, since it more novel.

11. Gregory has a praiseworthy method, one that operates through figures of the Old Testament, tangible examples, and entreaties. He devotes his whole discourse to a gospel or something pertaining to faith.

Frequently he multiplies authorities for the same matter and frequently divides one noun into many significations. The latter two devices are allowed only within reason in common sermons to lay people, nor are they used much. He also adds to his discourse edifying stories.

12. The method of St. Bernard is without method, exceeding the style and capability of almost all men of genius. He more than all the rest stresses scripture in all his sayings, so that scarcely one statement is his own which does not depend upon an authority in the Bible or on a multitude of authorities. His procedure is always devout, always artful. He takes a certain theme[4] or something in place of it and begins it artfully, divides it into two, three, or many members, confirms it and ends it, using every rhetorical color so that the whole work shines with a double glow, earthly and heavenly; and this, it seems to me, invites to devotion those who understand more feelingly, and helps more in the novel methods which we are now discussing. No one has so effectively joined the two at the same time.

13. It is therefore reprehensible to say that preaching ought not to shine with false verbal embellishments, for in very many sermons of St. Bernard the whole is almost always rich in colors. The same is true in the sermons of other saints, as is clear to one who knows rhetoric and examines these sermons. Further, Pope Leo says, this is the virtue of eloquence, that there is nothing foreign to it that cannot be extolled. Who will hesitate to say that wisdom and eloquence together move us more than either does by itself? Thus we must insist upon eloquence and yet not depart from wisdom, which is the better of the two. If both cannot be achieved, then neither can wisdom be achieved. It remains then that it is better to have eloquence than to lack every good. For of what use would an opinion be in which there was neither eloquence nor wisdom? Therefore let those who are not productive through wisdom strive to be eloquent. It is without doubt very blameworthy that one should preferably strive after eloquence when he can have wisdom by the striving, as St. Augustine teaches in *De doctrina christiana,* where he wants a preacher to strive to teach, please, and move. About those who try only to please so that they neither teach nor move, he says that their eloquence is the more damnable the finer eloquence it is. Therefore they are better when joined, and are a sweet mixture of good things.

14. There are twenty-two ornaments employed in the most carefully contrived sermons:

(1) Invention of the Theme
(2) Winning Over of Audience
(3) Prayer
(4) Introduction
(5) Division
(6) Statement of Parts
(7) Proof of Parts
(8) Amplification
(9) Digression, or "Transition"
(10) Correspondence
(11) Agreement of Correspondence
(12) Circuitous Development
(13) Convolution
(14) Unification
(15) Conclusion
(16) Coloration
(17) Modulation of Voice
(18) Appropriate Gesture
(19) Humor
(20) Allusion
(21) Firm Impression
(22) Weighing of Subject Matter

The first fifteen of these are inserted into their proper places once, or at any rate into a few places; the remainder, and generally Allusion and Firm Impression, can be placed almost anywhere. The element that follows after these, Humor, ought to be used in a few places and very sparingly. All these, when concurring, embellish a sermon elegantly, and so can be called the ornaments of a sermon.

15. For a good Invention of the Theme, the following are required:

(1) that it concur with the feast
(2) that it beget full understanding

(3) that it be on a Bible text which is not changed or corrected

(4) that it contain not more than three statements or a statement convertible to three

(5) that sufficient concordances can be found on these three ideas, even if only verbal

(6) that the theme itself can serve in place of the antetheme or protheme

[16–23. Discussion of the six criteria for selecting themes.]

24. The second ornament is Winning Over the Audience. The preacher ought to attract the minds of the listeners in such a way as to render them willing to hear and retain. This can be done in many ways:

(1) by placing at the beginning something subtle and interesting, as some authentic marvel which can be fittingly drawn in for the purpose of the theme

(2) by using an unknown cause of some saying (e.g., by explaining why the eye does not have a definite color: it would perceive only that one color)

(3) by frightening them with some terrifying tale or example (a tale from Jacques de Vitry)

(4) by showing by example or story that the devil always tries to hinder the word of God and the hearing of it

(5) by showing that the word of God is a great sign of predestination of good for listeners

(6) by telling the audience that he preaches only to convert them (not to beg from them)

25. In the beginning it is also customary to offer a prayer, and that is well, because as Plato says in the *Timaeus,* divine help should be implored in the smallest things. Since even the smallest things cannot occur without its influence, how much more should it be implored in the greatest? St. Augustine in *De doctrina christiana* urges that the preacher should be first a man of prayer before a talker. To me it seems good to propose the theme, and to immediately make a prayer about it. I have not seen it mentioned in any genuine author that such a prayer ought to

be said before the theme. Yet I have frequently seen it done. It is proper in either place, since both theme and prayer belong at the beginning. It should also be noted here that the prayer which is at the end of the antetheme ought always to depend upon what has preceded, so that it contains something which pertains to the prayer and at the same time contains a word of the theme even vocally, and especially that word on which depends the persuasion to prayer; this is the method of the Oxonians.

26. A theme may be taken from any authentic book of the scriptures; they are in error who say that themes should be taken only from the Gospels, the Psalms, the Epistles of Saint Paul, and the Books of Solomon. It must be understood that all the books in the Bible are authentic except the third and fourth books of Esdras, a psalm of David found in some Bibles, the Book of the Pastor,[5] and the letter to the Laodiceans.

27. Some preachers take their themes only from the gospel or epistle of the feast on which they preach; this is commendable, but it can be done as above.[6]

28. [Examples of themes which can be adduced for the more famous saints.]

29. It is also always useful to have prepared a few sermons which can provide for every saint and for the dedication of a church because it frequently happens that the church or place where the preacher happens to be preaching solemnizes a saint or the dedication, of which he had not even a thought. [Examples of such themes.]

30. It is now appropriate to specify what themes can be taken for incidental material, as on visitations, at elections, in synods, in processions, in disaster, on solemnities, . . . to religious, . . . at a council, . . . to the sick, . . . to merchants, . . .

31. And now according to the order set out in chapter 15, we shall consider the ornaments of the theme, of which the first is Introduction and which in the whole is the fourth ornament. It must be known that after the prayer the same theme must be resumed . . . and the book and chapter must be quoted. This ought to be done on principle in the antetheme, and, following the modern method, nothing must be quoted regarding the chapters. The theme must be quoted again in full, especially on account of some who by accident, as frequently happens, were

not present for the antetheme. In the third place [i.e., third place in the sermon] comes the Introduction, which can be formed in three ways:

(1) by authority
(2) by argument
(3) by both together

Authority is a method used more commonly in the antetheme than afterwards; no other introduction must be made in the antetheme for fear of prolixity; indeed the antetheme can exist without it, so that Introduction is not postulated as an ornament of the antetheme. An authority forming an Introduction can come from:

(1) something original
(2) a philosopher
(3) a poet
(4) someone with authority
(5) not from the Bible

The second method is through argument, and it is appropriate to form the Introduction in as many ways as there are kinds of argument:

(1) by induction
(2) by example
(3) by syllogism
(4) by enthemyme [*sic*]

Induction accounts for particular details to support the theme. Example may be used in three different ways:

(1) examples in nature
(2) examples in arts
(3) examples in history

In using a syllogism, the major premise ought to be proved immediately if it is not self-evident. Then the minor premise must be given with its proof; if the proofs be too extended, after the proofs of the major and the minor the premises must be stated again, and the theme immediately concluded by saying that it has already been proved. Enthemymes [*sic*] are of two kinds:

(1) "compelling" (described in Aristotle's *Prior Analytics*)

(2) "probable" (described in Boethius's *Topics*)

The Oxonians use all seven of these methods. The Parisians use an eighth method, a better one, in that no matter what kind of argument they use for the Introduction, all parts are confirmed with the authority of Holy Writ. Anyone may use all of these methods of forming an Introduction in themes that are comprised of two statements or more. But when a theme is comprised of only one explicit statement, it is not convenient to use all these methods indiscriminately.

32. I think a more elegant mode of forming an Introduction of such a theme occurs if a theme is first introduced by an authority, so that from the authority three members which correspond to the feast and the theme can be immediately drawn. [Then follows a lengthy example based on the theme "understand." In the city of God, the manner in which man, the angels, and God understand things is revealed as a correspondence to the excellences of Peter's understanding.]

33. Division is the fifth ornament. Though not expressed, the force of a word should be expressed first; that is, the divisions of a word should put the same idea into different words without repeating the same word which was originally divided. If it should happen that it is not possible to find an authority to fit the force of the word, it is acceptable to add adjectives or other determinants so that the authority will fit. The division of the second word should not be placed before the division of the first. The division ought to occur in one of three ways:

(1) according to the thing done

(2) according to the order of construction

(3) according to the order of delivery

It is very artistic if by a single division, Division is according to the order of construction and at the same time according to the order of material.

34. The sixth ornament, Statement of Parts, ought to show the distinction of parts in one of three ways:

(1) by showing parts of a virtual whole

(2) by showing parts of a universal whole

(3) by some other way

The statement can be made by means of different parts of speech, except that pronouns, conjunctions, and interjections cannot ordinarily administer to this purpose. Statement of Parts can be made especially with a substantive:

(1) through its accidents

(2) comparison

(3) case

(4) by means of adjectives without comparison

35. The seventh ornament, Proof of Parts, follows immediately after the preceding. This is done in various ways. The Parisians supply an authority for each part which is divisible into three; some, however, divide the first authority of verification into three, the second into two, and merely explain the third. Other methods aim at producing verbal correspondences between the divisions of the authorities and the divisions of the theme or its parts. It is obvious that consummate artistry resides in these methods:

(1) It verifies the division of the first member by a verbal and real authority.

(2) The further division is taken from something real.

(3) The proposition is verified by a corresponding verbal authority either by means of allusion or direct expression.

36. [A long example of the Parisian method.] Whoever understands this method, understands the more famous methods used at Paris in respect to antethemes. He understands that there is a short Introduction with an example for the same; how that example is verified by Scripture; how both the verification and the example are concluded by one authority which agrees with both; how every theme agrees with the three

aforementioned things; how the theme is divided; how all parts are stated with sensible examples and verified with agreeing authorities; how the last authority agrees with the first, that is, the authority of the Introduction; how one proceeds from the authority to the prayer.

37. Further exemplification of Parisian method.

38. Some preachers, especially in England, do not follow this method of developing the parts, but multiply the statement in such a way that they add to the division of the theme a double statement of the parts without authorities, and afterwards a third statement of the parts and an expression of the words of the theme, and then immediately add to this third statement of parts a brief verification of the parts. Some add to this mode, after verification by biblical authority, verification by an original authority, and this is elegant if it agrees with and explains the authority to which it is added. In using this method it is important to repeat the explicit statement before giving its verification, since some of the hearers may have forgotten the statement which was made earlier.

39. The eighth ornament, Amplification, has eight main species or methods:

(1) by discussing a noun by giving its definition or its opposite

(2) by division

(3) by reasoning or argumentation

a. by resolution of contraries

b. by enthymeme, asking the hearer to draw a conclusion

c. by examples

(4) by concordances

a. when authorities with different meanings come together in one statement

b. when authorities come together in meaning but not in expression

c. when one authority speaks fully and another speaks more fully

(5) through those things which agree in essence but differ in accidents

(6) by devising metaphors through the properties of things

(7) by expounding the theme in various ways

a. historically, when the literal fact is understood

b. allegorically, when one part is understood by another

c. morally, when one deed that must be done is understood through another

d. anagogically, when by some deed on earth is understood another that must be done in heaven or in the church triumphant

(8) by causes and effects

40. Because the method of the Oxonians is more commonly used, we must illustrate it more specifically. This method consists of adding a division, called Subdivision, immediately after the verification of parts of the theme once the theme has been divided and the parts stated. [Then follows a long example on the term "just."] This method is very artistic. Preachers using this method should make sure that when they divide themes they make a general description of the first division; thus in the subdivision descend as it were from genus to species or from some whole to its parts.

41. The ninth ornament is Digression, which is equivalent to Transition. It occurs when one proceeds artistically from one part to another. One who looks at the *Rhetoric* of Cicero (*De inv.* 1.51.97) can see that this is improperly called digression. If digression is considered as something incidental, it does not belong in a sermon. But the digression which we are discussing here consists of a certain skillful connecting of two principal statements, by verbal and real concordance.

42. The tenth ornament is Correspondence, or the express agreement of parts among themselves, as, for instance, when the first principal part is divided into a *b c,* the second into *d e f,* and the third into g *h i.* Then, according to this ornament, there must be agreement among *a d g, b e h,* and *c j i.*

43. The eleventh ornament, Agreement of Correspondence, is the completion of the former ornament. It is a clause or statement expressing the substance of the connection made between the parts of the principal statements.

44. The twelfth ornament is called Circuitous Development. It is nothing else beyond Correspondence than an artificial linking of the first part of the last principal statement with the second part of the first principal

statement, namely g to *b*, and again the linking of the second part of the last principal statement, namely *h*, to the third part of the first principal set (a *b c*), namely *c*. This ornament is in the image of a circle where the end and the beginning are the same. Some doubt the usefulness of this ornament. I know that it is more decorative than useful, because it dulls the mind of the listener by making an unsolvable labyrinth.

45. The thirteenth ornament is called Convolution, in which any part of a statement corresponds to every part of every other statement. It is called Convolution because there is not the determined application of one part to one part, but of all parts to all parts. One cannot easily use this ornament. [No example is cited.]

46. The fourteenth ornament is Unification, which is a period or *clausula* which contains in a unit what has been said separately in the development. It is useful following Convolution or Circuitous Development. If possible, some authority should be employed which verbally contains all the statements treated in the sermon.

47. Finally, there must be a Conclusion. This is a prayer ending the sermon and directing the mind to God as towards an end. Just as nature, if bent from its natural path by violence, always returns to its original state, so the sermon must end as it began. The more the end is like the beginning, so much the more elegantly does it end.

48. There are some other modes of preaching besides those I have mentioned, and it would be well to mention them briefly. [A description then follows of various methods used in dividing themes.]

49. There remain still two more methods. The first, suitable in any vulgar idiom to the ordinary people, is partly Parisian and partly Gregorian; it consists in choosing three materials suited to the listeners, and then developing the theme in each three parts as follows:

(1) by some proof from nature or arts

(2) by some proof from Scripture

(3) by some authoritative narrative

It seems superfluous to me and incorrect to handle more than three figures in one sermon, and likewise to adduce more than three narratives. It should be noted that stories may be taken not only from the Bible but from other authors like Augustine, Gregory, Helinandus, Valerius, Seneca, or Macrobius.

50. The second method should be used only before the most intelligent people.

We have dispatched all fifteen ornaments which directly apply to the form or execution of the sermon. There remain seven more which are extrinsic, but which serve for beauty:

(1) Coloration

a. in the number of terminations of the statements

b. in cadence, which occurs in pauses or at the end of clauses

c. in rhetorical colors, which can occur anywhere; it is sufficient to use those which appear in the last book of Cicero's *Rhetoric Secunda*

(2) Voice Modulation, as Augustine teaches in *De doctrina christiana.*

(3) Appropriate Gesture, as Hugh [of St. Victor] teaches in his *De institutione novitiorum.*

(4) Opportune Humor, according to Cicero, occurs when we add some thing jocular which will give pleasure when the audience is bored. This must be used especially when they begin to sleep.

(5) Allusion, when Scripture is touched upon but not adduced, but not in the same way it is written.

(6) Firm Impression, when allusion occurs in many places, or continually.

(7) Reflecting on the Subject Matter, which is the consideration of who, to whom, what, and how much is to be spoken.

To these fifty chapters I will add one of silence.

AN EXAMPLE FROM A HANDBOOK FOR PREACHERS

The Fasciculus morum *is a collection of what look to modern eyes like sermons on vices and virtues. These, however, are not transcriptions of something that was preached, but are, rather, aids for preachers to use in preparing their own sermons. That this is the case is shown both in the way that the treatments of vices and virtues in it are not based on divisions of a theme and in the cross-references that are made to other parts of the book ("as was explained above in the sixth chapter of part 2").*

The passage below is from the section on Envy and deals with Christ's passion as the remedy for it. The resources it offers a preacher looking for material include, first of all, biblical verses to be used as "authorities" proving a thesis advanced. The interpretation of these verses is allegorical or, more accurately, moral. There are also authoritative statements given from church fathers such as Augustine and from pagan writers. Exempla are taken from Ovid, a bestiary, and Middle English verse. This must have been a very useful homiletical aid. The translation is from Fasciculus Morum: A Fourteenth-Century Preacher's Handbook, *ed. and trans. Siegfried Wenzel (University Park: Pennsylvania State University Press, 1989), 201-13 [on facing pages with the Latin]. (For a discussion of preaching aids,* ***see Vol. 1, pp. 224-31.****)*

Part III: Envy

3.10: On Christ's Passion

In the fourth and last place it remains to see how this charity, when it has been driven away and is almost completely lost, may be found again and recovered. Verily thus: if man would diligently consider and intently weigh within him what love Christ has shown us, not only in his blessed incarnation but also in his cruel Passion, from which nothing could hold him back that he might hear or see or understand or fear so that he would not want to suffer death for us in order to free us from eternal death and the power of the devil.

For Christ wanted to show his exceedingly great love, than which there is none greater, when he offered his soul to God the Father for our redemption and gave his body most humbly and without guilt over to death, after the word of John 15: "Greater love than this no man has, that a man lay down his life for his friends."

Therefore, if we were to reflect on this love intently with our mind and heart, if indeed we are true children of God, we shall naturally find that love again that has been driven away. There is a common saying: "I love those that love me." But Christ has loved us first, as is said in Revelation 1, "and has washed us from our sins in his blood." This Passion, then, which he suffered for us will lead us back to perfect love. I will treat of it as follows: first, why he shed his blood; second, on what day, and where he suffered; third, at what hour, what age, and what time; fourth, by whom he was accused and how much he was taunted; and fifth, of the mystery and power of his cross.

Concerning the first point we should know that he shed his blood in the first place that it might be a help to sinners and a remedy against our spiritual enemies and fleshly sins. Notice that shedding his blood is a very strong remedy because it leads the sinner to the sorrow of contrition, to the shame of confession, and to the labor of satisfaction. In token of which we read that at Christ's Passion the rocks, that is, hardened hearts, were cleft in contrition; the graves were opened, in confession; and finally many bodies of saints arose, in satisfaction. Of these things we shall speak later, in part 5.

Notice also that in his Passion he undertook a great war for mankind against its enemies which is prefigured in the war that David took upon himself against the Philistine giant Goliath, as is recorded in Kings 17. David, whose name means "strong of hand," stands for Christ, the very strong champion, who took upon himself the cross as a staff so that he might overcome that giant Goliath, that is, the devil. The staff of the cross looks like the staff of a warrior that is called *bipennis*, a double-edged battle-ax, because it has two points at its end; Habakkuk 3 says of it: "And horns in his hands." But notice: among men, when one nobleman plans to fight another, he does not wait for his enemy's attacks but, in order to gain victory more quickly, marches to his opponent's place; thus our champion, Christ, knowing that our enemies the devils have their dwelling place in this dark air, and wanting to fight them and the powers of the air so to speak in their own camp, wished to be raised into the air on the cross on which he would defeat them.

That victory in battle, won over the devil for our redemption by Christ, is prefigured in the dream of Mordecai, Esther 10, where it is said that "a small wellspring grew into a large river," and that Mordecai saw two large dragons fight together at the wellspring, and one dragon overcame the other. When he later explained his dream, he said that these dragons were Haman and Mordecai. O blessed dream about our redemption and help! For spiritually speaking, that small wellspring was the blood of Christ, still shut in between flesh and skin; but it certainly grew into a large river when the spear opened his side and immediately there came out blood and water, and not only this, but his blood flowed and welled out through his hands and feet and whole body.

At that fountain two dragons were fighting, that is, the twofold love of Christ, which on one hand longed for his own life, but on the other for our salvation; the former love belonged to nature, the latter to grace. His natural love, that is, the love Christ had for his own life, was great, and justly so, for any wise person loves an object as much as it is worth, and Christ's life was of the greatest value, therefore he had to love it of necessity. But certainly the love of grace which he had for our souls was very strong and firm. And thus these two loves fought so violently during Christ's Passion that, when they clashed, they drove forth a sweat of blood. Yet finally the love of grace overcame the love of nature, so that Christ chose rather to die for mankind than to spare his own body. Whence Bernard says: "He would never have given himself for me, had he not, in some way, loved me more than himself."

But notice that in this battle within Christ there was no conflict that would bring guilt with it, for he submitted both loves or wills to the will of his Father, saying the words in Matthew: "Not my will but yours be done." And so it was done. For Haman, who was second to the king—that is, Christ, the Son of God, who is the second person in the Blessed Trinity—was hanged on the gallows. Mordecai, by whom I understand human nature or man who had been sentenced to eternal death, was received into the grace of the king, that is, of the Almighty Father, and made second to the king, when our nature, united with the Son of God, sits at God's right hand, raised higher than the angels.

Therefore, when we see such burning love for us, it is right and only natural for us to love him back from our whole heart; as Blessed Augustine says: "Behold his wounds as he hangs on the cross, his blood as he is dying, his scars as he rises from death, the price he is paying, and his bargain as he redeems us. Weigh how much these are worth and place them in the scales of love, so that he may be wholly enclosed in our heart who for us was wholly put on the cross." To love this love always, one may cry out with the Apostle: "If any man does not love our Lord Jesus Christ, let him be anathema," etc.

Christ suffered and shed his blood for us secondly that he may draw us to his love and charity. As an example: a hunting dog is sometimes given the blood of some prey to lick so that he may be more easily drawn to the chase. In the same manner we are given the blood of Christ; as the Psalmist has it: "That your foot may be dipped," that is, your affect, "in the blood" of Christ, that you may follow him more eagerly in love.

Far be it, then, that we be ungrateful to him, as someone once was ungrateful to his friend, of whom the following story is told. Virgil reports in the *Aeneid,* and likewise the commentator on Alexander the Great, books 5 and 6, how Aeneas burned so much with love for a girl that he would humble himself by becoming poor for her sake and exalt her with rich gifts. And this he did. Some day it happened that, as he returned greatly wounded from fighting a battle for her, he came back hardly alive. He went to her confidently as to a safe refuge, because he had loved her more than anyone else and had exalted her by becoming poor. But in her ingratitude she shut her doors and steadfastly denied him entrance.

Upon this he wrote to her his mishap in the words of Ovid's *Metamorphoses* and told her:

> Behold my wounds, which traces are of ancient fight.
> Whate'er thou hast, I gained it with my blood.
>
> Behold my wounds, my painful plight.
> All the wealth you own I won in fight.
> I am sorely wounded, behold my skin.
> Dear life, for my love let me now come in.[7]

Spiritually speaking, this knight Aeneas is Christ, who loved this girl, man's soul, so much that in order to make her rich and noble he took on him our nature and became poor and entered a fierce war for her sake against the enemy of mankind. In it he was so terribly wounded that, as Isaiah says, "From the sole of his foot to the top of his head there is no soundness in him." As he issued from this war hardly alive, he confidently approached the door of the Soul for whom he had suffered so much, so that she, moved above all else by love and compassion might comfort and refresh him in his need.

Then he knocks that he may be let in, as is said in Revelation 3: "See, I stand at the gate and knock." What else? Indeed there he calls out loudly the words of Canticles: "Open, my sister, my friend, my turtledove." But alas, I fear that, ungrateful and forgetful as she is of all his favors, she firmly shuts the doors of the soul, which are love, compassion and similar good sentiments; this the soul does when she ungratefully locks him out by committing sin. Yet nonetheless, as a most gracious and faithful knight he does not cease to knock and to cry: "Behold my wounds" and so forth.

O, human soul, blush then, and according to the Psalmist, "Open the gates of justice," that is to say, the soul's affections for God and his favors, which are so firmly shut through sin, and do so with the keys of contrition, confession love, and charity. When you do this, the King of Glory will surely enter and speak the words of the Psalm: "This is my rest for ever and ever; here will I dwell, for I have chosen it."

In the third place, Christ suffered and shed his blood so that he might call back the fugitives and exiles to the land of peace. This was fittingly prefigured in Numbers 35, where it is said: "The fugitive ought to have stayed in the city until the death of the high priest," and afterwards: "The banished and fugitives before the death of the high priest may by no means return into their own cities," but as it is written in Joshua 10:

"Then shall the man-slayer return and go into his own city and house from where he had fled."

Spiritually speaking, the "manslayer" was our first parent, who wounded himself and us to the death; he fled from "his own city and house" when he left paradise and came to this valley of misery. But after Christ our high priest's death he could bravely return, leaving all fear behind.

The reason for this is that fear of the sword that was drawn out of its sheath behind him compelled him to flee; Genesis 3: "He cast out Adam and placed before the paradise of pleasure Cherubim and a flaming sword." But this fear has been taken away through Christ's death, because blood has the power to quench fire. And as warm blood is said to have the natural power to dull the sharpness of a sword, thus Christ's blood, when it was newly shed in his death, rendered the flaming sword useless; as the Psalmist says: "From the malicious sword deliver me." Therefore we should swiftly return to our home leaving all fear behind us; Jeremiah: "Return, O virgin of Israel, return to your cities."

In the fourth place, Christ shed his blood so that he might wash us from the sickness of guilt. For he taught as a true physician and left the prescription that, however much we are in the grips of a spiritual illness, we are to be bled and thus healed. For Christ was bled as an example for us, yet not in the same way that other men practice, that is, in the arm alone, but rather in his entire body, for as is said in Isaiah: "From the sole of his foot to the top," etc. And his blessed body was certainly well heated when he was fiercely scourged at the column; likewise, it was tightly bound, because it was tightly nailed to the cross by its hands and feet; and likewise, a deep incision was made, because it was pierced in its side with a spear to his very heart.

But the consolation which is wont to be shown to people who are bled, he went totally without. Noblemen and religious are bled in pleasant and secret surroundings and receive better food and drink. But Christ was openly put to show before all men on Mount Calvary and was given gall and vinegar to drink, so that we should let our blood spiritually in the same way for his love and our own salvation, that is, we should abstain from sinful deeds to which we are moved by the fleshly nature of our blood; for as Bernard says: "A brave soldier does not feel his wounds when he sees those of his generous leader."

Thus Christ became like the pelican, who kills his own offspring when he gets angry, but afterwards, moved by compassion, he pierces his own body to his heart with his beak, and his offspring, sprinkled with his blood, come to life again. In the same way, by shedding the blood of his blessed heart Christ has brought sinners back to the life of grace after they had spiritually died by offending God, because he was moved in his compassion since he "does not want the death of the sinner."

Therefore Augustine says to Severinus: "Love is as strong as death, for it made death itself die in the death of the Redeemer." And Augustine says farther: "Let man know what he is worth and how much he owes; and when he thinks of his value, let him altogether stop being a slave. For he is guilty, not of a little money, but of the sweet blood of Christ when he stains his soul and violates it after it has thus been washed in the blood of Christ."

But I fear that with many people it goes as it does with a deranged child: the more his loving mother worries about his illness, the more he laughs and roars without any feeling for his mother. In the same way, when Christ sheds his tears and is bled for the sake of sinners, the latter not merely forget his Passion like ungrateful people, but like deranged persons laugh at him and blaspheme by tearing him to pieces with their horrible oaths and by taunting him for the Passion he suffered for us. Whence he says through the Psalmist: "They repaid me evil for good and hatred for my love." Notice what has been said above in chapter 3 against such people.

We must not act thus, beloved, but instead have compassion with his suffering, together with all creation. For at his death the sun had compassion and withdrew its rays, the earth quaked, rocks were split, tombs opened up, and the bodies of the saints rose, as is reported in Matthew.

In his *Letters* Ovid tells us that a young man called Acontius was in love with a maiden; though he had asked her often for her love, he found her to be unusually difficult. In his frustration he came up with the following trick. He took a very beautiful apple and wrote in it a marriage vow, thinking and hoping that if she read out the vow aloud, she would thereby be held to marry him, that is, by virtue of her reading it. The writing therefore was as follows:

> I swear to you, by the holy rites of Diana, That I will be your wedded spouse and your wife.

This apple he threw in a place where she always stayed, namely the temple of Diana, her god [*sic*], so that she could in no way overlook it but should find the writing and read it. And so it happened. But when she had read out the writing, she understood at once that she must of necessity marry him. Nonetheless, she did not agree at all. But in the end, after being attacked by fever and having received letters from heaven, she was compelled to consent and married the young man.

Morally interpreted, that maiden is the soul of man; her lover, our heavenly Father, of whom is said in Wisdom 11: "You spare all, O Lord, because all things are yours, who love souls."

This lover thought of many ways how he might draw the love of this maiden, that is, the soul, to himself—now by gifts, now by promises, both in the Old Law and in the state of natural law. In the end he used this trick: since he found that she rejected him so much, he took a very beautiful apple, namely Christ his Son made flesh, in whose body he wrote a promise when he allowed his blessed body to be carved and inscribed with many wounds as with so many large and small clear letters. This inscription indeed contains a promise of marriage between God and the soul, a promise so great and powerful that it is impossible to read what is thus written in this apple without consenting at once to his love and realizing fully that one must love him who has shown so many signs of love. Proverbs 12: "There is one who promises, and the conscience is pricked as if with a sword." What more, I ask, could he have done to attract your love? Did he not offer his body and soul for you?

According to some writers, the soul of man resides in his blood; and thus, according to Jerome, Christ shed all his blood in order to indicate that he was likewise giving his soul for us. According to others, the soul resides in the brain; and therefore Christ suffered much injury to his head. But according to yet others it resides in the heart; and thus Christ wanted to be pierced with a spear through the middle of his heart. Whence Jerome says: "I gave my beloved soul," to show his true love, so that we might love him in like manner for he loved us first and gave his soul for us.

But since many of us, although we should marry Christ after the voice of our conscience resist doing so in fact, he frequently compels us to suffer the fevers of worldly tribulation, through which, as it were, we must of necessity love him. We find a type of this in Luke 4, when Christ came to the house of Simon, where Simon's mother-in-law was held by a strong fever; Christ commanded it and the fever left her, and she got up at once and served them. Christ sends many people tribulations through which they are taught the better to call on Christ, and when the tribulations are over, to serve him more fervently in love.

Thus we see how this apple, that is, Christ, the Son of God made flesh, was inscribed with manifold wounds as if with a marriage vow, so that we may marry and firmly love him. That apple has been put in so many places that we absolutely cannot overlook it, for it is present in every church of the faithful, so that it can be read by everyone. For in Daniel 5 it is said: "Whoever shall read this writing and shall make its meaning known to me, shall be clothed with purple."

And in the fifth place, Christ suffered and shed his blood so that he might exclude the devil from purchasing us. By his trick the devil had bought mankind from our first parents for less than its regular price—as it were, for an apple of very little value. But notice: we see everyday that he who offers more obtains the goods more easily. But Christ offered and gave more than the devil: not just an apple but his body and soul all together, that he might thus free us from the devil's hard and cruel power through his bitter and terrible death. As a result, we are his children and not the devil's. On that exchange he left a most reliable charter for us.

Notice that a charter that is written in blood carries with it extreme reliability and produces much admiration. Just such a charter did Christ write for us on the cross when he who was "beautiful above the sons of men" stretched out his blessed body, as a parchment-maker can be seen to spread a hide in the sun. In this way Christ, when his hands and feet were nailed to the cross, offered his body like a charter to be written on. The nails in his hands were used as a quill, and his precious blood as ink. And thus, with this charter he restored to us our heritage that we had lost, as was explained above, in the sixth chapter of part 2.

And not only this, but whereas once we were banished from our inheritance, we can now say with the Psalmist: "Let us possess the sanctuary of God for an inheritance." And there he certainly destroyed the contract which our first parents made with the devil, of which Augustine says: "Eve borrowed sin from the devil, wrote out a contract, and found a person to give security, from which the interest of her sin grew for her posterity." For Eve borrowed sin from the devil when she most wickedly consented to the devil's suggestion against God's commandment; she wrote out a contract when she stretched out her hand for the apple; she found a person to give security when she caused Adam to consent to sin; and in this fashion the interest grew for her offspring. But truly Christ canceled this servitude totally when he left his whole body for us on the cross as a charter. For Christ says:

I am on the cross for you. Why sin? Cease for my sake! Cease, and I give you grace; confess, and I spare your pain.

In English:

I honge on cros for loue of the . . .

And thus our first point is dealt with, why Christ shed his blood for us.

AN EXAMPLE OF A THEMATIC SERMON

The artes praedicandi *and model sermons were aids to assist preachers in preparing thematic sermons. These sermons were based on a single verse from the Bible (the theme), which was divided into several points. These points were then confirmed by the citation of "authorities" primarily from the Bible, but from the Fathers and pagan authors as well. The sermon below was the work of Jean de Saint-Gilles, an Englishman who in the thirteenth century taught at Oxford, Paris, and Montpellier before becoming a Dominican. The sermon was for a Sunday in the church calendar, and its theme is taken from the beginning of the gospel pericope for that feast. An effort has been made to indicate the structure of the sermon typographically. The translation is taken from* No Uncertain Sound: Sermons That Shaped the Pulpit Tradition, *ed. with intro. Ray C. Petry (Philadelphia: Westminster, 1948), 199-204. (For a discussion of thematic preaching,* ***see Vol. 1, pp. 217-20.****)*

Jean de Saint-Gilles: "Be Ye Merciful"
(A Sermon for the Fifth Sunday after Pentecost)

THEME: Be ye merciful as your Father is merciful (Luke 6:36).
PROTHEME: The merciful man deals well with his soul (Prov. 11:17).

(**Theme and Explanation**) It is written in the sixth chapter of Luke: *Be ye merciful as your Father is merciful* (vs. 36). Then the Lord touches upon **four opposites of mercy**, that we may avoid them.

The **first** is: **Judge not** (vs. 37), and is directed against slanderers who destroy men with the sword of evil speaking. The **second** is: **Condemn not** (ibid.). This is directed especially against those of the clergy who condemn the innocent, against whom it is written in Exodus: *An innocent and just man thou shalt not kill* (23:7). By their bad example in accumulating prebends, seeking inheritances, planting vineyards, and acquiring riches and honors, they corrupt and condemn the little ones, that is, the laity. This directly contradicts compassion, whose property it is to scatter freely and not to amass. Furthermore there are those so severe that when they discover a man in mortal sin, they immediately condemn him. Thus they exclude everyone from the way of penitence. In opposition to this Augustine said: "No one ought to be despaired of while yet he lives." Such men, with David, by the sword of the sons of Ammon, which signifies the riotous mob, slew Uriah, who represents the light of the Lord. The **third** is: **Forgive** ... (Luke 6:37), that is, forgive the faults, penalties, conflicts, hate, pride, and everything of whatever sort they do not wish to forgive. They are like the devil, of whom it is said: He is cruel and he will not have mercy, even though the Lord says: *I do not say to you seven, but seventy times seven* (Matt. 18:22). They do not wish to release those they have imprisoned, even though it says in the Paralipomenon:[8] *Let the oppressed go free* (Isa. 58:6). For even if he is a poor man, he keeps his own prisoners. Thus in Job: *And if they are in chains, and bound in the cords of poverty, Thou showest them their works, that they have been guilty of violence* (36:8-9). The **fourth** injunction is: **Give** ... (Luke 6:39), that is, give both spiritual and temporal things. But we, gladly giving spiritual things, reserve for ourselves the temporal things, and give nothing to others. And likewise nothing shall be given to us, just as not even a drop of water was given to the rich man in the fifteenth chapter of Luke. Therefore, it happens that he who is unmerciful and cruel wrongs himself before he wrongs others. But those who claim that they are merciful, our preachers and teachers who say that they preach and teach because of their zeal for souls and so are merciful in their own eyes, these, nevertheless, are unwilling to show mercy to their own souls, although we read in Proverbs: *The merciful man deals well with his own soul* (11:17).

(**Protheme**) It is written in the Second Epistle to Timothy: *It is fitting that the farmer who labors should be the first to partake of the fruits ...* (2:6); likewise in Ecclesiasticus: *Have pity on thy own soul, pleasing God* (30:24).

(**Exposition**) The same apostles make the statement: "I am rich and made wealthy and have need of nothing" (Rev. 3:17), as if to say: I am without sin. But contrarily John says: *If we say that we have no sin, we deceive ourselves, and the truth is not in us* (1 John 1:8). And this is because, as it says in Ecclesiasticus: *He shall discern every plague, but not the plague of the soul* (25:18). In the book of Wisdom it is written: *He pleased God and was beloved* (4:10). Living among sinners he was translated, that is to say, from the world to the cloister, because it is perilous to dwell among sinners. "Who can steal away fire in his breast, without setting his clothing afire?" Obviously, no one. Likewise in Ecclesiasticus: *He that toucheth pitch is defiled with it* (13:1), and *Confession of faith perishes from* [is impossible to] *the dead as if they were nothing* (17:26). By living [in the world] you confess yourself to possess less discernment than by entering the cloister. But someone will say: "It is easier to remain in the world than to enter the cloister." Yet it is written of Lot in Genesis: *For Lot abode in the mountain* (19:30), by which is signified the cloister, and we do not read that he remained in Sodom, which signifies the world. Further, we can answer that if he had remained there, he would have been consumed. The angel particularly commanded Lot to depart from Sodom; but you, contrary to the angel's instruction, wish to remain in the world. Beware, therefore, lest you perish there with the Sodomites, that is, sinners. But have compassion upon yourselves and depart from the world. For this reason we read: *Be ye merciful,* both to yourselves and others, *as your Father is merciful* (Luke 6:36). To do this signifies, not identification with him, but imitation of him.

(**Part I**) The Lord has compassion upon us in **five benefits** which he has conferred upon us.

(**Consideration 1**) The first is the truest and highest benefit, namely, that he bestowed upon us his divinity, and that is **his Son, the price of our redemption.** And, in consequence, he conferred upon us the heavenly kingdom. Thus it was written to the Romans: *He who did not spare his own Son, but gave him for us all, has he not also with him given us all things?* (8:32). That is to say: Certainly he has.

(**Consideration 2**) The second benefit is that he has given us **the world.** As in First Corinthians: *All things are yours* . . . (3:21). But some one might say that this world is the devil's, according to that statement: *The prince of this world has come and in me he has nothing* (John 14:30). And again: *Now the prince of this world shall be cast out* (12:31). To this we answer that there are three things in the world—nature, corruption, and utility. Nature is of God, corruption of the devil, and utility belongs to man. As a certain saint says: "That we live in the world, this is of God; but that we sin, that is of the devil." Also Augustine says: "The sun serves Him, and the moon, and the sea, and the earth, and wherefore do I not serve Him?" We are all debtors of God, awaiting the payment of the price of recompense. For the Apostle says: *The creature itself shall be freed from the bondage of corruption, into the glorious liberty of the sons of God* (Rom. 8:21). The sun and the moon await the price of their servitude: *The light of the moon shall be as the light of the sun* (Isa. 30:26). Likewise the sea does service, about which it was said: *Here shall your swelling waves be stayed* (Job 38:11). And also the earth serves: *Let the earth bring forth green grass* (Gen. 1:11). When we, therefore, are unwilling to serve, we wrong the elements.

(**Consideration 3**) The third benefit is that he has given **angels** to watch over us, as in the Epistle to the Hebrews: *Firstly they are all ministering spirits* . . . (1:14).

(**Consideration 4**) The fourth is that he has made us in **his image,** as it is stated in Genesis, and this applies especially to those of the clergy who have a greater knowledge of him, and in proportion a higher obligation to serve him, because a servant who knows the will of his lord and does not do it will be severely chastised.

(**Consideration** 5) The fifth is that he has given us an **eternal heritage,** bestowing upon us hope of it in the present and its reality in the future. Therefore no one need despair as did Cain: *My sin is greater* ... (Gen. 4:13).

(**Confirmation 1**) To the first benefit the martyrs testify, having given themselves to suffer for Christ. (**Confirmation 2**) To the second, the people of the early Church, who, having sold everything, laid all that they had at the feet of the apostles. (**Confirmation 3**) To the third, Abraham and Lot testify, who, having offered hospitality, ministered to angels and angelic men (Gen. 18:16); as in 1 Peter: *If anyone ministers, it is as if by the strength which God imparts* (4:11). (**Confirmation 4**) To the fourth, the hermits testify who continually contemplate the Lord; as the Apostle said: *I have determined to know nothing but Jesus Christ and him crucified* (1 Cor. 2:2). (**Confirmation 5**) To the fifth, the men of sanctity are witnesses, who diligently cultivate their eternal heritage; as in Proverbs: *Diligently till thy ground* ... (24:27).

(**Part II**) Similarly we, having received these benefits, now ought to make **return. First,** in that we should give to God, not only our alms and goods, but **ourselves;** as in Genesis: *The Lord had respect to Abel,* that is, first, *and to his gifts,* afterward (4:4); likewise the Apostle: *I do not seek the things that are yours, but you* (2 Cor. 12:14). Thus of those who give themselves in part to the Lord, Hosea says: *Their heart is divided; now they shall perish* (10:2). For even if you give yourself whole to God, you are not worthy of him; as in Tobias: *If I give myself to be a servant, I am not worthy of thy providence* (9:2).

(**Consideration 2**) For the second benefit, we ought to make return by expending **our worldly wealth for the poor;** as in Luke: *Give and it shall be given to you* (6:38). For this reason James says: *Your gold and silver have rusted, and their rust shall bear witness against you, and it shall eat away your flesh* (5:3). Because of this, it is a good thing to give your possessions for the poor. Thus the Apostle: *Let a man so account of us, as of the ministers of Christ* ... (1 Cor. 4:1). Otherwise God would require of us the talent entrusted to us and cast us into outer darkness.

(**Consideration 3**) For the third we ought to make return by doing **service to God and to his own;** as in the Gospel: *I was in prison and you came to me; I was sick and you visited me* (Matt. 25:36). But often a man, being a nobleman, is unwilling to visit the sick, saying with the devil in Ezekiel: *I have made myself* (29:3). Let such a one listen to the saying of Job: *I have addressed corruption* ... (17:14), and *I have been* *eyes to the blind* (29:15), and likewise to the Lord in the Gospel: *"If you have done this to one of the least of these, you have done it unto me"* (Matt. 25:40).

(Consideration 4) For the fourth we should make return, in order **to obtain the benefit of the wisdom and knowledge of God.** *He who loves God is known by him* ... (cf. 1 John 5:2). We ought not, therefore, to be overwhelmed by present things nor by the love of mortal friends. *For if I do not go away [the Paraclete will not come to you]* ... (John 16:7).

(Consideration 5) In return for the fifth, we should strive toward **our eternal heritage,** even though Solomon says in contradiction: *A man has nothing more under the sun except that he eats and drinks* (Eccles. 8:15). For all the labor of a man is in God's sight. On this account the Lord said to the idle ones: *You also come into my vineyard* (Matt. 20:4).

(Conclusion) On account of all these things, therefore, we ought to be merciful, leading a life that is worthy of God.

Notes

1. For a full translation by Leopold Krul, O.S.B., see *Three Medieval Rhetorical Arts,* ed. James J. Murphy (Berkeley and Los Angeles: The University of California Press, 1971), 114-215.
2. Determining questions is the form of reasoning done by Scholastic theologians.
3. That is, a liturgical pericope from a gospel rather than the entire book.
4. That is, a biblical verse or text.
5. The *Shepherd* of Hermas.
6. Charland and the translator omit examples of themes that appear in this and the next three chapters.
7. The first translation is of Ovid's Latin, the second is of a Middle English verse translation of the Latin.
8. Title the Vulgate gives to the books of Chronicles. The passage cited, however, is actually from Isaiah.

CHAPTER 10

A HOMILETIC MISCELLANY

HUMBERT OF ROMANS: FROM *ON THE FORMATION OF PREACHERS*

Humbert, the fifth master of the Dominican order, wrote this treatise to delineate the spirituality implied in being a member of the Order of Preachers. The section included here is the second of the seven that make up the book. It deals with "what a preacher needs if he is to do his job" (Prologue). The development is similar to that used in thematic preaching. A thesis is advanced, it is proved by the quotation of a biblical "authority," which is often interpreted by a quotation from one of the Fathers taken from the "annotated Bible" of the period, the Glossa Ordinaria. *The reader who can put aside historical-critical biblical interpretation for a while can discover here many spiritual principles important for anyone with a vocation to preach. The translation is taken from* Early Dominicans: Selected Writings, *ed., trans., intro. Simon Tugwell, pref. Vincent de Couesnongle, Classics of Western Spirituality (New York: Paulist, 1982). (For a discussion of this treatise,* **see Vol. 1, pp. 239-42.***)*

Things That a Preacher Needs

(VIII) In Part Two we must consider the things that are necessary for a preacher. And these fall under six general headings:

(i) the quality of his life;
(ii) his knowledge;
(iii) his speech;
(iv) his merits;
(v) his person;
(vi) things signified symbolically in scripture.

The Quality of a Preacher's Life

(99) Goodness of life is necessary for every preacher. "Anyone who speaks the word of God must first consider his own manner of life," as Gregory says. Now there are many things involved in goodness of life, all of which a preacher must have. One is a holy conscience. The reason for this is that he must be able to speak boldly, and a bad conscience prevents this. "A man whose conscience trips up his tongue will find that his teaching becomes less confident," as Gregory says.

(100) Another thing he needs is that his life should be beyond reproach. How can a man rebuke others when he himself needs rebuking? So it says in Philippians 2:15-6, "You must be without reproach in the midst of a crooked and perverse people, carrying the word of life"; you, that is, who are carriers of the word of life.

(101) Another factor is austerity of life, like that of John, the preacher of penance. "I beat my body and reduce it to servitude, in case, after preaching to others, I myself might be found reprobate" *(1 Cor. 9:27).*

(102) Another thing is a certain pre-eminence of life. A preacher stands in a high place to preach, and he ought similarly to be in a high condition of life. "Go up on to a high mountain, you who preach good news to Zion" *(Isaiah 40:9).*

(103) Another thing is a certain radiance about his life. It is not enough for a preacher to lead a good life in private; his life is meant also to shine before men in such a way that he preaches by his example as well as by word of mouth. "Among whom you shine like lights in the world, carrying the word of life" *(Phil. 2:15-6);* you, that is, who are carriers of the word of life.

(104) Another thing is that his actions should be in harmony with his

words. Jerome says, "Do not let your deeds thwart your words. Otherwise, when you are speaking in church, your hearers will tacitly retort, 'Why do you not put your own words into practice?'"

(105) Another thing is a reputation which spreads like perfume, so that he can join the apostle in being a "good odour of Christ" which attracts others. "Judas was renowned to the very ends of the earth" (*1 Macc. 3:9*). The Gloss explains that this applies to a preacher.

The Knowledge a Preacher Needs

(IX 106) A preacher ought to be knowledgeable, since he has to teach others. This is why 1 Timothy 1:7 reproaches some people with the words, "Wanting to be teachers of the law, they understand neither what they are saying nor the things which they speak so dogmatically about."

Now there are many kinds of knowledge which are necessary for preachers. One is knowledge of the holy scriptures, because all preaching ought to be taken from them, as it says in Psalm 103:12, "From the middle of the rocks they will give utterance," the rocks meaning the two testaments, and preachers cannot do this unless they have knowledge of the two testaments. So this kind of knowledge is necessary. Even though the Lord called simple, uneducated people to be preachers, he still gave them knowledge of the holy scriptures, as we can see from their writings, in which they often adduce arguments from the Old Testament. As Jerome says, "The benefits which others acquire by training and daily meditation on the law were supplied to them by the Holy Spirit and they were, as scripture says, 'taught by God.'"

(107) Then there is knowledge of creatures. God has poured out his wisdom over all his works, and this is why St. Anthony said that creation is a book. Those who know how to read this book well draw from it many things which are very serviceable for helping people to grow. The Lord made use of this kind of knowledge in his preaching, when he said, "Consider the birds of the air" and "Consider the lilies of the field" (*Matt. 6:26, 28*).

(108) Then there is knowledge of historical stories. There are many stories told not only among believers but also among unbelievers, which can sometimes be very useful and edifying in a sermon. The Lord made use of some of them when he said of those who resisted the word of God, "The queen of the south will arise at the judgment with the men of this generation and condemn them, because she came from the ends of the earth to hear the wisdom of Solomon, and see, there is something more than Solomon here now," and when he said against people who would

not repent, "The men of Nineveh will rise at the judgment with his generation" *(Luke 11:31-2)*.

(109) Then there is knowledge of the church's precepts, which is important because people need to be instructed about many of them. "Paul went round Syria and Cilicia strengthening the church, bidding them observe the precepts of the apostles and elders" *(Acts 15:41)*.

(110) Then there is knowledge of the church's mysteries. The apostle is referring to this when he says, "If I knew all mysteries." The church is full of mystical symbols, and it contributes greatly to people's edification to have these expounded to them, and so it is helpful if the preacher understands them. That is why it says, "In the middle of the church he opened his mouth" (the preacher's mouth, that is) "and filled him with the spirit of wisdom and understanding" *(Ecclus. 15:5)*. The "spirit of understanding" refers to that spirit which enables a man to understand what is hidden under the symbols, because to "understand" means to take your "stand under" the symbolic surface.

(111) There is also experiential knowledge. People who have had much experience in dealing with the state of man's soul can say much more about the affairs of the soul. "A man who is experienced in many things will think many things, and a man who has learned much will declare understanding" *(Ecclus. 34:9)*.

(112) There is also the kind of knowledge which is called discretion. This enables a man to know to whom the word of God ought not to be preached—it ought not to be preached to swine or dogs—and to whom it ought to be preached. It also enables him to know when he ought to preach and when not, because "there is a time for keeping silent and a time for speaking." It also enables him to know what to say to whom, in accordance with Gregory's teaching in the *Pastoral Rule,* where he identifies thirty-six different situations. It also enables him to know how to refrain from going on too long and from talking too loudly, from gestures that would not be seemly and from saying things in a disorderly way, and from all the other things of this sort which can go wrong in preaching. So discretion is one of the things that belong to the job of being a preacher. Gregory says, "'The sole of their feet is the sole of a calf's foot' because every preacher has his 'divided hoof' in the form of discretion."

(113) Finally there is knowledge of the Holy Spirit. This was the kind of kind of knowledge which the first apostles had, and it taught them everything, and they spoke according to the way it taught them. "The apostles spoke in various tongues, as the Holy Spirit gave it to them to speak" *(Acts 2:4)*. Happy would he be who had such knowledge! It is this that makes up for what is lacking in all the other kinds of knowledge.

The Preacher's Speech

(X 114) A preacher must have the appropriate ability to speak, sufficient to ensure that he is not rendered unintelligible by any deficiency in his way of speaking. When Moses excused himself to the Lord because of his defective speech, he was given the help of his brother Aaron, who was an able speaker, to speak for him to the people. "The Lord said to Moses, 'I know that your brother Aaron, the Levite, is a capable speaker. . . . He will speak for you to the people and will be your mouth, but you will be to him in the place of God" *(Exod. 4:14-6)*.

(115) He must also have a good facility with words. The first preachers in the church were given all kinds of tongues for the sake of their preaching, so that they would have an abundance of words for everyone; so it is very unfortunate when a preacher sometimes runs out of words, whether because he has a bad memory or because he does not know enough Latin or whatever modern language it may be, or for any other reason. Over against this kind of deficiency, it says in Apocalypse 1:15, "His voice" (Christ's that is) "was like the voice of many waters," because the preacher, who is Christ's voice, ought to be overflowing with words.

(116) He must also have a sonorous voice. A great deal of the effectiveness of a sermon is lost if the preacher's voice is so thin and feeble that he cannot be heard clearly. This is why scripture often compares the voice of a preacher to the sound of a trumpet, because it ought to sound powerfully and clearly like a trumpet. "Let there be a trumpet in your throat" *(Hosea 8:1)*. This is said to a preacher.

(117) He must also have a fluent style of speech, so that he is easy to understand. In his book *On Christian Teaching*, Augustine says that men who are difficult to understand should never or hardly ever, and then only if it is absolutely necessary, be sent out to speak before the people. It is to make this point that it says, "The teaching of wise men is easy" *(Prov. 14:6)*.

(118) His enunciation must be balanced too; that is to say, not too fast and not too slow. If he speaks too quickly, it makes it hard for people to understand, but if he speaks too slowly, it makes for boredom. So Seneca says, "The philosopher's enunciation, like his life, ought to be orderly. But where there is precipitate haste, there is always disorder." He also says, "I want him to dribble his words as little as I want him to run. He should neither stretch men's ears nor swamp them." Now if this is required of a philosopher simply for the sake of worldly reputation, how much more is it required of a preacher for the sake of the good of souls?

(119) He must also be able to speak concisely. As Horace says,

Whatever you command, be brief, that what you say
Men's learning minds may quickly grasp and store away.

Accordingly it says in the Canticle 4:3, "Your lips are like a scarlet headband." The Gloss says this refers "to preachers," who are the lips of the church. And just as a headband restrains overflowing hair, so these lips ought to avoid any overflowing excess of words.

(120) His speech must also be simple, without fancy rhetorical flourishes, so that, like Shamgar, he can be said to take only a plowshare as his weapon. As Augustine says, "We must be careful not to detract from the weight of sacred and serious pronouncements by giving them cadences." By "cadences" he means measured rhythms, metres, and rhetorical embellishments. It is not surprising that the saints should say this, since the philosophers are of exactly the same mind. Seneca says, "A speech which is concerned with truth ought to be simple and straightforward." Other arts are a matter of ingenuity, but in this art of preaching there is a serious business for the mind to deal with. A sick man does not look for an eloquent doctor. If the doctor who can cure him can also make an elegant speech about what has to be done, that is like having an expert helmsman who is also handsome.

(121) He must also be sensible about saying different things to different people. Gregory says, in his *Register of Letters,* "Our speech should be a consolation to the good and a sting to the wicked, it should deflate the puffed-up and bridle the angry, it should stir up the lazy and set fire to the slack with its encouragement; it should seek to convince those who are running away, soothe those who are rough and comfort those who are in despair." This is the meaning of Isaiah 50:4, "The Lord gave me a learned tongue."

(122) Finally, since all of these will be of little value unless there is a graciousness upon the lips, in accordance with what it says in Ecclesiasticus 20:21, "A man without grace is like an idle tale," above everything else it is necessary for a preacher to have grace in his speaking, grace to season everything. This is what is said of the best preacher of all in Psalm 44:3 [Vulg.], "Grace is poured upon your lips."

The Preacher's Merit

(XI 123) Provided that he does his job in a praiseworthy fashion, the preacher gains much merit from his preaching over and above the merit of his own good life. "He who acts and teaches will be called great in the kingdom of heaven" *(Matt. 5:19)*.

But there are many ways in which this merit can be cancelled out or diminished. One is if anyone preaches without authority. "How shall they preach unless they are sent?" *(Rom. 10:15)*.

(124) Another is if someone preaches when he is guilty of some notorious sin. "God said to the sinner, 'Why do you declare my judgments and take up my covenant in your mouth?'" *(Psalm 49:16)*. This refers to notorious sinners.

Another is when somebody departs from the truth in his preaching, for whatever reason, like those who are spoken of in Ezekiel 13:19, "They have violated me" (who am the truth, that is) "before the people, for the sake of a fistful of barley and a piece of bread, to give life to souls which are not alive and to kill souls which are not dying, deceiving a people who give ear to their lies." As Augustine says in his book *On Christian Teaching,* "Maybe people will not understand so much, maybe they will not like it so much, maybe they will not be so moved, but still you should only speak what is true and just."

(126) Another is when the preacher does not practice what he preaches, making his deeds conform to his words. "Bind them round your throat," as it says in Proverbs 3:3, on which the Gloss comments, "in encouraging others to live good lives, the preacher binds himself to live a good life." This is why it says, "You teach others, do you not teach yourself? You preach a ban on thieving; do you then go and thieve?" *(Rom. 2:21)*.

(127) Another is when worldly results are given precedence over spiritual results, contrary to the example of the apostle, who was not looking for gifts, but for results *(Phil. 4:17)*. He was not after the goods of the people he was speaking to, he was after themselves *(2 Cor. 12:14)*. Gregory says in his *Morals on Job,* "Good preachers do not preach in order to receive their livelihood, they accept their livelihood in order to be able to preach. And when their hearers give them the necessities of life, they are not only pleased with the material gift, they are pleased with the generosity of the givers."

(128) Another is when a preacher does not seek what belongs to God, but what belongs to himself, such as reputation or honour, preaching himself and not our Lord Jesus Christ, contrary to the example of the apostle *(2 Cor. 4:5)*. Gregory says, in his *Homilies on Ezekiel,* "To seek only a passing moment of fame from the labour of preaching is to sell a precious treasure for a pittance."

(129) Another is when Christ is preached from a desire to do other people down, instead of with good will. "Some preach Christ out of envy and a spirit of competition, but others from good will" *(Phil. 1:15)*.

(130) Another is when a preacher upsets people by his rough way of speaking. "A mild tongue is a tree of life," because it brings forth good fruit; "but an unbridled tongue will wear a man's spirit away," the spirit of his hearer, that is *(Prov. 15:4).*

(131) Another is when an indiscreet preacher inveighs against one fault in such a way as to give occasion to another fault. What Gregory teaches in his *Pastoral Rule* is quite different:

> Humility must be preached to the proud in such a way that the timid do not become more fearful; confidence must be imparted to the timid in such a way that the proud do not become even more arrogant. Concern for good works must be preached to the idle without giving the restless any excuse for excessive activity; a limit must be set to the activity of the restless without making the idle complacent in their sloth. The anger of the intolerant must be quenched without encouraging the indifference of the lazy and slack; those who are too slack must be fired with zeal, but without adding fuel to the fury of others. Misers must be urged to be more generous in giving, without allowing full rein to the extravagant; the extravagant must be taught how to save, without fostering the misers' possessiveness about their perishable goods. Marriage should be commended to the promiscuous, without leading those who are chaste into sexual indulgence; bodily virginity must be commended to the chaste without making married people come to despise the fruitfulness of the flesh. Good must be preached in such a way that evil is not preached too by implication. The highest values must be commended in such a way that lower values are not disparaged; lower values must be fostered in such a way as not to give the impression that they are sufficient in themselves or to stop men aspiring to the higher values.

(132) Another way in which the preacher may reduce his merit is by not displaying any signs of penance. Jerome says,

> What an embarrassment, what a humiliation, to preach Jesus our Master, who was poor and hungry, with our own bodies stuffed full, and to proclaim the teaching of the fasters with our ruddy cheeks and our mouths full! If we occupy the place of the apostles, let us not only imitate their words, but also their way of life and their abstinence.

(133) Another is when the preaching is not motivated by charity. "If I speak with the tongues of men and of angels, but do not have charity, I have become like a tinkling cymbal or a booming gong" *(1 Cor. 13:1).* The tinkling cymbal benefits others, but wears itself away.

(134) So if preaching is to be meritorious for the preacher as well as being beneficial to those who listen to it, the preacher must avoid preaching without authority, he must not be a notorious sinner, he must not deviate from the truth, what he does must accord with what he says, he must be more interested in spiritual gain than in worldly profit, he must seek what belongs to God rather than what belongs to himself, he must not preach with a view to doing other people down, he must not upset his hearers with foolish words, he must not give occasion for any evil, he must not be without some evidence of doing penance, and his motivation must not lack charity.

The Preacher's Person

(XII 135) In connexion with the preacher's person, we should notice that he must be of male sex. "I do not permit a woman to teach" *(1 Tim. 2:12)*. There are four reasons for this: first, lack of understanding because a man is more likely to have understanding than a woman. Secondly, the inferior status imposed on women; a preacher occupies a superior position. Thirdly, if a woman were to preach, her appearance would inspire lustful thoughts, as the Gloss on this text says. And fourthly, as a reminder of the foolishness of the first woman, of whom Bernard says, "She taught once and wrecked the whole world."

(136) Next, he must not have any obvious or remarkable bodily deformity. People whose bodies are disfigured in this way are debarred from the Lord's service in Leviticus 21:17ff., and similarly the church has banned them from public office, for fear of popular scandal and ridicule.

It is also useful to him to be strong in body, so that he can stay up late at night studying, speak loudly when he is preaching, endure the labours of travelling, and the poverty of not having things he needs, and many other such hardships, as the apostles did. "They will be truly patient," that is, truly strong in endurance, "so that they may proclaim" *(Psalm 91:15-6)*.

(137) He also ought to be of suitable age. Gregory says, "Our Redeemer reigns in heaven as Creator, and he has always been the teacher of the angels by the display of his power, yet he refused to become the teacher of men until he was thirty. In this way he wanted to instil a healthy timidity into the over-hasty by letting them see that even he who cannot fail did not preach the grace of the fulness of life until he had reached the fulness of maturity in years."

(138) He also ought to have some superiority over the other people present, in his position or education or religious life or something of the

kind, except that occasionally it may be useful for a man to preach in the presence of his superiors, as a kind of exercise. This is why preaching is not the job of a layman, because the laity occupy the lowest rank. "How beautiful on the mountains are the feet of him who proclaims and preaches" *(Isaiah 52:7)*. This implies that a preacher ought to be high up, in some way, as on a mountain.

(139) Finally, he ought not to be in any way contemptible, for fear that his preaching too will be despised. Gregory says, "If a man's life is despised, it will follow that his preaching too is despised."

The Scriptural Symbols of the Preacher

(XIII 140) The scriptural figures which symbolize preachers are almost beyond counting, as we can see from the Gloss. This is in order to make preachers realise what they have to do and so bring forth fruit of all the different kinds indicated by the various symbols.

"If you separate the valuable from the cheap, you will be a kind of mouth for me" *(Jer. 15:19)*. This is glossed, "Separate: with your words, that is." And this is what a preacher does. This shows that he is a kind of mouth of the Lord.

"The light of my face did not fall to the ground" *(Job 29:24)*. This is glossed, "The light of the Lord's face does not fall to the ground, because the church does not preach her radiant mysteries to earthly men." This shows that the preacher is called God's face.

"I will honour the place of my feet" *(Is. 60:13)*. This is glossed, "Preachers are called the Lord's feet."

So, since preachers are called the Lord's mouth, the Lord's face and the Lord's feet, they must make sure that nothing comes from their mouth which is unworthy of the mouth of the Lord, and that nothing can be seen in them which is unworthy of the face of God, and that wherever they go they carry God with them, as feet carry the rest of the body to which they belong.

(141) Preachers are also called angels. "The seven angels prepared to blow the trumpet" *(Apoc. 8:6)*. This is glossed, "The whole company of preachers." So every preacher must ensure that there is nothing demonic or bestial in him; he must rather conduct himself in a way that is suitable for angels, above the common nature of men.

(142) They are also called the eyes and teeth and neck and breasts of the church, and other similar things, as we see from Cant. 4:1-5. This is because of the various functions which belong to them, as the Gloss on Cant. 4:5 says: "Preachers are called eyes, because they are on the watch

for hidden things, and teeth because they seize the wicked and drag them into the belly of the church, and neck because they supply the breath of life through preaching the joys of heaven and they also supply the food of doctrine, and breasts because, in Christ, they give milk to the little ones."

(143) They are also called heaven. "His Spirit adorned the heavens" *(Job 26:13)*. This is glossed "Preachers." So the preacher must take care to shine like the sky with all the different virtues which ought to adorn him.

(144) They are also called stars. "He enclosed the stars" *(Job 9:7)*. This is glossed, "Stars: preachers," and so they ought to shine on the earth in the darkness of this world, like the stars.

(145) They are also called doors of heaven. "He opened the doors of heaven" *(Psalm 77:23)*. This is glossed, "The doors of heaven are the preachers," and so they ought to see to it that men enter heaven through them, and that the things of heaven come into the world through them.

(146) They are also called clouds, because, like clouds, they are sent to travel about over the whole world. "Clouds give light to everything throughout their course" *(Job 37:11-12)*. This is glossed, "The clouds of God give light to everything throughout their course because they enlighten the ends of the world with the light of their preaching."

(147) They are also called snow. "He commanded the snow to descend upon the earth" *(Job 37:6)*. This is glossed, "Water is packed together in the sky above to become snow; when the snow falls to the earth it melts again and changes back into water. So snow falls from heaven to earth when the lofty minds of the saints, nourished on a contemplation that is well packed and solid, descend to the lowly words of preaching out of love for their brethren."

(148) Then again, they are called thunder. "When the seven thunders had spoken" *(Apoc. 16:4)*. This is glossed, "Thunders, that is, preachers." They are called thunder because it is their job to instil the fear of God. So Gregory says in his *Morals on Job,* "Thunder refers to the preaching of the fear of heaven; when the hearts of men hear it, they quake."

(149) Again they are called precious stones. "The king commanded them to bring great stones, precious stones, to set in the foundations of the temple" *(3 Kings 5:17)*. This is glossed, "The layers of stones which come higher up are the teachers whose preaching makes the church grow and whose virtues adorn her."

(150) They are also called mountains, because, like mountains, they are the first to receive the bounty of heaven, which they then transmit to the places below. "Let the mountains receive peace for the people, and the hills justice" (Ps. 71:3). This is glossed, "Mountains, that is, preachers."

(151) They are also called fountains, because they gush like fountains. "You made fountains burst forth" *(Psalm 73:15)*. This is glossed, "Fountains, that is, preachers, and you made them burst forth so that they would pour forth their flow of wisdom."

(152) They are also called eagles, because, just as eagles fly to corpses, so they fly to those who are dead in their sins. "Wherever there is a corpse, there will soon be an eagle" *(Job 39:30)*. This is glossed, "A holy preacher flies with eager haste to wherever he considers there are sinners, to show forth the light of new life to those who are lying dead in their sins."

(153) They are also called cocks. "Who gave the cock understanding?" *(Job 38:36)*. This is glossed, "Cocks are the preachers, who, in the darkness of this present life, zealously proclaim the light that is to come, by 'crowing' or, in other words, preaching."

(154) They are also called ravens, because of certain good qualities which they have. "Who prepared his food for the raven, when his little ones cry to God?" *(Job 38:41)*. This is glossed, "The raven is a preacher, from whom the chicks, cheeping in the nest, wait open mouthed to receive their food. Because of this discretion of his, God gives the raven a greater abundance; he receives more, because he receives not only for himself, but also for those whom he feeds."

(155) They are also called dogs. "Dumb dogs which cannot bark" *(Is. 56:10)*. This is glossed, "Bark, that is, preach." So the preacher is called a dog, and therefore he ought to wander round hither and thither like a hungry dog, eager to swallow up souls into the body of the church. "They will feel hunger like dogs and go about the city" *(Psalm 58:7)*.

(156) They are also called horses. "Will you give strength to the horse or put his whinnying in this throat?" *(Job 39:19)*. This is glossed, "In this passage the holy preacher is referred to under the name of a horse. For the preacher first of all receives strength by extinguishing vice in himself, and then moves on to the utterance of preaching in order to educate others."

(157) They are also called oxen. "A thousand yoke of oxen" *(Job 42:12)*. This is glossed, "Oxen: preachers." So they ought to work the fields energetically to show their strength. "Where there are no oxen, the manger is empty. Where there is an abundant harvest to be seen, it proves the strength of the oxen" *(Prov. 14:4)*.

(158) Also they are the standard-bearers of the army of the king of heaven, carrying his banner. "Lift up a sign for the people" *(Is. 62:10)*. This is glossed, "Lift up, by preaching, a sign, namely the cross, by proclaiming the Passion and the Resurrection."

(159) They are also the messengers of that Ahasuerus who is our joy,

carrying his letters and commands throughout all his provinces. "King Ahasuerus sent letters throughout all the provinces of his realm" *(Esther 1:22)*. This is glossed, "Through his preachers he sent out instructions and rebukes."

(160) They are also the strong men of David, through whom he accomplished mighty deeds in the world. "I have called my strong men in my wrath" *(Is. 13:3)*, on which the Gloss says, "Paul, for example." The text goes on: "The Lord of hosts has given the word to the army which fights his war." This is glossed, "He has given the word to the preachers, who are equipped with the armour of the apostle, to kill all those who raise themselves up against the knowledge of God."

(161) Then again they are the officers of the true Solomon, who carefully see to the food for his table. "The Officers, with immense care, supplied what was needed for the table of King Solomon at the appropriate time" *(3 Kings 4:27)*. This is glossed, "To ensure that there is nothing lacking in the king's house, the order of preachers labours, in writing and in speech, to make plentiful provision on the Lord's table for the nourishment of the faithful."

(162) They are also bricklayers, who work with Ezra to repair the temple of the living God. "They gave money to bricklayers" *(Ezra 3:7)*. This is glossed, "The bricklayers are preachers, who build men up in good works and bind them together with the bond of charity, as if they were cementing together cut and polished stones, to keep them in place in the whole construction."

(163) They are also the watchmen of the house of Israel, that is, the church, to tell it what they see coming. "Son of man, I have appointed you watchman to the house of Israel" *(Ezek. 3:17)*. This is glossed, "He calls the preacher a watchman because his way of life should be such as to set him up on high, where he can be useful by being able to see into the distance."

(164) Notice that all these symbols fall into nine sections, with reference, respectively, to: God, angels, the church, heaven, the sky, the earth, things that fly, earth-bound creatures, and human responsibilities. Happy the preacher who realises in himself all the symbols which apply to his office!

MEISTER ECKHART: SERMON ON LUKE 10:38

In the Rhineland in the late thirteenth and early fourteen centuries there developed a type of preaching in which a mystical theology was taught that encouraged a kind of religious experience in which the soul attained immediate knowledge of God in this life. Most of those engaged in such preaching were Dominicans and their primary audiences were the friars and nuns of their order. Their genre was the homily rather than the thematic sermon, so their preaching differed from the monastic preaching of Bernard and his contemporaries largely in the spirituality taught. (For a discussion of the theology and those who taught it, **see Vol. 1, pp. 242-45.***) This translation is taken from:* Meister Eckhart: The Essential Sermons, Commentaries, Treatises, and Defense, *trans. with intro. Edmund Colledge and Bernard McGinn, pref. Huston Smith, Classics of Western Spirituality (New York: Paulist, 1981), 177-81.*

Sermon 2

Intravit Jesus in quoddam castellum et mulier quaedam, Martha nomine, excepit illum in domum suam (Lk. 10.38).

I have begun with a few words in Latin that are written in the gospel; and in German this means: "Our Lord Jesus Christ went up into a little town, and was received by a virgin who was a wife."

Now notice carefully what this says. It must necessarily be that the person by whom Jesus was received was a virgin. "Virgin" is as much as to say a person who is free of all alien images, as free as he was when he was not. Observe that people may ask how a man who has been born and has advanced to the age of reason could be as free of all images as when he was nothing; he who knows so many things that are all images: How then can he be free? Keep in mind this distinction, which I want to make clear for you. If I were so rational that there were present in my reason all the images that all men had ever received, and those that are present in God himself, and if I could be without possessiveness in their regard, so that I had not seized possessively upon any one of them, not in what I did or what I left undone, not looking to past or to future, but I stood in this present moment free and empty according to God's dearest will, performing it without ceasing, then truly I should be a virgin, as truly unimpeded by any images as I was when I was not.

But I say that because a man is a virgin, that does not deprive him at all of any of the works he has ever done; but all this permits him to remain, maidenly and free, without any obstacles between him and supreme truth, just as Jesus is empty and free and maidenly in himself. As the authorities say that only between equals can unity be produced, so must a man be a maid and a virgin who is to receive the maidenly Jesus.

Now mark what I say and pay careful attention! For if a man were to be a virgin forever, no fruit would come from him. If he is to become fruitful, he must of necessity be a wife. "Wife" is the noblest word one can apply to the soul, much nobler that "virgin." That a man conceives God in himself is good, and in his conceiving he is a maiden. But that God should become fruitful in him is better; for the only gratitude for a gift is to be fruitful with the gift, and then the spirit is a wife, in its gratitude giving birth in return, when he for God gives birth again to Jesus into the heart of the Father.

Many good gifts are received in virginity and are not born again in wifely fruitfulness with grateful praise to God. The gifts all spoil and turn to nothing, so that the man is no better or more blessed because of them. So his virginity is no profit to him, because he is not, in addition to his virginity, a wife with all her fruitfulness. That is where the trouble is. That is why I have said: "Jesus went up into a little town, and was received by a virgin who was a wife." This must necessarily be so, as I have shown.

Married people seldom produce in a year more than one fruit. But I am now talking about a different kind of married people, about all those who are possessively attached to prayer, to fasting, to vigils, and to all kinds of exterior exercises and penances. Every attachment to every work deprives one of the freedom to wait upon God in the present and to follow him alone, free and renewed in every present moment, as if this were all that you had ever had or wanted or could do. Every attachment or every work you propose deprives you again and again of this freedom, and is what I now call a "year" because your soul produces no fruit unless it performs the work to which you have been so attached; and you have not trust, not in God or in yourself, unless you have performed the work on which you seized with such possessiveness, and otherwise you have no peace. That is why you too produce no fruit, unless you perform your work. That is what I reckon as a "year," and your fruit is small indeed, because it has been produced out of attachment to the work and not out of freedom. And I call these married people, because they are pledged to possessiveness. They produce little fruit, and what they do produce is small indeed, as I have said.

A virgin who is a wife is free and unpledged, without attachment; she is always equally close to God and to herself. She produces much fruit, and it is great, neither less nor more than is God himself. This virgin who is a wife brings this fruit and this birth about, and everyday she produces fruit, a hundred or a thousand times, yes, more than can be counted, giving birth and becoming fruitful from the noblest ground of all—or, to put it better, from that same ground where the Father is bearing his eternal Word, from that ground is she fruitfully bearing with him. For Jesus, the light and the reflection of the Fatherly heart—Saint Paul says that he is the glory and the reflection of the Fatherly heart, and with his power he illumines completely the Fatherly heart (Heb. 1:3)—this Jesus is united with her and she with him, and she shines and glows with him as one in oneness and as a pure bright light in the fatherly heart.

And, I have often said that there is a power in the soul that touches neither time nor flesh. It flows from the spirit and remains in the spirit and is wholly spiritual. In this power God is always verdant and blossoming in all the joy and the honor that he is in himself. That is a joy so heartfelt, a joy so incomprehensible and great that no one can tell it all. For it is in this power that the eternal Father ceaselessly brings his eternal Son so to birth, that this power also is bearing the Son of the Father, and bearing itself, that same Son in the single power of the Father. If a man possessed a whole kingdom, or all the riches of the heart, and gave up the whole of it for the love of God and became one of the poorest men that ever lived on earth, and if God then gave him as much to suffer as he has ever given any man, and if he suffered it all until his death, and if God then gave him one single glimpse of what he is in this power, his joy would be so great that all this suffering and poverty would be too little. Yes, even if after this God never gave him the kingdom of heaven, he still would have received a reward great enough for all that he had ever suffered, for God is present in this power as he is in the eternal now. If the spirit were always united with God in this power, the man could never grow old; for that now in which God made the first man, and the now in which the last man will have his end, and the now in which I am talking, they are all the same in God, and there is not more than the one now. Now you can see that this man lives in one light with God, and therefore there is not in him either suffering or the passage of time, but an unchanging eternity. From this man, truly, all wonderment has been taken away, and all things are essentially present in him. Therefore nothing new will come to him out of future events or accidents, for he dwells always anew in a now without ceasing. Such a divine lordship is there in this power.

There is another power that is also not of the body; it flows out of the spirit and remains in the spirit and is wholly spiritual. In this power God is ceaselessly gleaming and burning with all his riches, with all his sweetness and with all his joy. Truly, there is such delight and such great, immeasurable joy in this power that no one can tell or reveal it all. But I say: If there were a single man who were to contemplate rationally and truly in this for an instant the joy and the delight that is there, everything that he could have suffered and that God would have wished him to suffer would be for him too little and, indeed, nothing; and I say more—it would always be his joy and his ease.

If you really want to know whether your sufferings are your own or are God's, this is what you should observe. If you suffer for your own sake, however this may be, the suffering hurts you and is hard for you to bear. But if you suffer for God's sake and for his sake alone, the suffering will not be hard for you, because God is carrying the burden. This is really true! If there were a man who wanted to suffer for the love of God and purely for God alone, if all the suffering came down on him at once that all men have ever suffered and the whole world has as its common lot, that would not hurt him or be hard for him, because it would be God who was carrying the burden. If someone loaded a hundredweight on my neck and then someone else supported it on my neck, I should be as glad to carry a hundred of them as one, because it would not be hard for me, nor would it hurt me at all. In a few words: Whatever a man suffers for the love of God and for him alone, God makes this easy and sweet for him, as I said at the beginning, when we started our sermon: "Jesus went up into a little town, and was received by a virgin who was a wife." Why? It must necessarily be that she was a virgin and also a wife. Now I have told you that Jesus was received, but I have not said to you what the little town is; but now I want to talk about that.

I have sometimes said that there is a power in the spirit that alone is free. Sometimes I have said that it is a guard of the spirit; sometimes I have said that it is a light of the spirit; sometimes I have said that it is a spark. But now I say that it is neither this nor that, and yet it is a something that is higher above this and that than heaven is above the earth. And therefore I now give it finer names than I have ever given it before, and yet whatever fine names, whatever words we use, they are telling lies, and it is far above them. It is free of all names, it is bare of all forms, wholly empty and free, as God in himself is empty and free. It is so utterly one and simple, as God is one and simple, that man cannot in any way look into it. The same power of which I have spoken in which God is verdant and growing with all his divinity, and the spirit in God—with this same power is the Father bringing to birth his Only-Begotten Son as truly as in himself, for he truly lives in this power, and the spirit with the Father brings to birth the same Only-Begotten Son, and it begets itself the same Son, and is the same Son in this light, and it is the truth. If you could look upon this with my heart, you would well understand what I say, for it is true, and it is Truth's own self that says it.

And now see and pay heed! This little town, about which I am talking and which I have in mind, is in the soul so one and so simple, far above whatever can be described, that this noble power about which I have spoken is not worthy even once for an instant to look into this little town; and the other power too of which I spoke, in which God is gleaming and burning with all his riches and with all his joy, it also does not ever dare to look into it. This little town is so truly one and simple, and this simple one is so exalted above every manner and every power, that no power, no manner, not God himself may look at it. It is as true that this is true and that I speak truly as that God is alive! God himself never for an instant looks into it, never yet did he look on it, so far as he possesses himself in the manner and according to the properties of his Person. It is well to observe this, because this simple one is without manner and without properties. And therefore, if God were ever to look upon it, that must cost him all his divine names and the properties of his Persons; that he must wholly forsake, if he is ever once to look into it. But as he is simply one, without any manner and properties, he is not Father or Son or Holy Spirit, and yet he is a something that is neither this nor that.

Observe that as he is one and simple, so he comes into the one, which in the soul I have called a little town, and he does not come into it in any other way; but so he comes there, and so he is there. In this part the soul is like to God, and otherwise not. What I have said to you is true; I call the truth to witness this, and I lay my soul as a pledge.

That we may also be a little town into which Jesus may come and be received, and remain forever in us in the way that I have said, may God help us to this. Amen.

A WYCLIFFITE SERMON IN ENGLISH

While it used to be thought that John Wyclif translated the Bible into English, preached many vernacular sermons himself that have been preserved, and sent out wandering Lollard preachers to spread his views, it is now recognized that none of that is true. **(See Vol. 1, pp. 247-55,** *for discussion of these questions.) While he came to favor most of these things, the translations were made by his disciples, his surviving sermons are in Latin, and the English sermons date from after his death. Rather than transcripts of sermons delivered by itinerants, they come from one author or supervising editor and were prepared for established and affluent congregations of people who had come to accept the views at which Wyclif had arrived by the end of his life and others later developed by those inspired by him. The sermon below, an attack on the* *avarice of clergy based on the Gospel story of Jesus cleansing the Temple, is typical of this collection, although attacks on sins of the clergy were common in most late medieval preaching, whether inspired by Wyclif or not. The Middle English text appears in* English Wycliffite Sermons, *vol. 1, ed. Anne Hudson (Oxford: Clarendon, 1983). I have translated/transliterated it into a sort of King James-y English in an effort to make it more readable while preserving as much of the flavor of the original as possible, and my translation has been amended by Professor Robert F. Yeager.*

Sermon 10

On the Gospel for the Tenth Sunday after the Feast of Trinity

Cum appropinquaret Jesus Jerusalem. Luce 19.1

This gospel telleth generally what sorrow men should have for sin, since Christ that might not do sin wept so often for sin; for we read that Christ wept thrice, and each time he wept for sin. And so telleth our belief in the story of the gospel that Jesus seeing Jerusalem wept thereon for the sin of it, and said that if thou knew sin thus, thou shouldest weep as I do now; and certainly in this day that should be coming in peace to thee, if thou wouldest receive this day and the peace of it as thou shouldest. For all these things that thou shouldest ken[2] be now hidden from thine eyes, for days shall come on thee for the sin that thou shalt do to me; and thine enemies shall surround thee as a palace all about and bar thee in Jerusalem as sheep be barred in a fold. And they shall fell thee to the earth and thy children; and they shall not leave for thee stone lying upon stone, that they shall not remove and all thy walls destroy. And the cause of all this shall be thine unnatural ignorance, that thou wilt not know the time that God by grace hath visited thee.

All these words were showed by means of deeds performed, and Josephus maketh us aware of how Titus and Vespasian, the second-and-fortieth year after that Christ ascended to heaven, came at the solemnity of Pasch, and besieged Jerusalem and destroyed the men and walls utterly that they found there. And this is like the secret sin with which the Fiend blindeth men, so that they sorrow not more for sin than they do for other harm, for thus their will is misdirected and men fail to serve God. And herefore Christ teacheth his apostles that they should not be afraid for perils that should come for to avenge sin that is done; but the most dread of all should be to fall into sin, for that is worse than the pain that God ordaineth to ensue hereof. And thus in miserable affections that be grounded in man's will standeth all man's sin that he doth against God: for, if the sorrow and joy of a man and hope and dread were ruled well, his will would be ordained unto God to serve him as it should do.

After this telleth the story how Christ went into the Temple, and cast out both sellers and buyers, and said to them that "It is written, 'my house should be a house of prayer,' but ye have made it a den of thieves." And for a long time after he was each day teaching in the Temple. And in this deed that Christ did he teacheth his church to begin to purge his sanctuary, because it be the priests and clerics thereof that be the most cause of sin, and then purge other parts when the root is destroyed. And this told Christ wending into the Temple using these words, as if he would say in his working, "The cause of sin that I have told is wickedness of priests and clerics, and therefore I begin at the Temple—not to destroy them in their persons, but to take from them the cause of their sin, and arrange the church in respect to temporal goods as I have ordered them to live."

And it is the same to say that these goods be thus sacred and given to priests so that no man may take them from these priests, and to say that Antichrist hath so wedded these goods with priests that none may separate them, because priests are incorrigible. But this defamation should priests flee with all their might, and pray that they might be amended by the ordinance of Christ, for reason should teach them that they are worse than frantics, and so ought to be chastised till this passion were from them.

For what man would by reason, keeping a man in franticness,[3] give him a sword or a knife by which he would slay himself? Or who that kept a man in fever, and wist well how he should be ruled and that this meat[4] or this wine were contrary to his help, would give him at his will this food that should annoy him? So, since priests have goods of men, both of lords and of commons, and they misuse them thus, they might and should by charity withdraw these swords that thus do harm to priests, and in measure and manner give these goods to priests that Christ himself hath ordained as his, to have such goods. And this may by charity be withdrawn by the givers thereof, since no man may do evil to men and not also be able to do good to the same men, unless he were a living fiend—one that we should not trust with seculars.[5]

And to this end should clerics travail and procure that this thing were done, both for love of God's law, for love of clerics, and of commons. And if the fiend by envy, who is the enemy of charity, saith that this thing may not be done by the law that now is set, then he is saying that

Antichrist's law founded against God's law is stronger than charity, and Antichrist stronger than Christ. For this end should clerics weep and pray to God, that his ordinance may be kept in his strength and Antichrist's law put aback.

Notes

1. "When Jesus drew near to Jerusalem" (Lk. 19).
2. Know.
3. That is, being in charge of an insane person.
4. Food of any sort.
5. That is, laypeople.

PART III

FROM THE RENAISSANCE AND REFORMATION TO THE ENLIGHTENMENT

CHAPTER 11

ERASMUS AND THE HUMANISTS

ERASMUS: A RÉSUMÉ OF *ECCLESIASTES*

This first homiletics textbook fully to incorporate the principles of classical rhetoric deserves to be savored in itself. Its great length, however—in its parts as well as in its totality—militates against excerpting entire sections here. The most useful way of communicating a sense of the whole seems to be to provide a summary of the entire work. The one chosen is that of Manfred Hoffmann from his book Rhetoric and Theology: The Hermeneutic of Erasmus *(Toronto: University of Toronto, 1994), 39-55. (For a discussion of Ecclesiastes,* **see Vol. 1, pp.** *274-79.*)

Ecclesiastes sive de ratione concionandi

As this treatise is quite lengthy, we must be content with sketching its broad outline and paraphrasing its content with regard to our theme. The text is not readily analysable. Erasmus repeatedly interrupts his train of thought with digressions, more often than not caused by word associations within running commentaries on select biblical texts. One thing leads to another so that Erasmus time and again has to remind himself to return to the subject after lengthy disquisitions. Yet an overall structure emerges if we compare the layout of the first three books with the sequence of Quintilian's *Institutio oratoria: ars, artifex,* and *opus.*

Erasmus begins in book I with *artifex,* the preacher, and then deals, in books II and III, with *opus,* that is, the *officia in dicendo* and the *partes operis.* However, he relinquishes "the heading of art because those who have written about the precepts of eloquence themselves are uncertain whether rhetoric is an art, and because that supreme parent of eloquence acknowledged that it is the chief point of art to conceal art." In book IV he presents an index of theological *loci.* This sequence is indicated by Erasmus himself in the dedicatory letter: "We divide the main argument into four books. In the first we point out the dignity of the office and the virtues that must be at the preacher's command. In the second and third we accommodate the precepts of the rhetoricians, dialecticians, and theologians to the use of preaching. The fourth is like a catalogue and shows which ideas *(sententiae)* the preacher ought to derive from which places *(loci)* in Scripture."

BOOK I. ON THE DIGNITY, PURITY, PRUDENCE, AND THE OTHER VIRTUES OF THE PREACHER (ASD V-4 35:1; CF. 246:160)

Introduction (35:6–36:47):

The Greek word *ecclesia* means in Latin *concio:* an assembly of people called out to hear speeches on the affairs of the republic. *Ἐκκλησια[σ]τής* signifies the person who publicly speaks to the multitude. There are two republics, the profane and the sacred, with two *ecclesiastae,* performing different but not contrary functions, serving each other but aiming at the same goal: the tranquillity of both civic peace and Christian piety. In the sacred assembly the preacher explains sacred Scripture to the people.

I. The Preacher

1. Word, heart, spirit, and speech (36:48–44:186): The preacher speaks the word of heavenly philosophy, Jesus Christ, the *verbum sive sermo Dei.* Flowing from the Father's heart, Christ is the most certain expositor of the divine mind; through him God speaks to us. The word of human beings, too, springs from their spirit: "As is our word, so is our spirit." Thus we cannot approach God other than through our spirit and

language, for "the mind is the source, the word is the image flowing forth from the source." Just as Christ is the image of the Father so our speech mirrors what is conceived in the mind. Our words carry the power of their source, reproducing its useful or harmful affection. It makes all the difference, then, whether God or the devil rules the heart.

2. (44:187–54:388): In preparation for the ecclesiastical office, the student must acquire a profound knowledge of Scripture, practice literary composition, read diverse doctors, develop a sound judgment and uncommon prudence, nurture a sincere and strong mind, learn the precepts and practice of speaking, assemble *copia* of words and ideas, etc. The foremost source of ecclesiastical eloquence, however, is a clean heart. Renewed by the heavenly Spirit, it is able to understand Scripture, for the Bible was committed to writing by the same Spirit. "The fountain of right speaking is wisdom." Wisdom differs from knowledge in that a wise person, instead of knowing everything, is not only learned in the things that concern true happiness but also is transfigured by them. As often as we eat the food of evangelical doctrine, it goes over into the inmost parts of our mind, becomes our nature, and strengthens our spirit.

3. (54:389–58:497): Part of the clean heart is the purity of life. From the preacher's heart the virtues of Christ's innocence, mildness, and benevolence must shine forth in word, life, and face, whereas vices, even the appearance of evil, are detrimental to ministerial authority.

4. (60:498–68:684): "Faith pertains to dove-like simplicity, prudence to serpent-like caution." Faithful are those who teach nothing but God's commandments and everywhere look to both the glory of God and the advantage of the sacred flock. It is the function of prudence, however, "to discern from the circumstances of times, places, and persons what is to be applied to whom, when, and with what moderation." Therefore, the ecclesiastic must learn how to accommodate to the variety of gender, age, conditions, natural dispositions, opinions, institutions of life, and customs. According to the rhetoricians, the precepts of art must yield to prudence, which they divide into *judicium* and *consilium.* While sacred orators receive prudence as a gift of the Holy Spirit, the Spirit yet accommodates to their natural disposition. "The Holy Spirit does not remove the innate power of nature but perfects it."

5. (68:685–76:875): The preacher's *scopus* is a heart clean and prudent to discern "what is to be left unsaid, what to be said, before whom, at which time, and in what way speech should be moderated, knowing like

Paul to change one's voice and to become all to all, whenever it seems expedient to the salvation of the hearer." This faculty must be asked from God by prayer and sought by pious works. There are two kinds of good works: ceremonies (or corporeal exercises) and the spiritual works of piety. To exercise the body is useful only insofar as it enhances the spirit. Just as the pagan philosophers advised against *supercilium, superstitio, praeposterum judicium,* and *oblivio mediocritatis* in the body's training for endurance, so Christians should take the middle road by avoiding that immoderate severity to the body which is useless for spiritual growth.

II. The dignity of the teaching office

1. (76:876–77:937): Learned are all who believe the gospel, glean the heavenly philosophy from the Apostles' Creed, and keep the commandments of both laws, who are taught by Christ how to pray and in which way to pursue the goal of happiness. Still, among the learned ones stand out the doctors who have received the special gifts of the Spirit to teach righteousness to many.

2. (77:938–84:50): The dignity of office is a gift of God. Preachers have received a tongue instructed in the words of the Lord, not in philosophical syllogisms or rhetorical flourishes. They hear the voice of the Spirit in the mind's ears—human ears, to be sure, but perfected by God and fortified through faith and obedience. While preparation in the human disciplines is helpful, the student must not grow old in them but early on advance to secret wisdom. The pastoral office serves to root out the depraved opinions and impious doctrines from the hearers' minds and to plant the good seed by means of a tongue that is instructed in the word of God, which is Scripture divinely inspired.

3. (84:51–114:661): To persuade effectively, one must love what one teaches. The heart itself provides the lover with the ardour of speech, and doctrine is the more efficacious the more teachers excel in what they teach others. Since burning comes before shining, the flame of the mind shines forth in the light of doctrine. True charity accompanies sincere faith.

The external characteristics of Old Testament priesthood (such as consecration, sacrifice, anointing, and vestments) reveal hidden meanings if interpreted spiritually. Purity signifies cleansing from human desires and adorning with the heroic virtues.

From the (anointed) head comes the wisdom of sound doctrine, from the heart proceed voice and speech. It is not sufficient for the priest to know what is right and pious, unless there is the faculty of teaching others. It consists of a double word: the Old Testament hidden under the cover of figures and enigmas, and the New Testament revealing the mysteries and making known the manifest truth. The same is true of the twofold sense of the entire Scripture, the lower and the allegorical or higher one. To explain these properly, truth *(ἀλήθεια)* must be present so that doctrine contains no error, but also clarification (δήλωσις) so that the hidden message of Scripture becomes perspicuous even to the unschooled.

One must not rush into office but spend much time preparing in one's heart the ability to teach. We cannot teach others what to believe and how to live unless our life and morals reflect what we are talking about. That Jesus acted before he taught tells us that the most efficacious kind of doctrine is that which declares piety in life. Two things guard the pastor's innocence of life: fear and love. Fear as the beginning of wisdom means to draw back from evil; love is to do good.

There is also a distinction between Old and New Testament doctrine. While Aaron instructed how to use God's law, the New Testament teaches that inerrant philosophy which the son of God has brought from the Father's heart to earth. Of course, it is difficult to explain the secret Scriptures, but the harder the task, the greater is the gift of the spirit. Although this gift is given freely, it does not eliminate our industry, prayers, and good works. Natural gifts (a healthy body) and the natural endowments for speaking (a good voice, articulate language, quick mind, and trustworthy memory) are faculties made ready by human industry. But just like the professional skills (expertise in dialectical arguments, proficiency in the rhetorical power of speech, and the knowledge of natural things), they are not destroyed by the Spirit but perfected. Furthermore, moral education through parents and educators, just as preparation in the best of the secular disciplines, enhances the faculty of teaching.

III. The authority of the teaching function

1. (114:662–180:924): The highest church office is that of bishop, and among the ecclesiastical functions the highest is teaching the heavenly philosophy, a mandate which the bishop delegates to presbyters. But to desire the vocation of preacher is not wrong, for "to desire a good office is of charity." In the following, Erasmus deals with the qualifications of clergy, their functions, jurisdiction, selection, and removal, and the

abuses of the present time. Model bishops mentioned are Warham, Fisher, and Gregory I. This episcopal ideal is then set against the sorry state of contemporary Christian religion. The next section declares the bishop's office as superior to the prince's, and the work of parish priests as more difficult than monastic life.

2. (180:925–190:62): "Next to God's authority comes the sublimity of the prophets, whom God endowed with a special dignity and through whom as interpreters he wished to disclose his inscrutable will to mortals." Old Testament prophecies uncovered the past, foretold the future, or explained the divine secrets for the present without discriminating the times. But they yielded little by little to the evangelical light, becoming either lifeless or better when changed into a more sublime kind. The New Testament prophecy brings to light the mysteries of Scripture according to the spiritual sense. It depends on the spiritual prophets, then, whether the church grows or diminishes. As the Spirit leads them into all truth, nothing remains hidden until the last day. Now the mystical Scripture provides the living food and water, to be dispensed according to the circumstances of the hearers.

3. (190:63–198:228): Evangelical prophets are even more excellent than John the Baptist, the prophet in the middle between the old and the new prophecy. For expressing the gospel with the tongue is more felicitous than pointing to it with the finger. Certainly, the Spirit remains the same, but it is differently dispensed according to the times. As the Spirit now perfects faith, it destroys the external signs which were earlier necessary because of infirmity and unbelief. The law served as a pedagogue to Christ. But when the sun of the gospel arose, the minor lights darkened; the interior overshadowed the exterior. The miracle of God calling from death to life surpasses the old miracles, and the resurrection in the forgiveness of sins supersedes the resurrection of the body.

4. (198:229–206:380): The five special duties of bishops/priests are administering the sacraments of the new law, praying for the people, judging, ordaining, and, the highest, teaching, which surpasses even the celebration of the Eucharist. Erasmus insists that he has nothing against monasticism or priesthood, but to put second things first is a perverted judgment *(praeposterum judicium)*. Inverted choices are the fountain of all moral ruin. So also in ministry, the highest (teaching) must not be consigned to the lowest place, but the lowest must be raised to the highest. Consequently, humility rather than pride marks the excellent dignity of the minister.

5. (206:381–220:640): Since the church resides on the mountain of heroic virtues, teaching the gospel is like climbing up the mountain. As a lookout on the mountaintop, the preacher is both the custodian of doctrinal harmony and the guardian against the enemies, the most dangerous of which are the capital vices. Sacred rhetoric not only heals those good if weak folk who have fallen, but also removes those who are incurable. Since the saving doctrine is not earthly but heavenly, preachers must proceed from the letter of Scripture to its mystical sense, from the carnal to the spiritual, comparing spiritual things with spiritual things. Human wisdom exhibits on the outside some quite great and admirable things but looked at more deeply they turn out to be coal rather than gold. The evangelical philosophy, on the contrary, keeps its more splendid treasure in its inner recesses.

6. (222:641–240:27): Two things help teachers to render hearers teachable *(docilis):* Love makes them listen with pleasure rather than boredom; authority causes them to acknowledge the truth of what is taught. But both, love and authority, must be tempered by a prudence which so accommodates to the hearers' circumstances as to insure their advantage *(commodum)*, their advancement toward piety. While preachers should strive in love to please all, they must nonetheless have Paul's word in mind: "All is allowed, but not all is expedient." Likewise, the preacher's authority must not offend the people's backwardness or customs. Rather, the prudent ecclesiastic will dissemble in order to temper the license of the people. As to remuneration, the teacher's love gives freely and cheerfully; it earns well from everyone, benefits all, but does not ask benefaction from anyone in return. Nevertheless, heroic virtue does not reject the service of human gifts, whether innate or added by education and industry. Rather, natural dispositions are accommodated to the service of love. After all, perfect love makes all things common.

7. (240:28–246:159): Except for a brief admonition concerning faithful hearers, Erasmus' comments on the hearers are virtually all negative. Expecting histrionics from the preachers, the impious crowd *(vulgus)* behaves in the Christian assembly without decorum. Erasmus admonishes the people to listen to the preacher as if they hear Christ.

Conclusion. (246:160–63): The subject of this volume was the dignity, difficulty, purity, fortitude, utility, and reward of the faithful ecclesiastic. The rest will be presented in the next volume.

Book II

Introduction (247:4–252:137):

A heart created new by the generous God hardly needs copious rules for speaking. For it is the sincere disposition of the mind that prompts readiness of speech, an apposite delivery, and decent gestures. "The chief point of (rhetorical) art is to conceal art." Indeed, for certain ancient authors, "rhetoric is nothing else than prudence of speaking." Many of them were most eloquent without knowing art at all. Even so, the arts, taught early and moderately, develop the skilfulness of one's natural disposition. Rules and exercises aid our natural weakness. While practice translates art into experience, precepts enable a more certain and mature faculty of speaking. But precepts must "through frequent use pass over into habit as if into nature." To speak well, then, one must "put little value on art, but only after the faculty of speaking has been developed by the use of art."

I. Grammar

1. (252:138–260:302): Grammar, the foundation of all other disciplines, is "the art of speaking correctly *(emendate)*." It is acquired by reading the most eloquent ancient authors and requires the knowledge of words, of the orderly arrangement of ideas, and of natural things in their variety of species. Moreover, grammar includes history, poetry, and the knowledge of antiquity. History is blind without cosmography and arithmetics.

2. (260:303–262:339): Four things are essential to the faculty of speaking: "nature, art, imitation or example, and use or practice." So powerful is nature that nothing is more important for poetry and rhetoric, for "what is cognate is immediately apprehended." Children are naturally teachable because of their willingness to imitate. But shyness or natural timidity render teaching useless, unless these impediments are overcome by zeal and practice.

3. (262:340–264:415): The three languages (Greek, Latin, and Hebrew) serve to unlock the books of the ancients. They also provide access to the sources of the divine books. Furthermore, expertise in the vernacular is necessary for preaching.

4. (264:416–268:483): Readings from profane authors include Demosthenes, Cicero, Aristotle, Plato, Livy, Virgil, the tragedians, Tacitus, Seneca, and Plutarch; from the ecclesiastical authors, Basil,

Athanasius, Chrysostom, Gregory Nazianzen, and Origen; Tertullian, Hilary, Cyprian, Ambrose, Jerome, Augustine, Pope Gregory, Prudentius, Bernard, Pope Leo, Maximus, and Fulgentius. John Gerson is not very useful, Thomas Aquinas more so for philosophy and argumentation. Scotus and his kind are useful for the cognition of things but not for speaking. Add the more recent preachers. While no book is so bad that it will not yield some profit, the student should seek examples from the best.

II. Rhetoric

1. (268:484–274:594): Selecting some rhetorical precepts insofar as they are suitable for the preacher's office, Erasmus focuses his attention first on the triad of art, artist, and work. "While we admit that the eloquence of the preacher does not rest on art, we recognize that there must be some reason and prudence for speaking, which relies on judgment and counsel." Enough has been said in the first volume about the artist, the preacher. Now it is in place to touch on the duties *(officia)* of speaking, then on the parts of the work *(partes operum)*. The *materia* of rhetoric comes in three *genera:* the *genus forense,* which is remote from the preaching office; the *genus suasorium,* which for the preacher consists of teaching, persuading, exhorting, consoling, counselling, and admonishing; and the *genus encomiasticum,* which concerns doxology and thanksgiving.

2. (274:595–280:723): The *officia* of the preacher are *docere, delectare,* and *flectere.* Teaching is fundamental because it makes for understanding and persuasion. No one is delighted or moved by that which is neither understood nor believed. Delight comes from the *jucunditas* or rather *gratia* of speech. Eloquence is most powerful, however, if it changes *(flectere),* i.e., if it seizes *(rapere)* the affections of the hearers. The singular offices of the orator are *inventio, dispositio, elocutio, memoria,* and *pronuntiatio.*

3. (280:724–470:546): The *partes operis* are *exordium, narratio, divisio, confirmatio, confutatio,* and *conclusio.*

3.1 (280:727–304:362): *Exordium* (or the beginning of a speech) can arise, from Scripture; from history; from parables (narration in the *exordium; adfectus* in narration); from living nature; from present things; from similitude; from transition; from *sententia;* the material of introduction; invocation.

3.2 (304:365–310:524): *Divisio* either announces in a preliminary outline the order of things to come or, in a wider sense, shows the disposition of the work interspersed throughout the parts of speech.

3.2.1 (310:525–312:591): *Inventio partium principalium.* Partition must be distinct, clear, brief, and coherent. As the whole business of inventing the principal parts and arranging the inventory in a proper order is quite difficult, Erasmus touches here only on what the rhetoricians taught about the suasory and laudatory genre and adds what seems to be special about exhortation, consolation, and objurgation. The main point about the *genus suasorium* is to consider the subject matter and objective of persuasion, the audience, and the speaker. While preachers persuade to nothing but honest things, they persuade different people differently.

3.2.1.1 (312:592–316:719): The parts of the *genus suasorium* provide both the division and the propositions of the entire speech. While the Stoics contended that there is but one proposition, *honestum,* others separate utility from honesty. The concept *honestum* includes what in itself is right, beautiful, and decorous.

3.2.1.2 (316:720–328:20): The parts of the *genus laudatorium* (doxology; *bona externa: corpus, patria, parentes; bona animi: virtutes* and by comparison *vitia*) extol God and teach what is conducive to good living.

3.2.1.3 (328:21–332:138): *Exhortatio* is part of the *genus suasorium,* for persuasion teaches through arguments, exhortation stimulates the affections. The foremost parts of exhortation are *laus, expectatio publica, spes victoriae, spes gloriae* vs. *metus ignominiae, magnitudo praemii* vs *horror poenae,* and *commemoratio illustrium.* Exhortation can also be derived from *miseratio, odium, amor, invidia,* and *aemulatio.*

3.2.1.4 (332:139–334:205): The parts of *consolatio* have to do with private and public suffering in persecution, war, pestilence, and famine.

3.2.1.5 (334:206–341:371): *Admonitio* must not be satisfied with arguing against vices but persuade that they are abominations, demonstrate the reasons for correcting evil deeds, and show how much more righteous and pleasant it is to walk in the way of virtue until perfection.

3.2.2 (341:372–344:451): *De statibus sive constitutionibus.* "Status is the essential point of a case or a question on which the speaker focuses everything and to which the hearer especially looks." Used foremost in legal cases, status a) as *status conjecturalis sive inficialis* seeks the truth by inference from a comparison of facts; b) as *status qualitatis sive jurisdicialis* inquires whether a fact was done lawfully; c) as *status finis sive definitivus* seeks by definition to name the fact. The preacher too should focus everything on a *scopus,* for anyone speaking in public must have an intentional goal.

3.2.3 (344:452–356:798): *Inventio partium sive propositionum* draws on the parts and circumstances of the total case. A proposition can serve either as the beginning of an argument, or after the argument as *conclusio* or *collectio (propositio probata).* To invent partition and arrange propositions in the order *(gradus)* of an argument, it is useful to know the *status, loci,* and *circumstantiae* of the case, plus the art of law, philosophy, and theology. The rest comes from natural talent and exercise.

3.3 (356:799–370:106): *Argumentatio sive probatio.* Aristotle found that three things give credence to the speaker: *prudentia, virtus,* and *benevolentia.* It is the task of proof to confirm the argument and to refute the opposite. Proofs are either *artificiales (praejudicia, rumores, tormenta, tabulae, jurisjurandum, testimonia)* or *inartificiales* (*signa, necessaria,* and *probabilia*). Before going into arguments, it must be mentioned that there are certain propositions confessed to such a degree that they do not need proof, such as the essentials of the Christian faith. The *nativa vis ingenii* is very useful for the invention of proof, because the faculty of reasoning comes before the art of dialectic.

3.3.1 (370:107–400:850): *Circumstantiae.* Arguments arise partly from natural disposition, partly from art. But we invent arguments more quickly and easily if we know the rhetorical places from which they are to be derived. Any proof is taken from the circumstances of persons and things. *Circumstantiae personae* include *genus, natio, patria, sexus, aetas, educatio sive disciplina, habitus corporis, fortuna, conditio, animi natura, studia, adfectatio, antedicta,* and *antefacta, commotio, consilium, nomen. Circumstantiae rei* are subdivided into *causa (efficiens, materialis, formalis,* and *finalis)*; *locus; tempus*; *casus; facultas; instrumentum;* and *modus.*

3.3.2 (400:851–424:433): *Loci (topoi). Loci communes* serve to argue both ways, as for instance by amplifying virtues and exaggerating vices. Commonplaces are also used as a base for arguing single causes. Finally, *loci generales* make clear what happens generally to everything and how arguments, partly necessary and partly probable, are derived from single things. The general division of all questions is, "Whether something is, what it is, and of what kind it is." *Definitio* consists of *genus, species,* and *differentia. Divisio* and *partitio* include *exordium, incrementum,* and *summa. Similitudo* (with its subcategories: *fictio, analogia, exemplum,* and *imago*) is not only useful for proof but also lends much light and dignity to oratory. *Dissimilia* include *pugnantia, opposita, contraria, privativa, relativa, contradictoria, repugnantia, consequentia.* The next *loci* are *causae* and *effecta* with *generatio, corruptio,* and *comparatio.*

(424:434–427:489): *Catalogus* repeating the points of argumentation, the circumstances of persons and things, and the *loci.*

(427:490–462:347): The observation of loci is not only valuable for proving by argument in order to persuade but also for teaching the complete knowledge of any subject of art so that the student understands. Erasmus turns now to the subject of teaching and shows how the *loci* from *definitio* to *comparatio* apply to theological subject matter.

(462:348–468:484): *Argumentatio* consists of *propositio, ratio, confirmatio, exornatio,* and *complexio,* or, in the shorter version, of *propositio, ratio,* and *complexio.*

3.4 (468:485–470:546): The *Epilogus* refreshes the hearer's memory, presents the entire cause, and adds more solid arguments. Another kind of peroration is the *conclusio* which appeals to the affections, that is, in the Christian congregation, to piety. The next volume will deal with *amplificatio, orationis jucunditas,* and *vehementia.*

Book III

I. The single offices

1. (LB V 951E–955B): So far Erasmus has covered only one of the orator's five offices, *inventio.* Now he returns to the broader subject and adds what seems to have been omitted. Next to *inventio* comes *elocutio. Dispositio sive ordo,* about which he began to speak when discussing *divisio,* functions in four ways: a) as symmetry and proportion of words *(commoditas)* providing speech not only with perspicuity and rhythmic measure *(modulatio)* but also with sharpness *(acrimonia);* b) as the order of the principal propositions of speech; c) as the order of the individual arguments; d) as the division of the whole speech into *exordium, incrementum,* and *summa.*

2. (955C–956B): If one learns by rote and anxiously depends on loci and images, *memoria* becomes artificial, that is, completely dependent on art, and thus hinders more than aids. The natural talent becomes dull, the ardour of speaking cools off, and the natural power of memory (which is most capable of many things, especially if intelligence, care, practice, and order enhance the felicitous nature of a human being) is stunted.

3. (956B–967A): *Actio sive pronuntiatio* has to do with the moderation of voice, of facial expression, and of the whole body, all of which are to be adapted to the respective subject matter. Also in this regard,

reason and use perfect nature. Therefore, imitate the decorous, avoid the unbecoming, and above all observe what is decent.

II. Virtutes orationis

1. (967A–968E): Now Erasmus returns to those things which he had postponed and shows what makes speech powerful *(vehemens),* delightful *(jucunda),* and abundant *(copiosa). Loci communes* contribute to both the vehemence and the copiousness of speech. Commonplaces are those recurring meanings which, if amplified, help toward persuasion, whether through praise or blame. But more frequently they occur in the demonstrative genre. *Loci* are derived a) from *genera* and *partes* of virtues and vices; b) from meanings drawn from them and enforcing them; c) from common life.

2. (968F–976D): *Ampliftcatio* increases or diminishes either things or words. Amplification of things makes for *adfectus;* amplification of words produces rhythm and measure *(modus):* amplification a) of words; b) through gradual increment; c) through comparison; d) through reasoning *(ratiocinatio);* e) from means *(instrumentum);* f) from occasion, circumstances, and places; g) through *emphasis;* h) through congeries; i) through augmentation and diminution.

3. (976D–987E): *Adfectus* are divided into two kinds, the milder (comic) and the more severe (tragic), with neutral affections residing in the middle. Both kinds of affections are derived from the circumstances of persons and things. The affections can be aroused in three ways: a) through imagination or fantasy, whereby the speaker reproduces the images of things; b) by evidence, whereby the total view of the thing is so presented to the hearer's mind that it seems to be displayed to the eyes rather than spoken; c) through prayerful reading of those scriptural passages that are most conducive to inflaming the heart.

4. (987F–1005E): The *schemata (figurae)* conducive to sharp, powerful, and serious speech *(acrimonia, vehementia, gravitas)* are enumerated along with the figures suitable to delightful, clear, brilliant, pleasant, and charming speech *(jucunditas, perspicuitas, splendor, festivitas, venustas).*

5. (1005E–1008B): *Sententiae* express in appropriate brevity either what one should do in life or what usually happens.

6. (1008B–1011D): Nothing persuades more effectively, presents the subject matter more evidently, moves more potently the affections, and makes speech more dignified, attractive, or pleasant than *metaphora,* if

examples are drawn above all from Scripture, but also from nature. *Similitudo* or *collatio* is an explained metaphor. *Imago* is a species of *similitudo. Similitudo* can also be useful for reasoning *(ratiocinatio),* as for instance to show the absurdity of a heretical position.

7. (1011D–1016F): The quality of similitude changes the *character orationis (jucundus, grandis, acris, mediocris, humilis).* But beyond the three traditional *genera elocutionis (humile, mediocre, grande)* there are others. A section is added here to exemplify the use of *schemata* in a biblical text (Matt 9; Luke 5) to effect *jucunditas, splendor, vehementia, adfectus.*

8. (1016F–1019A): There are other tropes in Scripture, like *hypallage, enallage, heterosis,* and *synecdoche.*

III. Allegory

1. (1019A–1025F): No trope causes more work than allegory. While the exegete must always be careful not to distort the genuine sense of Scripture, there are linguistic idioms that render the plain sense absurd. Therefore, the preacher must look at the interpretation of the Fathers, compare places *(collatio locorum),* consider times and persons, identify the context in Scripture or in various interpretations, and meditate at length in faithful prayer. To twist the text to human affections and impious meanings is to remove the authority of Scripture.

2. (1026A–1033F): To accommodate Scripture appropriately to the subject matter, it is not enough to cull opinions from modern anthologies. Rather, one must return *ad fontes* and elicit the genuine meaning from the scriptural context. The ancient interpreters should be read with discretion and judgment, their authority resting on their proximity to the origin *(vetustas).* Still, the authority of the patristic *consensus* can neither measure up to Scripture itself nor rival the apostles. Therefore, one must dissent from the Fathers if they overallegorize, for the letter is the basis upon which the superstructure of allegory is built.

3. (1033F–1037D): *De ratione allegoriarum.* Metaphor is the fountain of several tropes: *collatio, imago* and *abusio, aenigma, allegoria, proverbium,* and *apologus.* Metaphor is a brief similitude, while similitude or *collatio* is a metaphor unfolded and accommodated to the subject matter. The rhetoricians defined *allegory* simply as a continuous metaphor, whereas in sacred literature and with the doctors of the church the term has received a wider meaning, sometimes standing for *tropus,* sometimes for *typus.* The modern theologians teach a fourfold sense of Scripture:

historicum sive grammaticum, tropologicum, allegoricum, and *anagogicum.* The ancient doctors knew only two senses: grammatical (or literal, or historical) and spiritual (which they variously called tropological, allegorical, or anagogical).

4. (1037D–1051D): Allegorical interpretation. One must neglect neither the literal nor the allegorical and tropological sense in Scripture. Nevertheless, necessity or utility compels us at times to draw back from the historical or literal sense. Even if the truth sometimes resides in the lowest sense and the words neither are absurd nor otherwise run counter to sound doctrine, the letter kills if we keep hanging on to it. The mysteries of celestial philosophy are hidden to impious folk but open to teachable people, whom they encourage, by attracting them pleasantly, to make a more avid effort. For the truth is more delightful if shining through allegories than revealed through simple narration, just as it is more powerfully imprinted in the mind.

5. (1051D–1058F): In explaining Scriptures, speech must be clear of obscurity. The obscurity of Scripture is due not only to the nature of tropes but also to other causes, such as incorrect translation; poor knowledge of antiquity; the use of words with different meanings but similar sounds; the use of the same noun to refer to different things; punctuation; pronunciations; contradiction, untruth, absurdity; and the difficulty of indicating the person in whose name a discourse proceeds.

6. (1058F–1062D): Rules of interpretation. Augustine related the seven rules of Tychonius concerning a) Christ and his mystical body, the church; b) the body of Christ divided in two parts, pious and impious; c) promises and law (letter and spirit; grace and commandment); d) genus and species, or the whole and the part; e) the quantity of time, or numbers; f) recapitulation; g) the devil and his body as one person. Augustine also said that Scripture can be interpreted in four ways: according to history, aetiology, analogy, and allegory. Instead of presenting more rules from ancient and modern authors, however, Erasmus advises, with Augustine, that the most efficacious rule of all is that "we should love sacred letters before we learn, being truly persuaded that there is nothing written in them that is false, trifling, or human-minded, but everything replete with heavenly philosophy and worthy of the Holy Spirit in whatever form it appears, if it is properly understood. With this in mind, then, the whole corpus of Scripture should be attentively read and appropriated by long meditation."

Conclusion (1062D–1072A): Erasmus returns to the question of *judicium* and *concilium,* which are applicable not only in invention but also in all offices of the orator. They adjust the address to the hearer's disposition, power of comprehension, and affections. Judgment determines what cause, person, time, place, and usage require, and sometimes, also, what is decent. Counsel makes the oratory persuasive. So preachers should be circumspect in accommodating to their audience in order to be beneficial to all.

Book IV

1. God and Satan (1071C–1074D): The following *elenchus* will aid those preachers who fail to develop an *index materiarum* for themselves. Two persons (God and Satan) are set up like columns of a building in which everything can be arranged in its proper place. The triune God who speaks to us in Scripture presides as the highest monarch over the celestial, ecclesiastical, and political hierarchies. Satan, by contrast, is the prince of darkness and author of evil whose malice God uses to tempt the elect and to punish the wicked. Turning the Trinity into its opposite, the devil corrupts what is created, incites humanity to sin, returns the redeemed to servitude, and heads a body of befouled members. His highest power is to hurt, his highest craft to destroy, and his highest malice to seduce and turn the order upside down. Where the Spirit binds and holds everything together, Satan breaks up and scatters everything.

2. Law (1074D–1078E): Although the law of God is always the same, it is variously revealed according to the variety of times and persons: the natural law for the created world, the law of Moses for fallen humankind, and the evangelical law for those who are restored and move on to perfection. Right in the beginning, Satan's law counteracted the divine law by the law of the flesh with its attendants, sin and death. Several *loci* arise from the law: on the difference between the old and new law; on the sacraments of both; on the consonance of both and how far the old is abrogated by the new; on the authority of canonical Scripture and how far it extends.

3. Virtues and vices (1078E–1083E): The law engenders the *locus* of the two kinds of sin and two kinds of death. Under the rubric of sin fall all kinds of vices. Opposed to vices are the virtues, the first among which are faith, hope, and love. As heroic virtues they are, respectively, correlated to the general virtues: prudence, fortitude, and justice, whereby temperance becomes a subspecies of justice. The virtues in general are focused on piety as the natural affection toward God, country, parents,

teachers, physicians and clergy. Next, the *officia caritatis* are arranged in stages, with respective *loci* and *contraria* listed in order. The *chorus temperantiae-intemperantiae* is followed by *loci* concerning Christian fortitude, and the entire section ends with the *clausula:* the extreme point of virtues and vices, the end of virtuous life in the glory of Christian death versus the end of vices in eternal despair.

4. In the following *Tituli* (1083E–1087F), Erasmus lists in outline the major headings and sections of the *elenchus*. In the *Syvlva* (1087F-1100C), he makes an (eventually abortive) attempt at amplifying, specifying, and adding to that material. After an admonition to the theologians to excerpt their own commonplaces from Scripture as well as an exhortation to concord, the work comes to an abrupt and, as the author himself admits, incomplete end.

CHAPTER 12

THE REFORMATION PREACHING OF LUTHER AND MELANCHTHON

MARTIN LUTHER: SERMON ON 2 CORINTHIANS 3:4-6

While Luther abandoned the thematic sermon form of the High Middle Ages, he did not revert precisely to the patristic homily. Instead of doing verse-by-verse commentary, he looked for the Sinnmitte *(center of meaning),* Hertzpunkt *(heart point), or* Kern *(kernel) of the passage from which he was preaching (usually a lectionary pericope) and built his* Konzept, *his outline, around that. In the sermon reproduced here, he finds great empathy with Paul's difficulty in dealing with the recalcitrant Christians at Corinth, and thus ends up preaching a sermon about preaching. The translation is taken from* Luther's Works: Vol. 51, Sermons (1), *ed. and trans. John W. Doberstein, (Philadelphia: Muhlenberg, 1959), 221-27. (For a discussion of Luther's method of preaching,* **see Vol. 1, pp. 294-98.**)

Sermon on the Epistle for the Twelfth Sunday after Trinity, (2 Cor. 3:4-6) Preached on the Afternoon of August 27, 1531

This is the Epistle for today and it is our custom to preach on it, but I do not like to preach on this Epistle because it is not for the people who cannot follow it. However, in order not to disturb the order, I shall deal with it briefly.

This was the situation at the time after Paul had preached at Corinth: When he turned his back, other preachers had come in his place, and everything he had planted they rooted out and did much better. But there were also some sincere hearts there, who remained in the doctrine which Paul had given them, though many defected. And yet they were few and therefore the sectarians entered in force, as we read in the First Epistle. This is what happened to Paul, and in the very church where he himself had preached and installed preachers. It grieved him and it was a rotten business, for he did not know what to do. If he kept silent, this would not be good; if he said nothing concerning his office, it would be regrettable; if he were to praise himself, it would not sound well. Meanwhile the godless went on extolling themselves. This is the general meaning of what he outlines in this chapter: he lauds himself but yet does not laud himself and then lashes out and gives the false apostles a slap. In short, the office of preaching is an arduous office, especially when it is like what Paul encountered here. I have often said that, if I could come down with good conscience, I would rather be stretched upon a wheel or carry stones than preach one sermon. For anyone who is in this office will always be plagued; and therefore I have often said that the damned devil and not a good man should be a preacher. But we're stuck with it now. Our Lord God was a better man than we are. And so it was with Jeremiah [Jer. 20:14-18]. If I had known I would not have let myself be drawn into it with twenty-four horses. Ingratitude is our reward; and after that we still have to bother ourselves with the sectarians and give an account to God on the last day. And for this we have let the peasants and the noblemen starve us until we feel like turning in our key and saying, "Go, preach yourselves, in the name of all the devils!"

So Paul here hardly knows what to do. "Do we need, as some do, letters of recommendation to you, or from you? You yourselves are our letter of recommendation" [2 Cor. 3:1-2]. His words are kindly for the sake of the devout, who have the gospel in their hearts and have not been defected, not for those who are evangelical in name but are devils nevertheless. But he says, "Such is the confidence that we have through Christ toward God" [2 Cor. 3:4]. And that we can set down and let stand. If I can't convert the whole crowd, then I'll gain one or two. This is our confidence: when we have preached, it will not have been in vain. If the townsmen, peasants, and the big fellows don't want it, let them leave it; let them go; they will see for themselves that they will regret it. And then there are some who always know better, like the sectarians and our young noblemen, who can handle it better than we can. But when it comes to a showdown, they turn out to be scamps and traitors. The townsmen, the fellows who, when they have read one book are full of the Holy Spirit, are the worst. If I were to follow my own impulse I would say, "Let the damned devil be your preacher!" So I have often thought, but I cannot bring myself to do it. But then confidence returns and we say, let happen what may, we still have our confidence through Christ.

"Not that we are sufficient of ourselves" [2 Cor. 3:5]. We have something else in which we put our confidence and that's the end of it. I cannot boast of anything higher except that I am preaching by God's command and will; it is his will and I know that it is not fruitless. Nevertheless, it is disgusting for me to have to look at the pope, the sectarians, and our own people chewing up the gospel. But we must shut our eyes and look to Him and remember that I did not invent this Word of God and this office. It is God's Word, God's work, his office. There we two [i.e., God and I] are at one in the cause. It didn't grow in my garden. If he that is above is pleased, what can the world do to me? And I lump them all together: the wise, the powerful, and the hypocrites. It is our confidence, no matter how much the world may boast, that God has qualified us to be ministers, and, secondly, that it is not only pleasing to the heart of God but also that we shall not preach in vain and that this ministry will lift to heaven some few who receive the Word. So Paul comforted himself, since he was having the same trouble that we are. All of Asia defected from Paul to the false apostles, as most of Germany now. What should he do? Should he fall into desperation and disputation as to whether God had really sent him? No, he says, "Fall away who will, be wise who will, we have confidence through Christ toward God." But quickly he turns and says, "Not that we are sufficient of ourselves." Before he says, "Such confidence have we," he says, "It has pleased God to call me to the ministry. I have taught the Corinthians rightly and God sent me and qualified me. But they do not consider me qualified. Therefore we have confidence that God has qualified us. If he does so, that's all that matters. If the world does not consider us qualified, so be it!" So Paul lays about him. "Not that we are sufficient of ourselves." As if he were saying: This is what the others, the noblemen, are doing; they qualify themselves, just like my little squires, the dunces who do not even have one little spark of faith and haven't even begun with works. We can't do things right for them; they can do much better, these fellows who know nothing and yet dispute our preaching. And it is true, when they come to make a speech they can talk a lot, but when you examine it by daylight it's nothing but chaff. So they are sufficient of themselves. And Paul says: These godless people, whom God did not send and who are not qualified by God and do not have the Holy Spirit, are self-qualified and what they preach, they think is right. So he gives them a slap. The truth is that no matter how learned a man may be, if he has no sure call and does not rightly teach the Scriptures, he may talk as he will but there is nothing behind it. And the same is true of those who want to judge others; if they understand a single word, then the devil take me!

So there you have two kinds of preachers. First those who qualify themselves and preach whatever they please. But Paul says: Such we do not want to be. We are not sufficient of ourselves, but God has made us sufficient, so that we know what the whole world does not know. So poor Paul is obliged to praise himself and rebuke others, even though it is courteously spoken. They speak as they please. That is politely said but nevertheless it is a rough slap. And this is high praise to say, God has qualified me; nor can I be censured by those who say God does not praise me and has not qualified me. Therefore anybody who wants to be a preacher, and especially one who is going to fight the battle, must learn this. We shall have these two kinds, Mr. Wiseacre and the good preachers, if not here, then outside. If they dared to do it, they would stop my mouth and that of all the learned men here. So it's a rotten office to have to deal with these people, not to speak of having to suffer such physical misery and give an accounting on the last day, that a man would rather be a swineherd. But this is our consolation, I can boast to them: if it pleases God, good enough; if it does not please him, let it fall. I wouldn't risk a hair of my head to uphold my office. But if it pleases God, I'd like to see the fellow who would knock it down.

"Our sufficiency is from God" [2 Cor. 3:5]. What Paul means is that whatever good we do in preaching is done by God; when we preach it is God's work if it has power and accomplishes something among men. Therefore if I am a good preacher who does some good, it isn't necessary for me to boast. It's not my mind, my wisdom, my ability. Otherwise at this hour all of you would be converted and the godless would be damned and all the wiseacres, anti-sacramentalists, sectarians, and Anabaptists who say, "The gospel in Wittenberg is nothing, because it does not make people holy," would be checked. Let Paul give the answer here! "If I were the one who could make people holy, I would begin with myself and make everybody else holy. I do not ascribe this to myself but to God. If my ministry is profitable, I ascribe it to God. If it produces fruit, I do not glory in myself; this is not my work, but the mercy of God, who has used me as his instrument. This the false scholars, wiseacres, and fanatics cannot do." These are real blows, thunder and lightning hurled against the false apostles, who also were boasting that they would make the people holy and who today are saying, "A good beginning has been made but we're going to do better." But the answer to that is that what we have done was done by God. If anybody can do it better, then by God's grace I have the humility to say: If somebody else can do better, we will follow him. There are many who want to do it, but how many are able? I would help to pay him myself, if there were such a person. I know what preaching is.

"Who has qualified us to be ministers of a new covenant, not in a written code but in the Spirit; for the written code kills, but the Spirit gives life" [2 Cor. 3:8]. These are all words of attack and they are all aimed at vile preaching. We know nothing; you know everything, as he says in 1 Cor. 4[:10], "We are fools for Christ's sake, but you are wise in Christ." If I say, I am more learned than you, I am a proud dunce. If I humble myself, then nobody will want to learn from me. Therefore I say, I am utterly nothing, God knows it. But when I accomplish anything through God, I do it not for the sake of the crowd but to commend our office, that is, good luck to you, but we still preach better than you; we preach the New Testament. Here he sets up a mark for them. Emulate me in this! You are preachers and learned men. We know the New Testament and preach it; you preach the Old Testament.

"Not in a written code but in the Spirit." These are Pauline words. You have heard that Paul exalted his office over against those who have put themselves forward and gloried in its fruits over against the sectarians. Now he also glories in the doctrine. And this is the controversy: We preach the Spirit and the New Testament, you the letter and the Old Testament. None of you preach the Spirit and no wiseacre teaches the New Testament; you all preach the letter and the Old Testament, that is, the law. Nobody preaches the New Testament except those whom God has qualified. In all the apostles who taught at that time you can see how they fought against the false apostles who taught the Old Testament. And look at the Anabaptists today. When they rise up they say, We must follow Christ's example, leave wife and child. That has a fine shine on it, but if you examine it you see that this is only preaching about what I should do. Likewise the anti-sacramental fanatics will not admit that there is forgiveness of sins in the sacrament and insist that it is only a work. The pope, too, says the mass is a good work. One who makes himself wise can never preach the New Testament, no matter how he preaches. In short, it is impossible for a sectarian to preach the New Testament. Therefore we can boast that we have not only the ministry and the fruits which proceed from it but also the doctrine; for I know that nobody except us proclaims this doctrine. They do not know what the New Testament is. Even though they talk about it they still run out into juridical legalism. They preach what magistrates and kings should be preaching. But Paul calls all this the "letter" which "kills." All doctrine which does not preach the New Testament, the Spirit, he calls the "letter." Ah, dear Paul, you are a vexing preacher when you hurl back these fellows and say that when they preach long sermons it still is nothing but words in a man's mouth and letters in a book. All their blabbering is like a letter in a book; it produces nothing. He who lacks the New Testament loves not God, believes not, hears and teaches not God's Word, and there is nothing there but what is written in a book. It is letter and remains letter, it produces nothing, and a man remains an angry, envious man, a thief, rascal, backbiter, adulterer. That's what it means to preach the letter, which teaches nothing more than what I should do. Then I and the preacher have nothing but letters and a book has just as many of them as we do. It lies like a dead letter in the heart, but I do not accept it for myself; it is a dead letter in a book. Therefore where the only preaching is, "Do this," it remains only a letter. So Paul is against the false apostles who disparaged and reviled him. He could not please anybody. In short, they preach the letter, but they themselves neither hear nor perform what they preach, they remain without God and with the Spirit. Hence there is no fear, no faith, no obedience to God, no chaste hearts, no humility.

Therefore we preach something better: the Spirit and the New Testament, which is that Jesus Christ has come for your sake and taken your sins upon himself. There you hear, not what you should do, but what God is doing through Christ, which means, of course, that he works faith and bestows the Holy Spirit. This is what it means to preach the New Testament and the Holy Spirit. But nobody who wants to make people good through laws is practicing this preaching. That's Moses' and the hangman's business. Otherwise all people would long since have been good; for I preach daily that you should be good and not steal, but the more you hear it the worse you become; you remain the same rascals you were before. Therefore it remains merely letter. When the hangman comes he can chop off a finger, but the heart remains a rogue. I don't want to talk in subtleties about the law and how it frightens people, but only crassly. We have the confidence to say that we preach rightly, that we are sufficient and the fruit follows, that our doctrine is true, and that our ministry is pleasing to God. If we have these three things, then I who preach and you who hear have enough. If the vulgar crowd departs, what is that to me? I might well be angry on account of ingratitude and the fanatics, but I must let it be, as Paul did. If it does not please the world, it is enough that it pleases God. If it does not produce fruit in all, it is enough that it produces fruit in some. If the doctrine be true, let those who preach falsely go. There I can defend myself against spite and vexation. But that I should wish to stop their mouths and persuade the people not to despise me and to be grateful, this confidence we must not have. God is my Lord, the world is my enemy. The fruit will come and the third[1] will come too. So in the fourth chapter also, Paul comforts himself and his followers, admonishing them not to be offended when it appears that our doctrine is lost, if only it please the One who is above.

MELANCHTHON: THE DIDACTIC GENUS IN *ELEMENTORUM RHETORICES*

A far greater influence on the preaching of Lutherans than the example of the Reformer was the rhetorical writings of his closest disciple, Philip Melanchthon. (For a discussion of this, **see Vol. 1, pp. 298-300.***) Recognizing that none of the* genera dicendi *of classical rhetoric made provision for the biblical interpretation that is so important an element of preaching, Melanchthon invented a fourth genus for the pulpit and for classroom lectures as well, a genus he called the "Didascalic" or "Didactic." In doing so, he reflected Luther's understanding that preaching was teaching doctrine in a way that urged people to accept it and live by it. This genus borrows heavily from dialectic, the method used for investigating philosophical truth. Sermons or lectures were to be based on the* loci *of What is the thing? What are its parts or species? What are its causes? What are its effects? What things are related to it and what things are opposed to it? By asking these questions of the subject at hand, the preacher or teacher can "invent" or discover what should be said in a sermon or lecture on the subject. Melanchthon illustrates this method by asking these questions about virtue, penance, and faith. The translation is taken from Sister Mary Joan La Fontaine, "A Critical Translation of Philip Melanchthon's* Elementorum Rhetorices Libri Duo*" (Ph.D. diss., University of Michigan, 1968), 88-111.*

Generally three kinds of case[2] are listed: 1) Declamatory,[3] which engaged in praise and blame, 2) Deliberative, which is engaged in persuading and dissuading, 3) Judicial, which treats of forensic controversies. I myself recommend adding a fourth kind, and borrow the name for it from the Greek and call it Didactic. This, indeed, is concerned with Dialectics. However, wherever various kinds of things are re(viewed?) it should not be ignored, especially in these days when it is a great use in church matters where it is not so much a matter of platform speaking, but where wise men of dialectics can teach the dogmas of religion so that they are to be understood.

It is, moreover, this Didactic method, rooted as it is in dialectics, which rhetoricians use in defining the state of the case. The laudatory type is based on the Didactic method. For it is not by definition alone, but also by oratorical embellishment, the painting of a picture, so to speak, by which things can be understood more clearly with no experience of life. For example, he who praises the laws and speaks from authority, will define the laws and will amplify the definition.

The Psalm [110], says the master, will rightly be placed in this class, for it praises Christ. And this statement of praise is a certain kind of definition for it praises the person of Christ. It recalls his various prerogatives, it explains that he is the lord who sits at the right hand of God, that is, that he rules with God as an equal; it adds where he has shown himself plainly, namely in Sion, and that he is superior to his enemies. There will be a priest, it says, through whom God will be appeased. And he adds: "This priest will be eternal, not as the priesthood of Leviticus, but a priest who will bless and who will announce the remission of sins." It goes on to describe the supplications of the impious who resist the Lord. And at the end it indicates that even the Lord himself will be subjected to the common afflictions of mankind, but that he will revive from them.

If anyone, in this manner will consider the Psalm to be a description of Christ and will realize that the singular parts referred to are dialectical definitions, he will clearly understand the Psalm, and he will more easily illustrate the sequence of everything through definition and will be able to amplify on it.

But there are many other kinds of method such as this, which it is not necessary to enumerate here. It is easy to determine which method fits each case. The speech of thanks belongs in the category of the Demonstrative, for we are extolling our blessings. Such is [Cicero's] speech *In Behalf of Marcus Marcellus*. Under the Deliberative category come petitions, commendations, imprecations, consultations, objurgations, and many other things which Erasmus examines in *The Art of Writing*.

Knowledge of Classes of Cases

In order that young people might know when they should look for topics of invention, let them remember in the first place that the topics are of no use in discovering the subject or question at issue. In cases of litigation the circumstances furnish the material when the litigant brings his problems to the advocate. For one teaching in the church, a definite subject matter is prescribed in sacred scripture that needs explaining. Various occasions for writing letters give rise to different arguments. So the art is not abandoned nor are the rules for investigating affairs. Rather they offer themselves and even should be pursued when they elude us.

Art is to be thought of as assisting us in explaining the serious, important and obscure matters of public concern rather than indolently pursuing those affairs. Therefore, when the matter is undertaken, there must be thought given at the very outset to which category the affair pertains. There are distinct categories and the principles (places *[topoi/loci]*) are not to be found among the uneducated. Because of this, when I have ascertained the specific kind of case, immediately certain principles (places) come to mind for bringing it to light and for dealing with material that will be useful. So it is useful to understand the particular kind of case because once that is known a person is in a position to perceive the finality[4] of the speech, that is, the principal intent and the main arguments, or as they say, the scope of the speech.

For the chief thing in any speech about any subject is to know the purpose, or in other words, to know what usefulness can be expected from it. For every oration has another purpose besides giving knowledge, namely, a prescription for action. Persuasive orations demand that something be done, such as persuading a man to undertake the war with the Turks. The Psalms are of the deliberative type, which either give principles or console, or condemn and ask that something be done.

But the end of the demonstrative[5] species is knowledge, as when we praise Alexander [the Great] we tell how he manages his affairs wisely, courageously and happily, and thus we teach the listener. Even though examples to be imitated are proposed in the case, yet in this kind of oration we ask for nothing openly from our listeners[6] except that they contemplate and admire the wisdom, the virtue and the happiness of much a man.

So the purpose of the didactic kind of instruction is to produce knowledge in individuals, as for instance when someone teaches what the gospel is, how we can bring it about that God should think and pronounce us righteous, what faith is, such a person must propose this purpose in his teaching, that he may teach his listeners; and even if later the knowledge can be put to use, yet didactic oratory differs from that which tells people how to put teaching into practice.

The Greeks in the very beginning of all their books ask what the purpose is of the work at hand and what is its scope, as they call it. The rhetoricians do the same thing when they determine the kind of case; what is the meaning of the speech and what it calls for. In other words, whether it is concerned merely with knowledge or whether in addition to information it calls for action. So it is necessary to examine the speech carefully and to seriously consider what use we may derive from the speech. Nor is the mind of the simple listener first aroused unless he gives some thought to the purpose of the oration. For this reason I have spoken on this matter at great length that I might indicate these principles are of great value for forming and sharpening judgments.

In addition to this, young people are warned about this lest they sometimes confuse the various kinds of case. Although each affair is to be referred principally to one category, often another type develops in certain instances as in Cicero's oration *Pro Archia* where almost the entire speech is concerned with legal matters. But in proceeding with the case, he leans heavily on the principles of declamation, not about the point in question but about the person of Archias whose praises he sings in order to win a favorable judgment. Demosthenes, too, when trying to convince, relies on the demonstrative type, as when he inveighs against Philip of Macedon.

Concerning the Didactic Kind

If anyone would desire in this matter more lengthy principles, he should return to Dialectics, which science alone spells out the reason for teaching. For Dialectics is, properly speaking, the very art of good teaching. It carries the greatest force and the greatest usefulness. Often men must be taught religion, matters of equity, and other obligations, and without the use of this method things cannot be properly explained. And we ourselves cannot ever learn to properly grasp difficult and complicated material unless we follow this method, which is very easy provided one has little practice in it.

But there are twofold questions also. Some questions are simple. For instance, when it concerns a single word. What is virtue! what is penitence? However, other questions are composite, as when a particular statement is to be either affirmed or denied. For instance: Should a Christian divest himself of property or not!

Simply the principles are these:

What is the thing?

What are its parts or species?

What are its causes?

What are its effects?

What things are related to it

and what things are opposed to it?

These principles (places, topics) should be consulted when we wish to teach men. And minds must be trained in such a way that immediately there will come to mind those principles that will tell them where to look and how to select things from the great store of material and in what order it should be set out. For the places of invention both among the dialecticians and the rhetoricians so much assist the discovery of material, and in its ordering after a great store has been provided by some other technique or from the affairs themselves.

First, there must always be the definition. This question must be asked and determined: what is it? However, we must discuss the terminology, and the significance of the word must be pointed out: for it is generally agreed that there are innumerable verbal disputes and quarrels over terminology. In the beginning then we must have the exact meaning and definition of terms so that there may be no chance for ambiguity.

Certainly in this connection in the disputatious of the theologians the phrasing of sacred literature is deserving of notice, for we employ Hebraic figures of speech and if they are not translated correctly, many errors will creep in as in the case of Pelagius who said that grace was only the result of the known law and doctrine. But Paul long distinguished between grace and law. Paul calls grace reconciliation, that is, remission of sins and the divine acceptance to which it is joined as a gift of the Holy Spirit. But Pelagius shamefully corrupted Paul's teaching.

But because the principles are handed down to us for teaching in our little textbooks of Dialectics, I shall here, for the sake of brevity, give one or two examples.

What is virtue? It is a habit of the will inclining me to be obedient to the judgment of right reason. I examine closely the one usual definition of the philosophers.

What are the parts? Speaking dialectically, we can say that they are defined according to kind and difference. But suppose it is asked: what things exist in the soul, what are their activities, then the species must be determined. For diverse species have diverse habits.

Many kinds *[species]* can be named: piety, justice, fortitude, modesty, etc.

What are the causes of the habits? Simply repeated honest actions. Such actions are the result of right mental judgment with the assent of the will.

What are the effects of the habits? Rewards[7] proposed by God, such as: "Honor your father and mother if you wish to live long upon the earth."

What are connected things? Bodily virtue (a good inclination in one's nature) is connected with virtue, which is a habit.

What is opposed to it? The pretense of virtue, and the openly shameful disregard of virtue, such as the crimes of Nero and of similar people.

So dialectics shows the depths and heights which supply great preponderance of things if you wish to explain completely single propositions.

Another Example

What is penance! First, what does the word itself mean? In the language of the church it is usually described as the turning of the will to true piety.

That is the definition. Penance is contrition and it is also faith by which we believe that our sins are forgiven because of Christ, and this faith leads to a new obedience towards God.

What are the parts (of penance)? True conversion has two parts just as there are two movements of the mind—contrition which is the admission of sin or the subsequent fear and sorrow because of sin.

But the other part is faith which strengthens and consoles the frightened soul when it accepts the remission of sin as a gift through Christ.

And really in this instance there is a third part which is truly an effect of the first, namely, a new obedience.

What are the causes of penance? The causes are as diverse as the motives. Contrition is this: the causes of fears is the law which exposes the sin and impelling the will through the efficacious action of the Holy Spirit through the law. The will assenting and not blocking the Holy Spirit, the individual rejects his sin and is repentant.

The causes of faith are the gospels announcing remission through Christ and the efficacious action of the gospel moving the will to action. The will gives assent and does not block the Holy Spirit.

What are the relationships (allied factors)? Allied to contrition is the virtue that we call the fear of God. And allied to faith is hope and love.

What are opposed to it? Profane security or contempt of the judgment of God, and pretended faith, which is profane security and contempt for the judgment of God, is contrary to faith.

What are the effects of true penitence? New spiritual life, good works, and what I call the effects, all which follow with certainty, within which I include even eternal life.

Another Example

What is faith? First, let me consider the meaning of the word faith. Sometimes faith simply signifies an acknowledgment of the historical story of Christ. But elsewhere in the writings of the prophets and apostles, faith means faithfulness, by which we give assent to the promises of God as in St. Paul to the Romans. For here he openly affirms when speaking about faith that we give assent to a promise. He says: "For through faith is the promise truly made strong."

It is faith therefore by which we give assent to the promise of God that Christ would be a sacrifice (propitiation) for us. This faith embraces two things: the acknowledgment of history and faithfully assenting to a promise to which that history refers.

Now what are the parts? Just as the movement of the eyes cannot be divided into parts, so also neither the movement of the mind or the will can be divided, and yet faith brings together the acknowledgment (of Christ) in both the intellect and will and leads it to accept the proffered blessing, namely, assent to promise.

The kinds of faith can always be determined because faith either concerns itself about the promises of corporal blessings or about the promises of grace and eternal things. However, the promises of corporal things remind us of the other promise which is the principal one. For this reason holy people concerned with the promise of corporal blessings are always concerned with the promise of grace or reconciliation.

What are the causes? The object of faith is mercy promised through Christ, by which God pronounces us just people, not because of the law or our dignity or our good works, but because of Christ who willed to be our Savior. And this mercy is revealed to us through the Word, namely the gospel or the promises, which are clearly revealed in the gospel. I have spoken concerning the object of faith; the instrument of faith that works in us is the Word itself. The efficient cause is the Holy Spirit which is effective through the word and works on the mind and will of man. And the will assents or does not struggle.

The subject in which these things occur is in man's soul itself, in his mind and will.

What are the effects? I call all those things effects which necessarily follow true faith.

Justification follows faith from the covenant of God, that is, reconciliation or the imputation of justice. This could be called the special characteristic of faith or a corollary to faith because it is something that necessarily comes from the covenant of God, and once joined to faith, it shows that we can no longer assent to the promise except by faith. The promised reconciliation comes about, not because of our works or our dignity or our virtues, but because of Christ. And nevertheless it ought to be something we accept as a blessing. We accept it, therefore, by faith. And so justification, or reconciliation, is not the effect of faith, but proper to it or correlative to it. It is even the movement of faith.

The effects can truly be listed as tranquillity and joy of conscience because by faith fear and terror are overcome. Invocation (prayer) and delight follow this effect because we ask for that which we highly esteem. And because I list as effects all things that certainly follow, I include eternal life. Likewise, freedom as well, as all events followed the faith of Ezekiel.

What are the similarities? The hope of expecting freedom in the future, prayer and love.

The things against it? False faith, despair and unholy fear.

When in this fashion all the subject matter is encompassed in the boundaries of the art, comprehension will be more sure. And the individual proofs supply a huge body of matter in explanation. Therfore, this diligence is a great help both in making judgment about obscure matters and in explaining and illustrating them. There is no doubt but that in Plato these numerous places praising the method should commend to us this same practice of reviewing in accordance with these goals the questions we are going to treat.

Notes

1. That is, that my ministry shall please God.
2. *Causa* here refers to *genus dicendi.*
3. That is, epideictic.

4. The final cause, in Aristotelian/Scholastic terminology; the purpose.

5. La Fontaine reads "deliberative" but the Latin is *demonstrativi,* so this is a typographical error.

6. La Fontaine translates this word as "literature," but the Latin is *audientibus.*

7. Latin: *praemia;* La Fontaine reads "commands."

CHAPTER 13

CALVIN AND THE REFORM TRADITION

JOHN CALVIN: SERMON 9 ON JOB 19:26-29

Calvin believed that everything God has to say to human beings is revealed in Scripture and that everything in Scripture is a perfect part of that revelation. Thus preaching seeks to make known the teaching of Scripture about what God has done for human beings and what God wills them to do. Such preaching, through the action of the Holy Spirit, communicates God's word to Christians. The sole purpose of preaching is to present that word and apply it to the lives of the congregation. Preaching consists of explaining what a passage means and then noting its implications for those who hear. And it should be done by course preaching through every verse of every book in the Bible.

The sermon presented here is not the one outlined in **Vol. 1, pp. 315-22,** *because there is no readily accessible translation of that sermon into modern English. Yet this one is on the same book of the Bible, from the same section of the book, and it reflects the same method. This translation is taken from* Sermons from Job by John Calvin, *sel. and trans. Leroy Nixon, intro. Harold Dekker (Grand Rapids, Mich.: Eerdmans,*

1952), 120-35. In order to make the sermon more understandable, I have broken it up into more paragraphs and changed some of Nixon's punctuation. The only words that are not his, however, are a very few that are inserted in brackets to clarify the meaning.

Sermon 9

On Job 19:26-29

From My Flesh I Shall See God[1]

(26) Though after my skin worms have worn this away, from my flesh I shall see God. (27) I, myself, shall contemplate him, my eyes shall see him, and none other; my reins have decayed in my bosom. (28) And you have said, "Wherefore is he persecuted?" And the root of the remark is found in me. (29) Fear the presence of the sword; for the wrath of affliction is with the sword, in order that you may know that there is judgment. [Job 19:26-29[2]]

Recapitulation of Previous Day's Sermon

We saw yesterday the protest Job made of having regard to God and not being at all attached to men. Because those whose interest is confined to this world below do not voluntarily search their consciences to condemn themselves as they ought, and to realize their sins, in order that they may ask God to pardon them, confessing that they have transgressed.

For we see, as soon as we are set on the approval of men, that we ask only to surpass them, whether by truth or by falsehood. This is the cause why we do not properly think of God, and consequently we take no pains to correct our faults, as we ought. Briefly, there is only hypocrisy.

Therefore Job says that he knows that his Redeemer is living, as if he said that he has not pleaded thus far to be thus justified before men, that this was not his purpose. For he knew that he must come before God, and there be judged, and render account of all his life.

Then he adds that God will stand upright at the last day upon the dust, as if he said, "When men will be decayed, as the world must perish, God is permanent. So I shall commit great folly by wishing to excuse myself before men while God condemns me, for those who are now my judges, or who wish to confer this honor—they must perish with me, and God will remain always. So then, it is sufficient for me to surrender myself to him, and to hear that which it will please him to ordain."

Now when he says, "God will stand upright upon the dust," [Job] signifies that [God] is not like men. For we must forfeit everything when we are annihilated, we know that we must return to that from which we came, in corruption, in rottenness. "But God," says he, "cannot forfeit in the manner of men, but he will always be in his condition." Besides, let us note that Job wished to signify that God will pour out the power which is in him upon the dust, that is to say, upon men who are nothing, and who have no power in themselves.

Now this title which he attributed to God implies much, that [God] is his guarantor, and he by whom he is maintained. If God wished, he could surely remain whole, and yet we shall perish. But he wishes to make us partakers of his power, and to make us experience it. So, he stands thus upright upon the dust, he makes the dust to completely revive, and thereupon he restores it. For without this, in vain he would be called both "Redeemer" and "Guarantor."

Let us note well that Job wished to express that God does not only keep His power enclosed in his essence, but that it is poured out upon men. This is a good doctrine for us. For in the first place we are admonished what vanity it is to wish only to please men and to be approved by them. What do we gain? For everything here below must pass away. Let us learn, then, to have our eyes fixed on God, in order that he may own us, and that we may be able to be approved by him. This is where we must apply all our study.

However, in order not to be attached to this world, in order not to be wrapped up in the hypocrisy which is by nature too deeply rooted in us, let us know that God [is] our guarantee. That is to say that it belongs to him alone to maintain the integrity of men, when they will have walked in pure conscience before him. That he will be their judge once for all, and he will stand upright upon the dust; and although all that we see around us may be frail and worthless, God is not that way, his condition is much higher. And not only for himself, but in order to put all creatures back in their condition when they shall have expired.

And it is an inestimable consolation for believers when they are seen to be oppressed by slander in this world and, although they have tried to walk uprightly, [the slanderers] never stop annoying them and biting them falsely. Then they can commit themselves to God and call upon him for their guarantee, they lean upon the certainty that God will be standing when men will be annihilated.

Well, those who today presume to condemn us and to speak against us, must fall down, and things will surely be reversed, for God will then be our Redeemer. Men today by their temerity usurp the power of God, they undertake what is not lawful for them, but it must be that God will show in the end his position, both that he may be exalted and that we may know that it belongs to him to maintain us. This is what we ought to keep in mind whenever anyone speaks against us falsely: both that we shall have good testimony before God, and that it will be sufficient that he approves us, although we may be rejected by all the world.

Verses 26 and 27

We come to what Job says. He says, that worms—for although the word may not be expressed, yet it is clearly seen that he intends all vermin and corruption—that worms, after they have eaten the skin, will nibble away and wear away what is left. But though he hopes to see God, and to see him, he says, "from my flesh," that is to say, to be restored.

"Yes, I shall see him, and no other, although my reins have decayed within me." That is to say, all my power is dissolved and abolished. Here is an affirmation worthy of being noted, when Job declares that he will have his attention fixed on God, and no other, indeed, although he may be entirely consumed. As if he said that the hope that he has in God he will not measure according to what he can see, but that when nothing appears, yet he will not cease to look to God.

How so? If a man finds himself as it were forsaken by God, that he perceives only all manner of despair, that death threatens him from all sides, even that it swallows him up, and yet nevertheless he perseveres. He is constant in the faith, to say, "So, I shall call upon my God, and I shall still experience his power. Only his power can give me strength, and that will happen, even when it seems that I shall be lost." Here is a man who surmounts things present. He does not show then the faith and the hope that he has in God because he can see and comprehend by his natural senses, but he passes beyond the world. As it is said, we ought to hope beyond hope, and hope is of things hidden.

Now we see the intention of Job. It is true that he does not speak here explicitly and simply of the resurrection. Yet these words cannot be expounded unless it is recognized that Job wished to attribute to God a power which is not seen today in the common order of nature. It is as if he said that God wishes to be known by us not only while he does us good, preserves, and nourishes us. But when he apparently fails us and we see only death before us, we must be resolved that our Lord will not cease to be our guarantee, and that, being his own, we shall be maintained through his protection.

But in order to profit better by this passage, let us weigh well what Job says. "Although what remains here," he says, "may be worn away after my skin, yet I shall see my God." This is not believing in God only because he causes the earth to produce corn and wine, as we see many brutish persons who have no taste or feeling that there is a God in heaven unless he feeds them and fills their bellies. When they are asked, "Who is God?" they answer, "He is the one who nourishes us." It is true that we surely must understand the goodness and the power of our God in all the benefits which he bestows upon us, but we must not stop there. For, as I have already said, our faith must rise above all that can be seen in this world.

And so, let us not say, "I believe in God, because he sustains me, because he gives me health, because he nourishes me." But let us say, "I believe in God, since already he has given me some taste of his goodness and of his power when he cares for this body which is only corruption. In that I see that he declares himself Father, in that I subsist by the power of his Spirit.

"But I believe in him alone, since he calls me to heaven, since he did not create me like a bull or an ass to live here some space of time, but he has formed me in his image in order that I may hope in his kingdom to be partaker of the glory of his Son. I believe that daily he invites me there, in order that I may not doubt that when my body shall be cast into the sepulcher, that it will be there, as it were, annihilated, nevertheless it will be restored at the last day. And that meanwhile my soul shall be in safekeeping and secure, when after death God will have me in his protection, and that even then I shall contemplate better than I do now the life which has been acquired for us through the blood of our Lord Jesus Christ."

This, then, is what ought to be our creed in order to be well ruled. Now when we shall be thus well disposed, we shall be able to say with Job, "Well, it is true that I see that my body is passing away into decadence. If there is some vigor, it is decreasing day by day, and I contemplate death without going to seek it ten leagues away. For I can see so little but infirmity in my flesh, that it is already a message of death. Yet I shall see my God." And if we can speak thus when we see that our power declines and vanishes little by little, if it pleases God to afflict us in such wise that we are, as it were, half rotted, thus was Job. For he says, "My skin is eaten and consumed." He was, as it were, a corpse, and nevertheless he protests, "So, I shall not cease to behold my God." Let us not cease to hope in God according to the example of Job.

This, then, is how the greatness of the afflictions that God will send us will not be to astonish us, provided that we are taught to recognize him as he is toward us: namely, to consider well to what end he has created us and maintains us in this world.

Besides, when Job says that he will see his Redeemer from his flesh, he intends (as we have already said) that he will be restored in a new state, his skin having been so eaten. For he says that even his bones will be consumed and that nothing will remain whole. And then he adds, "From my flesh I shall see God." And how will he see him from his flesh? That is to say, "I shall be restored as I was previously, and I shall yet see my God." And so he confesses that God will be powerful enough to raise him up, though he has entirely consumed him and plunged him into the depths. This is the condition for which we ought to hope in God: it is that when he will have cast us into the sepulcher, we may know that he extends his hand to withdraw us from it.

Let us not say, then, "I hope in God, because I see that he assists me and he fails me in nothing." But when God fails us, that he is, as it were, far away from us, let us say with Job, "I shall see him from my flesh. I am now nothing, it seems that I am a shadow, that my life is quickly vanishing. Yet my God will declare himself so powerful toward me that I shall see him."

So Job spoke thus from the time when there was not yet great doctrine, when possibly the Law was not written. But let us suppose it was written, the prophets were not yet. There was only Moses, for the prophets mention Job as a man from ancient time.[3] So, then, having only a little spark of light, he was so strengthened in his afflictions, and not only when he saw a species of death, but when it seemed that God had given him a constitution like a monster among men—a terrible and frightful thing—yet he could say, "So is it that I shall see my God."

What excuse will there be today, when God declares the Resurrection to us so exactly and so explicitly and he gives us such beautiful promises of it? And even considered that we see the mirror and the substance of it in our Lord Jesus Christ, that he was raised in order to show us that we must not doubt that we are at once partakers of this immortal glory. If then, after such confirmations, we cannot have the knowledge that was in Job, must it not be imputed to our ingratitude? For if we could receive the promises of God in true faith, would they not have enough power to make us surmount all the temptations which thus rule over us.

So then, let us note well this passage in order to be able to say also with St. Paul, "For if this hut, which is our body, goes away (for by a "hut" he means something made of leaves, some hovel that amounts to nothing), we have a building which is prepared, much better and more excellent, in heaven. If this exterior man (that is to say, all that which is of the present life and which appeared) is annihilated, yet God wishes to renew us, and to make us already somehow to contemplate our resurrection, when we see our body thus failing" (2 Cor. 5:1). As also Saint Paul in the other passage reminds us of the seed which is cast into the ground, saying that it cannot germinate to have a live root and to bear fruit unless it is first changed into rottenness (1 Cor. 15:36).

Do we see, then, that death begins to rule over us? Let us note that God wishes to give us true life: namely, the heavenly life which was acquired for us through the precious blood of his Son. Now without this we must be conquered by the least temptation of the world, for, as I have already said, all the miseries that we have to suffer are so many messages of death. Now, seeing death and supposing that we shall be consumed by it, must we not despair entirely? There is, then, no other means to comfort us in our afflictions except this doctrine: it is that when all that which is in us will be consumed, we shall not cease to see our God, indeed, to see him from our flesh.

And then it is said, "My eyes will contemplate him, and none other." Job adds this, following the proposition that he had held, namely, "Since God has given me the certainty that he will restore me to power, I shall commit myself entirely to him. I must no longer be bewildered, nor be distracted, this way, or that way, for I must commit myself to him alone." "My eyes," then, "will contemplate him, and none other." Here is still a beautiful doctrine. What he said not long ago, namely, that he will see God from his flesh, refers to the experience when God will stand him as it were upon his feet. What he says this time is spoken from another consideration, namely, from a consideration of hope.

For God is regarded by us in two manners: (1) we regard him when he shows himself to be Father and Savior by experience and when he gives us a noteworthy experience of it. There is my God who will have withdrawn me from such a sickness that it will be like a resurrection; it is a testimony that he has put his hand upon me to help me. I contemplate him then, and I contemplate him by experience. Now, while I am sick, though there is no more hope, I do not cease to contemplate God, for I put my confidence in him. Afterwards, I await in patience the issue which he wishes to give me, and I do not doubt that, though he may withdraw me from the world, I am his own.

(2) There is still another manner of contemplating God. Job, then, said that he will contemplate God by experience when he will be restored to his condition. He adds in the second place that he will not cease to contemplate him, though he may be completely crushed by evils. "My eyes," he says, "will be fastened on him, I do not wish to turn them away."

Now here we see the nature of faith: namely, to so reflect on God that it does not go astray, that it has no such distractions as we are accustomed to having. I pray you, what is the cause why we cannot rest ourselves in God as it would be required? It is because we separate the office of God and all his virtue into so many pieces and bits that there is almost nothing left of him. We shall well say that it is God to whom it belongs to sustain us. However, we do not cease to traipse high and low, before and behind, to seek the means of our life, not as being given by God and proceeding from him, but we attribute to them even the power of God, and we make as it were idols of them.

That is how we can regard God with pleasure and yet cannot also have rest or contentment in him. Let us note well, then, the word which Job uses. It is that his eyes will contemplate God, and none other—as if he said, "I will cling to this, I shall no longer be so agitated as men are, but I shall commit myself entirely to my God by saying, 'It is thou, Lord, indeed thou alone from whom I hold my life, and when I shall decay now, thou wilt restore me as thou hast promised.'"

Now let us always make the comparison between Job and us, that if Job, not having such a testimony of the goodness of God, not having a doctrine one one-hundredth as familiar as we have, nevertheless said that he would contemplate God—and we, shall we be excused when we shall have gone astray this way and that way? Indeed, after our Lord Jesus Christ presents himself to us, in whom dwells all fullness of divine glory, and all the power of the Holy Spirit is shown in him when he is raised from the dead? And it is not even necessary for us to extend our view very far to contemplate him, for the gospel is a good mirror, where we see him face to face. Since it is so (as I have mentioned) let us be advised not to be guilty of such ingratitude that we may not have condescended to look at him who presented himself to us so meekly. This, in summary is what we have to note from this passage.

Job adds further, "Although my reins may be decayed within me," that is to say, "though there may no longer be power or rigor in me." In summary (following the proposition that he had already maintained) he shows that he does not look to God because God has treated him gently, because God has granted him all his wishes, because he is preserved from afflictions, but it is entirely the reverse. "Although," he says, "I am in such anguish, though it seems that God is beating down upon me, though there is no longer any vigor in me, yet I shall contemplate my God with my eyes, and I shall cling to him alone, and I know that I shall yet see him as my Redeemer and Guarantor, after he will have thus consumed me."

Verse 28

Now he says in conclusion to his friends, "You have said, 'Why is he persecuted?' (or 'Why shall we persecute him?') For the root of the case (or of the proposition) is found in me." This passage is a little obscure because the word can be taken in two ways: "Why is he persecuted?" or, "Why shall we persecute him?" If we take it "Why is he persecuted?" it is that the friends of Job are astonished because God had treated him so harshly, and yet they conclude that they must say that he is a man entirely reprobate. If it is translated "How shall we persecute him?" it will be that they have come out of deliberate malice to find fault and to bite at him. But although there is diversity as to the words, yet the sense comes out the same.

Let us look at the doctrine that we have to gather from it, for it is the principal thing, even the whole thing. Job, then, reproaches his friends that they have judged poorly of his affliction. And why so? For from the very first they rushed there, saying: "Oh, he must be a wicked man! If he had walked in good and pure conscience, he would not be thus afflicted." Now on the contrary, Job says that the root of the proposition is found in him. It is true that this word sometimes means "thing" and sometimes "word," but Job here signifies that he has a good and firm foundation, and that when he will have been properly sounded, it will be found that his case is not such as the others had falsely estimated it.

Let us look now to what purpose this tends, and what profit we can receive from it. When Job proposes to his friends that they have said, "Why is he persecuted?" he shows that it is cruelty in men to look for the sins of another as soon as they see someone beaten by the rods of God, saying, "This man must he wicked. Let us then peck him to death." For this is the end where we must begin. It is true (as was said more fully before) that in all the stripes and corrections that God sends, we must always contemplate his judgment upon the sins of men, but it is to condemn us. We must not be judges of another by sparing ourselves; let us begin, let us begin with ourselves. We see, then, the usefulness of this doctrine: namely, that if a man is oppressed by evils, we should not be so hasty to condemn him, and indeed we should not be inclined on that account to find crimes in him. But rather we should look to God, who shows himself judge both of us and of him, and who constrains us to recognize that we must have pity and compassion for him who endures, and that we must do it willingly, although we may know his faults. But we should be advised rather to bring him some medicine that he may get well.

Let us guard against putting the plow before the oxen, that is, against making judgment before having understood the case, as we are accustomed to do. Already it has been said oftentimes, that God will not afflict men always for the same purpose. Sometimes he will punish their sins, sometimes he will wish to prove their patience, or there will be some other reason.

Then, let us not be too hasty or bold to judge before we have known all the facts, for we see what happened to the friends of Job. As soon as they see him afflicted they say, "He must be wicked." But blessed is the man who judges prudently upon the afflicted, as it is said in the Psalm (106:3). Was not David oppressed by the hand of God as harshly as ever any man was? Yet [God] says, "I have found David my servant according to my heart, I have anointed him with the oil of joy."[4] Behold God who takes David as it were into his bosom, and yet we see how he is treated. If we are bold to judge it, we shall condemn both David and Abraham, and all the holy patriarchs. And will not this judgment come back to the dishonor of God? Certainly! So then, let us be sober and modest when we see that our neighbors are afflicted, and let us recognize the hand of God, in order that it may not happen to us as it happened to the friends of Job.

Now he says especially that the "root of the case is found in him" (Job 19:28*b*), or "root of the proposition," or "effect and substance." By this he indicates that we must inquire before we judge. Now in fact, each one will surely confess that if we made this mistake willingly, it would be foolish presumption and arrogance in us. And this proverb is quite common, "From a foolish judge, a brief sentence." Yet let us not hazard such a guess without having sounded and examined what the thing is. Let us note well, then, that we must come to the root before passing any judgment. And let us not judge suddenly, fearing to appear ignorant, for this is what compels men to be too hasty: it is that they are ashamed not to be keen enough to judge immediately. For if I do not give my account of it, I shall not be esteemed. Now God mocks this ambition. Let us contain ourselves, then, in soberness and modesty until God has declared to us why he punishes one rather than another; let us not get ahead of God. It is true, when we shall have inquired, when we shall have come to the root, we shall then be able to judge freely. For the judgment will not be from us, it will be taken from God, since it will be founded upon his Word, and it will be governed by his Holy Spirit. But above all we must come to the root which is here mentioned.

Verse 29

And then Job says, "Fear the presence of the sword, for the indignation of iniquity [or of affliction] of the sword is near, in order that you may know that there is judgment." This proposition is obscure enough, because the words are chopped. But in summary Job wished to say, "Fear before the sword," as if he said, "You speak here as in darkness, you make sport like those who have nothing else to do, and who are at their leisure." Such people will be able to dispute, as there are no people who make war better than those who are far from the front lines. They will direct the battle, they will besiege cities, they kill, they pillage, they sack. It is marvelous! But when they will have chatted well, and drunk in the marketplace, they need only hear the sound of a drum, [and] they are scattered. Job, then, reproaches his friends that they have disputed about his case as it were at leisure, but that they must apprehend the judgment of God and fear the sword, as if already he had showed himself upon them.

And then he says "the indignation of iniquity." This word denotes the cruelty for which he had already previously blamed them. "The indignation," then, as if to say, "You are here hot with anger against me, indeed, to afflict me." For the Hebrew word can mean "iniquity" and also "affliction." But Job here declares that his friends have not come to him as having some compassion for his trouble. Rather that they have come to him hot with anger, indeed, to afflict him and to molest him further.

And what does he mean by this? "The sword," he says. That is to say, "God will not leave such a rage unpunished, for although I have offended you, yet you must be more humane toward me. But by condemning me without cause you show only greater severity toward me. The sword of God, then, must be displayed upon you, indeed, in order that you may recognize that there is judgment."

Here is a noteworthy and very useful sentence, for Job in thus rebuking his friends is as it were a prophet of God who addresses himself to all in common and in general. He warns us, then, that we have to fear the sword of God, if we are so malicious as to judge evil of the good, and if we are so inhumane as to torment and afflict those who are already miserable enough. It is said, "Cursed are you who say evil is good, and good is evil" (Isa. 5:20), and yet we see that this vice has reigned from all time, and still reigns today.

Those who are led by their passions—what scruple will they have against defying God openly? They know well enough, "Here is a case good in itself, and yet I shall go against it." "Here is a man who asks to serve God, I shall hinder him." "Here is something that could be to the edification of the church which could serve the community of men, to the public welfare, and I shall ruin it completely." For there will be seen even those who are seated on the throne of justice who will be there like devils incarnate to defy God, to upset all equity and uprightness, and who will be full of corruption and excess. When we see this, what can we say, except that we have come to the top of the heap of every iniquity? So it is with others. It is seen that there is neither great nor small who does not defy God.

So then, must we not say that the devil possesses men, when they are so given to upsetting the good, to maintaining the evil, even since this horrible curse has been pronounced by the prophet against all those who will call evil good and good evil? And this is what Job here claimed, saying, "Fear the sword." To whom does he speak? To those who are inflated against God and against all uprightness. For against whom do we wage war except against God when we wish to change the light into darkness, when we wish to oppress a good cause? Here is God who is assailed by us.

So then, we have good occasion to fear, even when we shall afflict a single poor man, and when we shall molest him anew. For here is God who is opposed to it. He says that he does not wish to bear these acts of violence, these extortions. When someone wishes to commit some outrage and injury to poor people, he goes before, and shows that he is their protector. When, then, we are tempted to offend and to molest the poor and those who are already in affliction, ought not these words to make us tremble when they come back into our memory, that the sword of God is unsheathed against all those who wish to afflict further those who are already too much afflicted?

Here, then, is God who defies all those who are given to injuries, acts of violence and extortion, or such things, and he summons them to fire and blood. And so, when it is a matter of some poor afflicted person, and [one] who will have no support, let us fear to tread upon him, and to molest him, and to put him to shame. And why so? For here is God who pronounces that he has his sword unsheathed against all those who will have thus tormented the good and the innocent.

This is what Job says in conclusion, that "the indignation of iniquity will bring down the sword." As if he said, "It is true that men, when now they burst forth to molest the good, it seems to them that they will remain unpunished, they fear neither God nor his judgment. Indeed, but the sword [he says] is ready for them." Let us not, then, be so presumptuous as to promise ourselves that the hand of God cannot approach us, when we shall have so tormented poor people, who asked only to be peaceable, and who have not offended us in anything. When we shall come to sting them, and when we shall act toward them in sourness, God will be to us a hundred thousand times yet more sour. And we shall experience him in such manner when we shall have come before him as before our judge.

Now if this were well pondered, it is certain that things would be better in the world than they are. We see princes who through their ambition will go to sack the country, burn down houses, destroy cities, steal, ravish, pillage and ruin everything, so that it is horrible. And why? All this is lawful to them under the title of war. But they ought first to consider whether they are constrained to stir up such troubles and to wage war thus through all the world. But since it is only their ambition which inflames them to it, and since so many evils must be produced by this rage by which they are moved—do they think that the sword is not ready for them? And then those who serve them in their cupidity, and who nourish them in it—do they also suppose that God ought not to unsheathe his sword upon them? But let us consider not only those, for we see those who are neither kings nor princes, and who will not have the power to upset the country and to go there by force, who yet will not cease to have as much malice or more than the others. For they will be like little scorpions which shoot out their poison through the tail when they can do no other damage and we see that each one asks only to sting and to molest.

Must not, then, what is here said be experienced, namely, that the sword is unsheathed against all such people? And that is why Job says especially, "in order that you may know." It is true that these were not blockheads, that they knew that there was a God in heaven who was judge of the world. They were learned and well-trained people, as we have seen by their statements, and, as we shall yet see, pleasing to God. And why is it, then, that Job says to them, "in order that you may know"? It is that when men are blinded by their evil afflictions they do not recognize God. That it seems to them that, when they will have put up a veil of partition, God ought no longer to see a drop, and that he ought not to punish them as they have deserved.

Let us contemplate, then, the sword, although now we do not see it with the eye. That is to say, although God does not yet show us such signs that he wishes to afflict us to make us recognize that he is judge of the world. And let us show us that he does not wish to use excessive strictness toward us, indeed, when we shall not have been strict toward our neighbors. And besides, let us know that it is not yet enough to abstain from every evil, but we must be advised to help all those who are in affliction. For when a man will be able to protest that he has abstained from every wrong and injury, still he will not be acquitted before God on that account. And why not? For he ought to aid and help those who had need of his help. Now if those who have abstained from evil are not absolved before God, but are held as guilty, I pray you, what shall we say of those who invent only malice day and night, who consider, "How shall I be able to sting now this one, then that one?" When there will be such wicked people who will sharpen themselves thus on deliberate purpose to destroy their neighbors, surely must not the sword of God be all the more sharpened against them?

Let us consider, then, ourselves, and not only let us be ready to relieve those whom we see to be afflicted, but also, since there are so many miseries and calamities throughout all the world, let us have pity and compassion for those who are far away, and let our view be extended that far (as charity ought to embrace all mankind) and let us pray to God that it may please him to pity those who are so anguished. And that, after having chastised them with his rods, he may lead them back to himself, and cause that all this may be converted to their salvation, so that, instead of our now having occasion to groan, we may then be able to rejoice all together and to bless his name with one accord.

Bidding to Prayer

Now we shall bow in humble reverence before the face of our God.

Notes

1. Sermon 72 in *Calvini Opera, Corpus Reformatorum,* vol. 34, pp. 127-39.
2. Nixon's translation of Calvin's translation of the text. At various points in the sermon Calvin proposes alternative translations of particular passages.
3. Ezekiel 14:14-20.
4. Not an actual quotation, but a summary of Psalm 89:20; 1 Chronicles 17:19; and Psalm 45:7.

CHAPTER 14

THE PREACHING OF CATHOLIC REFORM

A FRENCH BAROQUE SERMON ON CHARLES BORREMEO

A sermon for the feast day of St. Charles Borromeo, Cardinal Archbishop of Milan, is an appropriate choice as an example of Catholic Reform preaching, since no one did more than he to encourage the implementation of the Council of Trent's decrees concerning the duty to preach. He was indefatigable in his own proclamation of the Word, he encouraged his clergy to preach and issued an instruction to them on the subject, he commissioned others to write textbooks on homiletics, and he imported excellent preachers into his see to serve as examples for others.

The sermon was preached by Jean-Pierre Camus, one of the most innovative homileticians of the French Baroque period. (For a discussion of French Baroque preaching, **see Vol. 1, pp. 343-45.***) This was the time when the ideals of Trent and Borromeo were being implemented in France. One effect of the Renaissance in France, as in the rest of Europe, was a recovery of classical rhetoric, which restored it to its former place as the basis of education. A side effect of that was to heighten the* *medieval enthusiasm for homiletical reference books containing illustrations, anecdotes, and analogies for all occasions. A style of preaching was developed called "thesaurus" preaching, which was so named because of its dependence on these compendia. The style, however, was laborious, because those who practiced it felt obliged to spell out in detail all the connections between their illustration and what it was supposed to illustrate.*

To avoid such tedium, Camus created a sermon form that was a "nonchalant linking together of strings of analogies, allusions, anecdotes, scriptural figures, and quotations" combined to form a poetic prose.[1] *Thus these figures furnish both the argument and the ornamentation of his sermon. This style of preaching is designated as "catenary" from this linking of images. While Camus knew that his published sermons, like others of the time, would be plundered by others in the construction of their own, he felt that his supplied an outline that borrowers would have to fill in for themselves.*

The main justification for this sort of preaching, however, was the realization that most of the biblical, theological, liturgical, and spiritual content of sermons at the time was familiar to those who heard it from their deep formation in the faith. The challenge was in enabling them to experience anew what had become familiar and trite. Camus's way of dealing with that challenge was to surprise his hearers with unexpected ways of stating the familiar faith. What may appear to modern readers as an affected toying with the gospel was, at the time it appeared, a sincere and sophisticated strategy to assist people in, as a recent book title has it, "meeting Jesus again for the first time."

The French text of this sermon, which was delivered in the Church of Saint Jacques, Paris in 1618, appears in Peter Bayley, Selected Sermons of the French Baroque (1600–1650) *(New York and London: Garland, 1983). I am deeply indebted to Professor Waring McCrady, who translated it for this volume. I am also grateful to Professor Bayley for helpful advice.*

Jean-Pierre Camus: Third Panegyric Commemorating Saint Charles Borromeo

Translated by James Waring de Bernières McCrady

Introductory thoughts on fire and light[2]

His lamps are entirely fire and flames (Song of Songs 8:6)

> The lamps of my Spouse, says the Divine Beloved, are lamps made entirely of fire and flame, of heat and light.

Unique and admirable lamps!—such as only Divine Love could produce! For if you, my listeners, will consider the hanging lamps that are usually found in houses of worship—whether they be of crystal, of silver, of gold, or of any other metal—, you will see that their actual light is in fact not bright but consists of an ordinary flame burning at the tip of a wick. The wick is floated in oil, the oil held in some container, the container steadied by circular devices, and these circles suspended by a few chains, so that in the final result the actual flame is the smallest aspect of the whole apparatus.

Think of that great lampstand, one of the treasures of the Tabernacle, that [in the Old Testament] shone night and day before the Mercy Seat. Though it was wrought in solid gold and had seven branches sculpted with lilies and olive motifs, and though the seven containers at the ends of these branches were kept filled with aromatic oil, yet can you not see that the parts actually emitting the light, however bright it was, were in themselves tiny in comparison to the whole of that magnificent work?

How different are the lamps of Divine Love!—for in their case the chains, the circular fixtures, the oil containers, the wicks, all these parts are themselves ablaze with light, brilliant and clear, and with fire in all its warmth. In like manner do the holy saints who shine with the flame of God carry in their hearts a veritable brazier, wherein Love, like the Phoenix reduced to ashes, may be kindled anew and grow.

And such were the lamps of love burning in that veritable tabernacle of the Holy Spirit, the great Saint Charles Borromeo, whose memory we venerate today. He was like a lamp in Israel, both burning and shining, equally as filled with light as with warmth, with warmth as with light. In fact, was it not to honor the extraordinary breadth of his Charity that the citizens of Milan (as I myself had occasion to witness a few years ago in the cathedral of that beautiful city on the very day of his feast) suspended in the midst of their metropolitan church a large and magnificent lamp ingeniously constructed to resemble a Cardinal's hat, in order to witness that the Charity radiating from their blessed bishop—for whom Charity was his crown and the pinnacle of his perfection—was a love both burning with heat and shining with light?

Certainly the red which dyes the hats of the illustrious Cardinals of the Holy Roman Church serves to recall to those who wear them that it is their duty to surpass others as much in Charity as they do in ecclesiastical dignity. Theirs must be a Charity willing to shed life's blood in order to sustain the Church of which they are the supporting columns. But our blessed Cardinal Archbishop, not satisfied by the double purple of his office, demonstrated that the intensity of his Charity was as much more lively and dazzling as the splendid red of genuine fire surpasses the brilliance of the cardinal's scarlet, even were such vestment material (like that of the Temple curtains) to be twice submerged in the dye.

On the Isle of Chios the ancients used to collect a mineral substance called Asbestos which when set on fire would shine as brightly as any flaming torch but without consuming itself or burning out. The inhabitants of the island divided up their store of asbestos, placing one half of it in their Temple of Diana and the other half on the peaks of their lighthouses to guide their sailing vessels in the dark of night. Now Saint Charles was obviously a living stone in the structure of God's House, but we may say that he was veritably one of those asbestos stones, in that having once taken on the holy ardor of Charity as poured into his heart by the Holy Spirit, he not only never allowed it to be extinguished but continually cast forth its beams of light and communicated its warmth into the dark and cold places of his times. His light did not falter in the darkness of that corrupt age but rather shone like a guiding star in the midst of a storm. Nor was the light of his lamp felt only in his own diocese, like the effect of a gossiper who reaches an audience only within his provincial sway. On the contrary, his voice could be heard from far outside the diocese of Milan, like a beacon guiding the despondent into the port of salvation and harbor of grace which is the holy Church. He was the very illumination of his time, a mirror of reflection for the guidance of prelates, a vessel of solid gold adorned with precious stones, an exemplar of piety, even of perfection itself. Ah, dear friends, would that I could give forth such light and such ardor!—I, who am forever deficient in warmth and lacking in beams of clarity!

> O Eternal Father, Father of all light, even light without shadow, you who are the very essence of flame and the all-consuming fire—you who make your presence known in burning bushes, in radiant mountains, in fiery furnaces—enlighten my darkness, fill with your warmth the coldness of my nature!—but let me be not like the sun which while heating all else stands too distant to know its own warmth, not like a torch giving light to others while remaining in darkness to itself, not like a lute which can fill all ears with harmony yet cannot hear itself! Grant rather that the words of fire which you speak to others through my mouth may equally bring enlightenment and warmth to my inmost being, that as a torchbearer bringing light to others I may likewise enlighten myself. May true warmth be kindled in me by the fervor of this meditation.

O Son Divine, O Admirable Jesus, who came to bring new fire to the earth, who fanned so devotedly the feeble fires of human hearts that you never ceased to sigh in your labors even unto death on the Cross, impart to me the merest spark of your sacred fire that I may kindle the hearts of all before whom I speak today.

O Holy Spirit, living source of light and of love, of fire and of Charity, grant that your spiritual anointing may pour life into this discourse on fire and on Charity. Shine forth your light upon our senses and spread your love throughout our hearts.

And you, our Mother in holy affection,
lead us now by your sacred direction.
Ave!

Exordium, Part I: Apology for the Insufficiency of the Preacher

So here I am, my beloved Parish of Saint Jacques, having climbed for a third time into your pulpit to sound praises before you concerning the great Saint Charles Borromeo, patron of this famous Brotherhood of Charity under whose banner so many devout people of this great town have united to fight for the Faith. My mind from the start has been divided along two paths of thinking which result in two difficulties. The first is to wipe clean with the sweeping sponge of oblivion, the ideas and concepts which I have spread before you at other times on this subject, in order not to fall into lamentable repetitions. The second is to gather what new thoughts I can bring you, in order to say what I have not said before, and not to say again what has already been said.

But even had it pleased God, dear friends, that the lowliness of my mind should have been better proportioned to the extent of the materials at hand, still my fears of lacking appropriate materials would be easily overcome by the voluminous richness of our subject.

On the other hand, just as a large and abundant spring can release little water by means of one narrow streambed (not that it lacks the will, but that the way is so restricted), and as the splendor of the Sun can enter an enclosed space only in accordance with the size of the window or the crack in the wall, so does this ample subject find itself constrained and restricted by the limits of my capacity.

I would gladly request of this modern-day Moses that he should cover his face, for my eyes are too feeble to stand the light that shines from it in such bright rays.

Consider also that no matter how great a fire may be, if you have only a modest candle to light from it you can bear away with you only as big a flame as your taper can handle.

Consider again that whether you climb to the top of a tower or to the peak of a mountain, no matter how high you go, you will never be able to see more than half of the Heavens, for the horizon will necessarily rob the other hemisphere from your sight. If you would see the whole of the sky, your travel must encompass the full circle of the globe.

Elevated subjects are far too rich and complex to be easily digested by little minds. For these latter, as they said in ancient times, it must suffice to try and to dare, for at least to have desired great things is to be not quite so little. Our would-be wings call us to fly, but our weight holds us down.

Select along the coast whatever high precipice, whatever rocky peak you will, but though you survey all that can be seen from there, you will never be able to view the ocean in its entirety.

Count if you can the stars in the heavens, said God to Abraham. And I say the same of the perfections of the saint whom we wish to honor today: however much we may cover, we will fall greatly short of encompassing his worth.

Nonetheless, we should not succumb to discouragement, we should not be overwhelmed by the extent of what there is to say—we must dare to do what we can. Even though our subject far surpasses our praise, even though we are incapable of worthily lifting him up, if we do what it is in our power to do, we will have done our duty.

So now, over this vast ocean before our eyes, let us imitate the gentle dove of Noah which, though it found no land to stand on, did return to the ark bearing a single sprig from an olive tree. From the ocean of virtues that encompass the worthiness of our Saintly subject, unable to select them all I have decided to hold before you the one denoted by the olive branch, and that is holy Charity—the single virtue that within its unity contains the universality of all the others.

So,

May words lift high in saintly fame,
Through this discourse of piety,
The holy and life-giving flame
Of Charles's perfect Charity.

Exordium, Part II: Why Charity Is a Most Appropriate Subject

Now just as [the traditional element of] fire not only surpasses in rank the other classical elements [of earth, air, and water] so that it can even enclose them within its sphere, likewise in discussing Borromeo's virtue of Charity we will fully include and hold within it all his other virtues.

I feel obligated to speak to you of the Charity of Saint Charles for two reasons; first because his very name invites me to it; and second, because of the name of our organization, that is, the Confraternity of the Charity of Saint Charles.

Please notice, dear fellow-members, that the name "Charles" even in our own language seems to derive its etymology from the word "Charity" and recalls to us both light and warmth. And what sort of Charity can it be, poured into our hearts by the Holy Spirit, if not a luminous warmth, a warm luminosity given from above by the Father of light and all virtues? And this same name in the Latin language resounds as well as in our own with the clarity of light, or the light of Charity. The suggestion is so salient that our great prelate bears by his name alone a motto for all good pastors and Apostolic leaders, who are at once "the light of the world" by their doctrine and "the salt of the earth," salt whose sharp heat denotes piety and the good and exemplary life.

Thus when I consider the name of our organization, how better could I teach the members of the Charity of Saint Charles than by reviewing the Charity of their dear patron saint? It is a love in which they are not merely brought together but are literally "made One" in Jesus Christ our Lord.

Therefore, I am convinced that the very voice from heaven which in the Apocalypse struck the ear of the Bishop of Laodicea is even now touching mine. By this voice I counsel you to pile up treasures of pure gold if you would seek to attain wealth. And what is this pure gold if it is not the Charity of the Beloved whose head is pure gold in the Song of Songs?

Now if gold is the standard of value not only for other metals but essentially for anything that can be bought, likewise Charity, the bond of perfection, encompasses entirely the value of all worthy acts.

Charity is like the wellspring of Eden that flows out into various rivers, and the microcosm of our interior life is watered by it. It casts prudence over judgment, justice over the will, restraint over irascible appetite, and temperance over concupiscence.

But however many sowings we may cast over a new-plowed field, if the sweet warmth of the sun caressing the ground at planting time does not suckle the seeds enclosed in the maternal breast of the earth, our intended plants will never grow. They will not even germinate. They will produce absolutely nothing. And so it is with such virtues as are exercised outside of grace, that grace which can only be found in Charity, they cannot produce a single fruit unto eternal life if they are deprived of this vital warmth.

According to Saint Paul's teaching, if all other virtues are taken together but have not Charity, they amount to nothing, yet Charity alone suffices in default of all the others. It was this virtue that brought the Magdalene to the peak of perfection and drew her out of the depths of perdition.

With Charity, all vices can be conquered, all desires of the soul made subservient, just as with the jawbone of an ass Samson brought down the Philistines and then found in that bone a spring to quench his tormenting thirst.

One could even apply to Charity the very words that Solomon applied to Wisdom, that with it come all other good things.

Charity is a true honey, containing in itself the juice and quintessence of the flowers of all virtues.

He who loves, says Scripture, accomplishes all the Law.

And as a single gust of wind can carry a boat further on the sea than could a hundred strokes of the oars, so likewise can Charity alone move us further towards perfection than could the practice of all the other virtues—which without love are without life.

Exordium, Part III: How This Sermon Is to Be Constructed

And now, in order to speak clearly of this Charity which is confected in the very winepresses of the Beloved, I thought I should begin by showing that Charity is a virtue not only useful but essential to those whom God calls to the high orders of his Church. Then I will focus more specifically on the love that God poured into Saint Charles, reviewing some traits of Charity not only in his life but also in the welcome circumstances that brought about his blessed death and carried him into eternal felicity.

I. CHARITY, AN ESSENTIAL FOR GOD'S LEADERS

When God wishes to attain some effective and powerful end, he very efficiently applies the necessary means. Now if he has a particularly strong desire to bring about the salvation of certain souls, he customarily effects in those whom he calls to lead them—whom he has specifically commissioned to guide them—an overpowering sense of Charity. Thus armed, the chosen leaders can better take on the guidance of such souls to perfection and into union with God himself, who is Love. He sets on guard over the earthly Paradise an angel with a sword of fire, symbol of the pastors of the Church (which is the true Eden of the Beloved Spouse) who must guard the souls assigned to them with an ardent and fiery zeal.

Once Moses is chosen to lead his people, appreciate how he espouses the cause of the Israelites and protects them from the wrath of God! Can you picture him killing the Egyptian and hiding him under the sand? Imagine him massacring the idolaters!—so much was he fired by zeal both for God and for his neighbor. And ultimately you see him luminous and dazzling from his Charity.

Likewise when Elias is sent to be a prophet in Israel, he in turn becomes all fire, zealous for the Lord of Hosts. By prayer he brings down fire from Heaven, and ultimately it is in a fiery chariot that he is carried off by his Charity.

Ezekiel speaks repeatedly of wheels of fire.

Isaiah declares that the fire of heaven has entered into his very bones.

The angels by which God governs the world are called fiery servants.

And when the moment comes for sending forth the Apostles to preach the gospel to the ends of the earth, their commission is sealed with tongues of fire. Read their accomplishments in the book of Acts and you will see that they are carried on wings of zeal—zeal flaming with the fire of Charity. They are like soaring fireworks, leaping into action when ignited by the spark of holy fire.

This same fire transported Saint Paul through many travels and caused his concern for all the churches to press relentlessly in his heart. This same zeal that eventually caused him willingly to become anathema to his family, this zeal which—when at first misguided—had formerly moved him to defend the traditions of his forefathers, was by his conversion made legitimate and knowledgeably re-aligned, so that it effected marvelous results to the glory of God.

Consider also that it was because of his great Charity that Saint Peter received from the Savior his vicarage on earth, his role as universal shepherd of Christ's flock; and to bring life into the labors of this pastoral charge, at the transfiguration Christ showed himself to Peter on Mount Tabor, luminous and ardent like a mirror of Charity, an experience of perfection.

So also did the Savior show himself to Saint John [of Patmos] in his Revelation, appearing in the midst of candlesticks, surrounded by stars, his eyes gleaming like flame, and his feet like molten metal, as though burned in a furnace—the very hieroglyph of Charity and of the exemplary life that should shine and burn in the hearts of all who are called to important ecclesiastical office. Such prelates, like stars in the firmament of the Church, should show forth their light both by continuous shining and by occasional lightning flashes, showering good influence over their flocks by word and by deed.

And who could express what a furnace of Charity was in the breast of Saint Martin, who was seen many times environed with sacred flame, as was also the heart of Blessed Philip Neri whose breast ultimately burst from the vehemence of his love. And how beyond measure was the zeal of Saint Ambrose, who displayed already at his birth a ray of light on his forehead and a line of honey across his lips, witnessing thereby that the splendor of truth was to flow from those lips, smoother than honey and nectar!

Now note that this very Ambrose was the great predecessor of and a perpetual example to our own Saint Charles, a model so closely followed by the latter that if in some aspects the original was superior to the copy, one can also say truthfully that in others the copy surpassed the original. Thus when Saint Charles came into the world, as we have mentioned on an earlier occasion, in order to presage the fire and flame that his lamp was to give, there appeared a great light throughout the entire room where his mother was giving birth. Now consider the untrustworthy astrologers who deduce so many uncertain and misleading conclusions from the stars, interpreting merely from the position of the sky at the moment of a birth. If they can conjecture from so little the adventures which are to menace men throughout their days, how much more confidently should we expect marvels of greatness and accomplishment in the case of Saint Charles!—since not only his person but the very place where he was born (even while darkness reigned throughout our hemisphere, the birth being at three o'clock in the morning) became resplendent with light! O admirable horoscope, presided over by such a supernatural ascendant!

Thus it was Charity, that warmth divine spread by the Holy Spirit in our hearts, which was the guide of his life, the torch which illumined his actions, and the sacred escort of his mortal pilgrimage. During his lifetime he appeared among men with the characteristic quality attributed by scripture to the great forerunner of the Messiah, ardent in times of contemplation, fiery in times of action,—a lamp burning and shining for others; fire warming all his inmost being while glowing through his exterior works, because he remained ever ardent in his sincerity of heart and conscience, and brilliant in his good example. So outstanding was this effect that one could call his light resplendent among the shadows of his century, reflecting to us the song of the divine psalmist who proclaimed a light among the shadows, arisen for those upright in heart.

If Saint Francis of Paula, founder of the Order of Minims, was held to rank high in Charity because he was seen several times during his life surrounded by sacred flames, what less should we expect from our Saint Charles, who even before he had accomplished any act of goodness was distinguished by God—like a new Jacob—through the singular blessing of the miracle accompanying his birth?

We know that when the grass called Aproxis catches fire it cannot be extinguished by water, or by vinegar, or by any other means save by the total consumption of the plant. Likewise, from the moment sacred flame first kindled itself in the heart of our saint, neither the waters of abundant prosperity, nor the vinegar of adversity, nor any other turn of fate, could quench its fervor. It was this fire that nourished the perpetual activity which kept indefatigable Charles's service to God, this fire that caused him ceaselessly to seek whatever subject he could employ for the advancement of the glory of his great Master or for the salvation of his neighbor. We know that fires here on earth will die out if they are not nourished by a continual feeding of wood or some other combustible fuel, but there exist heavenly fires which feed themselves, whose burning is their very center and identity. Thus does the Charity of saintliness maintain itself without other support than fixing on some desirable sovereign good, and loving the sovereign good so clearly and deliciously sighted. Nonetheless, in this mortal life, even such divine fire lasts in human breasts only so long as good actions give occasion for it to fuel itself and be nourished.

Where love is, says an ancient church father, works will be found, and where there are no works there is no love. Tirelessly, true Charity puts gentle pressure on the heart, and the heart is so stimulated in response that it will produce some act in testimony to express to the Beloved how agreeable are the tasks endured for his sake. Just as Rebecca said to her husband, "Give me children, lest I die of boredom and ordinary irritations," so also does delight, when it is true, say to the heart loving truly and with unfeigned Charity, "Do something in favor of the one you love, lest I perish and remain no longer within you."

Certainly, when we read in the life of our saint the many great deeds which he performed in the service of the One who is served by all, we have difficulty in appreciating how in the short time he had on this earth[3] he could have accomplished so many remarkable things.

Fire, through its naturally outreaching flames, holds always to its own center. So also it was with the excellent Charity of our Holy Archbishop. For his heart, even amidst the travels imposed on him by the requirements of the Universal Church, served like the needle in a compass of true delight, pointing steadfastly toward his beloved official residence as the only place of real repose—the dwelling that he had chosen as his normal habitation. It was there that he blessed widows and gave them solace; there that he distributed most willingly his alms for the poor; when seated there he could pour out grace from his Horn of Plenty; and when residing there he became most effectively a beautiful lamp set in the house of God.

Though the sun, while running through its twelve houses, visits with its eye the entirety of the earth, nonetheless there are certain places on which it seems to smile most favorably—there are particular flowers for which it seems to have more concern than for others. So also could our saint say, with the great Apostle, that he carried concerns for all churches, being himself one of the columns of the Roman Church, mother and matrix of all other churches spread throughout the universe, and yet his special solicitude remained for the church in Milan, his own particular vine, to the cultivating of which he was committed in singular vigilance.

II. THE CHARITY THAT GOD POURED INTO SAINT CHARLES

Let us now consider the special features of Saint Charles's work in his own territory, which so appreciated having in him such a wonderful family father. Who does not know how many thorns and wild bushes of ignorance and of evil living were tangled into this vine at the time our good Laborer was sent to trim it? The riches and abundance of the famous town of Milan had rendered it all too like another city which Scripture shows us to have been execrable, so full of debauchery and disorder that it was in total chaos from one end to the other. From lowliest citizen to most mighty, there was no health and even less sanctity. Corruption ruled, with offices left unfilled and deprivation resulting for all sorts and conditions. Parts of the diocese that were healthy as to their faith were so infected by bad behavior that one could only expect their near ruin. Into other areas there had slipped the infection of error through the neglect of the clergy; it was a true case of abomination and desolation. In emphasizing such deplorable qualities I do not mean to find fault with the flourishing city-state of Milan but rather to recall the words of a certain prophet, that if God, by inspiration, did not scatter the seeds of good works into our hearts, those who might seem the most virtuous could actually end up worse off than the inhabitants of Sodom. I stress the excessive degree of the sickness only in order to bring out the skill and excellence of the Doctor, and also so that the Diocese of Milan might render unceasing thanks to God for having sent them such an individual—a person capable of helping, a person who could trouble their waters as did the angel at Bethesda, and who knew how to throw into the pool those who were afflicted by the paralysis of inveterate sins.

And so, to this town came Saint Charles, appearing like Saint Elmo's fire amidst the storm and tempest which was menacing so many souls with eternal shipwreck.

He was that man divinely raised up to oppose God's own just wrath.

He was a clear and shining lamp in a shadowy place.

He was a full moon in the night of the shadows of death, in the darkness of sin itself. And just as stars are never so clear or so bright as when the night itself is blackest, so is the brilliance of love brought out when it is pure amidst so much impurity and just amidst so much injustice. Saint Gregory reminds us that it is not so laudable an achievement to be good among good people, but that it is a signal perfection to be good in an evil society. Such was Abraham among the Canaanites, or Job in the land of Uz, or Lot in his town made so abysmal by excess.

God, in his mysterious ways, having provided a wife, Jacob, upright and full of justice, did not cease to love Leah though she was repulsive and ugly. Nor did Moses refuse the dark Egyptian woman, or Hosea his lawless pagan, when God provided them for marriage. And our holy prelate did not refuse to take onto his shoulders the burden of the Church of Milan, though he saw and knew the heaviness of the assignment, and though he sensed how long he would have to struggle in that place for the name of Jesus Christ. He took on himself this totally deformed wife in order to reform her; he accepted her unruly that he might rule her; disorderly that he might give her better order; disfigured that he might restore the luster of her first beauty and re-establish the worthy traits by which Saint Ambrose had once made her admirable. As dirty as she was, Borromeo never tired of seeing her beauty and remained inviolably faithful to her unto death. He behaved towards her as did the prudent laborer, who seeing an abandoned field that produced only brush and thistles, set about cleaning and pruning in hopes that once properly cleared of roots and cultivated it would as easily produce good grain as it had useless weeds. Recognizing (since he was originally from the area) a natural goodness in the souls of the Milanese, he believed—nor was he confounded in this attempt or frustrated in this hope—that a docility called divine by the Apostle could render these people susceptible to a better example than that of their dissoluteness.

Oh who could express the ardent love that moved him so passionately for his dear city of Milan!—for his diocese, for his province, to which he was attached like a planet, orbiting constantly but never straying from its appointed sphere. No hen ever devoted more attention to her little ones or did so with greater fervor; no gentle mother ever cherished her child with more tenderness, than did this good Prelate in his dedication to those committed to his charge. He was ever vigilant, ever concerned to give account of their souls, knowing that some day God would hold him responsible for the blood of any lost sheep. And in consequence of this intense concern it would be impossible to number the visitations he made, almost as though his whole life became one perpetual visit. God had placed him like a sentinel over Jerusalem, and there he made his continual round, never ceasing to cry out day and night, challenging, begging, conjuring his people in patience and in doctrine.

Oh who could worthily describe the difficult and dangerous visits he made into the most forbidding and dangerous of the Gridone mountains, where making his way along frightful precipices, his hands and feet depending on crampons of iron, he faced death at every step! Yet this he did because he was so desirous of leading his flock into eternal life. When people would ask him what took him into such wild places, he answered with the unaffected gentleness of little Joseph commanded by his father Jacob to find his siblings, "Alas, I seek my brethren." Such exemplary Charity so vividly touched the hearts of some of these mountain people—who had been perverted by heresy—that they were gently constrained to return to the breast of the Church they had so miserably abandoned, the church outside of which there is no salvation.

If in describing these difficult visits we were to add the other qualities that accompanied them, we would never finish. So thorough and exacting was Saint Charles, it was like searching Jerusalem by lamplight. He would examine the very slightest details, not content merely to bring back the lost sheep, as did the Shepherd in the parable, but sweeping every corner to search for the lost coin, knowing that great faithfulness is measured by its tiniest diligence.

And not only was he scrupulous in his visitation of the various locales, but he was also diligent and active in maintaining personal contacts. Should one of his fellow bishops, whether nearby or more distantly in his province, fall sick with some illness menacing death—no matter the season at hand or the threats of the weather—, abruptly would he depart to go and render succor in the final passage of this brother and help him in a holy death, knowing well that Christian dedication, true and sincere, is especially witnessed in times of present necessities.

Again, who does not know of the happy visit that he made to Vercelli in order to be present to that valorous prince, the Most Serene Charles Emanuel, duke of Savoy, who, though in early youth at the time, was yet threatened by the extremes of a disease from which no other release could be expected than death? And who likewise knows not that in recalling him virtually from the tomb by his prayers, he resuscitated the hopes of all Savoy, hitherto swaddled in the dread of losing this singular child, born of one of the most excellent pearls of our own France?

Add to his visitations his pilgrimages, so austere and so laborious that, not content with making them on foot, he often laid upon himself some further burden in order to heap pain upon pain, mortification upon mortification, suffering upon suffering. At one time, for instance, though already besieged by fatigues and infirmities, he set himself the object of bathing with his own tears the Holy Shroud, already dipped in the blood of the Savior and preserved at that time in the capital city of Savoy; which pious act to perform, he proposed traversing on foot the forbidding mount Cenis, the upper reaches whereof were covered in perpetual snow as though by a woolen cloak, and strewn besides by mists and fogs like clouds of ashes; and then to follow the steep and rugged paths of the Maurienne to reach his goal. [And this he would have done,] had not the sovereign of those States thwarted the penitential proposal by transporting the precious Relic in question, the great treasure of his house, into his own piedmontese capital of Turin.

We have not time to detail Saint Charles's frequent devotions at the shrine of the hallowed but difficult mountain of Varallo, where upon arrival he would veritably consume himself in prayers and mortification until, like a new phoenix on the highest summits of a blessed Araby, he would emerge blazing and transformed.

It is from such wellsprings of the fire of his Charity that sprang the astonishing activity by which he assembled so many Synods and celebrated so many Provincial Councils; suffice it to say that it was by his persistence that the Council of Trent was brought to an end and closed, and that it was by his diligence that the decisions of that Ecumenical Council were first received and practiced in his diocese, and from there throughout his province, and then throughout Italy and ultimately in more distant regions.

This same Charity, which "seeketh not her own" but rather the interests of Jesus Christ, caused him betimes to deplete himself, as would the Spouse of the Song of Songs, pressed by the ardors of the Sun of his soul, the Crucified Spouse. Who without marveling could peruse in the accounts of his life the quantity of material goods which he expended on pious foundations? How many colleges, how many seminaries did he found, from which, as from so many seeded nurseries, have arisen young plants that in good time formed orchards for the Church, bearing their fruit in due season? How many monastic establishments for both one sex and the other, did he not establish and endow, which at once are lamps of continuous fire before God, appeasing his wrath through prayer, and so many fortresses for maintaining the spiritual state of the Church against her adversaries? Theatines, Barnabites, Jesuits, and Capuchins acknowledge him as their founder not only in Milan but in divers places both in his diocese and throughout his province as well; not to mention that holy congregation of the Ursulines, now so universally established, of which he was the institutor.

Nor did he stop with his concern for setting apart so many good souls; for knowing yet (and in accordance with the doctrine of Saint Bernard) that the shepherd of souls must look out not only for those who are whole but even more for those who are sick, his solicitude reached out further to the rescue of fallen women, for whom he established the pious House of Mercy, a place where modern Magdalenes may gently weep at the feet of Jesus Christ, having no other weapons than their tears to overcome the rigors of his Justice and to provoke an outpouring of Grace where guilt had formerly overflowed.

How many hazards did he risk and to what perils did he not expose himself, in order to rescue from error and vice—which are the very jaws of ravishing wolves and the yawning gates of hell—the souls which had been taken in? And how many times might erring Sinners have succeeded in their schemes to bring him down, had not God been his one sure defense? The attempt on his life when he reformed the Penitents might have passed under the shroud to the tomb of Oblivion, had not its cruel trigger-man attained fame as a new Herostratus. But how joyously did Saint Charles drink in that other horrible affront, imposed on him during a visit to the Church of La Scala, giving thanks like a true Apostle at having occasion to suffer before everyone such ignominy for the Love of Jesus Christ. Though it is true that the memorable sentence from the Holy See made full reparation, that did not in any way diminish the joy sensed by our Saint at having patiently endured such a palpable outrage.

Again, it was his selfsame Charity which rendered him indefatigable in the office of Evangelist, where he often joined his voice with that of the Apostle to say "Woe is unto me if I preach not!" and with that of the Prophet to say "Woe is me if I do not speak: for it is to those of my condition that is addressed the commandment, 'Cry without ceasing, raise up your voice as though you were sounding the trumpet, and lay out before my people their prevarications that they may correct themselves'"—

to fulfill this function his voice was always ready, like that of Saint Paul in addressing the Corinthians.

But know also that if his mouth was readily opened by the communication of spiritual riches and by the dispensation of the treasures of the divine knowledge which lay within him, no less was his purse readily open for the distribution of temporal riches; for this he believed to be true Economics: that he was the householder and not the proprietor, that the goods which he possessed were in fact the patrimony of the poor; and that any ecclesiastical worthy possessed of a just and reasonable soul should do likewise, imitating by such acts the wise Patriarch Joseph, faithful dispenser of the grain of his master, the King of Egypt. How often did Saint Charles find himself reduced to material poverty, after having sold everything, down to the very straw of his bed, to solace the needs of the poor, giving away even his personal houserobe and reserving to himself only such garments as were necessary for him to appear in public. Thus arrayed, he could say with the holy Spouse, that the Sun had stripped him (as it is worded not in the Vulgate version but in another one equally true to the original text).

Consider now that the more the Sun rises above the horizon, the more effectively it heats. Just so it was that the more Charity arose in this Apostolic man, the more ardent did that virtue become. Who, for instance, could worthily assess the outpourings of St. Charles's Christian concern when the Plague appeared and for the space of two whole years incessantly afflicted his diocese? How many high feats of spiritual warfare did he accomplish during that time, visiting in person the sick and the dying, braving a thousand hazards which can more easily be admired than expressed? On as many occasions did he, during that time, take both his life and his dignity and offer them up to the glory of the Savior and to the well being and salvation of his flock. Could one possibly find a greater act of Charity than that of exposing his life to so manifest a peril for the sake of those he loved? He might justly have applied to himself the words of the Great Apostle, "What ailing person is there with whom I do not suffer?—and what sufferer for whom I am not filled with compassion?"

III. THE DEATH OF SAINT CHARLES

The salamander may well live in the midst of the fire, but it also dies there. Saint Charles lived in Charity, and it was his also to die in Charity. And he died not merely in Charity but, we may piously believe, as a result of Charity. In the case of a saint who had so much loved throughout his life, of what else could he have died but of Love? And such a death is holy and desirable above all others—since that is how the Savior died, since that is how his holy Mother died, and since the Angels themselves would willingly desire to be mortals in order so to die. It is certain that anyone who would be saved must die in Charity, for whoever is found without Love at the end of this earthly life will be sent by a temporal death into an eternal one. As it is written, the one who is without love lives in death, and by contrast, those who love will be transported from death into life.

In my opinion, it would not be sufficient to say that Saint Charles Borromeo, gifted with so many extraordinary perfections, should have gone to a better life by an ordinary passage common to all such as are introduced into the dwelling-place of the redeemed. Nay, let us say rather, for the greater glory of the Good God who received him into the plenitude of the Saints, that just as his predecessor Saint Ambrose died in an assault of divine Dilection (which so seized his heart upon his receiving the blessed Viaticum that—his natural being already so debilitated by age and by sickness as not to be able to support this supernatural impetuosity—his soul was sweetly constrained to depart from the dwelling-place of his body and thence to proceed to the sojourn that was the dear object of all his desire), in a like fashion was our Saint Charles so tenderly moved by the effects of a depiction of the Savior's agony in the Garden of Gesthsemene—upon which he continually held his eyes fixed until his last breath—that it is entirely probable his soul, liquefied and exhaled from his body like vapor, mixed itself into that precious liqueur of his Master's tears seen flowing in great streams to the ground, and that thus he died—not merely *in* a state of Love, but *through* that state of Love.

O Death, worthy crown of so beautiful a life, excellent closure of so rare a running of days! Oh how desirable is the death of the Just, and how much to be desired—for souls in hope of salvation—an ending such as theirs!

> Oh how precious and dear is the death of his Saints
>
> In the sight of the Lord, so gentle and so good!

May I take the liberty of closing all this discourse on the Charity of Saint Charles—speaking as I am to those who have given not only their names but also their hearts to this holy Confraternity which carries the title of Charity—may I be permitted, I say, to close with these shining words from the great Saint Augustine (that burning light of the Holy Church):

O fire eternally burning yet never extinguished, Charity eternal and God to me (for God is Charity), set me on fire that I may give myself totally to the One who has entirely given himself to me, and thus let me die for the Love, in the Love, and by means of the Love of the One who died on the Cross for the Love and by the Love of my Love. Amen.[4]

Notes

1. Bayley, *French Pulpit Oratory*, 85.
2. These boldfaced section titles are not in the original French.
3. Forty-six years (1538–84).
4. Augustine, *Confessions*, 10:40.

CHAPTER 15

UPHEAVAL IN BRITAIN

HUGH LATIMER: SIXTH SERMON BEFORE EDWARD VI

The first great preacher of the Reformation in England was Hugh Latimer, who taught at Cambridge at the time. His fortunes went up and down with royal favor, being made a bishop under Henry VIII and then sent to the Tower of London by him. He was popular under Edward and burned under Mary. His sermons still show some qualities of medieval sermons, including the quotation of scripture from the Latin Vulgate even though English Bibles had been required in every parish church from 1539. For the most part, though, he did expository preaching that followed the text, except for his frequent digressions. He was a great popular preacher, unique in his style, which included broad humor, stories about himself and others, and vivid language. Yet his content was always serious. He was devoted to the Reformation cause in its English Erasmian tradition, and he had a strong social conscience.

The sermon included here shows his high doctrine of Scripture and his sense that sermons must be biblically based (**see Vol. 1, pp. 360-63**)*. It also reveals his belief in the religious significance of work. While his sermons first appeared in print shortly after his death, a convenient collection that includes the following sermon is* Selected Sermons of Hugh

Latimer, *ed. Allan G. Chester, Folger Documents of Tudor and Stuart Civilization (Charlottesville: University Press of Virginia for the Folger Shakespeare Library, 1968).*

THE SIXTH SERMON OF MASTER HUGH LATIMER, WHICH HE PREACHED BEFORE THE KING'S MAJESTY WITHIN HIS GRACE'S PALACE AT WESTMINSTER THE TWELFTH DAY OF APRIL (1549)

Quaecumque scripta sunt ad nostram doctrinam scripta sunt. (Romans 15:4)

"All things that are written, are written to be our doctrine."

What doctrine is written for us in the eighth chapter of the first book of the Kings I did partly show unto you, most honorable audience, this day sennight,[1] of that good man, father Samuel, that good judge, how good a man he was, what helpers and coadjutors he took unto him to have his office well discharged. I told you also of the wickedness of his sons, how they took bribes and lived wickedly, and by that means brought both their father and themselves to deposition; and how the people did offend God in asking a king in father Samuel's time; and how father Samuel was put from his office, who deserved it not. I opened to you also how father Samuel clears himself, that he knew not the faults of his sons. He was no bearer with his sons; he was sorry for it when he heard it, but he would not bear with them in their wickedness. *Filii mei vobiscum sunt,* "My sons are with you" (I Sam. 12:2), saith he, "do with them according to their deserts. I will not maintain them nor bear with them." After that, he clears himself at the King's feet, that the people had nothing to burden him withal, neither money nor money worth.

In treating of that part I chanced to show you what I heard of a man that was slain, and I hear say it was not well taken. Forsooth, I intend not to impair any man's estimation or honesty, and they that enforce it to that enforce it not to my meaning. I said I heard but of such a thing, and took occasion by that that I heard to speak against the thing that I knew to be naught, that no man should bear with any man to the maintenance of voluntary and prepensed murder. And I hear say since the man was otherwise an honest man, and they that spake for him are honest men. I am inclinable enough to credit it. I spoke not because I would have any man's honesty impaired. Only I did as St. Paul did, who, hearing of the Corinthians that there should be contentions and misorder among them, did write unto them that he heard; and thereupon by occasion of hearing he set forth the very wholesome doctrine of the Supper of the Lord. We might not have lacked that doctrine, I tell you. Be it so, the Corinthians had no such contentions among them as Paul wrote of; be it so, they had not misordered themselves. It was neither off nor on to that that Paul said; the matter lay in that, that upon hearing he would take occasion to set out the good and true doctrine.

So I did not affirm it to be true that I heard; I spake it to advertise you to beware of bearing with willful and prepensed murder. I would have nothing enforced against any man; this was my intent and meaning. I do not know what ye call chance-medley in the law; it is not for my study. I am a scholar in scripture, in God's book; I study that. I know what voluntary murder is before God. If I shall fall out with a man, he is angry with me and I with him, and, lacking opportunity and place, we shall put it off for that time; in the mean season I prepare my weapon and sharp it against another time; I swell and boil in this passion towards him; I seek him, we meddle together; it is my chance, by reason my weapon is better than his and so forth, to kill him; I give him his death stroke in my vengeance and anger: this call I voluntary murder in scripture. What it is in the law I cannot tell. It is a great sin, and therefore I call it voluntary.

I remember what a great clerk writeth of this: *Omne peccatum adeo est voluntarium, ut nisi sit voluntarium non sit peccatum.* "Every sin," saith he, "is so voluntary that if it be not voluntary it cannot be called sin." Sin is no actual sin if it be not voluntary. I would we would all know our faults and repent. That that is done, is done; it cannot be called back again. God is merciful; the King is merciful. Here we may repent; this is the place of repentance. When we are gone hence, it is too late then to repent. And let us be content with such order as the magistrates shall take. But sure it is a perilous thing to bear with any such matter. I told you what I heard say; I would have no man's honesty impaired by my telling. I heard say since of another murder, that a Spaniard should kill an Englishman and run him through with his sword; they say he was a tall man. But I hear it not that the Spaniard was hanged for his labor; if I had, I would have told you it too.

They fell out, as the tale goeth, about a whore. O Lord, what whoredom is used nowadays, as I hear by the relation of honest men, which tell it not after a worldly sort, as though they rejoiced at it, but heavily, with heavy hearts, how God is dishonored by whoredom in this city of London; yea, the Bank when it stood was never so common! If it be true that is told, it is marvel that it doth not sink and that the earth gapeth not and swalloweth it up. It is wonderful that the city of London doth suffer such whoredom unpunished. God hath suffered long of His great lenity, mercy, and benignity; but He will punish sharply at length if we do not repent. There is some place in London, as they say, "Immunity, impunity." What should I call it? A privileged place for whoredom. The Lord Mayor hath nothing to do there; the sheriffs they cannot meddle with it; and the quest they not inquire of it. And there men do bring their whores, yea, other men's wives, and there is no reformation of it.

There is such dicing houses also, they say, as hath not been wont to be, where young gentlemen dice away their thrift. And where dicing is, there are other follies also. For the love of God let remedy be had; let us wrestle and strive against sin. Men of England, in times past, when they would exercise themselves—for we must needs have some recreation; our bodies cannot endure without some exercise—they were wont to go abroad in the fields ashooting; but now is turned into glossing, gulling, and whoring within the house. The art of shooting hath been in times past much esteemed in this realm. It is a gift of God that He hath given us to excel all other nations withal; it hath been God's instrument whereby He hath given us many victories against our enemies. But now we have taken up whoring in towns instead of shooting in the fields. A wondrous thing, that so excellent a gift of God should be so little esteemed! I desire you, my lords, even as ye love the honor and glory of God and intend to remove His indignation, let there be sent forth some proclamation, some sharp proclamation to the justices of peace, for they do not their duty. Justices now be no justices. There be many good acts made for this matter already. Charge them upon their allegiance that this singular benefit of God may be practiced and that it be not turned into bolling, glossing, and whoring within the towns; for they be negligent in executing these laws of shooting. In my time my poor father was as diligent to teach me to shoot as to learn any other thing; and so I think other men did their children. He taught me how to draw, how to lay my body in my bow and not to draw with strength of arms, as other nations do, but with strength of the body. I had my bows bought me according to my age and strength; as I increased in them, so my bows were made bigger and bigger. For men shall never shoot well except they be brought up in it. It is a goodly art, a wholesome kind of exercise, and much commended in physic.

Marcilius Ficinus, in his book *De triplici vita*—it is a great while since I read him now—but I remember he commendeth this kind of exercise and saith that it wrestleth against many kinds of diseases. In the reverence of God let it be continued; let a proclamation go forth charging the justices of peace that they see such acts and statutes kept as were made for this purpose.

I will to my matter. I intend this day to entreat of a piece of scripture written in the beginning of the fifth chapter of Luke. I am occasioned to take this place by a book sent to the King's Majesty that dead is by Master Pole. It is a text that he doth greatly abuse for the supremity; he racks it and violents it to serve for the maintenance of the Bishop of Rome. And as he did enforce the tother place that I entreated of last, so did he enforce this also to serve his matter. The story is this. Our Saviour Christ was come now to the bank of the water of Gennesaret. The people were come to Him and flocked about Him to hear Him preach. And Jesus took a boat that was standing at the pool (it was Simon's boat) and went into it. And sitting in the boat He preached to them that were on the bank. And when He had preached and taught them, He spake to Simon and bade him launch out further into the deep and loose his nets to catch fish. And Simon made answer and said, "Master, we have labored all night, but we caught nothing; howbeit at Thy commandment, because Thou biddest us, we will go to it again" (Luke 5:5). And so they did and caught a great draught, a miraculous draught, so much that the net brake; and they called to their fellows that were by—for they had two boats—to come to help them; and they came and filled both their boats so full that they were nigh drowning.

This is the story. That I may declare this text so that it may be to the honor of God and edification of your souls and mine both, I shall desire you to help me with your prayer, in the which, etc.

Factum est autem (saith the text) *cum turba irrueret in eum.* St. Luke tells the story, "And it came to pass when the people pressed upon Him" (Luke 5:1), so that He was in peril to be cast into the pond, they rushed so fast upon Him and made such throng to Him. A wondrous thing! What a desire the people had in those days to hear our Saviour Christ preach! And the cause may be gathered of the latter end of the chapter that went before. Our Saviour Christ had preached unto them and healed the sick folks of such diseases and maladies as they had, and therefore the people would have retained Him still. But He made them answer and said, *Et aliis civitatibus oportet me evangelizare regnum Dei, nam in hoc missus sum,* "I must preach the kingdom of God to other cities also; I must show them My Father's will, for I came for that purpose; I was sent to preach the Word of God" (Luke 4:43). Our Saviour Christ said how He must not tarry in one place, for He was sent to the world to preach everywhere.

Is it not a marvelous thing that our unpreaching prelates can read this place and yet preach no more than they do? I marvel that they can go quietly to bed and see how He allureth them with His example to be diligent in their office. Here is a godly lesson also how our Saviour Christ fled from glory. If these ambitious parsons that climb to honor by bywalks inordinately would consider this example of Jesus Christ, they should come to more honor than they do; for when they seek honor by such bywalks, they come to confusion. Honor followeth them that flee from it. Our Saviour Christ gat Him away early in the morning and went unto the wilderness. I would they would follow this example of Christ and not seek honor by such bywalks as they do. But what did the people when He had hid Himself? They smelled Him out in the wilderness and came unto Him by flocks and followed Him a great number. But where read you that a great number of scribes and Pharisees and bishops followed Him?

There is a doctor that writeth of this place; his name is Doctor Gorham, Nicholas Gorham. I knew him to be a school doctor a great while ago, but I never knew him to be an interpreter of scripture till now of late. He saith thus: *Major devotio in laicis vetulis quam in clericis, etc.* "There is more devotion," saith he, "in lay folk and old wives, these simple folk, the vulgar people, than in the clerks." They be better affect to the word of God than those that be of the clergy. I marvel not at the sentence, but I marvel to find such a sentence in such a doctor. If I should say so much, it would be said to me that it is an evil bird that defiles his own nest; and, *Nemo laeditur nisi a seipso,* "There is no man hurt but of his own self." There was verified the saying of our Saviour Christ which He spake in another place: *Ubicumque fuerit cadaver, ibi congregabuntur aquilae,* "Wheresoever a dead carrion is, thither will the eagles gather" (Matt. 24:28). Our Saviour Christ compares Himself to a dead carrion, for where the carrion is there will the eagles be. And though it be an evil smell to us and stinks in a man's nose, yet it is a sweet smell to the eagles; they will seek it out. So the people sought out Christ; they smelt His savor; He was a sweet smell to them. He is *odor vitae ad vitam,* "the smell of life to life." They flocked about Him like eagles. Christ was the carrion and the people were the eagles. They had no pleasure to hear the scribes and the Pharisees; they stank in their nose; their doctrine was unsavory; it was but of lolions, of decimations, of aniseed and cummin, and such gear. There was no comfort in it for sore consciences; there was no consolation for wounded souls. There was no remedy for sins as was in Christ's doctrine. His doctrine eased the burden of the soul; it was sweet to the common people and sour to the scribes. It was such comfort and pleasure to them that they came flocking about him.

Wherefore came they? *Ut audirent verbum Dei* (Luke 5:1). It was a good coming; they came to hear the word of God. It was not to be thought that they came all of one mind to hear the word of God. It is likely that in so great a multitude some came of curiosity to hear some novels; and some came smelling a sweet savor, to have consolation and comfort of God's word. For we cannot be saved without hearing of the word; it is a necessary way to salvation. We cannot be saved without faith, and faith cometh by hearing of the word. *Fides ex auditu.* "And how shall they hear without a preacher?" (Romans 10:14). I tell you it is the footsteps of the ladder of heaven, of our salvation. There must be preachers if we look to be saved. I told you of this gradation before in the tenth to the Romans; consider it well. I had rather ye should come of a naughty mind to hear the word of God for novelty or for curiosity to hear some pastime than to be away. I had rather ye should come as the tale is by the gentlewoman of London. One of her neighbors met her in the street and said, "Mistress, whither go ye?" "Marry," said she, "I am going to St. Thomas of Acres to the sermon; I could not sleep all this last night, and I am going now thither; I never failed of a good nap there."

And so I had rather ye should go anapping to the sermons than not to go at all. For with what mind soever ye come, though ye come for an ill purpose, yet peradventure ye may chance to be caught ere ye go; the preacher may chance to catch you on his hook. Rather than ye should not come at all, I would have you come of curiosity, as St. Augustine came to hear St. Ambrose. When St. Augustine came to Milan (he tells the story himself, in the end of his book of Confessions), he was very desirous to hear St. Ambrose, not for any love he had to the doctrine that he taught, but to hear his eloquence, whether it was so great as the speech was and as the bruit went. Well, before he departed St. Ambrose caught him on his hook and converted him, so that he became of a Manichee and of a Platonist a good Christian, a defender of Christ's religion and of the faith afterward. So I would have you come to sermons. It is declared in many mo [*sic*] places of scripture how necessary preaching is, as this, *Evangelium est potentia Dei ad Sa[lutem] omni credenti,* "The preaching of the gospel is the power of God to every man that doth believe" (Romans 1:16). He means God's word opened; it is the instrument and the thing whereby we are saved.

Beware, beware ye diminish not this office, for if ye do ye decay God's power to all that do believe. Christ saith, consonant to the same, *Nisi quis renatus fuerit e supernis, non potest videre regnum Dei,* "Except a man be born again from above, he cannot see the kingdom of God" (John 3:3). He must have a regeneration. And what is this regeneration? It is not to be christened in water, as these firebrands expound it, and nothing else. How is it to be expounded then? St. Peter showeth that one place of scripture declareth another. It is the circumstance and collation of places that make scripture plain. *Regeneramur autem,* saith St. Peter, "and we be born again." How? *Non ex semine mortali, sed immortali,* "Not by a mortal seed, but by an immortal." What is this immortal seed? *Per sermonem Dei viventis,* "By the word of the living God" (I Peter 1:23). By the Word of God preached and opened. Thus cometh in our new birth.

Here you may see how necessary this office is to our salvation. This is the thing that the devil wrestleth most against; it hath been all his study to decay this office. He worketh against it as much as he can; he hath prevailed too much, too much in it. He hath set up a state of unpreaching prelacy in this realm this seven hundred year, a state of unpreaching prelacy. He hath made unpreaching prelates; he hath stirred up by heaps to persecute this office in the title of heresy. He hath stirred up the magistrates to persecute it in the title of sedition; and he hath stirred up the people to persecute it with exprobations and slanderous words, as by the name of "new learning," "strange preaching." And with impropriations he hath turned preaching into private masses. If a priest should have left mass undone on a Sunday within these ten years, all England should have wondered at it; but they might have left off the sermon twenty Sundays and never have been blamed. And thus by these impropriations private masses were set up and preaching of God's word trodden under foot. But what doth he now? What doth he now? He stirs men up to outrageous rearing of rents, that poor men shall not be able to find their children at the school to be divines.

What an unreasonable devil is this! He provides a great while beforehand for the time that is to come. He hath brought up now of late the most monstrous kind of covetousness that ever was heard of. He hath invented fee farming of benefices, and all to decay this office of preaching, insomuch that when any man hereafter shall have a benefice he may go where he will, for any house he shall have to dwell upon or any glebe land to keep hospitality withal. But he must take up a chamber in an alehouse and there sit and play at the tables all the day. A goodly curate! He hath caused also, through this monstrous kind of covetousness, patrons to sell their benefices. Yea, what doth he more? He gets him to the university and causeth great men and squires to send their sons thither and put out poor scholars that should be divines, for their parents intend not they shall be preachers but that they may have a show of learning. Tut, it were too long to declare unto you what deceit and means the devil hath found to decay the office of salvation, this office of regeneration.

But to return to my matter. The people came to hear the word of God. They heard Him with silence. I remember now a saying of St. Chrysostom, and peradventure it might come hereafter in better place, but yet I will take it whilst it cometh to my mind. The saying is this, *Et loquentem eum audierunt in silentio, seriem locutionis non interrumpentes*. "They heard Him," saith he, "in silence, not interrupting the order of his preaching." He means they heard him quietly, without any shuffling of feet or walking up and down. Surely it is an ill misorder that folk shall be walking up and down in the sermon time, as I have seen in this place this Lent; and there shall be such huzzing and buzzing in the preacher's ear that it maketh him oftentimes to forget his matter. Oh, let us consider the King's Majesty's goodness! This place was prepared for banqueting of the body; and His Majesty hath made it a place for the comfort of the soul and to have the Word of God preached in it, showing hereby that he would have all his subjects at it if it might be possible.

Consider what the King's Majesty hath done for you; he alloweth you all to hear with him. Consider where ye be. First, ye ought to have a reverence to God's word; and though it be preached by poor men, yet it is the same word that our Saviour spake. Consider also the presence of the King's Majesty, God's high vicar in earth. Having a respect to his personage, ye ought to have reverence to it and consider that he is God's high minister and yet alloweth you all to be partakers with him of the hearing of God's word. This benefit of his would be thankfully taken, and it would be highly esteemed. Hear in silence, as Chrysostom saith. It may chance that some in the company may fall sick or be diseased; if there be any such, let them go away with silence; let them leave their salutations till they come in the Court; let them depart with silence. I took occasion of Chrysostom's words to admonish you of this thing.

What should be the cause that our Saviour Christ went into the boat? The scripture calleth it *navis* or *navicula,* but it was no ship. It was a fisher's boat; they were not able to have a ship. What should be the cause why He would not stand on the bank and preach there, but He desired Peter to draw the boat somewhat from the shore into the midst of the water? What should be the cause? What should be the cause? One cause was for that He might sit there more commodiously than on the bank. Another cause was for that He was like to be thrust into the pond of the people that came unto Him. Why, our Saviour Christ might have withstood them; He was strong enough to have kept Himself from thrusting into the water. He was stronger than they all, and if He had listed He might have stood on the water as well as He walked on the water. Truth it is, so might He have done indeed. But as it was sometime

His pleasure to show the power of His Godhead, so He declared now the infirmity and imbecility of His manhood.

Here He giveth us an example what we shall do. We must not tempt God by any miracles, so long as we may walk by ordinary ways. As our Saviour Christ, when the devil had Him on the top of the temple and would have had Him cast Himself down, He made him this answer, *Non tentabis Dominum Deum tuum,* "Thou shalt not tempt thy Lord God" (Luke 4:12). As if he should have said, "We may not tempt God at all." It is no time now to show any miracles; there is another way to go down by grecings. Thus He did to show us an example that we must not tempt God, except it be in extreme necessity, and when we cannot otherways remedy the matter to leave it all to God. Else we may not tempt the majesty of his Deity. Beware tempting of God.

Well, He comes to Simon's boat. And why rather to Simon's boat than another? I will answer as I find in experience in myself. I came hither today from Lambeth in a wherry; and when I came to take my boat, the watermen came about me, as the manner is, and he would have me, and he would have me. I took one of them. Now ye will ask me why I came in that boat rather than in another? Because I would go into that that I see stand next me; it stood more commodiously for me. And so did Christ by Simon's boat; it stood nearer for Him; He saw a better seat in it. A good natural reason. Now come the papists and they will make a mystery of it; they will pick out the supremacy of the Bishop of Rome in Peter's boat. We may make allegories enough of every place in scripture, but surely it must needs be a simple matter that stands on so weak a ground.

But ye shall see further. He desired Peter to thrust out his boat from the shore. He desired him. Here was a good lesson for the Bishop of Rome and all his College of Cardinals to learn humility and gentleness. *Rogabat eum,* "He desired him" (Luke 4:3). It was gently done of Him, without any austerity, but with all urbanity, mildness and softness, and humility. What an example is this that He gives them here! But they spy it not. They can see nothing but the supremacy of the Bishop of Rome. A wondrous thing, what sight they have; they see nothing but the supremacy of the Bishop of Rome! *Imperabatis ovibus meis,* saith Ezekiel, *cum avaritia et austeritate, et dispersae sunt absque pastore,* "Ye have ruled my sheep, and commanded them with great lordliness, austerity, and power; and thus ye have dispersed my sheep abroad" (Ezek. 34:4-5). And why? There was no shepherd. They had wanted one a great while. Rome hath been many hundred years without a good shepherd. They would not learn to rule them gently; they had rule over them, but it was with cursings, excommunications, with great austerity and thunderbolts and the devil and all, to maintain their unpreaching prelacy. I beseech God open their eyes that they may see the truth and not be blinded with those things that no man can see but they.

It followeth in the text, *Sedens docebat de navi,* "He taught sitting" (Luke 5:3). Preachers, belike, were sitters in those days. As it is written in another place, *Sedent in cathedra Moysi,* "They sit in the chair of Moses" (Matt. 23:2). I would our preachers would preach sitting or standing, one way or other. It was a godly pulpit that our Saviour Christ had gotten Him here, an old rotten boat, and yet He preached his Father's will, his Father's message, out of this pulpit. He regarded the people more than the pulpit. He cared not for the pulpit so He might do the people good. Indeed, it is to be commended for the preacher to stand or sit, as the place is. But I would not have it so superstitiously esteemed but that a good preacher may declare the Word of God sitting on a horse or preaching in a tree. And yet if this should be done, the unpreaching prelates would laugh it to scorn. And though it be good to have the pulpit set up in churches, that the people may resort thither, yet I would not have it so superstitiously used but that in a profane place the Word of God might be preached sometimes; and I would not have the people offended withal, no more than they be with our Saviour Christ's preaching out of a boat. And yet to have pulpits in churches, it is very well done to have them, but they would be occupied; for it is a vain thing to have them as they stand in many churches.

I heard of a bishop of England that went on visitation, and, as it was the custom, when the bishop should come and be rung into the town, the great bell's clapper was fallen down; the tyall was broken, so that the bishop could not be rung into the town. There was a great matter made of this, and the chief of the parish were much blamed for it in the visitation. The bishop was somewhat quick with them and signified that he was much offended. They made their answers and excused themselves as well as they could. "It was a chance," said they, "that the clapper brake, and we could not get it amended by and by. We must tarry till we can have done it; it shall be amended as shortly as may be." Among the other, there was one wiser than the rest and he comes me to the bishop. "Why, my lord," saith he, "doth Your Lordship make so great matter of the bell that lacketh his clapper? Here is a bell," saith he, and pointed to the pulpit, "that hath lacked a clapper this twenty years. We have a parson that fetcheth out of this benefice £50 every year, but we never see him." I warrant you the bishop was an unpreaching prelate. He could find fault with the bell that wanted a clapper to ring him into the town, but he could not find any fault with the parson that preached not at his benefice. Ever this office of preaching hath been least regarded; it hath scant had the name of God's service. They must sing *Salve festa dies* about the church, that no man was the better for it but to show their gay coats and garments.

I came once myself to a place, riding on a journey homeward from London, and I sent word overnight into the town that I would preach there in the morning, because it was holiday and methought it was an holiday's work. The church stood in my way, and I took my horse and my company and went thither. I thought I should have found a great company in the church, and when I came there the church door was fast locked. I tarried there half an hour and more. At last the key was found, and one of the parish comes to me and says, "Sir, this is a busy day with us. We cannot hear you; it is Robin Hood's Day. The parish are gone abroad to gather for Robin Hood. I pray you let them not." I was fain there to give place to Robin Hood. I thought my rochet should have been regarded, though I were not; but it would not serve, it was fain to give place to Robin Hood's men. It is no laughing matter, my friends; it is a weeping matter, a heavy matter; a heavy matter, under the pretense for gathering for Robin Hood, a traitor and a thief, to put out a preacher, to have his office less esteemed, to prefer Robin Hood before the ministration of God's word. And all this hath come of unpreaching prelates. This realm hath been ill provided for, that it hath had such corrupt judgments in it to prefer Robin Hood to God's word. If the bishops had been preachers, there should never have been any such thing. But we have a good hope of better. We have had a good beginning. I beseech God to continue it! But I tell you, it is far wide that the people have such judgments; the bishops they could laugh at it. What was that to them? They would have them continue in their ignorance still and themselves in unpreaching prelacy.

Well, sitting, sitting. "He sat down and taught." The text doth tell us that He taught, but it doth not tell us what He taught. If I were a papist, I could tell what He said; I would, in the Pope's judgment, show what He taught. For the Bishop of Rome hath *in scrinio pectoris sui* the true understanding of scriptures. If he call a council of College of Cardinals, he hath authority to determine the supper of the Lord, as he did at the Council of Florence! And Pope Nicholas and Bishop Lanfranc shall come and expound this place and say that our Saviour Christ said thus: "Peter, I do mean this by sitting in thy boat, that thou shalt go to Rome and be bishop there five-and-twenty years after mine ascension; and all thy successors shall be rulers of the universal church after thee."

Here would I place also holy water and holy bread and all unwritten verities, if I were a papist, and that scripture is not to be expounded by any private interpretation but by our holy father and his College of Cardinals. This is a great deal a better place than *Duc in altum* (Luke 5:4). But what was Christ's sermon? It may soon be gathered what it was. He is always like Himself. His first sermon was, "*Paenitentiam agite,*" "Do penance; your living is naught; repent." Again, at Nazareth, when He read in the temple and preached remission of sins and healing of wounded consciences, and in the long Sermon in the Mount, He was always like Himself. He never dissented from Himself.

Oh, there is a writer hath a jolly text here, and his name is Dionysius. I chanced to meet with his book in my Lord of Canterbury's library. He was a monk of the Charterhouse. I marvel to find such a sentence in that author. What taught Christ in this sermon? Marry, saith he, it is not written. And he addeth more unto it: *Evangelistae tantum scripserunt de sermonibus et miraculis Christi quantum cognoverunt, inspirante Deo, sufficere ad aedificationem ecclesiae, ad confirmationem fidei, et ad salutem animarum.* It is true. It is not written. All His miracles were not written, so neither were all His sermons written; yet for all that the evangelists did write so much as was necessary. "They wrote so much of the miracles and sermons of Christ as they knew by God's inspiration to be sufficient for the edifying of the church, the confirmation of our faith, and the health of our souls." If this be true, as it is indeed, where be [un]written verities? I marvel not at the sentence, but to find it in such an author. Jesus! what authority he gives to God's word! But God would that such men should be witness with the authority of His book, will they nill they.

Now to draw towards an end. It followeth in the text, *Duc in altum.* Here comes in the supremity of the Bishop of Rome. When our Saviour Christ had made an end of His sermon and had fed their souls, He provided for their bodies. First He began with the soul; Christ's word is the food of it. Now He goeth to the body. He hath charge of them both; He giveth food for them both. We must commit the feeding of the body and of the soul to Him. Well, He saith to Peter, *Duc in altum;* "Launch into the depth; put forth thy boat farther into the deep of the water; loose your nets; now fish" (Luke 5:4). As who would say, "Your souls are now fed; I have taught you My doctrine; now I will confirm it with a miracle." Lo, sir, here is *Duc in altum.* Here Peter was made a great man, say the papists, and all his successors after him. And this is derived of these few words, "Launch into the deep." And their argument is this: He spake to Peter only, and He spake to him in the singular number; *ergo,* He gave him such a pre-eminence above the rest. A goodly argument! I ween it be a syllogismus, *in quem terra pontus.*

I will make a like argument. Our Saviour Christ said to Judas, when he was about to betray Him, *Quod facis fac citius* (John 13:27). Now when He spake to Peter there were none of His disciples by but James and John, but when He spake to Judas they were all present. Well, He said unto him, *Quod facis fac citius,* "Speed thy business that thou hast in thy head; do it." He gave him here a secret monition that He knew what he intended, if Judas had had grace to have taken it and repented. He spake in the singular number to him; *ergo,* He gave him some pre-eminence. Belike He made him a cardinal; and it might full well be, for they have followed Judas ever since. Here is as good a ground for the College of Cardinals as the other is for the supremity of the Bishop of Rome. "Our Saviour Christ," say they, "spake only to Peter for pre-eminence because he was chief of the apostles, and you can show none other cause; *ergo,* this is the cause why He spake to him in the singular number." I daresay there is never a wherryman at Westminster Bridge but he can answer to this and give a natural reason of it. He knoweth that one man is able to shove the boat, but one man was not able to cast out the nets. And therefore He said in the plural number, *Laxate retia,* "Loose your nets" (Luke 5:4). And He said in the singular number to Peter, "Launch out the boat." Why? Because he was able to do it. But He spake the other in the plural number because he was not able to convey the boat and cast out the nets too. One man could not do it. This would the wherryman say, and that with better reason than to make such a mystery of it as no man can spy but they. And the cause why He spake to all was to show that He will have all Christian men to work for their living. It is He that sends food both for the body and soul, but He will not send it without labor. He will have all Christian people to labor for it; He will use our labor as a mean whereby he sendeth our food.

This was a wondrous miracle of our Saviour Christ, and did it not only to allure them to His discipleship but also for our commodity. It was a seal to seal His doctrine withal. Now ye know that such as be keepers of seals, as my Lord Chancellor and such other, whatsoever they be, they do not always seal; they have a sealing time. For I have heard poor men complain that they have been put off from time to time of sealing to another, till all their money were spent. And as they have times to seal in, so our Saviour Christ had His time of sealing. When He was here in earth with His apostles, and in the time of the primitive church, Christ's doctrine was sufficiently sealed already with seals of His own making. What should our seals do? What need we to seal His seal? It is a confirmed doctrine already.

Oh, Luther, when he came into that world first and disputed against the Decretals, the Clementines, Alexandrines, Extravagantines, what ado had he! But ye will say, "Peradventure he was deceived in some things." I will not take upon me to defend him in all points. I will not stand to it that all that he wrote was true; I think he would not so himself. For there is no man but he may err. He came to further and further knowledge, but surely he was a goodly instrument. Well, I say, when he preached first, they called upon him to do miracles. They were wrought before, and so we need to do no miracles. Indeed, when the popish prelates preached first they had need of miracles, and the devil wrought some in the preaching of purgatory. But what kind of miracles these were all England doth know. But it will not know. A wonderful thing that the people will continue in their blindness and ignorance still! We have great utility of the miracles of our Saviour Jesus Christ. He doth signify unto us by this wonderful work that He is Lord as well of the water as of the land. A good comfort for those that be on the water, when they be in any tempest or danger, to call upon Him.

The fish here came at His commandment. Here we may learn that all things in the water are subject to Christ. Peter said, "Sir, we have labored all night and have not caught one fin; howbeit at your word we will to it afresh" (Luke 5:5). By this it appeareth that the gain, the lucre, the revenues that we get must not be imputed to our labor; we may not say, "Gramercy, labor." It is not our labor; it is our Saviour Christ that sendeth us living. Yet must we labor, for He that said to Peter, "Labor," and He that bade the fishers labor, bids all men to labor in their business. There be some people that ascribe their gains, their increase gotten by any faculty, to the devil. Is there any, trow ye, in England would say so? Now if any man should come to another and say he gat his living by the devil, he would fall out with him. There is not a man in England that so saith, yet is there some that think it. For all that get it with false buying and selling, with circumvention, with usury, impostures, mixed wares, false weights, deceiving their lords and masters—all those that get their goods on this fashion, what do they think but that the devil sends them gains and riches? For they be his, being unlawfully gotten. What is this to say but that the devil is author of their gains when they be so gotten? For God inhibits them. *Deus non volens iniquitatem tu es,* "God will no iniquity." These folk are greatly deceived.

There be some, again, impute all to their labors and works. Yea, on the holy day they cannot find in their hearts to come to the temple to the blessed Communion; they must be working at home. These are wide again on the other side. And some there be that think if they work nothing at all they shall have enough. They will have no good exercise, but gape and think that God will send meat into their mouths. And these are far wide. They must work. He bade the fishers work; our Saviour Christ bade Peter work; and He that said so to them says the same to us, every man in his art. *Benedictio Dei facit divitem,* "The blessing of God maketh a man rich" (Prov. 10:22). He lets His sun shine upon the wicked, as well as upon the good; He sends riches both to good and bad. But this blessing turns to them into a malediction and a curse; it increaseth their damnation. St. Paul, writing to the Thessalonians, did put an order how every man should work in his vocation: *Cum essemus apud vos, hoc praecipiebamus vobis, ut si quis nollet operari is nec edat.* "When I was among you," saith he, "I made this ordinance, that whosoever would not do the work of his vocation should have no meat" (2 Thess. 3:10). It were a good ordinance in a commonweal that every man should be set on work, every man in his vocation. "Let him have no meat."

Now he saith, furthermore, *Audivimus quosdam inter vos versantes inordinate nihil operis facientes,* "I hear say there is some amongst you that lives inordinately" (*ibid.,* 3:11). What is that word "inordinately"? Idly, giving themselves to no occupation for their living; *curiose agentes,* curious men, given to curiosity, to searching what other men do. St. Paul saith "he heard say"; he could not tell whether it were so or no. But he took occasion of hearing say to set out a good and wholesome doctrine: *His autem qui sunt ejusmodi praecipimus et obsecramus.* "We command and desire you, for the reverence of God, if there be any such, that they will do the works of their vocation and go quietly to their occupation and so eat their own bread" (*ibid.,* 3:12). Else it is not their own; it is other men's meat.

Our Saviour Christ, before he began His preaching, lived of His occupation; he was a carpenter and gat His living with great labor. Therefore let no man disdain or think scorn to follow Him in a mean living, a mean vocation, or a common calling and occupation. For as He blessed our nature with taking upon Him the shape of man, so in His doing He blessed all occupations and arts. This is a notable example to signify that He abhors all idleness. When He was a carpenter, then He went and did the work of His calling; and when He was a preacher, He did the works of that calling. He was no unpreaching prelate. The Bishop of Rome should have learned that of Him. And these gainers with false arts, what be they? They are never content with that they have, though it be never so much. And they that are true dealers are satisfied with that God sends, though it be never so little. *Quaestus magnus pietas cum animo sua sorte contento,* "Godliness is great gain; it is lucre enough, it is vantage enough, to be content with that that God sends" (1 Tim. 6:6). The faithful cannot lack; the unfaithful is ever lacking, though he have never so much.

I will now make an end. *Labores manuum tuarum;* let us all labor. Christ teacheth us to labor; yea, the Bishop of Rome himself He teacheth him to labor, rather than to be head of the church. Let us put our trust in God; *Labores manuum tuarum.* "Cast thy care upon the Lord, and He will nourish thee and feed thee" (Psalm 55:22). Again, the prophet saith, *Nunquam vidi justum derelictum, nec semen ejus quaerens panem,* "I never saw the righteous man forsaken nor his seed to seek his bread" (Psalm 37:25). It is infidelity, infidelity, that mars all together.

Well, to my text: *Labores manuum tuarum quia manducabis, beatus es, et bene tibi erit, etc.,* "Because thou eatest the labors of thy hands, that that God sends thee of thy labor" (Psalm 128:2). Every man must labor; yea, though he be a king yet he must labor. For I know no man hath a greater labor than a king. What is his labor? To study God's book, to see that there be no unpreaching prelates in his realm nor bribing judges, to see to all estates, to provide for the poor, to see victuals good cheap. Is not this a labor, trow ye? Thus if thou dost labor, exercising the works of thy vocation, thou eatest the meat that God sends thee. And then it followeth, *Beatus es,* "Thou art a blessed man in God's favor," *et bene tibi erit,* "and it shall go well with thee in this world," both in body and soul, for God provides for both. How shalt thou provide for thy soul? Go hear sermons. How for the body? Labor in thy vocation. And then shall it be well with thee, both here and in the world to come, through the faith and merits of our Saviour Jesus Christ, to Whom with the Father and the Holy Ghost be praise for ever and ever, world without end. Amen.

THE END OF THE SIXTH SERMON

LANCELOT ANDREWES: FIFTEENTH NATIVITY SERMON

Lancelot Andrewes received many honors in his lifetime indicating the high esteem in which he was held by Queen Elizabeth and King James I. He was one of the best scholars in England in his day and, among other things, headed the London group of Old Testament scholars working on the King James version. The style of his preaching is called "witty" and "metaphysical" (for a discussion of metaphysical preaching, **see Vol. 2, pp. 370-79***), the first meaning that he used surprising analogies, and the second that he was of the generation of the metaphysical poets—at least two of whom, John Donne and George Herbert—were priests and* *preachers. The taste for such preaching has varied over the centuries; T. S. Eliot was an enthusiastic partisan for Andrewes's sermons. It helps to remember that Andrewes was a contemporary of Shakespeare; both appealed to the same taste in the use of language. It also helps to know that he spent a number of hours each day in prayer.*

The sermon below influenced Eliot's poem "The Journey of the Magi." It is taken from Lancelot Andrewes, Seventeen Sermons on the Nativity, *The Ancient and Modern Library of Theological Literature (London: Griffith, Farran, Okeden, & Welsh, n.d.). The original spelling and capitalization are retained as contributing to the flavor of the sermon.*

Sermon XV

A Sermon Preached before the King's Majesty, at Whitehall on Wednesday, the Twenty-fifth of December, A.D. MDCXXII, being Christmas day.

Behold there came wise men from the East to Jerusalem Saying where is the King of the Jews that is born? For we have seen His star in the East, and are come to worship Him. *Matthew 2:1-2.*

[Ecce magi ab Oriente venerunt Jerosolymam, dicentes, Ubi est Qui natus est Rex Judaeorum? Vidimus enim stellam Ejus in Oriente, et venimus adorare Eum. Latin Vulg.*]*

There be in these two verses two principal points, as was observed, when time was;[2] 1. The persons that arrived at Jerusalem, 2. and their errand. The persons in the former verse, whereof hath been treated heretofore. Their errand in the latter, whereof we are now to deal. Their errand we may best learn from themselves out of their *dicentes &c.* Which, in a word, is to worship Him. Their errand our errand, and the errand of this day.

This text may seem to come a little too soon, before the time; and should have stayed till the day it was spoken on,[3] rather than on this day. But if you mark them well, there are in the verse four words that be *verba diei hujus* "proper and peculiar to this very day." 1. For first, *natus est* is most proper to this day of all days, the day of His Nativity. 2. Secondly, *vidimus stellam;* for on this day it was first seen, appeared first. 3. Thirdly, *venimus;* for this day they set forth, began their journey. 4. And last, *adorare Eum;* for "when He brought His only-begotten Son into the world, He gave in charge, Let all the Angels of God worship Him" (Heb. 1:6). And when the Angels to do it, no time more proper for us to do it as then. So these four appropriate it to this day, and none but this.

The main heads of their errand are 1. *Vidimus stellam*, the occasion; 2. and *Venimus adorare*, the end of their coming. But for the better conceiving it I will take another course, to set forth these points to be handled.

I. Their faith first: faith—in that they never ask "Whether He be," but "Where He is born"; for that born He is, that they steadfastly believe.

II. Then the work or service (Phil. 2:17) of this faith, as St. Paul calleth it; "the touch or trial," "*dokimion*" (1 Peter 1:7), as St. Peter; the *ostende mihi* (James 2:18), as St. James; of this their faith in these five. 1. Their confessing of it in *venerunt dicentes. Venerunt,* they were no sooner come, but *dicentes,* they tell it out; confess Him and His birth to be the cause of their coming. 2. Secondly, as confess their faith, so the ground of their faith; *vidimus enim,* for they had "seen" His star; and His star being risen, by it they knew He must be risen too. 3. Thirdly, as St. Paul calls them in Abraham's, *vestgia fidei,* "the steps of their faith" (Rom. 4:12), in *venimus,* "their coming"—coming such a journey, at such a time, with such speed. 4. Fourthly, when they were come, their diligent enquiring Him out by *ubi est?* for here is the place of it, asking after Him to find where He was. 5. And last, when they had found Him, the end of their seeing, coming, seeking; and all for no other end but to worship Him. Here they say it, at the 11th verse they do it in these two acts; 1. *procidentes,* their "falling down," 2. and *obtulerunt,* their "offering" to Him. Worship Him with their bodies, worship Him with their goods; their worship and ours the true worship of Christ.

The text is of a star, and we may make all run on a star,[4] that so the text and day may be suitable, and Heaven and earth hold a correspondence. St. Peter calls faith "the day-star rising in our hearts" (2 Peter 1:19), which sorts well with the star in the text rising in the sky. That in the sky manifesting itself from above to them; this in their hearts manifesting itself from below to Him, to Christ. Manifesting itself by these five: 1. by *ore fit confessio*, "the confessing of it" (Rom. 10:10); 2. by *fides est substantia,* "the ground of it" (Heb. 11:1); 3. by *vestigia fidei,* "the steps of it" (Rom. 4:12) in their painful coming; 4. by their *ubi est?* "careful enquiring"; 5. and last, by *adorare Eum,* "their devout worshipping." These five, as so many beams of faith, the day-star risen in their hearts. To take notice of them. For every one of them is of the nature of a condition, so as if we fail in them, *non lucet nobis stella haec,* "we have no part in the light, or conduct of this star." Neither in *stellam,* "the star itself," nor in *Ejus,* "in Him Whose the star is"; that is, not in Christ neither.

We have now got us a star on earth for that in Heaven, and these both lead us to a third. So as upon the matter three stars we have, and each his proper manifestation. 1. The first in the firmament; that appeared unto them, and in them to us—a figure of St. Paul's *"Epiphanē charis,"* "the grace of God appearing, and bringing salvation to all men" (Tit. 2:11), Jews and Gentiles and all. 2. The second here on earth is St. Peter's *Lucifer in cordibus;* and this appeared in them, and so must in us. Appeared 1. in their eyes—*vidimus;* 2. in their feet—*venimus;* 3. in their lips—*dicentes ubi est;* 4. in their knees—*procidentes,* "falling down"; 5. in their hands—*obtulerunt,* "by offering." These five every one a beam of this star. 3. The third in Christ Himself, St. John's star. "The generation and root of David, the bright morning Star, Christ." And He, His double appearing. 1. One at this time now, when He appeared in great humility; and we see and come to Him by faith. 2. The other, which we wait for, even "the blessed hope, and appearing of the great God and our Saviour" (Tit. 2:13) in the majesty of His glory.

These three: 1. The first that manifested Christ to them; 2. The second that manifested them to Christ; 3. The third Christ Himself, in Whom both these were as it were in conjunction. Christ "the bright morning Star" of that day which shall have no night; the *beatifica visio,* "the blessed sight" of which day is the *consummatum est* of our hope and happiness for ever.

Of these three stars the first is gone, the third yet to come, the second only is present. We to look to that, and to the five beams of it. That is it must do us all the good, and bring us to the third.

I. St. Luke calleth faith the "door of faith" (Acts 14:27). At this door let us enter. Here is a coming, and "he that cometh to God," and so he that to Christ, "must believe, that Christ is": so do these. They never ask *an sit,* but *ubi sit?* Not "whether," but "where He is born." They that ask *ubi Qui natus?* take *natus* for granted, presuppose that born He is. Herein is faith—faith of Christ's being born, the third article of the Christian Creed.

And what believe they of Him? Out of their own words here; 1. first that *natus,* that "born" He is, and so Man He is—His human nature. 2. And as His nature, so His office in *natus est Rex,* "born a King." They believe that too. 3. But *Judaeorum* may seem to be a bar; for then, what have they to do with "the King of the Jews"? They be Gentiles, none of His lieges, no relation to Him at all: what do they seeking or worshipping Him? But weigh it well, and it is no bar. For this they seem to believe: He is so *Rex Judaeorum,* "King of the Jews," as He is *adorandus a Gentibus,* "the Gentiles to adore Him." And though born in Jewry, yet Whose birth concerned them though Gentiles, though born far off in the "mountains of the East." They to have some benefit by Him and His birth, and for that to do Him worship, seeing *officium fundatur in beneficio* ever. 4. As thus born in earth, so a star He hath in Heaven of His own—*stellam Ejus,* "His star"; He the owner of it. Now we know the stars are the stars of Heaven, and He that Lord of them Lord of Heaven too; and so to be adored of them, of us, and of all. St. John puts them together; "the root and generation of David," His earthly; and "the bright morning star" (Rev. 22:16), His Heavenly or Divine generation. *Haec est fides Magorum,* this is the mystery of their faith. In *natus est,* man; in *stellam Ejus,* God. In *Rex,* "a King," though of the Jews, yet the good of Whose Kingdom should extend and stretch itself far and wide to Gentiles and all; and He of all to be adored. This, for *corde creditur,* the day-star itself in their hearts. Now to the beams of this star.

II. Next to *corde creditur* is *ore fit confessio,* "the confession" of this faith. It is in *venerunt dicentes,* they came with it in their mouths. *Venerunt,* they were no sooner come, but they spake of it so freely, to so many, as it came to Herod's ear and troubled him not a little that any King of the Jews should be worshipped beside himself. So then their faith is no bosom-faith, kept to themselves without ever a *dicentes,* without saying any thing of it to any body. No; *credidi, propter quod locutus sum,* "they believed, and therefore they spake" (Psa. 116:10). The star in their hearts cast one beam out at their mouths. And though Herod, who was but *Rex factus,* could evil brook to hear of *Rex natus,*—must needs be offended at it, yet they were not afraid to say it. And though they came from the East, those parts to whom and their King the Jews had long time been captives and their underlings, they were not ashamed neither to tell, that One of the Jews' race they came to seek; and to seek Him to the end "to worship Him." So neither afraid of Herod, nor ashamed of Christ; but professed their errand, and cared not who knew it. This for their confessing Him boldly.

But faith is said by the Apostle to be *hypostasis,* and so there is a good "ground"; and *elenchos,* and so hath a good "reason" for it (Heb. 11:1). This puts the difference between *fidelis* and *credulus,* or as Solomon terms him, *fatuus qui credit omni verbo* (Pro. 14:15); between faith and lightness of belief. Faith hath ever a ground; *vidimus enim,*—an *enim,* a reason for it, and is ready to render it. How came you to believe? *Audivimus enim,* "for we have heard an Angel" (Luke 2:20), say the shepherds. *Vidimus enim,* "for we have seen a star," say the Magi, and this is a well-grounded faith. We came not of our own heads, we came not before we saw some reason for it—saw that which set us on coming; *Vidimus enim stellam Ejus.*

Vidimus stellam—we can well conceive that; any that will but look up, may see a star. But how could they see the *Ejus* of it, that it was His? Either that it belonged to any, or that He it was it belonged to. This passeth all perspective; no astronomy could shew them this. What by course of nature the stars can produce, that they by course of art or observation may discover. But this birth was above nature. No trigon, triplicity, exaltation[5] could bring it forth. They are but idle that set figures for it. The star should not have been His, but He the star's, if it had gone that way. Some other light then, they saw this *Ejus* by.

Now with us in Divinity there be but two in all; 1. *Vespertina,* and 2. *Matutina lux. Vespertina,* "the owl-light" of our reason or skill is too dim to see it by. No remedy then but it must be as Esay calls it, *matutina lux,* "the morning-light," the light of God's law must certify them of the *Ejus* of it. There, or not at all to be had whom this star did portend.

And in the Law, there we find it in the twenty-fourth of Numbers (Num. 24:17). One of their own Prophets that came from whence they came, "from the mountains of the East," was ravished in spirit, "fell in a trance, had his eyes opened," and saw the *Ejus* of it many an hundred years before it rose. Saw *orietur in Jacob,* that there it should "rise," which is as much as *natus est* here. Saw *stella,* that he should be "the bright morning-Star," and so might well have a star to represent Him. Saw *sceptrum in Israel,* which is just as much as *Rex Judaeorum,* that it should portend a King there—such a King as should not only "smite the corners of Moab," that is Balak their enemy for the present; but "should reduce and bring under Him all the sons of Seth," that is all the world; for all are now Seth's sons, Cain's were all drowned in the flood. Here now is the *Ejus* of it clear. A Prophet's eye might discern this; never a Chaldean of them all could take it with his astrolabe. Balaam's eyes were open to see it, and he helped to open their eyes by leaving behind him this prophecy to direct them how to apply it, when it should arise to the right *Ejus* of it.

But these had not the law. It is hard to say that the Chaldee paraphrase was extant long before this. They might have had it. Say, they had it not: if Moses was so careful to record this prophecy in his book, it may well be thought that some memory of this so memorable a prediction was left remaining among them of the East, his own country where he was born and brought up. And some help they might have from Daniel too, who lived all his time in Chaldea and Persia, and prophesied among them of such a King, and set the just time of it.

And this, as it is conceived, put the difference between the East and the West. For I ask, was it *vidimus in Oriente* with them? Was it not *vidimus in Occidente?* In the West such a star—it or the fellow of it was seen nigh about that time, or the Roman stories deceive us. Toward the end of Augustus' reign such a star was seen, and much scanning there was about it. Pliny saith it was generally holden, that star to be *faustum sydus,* a "lucky comet," and portended good to the world, which few or no comets do. And Virgil, who then lived, would needs take upon him to set down the *ejus* of it, . . . *Ecce Dionoei, &c.*—entitled Caesar to it. And verily there is no man that can without admiration read his sixth Eclogue, of a birth that time expected, that should be the offspring of the gods, and that should take away their sins. Whereupon it hath gone for current—the East and West, *Vidimus* both.

But by the light of their prophecy, the East, they went straight to the right *Ejus.* And for want of this light the West wandered, and gave it a wrong *ejus;* as Virgil, applying it to little Salonine: and as evil hap was, while he was making his verses, the poor child died; and so his star shot, vanished, and came to nothing. Their *vidimus* never came to a *venimus;* they neither went, nor worshipped Him as these here did.

But by this we see, when all is done, hither we must come for our morning-light; to this book, to the word of prophecy. All our *vidimus stellam* is as good as nothing without it. That star is past and gone, long since; "Heaven and earth shall pass, but this word shall not pass." Here on this, we to fix our eye and to ground our faith. Having this, though we neither hear Angel nor see star, we may by the grace of God do full well. For even they that have had both those, have been fain to resolve into this as their last, best, and chiefest point of all. Witness St. Peter: he, saith he, and they with him, "saw Christ's glory, and heard the voice from Heaven in the Holy Mount" (2 Peter 1:17-19). What then? After both these, *audivimus* and *vidimus,* both senses, he comes to this, *Habemus autem firmiorem, &c.* "We have a more sure word of prophecy" than both these; *firmiorem,* a "more sure," a more clear, than them both. And *si hîc legimus*—for *legimus* is *vidimus,* "if here we read it written," it is enough to ground our faith, and let the star go.

And yet, to end this point; both these, the star and the prophecy, they are but *circumfusa lux*—without both. Besides these there must be a light within in the eye; else, we know, for all them nothing will be seen. And that must come from Him, and the enlightening of His Spirit. Take this for a rule; no knowing of *Ejus absque Eo,* "of His without Him," Whose it is. Neither of the star, without Him That created it; nor of the prophecy, without Him That inspired it. But this third coming too; He sending the light of His Spirit within into their minds, they then saw clearly, this the star, now the time, He the Child That this day was born.

He That sent these two without, sent also this third within, and then it was *vidimus* indeed. The light of the star in their eyes, the "word of prophecy " in their ears, the beam of His Spirit in their hearts; these three made up a full *vidimus*. And so much for *vidimus stellam Ejus,* the occasion of their coming.

Now to *venimus,* their coming itself. And it follows well. For it is not a star only, but a load-star; and whither should *stella Ejus ducere,* but *ad Eam*? "Whither lead us but to Him Whose the star is?" The star to the star's Master.

All this while we have been at *dicentes,* "saying" and seeing; now we shall come to *facientes,* see them do some-what upon it. It is not saying nor seeing will serve St. James; he will call, and be still calling for *ostende mihi,* "shew me thy faith by some work" (James 2:18). And well may he be allowed to call for it this day; it is the day of *vidimus,* appearing, being seen. You have seen His star, let Him now see your star another while. And so they do. Make your faith to be seen; so it is—their faith in the steps of their faith. And so was Abraham's first by coming forth of his country; as these here do, and so "walk in the steps of the faith of Abraham" (Rom. 4:12), do his first work.

It is not commended to stand "gazing up into Heaven" (Acts 1:11) too long; not on Christ Himself ascending, much less on His star. For they sat not still gazing on the star. Their *vidimus* begat *venimus;* their seeing made them come, come a great journey. *Venimus* is soon said, but a short word; but many a wide and weary step they made before they could come to say *Venimus,* Lo, here "we are come"; come, and at our journey's end. To look a little on it.

In this their coming we consider, 1. First, the distance of the place they came from. It was not hard by as the shepherds—but a step to Bethlehem over the fields; this was riding many a hundred miles, and cost them many a day's journey. 2. Secondly, we consider the way that they came, if it be pleasant, or plain and easy; for if it be, it is so much the better. 1. This was nothing pleasant, for through deserts, all the way waste and desolate. 2. Nor secondly, easy either; for over the rocks and crags of both Arabias, specially Petraea, their journey lay. 3. Yet if safe—but it was not, but exceeding dangerous, as lying through the midst of the "black tents of Kedar" (Cant. 1:5), a nation of thieves and cut-throats; to pass over the hills of robbers, infamous then, and infamous to this day. No passing without great troop or convoy. 4. Last we consider the time of their coming, the season of the year. It was no summer progress. A cold coming they had of it at this time of the year, just the worst time of the year to take a journey, and specially a long journey in. The ways deep, the weather sharp, the days short, the sun farthest off, *in solstitio brumali,* "the very dead of winter." *Venimus,* "we are come," if that be one, *venimus,* "we are now come," come at this time, that sure is another.

And these difficulties they overcame, of a wearisome, irksome, troublesome, dangerous, unseasonable journey; and for all this they came. And came it cheerfully and quickly, as appeareth by the speed they made. It was but *vidimus, venimus,* with them; "they saw," and "they came"; no sooner saw, but they set out presently. So as upon the first appearing of the star, as it might be last night, they knew it was Balaam's star; it called them away, they made ready straight to begin their journey this morning. A sign they were highly conceited of His birth, believed some great matter of it, that they took all these pains, made all this haste that they might be there to worship Him with all the possible speed they could. Sorry for nothing so much as that they could not be there soon enough, with the very first, to do it even this day, the day of His birth. All considered, there is more in *venimus* than shews at the first sight. It was not for nothing it was said in the first verse, *ecce venerunt;* their coming hath an *ecce* on it, it well deserves it.

And we, what should we have done? Sure these men of the East shall rise in judgment against the men of the West (Matt. 8:11), that is us, and their faith against ours in this point. With them it was but *vidimus, venimus;* with us it would have been but *veniemus* at most. Our fashion is to see and see again before we stir a foot, specially if it be to the worship of Christ. Come such a journey at such a time? No; but fairly have put it off to the spring of the year, till the days longer, and the ways fairer, and the weather warmer, till better travelling to Christ. Our Epiphany would sure have fallen in Easter-week at the soonest.

But then for the distance, desolateness, tediousness, and the rest, any of them were enough to mar our *venimus* quite. It must be no great way, first, we must come; we love not that. Well fare the shepherds, yet they came but hard by; rather like them than the Magi. Nay, not like them neither. For with us the nearer, lightly the farther off; our proverb is you know, "The nearer the Church, the farther from God."

Nor it must not be through no desert, over no Petraea if rugged or uneven the way, if the weather ill-disposed, if any never so little danger, it is enough to stay us. To Christ we cannot travel, but weather and way and all must be fair. If not, no journey, but sit still and see farther. As indeed, all our religion is rather *vidimus,* a contemplation, than *venimus,* a motion, or stirring to do aught.

But when we do it, we must be allowed leisure. Ever *veniemus,* never *venimus;* ever coming, never come. We love to make no very great haste.

To other things perhaps; not to *adorare,* the place of the worship of God. Why should we? Christ is no wildcat. What talk ye of twelve days? And if it be forty days hence, ye shall be sure to find His Mother and Him; she cannot be churched till then. What needs such haste? The truth is, we conceit Him and His birth but slenderly, and our haste is even thereafter. But if we be at that point, we must be out of this *venimus;* they like enough to leave us behind. Best get us a new Christmas in September; we are not like to come to Christ at this feast. Enough for *venimus.*

But what is *venimus* without *invenimus?* And when they come, they hit not on Him at first. No more must we think, as soon as ever we be come, to find him straight. They are fain to come to their *ubi est?* We must now look back to that. For though it stand before in the verse, here is the right place of it. They saw before they came, and came before they asked; asked before they found, and found before they worshipped. Between *venimus,* "their coming," and *adorare,* "their worshipping," there is the true place of *dicentes, ubi est?*

Where, first, we note a double use of their *dicentes,* these wise men had. 1. As to manifest what they knew, *natus est,* "that He is born," so to confess and ask what they knew not, the place where. We to have the like.

2. Secondly, set down this; that to find where He is, we must learn of these to ask where He is, which we full little set ourselves to do. If we stumble on Him, so it is; but for any asking we trouble not ourselves, but sit still as we say, and let nature work; and so let grace too, and so for us it shall. I wot well, it is said in a place of Esay, "He was found," *a non quaerentibus,* "of some that sought Him not" (Isa. 65:1), never asked *ubi est?* But it is no good holding by that place. It was their good hap that so did. But trust not to it, it is not every body's case, that. It is better advice you shall read in the Psalm, *haec est generatio quaerentium,* "there is a generation of them that seek Him" (Ps. 24: 6). Of which these were, and of that generation let us be. Regularly there is no promise of *invenietis* but to *quaerite,* of finding but to such as "seek." It is not safe to presume to find Him otherwise.

I thought there had been small use now of *ubi est?* Yet there is except we hold the ubiquity, that Christ is *ubi non,* "any where." But He is not so. Christ hath His *ubi,* His proper place where He is to be found; and if you miss of that, you miss of Him. And well may we miss, saith Christ Himself, there are so many will take upon them to tell us where, and tell us of so many *ubis. Ecce hîc,* "Look you, here He is"; *Ecce illîc;* nay then, "there." *In deserto,* "in the desert." Nay, *in penetralibus,* "in such a privy conventicle" (Matt. 24:23), you shall be sure of Him. And yet He, saith He Himself, in none of them all. There is then yet place for *ubi est?* I speak not of His natural body but of His mystical—that is Christ too.

How shall we then do? Where shall we get this "where" resolved? Where these did. They said it to many, and oft, but gat no answer, till they had got together a convocation of Scribes, and they resolved them of Christ's *ubi*. For they in the East were nothing so wise, or well seen, as we in the West are now grown. We need call no Scribes together, and get them tell us, "where." Every artisan hath a whole Synod of Scribes in his brain, and can tell where Christ is better than any learned man of them all. Yet these were wise men; best learn where they did.

And how did the Scribes resolve it then? Out of Micah. As before to the star they join Balaam's prophecy, so now again to His *orietur,* that such a one should be born, they had put Micah's *et tu Bethlehem,* the place of His birth. Still helping, and giving light as it were to the light of Heaven, by a more clear light, the light of the Sanctuary.

Thus then to do. And to do it ourselves, and not seek Christ *per alium;* set others about it as Herod did these, and sit still ourselves. For so, we may hap never find Him no more than he did.

And now we have found "where," what then? It is neither in seeking nor finding, *venimus* nor *invenimus;* the end of all, the cause of all is in the last words, *adorare Eum,* "to worship Him." That is all in all, and without it all our seeing, coming, seeking, and finding is to no purpose. The Scribes they could tell, and did tell where He was, but were never the nearer for it, for they worshipped Him not. For this end to seek Him.

This is acknowledged: Herod, in effect, said as much. He would know where He were fain, and if they will bring him word where, he will come too and worship Him, that he will. None of that worship. If he find Him, his worshipping will prove worrying; as did appear by a sort of silly poor lambs that he worried, when he could not have his will on Christ (Matt. 2:16). Thus he at His birth. And at His death, the other Herod, he sought Him too; but it was that he and his soldiers might make themselves sport with Him (Luke 23:11). Such seeking there is otherwhile. And such worshipping; as they in the judgment hall worshipped Him with *Ave Rex,* and then gave Him a bob blindfold (John 19:3). The world's worship of Him for the most part.

But we may be bold to say, Herod was "a fox" (Luke 13:32). These mean as they say; to worship Him they come, and worship Him they will. Will they so? Be they well advised what they promise, before they know whether they shall find Him in a worshipful taking or no? For full little know they, where and in what case they shall find Him. What, if in a stable, laid there in a manger, and the rest suitable to it; in as poor and pitiful a plight as ever was any, more like to be abhorred than adored of such persons? Will they be as good as their word, trow? Will they not step back at the sight, repent themselves of their journey, and wish themselves at home again? But so find Him, and so finding Him, worship Him for all that? If they will, verily then great is their faith. This, the clearest beam of all.

"The Queen of the South" (Matt. 12:42), who was a figure of these Kings of the East, she came as great a journey as these. But when she came, she found a King indeed, King Solomon in all his royalty. Saw a glorious King, and a glorious court about him. Saw him, and heard him; tried him with many hard questions, received satisfaction of them all. This was worth her coming. Weigh what she found, and what these here—as poor and unlikely a birth as could be, ever to prove a King, or any great matter. No sight to comfort them, nor a word for which they any whit the wiser; nothing worth their travel. Weigh these together, and great odds will be found between her faith and theirs. Theirs the greater far.

Well, they will take Him as they find Him, and all this notwithstanding, worship Him for all that. The Star shall make amends for the manger, and for *stella Ejus* they will dispense with *Eum*.

And what is it to worship? Some great matter sure it is, that Heaven and earth, the stars and Prophets, thus do but serve to lead them and conduct us to. For all we see ends in *adorare. Scriptura et mundus ad hoc sunt, ut colatur Qui creavit, et adoretur Qui inspiravit;* "the Scripture and world are but to this end, that He That created the one and inspired the other might be but worshipped." Such reckoning did these seem to make of it here. And such the great treasurer of the Queen Candace. These came from the mountains in the East; he from the uttermost part of Ethiopia came (Acts 8:27), and came for no other end but only this—to worship; and when they had done that, home again. *Tanti est adorare.* Worth the while, worth our coming, if coming we do but that, but worship and nothing else. And so I would have men account of it.

To tell you what it is in particular, I must put you over to the eleventh verse, where it is set down what they did when they worshipped. It is set down in two acts *proskunein,* and *prospherein,* "falling down," and "offering." Thus did they, thus we to do; we to do the like when we will worship. These two are all, and more than these we find not.

We can worship God but three ways, we have but three things to worship Him withal. 1. The soul He hath inspired; 2. the body He hath ordained us; 3. and the worldly goods He hath vouchsafed to bless us withal. We to worship Him with all, seeing there is but one reason for all. If He breathed into us our soul, but framed not our body, but some other did that, neither bow your knee nor uncover your head, but keep on your hats, and sit even as you do hardly. But if He hath framed that body of yours and every member of it, let Him have the honour both of head and knee, and every member else.

Again, if it be not He That gave us our worldly goods but somebody else, what He gave not, that withhold from Him and spare not. But if all come from Him, all to return to Him. If He send all, to be worshipped with all. And this in good sooth is but *rationabile obsequium,* as the Apostle calleth it (Rom. 12:1). No more than reason would, we should worship Him with all.

Else if all our worship be inward only, with our hearts and not our hats as some fondly imagine, we give Him but one of three; we put Him to His thirds, bid Him be content with that, He gets no more but inward worship. That is out of the text quite. For though I doubt not but these here performed that also, yet here it is not. St. Matthew mentions it not, it is not to be seen, no *vidimus* on it. And the text is a *vidimus,* and of a star; that is, of an outward visible worship to be seen of all. There is a *vidimus* upon the worship of the body, it may be seen—*procidentes.* Let us see you fall down. So is there upon the worship with our worldly goods, that may be seen and felt—*offerentes.* Let us see whether, and what you offer. With both which, no less than with the soul, God is to be worshipped. "Glorify God with your bodies, for they are God's" (1 Cor. 6:20), saith the Apostle. "Honour God with your substance, for He hath blessed your store" (Prov. 3:9), saith Solomon. It is the precept of a wise King, of one there; it is the practice of more than one, of these three here. Specially now; for Christ hath now a body, for which to do Him worship with our bodies. And now He was made poor to make us rich, and so *offerentes* will do well, comes very fit.

To enter farther into these two would be too long, and indeed they be not in our verse here, and so for some other treatise at some other time.

There now remains nothing but to include ourselves, and bear our part with them, and with the Angels, and all who this day adored Him.

This was the load-star of the Magi, and what were they? Gentiles. So are we. But if it must be ours, then we are to go with them; *vade, et fac similiter,* "go, and do likewise" (Luke 10:37). It is *Stella gentium,* but *idem agentium* "the Gentiles' star," but "such Gentiles as overtake these and keep company with them." In their *dicentes,* "confessing their faith freely"; in their *vidimus,* "grounding it throughly"; in their *venimus,* "hasting to come to Him speedily"; in their *ubi est?* "enquiring Him out diligently"; and in their *adorare Eum,* "worshipping Him devoutly." *Per omnia* doing as these did; worshipping and thus worshipping, celebrating and thus celebrating the feast of His birth.

We cannot say *vidimus stellam;* the star is gone long since, not now to be seen. Yet I hope for all that, that *venimus adorare,* "we be come thither to worship." It will be the more acceptable, if not seeing it we worship though. It is enough we read of it in the text; we see it there. And indeed as I said, it skills not for the star in the firmament, if the same Day-Star be risen in our hearts that was in theirs, and the same beams of it to be seen, all five. For then we have our part in it no less, nay full out as much as they. And it will bring us whither it brought them, to Christ. Who at His second appearing in glory shall call forth these wise men and all that have ensued the steps of their faith, and that upon the reason specified in the text; for I have seen their star shining and shewing forth itself by the like beams; and as they came to worship Me, so am I come to do them worship. A *venite* then, for a *venimus* now. Their star I have seen, and give them a place above among the stars. They fell down: I will lift them up, and exalt them. And as they offered to Me, so am I come to bestow on them, and to reward them with the endless joy and bliss of My Heavenly Kingdom.

To which, &c.[6]

Notes

1. "Seven nights" (i.e., a week ago).
2. That is, in a previous sermon.
3. The feast of the Epiphany, January 6.
4. A reference to his dividing many discussions into five points, corresponding to the five points of a star.
5. Astrological terms.
6. A formulaic ending, such as the one for the previous sermon: "To which He grant that we may come, that this day came to us in earth that we thereby might come to Him and remain with Him for ever, 'Jesus Christ the Righteous.'"

PART IV

THE MODERN ERA: FROM THE RESTORATION TO WORLD WAR I

CHAPTER 16

THE DAWN OF MODERNITY (A)

THE RESTORATION AND THE AGE OF REASON

JOHN TILLOTSON: SERMON 48, "THE UNITY OF THE DIVINE NATURE AND THE BLESSED TRINITY"

England's Civil War between Royalists and Parliamentarians was also one of the religious wars of that period, with what became Anglicans on one side and Puritans and Independents on the other. After the Restoration of the monarchy under Charles II in 1660, the people were ready to be broad-minded about theological questions—to become latitudinarians. Then, too, the Age of Reason was dawning, and with it the rise of natural science. In this rise of modernism, a new sort of religious expression was expected: one that was less emotional and more rational in its appeal, one calmer, plainer, and clearer in its expression. A type of preaching arose that was to become extraordinarily popular—so much so that volumes of sermons sold more copies than the works of the best writers of creative literature of the day. Indeed, some of the most influential thinkers in every area of thought were numbered among the sermon writers.

No one did more to set this style than John Tillotson (**see Vol. 1, pp. 411-14**), *who was archbishop of Canterbury from 1691 to 1694. Although religious doubt was on the rise, the following sermon shows that latitudinarianism by no means meant disloyalty to the creeds. The sermon also shows the calmness and reasonableness of his approach, and his irenic attitude toward other Christians—with the exception of Roman Catholics. In Tillotson, the English sermon took a decisive turn in the direction of the essay. The sermon is taken from* The Works of Dr. John Tillotson, Late Archbishop of Canterbury. With the Life of the Author, by Thomas Birch, M.A. Also, a Copious Index, and the Texts of Scripture Carefully Compared. In Ten Volumes *(London: J. F. Dove for Richard Priestley, 1820), 3:409-38.*

Sermon 48

Concerning the Unity of the Divine Nature, and the Blessed Trinity, &c.

For there is one God. 1 Tim. 2:5

The particle *for* leads us to the consideration of the context and occasion of these words, which in short is this. The design of this Epistle is to direct Timothy, to whom St. Paul had committed the government of the church of Ephesus, how he ought to demean himself in that great and weighty charge. And at the beginning of this chapter he gives direction concerning public prayers in the church; that prayers and thanksgiving be made for all men, and for all ranks and orders of men; especially for kings and all that are in authority, that under them Christians might lead a quiet and peaceable life in all godliness and honesty.

And this he tells us was very suitable to the Christian religion, by which God designed the salvation of mankind; and therefore it must needs be very acceptable to him, that we should offer up prayers and thanksgivings to him in behalf of all men: "For this (saith the apostle) is good and acceptable in the sight of God our Savior, who will have all men to be saved, and to come to the knowledge of the truth."

And then it follows in the next words, "For there is one God, and one mediator between God and men, the man Christ Jesus, who gave himself a ransom for all," as if he had said—This universal charity of Christians, in praying for all men, must needs be very acceptable to him to whom we put up our prayers, God the Father, who sent his Son for the salvation of all men: and to him likewise by whom we offer up our prayers to God, and is amongst us Christians the only mediator between God and man, in virtue of that price and ransom which be paid for the redemption of all mankind; I say, for this reason it must needs be very acceptable to him, that we should pray for all men, because he died for all men, and now that he is in heaven at the right hand of God intercedes with him for the salvation of those for whom he died: "There is one God, and one mediator between God and men, the man Christ Jesus, who gave himself a ransom for all."

Which words, though they be brought in to prove more immediately, that it is acceptable to God our Savior, that we should put up our prayers to him for all men, because he desires the salvation of all men, and hath sent his Son to purchase the salvation of all men, by the sacrifice of himself; and in virtue of that sacrifice to be the only mediator between God and us: I say, though this be the immediate scope and design of these words, yet they are likewise a direction to us, unto whom we ought to address our prayers—namely, to God; and by whose mediation and intercession we ought to put up our prayers to God the Father, namely, by his Son Jesus Christ, who is constituted the only mediator between God and men.

There are several propositions contained in this and the following verse; but I shall at present confine myself to the first; namely, that "there is one God"; that is, "but one," as St. Paul elsewhere expresseth it, "there is none other God but one" (1 Cor. 8:4). And Moses lays this as the foundation of the natural law as well as of the Jewish religion: "the Lord he is one God, and there is none besides him" (Deut. 4:35); that is, besides Jehovah, whom the people of Israel did worship as the only true God. And this the prophet Isaiah perpetually declares in opposition to the polytheism and variety of gods among the heathen: "I am the first and I am the last, and besides me there is no God" (Isa. 44:6). And again, "Is there any god besides me? There is no god, I know not any" (vs. 8): he who hath an infinite knowledge and knows all things, knows no other god. And our blessed Savior makes this the fundamental article of all religion, and the knowledge of it necessary to every man's salvation: "This (says he) is life eternal, to know thee the only true God."

The unity of the Divine nature is a notion wherein the greatest and the wisest part of mankind did always agree, and therefore may reasonably be presumed to be either natural, or to have sprung from some original tradition delivered down to us from the first parents of mankind—I mean, that there is one Supreme Being, the author and cause of all things, whom the most ancient of the heathen poets commonly called "the

Father of Gods and Men." And thus Aristotle in his Metaphysics defines God, "the eternal and most excellent, or best of all living beings." And this notion of one Supreme Being, agrees very well with that exact harmony which appears in the frame and government of the world, in which we see all things conspiring to one end, and continuing in one uniform order and course; which cannot reasonably be ascribed to any other but a constant and uniform cause; and which to a considering man does plainly show, that all things are made and governed by that one powerful principle, and great and wise mind, which we call God.

But although the generality of mankind had a notion of one supreme God, yet the idolatry of the heathen plainly shows that this notion, in process of time, was greatly degenerated, and corrupted into an apprehension of a plurality of gods; though in reason it is evident enough that there can be no more gods than one; and that one, who is of infinite perfection, is as sufficient to all purposes whatsoever, as ten thousand deities, if they were possible, could possibly be—as I shall show in the following discourse.

Now this multitude of deities, which the fond superstition and vain imagination of men had formed to themselves, were, by the wiser sort, who being forced to comply with the follies of the people endeavored to make the best of them, supposed to be either parts of the universe, which the Egyptians, as Plutarch tells us, thought to be the same with God; but then the more considerable parts of the universe they parceled out into several deities; and as the ocean hath several names, according to the several coasts and countries by which it passeth, so they gave several names to this one deity, according to the several parts of the world which several nations made the objects of their worship.

Or else, they adored the several perfections and powers of the one supreme God under several names and titles, with regard to the various blessings and benefits which they thought they received from him.

Thus the Indian philosophers, the Brachmans,[1] are said to have worshiped the sun as the supreme Deity; and he certainly is the most worshipful of all sensible beings, and bids fairest for a deity; especially if he was, as they supposed, animated by a spirit endued with knowledge and understanding. And if a man who had been bred in a dark cave, should all on the sudden be brought out at noonday to behold this visible world; after he had viewed and considered it a while, he would in all probability pitch upon the sun as the most likely, of all the things he had seen, to be a deity. For if such a man had any notion of a God, and were to choose one upon sight, he would without dispute fix upon the sun, and fall down before him and worship him.

And Macrobius manageth this as his main plea for the idolatry of the heathen: that under all the several names of their gods they worshiped the sun: and this diversity of names was but a more distinct conception and acknowledgment of the many blessings and advantages which mankind received from him, and a more particular and express adoration of the several powers and perfections which were in him. And this was the very best defense, and all the tolerable sense which the wisest among the heathen could make, of the multitude of their deities.

And yet whilst they generally owned one Supreme Being that was the principle and original of all things, they worshiped several subordinate deities as really distinct from one another. Some of these they fancied to be superior to the rest, and to have their residence in heaven; by which Marcilius Ficinus supposes Plato to mean no more but the chief of the angels. These were called *theoi, Dei Superi* and *Dii Caelestes,* "superior" and "heavenly gods": the Scripture terms them the "host of heaven," meaning the sun, moon, and stars, which they supposed to be animated, or at least to be inhabited by angels, or glorious spirits, whom they called gods.

Other of their deities were accounted much inferior to these, being supposed to be the souls of their deceased heroes, who, for their great and worthy deeds, when they lived upon earth, were supposed after death to be translated into the number of their gods. And these were called *Semidei* and *Deastri,* that is, "half-gods," and a "sort of gods." And as the other were "celestial," so these were *Daimones epichthonioi,* a kind of "terrestrial" spirits, that were presidents and procurators of human affairs here below; that is, a middle sort of divine powers that were mediators and agents between God and men, and did carry the prayers and supplications of men to God, and bring down the commands and blessings of God to men.

But in the midst of all this crowd and confusion of deities, and the various superstitions about them, the wiser heathen, as Thales, Pythagoras, Socrates, Plato, Aristotle, Tully, Plutarch, and others, preserved a true notion of one supreme God, whom they defined an Infinite Spirit, pure from all matter, and free from all imperfection: and all the variety of their worship was, as they pretended in excuse of it, but a more particular owning of the various representations of the Divine power and excellencies which manifested themselves in the world, and of the several communications of blessings and favors by them imparted to men: and Tertullian observes, that even when idolatry had very much obscured the glory of the sovereign Deity, yet the greater part of mankind did still, in their common forms of speech, appropriate the name of God, in a more especial and peculiar manner to one, saying, "If God grant," "If God please," and the like (*Adversus Marcionem* 1.10).

So that there is sufficient ground to believe, that the unity of the Divine nature, or the notion of one supreme God, Creator and Governor of the world, was the primitive and general belief of mankind: and that polytheism and idolatry were a corruption and degeneracy from the original notion which mankind had concerning God; as the Scripture history doth declare and testify.

And this account which I have given of the heathen idolatry doth by no means excuse it. For whatever may be said by way of extenuation in behalf of some few of the wiser and more devout among them, the generality were grossly guilty both of believing more gods and of worshiping false gods.

And this must needs be a very great crime, since the scripture every where declares God to be particularly jealous in this case, and that "he will not give his glory to another, nor his praise to graven images": nay, we may not so much as make use of sensible images to put us in mind of God, lest devout ignorance, seeing the worship which wise men paid towards an idol, should be drawn to terminate their worship there, as being the very Deity itself, which was certainly the case of the greatest part of the heathen world.

And surely those Christians are in no less danger of idolatry who pay a veneration to images by kneeling down and praying before them; and in this they are much more inexcusable, because they offend against a much clearer light; and yet when they go about to justify this practice, are able to bring no other nor better pleas for themselves than the heathen did for their worshiping of images, and for praying to their inferior deities, whom they looked upon as mediators between the gods in heaven and men upon earth.

There is but one objection, that I know of, against the general consent of mankind concerning the unity of God, and it is this: that there was an ancient doctrine of some of the most ancient nations that there were two first causes or principles of all things, the one the cause of all good, and the other of all the evil that is in the world: the reason whereof seems to have been, that they could not apprehend how things of so contrary nature as good and evil could proceed from one and the same cause.

And these two principles in several nations were called by several names. Plutarch says, that among the Greeks the good principle was called God, and the evil principle *Daimōn*, or the devil. In conformity to which ancient tradition the Manichees, a sect which called themselves Christians, did advance two principles, the one infinitely good, which they supposed to be the original cause of all the good which is in the world, the other infinitely evil, to which they ascribed all the evils that are in the world.

But all this is very plainly a corruption of a much more ancient tradition concerning that old serpent, the devil, the head of the fallen angels, who, by tempting our first parents to transgress a positive and express law of God, brought sin first into the world and all the evils consequent upon it—of which the Scripture gives us a most express and particular account.

And as to the notion of a being infinitely evil, into which this tradition was corrupted, after idolatry had prevailed in the world, besides that it is a contradiction, it would likewise be to no purpose to assert two opposite principles of infinite, that is, of equal force and power, for two infinites must of necessity be equal to one another; because nothing can be more or greater than infinite: and therefore, if two infinite beings were possible, they would certainly be equal, and could not be otherwise.

Now that the notion of a principle infinitely evil is a contradiction, will be very plain, if we consider that what is infinitely evil must, in strict reasoning and by necessary consequence, be infinitely imperfect; and therefore infinitely weak, and for that reason, though never so malicious and mischievous, yet being infinitely weak and foolish, could never be in capacity either to contrive mischief or to execute it.

But if it should be admitted, that a being infinitely mischievous could be infinitely knowing and powerful, yet it could effect no evil: because the opposite principle of infinite goodness, being also infinitely wise and powerful, they would tie up one another's hands. So that upon this supposition the notion of a Deity must signify just nothing, because, by virtue of the eternal opposition and equal conflict of these two principles, they would keep one another at a perpetual bay; and being just an equal match to one another, the one having as much mind and power to do good, as the other to do evil, instead of being two deities they would be but two idols, able to do neither good nor evil.

And having, I hope, now sufficiently cleared this objection, I shall proceed to show how agreeable this principle, that there is but one God, is to the common reason of mankind, and to the clearest and most essential notions which we have of God: and this will appear these two ways.

First, By considering the most essential perfections of the Divine nature.

Secondly, From the repugnancy and impossibility, the great absurdity and inconvenience, of supposing more gods than one.

First, By considering the most essential perfections of the Divine nature. Absolute perfection, which we ascribe to God as the most essential notion which mankind hath always had concerning him, does necessarily suppose unity; because this is essential to the notion of a being that is absolutely perfect, that all perfection meets and is united in such a being: but to imagine more gods, and some perfections to be in one and some in another, does destroy the most essential notion which men have of God, namely, that he is a being absolutely perfect, that is, as perfect as is possible: now to suppose some perfections in one god which are not in another, is to suppose some possible perfection to be wanting in God, which is a contradiction to the most natural and the most easy notion which all men have of God, that he is a being in whom all perfections do meet and are united: but if we suppose more gods, each of which hath all perfections united in him, then all but one would be superfluous and needless; and therefore by just and necessary consequence not only may, but of necessity must be, supposed not to be; since necessary existence is essential to the Deity: and therefore if but one God be necessary, there can be no more.

Secondly, From the repugnancy and impossibility, the great absurdity and inconveniency, of the contrary. For suppose there were more gods, two for example—and if there may be two there may be a million, for we can stop nowhere—I say, suppose two gods; either these two would be in all perfections equal and alike, or unequal and unlike: if equal and alike in all things, then, as I said before, one of them would be needless and superfluous, and if one, why not as well the other? they being supposed to be in all things perfectly alike; and then there would be no necessity at all of the being of a god; and yet it is granted on all hands, that necessary existence is essential to the notion of a god but if they be unequal, that is, one of them inferior to and less perfect than the other, that which is inferior and less perfect could not be God, because he would not have all perfection. So that which way soever we turn the thing and look upon it, the notion of more gods than one is by its own repugnancy and self-contradiction destructive of itself.

Before I come to apply this doctrine of the unity of God, I must not pass by a very considerable difficulty, which will most certainly arise in every man's mind, without taking particular notice of it, and endeavoring to remove it, if I can. And it is the doctrine of the blessed Trinity, or of three real differences or distinct persons in one and the same Divine nature.

And though this be not a difficulty peculiar only to the Christian religion, as by the generality of those who urge this objection against

Christians hath been inconsiderately thought; for it is certain that long before Christianity appeared in the world, there was a very ancient tradition, both among Jews and heathen, concerning three real differences or distinctions in the Divine nature, very nearly resembling the Christian doctrine of the Trinity, as I shall have occasion more fully to show by and by; yet it cannot be denied, but that this difficulty doth in a more especial manner affect the Christian religion; the generality of Christians, who do most firmly believe the Trinity, believing likewise at the same time, more steadfastly if it be possible, that "there is but one God." "To us (saith St. Paul, that is, to us Christians) there is but one God" (1 Cor. 8:6). But how can this possibly consist with the common doctrine of Christians concerning the Trinity, God the Father, Son, and Holy Ghost, to each of whom they attribute, as they verily believe the Scripture does, the most incommunicable properties and perfections of the Divine nature? And what is this less in effect than to say, that there are three Gods?

For the clearing of this difficulty I shall, with all the brevity I can, offer these following considerations: which I hope, to an impartial and unprejudiced judgment, will be sufficient to remove it, or at least to break the main force and strength of it.

I. I desire it may be well considered, that there is a wide difference between the nice speculations of the schools, beyond what is revealed in Scripture, concerning the doctrine of the Trinity, and what the Scripture only teaches and asserts concerning this mystery. For it is not to be denied, but that the schoolmen, who abounded in wit and leisure—though very few among them had either exact skill in the Holy Scriptures, or in ecclesiastical antiquity and the writings of the ancient fathers of the Christian church—I say, it cannot be denied, but that these speculative and very acute men, who wrought a great part of their divinity out of their own brain, as spiders do cobwebs out of their own bowels, have started a thousand subtleties about this mystery, such as no Christian is bound to trouble his head withal; much less is it necessary for him to understand those niceties, which we may reasonably presume that they who talk of them did themselves never thoroughly understand; and least of all is it necessary to believe them. The modesty of Christians is contented in Divine mysteries to know what God hath thought fit to reveal concerning them, and hath no curiosity to be wise above that which is written. It is enough to believe what God says concerning these matters; and if any man will venture to say more, every other man surely is at his liberty to believe as he sees reason.

II. I desire it may, in the next place, be considered, that the doctrine of the Trinity, even as it is asserted in Scripture, is acknowledged by us to be still a great mystery, and so imperfectly revealed as to be in a great measure incomprehensible by human reason. And therefore, though some learned and judicious men may have very commendably attempted a more particular explication of this great mystery by the strength of reason, yet I dare not pretend to that, knowing both the difficulty and danger of such an attempt, and mine own insufficiency for it.

All that I ever designed upon this argument was to make out the credibility of the thing from the authority of the Holy Scripture, without descending to a more particular explication of it than the Scripture hath given us; lest, by endeavoring to lay the difficulties which are already started about it, new ones should be raised, and such as may perhaps be much harder to be removed than those which we have now to grapple withal. And this I hope I have in some measure done in one of the former discourses (Sermon XLIV). Nor indeed do I see that it is any ways necessary to do more; it being sufficient that God hath declared what he thought fit in this matter, and that we do firmly believe what he says concerning it to be true, though we do not perfectly comprehend the meaning of all that he hath said about it.

For in this and the like cases I take an implicit faith to be very commendable; that is, to believe whatever we are sufficiently assured God hath revealed, though we do not fully understand his meaning in such a revelation. And thus every man who believes the Holy Scriptures to be a truly divine revelation, does implicitly believe a great part of the prophetical books of Scripture, and several obscure expressions in those books, though he do not particularly understand the meaning of all the predictions and expressions contained in them. In like manner, there are certainly a great many very good Christians who do not believe and comprehend the mysteries of faith nicely enough to approve themselves to a scholastical and magisterial judge of controversies, who yet, if they do heartily embrace the doctrines which are clearly revealed in Scripture and live up to the plain precepts of the Christian religion, will I doubt not be very well approved by the great and just, and by the infallibly infallible Judge of the world.

III. Let it be further considered, that though neither the word trinity, nor perhaps person, in the sense in which it is used by divines when they treat of this mystery, be anywhere to be met with in Scripture, yet it cannot be denied but that Three are there spoken of by the terms of Father, Son, and Holy Ghost, in whose name every Christian is baptized, and to each of whom the highest titles and properties of God are in scripture attributed: and these Three are spoken of with as much distinction from one another as we use to speak of three several persons.

So that though the word trinity be not found in Scripture, yet these Three are there expressly and frequently mentioned; and a trinity is nothing but three of anything. And so likewise, though the word person be not there expressly applied to Father, Son, and Holy Ghost, yet it will be very hard to find a more convenient word whereby to express the distinction of these Three. For which reason I could never yet see any just cause to quarrel at this term. For since the Holy Spirit of God in Scripture hath thought fit in speaking of these Three to distinguish them from one another, as we use in common speech to distinguish three several persons, I cannot see any reason why, in the explication of this mystery, which purely depends upon divine revelation, we should not speak of it in the same manner as the Scripture doth: and though the word person is now become a term of art, I see no cause why we should decline it, so long as we mean by it neither more or less than what the Scripture says in other words.

IV. It deserves further to be considered, that there hath been a very ancient tradition concerning three real differences or distinctions in the divine nature; and these, as I said before, very nearly resemble the Christian doctrine of the Trinity.

Whence this tradition had its original is not easy upon good and certain grounds to say; but certain it is, that the Jews anciently had this notion: and that they did distinguish the Word of God, and the Holy Spirit of God, from him who was absolutely called God, and whom they looked upon as the first principle of all things; as is plain from Philo Judaeus, and Moses Nachmanides, and others cited by the learned Grotius in his incomparable book of the Truth of the Christian Religion (Lib. V).

And among the heathen, Plato, who probably enough might have this notion from the Jews, did make three distinctions in the Deity by the names of essential goodness, and mind, and spirit.

So that whatever objections this matter may be liable to, it is not so peculiar a doctrine of the Christian religion as many have imagined, though it is revealed by it with much more clearness and certainty: and consequently, neither the Jews nor Plato have any reason to object it to us Christians; especially since they pretend no other ground for it but either their own reason, or an ancient tradition from their fathers:

whereas we Christians do appeal to express Divine revelation for what we believe in this matter, and do believe it singly upon that account.

V. It is besides very considerable, that the Scriptures do deliver this doctrine of the Trinity without any manner of doubt or question concerning the unity of the divine nature: and not only so, but do most steadfastly and constantly assert that there is but one God: and in those very texts, in which these three differences are mentioned, the unity of the divine nature is expressly asserted, as where St. John makes mention of the Father, the Word, and the Spirit, the unity of these Three is likewise affirmed—"there are Three that bear record in heaven, the Father, the Word, and the Spirit; and these Three are one."

VI. It is yet further considerable, that from this mystery, as delivered in Scripture, a plurality of Gods cannot be inferred without making the Scripture grossly to contradict itself: which I charitably suppose the Socinians would be as loath to admit as we ourselves are. And if either councils, or fathers, or schoolmen, have so explained this mystery as to give any just ground, or so much as a plausible color, for such an inference, let the blame fall where it is due, and let it not be charged on the Holy Scriptures; but rather, as the apostle says in another case, "Let God be true, and every man a liar."

VII. Lastly, I desire it may be considered, that it is not repugnant to reason to believe some things which are incomprehensible by our reason, provided that we have sufficient ground and reason for the belief of them: especially if they be concerning God, who is in his nature incomprehensible; and we be well assured that he hath revealed them. And therefore it ought not to offend us that these differences in the Deity are incomprehensible by our finite understandings, because the divine nature itself is so, and yet the belief of that is the foundation of all religion.

There are a great many things in nature which we cannot comprehend how they either are, or can be—as the continuity of matter, that is, how the parts of it do hang so fast together, that are many times very hard to be parted—and yet we are sure that it is so, because we see it every day. So likewise how the small seeds of things contain the whole form and nature of the things from which they proceed and into which by degrees they grow, and yet we plainly see this every year.

There are many things likewise in ourselves which no man is able in any measure to comprehend, as to the manner how they are done and performed—as the vital union of the soul and body: who can imagine by what device or means a spirit comes to be so closely united and so firmly linked to a material body that they are not to be parted without great force and violence offered to nature? The like may be said of the operations of our several faculties of sense and imagination, of memory and reason, and especially of the liberty of our wills: and yet we certainly find all these faculties in ourselves, though we cannot either comprehend or explain the particular manner in which the several operations of them are performed.

And if we cannot comprehend the manner of those operations which we plainly perceive and feel to be in ourselves, much less can we expect to comprehend things without us; and least of all can we pretend to comprehend the infinite nature and perfections of God, and every thing belonging to him. For God himself is certainly the greatest mystery of all other, and acknowledged by mankind to be in his nature, and in the particular manner of his existence, incomprehensible by human understanding. And the reason of this is very evident, because God is infinite, and our knowledge and understanding is but finite: and yet no sober man ever thought this a good reason to call the being of God in question.

The same may be said of God's certain knowledge of future contingencies which depend upon the uncertain wills of free agents: it being utterly inconceivable how any understanding, how large and perfect soever, can certainly know beforehand that which depends upon the freewill of another, which is an arbitrary and uncertain cause.

And yet the Scripture doth not only attribute this foreknowledge to God, but gives us also plain instances of God's foretelling such things, many ages before they happened, as could not come to pass but by the sins of men, in which we are sure that God can have no hand; though nothing can happen without his permission: such was that most memorable event of the death of Christ, who, as the Scripture tells us, "was by wicked hands crucified and slain"; and yet even this is said to have happened according to the determinate foreknowledge of God, and was punctually foretold by him some hundreds of years before. Nay, the Scripture doth not only ascribe this power and perfection to the Divine knowledge, but natural reason hath been coerced to acknowledge it, as we may see in some of the wisest of the philosophers. And yet it would puzzle the greatest philosopher that ever was, to give any tolerable account how any knowledge whatsoever can certainly and infallibly foresee an event through uncertain and contingent causes. All the reasonable satisfaction that can be had in this matter is this: that it is not at all unreasonable to suppose that infinite knowledge may have ways of knowing things which our finite understandings can by no means comprehend how they can possibly be known.

Again, there is hardly any thing more inconceivable than how a thing should be of itself, and without any cause of its being; and yet our reason compels us to acknowledge this; because we certainly see that something is, which must either have been of itself, and without a cause, or else something that we do not see must have been of itself, and have made all other-things: and by this reasoning we are forced to acknowledge a Deity, the mind of man being able to find no rest but in the acknowledgment of one eternal and wise Mind as the principle and first cause of all other things; and this principle is that which mankind do by general consent call God. So that God hath laid a sure foundation of our acknowledgment of his being in the reason of our own minds. And though it be one of the hardest things in the world to conceive how anything can be of itself, yet necessity drives us to acknowledge it, whether we will or no: and this being once granted, our reason, being tired in trying all other ways, will for its own quiet and ease force us at last to fall in with the general apprehension and belief of mankind concerning a Deity.

To give but one instance more: There is the like difficulty in conceiving how any thing can be made out of nothing, and yet our reason doth oblige us to believe it: because matter, which is a very imperfect being and merely passive, must either always have been of itself, or else, by the infinite power of a most perfect and active being, must have been made out of nothing: which is much more credible than that any thing so imperfect as matter is should be of itself: because that which is of itself cannot be conceived to have any bounds and limits of its being and perfection; for by the same reason that it necessarily is and of itself it must necessarily have all perfection, which it is certain matter hath not; and yet necessary existence is so great a perfection, that we cannot reasonably suppose any thing that hath this perfection to want any other.

Thus you see, by these instances, that it is not repugnant to reason to believe a great many things to be, of the manner of whose existence we are not able to give a particular and distinct account. And much less is it repugnant to reason to believe those things concerning God which we are very well assured he hath declared concerning himself, though these things by our reason should be incomprehensible.

And this is truly the case as to the matter now under debate: we are sufficiently assured that the Scriptures are a divine revelation, and that this mystery of the Trinity is therein declared to us. Now that we cannot comprehend it, is no sufficient reason not to believe it: for if this were a good reason for not believing it, then no man ought to believe that there is a God, because his nature is most certainly incomprehensible. But we are assured by many arguments that there is a God, and the same natural reason which assures us that he is, doth likewise assure us that he is incomprehensible; and therefore our believing him to be so, doth by no means overthrow our belief of his being.

In like manner, we are assured by divine revelation of the truth of this doctrine of the Trinity, and being once assured of that, our not being able fully to comprehend it, is not reason enough to stagger our belief of it. A man cannot deny what he sees, though the necessary consequence of admitting it may be something which he cannot comprehend. One cannot deny the frame of this world which he sees with his eyes, though from thence it will necessarily follow, that either that, or something else, must be of itself; which yet, as I said before, is a thing which no man can comprehend how it can be.

And by the same reason, a man must not deny what God says to be true; though he cannot comprehend many things which God says: as particularly concerning this mystery of the Trinity. It ought then to satisfy us, that there is sufficient evidence that this doctrine is delivered in Scripture, and that what is there declared concerning it doth not imply a contradiction. For why should our finite understandings pretend to comprehend that which is infinite, or to know all the real differences that are consistent with the unity of an infinite Being, or to be able fully to explain this mystery by any similitude or resemblance taken from finite beings?

But before I leave this argument, I cannot but take notice of one thing which they of the Church of Rome are perpetually objecting to us upon this occasion. And it is this: that by the same reason that we believe the doctrine of the Trinity, we may and must receive that of transubstantiation. God forbid: because of all the doctrines that ever were in any religion, this of transubstantiation is certainly the most abominably absurd.

However, this objection plainly shows how fondly and obstinately they are addicted to their own errors, how misshapen and monstrous soever, insomuch, that rather than the dictates of their church, how absurd soever, should be called in question, they will question the truth even of Christianity itself; and if we will not take in transubstantiation, and admit it to be a necessary article of the Christian faith, they grow so sullen and desperate, that they matter not what becomes of all the rest: and rather than not have their will of us in that which is controverted, they will give up that which by their own confession is an undoubted article of the Christian faith, and not controverted on either side—except only by the Socinians, who yet are hearty enemies to transubstantiation and have exposed the absurdity of it with great advantage.

But I shall endeavor to return a more particular answer to this objection, and such an one as I hope will satisfy every considerate and unprejudiced mind, that after all this confidence and swaggering of theirs, there is by no means equal reason either for the receiving or for the rejecting of these two doctrines of the Trinity and transubstantiation.

First, There is not equal reason for the belief of these two doctrines. This objection, if it be of any force, must suppose that there is equal evidence and proof from Scripture for these two doctrines: but this we utterly deny, and with great reason; because it is no more evident from the words of Scripture that the sacramental bread is substantially changed into Christ's natural body by virtue of those words, "This is my body," than it is, that Christ is substantially changed into a natural vine by virtue of those words, "I am the true vine" (John 15:1) or than that the rock in the wilderness, of which the Israelites drank, was substantially changed into the person of Christ, because it is expressly said, "That rock was Christ," or than that the Christian church is substantially changed into the natural body of Christ because it is in express terms said of the church that it "is his body" (Eph. 1:23).

But besides this, several of their own most learned writers have freely acknowledged that transubstantiation can neither be directly proved nor necessarily concluded from Scripture, but this the writers of the Christian church did never acknowledge concerning the Trinity and the Divinity of Christ, but have always appealed to the clear and undeniable testimonies of Scripture for the proof of these doctrines. And then the whole force of the objection amounts to this: That if I am bound to believe what I am sure God says though I cannot comprehend it, then I am bound by the same reason to believe the greatest absurdity in the world, though I have no manner of assurance of any divine revelation concerning it. And if this be their meaning, though we understand not transubstantiation, yet we very well understand what they would have, but cannot grant it; because there is not equal reason to believe two things, for one of which there is good proof, and for the other no proof at all.

Secondly, Neither is there equal reason for the rejecting of these two doctrines. This the objection supposes, which yet cannot be supposed but upon one or both of these two grounds: either because these two doctrines are equally incomprehensible or because they are equally loaded with absurdities and contradictions.

The first is no good ground of rejecting any doctrine, merely because it is incomprehensible, as I have abundantly showed already. But besides this, there is a wide difference between plain matters of sense, and mysteries concerning God; and it does by no means follow, that if a man do once admit anything concerning God which he cannot comprehend, he hath no reason afterwards to believe what he himself sees. This is a most unreasonable and destructive way of arguing, because it strikes at the foundation of all certainty, and sets every man at liberty to deny the most plain and evident truths of Christianity, if he may not be humored in having the absurdest things of the world admitted for true. The next step will be to persuade us that we may as well deny the being of God because his nature is incomprehensible by our reason as deny transubstantiation because it evidently contradicts our senses.

Secondly, Nor are these two doctrines loaded with the like absurdities and contradictions: so far from this, that the doctrine of the Trinity, as it is delivered in the Scriptures, and hath already been explained, hath no absurdity or contradiction either involved in it, or necessarily consequent upon it, but the doctrine of transubstantiation is big with all imaginable absurdity and contradiction. And their own schoolmen have sufficiently exposed it, especially Scotus—and he designed to do so, as any man that attentively reads him may plainly discover: for in his disputation about it he treats this doctrine with the greatest contempt as a new invention of the council of Lateran under Pope Innocent III. To the decree of which council concerning it he seems to pay a formal submission, but really derides it as contrary to the common sense and reason of mankind, and not at all supported by Scripture—as any one may easily discern that will carefully consider his manner of handling it and the result of his whole disputation about it.

And now, suppose there were some appearance of absurdity and contradiction in the doctrine of the Trinity as it is delivered in Scripture, must we therefore believe a doctrine which is not at all revealed in Scripture, and which hath certainly in it all the absurdities in the world, and all the contradictions to sense and reason, and which, once admitted, doth at once destroy all certainty? Yes, say they, why not? since we of the church of Rome are satisfied that this doctrine is revealed in Scripture, or, if it be not, is defined by the church, which is every whit as good. But is this equal, to demand of us the belief of a thing which hath always been controverted, not only between us and them, but even among themselves, at least till the council of Trent? And this upon such unreasonable terms that we must either yield this point to them or else renounce a doctrine agreed on both sides to be revealed in Scripture.

To show the unreasonableness of this proceeding, let us suppose a priest of the church of Rome pressing a Jew or Turk to the belief of transubstantiation, and, because one kindness deserves another, the Jew or Turk should demand of him the belief of all the fables in the Talmud, or in the Alcoran,[2] since none of these nor indeed all of them together are near so absurd as transubstantiation; would not this be much more reasonable and equal than what they demand of us? Since no absurdity, how monstrous and big soever, can be thought of, which may not enter into an understanding in which breach hath been already made wide enough to admit transubstantiation. The priests of Baal did not half so much deserve to be exposed by the prophet for their superstition and folly as the priests of the church of Rome do for this senseless and stupid doctrine of theirs with a hard name. I shall only add this one thing more: that if this doctrine were possible to be true, and clearly proved to be so, yet it would be evidently useless and to no purpose. For it pretends to change the substance of one thing into the substance of another thing that is already, and before this change is pretended to be made. But to what purpose? Not to make the body of Christ, for that was already in being; and the substance of the bread is lost, nothing of it remaineth but accidents, which are good for nothing, and indeed are nothing when the substance is destroyed and gone.

All that now remains is to make some practical inferences from this doctrine of the unity of the divine nature. And they shalt be the same which God himself makes by Moses, which text is also cited by our Savior: "Hear, O Israel, the Lord thy God is one Lord; and thou shalt love the Lord thy God with all thine heart, and with all thy soul, and with all thy mind, and with all thy strength: and thou shalt love thy neighbor as thyself" (Deut. 6:4; Mk. 12:29-31). So that, according to our Savior, the whole duty of man, the love of God and of our neighbor, is founded in the unity of the Divine nature.

I. The love of God: "the Lord thy God is one Lord," therefore "thou shalt love him with all thy heart, &c., this is the first and great commandment": and it comprehends in it all the duties of the first table as naturally flowing from it—as that we should serve him only, and pay no religious worship to any but to him. For to pay religious worship to any thing is to make it a god, and to acknowledge it for such: and therefore God being but one, we can give religious worship to none but to him only. And among all the parts of religious worship none is more peculiarly appropriated to the Deity than solemn invocation and prayer. For he to whom men address their requests at all times and in all places must be supposed to be always everywhere present, to understand all our desires and wants, and to be able to supply them; and this God only is, and can do.

So likewise from the unity of the Divine nature may be inferred that we should not worship God by any sensible image or representation, because God, being a singular being, there is nothing like him or that can, without injuring and debasing his most spiritual and perfect and immense being, be compared to him, as he himself speaks in the prophet, "To whom will ye liken me, saith the Lord, and make me equal?" (Isa. 46:5). And therefore with no distinction whatsoever can it be lawful to give religious worship, or any part of it, to any but God: we can pray to none but to him, because he only is everywhere present, and "only knows the hearts of all the children of men" (1 Kings 8:39), which Solomon gives as the reason why we should address our supplications to God only "who dwelleth in the heavens."

So that the reason of these two precepts is founded in the unity and singularity of the divine nature, and unless there be more gods than one, we must worship him only, and pray to none but to him: because we can give invocation to none but to him only whom we believe to be God, as St. Paul reasons: "How shall they call on him in whom they have not believed?" (Rom. 10:14).

II. The love likewise of our neighbor is found in the unity of the divine nature, and may be inferred from it: "Hear, O Israel, the Lord thy God is one Lord, therefore thou shalt love thy neighbor as thyself." And the apostle gives this reason why all mankind should be at unity among themselves: "There is one God and Father of all," and therefore we should "keep the unity of the Spirit in the bond of peace" (Eph. 4:6), that is, live in mutual love and peace. The prophet likewise assigns this reason why all mankind should be upon good terms with one another and not be injurious one to another: "Have we not all one Father, hath not one God created us? Why do we then deal treacherously every man against his brother?" (Mal. 2:10).

And therefore, when we see such hatred and enmity among men, such divisions and animosities among Christians, we may not only ask St. Paul's question, "Is Christ divided?" that we cannot agree about serving him—either all to serve him one way or to bear with one another in our differences: I say we may not only ask St. Paul's question, "Is Christ divided?" but may ask further, "Is God divided?" Is there not one God, and are we not his offspring? Are we not all the sons of Adam, who was the son of God? So that if we trace ourselves to our original, we shall find a great nearness and equality among men; and this equality, that we are all God's creatures and image, and that the one only God is the Father of us all, is a more real ground of mutual love, and peace, and equity in our dealings one with another, than any of those petty differences and distinctions of strong and weak, of rich and poor, of wise and foolish, of base and honorable, can be to encourage men to anything of insolence, injustice, and inequality of dealing one towards another. Because that wherein all agree—that we are the creatures and children of God, and have all one common Father—is essential and constant; but those things wherein we differ are accidental and mutable, and happen to one another by turns.

Thus much may suffice to have been spoken concerning the proposition in the text, "There is one God": to Him, Father, Son, and Holy Ghost, be all honor and glory, dominion and power, now and for ever. Amen.

Notes

1. That is, Brahmans.
2. The Koran *(Qur'ân)*.

CHAPTER 17

THE DAWN OF MODERNITY (B)

THE RECOVERY OF FEELING

GEORGE WHITEFIELD: SERMON ON JACOB'S LADDER

In the days before modern communication and transportation, George Whitefield was heard by more people than anyone who had lived before him (**see Vol. 1, pp. 431-37**). *Although crossing the ocean was a risky undertaking in the eighteenth century, the following sermon was delivered as a farewell to his English followers as he embarked on his thirteenth voyage to America. His preaching did much to launch the First Great Awakening in Britain's American colonies and the Evangelical Awakening in Great Britain. Whitefield possessed a number of qualities that enabled him to be heard by and move audiences that numbered in the thousands. Often his hearers were in the grips of powerful emotion, and many underwent conversion experiences. Fortunately, eighteen of his sermons were taken down in shorthand while they were being delivered, and it is thus possible for us to know exactly what he said on those occasions. The following is a case in point and a good example of the kind of sermon he preached. It is taken from* Eighteen

Sermons Preached by the Late Rev. George Whitefield, A.M. Taken in Verbatim Short-hand and Faithfully transcribed by Joseph Gurney, *rev. A. Gifford (Lexington, Ky.: Thomas T. Skillman, 1825), 281-301. Used by permission of the University of Missouri-Kansas City Libraries, Special Collections Department.*

Sermon 17: Jacob's Ladder

A Farewell Sermon

Genesis 28:12, &c.

And he dreamed, and behold, a ladder set upon the earth, and the top of that reached to heaven: and behold, the angels of God ascending and descending on it. And behold, the Lord stood above it, and said, I am the Lord God of Abraham thy father, and the God of Isaac; the land whereon thou liest, to thee will I give it, and to thy seed. And thy seed shall be as the dust of the earth; and thou shalt spread abroad to the West and to the East, into the North into the South; and in thee, and in thy seed, shall all the families of the earth be blessed. And behold, I am with thee, and will keep thee again into this land: for I will not leave thee, until I have done that which I have spoken to thee of.

The wise man observes, that *in the multitude of dreams, there is many vanities,* being often the effects of a peculiar disorder of body, or owing to some disturbance of the mind. They whose nervous system has been long relaxed, who have had severe domestic trials, or have been greatly affected by extraordinary occurrences, know this to be true by their experience; but however this may be, there have been, and possibly may be still, dreams that have no manner of dependencies on the indisposition of the body, or other natural causes, but seemed to bring a divine sanction with them, and make peculiar impressions on the party, though this was more frequent before the canon of scripture was closed, than now.

God spoke to his people in a dream, in a vision of the night; witness the subject of our present meditation, a dream of the patriarch Jacob's, when going forth as a poor pilgrim, with a staff in his hand, from his father's house, deprived of his mother's company and instruction, persecuted by an elder brother, without attendants or necessaries, only leaning on an invisible power.

I need not inform you in how extraordinary a way he got the blessing, which provoked his brother to such a degree, as determined him to be the death of Jacob, as soon as ever his aged father dropp'd: to what a height did this wicked man's envy rise, when he said, *the days of mourning for my father will come,* and what then? Why though I have some compassion for the old man, and therefore will not lay violent hands upon my brother while my father is alive, yet I am resolved to kill him before my father is cold in his grave. This is the very spirit of Cain, who talked to his brother, and then slew him; this coming to the ears of his mother, she tells the good old patriarch, her husband, who loving peace and quietness, takes the good advice of the weaker vessel, and orders Jacob to go to his mother's brother, Laban, and stay a little while out of Esau's sight (perhaps out of sight out of mind), and by and by probably, said he, thou mayst come to thy father and mother again in peace and safety.

Jacob though sure of the blessing in the end, by his father's confirmation of it, yet prudently makes use of proper means; therefore he obeyed parents: and wo, wo be to those who think a parent's blessing not worth their asking for! Having had his mother's blessing, as well as his father's, without saying, I will try it out with my brother, I will let him know that I am not afraid to him, he views it as the call of God, and like an honest, simple pilgrim, went out from Beersheba towards Haran.

Was it not a little unkind of his parents not to furnish him with some necessaries and conveniences? When the servant was sent to fetch a wife for Isaac, he had a great deal of attendance, why should not Jacob have it now; his father might have sent him away with great parade: but I am apt to believe this did not sit Jacob's real, pilgrim spirit; he was a plain man, and dwelt in tents, when perhaps he might have dwelt under cedar roofs; he chose a pilgrim's life, and prudence directed him to go thus in a private manner, to prevent increasing Esau's envy, and giving the fatal blow.

Methinks, I see the young pilgrim weeping when he took his leave of his father or mother; he went on foot, and they that are acquainted with the geography of the place, say that the first day of his journey he walked not less than forty English miles; what exercise must he have had all that way; no wonder, therefore, that by the time the sun was going down, poor Jacob felt himself very weary, for we are told, ver. 11, *that he lighted on a certain place, and tarried there all night, because the sun was set.* There is a particular emphasis to be put upon this term, *a certain place;* he saw the sun going down, he was a stranger in a strange land. (You that are born in England can have very little idea of it, but persons that travel in the American woods can form a more proper idea, for you may there travel a hundred and a thousand miles, and go through one continued tract of tall green trees, like the tall cedars of Lebanon; and that the gentlemen of America, from one end to the other, are of such an hospitable temper, as I have not only been told, but have found among them upwards of thirty years, that they would not let public houses be licensed, that they may have an opportunity of entertaining English friends: may God, of his infinite mercy, grant this union may never be dissolved.)

Well, Jacob got to a certain place, and perhaps he saw a good tree that would serve him for a canopy; however, this we are told, he tarried there all night because the sun was set, and he took of the stones of that place and put them for his pillow, and laid down in that place to sleep; hard lodgings for him who was used to lie otherwise at home: I don't hear him say, I wish I was got back to my mother again, I wish I had not set out; but upon the hard ground and hard pillow he lies down; I believe never poor man slept sweeter in his life, for it is certainly sweet sleep when God is near us; he did not know but his brother might follow and kill him while he was asleep, or that the wild beasts might devour him: (in America, when they sleep in the woods, and I expect to have some such sleeping times in them before a twelve-month is over, we are obliged to make a fire to keep the beasts from us: I have often said then, and I hope I shall never forget it, when I rise in the morning, this fire and the woods that keeps the wild beast from hurting us, is like the fire of God's love that keeps the devil from hurting us:) thus weary and solitary he falls asleep, and sweetly dreams, *and behold!*

I don't remember many passages of Scripture where the word *behold* is repeated so many times in so short a space as in the passage before us; doubtless, the Lord would have us particularly take notice of it, even us upon whom the ends of the world are come. Behold, *a ladder set upon the earth, and the top reached to heaven; and behold, the angels of God ascending and descending upon it;* and behold, *the Lord stood above it;* so here are three *beholds* in a very few lines. Was there anything very extraordinary in that? Perhaps the Deist would say, your patriarch was tired, and dreamed among other things of a ladder; yes, he did, but this dream was of God, and how kind was he to meet him at the end of the first day's journey, to strengthen and animate him to go forward in this lonesome pilgrimage.

This ladder is reckoned by some to denote the providence of God: it was let down as it were from heaven, particularly at this time to poor Jacob, that he might know that however he was become a pilgrim, and left his all, all for God's glory, that God would take care for his comfort, and give his angels charge over him to keep him in all his ways, which was denoted by the angels ascending and descending upon the ladder.

Some think that particular saints and countries have particular guardian angels, and therefore that the angels that ascended were those that had the particular charge of that place, so far as Jacob had come; that the angels that descended were another set of angels, set down from heaven to guard him in his future journey; perhaps, this is more a fancy than the word of God. However, I very much like the observations of good Mr. Burket, "Why should we dispute whether every individual believer has got a particular angel, when there is not one believer but has got guards of angels to attend him," which are a great deal better than a great many servants, that prove our plagues, and instead of waiting upon us, make as wait upon them.

But, my dear hearers, I don't know one spiritual commentator, but agrees that this ladder was a type of the Lord Jesus Christ; and that as Jacob was now banished from his father's house, and while sleeping upon a hard, cold stone, God was pleased not only to get him an assurance that he would be with him in the way, but gave him a blessed sight of Jesus Christ, in whom Jacob believed.

A ladder you know is something by which we climb from one place to another; hence, in condescension to our weak capacities, God ordered a ladder to be set down, to show us that Christ is the way to heaven: *I am the way, the truth and the life: I am the door,* says he; neither is there salvation in any other, for there is no other name given under heaven whereby we must be saved. The Deists, who own a God but deny his Son, dare go to a God out of Christ: but Jacob is here taught better: how soon does God reveal the gospel unto him; here is a ladder, by which God preaches to us; if you have a mind to climb from earth to heaven, you must get up by the Son of God; no one ever pointed out a proper way to heaven for us but himself.

When Adam and Eve fell from God, a flaming sword turned every way to keep them from the tree of life; but Jesus alone is a new and living way, not only to the Holy of Holies below, but into the immediate presence of God; and that we might know that he was a proper Savior, the top of it reached to heaven; if it had stopped short Jacob might have said, Ah! The ladder is within a little way of heaven, but does not quite reach it; if I climb up to the top I shall not get there after all; but the top reached to heaven, to point out the divinity and exaltation of the Son of God; such a savior became us who was God.

God overall, blessed for evermore: and therefore the Arian scheme is most uncomfortable and destructive; to talk of Christ as a Savior that is not God is no Christ at all. I would turn Deist tomorrow if I did not know that Christ was God; *but cursed is the man that builds his faith upon an arm of flesh*. If Christ is God, the Arians and Socinians, by their own principles, are undone for ever; but Jesus Christ is very God, and very man, begotten (and not made) of the Father: God, of his infinite mercy, write his divinity deep in our hearts!

The bottom of the ladder reached to the earth: this points out to us the humiliation of the blessed Lord: for us men he came down from heaven; we pray to and for a descending God. All the sufferings which our Lord voluntarily exposed himself to, were that he might become a ladder for you and I to climb up to heaven by. Come down from the cross, say they, and we will believe thee; if he had, what would have become of us? Did they believe on him when he was dead, buried, and risen again? No. Some people say, if Christ was here, O dear, we should love him; just as much as they did when he came down before. If he had come down from the cross, they would have hung him up again: O that you and I might make his cross a step to glory!

As the top of the ladder pointed out his exaltation, the bottom his humiliation, the two sides of the ladder being joined together, point out the union of the Deity and manhood in the person of Christ; and that as the ladder had steps to it, so blessed be God, Jesus Christ has found out a way whereby we may go, step after step, to glory. The first step is the righteousness of Christ, the active and passive obedience of the Redeemer; no sitting one foot upon this ladder without coming out of ourselves, and relying wholly upon a better righteousness than our own.

Again, all the other steps are the graces of the blessed spirit; therefore, you need not be afraid of our destroying inward holiness by preaching the doctrine of the imputation of Christ's righteousness, that one is the foundation, the other the superstructure; to talk of my having the righteousness of Christ imputed to my soul, without my having the holiness of Christ imparted to it, and bringing forth the fruits of the Spirit as an evidence of it, is only deceiving ourselves.

I would never preach upon imputed righteousness, without speaking of inward holiness, for if you don't take a great deal of care, you will unawares, under a pretense of exalting Christ, run into Antinomianism, depths that Calvin never went into; you will embitter others' spirits that don't agree with you, and at the same time hurt the fruits of the Spirit: may God give you clear heads, and at the same time warm hearts.

On the ladder Jacob saw the angels of God ascending and the descending;

what is that for? To show that they are ministering spirits, sent forth to minister to them that shall be heirs of salvation; therefore we find them attending upon Christ. We did not hear much of them after the canon of Scripture was closed, but as soon as ever Christ was born, the angels sang; till then we never heard of their singing below, as far as I can judge, since the creation; then the sons of God shouted for joy: but when Eve reached out her hand to pluck the fatal apple, and gave to Adam, earth groaned, and the angels hung, as it were, their hearts upon the willows; but when Christ, the second Adam, was born, the angels sang at midnight, *Glory to God in the highest.* I pray to God we may all die singing that anthem, and sing it to all eternity.

After his temptations, they came and ministered to him, as some think, food for his body, and wished him joy and comfort in his soul; and in his agonies in the garden, an angel strengthened him. After his resurrection two appeared again, one at the head and another at the foot of his sepulcher, to let those that looked into the sepulcher know, that they would not only wait upon the head but the foot; and the angels are glad to wait upon the meanest of the children of God. When our Lord departed, a cloud received him out of their sight, which probably was a cloud of the angels: having led his disciples out of the city, he blessed them, and then away he went to heaven: May that blessing rests upon you and your children! This intimates that God makes use of angels to attend his people, especially when they are departing into eternity; perhaps, part of our entertainment in heaven will be, to hear the angels declare how many millions of times they have assisted and helped us.

Our Lord says, angels do there behold the face of the Father, of his little ones; and therefore I love to talk to the lambs of the flock, and why should I not talk to them whom angels think it their honor to guard; and if it was not for this, how would any children escape the dangers they are exposed to in their tender age? It is owing to the particular providence of God, that any one child is brought to manhood; therefore I can't help admiring that part of the Litany, in which we pray, that God would take care not only of the grown people, but of children also: God take care of yours both in body and soul.

But what gave the greatest comfort to Jacob was, that the Lord was on top of the ladder, which I do not know whether it would have been so, if Jacob had not seen God there. It comforts me, I assure you, to think, that whenever God shall call for me, I shall be carried by angels into Abraham's bosom; and I have often thought that whenever that time comes, that blessed, long longed-for moment comes, as soon as ever they have called upon me, my first question will be to them, where is my dear

Master? Where is Jesus? Where is that dear Emanuel, who has loved me with an everlasting love, and has called me by his grace, and has sent you to fetch me home to see his face? But I believe you and I shall have no occasion to ask where he is, for he will come on to meet us, he will stand at the top of his ladder to take his pilgrims in; so God was at the top of the ladder; pray mind that.

He appears not sitting, as he is often represented in heaven, but standing, as much as to say, here, here, Jacob, thy brother wants to kill thee; here thou art come without a servant, art lying upon a hard bed, but here I am ready in order to preserve thee; I stand above, and I see thy weariness, I see the fatigue and hardships thou hast yet to undergo, though thou dost not see it thyself; thou hast thrown thyself upon my providence and protection, and I will give thee the word of a God that I will stand by thee; *the Lord stood above:* if he had said nothing, that would have been enough to have shewn his readiness to help.

But God speaks, *behold:* well might this be ushered in with the word *behold;* a ladder set on the earth, and behold the angels of God ascending and descending on it; and, above all, *behold* God speaking from it! What doth he say? *I am the Lord God of Abraham thy father.* Oh! Happy they that can say, the Lord God of my father; happy you that have got fathers and mothers in heaven.

I remember, about twenty-five years ago, as I was traveling from Bristol, I met with a man on the road, and being desirous to know whether he was serious or not, I began to put in a word for Christ, (and God forbid I should travel with anybody a quarter of an hour without speaking of Christ to them) he told me what a wicked creature he had been; but, sir, says he, in the midst of my wickedness people used to tell me, you have got a good many prayers upon the file for you, your godly father and mother have prayed very often for you; and it was the pleasure of God he was wrought upon, and brought to Christ. Lay in a good stock for your children, get a good many prayers in for them, they may be answered when you are dead and gone.

I am the God of Abraham thy father, not thy grandfather; to put him in mind what an honor God would put upon him, to make him as it were the father of the church. Though you have many instructors, says Paul, you have but one father: *and the God of Isaac; the land whereon thou liest, to thee I will give it, and to thy seed.* Amazing! amazing! You know very well when persons buy or come into an estate, they usually take possession of it by some ceremony, such as receiving or taking up a piece of dirt, or twig, in their hand, as a sign of their title. Now, says God, poor Jacob, thou dost little think that this very spot of ground that thou liest on tonight, cold and stiff, I intend to give to thee, and thy posterity, for an inheritance.

O my brethren, live all to God, and God will give all to you: who would have thought of this, probably Jacob did not: it is as if God took a pleasure in seeing his dear children lie on such hard ground; if he had been on a feather-bed, he might not have had such a visit: thou shalt have now a God to lean upon; *to thee will I give it, and to thy seed, which shall be as the dust of the earth, and thou shalt spread abroad to the West and to the East and to the North and to the South: and in thee and in thy seed, shall all the families of the earth be blessed.* Thus did heaven balance the loss of the comforts of his father's house, by the discovery of his and his offspring's prosperity, by an interest in the promised seed.

My particular circumstances call me to observe, and I believe God has done it on purpose to encourage me, that faith, resting on the promise, is easily resigned to the loss of the present good, whereas worldly hearts consider prosperity as a portion; they don't care if the devil takes them hereafter, so they have it now; and that makes carnal people wonder how we can give up things in this world, for the sake of those not yet born; but it is to glorify God, and lay a foundation for others' happiness. Here God gives Jacob to know, that hereafter his seed should spread on the East, West, North and South, his branches should multiply, and at last from his loins should Jesus Christ come; what for? *In whom all the families of the earth should be blessed:* God Almighty grant we may be blessed in him.

Then if Jacob should say in his heart, hast thou no promise for me? Here is another *behold* comes in; *Behold, I am with thee, and will keep thee in all places whither thou goest.* What a word is this! Thou hast nobody with thee, nothing but a staff (he could not carry much upon his back, like a poor soldier with a knapsack behind, and a little bread in his pocket), well, saith God, I do not despise thee because thou art destitute, but I love thee the better for it; thy brother Esau longs to kill thee, but if Esau stabs thee he shall stab thy God first; I will not only be with thee now, but I will watch every step thou takest, *I will be with thee in all places whither thou goest;* as much as to say, Jacob, thou art a pilgrim, thy life is to be a moving life, I don't intend thou shalt settle and keep in one place; thy life is to be a life of changes, thou art to move from place to place, but *I will be with thee in all places whither thou goest,* and thereby it shall be known that I am Jacob's God, and also by my bringing thee again into this land.

He not only assures him of a successful journey, whither he was now going, but promises to bring him back once more to see his dear father and mother, and relations again; *I will bring thee back to this land;* and to confirm his faith and hope, the great God adds, *I will not leave thee till I have done that I have spoken to thee of;* that is, all the good he had just now promised. Some people promise, but they cannot do it today, and they will not do it tomorrow. I have known the world, and have rung the changes of it ever since I have been here; but blessed be God, an unchangeable Christ having loved his own, he loveth them to the end; *I will not leave you till I have performed all things I have promised you:* may this promise come upon you and your children, and all that God shall call.

Thus spake the great Jehovah to poor Jacob, just setting out to a strange land, knowing not whither he went; but now God speaks not only to Jacob, but he speaks to you; and, blessed be the living God, he speaks to me also, less than the least of all; and as my design is (though I cannot tell but this may be the last opportunity) to speak something to you about my departure; yet, brethren, my grand design in preaching to you, is to recommend the Lord Jesus Christ to your souls: and, before I go, to make a particular, personal application.

Give me leave, therefore, to ask you, it may be the last time I ask many of you, whether you have ever set your foot upon this blessed ladder, the son of God! I ask you in the name of the Lord Jesus Christ, in the name of the Father, Son, and Holy Ghost, did you ever set your foot, I say, upon this ladder? That is, did you ever yet believe on Jesus Christ, and come to him as poor lost sinners, relying upon no other righteousness than that of the Son of God? Perhaps, if you was to speak, some of you would say, away with your ladder; and what will you do then? Why, say you, I will climb to heaven without it; what ladder will you climb upon? Oh, I think to go to heaven because I have been baptized; that ladder will break under you; what, a ladder made of water; what are you dreaming of? no; O, I think I shall go to heaven because I have done nobody any harm; what, a ladder made of negative goodness; no; I think to go, you'll say, by good works; a ladder made of good works, that has not Christ for its bottom, what is that? I think, say you, to go to heaven by my prayers and fastings; all these are good in their place; but, my brethren, don't think to climb to heaven by these ropes of sand. If you never before set your foot on Christ, this blessed ladder, God grant this may be the happy time.

I have been praying before most of you were up, I believe, that God would give me a parting blessing. I remember, soon after I left England last, that a dear Christian friend told me, that there was one woman, who came only out of curiosity, that dated her conversion from hearing my last sermon; and I bless God, I never once left England, but some poor soul has dated their conversion from my last sermon. When I put on my surplice, to come out to read the second service, I thought it was just like a person's being decently dressed to go out to be executed; I would rather, was it the will of God, it should be so, than to feel what I do in parting from you; then death would put an end to all; but I am to be executed again and again, and nothing will support me under the torture, but the consideration of God's blessing me to some poor souls. Do pray for me, ye children of God, that God would give us a parting blessing.

God help you, young people to put your foot on this ladder, don't climb wrong: the devil has got a ladder, but it reaches down to hell; all the devil's children go down, not up; the bottom of the devil's ladder reaches to the depths of the damned, the top of it reaches to the earth; and when death comes, then up comes the devil's ladder to let you down. For God's sake, come away from the Devil's ladder; climb, climb, dear young men. O, it delighted me on Friday night at the Tabernacle, when we had a melting parting sacrament; and it delighted me this morning to see so many young men at the table; God add to the blessed number! Young women, put your feet upon this ladder; God lets one ladder down from heaven, and the devil brings another up from hell. O, say you, I would climb up God's ladder, I think it is right, but I shall be laughed at; do you think to go to heaven without being laughed at? The Lord Jesus Christ help you to climb to heaven; come, climb till you get out of the hearing of their laughter. O trust not to your own righteousness, your vows, and good resolutions.

Some of you, blessed be God, have climbed upon this ladder, at least are climbing; well, I wish you joy; God be praised for setting your feet on this ladder; God be praised for letting down this ladder; I have only one word to say to you; for Jesus Christ's sake, and your own too, climb a little faster; take care the world does not get hold of your heels. It is a shame the children of God don't climb faster; you may talk what you please, but God's people's lukewarmness is more provoking to him than all the sins of the nation.

We cry out against the sins of the land; would to God we did cry out more of the sins of the saints; *I will spew you out of my mouth, because you are lukewarm,* says Christ; and if any of you say you cannot climb because you are lame-footed, look to Jesus Christ, my dear friends, and your afflictions shall make you climb; and if any of you are coming down, the ladder again, the Lord Jesus Christ bless the foolishness of preaching to help you up again. O, say you, I am giddy, I shall fall; here, I will give you a rope; so God lets down a promise: climb, climb, then, till you have got higher into a better climate, and God shall put his hand out by and by when you get to the top of the ladder to receive you to himself. Blessed be the living God, I hope and believe I shall meet many of you by and by.

And now, my brethren, it is time for me to preach my own funeral sermon; and I would humbly hope that, as a poor sinner, I may put in my claim for what God promised Jacob; and I do put in, with full assurance of faith that God will be with me. I am now going, for the thirteenth time, to cross the Atlantic; when I came from America, last, I took my leave of all the continent, from the one end of the provinces to the other, except some places which we had not then taken; I took my leave for life, without the last design of returning there again, my health was so bad; and the prospect of getting the orphan-house into other hands made me say when I first came over, I have no other river to go over than the river Jordan.

I thought then of retiring, for I did not choose to appear when my nerves were so relaxed that I could not serve God as I could wish to do; but as it hath pleased God to restore my health much, and has so ordered it by his providence, that I intend to give up the orphan-house, and all the land adjoining, for a public college.

I wished to have had a public sanction, but his grace the late Archbishop of Canterbury put a stop to it; they would give me a charter, which was all I desired, but they insisted upon, at least his grace and another did, that I should confine it totally to the church of England, and that no extempore prayer should be used in a public way in that house, though Dissenters and all sorts of people, had contributed to it: I would sooner cut my head off than betray my trust, by confining it to a narrow bottom; I always meant it should be kept upon a broad bottom, for people of all denominations, that their children might be brought up in the fear of God; by this means the orphan-house reverted into my hands; I have once more, as my health is restored, determined to pursue the plan I had fixed on.

And through the tender mercies of God, Georgia, (which about thirty-two years ago was a total desolate place, and when the land, as it was given me by the House of Commons, would have been totally deserted, and the colony have quite ceased, had it not been for the money I have laid out for the orphan-house, to keep the poor people together) that colony is arising to an amazing height; by the schemes now going on, public buildings are erecting. I had news last week of the great prosperity of the negroes.

And I hope by the twenty-fifth of March—which is the day, the anniversary day, I laid the first brick, in the year 1739—I say, I hope by that time, all things will be finished, and a blessed provision will be made for orphans and poor students that will be brought up there; it will be a blessed source of provision for the children of God in another part of the world.

This is the grand design I am going upon; this is my visible cause; but I never yet went to them, but God has been pleased to bless my ministration among them; and therefore after I have finished the orphan-house affair, I intend to go all along the continent by land, (which will keep me all the winter and spring) and when I come to the end of it, which will be Canada and New England, then I hope to return again to this place; for let people say what they will, I have not so much as a single thought of settling abroad on this side of eternity.

And I am going in no public capacity, I shall set out like a poor pilgrim, at my own expense, trusting upon God to take care of me, and to bear my charges; and I call God to witness and I must be a cursed devil and hypocrite, to stand here in the pulpit and provoke God to strike me dead for lying, I never had the love of the world, nor never felt it one quarter of an hour in my heart, since I was twenty years old. I might have been rich: but though the Chapel is built, and I have a comfortable room to lie in, I assure you I built it at my own expense, it cost nobody but myself anything. I have a watchcoat made me, and in that I shall lie every night on the ground, and may Jacob's God bless me.

I will not say much of myself, but when I have been preaching, I have read and thought of those words with pleasure, *Surely this is the house of God. And I will bring thee again to this land.* Whether that will be my experience or not, blessed be God, I have a better land in view; and my dear brethren, I do not look upon myself at home till I land in my Father's kingdom; and if I am to die in the way, if I am to die in the ship, it comforts me that I know I am as clear as the sun, that I go by the will of God. And though people may say, will you leave the world? Will you leave the Chapel? O, I am astonished that we cannot leave every thing for Christ.

My greatest trial is to part with those who are as dear to me as my own soul; and however others may forget me, as thousands have, and do forget me, yet I cannot forget them; and now may Jacob's God be with you; O keep close to God, my dear London friends; I do not bid you keep close to Chapel, you have done so always; I shall endeavor to keep up the word of God among you in my absence; I shall have the same persons that managed for me when I was out last, and they sent me word again and again, by letter, that it was remarkable, that the Tottenham-court people were always present when ordinances were there.

You see I went upon a fair bottom; I might have had a thousand a year out of this place if I had chose it; when I'm gone to heaven you'll see what I have got on earth; I do not like to speak now, because it may be thought boasting; but I'm sure there are numbers of people here if they knew what I have, would love me as much as they now hate me. When we come before the great Judge of quick and dead, while I stand before him, God grant you may not part with me then; it will be a dreadful parting then, it will be worse then to go into the fire, to be among the devil and his angels; God forbid it! God forbid it! God forbid it! O remember that my last words were, come, come to Christ; the Lord help you to come to Christ; come to Christ, come to Jacob's God; God give you faith like Jacob's faith.

You that have been kind to me, that have helped me when I was sick, some of whom are here that have been very kind to me; may God reward you, my friends, and God forgive my enemies; God, of his infinite mercy, bless you all; you will be amply provided for, I believe, here; may God spread the gospel everywhere; and may God never leave you, nor forsake you. Even so, Lord Jesus. Amen and Amen.

JOHN WESLEY: PREFACE TO *SERMONS ON SEVERAL OCCASIONS*

One of the means that John Wesley used to turn an amorphous revival into a tightly disciplined corps of dedicated Christians was to supply them with a complete library of all (in his opinion) they needed to know and think. At the heart of this library was a collection of sermons he had written, to which he added from time to time, and which covered the basic doctrines of the Christian faith as well as the special emphases of his teaching (see Vol. 1, pp. 448-50)*. Many of these sermons had never actually been preached; they were written entirely to fill gaps in the areas covered by the collection. The inspiration for this collection was the* Book of Homilies *of the Established Church, which had been created to catechize the English people about how the historic faith was understood by the English Reformers. Wesley's preface explains some of his purposes in writing this collection of catechetical material in sermonic form. The* *preface appears inter alia in* The Works of John Wesley, *vol. 5 (Grand Rapids, Mich.: Zondervan, n.d.), 1-6.*

Preface

1. The following Sermons contain the substance of what I have been preaching for between eight and nine years last past. During that time I have frequently spoken in public, on every subject in the ensuing collection; and I am not conscious, that there is any one point of doctrine, on which I am accustomed to speak in public, which is not here, incidentally, if not professedly, laid before every Christian reader. Every serious man who peruses these, will therefore see, in the clearest manner, what these doctrines are which I embrace and teach as the essentials of true religion.

2. But I am throughly sensible, these are not proposed in such a manner as some may expect. Nothing here appears in an elaborate, elegant, or oratorical dress. If it had been my desire or design to write thus, my leisure would not permit. But, in truth, I, at present, designed nothing less; for I now write, as I generally speak, *ad populum,*—to the bulk of mankind, to those who neither relish nor understand the art of speaking; but who, notwithstanding, are competent judges of those truths which are necessary to present and future happiness. I mention this, that curious readers may spare themselves the labor of seeking for what they will not find.

3. I design plain truth for plain people: Therefore, of set purpose, I abstain from all nice and philosophical speculations; from all perplexed and intricate reasonings; and, as far as possible, from even the show of learning, unless in sometimes citing the original Scripture. I labor to avoid all words which are not easy to be understood, all which are not used in common life; and, in particular, those kinds of technical terms that so frequently occur in Bodies of Divinity; those modes of speaking which men of reading are intimately acquainted with, but which to common people are an unknown tongue. Yet I am not assured, that I do not sometimes slide into them unawares: It is so extremely natural to imagine, that a word which is familiar to ourselves is so to all the world.

4. Nay, my design is, in some sense, to forget all that ever I have read in my life. I mean to speak, in the general, as if I had never read one author, ancient or modern (always excepting the inspired). I am persuaded, that, on the one hand, this may be a means of enabling me more clearly to express the sentiments of my heart, while I simply follow the

chain of my own thoughts, without entangling myself with those of other men; and that, on the other, I shall come with fewer weights upon my mind, with less of prejudice and prepossession, either to search for myself, or to deliver to others, the naked truths of the gospel.

5. To candid, reasonable men, I am not afraid to lay open what have been the inmost thoughts of my heart. I have thought, I am a creature of a day, passing through life as an arrow through the air. I am a spirit come from God, and returning to God: Just hovering over the great gulf; till, a few moments hence, I am no more seen; I drop into an unchangeable eternity! I want to know one thing,—the way to heaven; how to land safe on that happy shore. God himself has condescended to teach the way: For this very end he came from heaven. He hath written it down in a book. O give me that book! At any price, give me the book of God! I have it: Here is knowledge enough for me. Let me be *homo unius libri.*[1]

Here then I am, far from the busy ways of men. I sit down alone: Only, God is here. In his presence I open, I read his book; for this end, to find the way to heaven. Is there a doubt concerning the meaning of what I read? Does anything appear dark or intricate? I lift up my heart to the Father of Lights:—"Lord, is it not thy word, 'If any man lack wisdom, let him ask of God?' Thou 'givest liberally, and upbraidest not.' Thou hast said, 'If any be willing to do thy will, he shall know.' I am willing to do, let me know, thy will." I then search after and consider parallel passages of Scripture, "comparing spiritual things with spiritual." I meditate thereon with all the attention and earnestness of which my mind is capable. If any doubt still remains, I consult those who are experienced in the things of God; and then the writings whereby, being dead, they yet speak. And what I thus learn, that I teach.

6. I have accordingly set down in the following sermons what I find in the Bible concerning the way to heaven; with a view to distinguish this way of God from all those which are the inventions of men. I have endeavored to describe the true, the scriptural, experimental religion, so as to omit nothing which is a real part thereof, and to add nothing thereto which is not. And herein it is more especially my desire, First, to guard those who are just setting their faces toward heaven, (and who, having little acquaintance with the things of God, are the more liable to be turned out of the way,) from formality, from mere outside religion, which has almost driven heart-religion out of the world; and, Secondly, to warn those who know the religion of the heart, the faith which worketh by love, lest at any time they make void the law through faith, and so fall back into the snare of the devil.

7. By the advice and at the request of some of my friends, I have prefixed to the other sermons contained in this volume, three sermons of my own, and one of my Brother's, preached before the University of Oxford. My design required some discourses on those heads; and I preferred these before any others, as being a stronger answer than any which can be drawn up now, to those who have frequently asserted that we have changed our doctrine of late, and do not preach now what we did some years ago. Any man of understanding may now judge for himself, when he has compared the latter with the former sermons.

8. But some may say, I have mistaken the way myself, although I take upon me to teach it to others. It is probable many will think this, and it is very possible that I have. But I trust, whereinsoever I have mistaken, my mind is open to conviction. I sincerely desire to be better informed. I say to God and man, "What I know not, teach thou me!"

9. Are you persuaded you see more clearly than me? It is not unlikely that you may. Then treat me as you would desire to be treated yourself upon a change of circumstances. Point me out a better way than I have yet known. Show me it is so, by plain proof of Scripture. And if I linger in the path I have been accustomed to tread, and am therefore unwilling to leave it, labor with me a little; take me by the hand, and lead me as I am able to bear. But be not displeased if I entreat you not to beat me down in order to quicken my pace: I can go but feebly and slowly at best; then, I should not be able to go at all. May I not request of you, further, not to give me hard names in order to bring me into the right way. Suppose I were ever so much in the wrong, I doubt this would not set me right. Rather, it would make me run so much the farther from you, and so get more and more out of the way.

10. Nay, perhaps, if you are angry, so shall I be too; and then there will be small hopes of finding the truth. If once anger arise, *ēute kapnos* (as Homer somewhere expresses it,) this smoke will so dim the eyes of my soul, that I shall be able to see nothing clearly. For God's sake, if it be possible to avoid it, let us not provoke one another to wrath. Let us not kindle in each other this fire of hell; much less blow it up into a flame. If we could discern truth by that dreadful light, would it not be loss rather than gain? For, how far is love, even with many wrong opinions, to be preferred before truth itself without love! We may die without the knowledge of many truths, and yet be carried into Abraham's bosom. But, if we die without love, what will knowledge avail? Just as much as it avails the devil and his angels!

The God of love forbid we should ever make the trial! May he prepare us for the knowledge of all truth, by filling our hearts with all his love, and with all joy and peace in believing.

C. H. SPURGEON: LECTURE ON THE AIM OF PREACHING

Much of what made the sermons of Charles Haddon Spurgeon attractive to the thousands who assembled weekly to hear him at the Metropolitan Tabernacle in London during the last half of the nineteenth century is visible as well in the lectures that he gave to those studying for the ministry at the Pastor's College connected with his congregation. (For a discussion of these lectures, **see Vol. 1, pp. 460-62.***) Although the lecture reprinted here does not appear until the end of the second of the three series presented by Spurgeon, it reveals the theological core of his entire ministry. In addition, it is an excellent summary of his homiletical strategy. It appears in C. H. Spurgeon,* Lectures to My Students: A Selection from Addresses Delivered to the Students of the Pastors' College, Metropolitan Tabernacle, *three volumes in one (Grand Rapids, Mich.: Baker, 1977; reproduced by photolithoprint from the editions of 1875, 1877, and 1894), 2:179-92.*

Lecture X, Second Series

On Conversion as Our Aim

The grand object of the Christian ministry is the glory of God. Whether souls are converted or not, if Jesus Christ be faithfully preached, the minister has not labored in vain, for he is a sweet savor unto God as well in them that perish as in them that are saved. Yet, as a rule, God has sent us to preach in order that through the gospel of Jesus Christ the sons of men may be reconciled to him. Here and there a preacher of righteousness, like Noah, may labor on and bring none beyond his own family circle into the ark of salvation; and another, like Jeremiah, may weep in vain over an impenitent nation; but, for the most part, the work of preaching is intended to save the hearers. It is ours to sow even in stony places, where no fruit rewards our toil; but still we are bound to look for a harvest, and mourn if it does not appear in due time.

The glory of God being our chief object, we aim at it by seeking the edification of saints and the salvation of sinners. It is a noble work to instruct the people of God, and to build them up in their most holy faith:

we may by no means neglect this duty. To this end we must give clear statements of gospel doctrine, of vital experience, and of Christian duty, and never shrink from declaring the whole counsel of God. In too many cases sublime truths are held in abeyance under the pretense that they are not practical; whereas the very fact that they are revealed proves that the Lord thinks them to be of value, and woe unto us if we pretend to be wiser than he. We may say of any and every doctrine of scripture: "To give it then a tongue is wise in man." If any one note is dropped from the divine harmony of truth the music may be sadly marred. Your people may fall into grave spiritual diseases through the lack of a certain form of spiritual nutriment, which can only be supplied by the doctrines which you withhold. In the food which we eat there are ingredients which do not, at first appear to be necessary to life; but experience shows that they are requisite to health and strength. Phosphorus will not make flesh, but it is wanted for bone; many earths and salts come under the same description—they are necessary in due proportion to the human economy. Even thus certain truths which appear to be little adapted for spiritual nutriment are, nevertheless, very beneficial in furnishing believers with backbone and muscle, and in repairing the varied organs of Christian manhood. We must preach "the whole truth," that the man of God may be thoroughly furnished unto all good works.

Our great object of glorifying God is, however, to be mainly achieved by the winning of souls. We *must* see souls born unto God. If we do not, our cry should be that of Rachel, "Give me children, or I die." If we do not win souls, we should mourn as the husbandman who sees no harvest, as the fisherman who returns to his cottage with an empty net, or as the huntsman who has in vain roamed over hill and dale. Ours should be Isaiah's language uttered with many a sigh and groan: "Who hath believed our report? And to whom is the arm of the Lord revealed?" The ambassadors of peace should not cease to weep bitterly until sinners weep for their sins.

If we intensely desire to see our hearers believe on the Lord Jesus, how shall we act in order to be used of God for producing such a result? This is the theme of the present lecture.

Since conversion is a divine work, we must take care that we *depend entirely upon the Spirit of God,* and look to him for power over men's minds. Often as this remark is repeated, I fear we too little feel its force; for if we were more truly sensible of our need of the Spirit of God, should we not study more in dependence upon his teaching? Should we not pray more importunately to be anointed with his sacred unction? Should we not in preaching give more scope for his operation? Do we not fail in many of our efforts, because we practically, though not doctrinally, ignore the Holy Ghost? His place as God is on the throne, and in all our enterprises he must be first, midst, and end: we are instruments in his hand, and nothing more.

This being fully admitted what else should be done if we hope to see conversions? *Assuredly we should be careful to preach most prominently those truths which are likely to lead to this end.* What truths are those? I answer, we should first and foremost preach *Christ, and him crucified.* Where Jesus is exalted souls are attracted: "I, if I be lifted up, will draw all men unto me." The preaching of the cross is to them that are saved the wisdom of God and the power of God. The Christian minister should preach all the truths which cluster around the person and work of the Lord Jesus, and hence he must declare very earnestly and pointedly *the evil of sin,* which created the need of a Savior.

Let him show that sin is a breach of the law, that it necessitates punishment, and that the wrath of God is revealed against it. Let him never treat sin as though it were a trifle, or a misfortune, but let him set it forth as exceeding sinful. Let him go into particulars, not superficially glancing at evil in the gross, but mentioning various sins in detail, especially those most current at the time: such as that all-devouring hydra of drunkenness, which devastates our land; lying, which in the form of slander abounds on all sides; and licentiousness, which must be mentioned with holy delicacy, and yet needs to be denounced unsparingly. We must especially reprove those evils into which our hearers have fallen, or are likely to fall. Explain the Ten Commandments and obey the divine injunction: "show my people their transgressions, and the house of Jacob their sins." Open up the spirituality of the law as, our Lord did, and show how it is broken by evil thoughts, intents, and imaginations. By this means many sinners will be pricked in their hearts.

Old Robbie Flockhart used to say, "It is of no use trying to sew with the silken thread of the gospel unless we pierce a way for it with the sharp needle of the law." The law goes first, like the needle, and draws the gospel thread after it: therefore preach concerning sin, righteousness, and judgment to come. Let such language as that of the fifty-first Psalm be often explained: show that God requireth truth in the inward parts, and that purging with sacrificial blood is absolutely needful.

Aim at the heart. Probe the wound and touch the very quick of the soul. Spare not the sterner themes, for men must be wounded before they can be healed, and slain before they can be made alive. No man will ever put on the robe of Christ's righteousness till he is stripped of his fig leaves, nor will he wash in the fount of mercy till he perceives his filthiness. Therefore, my brethren, we must not cease to declare the law, its demands, its threatenings, and the sinner's multiplied breaches of it.

Teach the depravity of human nature. Show men that sin is not an accident, but the genuine outcome of their corrupt hearts. Preach the doctrine of the natural depravity of man. It is an unfashionable truth; for nowadays ministers are to be found who are very fine upon "the dignity of human nature." The "lapsed state of man"—that is the phrase—is sometimes alluded to, but the corruption of our nature, and kindred themes are carefully avoided: Ethiopians are informed that they may whiten their skins, and it is hoped that leopards will remove their spots. Brethren, you will not fall into this delusion, or, if you do, you may expect few conversions. To prophesy smooth things, and to extenuate the evil of our lost estate, is not the way to lead men to Jesus.

Brethren, *the necessity for the Holy Ghost's divine operations* will follow as a matter of course upon the former teaching, for dire necessity demands divine interposition. Men must be told that they are dead, and that only the Holy Spirit can quicken them; that the Spirit works according to his own good pleasure, and that no man can claim his visitations or deserve his aid. This is thought to be very discouraging teaching, and so it is, but men need to be discouraged when they are seeking salvation in a wrong manner. To put them out of conceit of their own abilities is a great help toward bringing them to look out of self to another, even the Lord Jesus. The doctrine of election and other great truths which declare salvation to be all of grace, and to be, not the right of the creature, but the gift of the Sovereign Lord, are all calculated to hide pride from man, and so to prepare him to receive the mercy of God.

We must also set before our hearers the justice of God and *the certainty that every transgression will be punished.* Often must we

> Before them place in dread array,
> The pomp of that tremendous day
> When Christ with clouds shall come.

Sound in their ears the doctrine of the Second Advent, not as a curiosity of prophecy, but as a solemn practical fact. It is idle to set forth our Lord in all the tinkling bravery of an earthly kingdom, after the manner of brethren who believe in a revived Judaism; we need, to preach the Lord as coming to judge the world in righteousness, to summon the nations to his bar, and to separate them as a shepherd divideth the sheep from the goats.

Paul preached of righteousness, temperance, and judgment to come, and made Felix tremble: these themes are equally powerful now. We rob the gospel of its power if we leave out its threatenings of punishment. It is to be feared that the novel opinions upon annihilation and restoration which have afflicted the church in these last days have caused many ministers to be slow to speak concerning the last judgment and its issues, and consequently the terrors of the Lord have had small influence upon either preachers or hearers. If this be so it cannot be too much regretted, for one great means of conversion is thus left unused.

Beloved brethren, we must be most of all clear upon the great soul-saving doctrine of the *atonement;* we must preach a real bona fide substitutionary sacrifice, and proclaim pardon as its result. Cloudy views as to atoning blood are mischievous to the last degree; souls are held in unnecessary bondage, and saints are robbed of the calm confidence of faith, because they are not definitely told that "God hath made him to be sin for us, who knew no sin, that we might be made the righteousness of God in him." We must preach substitution straightforwardly and unmistakably, for, if any doctrine be plainly taught in Scripture it is this: "The chastisement of our peace was upon him, and with his stripes we are healed." "He, his own self, bare our sins in his own body on the tree." This truth gives rest to the conscience by showing how God can be just, and the justifier of him that believeth. This is the great net of gospel fishermen: the fish are drawn or driven in the right direction by other truths, but this is the net itself.

If men are to be saved, we must in plainest terms preach *justification by faith,* as the method by which the atonement becomes effectual in the soul's experience. If we are saved by the substitutionary work of Christ, no merit of ours is wanted, and all men have to do is by a simple faith to accept what Christ has already done. It is delightful to dwell on the grand truth that "this man, after he had offered one sacrifice for sins for ever, sat down on the right hand of God." O glorious sight: the Christ sitting down in the place of honor because his work is done. Well may the soul rest in a work so evidently complete.

Justification by faith must never be obscured, and yet all are not clear upon it. I once heard a sermon upon "They that sow in tears shall reap in joy," of which the English was, "Be good, very good, and though you will have to suffer in consequence, God will reward you in the end." The preacher, no doubt, believed in justification by faith, but he very distinctly preached the opposite doctrine. Many do this when addressing children, and I notice that they generally speak to the little ones about *loving* Jesus, and not upon believing in him. This must leave a mischievous impression upon youthful minds and take them off from the true way of peace.

Preach earnestly *the love of God in Christ Jesus,* and magnify the abounding mercy of the Lord; but always preach it in connection with his justice. Do not extol the single attribute of love in the method too generally followed, but regard love in the high theological sense, in which, like a golden circle, it holds within itself all the divine attributes: for God were not love if he were not just, and did not hate every unholy thing. Never exalt one attribute at the expense of another. Let boundless mercy be seen in calm consistency with stern justice and unlimited sovereignty. The true character of God is fitted to awe, impress, and humble the sinner: be careful not to misrepresent your Lord.

All these truths and others which complete the evangelical system are calculated to lead men to faith; therefore make them the staple of your teaching.

Secondly, if we are intensely anxious to have souls saved we must not only preach the truths which are likely to lead up to this end, but we must *use modes of handling those truths which are likely to conduce thereto.* Do you enquire, what are they? First, you must do a great deal by way of *instruction.* Sinners are not saved *in* darkness but *from* it; "that the soul be without knowledge, it is not good." Men must be taught concerning themselves, their sin, and their fall; their Savior, redemption, regeneration, and so on. Many awakened souls would gladly accept God's way of salvation if they did but know it; they are akin to those of whom, the apostle said, "And now, brethren, I wot that through ignorance ye did it." If you will instruct them God will save them: is it not written, "the entrance of thy word giveth light"? If the Holy Spirit blesses your teaching, they will see how wrong they have been, and they will be led to repentance and faith.

I do not believe in that preaching which lies mainly in shouting, "Believe! Believe! Believe!" In common justice you are bound to tell the poor people what they are to believe. There must be instruction, otherwise the exhortation to believe is manifestly ridiculous, and must in practice be abortive. I fear that some of our orthodox brethren have been prejudiced against the free invitations of the gospel by hearing the raw, undigested harangues of revivalist speakers whose heads are loosely put together. The best way to preach sinners to Christ is to preach Christ to sinners. Exhortations, entreaties, and beseechings, if not accompanied with sound instruction, are like firing off powder without shot. You may shout, and weep, and plead, but you cannot lead men to believe what they have not heard, nor to receive a truth which has never been set before them. "Because the preacher was wise, he still taught the people knowledge."

While giving instructions it is wise to *appeal to the understanding.* True religion is as logical as if it were not emotional. I am not an admirer of the peculiar views of Mr. Finney, but I have no doubt that he was useful to many; and his power lay in his use of clear arguments. Many who knew his fame were greatly disappointed at first hearing him, because he used few beauties of speech and was as calm and dry as a book of Euclid; but he was exactly adapted to a certain order of minds, and they were convinced and convicted by his forcible reasoning. Should not persons of an argumentative cast of mind be provided for? We are to be all things to all men, and to these men we must become argumentative and push them into a corner with plain deductions and necessary inferences. Of carnal reasoning we would have none, but of fair, honest pondering, considering, judging, and, arguing the more the better.

The class requiring logical argument is small compared with the number of those who need to be pleaded with, by way of *emotional persuasion.* They require not so much reasoning as heart-argument—which is logic set on fire. You must argue with them as a mother pleads with her boy that he will not grieve her, or as a fond sister entreats a brother to return to their father's home and seek reconciliation: argument must be quickened into persuasion by the living warmth of love. Cold logic has its force, but when made red hot with affection the power of tender argument is inconceivable. The power which one mind can gain over others is enormous, but it is often best developed when the leading mind has ceased to have power over itself. When passionate zeal has carried the man himself away his speech becomes an irresistible torrent, sweeping all before it. A man known to be godly and devout, and felt to be large-hearted and self-sacrificing, has a power in his very person, and his advice and recommendation carry weight because of his character; but when he comes to plead and to persuade, even to tears, his influence is wonderful, and God the Holy Spirit yokes it into his service.

Brethren, we must *plead.* Entreaties and beseechings must blend with our instructions. Any and every appeal which will reach the conscience and move men to fly to Jesus we must perpetually employ, if by any means we may save some. I have sometimes heard ministers blamed for speaking of themselves when they are pleading, but the censure need not be much regarded while we have such a precedent as the example of Paul. To a congregation who love you it is quite allowable to mention your grief that many of them are unsaved, and your vehement desire, and incessant prayer for their conversion. You are doing right when you mention your own experience of the goodness of God in Christ Jesus, and plead with men to come and taste the same. We must not be abstractions or mere officials to our people, but we must plead with them as real flesh and blood, if we would see them converted. When you can quote yourself as a living instance of what grace has done, the plea is too powerful to be withheld through fear of being charged with egotism.

Sometimes, too, we must change our tone. Instead of instructing, reasoning and persuading, we must come to *threatening*, and declare the wrath of God upon impenitent souls. We must lift the curtain and let them see the future. Show them their danger, and warn them to escape from the wrath to come. This done, we must return to *invitation*, and set before the awakened mind the rich provisions of infinite grace which are freely presented to the sons of men. In our Master's name we must give the invitation, crying, "Whosoever will, let him take the Water of life freely." Do not be deterred from this, my brethren, by those ultra-Calvinistic theologians who say, "You may instruct and warn the ungodly, but you must not invite or entreat them." And why not? "Because they are dead sinners, and it is therefore absurd to invite them, since they cannot come." Wherefore then may we warn or instruct them?

The argument is so strong, if it be strong at all, that it sweeps away all modes of appeal to sinners, and they alone are logical who, after they have preached to the saints, sit down and say, "The election hath obtained it, and the rest were blinded." On what ground are we to address the ungodly at all? If we are only to bid them do such things as they are capable of doing without the Spirit of God, we are reduced to mere moralists. If it be absurd to bid the dead sinner believe and live, it is equally vain to bid him consider his state, and reflect upon his future doom. Indeed, it would be idle altogether were it not that true preaching is an act of faith, and is owned by the Holy Spirit as the means of working spiritual miracles.

If we were by ourselves, and did not expect divine interpositions, we should be wise to keep within the bounds of reason, and persuade men to do only what we see in them the ability to do. We should then bid the living live, urge the seeing to see, and persuade the willing to will. The task would be so easy that it might even seem to be superfluous; certainly no special call of the Holy Ghost would be needed for so very simple an undertaking. But, brethren, where is the mighty power and the victory of faith if our ministry is this and nothing more? Who among the sons of men would think it a great vocation to be sent into a synagogue to say to a perfectly vigorous man, "Rise up and walk," or to the possessor of sound limbs, "Stretch out thine hand." He is a poor Ezekiel whose greatest achievement is to cry, "Ye living souls, live."

Let the two methods be set side by side as to practical result, and it will be seen that those who never exhort sinners are seldom winners of souls to any great extent, but they maintain their churches by converts from other systems. I have even heard them say, "Oh, yes, the Methodists and Revivalists are beating the hedges, but we shall catch many of the birds." If I harbored such a mean thought I should be ashamed to express it. A system which cannot touch the outside world, but must leave arousing and converting work to others, whom it judges to be unsound, writes its own condemnation.

Again, brethren, if we wish to see souls saved, we must be wise as to *the times* when we address the unconverted. Very little common sense is spent over this matter. Under certain ministries there is a set time for speaking to sinners, and this comes as regularly as the hour of noon. A few crumbs of the feast are thrown to the dogs under the table at the close of the discourse, and they treat your crumbs as you treat them, namely, with courteous indifference. Why should the warning word be always at the hinder end of the discourse when hearers are most likely to be weary? Why give men notice to buckle on their harness so as to be prepared to repel our attack?

When their interest is excited, and they are least upon the defensive, then let fly a shaft at the careless, and it will frequently be more effectual than a whole flight of arrows shot against them at a time when they are thoroughly encased in armor of proof. Surprise is a great element in gaining attention and fixing a remark upon the memory, and times for addressing the careless should be chosen with an eye to that fact. It may be very well as a rule to seek the edification of the saints in the morning discourse, but it would be wise to vary it, and let the unconverted sometimes have the chief labor of your preparation and the best service of the day.

Do not close a single sermon without addressing the ungodly, but at the same time set yourself seasons for a determined and continuous assault upon them, and proceed with all your soul to the conflict. On such occasions aim distinctly at immediate conversions; labor to remove prejudices, to resolve doubts, to conquer objections, and to drive the sinner out of his hiding-places at once. Summon the church members to special prayer, beseech them, to speak personally both with the concerned and the unconcerned, and be yourself doubly upon the watch to address individuals. We have found that our February meetings at the Tabernacle have yielded remarkable results, the whole month being dedicated to special effort. Winter is usually the preacher's harvest, because the people can come together better in the long evenings, and are debarred from out-of-door exercises and amusements. Be well prepared for the appropriate season when "kings go forth to battle."

Among the important elements in the promotion of conversion are your own tone, temper, and spirit in preaching. If you preach the truth in a dull, monotonous style, God *may* bless it, but in all probability he will not; at any rate the tendency of such a style is not to promote attention, but to hinder it. It is not often that sinners are awakened by ministers who are themselves asleep.

A hard, unfeeling mode of speech is also to be avoided; want of tenderness is a sad lack, and repels rather than attracts. The spirit of Elijah may startle, and where it is exceedingly intense it may go far to prepare for the reception of the gospel; but for actual conversion more of John is needed: love is the winning force. We must love men to Jesus. Great hearts are the main qualifications for great preachers, and we must cultivate our affections to that end.

At the same time our manner must not degenerate into the soft and saccharine cant which some men affect who are forever *dearing* everybody, and fawning upon people as if they hoped to soft-sawder[2] them into godliness. Manly persons are disgusted, and suspect hypocrisy when they hear a preacher talking molasses. Let us be bold and outspoken, and never address our hearers as if we were asking a favor of them, or as if they would oblige the Redeemer by allowing him to save them. We are bound to be lowly, but our office as ambassadors should prevent our being servile.

Happy shall we be if we preach believingly, always expecting the Lord to bless his own word. This will give us a quiet confidence which will forbid petulance, rashness, and weariness. If we ourselves doubt the power of the gospel, how can we preach it with authority? Feel that you are a favored man in being allowed to proclaim the good news, and rejoice that your mission is fraught with eternal benefit to those before you. Let the people see how glad and confident the gospel has made you, and it will go far to make them long to partake in its blessed influences.

Preach very solemnly, for it is a weighty business, but let your matter be lively and pleasing, for this will prevent solemnity from souring into dreariness. Be so thoroughly solemn that all your faculties are aroused and consecrated, and then a dash of humor will only add intenser gravity to the discourse, even as a flash of lightning makes midnight darkness all the more impressive. Preach to one point, concentrating all your energies upon the object aimed at. There must be no riding of hobbies, no introduction of elegancies of speech, no suspicion of personal display, or you will fail. Sinners are quick-witted people, and soon detect even the smallest effort to glorify self. Forgo everything for the sake of those you long to save. Be a fool for Christ's sake if this will win them, or be a scholar, if that will be more likely to impress them. Spare neither labor in the study, prayer in the closet, nor zeal in the pulpit. If men do not judge their souls to be worth a thought, compel them to see that their minister is of a very different opinion.

Mean conversions, expect them, and prepare for them. Resolve that your hearers shall either yield to your Lord or be without excuse, and that this shall be the immediate result of the sermon now in hand. Do not let the Christians around you wonder when souls are saved, but urge them to believe in the undiminished power of the glad tidings, and teach them to marvel if no saving result follows the delivery of the testimony of Jesus. Do not permit sinners to hear sermons as a matter of course, or allow them to play with the edged tools of scripture as if they were mere toys; but again and again remind them that every true gospel sermon leaves them worse if it does not make them better. Their unbelief is a daily, hourly sin; never let them infer from your teaching that they are to be pitied for continuing to make God a liar by rejecting His Son.

Impressed with a sense of their danger, give the ungodly no rest in their sins; knock again, and again at the door of their hearts, and knock as for life and death. Your solicitude, your earnestness, your anxiety, your travailing in birth for them God will bless to their arousing. God works mightily by this instrumentality. But our agony for souls must be real and not feigned, and therefore our hearts must be wrought into true sympathy with God. Low piety means little spiritual power. Extremely pointed addresses may be delivered by men whose hearts are out of order with the Lord, but their result must be small. There is a something in the very tone of the man who has been with Jesus which has more power to touch the heart than the most perfect oratory: remember this and maintain an unbroken walk with God. You will need much night-work in secret if you are to gather many of your Lord's lost sheep. Only by prayer and fasting can you gain power to cast out the worst of devils. Let men say what they will about sovereignty, God connects special success with special states of heart, and if these are lacking he will not do many mighty works.

In addition to earnest preaching it will be wise to use other means. If you wish to see results from your sermons you must be accessible to enquirers. A meeting after every service may not be desirable, but frequent opportunities for coming into direct contact with your people should be sought after, and by some means created. It is shocking to think that there are ministers who have no method whatever for meeting the anxious, and if they do see here and there one, it is because of the courage of the seeker, and not because of the earnestness of the pastor. From the very first you should appoint frequent and regular seasons for seeing all who are seeking after Christ, and you should continually invite such to come and speak with you. In addition to this, hold numerous enquirers' meetings, at which the addresses shall be all intended to assist the troubled and guide the perplexed, and with these intermingle fervent prayers for the individuals present, and short testimonials from recent converts and others.

As an open confession of Christ is continually mentioned in connection with saving faith, it is your wisdom to make it easy for believers who are as yet following Jesus by night to come forward and avow their allegiance to him. There must be no persuading to make a profession, but there should be every opportunity for so doing, and no stumbling block placed in the way of hopeful minds. As for those who are not so far advanced as to warrant any thought of baptism, you may be of the utmost benefit to them by personal intercourse, and therefore you should seek it. Doubts may be cleared away, errors rectified, and terrors dispelled by a few moments' conversation; I have known instances in which a life-long misery has been ended by a simple explanation which might have been given years before. Seek out the wandering sheep one by one, and when you find all your thoughts needed for a single individual, do not grudge your labor, for your Lord in his parable represents the good shepherd as bringing home his lost sheep, not in a flock, but one at a time upon his shoulders, and rejoicing so to do.

With all that you can do your desires will not be fulfilled, for soul winning is a pursuit which grows upon a man; the more he is rewarded with conversions the more eager he becomes to see greater numbers born unto God. Hence you will soon discover that *you need help if many are to be brought in.* The net soon becomes too heavy for one pair of hands to drag ashore when it is filled with fishes; and your fellow-helpers must be beckoned to your assistance. Great things are done by the Holy Spirit when a whole church is aroused to sacred energy: then there are hundreds of testimonies instead of one, and these strengthen each other; then advocates for Christ succeed each other and work into each other's hands, while supplication ascends to heaven with the force of united importunity; thus sinners are encompassed with a cordon of earnest entreaties, and heaven itself is called into the field.

It would seem hard in some congregations for a sinner to be saved, for whatever good he may receive from the pulpit is frozen out of him by the arctic atmosphere with which he is surrounded: and on the other hand some churches make it hard for men to remain unconverted, for with holy zeal they persecute the careless into anxiety. It should be our ambition, in the power of the Holy Ghost, to work the entire church into a fine missionary condition, to make it like a Leyden jar charged to the full with divine electricity, so that whatever comes into contact with it shall feel its power. What can one man do alone? What can he not do with an army of enthusiasts around him?

Contemplate at the outset the possibility of having a church of soul-winners. Do not succumb to the usual idea that we can only gather a few useful workers, and that the rest of the community must inevitably be a dead weight: it may possibly so happen, but do not set out with that notion or it will be verified. The usual need not be the universal; better things are possible than anything yet attained; set your aim high and spare no effort to reach it.

Labor to gather a church alive for Jesus, every member energetic to the full, and the whole in incessant activity for the salvation of men. To this end there must be the best of preaching to feed the host into strength, continual prayer to bring down the power from on high, and the most heroic example on your own part to fire their zeal: then under the divine blessing a common-sense management of the entire force cannot fail to produce the most desirable issues. Who among you can grasp this idea and embody it in actual fact?

To call in another brother every now and then to take the lead in evangelistic services will be found very wise and useful; for there are some fish that never will be taken in your net, but will surely fall to the lot of another fisherman. Fresh voices penetrate where the accustomed sound has lost effect, and they tend also to beget a deeper interest in those already attentive. Sound and prudent evangelists may lend help even to the most efficient pastor, and gather in fruit which he has failed to reach; at any rate it makes a break in the continuity of ordinary services, and renders them less likely to become monotonous.

Never suffer jealousy to hinder you in this. Suppose another lamp should outshine yours, what will it matter so long as it brings light to those whose welfare you are seeking? Say with Moses, "Would God all the Lord's servants were prophets." He who is free from selfish jealousy will find that no occasion will suggest it; his people may be well aware that their pastor is excelled by others in talent, but they will be ready to assert that he is surpassed by none in love to their souls. It is not needful for a loving son to believe that his father is the most learned man in the parish; he loves him for his own sake, and not because he is superior to others. Call in every now and then a warm-hearted neighbor, utilize the talent in the church itself, and procure the services of some eminent soul-winner, and this may, in God's hands, break up the hard soil for you, and bring you brighter days.

In fine, beloved brethren, by any means, by all means, labor to glorify God by conversions, and rest not till your heart's desire is fulfilled.

Notes

1. "A man of one book."
2. Solder, used here metaphorically to mean "flatter."

CHAPTER 18

AMERICAN REVEILLE

JONATHAN EDWARDS: SERMON ON A DIVINE AND SUPERNATURAL LIGHT

Jonathan Edwards is known to most Americans as the preacher of "Sinners in the Hands of an Angry God," as a specialist in hellfire and damnation preaching. Thus he is regarded by many almost as a sadistic monster who took pleasure in frightening people. As a result, he is not recognized as one of the true geniuses this country has produced. Yet those who have studied his work recognize in him a profound philosophical mind. He was also an acute observer of nature and of human nature, a literary artist of great merit, one of the best theologians of his time, and a preacher effective enough to have launched the First Great Awakening.

The sermon below was chosen rather than the more notorious one mentioned above because it reflects his key principle of the excellency of God, which he saw as God's free choice to elect some to salvation and some to damnation (**See Vol. 1, pp.** *482-88*)*. He considered the ability to love and admire that sovereign freedom of God to be one of the fruits of election. It reflects what would be his defense against the charge that he took pleasure in terrifying people.*

First of all, he would say that the reprobate who heard his sermons would not be frightened by them because they would either be too doubting to care or, alternatively, would assume in their pride that they were among the elect. The elect, on the other hand, would recognize in the sermon the excellency of God and rejoice in it. The only ones who would be frightened would be those in whom God was working to effect their election. Thus their terror would be a sign of hope.

While predestination is not a popular idea today, it should be recognized that it has been believed in by some of the greatest minds in the history of the church, including Augustine, Luther, and Calvin. Thus it could hardly be so obviously untrue as is often supposed.

The text of the sermon is that of The Works of Jonathan Edwards, *rev. and corrected by Edward Hickman, 2 vols. (London, 1835: reprint, Edinburgh and Carlisle, Pa.: Banner of Truth Trust, 1979). It also appears in Stephen R. Yarbrough and John C. Adams,* Delightful Conviction: Jonathan Edwards and the Rhetoric of Conversion, *Great American Orators, no. 20 (Westport, Conn.: Greenwood, 1993), 109-23.*

A Divine and Supernatural Light,
Immediately Imparted to the Soul by the Spirit of God,
Shown to be Both a Scriptural and Rational Doctrine[1]

And Jesus answered and said unto him, Blessed art thou, Simon Barjona: for flesh and blood hath not revealed it unto thee, but my Father which is in heaven. Matthew 16:17.

Christ addresses these words to Peter upon occasion of his professing his faith in him as the Son of God. Our Lord was inquiring of his disciples, whom men said that he was; not that he needed to be informed, but only to introduce and give occasion to what follows. They answer, that some said he was John the Baptist, and some Elias, and others Jeremias, or one of the prophets. When they had thus given an account whom others said that he was, Christ asks them, whom they said that he was? Simon Peter, whom we find always zealous and forward, was the first to answer: he readily replied to the question, *Thou art Christ, the Son of the living God.*

Upon this occasion, Christ says as he does *to* him and *of* him in the text: in which we may observe,

1. That Peter is pronounced blessed on this account.—

Blessed art thou—"Thou art an happy man, that thou art not ignorant of this, that I *am Christ, the Son of the living God.* Thou art distinguishingly happy. Others are blinded, and have dark and deluded apprehensions, as you have now given an account, some thinking that I am Elias, and some that I am Jeremias, and some one thing, and some another, but none of them thinking right, all of them are misled. Happy art thou, that art so distinguished as to know the truth in this matter."

2. The evidence of this his happiness declared; *viz.* That God, and he *only,* had *revealed it* to him. This is an evidence of his being *blessed,*

First, As it shows how peculiarly favored he was of God above others: *q.d.* "How highly favored art thou, that others, wise and great men, the scribes, Pharisees, and rulers, and the nation in general are left in darkness, to follow their own misguided apprehensions; and that thou shouldst be singled out, as it were, by name, that my heavenly Father should thus set his love on *thee, Simon Bar-jona.—This* argues thee *blessed,* that thou shouldst thus be the object of God's distinguishing love."

Secondly, It evidences his blessedness also, as it intimates that this knowledge is above any that *flesh* and *blood* can *reveal.* "This is such knowledge as only my *Father which is in heaven* can give: it is too high and excellent to be communicated by such means as other knowledge is. Thou art *blessed,* that thou knowest what God alone can teach thee."

The original of this knowledge is here declared, both negatively and positively. *Positively,* as God is here declared the author of it. *Negatively,* as it is declared, *that flesh and blood* had *not revealed* it. God is the author of all knowledge and understanding whatsoever. He is the author of all moral prudence, and all of the skill that men have in their secular business. Thus it is said of all in Israel that were *wise-hearted,* and skilled in embroidering, that God had *filled* them *with the spirit of wisdom.* Exod. 28:3.

God is the author of such knowledge; yet so *that flesh and blood reveals it.* Mortal men are capable of imparting the knowledge of human arts and sciences, and skill in temporal affairs. God is the author of such knowledge by those means: *flesh and blood* is employed the *mediate* or *second* cause of it; he conveys it by the power and influence of natural means. But this spiritual knowledge spoken of in the text, is what God is the author of, none else: he *reveals it, and flesh and blood reveals it not.* He imparts this knowledge immediately, not making use of any intermediate natural causes, as he does in other knowledge.

What had passed in the preceding discourse naturally occasioned Christ to observe this; because the disciples had been telling how others did not know him, but were generally mistaken about him, divided and confounded in their opinions of him: but Peter had declared his assured faith, that he was the *Son of God.* Now it was natural to observe, how it was *not flesh and blood* that had *revealed it to him,* but God; for if this knowledge were dependent on natural causes or means, how came it to pass that they, a company of poor fishermen, illiterate men, and persons of low education, attained to the knowledge of the truth; while the Scribes and Pharisees, men of vastly higher advantages, and greater knowledge and sagacity, in other matters, remained in ignorance? This could be owing only to the gracious distinguishing influence and revelation of the Spirit of God. Hence, what I would make the subject of my present discourse, from these words, is this

Doctrine

That there is such a thing as a spiritual and divine light, immediately imparted to the soul by God, of a different nature from any that is obtained by natural means—And on this subject I would,

I. Show what this divine light is.

II. How it is given immediately by God, and not obtained by natural means.

III. Show the truth of the doctrine.

And then conclude with a brief improvement.

I. I would show what this spiritual and divine light is. And in order to it would show,

First, In a few things what it is not. And here,

1. Those convictions that natural men may have of their sin and misery is not this spiritual and divine light. Men in a natural condition may have convictions of the guilt that lies upon them, and of the anger of God, and their danger of divine vengeance. Such convictions are from the light of truth. That some sinners have a greater conviction of their guilt and misery than others, is because some have more light, or more of an apprehension of truth, than others. And this light and conviction may be from the Spirit of God; the Spirit convinces men of sin: but yet nature is much more concerned in it than in the communication of that spiritual and divine light that is spoken of in the doctrine; it is from the Spirit of God only as assisting natural principles, and not as infusing any new principles.

Common grace differs from special, in that it influences only by assisting of nature; and not by imparting grace, or bestowing any thing above nature. The light that is obtained, is wholly natural, or of no superior kind to that mere nature attains to, though more of that kind be obtained than would be obtained if men were left wholly to themselves: or, in other words, common grace only assists the faculties of the soul to do that more fully which they do by nature, as natural conscience or reason will by mere nature make a man sensible of guilt, and will accuse and condemn him when he has done amiss.

Conscience is a principle natural to men; and the work that it doth naturally, or of itself, is to give an apprehension of right and wrong, and to suggest to the mind the relation that there is between right and wrong and a retribution. The Spirit of God, in those convictions which unregenerate men sometimes have, assists conscience to do this work in a further degree than it would do if they were left to themselves. He helps it against those things that tend to stupefy it, and obstruct its exercise.

But in the renewing and sanctifying work of the Holy Ghost, those things are wrought in the soul that are above nature, and of which there is nothing of the like kind in the soul by nature; and they are caused to exist in the soul habitually, and according to such a stated constitution or law that lays such a foundation for exercises in a continued course as is called a principle of nature. Not only are remaining principles assisted to do their work more freely and fully, but those principles are restored that were utterly destroyed by the fall; and the mind thenceforward habitually exerts those acts that the dominion of sin had made it as wholly destitute of as a dead body is of vital acts.

The Spirit of God acts in a very different manner in the one case, from what he doth in the other. He may indeed act upon the mind of a natural man, but he acts in the mind of a saint as an indwelling vital principle. He acts upon the mind of an unregenerate person as an extrinsic occasional agent; for in acting upon them, he doth not unite himself to them; for notwithstanding all his influences that they may possess, they are still sensual, having not the Spirit. Jude 19. But he unites himself with the mind of a saint, takes him for his temple, actuates and influences him as a new supernatural principle of life and action.

There is this difference, that the Spirit of God, in acting in the soul of a godly man, exerts and communicates himself there in his own proper nature. Holiness is the proper nature of the Spirit of God. The Holy Spirit operates in the minds of the godly, by uniting himself to them, and living in them, and exerting his own nature in the exercise of their faculties.

The Spirit of God may act upon a creature, and yet not in acting communicate himself. The Spirit of God may act upon inanimate creatures;

as, *the Spirit moved upon the face of the waters,* in the beginning of the creation; so the Spirit of God may act upon the minds of men many ways, and communicate himself no more than when he acts upon an inanimate creature. For instance, he may excite thoughts in them, may assist their natural reason and understanding, or may assist other natural principles, and this without any union with the soul, but may act as it were, upon an external object. But as he acts in his holy influences and spiritual operations, he acts in a way of peculiar communication of himself; so that the subject is thence denominated spiritual.

2. This spiritual and divine light does not consist in any impression made upon the imagination. It is no impression upon the mind, as though one saw any thing with the bodily eyes. It is no imagination or idea of an outward light or glory, or any beauty of form or countenance, or a visible luster or brightness of any object. The imagination may be strongly impressed with such things; but this is not spiritual light. Indeed when the mind has a lively discovery of spiritual things, and is greatly affected by the power of divine light, it may, and probably very commonly doth, much affect the imagination; so that impressions of an outward beauty or brightness may *accompany* those spiritual discoveries. But spiritual light is not that impression upon the imagination, but an exceedingly different thing. Natural men may have lively impressions on their imaginations; and we cannot determine but that the devil, who transforms himself into an angel of light, may cause imaginations of an outward beauty, or visible glory, and of sounds and speeches, and other such things; but these are things of a vastly inferior nature to spiritual light.

3. This spiritual light is not the suggesting of any new truths or propositions not contained in the word of God. This suggesting of new truths or doctrines to the mind, independent of any antecedent revelations of those propositions, either in word or writing, is inspiration; such as the prophets and apostles had, and such as some enthusiasts pretend to. But this spiritual light that I am speaking of, is quite a different thing from inspiration. It reveals no new doctrine, it suggests no new proposition to the mind, it teaches no new thing of God, or Christ, or another world, not taught in the Bible, but only gives a due apprehension of those things that are taught in the word of God.

4. It is not every affecting view that men have of religious things that is this spiritual and divine light. Men by mere principles of nature are capable of being affected with things that have a special relation to

religion as well as other things. A person by mere nature, for instance, may be liable to be affected with the story of Jesus Christ, and the sufferings he underwent, as well as by any other tragical story. He may be the more affected with it from the interest he conceives mankind to have in it. Yea, he may be affected with it without believing it; as well as a man may be affected with what he reads in a romance, or sees acted in a stage-play. He may be affected with a lively and eloquent description of many pleasant things that attend the state of the blessed in heaven, as well as his imagination be entertained by a romantic description of the pleasantness of fairy land, or the like.

And a common belief of the truth of such things, from education or otherwise, may help forward their affection. We read in Scripture of many that were greatly affected with things of a religious nature, who yet are there represented as wholly graceless, and many of them very ill men. A person therefore may have affecting views of the things of religion, and yet be very destitute of spiritual light. Flesh and blood may be the author of this: one man may give another an affecting view of divine things with but common assistance; but God alone can give a spiritual discovery of them.—But I proceed to show,

Secondly, Positively what this spiritual and divine light is.

And it may be thus described: A true sense of the divine excellency of the things revealed in the word of God, and a conviction of the truth and reality of them thence arising. This spiritual light primarily consists in the former of these, *viz.* A real sense and apprehension of the divine excellency of things revealed in the word of God. A spiritual and saving conviction of the truth and reality of these things, arises from such a sight of their divine excellency and glory; so that this conviction of their truth is an effect and natural consequence of this sight of their divine glory. There is therefore in this spiritual light,

1. A true sense of the divine and superlative excellency of the things of religion; a real sense of the excellency of God and Jesus Christ, and of the work of redemption, and the ways and works of God revealed in the gospel. There is a divine and superlative glory in these things; an excellency that is of a vastly higher kind, and more sublime nature, than in other things; a glory greatly distinguishing them from all that is earthly and temporal. He that is spiritually enlightened truly apprehends and sees it, or has a sense of it. He does not merely rationally believe that God is glorious, but he has a sense of the gloriousness of God in his heart. There is not only a rational belief that God is holy, and that holiness is a good thing, but there is a sense of the loveliness of God's holiness. There

is not only a speculatively judging that God is gracious, but a sense how amiable God is on account of the beauty of this divine attribute.

There is a twofold knowledge of good of which God has made the mind of man capable. The first, that which is merely notional; as when a person only speculatively judges that any thing is, which by the agreement of mankind, is called good or excellent, *viz,* that which is most to general advantage, and between which and a reward there is a suitableness,—and the like. And the other is, that which consists in the sense of the heart as when the heart is sensible of pleasure and delight in the presence of the idea of it. In the former is exercised merely the speculative faculty, or the understanding, in distinction from the will or disposition of the soul. In the latter, the will, or inclination, or heart, are mainly concerned.

Thus there is a difference between having an *opinion,* that God is holy and gracious, and having a *sense* of the loveliness and beauty of that holiness and grace. There is a difference between having a rational judgment that honey is sweet, and having a sense of its sweetness. A man may have the former that knows not how honey tastes; but a man cannot have the latter unless he has an idea of the taste of honey in his mind. So there is a difference between believing a person is beautiful, and having a sense of his beauty. The former may be obtained by hearsay, but the latter only by seeing the countenance. When the heart is sensible of the beauty and amiableness of a thing, it necessarily feels pleasure in the apprehension. It is implied in a person's being heartily sensible of the loveliness of a thing, that the idea of it is pleasant to his soul; which is a far different thing from having a rational opinion that it is excellent.

2. There arises from this sense of the divine excellency of things contained in the word of God, a conviction of the truth and reality of them; and that, either indirectly or directly.

First, Indirectly, and that two ways.

1. As the prejudices of the heart, against the truth of divine things, are hereby removed; so that the mind becomes susceptive of the due force of rational arguments for their truth. The mind of man is naturally full of prejudices against divine truth. It is full of enmity against the doctrines of the gospel; which is a disadvantage to those arguments that prove their truth, and causes them to lose their force upon the mind. But when a person has discovered to him the divine excellency of Christian doctrines, this destroys the enmity, removes those prejudices, sanctifies the reason, and causes it to lie open to the force of arguments for their truth.

Hence was the different effect that Christ's miracles had to convince the disciples, from what they had to convince the scribes and Pharisees. Not that they had a stronger reason, or had their reason more improved; but their reason was sanctified, and those blinding prejudices, that the scribes and Pharisees were under, were removed by the sense they had of the excellency of Christ, and his doctrine.

2. It not only removes the hindrances of reason, but positively helps reason. It makes even the speculative notions more lively. It engages the attention of the mind, with more fixedness and intenseness to that kind of objects; which causes it to have a clearer view of them, and enables it more clearly, to see their mutual relations, and occasions it to take more notice of them. The ideas themselves that otherwise are dim and obscure, are by this means impressed with the greater strength, and have a light cast upon them; so that the mind can better judge of them. As he that beholds objects on the face of the earth, when the light of the sun is cast upon them, is under greater advantage to discern them in their true forms and natural relations, than he that sees them in a dim twilight.

The mind, being sensible of the excellency of divine objects, dwells upon them with delight; and the powers of the soul are more awakened and enlivened to employ themselves in the contemplation of them, and exert themselves more fully and much more to the purpose. The beauty of the objects draws on the faculties, and draws forth their exercises; so that reason itself is under far greater advantages for its proper and free exercises, and to attain its proper end, free of darkness and delusion.—But,

Secondly, A true sense of the divine excellency of the things of God's word doth more directly and immediately convince us of their truth; and that because the excellency of these things is so superlative. There is a beauty in them so divine and God-like, that it greatly and evidently distinguishes them from things merely human, or that of which men are the inventors and authors; a glory so high and great, that when clearly seen, commands assent to their divine reality. When there is an actual and lively discovery of this beauty and excellency, it will not allow of any such thought as that it is the fruit of men's invention. This is a kind of intuitive and immediate evidence. They believe the doctrines of God's word to be divine, because they see a divine, and transcendent, and most evidently distinguishing glory in them; such a glory as, if clearly seen, does not leave room to doubt of their being of God, and not of men.

Such a conviction of the truths of religion as this, arising from a sense of their divine excellency, is included in saving faith. And this original of it, is that by which it is most essentially distinguished from that common assent, of which unregenerate men are capable.

II. I proceed now to the *second* thing proposed, *viz*. To show how this light is immediately given by God, and not obtained by natural means. And here,

1. It is not intended that the natural faculties are not used in it. They are the subject of this light; and in such a manner, that they are not merely passive, but active in it. God, in letting in this light into the soul, deals with man according to his nature, and makes use of his rational faculties. But yet this light is not the less immediately from God for that; the faculties are made use of as the subject, and, not as the cause. As the use we make of our eyes in beholding various objects, when the sun arises, is not the cause of the light that discovers those objects to us.

2. It is not intended that outward means have no concern in this affair. It is not in this affair, as in inspiration, where new truths are suggested: for by this light is given only a due apprehension of the same truths that are revealed in the word of God; and therefore it is not given without the word. The gospel is employed in this affair. This light is the "light of the glorious gospel of Christ." 2 Cor. 4:4. The gospel is as a glass, by which this light is conveyed to us. 1 Cor. 3:12. "Now we see through a glass"—But,

When it is said that this light is given immediately by God, and not obtained by natural means, hereby is intended, that it is given by God without making use of any means that operate by their own power or natural force. God makes use of means; but it is not as mediate causes to produce this effect. There are not truly any second causes of it; but it is produced by God immediately. The word of God is no proper cause of this effect; but is made use of only to convey to the mind the subject-matter of this saving instruction: and this indeed it doth convey to us by natural force or influence. It conveys to our minds these doctrines; it is the cause of a notion of them in our heads, but not of the sense of their divine excellency in our hearts.

Indeed a person cannot have spiritual light without the word. But that does not argue, that the word properly causes that light. The mind cannot see the excellency of any doctrine, unless that doctrine be first in the mind; but seeing the excellency of the doctrine may be immediately from the Spirit of God; though the conveying of the doctrine or proposition itself may be by the word. So that the notions which are the subject-matter of this light, are conveyed to the mind by the word of God; but that due sense of the heart, wherein this light formally consists, is immediately by the Spirit of God. As for instance, the notion that there is a Christ, and that Christ is holy and gracious, is conveyed to the mind by the word of God; but the sense of the excellency of Christ by reason of that holiness and grace, is nevertheless immediately the work of the Holy Spirit.— I come now,

III. To show the truth of the doctrine; that is, to show that there is such a thing as that spiritual light that has been described, thus immediately let into the mind by God. And here I would show briefly, that this doctrine is both *scriptural* and *rational.*

First, It is scriptural. My text is not only full to the purpose, but it is a doctrine with which the Scripture abounds. We are there abundantly taught, that the saints differ from the ungodly in this, that they have the knowledge of God, and a sight of God, and of Jesus Christ. I shall mention but few texts out of many: 1 John 3:6. "Whosoever sinneth, hath not seen him, nor known him." 3 John 11. "He that doth good, is of God: but he that doth evil, hath not seen God." John 14:19. "The world seeth me no more; but ye see me." John 17:3. "And this is eternal life, that they might know thee, the only true God, and Jesus Christ whom thou hast sent." This knowledge, or sight of God and Christ, cannot be a mere speculative knowledge; because it is spoken of as that wherein they differ from the ungodly. And by these scriptures, it must not only be a different knowledge in degree and circumstances, and different in its effects; but it must be entirely different in nature and kind.

And this light and knowledge is always spoken of as immediately given of God; Mt. 11:25-27. "At that time Jesus answered and said, I thank thee, O Father, Lord of heaven and earth, because thou hast hid these things from the wise and prudent, and hast revealed them unto babes. Even so, Father, for so it seemed good in thy sight. All things are delivered unto me of my Father: and no man knoweth the Father, save the Son, and he to whomsoever the Son will reveal him." Here this effect is ascribed exclusively to the arbitrary operation and gift of God bestowing this knowledge on whom he will, and distinguishing those with it who have the least natural advantage or means for knowledge, even babes, when it is denied to the wise and prudent. And imparting this knowledge is here appropriated to the Son of God, as his sole prerogative.

And again, 2 Cor. 4:6. "For God who commanded the light to shine out of darkness, hath shined it in our hearts, to give the light of the knowledge of the glory of God, in the face of Jesus Christ." This plainly shows, that there is a discovery of the divine superlative glory and excellency of God and Christ, peculiar to the saints; and also, that it is as immediately from God, as light from the sun: and that it is the immediate effect of his power and will. For it is compared to God's creating the light by his powerful word in the beginning of the creation; and is said to be by the Spirit of the Lord, in the 18th verse of the preceding chapter.

God is spoken of as giving the knowledge of Christ in conversion, as of what before was hidden and unseen, Gal. 1:15, 16. "But when it pleased God, who separated me from my mother's womb, and called me by his grace, to reveal his Son in me"—The scripture also speaks plainly of such a knowledge of the word of God, as has been described, as the immediate gift of God; Ps. 119:18. "Open thou mine eyes, that I may behold wondrous things out of thy law." What could the psalmist mean, when he begged of God to open his eyes? Was he ever blind? Might he not have resort to the law and see every word and sentence in it when he pleased? And what could he mean by those wondrous things? Were they the wonderful stories of the creation, and deluge, and Israel's passing through the Red Sea, and the like? Were not his eyes open to read these strange things when he would? Doubtless by wondrous things in God's law, he had respect to those distinguishing and wonderful excellencies, and marvelous manifestations of the divine perfections and glory, contained in the commands and doctrines of the word, and those works and counsels of God that were there revealed. So the Scripture speaks of a knowledge of God's dispensation, and covenant of mercy and way of grace towards his people, as peculiar to the saints, and given only by God, Ps. 25:14. "The secret of the Lord is with them that fear him; and he will show them his covenant."

And that a true saving belief of the truth of religion is that which arises from such a discovery is also, what the Scripture teaches. As John 6:40. "And this is the will of him that sent me, that every one who seeth the Son, and believeth on him, may have everlasting life"; where it is plain that a true faith is what arises from a spiritual sight of Christ. And John 17:6, 7, 8. "I have manifested thy name unto the men which thou gavest me out of the world.—Now they have known that all things whatsoever thou hast given me, are of thee. For I have given unto them the words which thou gavest me, and they have received them, and have known surely that I came out from thee, and they have believed that thou didst send me"; where Christ's manifesting God's name to the disciples, or giving them the knowledge of God, was that whereby they knew that Christ's doctrine was of God, and Christ himself proceeded from him, and was sent by him. Again, John 12: 44, 45, 46. "Jesus cried and said, He that believeth on me, believeth not on me, but on him that sent me. And he that seeth me, seeth him that sent me. I am come a light into the world, that whosoever believeth on me, should not abide in darkness." There believing in Christ, and spiritually seeing him, are parallel.

Christ condemns the Jews, that they did not know that he was the Messiah, and that his doctrine was true, from an inward distinguishing taste and relish of what was divine, in Luke 41:56, 57. He having there blamed the Jews, that though they could discern the face of the sky and of the earth, and signs of the weather, that they could not discern those times—or as it is expressed in Matthew, the signs of those times—adds, "yea, and why even of your own selves, judge ye not what is right?" i.e., without extrinsic signs. Why have ye not that sense of true excellency, whereby ye may distinguish that which is holy and divine? Why have ye not that savor of the things of God, by which you may see the distinguishing glory, and evident divinity, of me and my doctrine?

The apostle Peter mentions it as what gave him and his companions good and well-grounded assurance of the truth of the gospel, that they had seen the divine glory of Christ.—2 Pet. 1:16. "For we have not followed cunningly devised fables, when we made known unto you the power and coming of our Lord Jesus Christ, but we were eye-witnesses of his majesty." The apostle has respect to that visible glory of Christ which they saw in his transfiguration: that glory was so divine, having such an ineffable appearance and semblance of divine holiness, majesty, and grace, that it evidently denoted him to be a divine person. But if a sight of Christ's outward glory might give a rational assurance of his divinity, why may not an apprehension of his spiritual glory do so too? Doubtless Christ's spiritual glory is itself as distinguishing, and as plainly shows his divinity, as his outward glory,—nay, a great deal more: for his spiritual glory is that wherein his divinity consists: and the outward glory of his transfiguration showed him to be divine, only as it was a remarkable image or representation of that spiritual glory. Doubtless, therefore, he that has had a clear sight of the spiritual glory of Christ, may say, I have not followed cunningly devised fables, but have been an eye-witness of his majesty, upon as good grounds as the apostle, when he had respect to the outward glory of Christ that he had seen. But this brings me to what was proposed next, *viz,* to show that,

Secondly, This doctrine is rational.

1. It is rational to suppose, that there is really such an excellency in divine things—so transcendent and exceedingly different from what is in other things—that, if it were seen, would most evidently distinguish them. We cannot rationally doubt but that things divine, which appertain to the Supreme Being, are vastly different from things that are human; that there is a high, glorious, and God-like excellency in them, that does most remarkably difference them from the things that are of

men; insomuch that if the difference were but seen, it would have a convincing, satisfying influence upon any one, that they are divine. What reason can be offered against it? Unless we would argue, that God is not remarkably distinguished in glory from men.

If Christ should now appear to any one as he did on the mount at his transfiguration; or if he should appear to the world in his heavenly glory, as he will do at the day of judgment; without doubt, his glory and majesty would be such as would satisfy every one, that he was a divine person, and that his religion was true: and it would be a most reasonable and well-grounded conviction too. And why may there not be that stamp of divinity, or divine glory, on the word of God, on the scheme and doctrine of the gospel, that may be in like manner distinguishing and as rationally convincing, provided it be but seen?

It is rational to suppose, that when God speaks to the world, there should be something in his word vastly different from men's word. Supposing that God never had spoken to the world, but we had notice that he was about to reveal himself from heaven, and speak to us immediately himself, or that he should give us a book of his own inditing; after what manner should we expect that he would speak? Would it be rational to suppose, that his speech would be exceeding different from men's speech, that there should be such an excellency and sublimity in his word, such a stamp of wisdom, holiness, majesty, and other divine perfections, that the word of men, yea of the wisest of men, should appear mean and base in comparison of it? Doubtless it would be thought rational to expect this, and unreasonable to think otherwise.

When a wise man speaks in the exercise of his wisdom, there is something in everything he says, that is very distinguishable from the talk of a little child. So, without doubt, and much more, is the speech of God to be distinguished from that of the wisest of men; agreeable to Jer. 23:28-29. God having there been reproving the false prophets that prophesied in his name, and pretended that what they spake was his word, when indeed it was their own word, says, "The prophet that hath a dream, let him tell a dream; and he that hath my word, let him speak my word faithfully: what is the chaff to the wheat? saith the Lord. Is not my word like as a fire? saith the Lord: and like a hammer that breaketh the rock in pieces?"

2. If there be such a distinguishing excellency in divine things; it is rational to suppose that there may be such a thing as seeing it. What should hinder but that it may be seen? It is no argument, that there is no such distinguishing excellency, or that it cannot be seen, because some do

not see it, though they may be discerning men in temporal matters. It is not rational to suppose, if there be any such excellency in divine things, that wicked men should see it. Is it rational to suppose, that those whose minds are full of spiritual pollution, and under the power of filthy lusts, should have any relish or sense of divine beauty or excellency; or that their minds should be susceptive of that light that is in its own nature so pure and heavenly? It need not seem at all strange, that sin should so blind the mind, seeing that men's particular natural tempers and dispositions will so much blind them in secular matters; as when men's natural temper is melancholy, jealous, fearful, proud, or the like.

3. It is rational to suppose, that this knowledge should be given immediately by God, and not be obtained by natural means. Upon what account should it seem unreasonable, that there should be any immediate communication between God and the creature? It is strange that men should make any matter of difficulty of it. Why should not he that made all things, still have something immediately to do with things that he has made? Where lies the great difficulty, if we own the being of a God, and that he created all things out of nothing, of allowing some immediate influence of God on the creation still? And if it be reasonable to suppose it with respect to any part of the creation, it is especially so with respect to reasonable intelligent creatures; who are next to God in the gradation of the different orders of beings, and whose business is most immediately with God; and reason teaches that man was made to serve and glorify his Creator.

And if it be rational to suppose that God immediately communicates himself to man in any affair, it is in this. It is rational to suppose that God would reserve that knowledge and wisdom, which is of such a divine and excellent nature, to be bestowed immediately by himself and that it should not be left in the power of second causes.

Spiritual wisdom and grace is the highest and most excellent gift that ever God bestows on any creature: in this the highest excellency and perfection of a rational creature consists. It is also immensely the most important of all divine gifts: it is that wherein man's happiness consists, and on which his everlasting welfare depends. How rational is it to suppose that God, however he has left lower gifts to second causes, and in some sort in their power, yet should reserve this most excellent, divine, and important of all divine communications, in his own hands, to be bestowed immediately by himself, as a thing too great for second causes to be concerned in.

It is rational to suppose, that this blessing should be immediately from

God, for there is no gift or benefit that is in itself so nearly related to the divine nature. Nothing which the creature receives is so much a participation of the Deity: it is a kind of emanation of God's beauty, and is related to God as the light is to the sun. It is therefore congruous and fit, that when it is given of God, it should be immediately from himself, and by himself, according to his own sovereign will.

It is rational to suppose, that it should be beyond man's power to obtain this light by the mere strength of natural reason; for it is not a thing that belongs to reason, to see the beauty and loveliness of spiritual things; it is not a speculative thing, but depends on the sense of the heart. Reason indeed is necessary in order to it, as it is by reason only that we are become the subjects of the means of it; which means I have already shown to be necessary in order to it, though they have no proper causal influence in the affair. It is by reason that we become possessed of a notion of those doctrines that are the subject matter of this divine light, or knowledge; and reason may many ways be indirectly and remotely an advantage to it. Reason has also to do in the acts that are immediately consequent on this discovery: for seeing the truth of religion from hence, is by reason; though it be but by one step, and the inference be immediate. So reason has to do in that accepting of and trusting in Christ, *that* is consequent on it.

But if we take *reason* strictly—not for the faculty of mental perception in general, but for ratiocination, or a power of inferring by arguments—the perceiving of spiritual beauty and excellency no more belongs to reason, than it belongs to the sense of feeling to perceive colors, or to the power of seeing to perceive the sweetness of food. It is out of reason's province to perceive the beauty or loveliness of anything: such a perception does not belong to that faculty. Reason's work is to perceive truth and not excellency. It is not ratiocination that gives men the perception of the beauty and amiableness of a countenance, though it may be many ways indirectly an advantage to it yet it is no more reason that immediately perceives it, than it is reason that perceives the sweetness of honey: it depends on the sense of the heart— Reason may determine that a countenance is beautiful to others, it may determine that honey is sweet to others; but it will never give me a perception of its sweetness.

I will conclude with a very brief improvement of what has been said.

First, This doctrine may lead us to reflect on the goodness of God, that has so ordered it, that a saving evidence of the truth of the gospel is such, as is attainable by persons of mean capacities and advantages, as well as those that are of the greatest parts and learning. If the evidence of the gospel depended only on history, and such reasonings as learned men only are capable of, it would be above the reach of far the greatest part of mankind. But persons with an ordinary degree of knowledge are capable, without a long and subtle train of reasoning, to see the divine excellency of the things of religion: they are capable of being taught by the Spirit of God, as well as learned men. The evidence that is this way obtained, is vastly better and more satisfying, than all that can be obtained by the arguing of those that are most learned, and greatest masters of reason. And babes are as capable of knowing these things, as the wise and prudent and they are often hid from these when they are revealed to those. 1 Cor. 1:26-27. "For ye see your calling, brethren, how that not many wise men after the flesh, not many mighty, not many noble, are called. But God hath chosen the foolish things of the world—."

Secondly, This doctrine may well put us upon examining ourselves, whether we have ever had this divine light let into our souls. If there be such a thing, doubtless it is of great importance whether we have thus been taught by the Spirit of God; whether the light of the glorious gospel of Christ, who is the image of God, hath shined unto us, giving us the light of the knowledge of the glory of God in the face of Jesus Christ; whether we have seen the Son, and believed on him, or have that faith of gospel-doctrines which arises from a spiritual sight of Christ.

Thirdly, All may hence be exhorted, earnestly to seek this spiritual light. To influence and move to it, the following things may be considered.

1. This is the most excellent and divine wisdom that any creature is capable of. It is more excellent than any human learning; it is far more excellent than all the knowledge of the greatest philosophers or statesmen. Yea, the least glimpse of the glory of God in the face of Christ doth more exalt and ennoble the soul, than all the knowledge of those that have the greatest speculative understanding in divinity without grace. This knowledge has the most noble object that can be, *viz,* the divine glory and excellency of God and Christ. The knowledge of these objects is that wherein consists the most excellent knowledge of the angels, yea, of God himself.

2. This knowledge is that which is above all others sweet and joyful. Men have a great deal of pleasure in human knowledge, in studies of natural things; but this is nothing to that joy which arises from this divine light shining into the soul. This light gives a view of those things that are immensely the most exquisitely beautiful, and capable of delighting the eye of the understanding. This spiritual light is the dawning of the light of glory in the heart. There is nothing so powerful as this to support

persons in affliction, and to give the mind peace and brightness in this stormy and dark world.

3. This light is such as effectually influences the inclination, and changes the nature of the soul. It assimilates our nature to the divine nature, and changes the soul into an image of the same glory that is beheld. 2 Cor. 3:18. "But we all with open face, beholding as in a glass the glory of the Lord, are changed into the same image, from glory to glory, even as by the Spirit of the Lord." This knowledge will wean from the world, and raise the inclination to heavenly things. It will turn the heart to God as the fountain of good, and to choose him for the only portion. This light, and this only, will bring the soul to a saving close with Christ. It conforms the heart to the gospel, mortifies its enmity and opposition against the scheme of salvation therein revealed: it causes the heart to embrace the joyful tidings, and entirely to adhere to, and acquiesce in the revelation of Christ as our Savior: it causes the whole soul to accord and symphonize with it, admitting it with entire credit and respect, cleaving to it with full inclination and affection; and it effectually disposes the soul to give up itself entirely to Christ.

4. This light, and this only, has its fruit in an universal holiness of life. No merely notional or speculative understanding of the doctrines of religion will ever bring to this. But this light, as it reaches the bottom of the heart, and changes the nature, so it will effectually dispose to an universal obedience. It shows God as worthy to be obeyed and served. It draws forth the heart in a sincere love to God, which is the only principle of a true, gracious, and universal obedience; and it convinces of the reality of those glorious rewards that God has promised to them that obey him.

Notes

1. Preached at Northampton, and published at the desire of some of the hearers, in the year 1734.

CHAPTER 19

THE SECOND CALL

FRANCIS ASBURY: JOURNAL SAMPLE PAGES

Francis Asbury, the first Methodist bishop in America, traveled more than a quarter of a million miles, mostly by horseback, first as a circuit rider and later during his episcopate. The journal he kept shows how valiantly he labored to spread the gospel under the most trying frontier conditions. The section copied below is from the days before he became bishop, but the main change that position made was in the area he covered rather than in the type of activities. Many aspects of his ministry come alive in these terse entries: not only the occasions and texts of his preaching, but his interactions with laypeople and other clergy, the hardships of travel, his health problems, and his efforts to acquire greater holiness as well. This passage is taken from The Journal and Letters of Francis Asbury in Three Volumes: Volume I, The Journal 1771 to 1793, *ed. Elmer T. Clark with T. Manning Potts and Jacob S. Payton (London: Epworth; Nashville: Abingdon, 1958), 248-51.*

Asbury's Journal

MARYLAND August 26, 1777

Tuesday, 26. Thomas Worthington informed me that they had made choice of me to preach in the Garrison Church.[1] But I shall do nothing that will separate me from my brethren. I hope to live and die a Methodist.

Wednesday, 27. Though it rained I rode twenty-five miles to Magothy; but was tempted and shut up in my wind, while endeavoring to announce, "If God be for us, who can be against us?" But the next day my soul was happy at Mr. Perigau's, and I admitted four persons into the society on trial. The militia were now collecting from all quarters. On the *Lord's day* my soul was much drawn out and blessed in preaching on 1 John 2:16,17. Perhaps it will not be in my power to preach much longer with a clear conscience. But if it should be so, my greatest concern would be for the people of God. For many of the poor sinners seem deaf to all entreaties; and I seem to be only a witness for God against them, that their damnation may be just, if they will not obey the Gospel.

Monday, September 1. The Lord refreshed my own spirit, while I encouraged the few faithful souls who were present, from the words of our Lord, "Fear not, little flock, for it is your Father's good pleasure to give you the kingdom." Brother Daniel Ruff, who had returned from Virginia, met me today.

Wednesday, 3. My soul was watered with the peaceful influence of Divine grace. But what I enjoyed was a stimulus urging me to groan for more. I spent much of my time in reading Law's *Serious Call,* and Baxter's *Call to the Unconverted;* and think the latter is one of the best pieces of human composition in the world, to awaken the lethargic souls of poor sinners.

My mind was under heavy exercises: so I fasted, and preached with much freedom at Mr. Joseph Taylor's; but it brought on a smart fever. Though I was much indisposed, necessity was laid upon me to preach twice on *Thursday,* which increased my fever; and with indifferent lodging and the noise of children, the night was very uncomfortable.

Lord's day, 7. After being blessed with a warm and comfortable season while preaching to a large company at Mr. Hunt's, I then rode to the widow P.'s, where the word went to the hearts of the people with Divine energy, while I exposed to their view the polluted state of the natural man, and pointed out the sovereign remedy.

Tuesday, 9. My mind was so intensely bent on seeking after more of God, that I devoted three hours to the exercise of private prayer and found myself much drawn out by the Spirit of grace, in holy wrestling and communion with God. Being informed that sister S. had slept in the Lord, I congratulated her felicity. Happy soul! She is taken away from the evil to come, and gone to Abraham's bosom, where the wicked cease from troubling, and where the weary are at rest. I have endeavored to banish all anxiety from my mind, and devote much of my time to prayer; and have reaped the gracious benefit thereof in my soul. On *Wednesday* I went to Magothy, and had a large congregation; but found that some of our members had begun to backslide, and that the society stood in need of purging.

Thursday, 11. By particular request I preached a funeral sermon at the burial of Mr. William Ridgely. There were a great many people; and some of them were cut to the heart while I enforced Eccl. 9:10. But afterward at Mr. P.'s my mind was somewhat embarrassed.

Friday, 12. In performing the last office for L. S., who was a Christian indeed, I declared, for the comfort of true believers, "The last enemy that shall be destroyed is death." Some attended on this occasion who had never heard a Methodist before; and the Lord gave me utterance and power.

Monday, 15. We have great commotions on every side. But in the midst of war, the Lord keeps my soul in peace. My heart was warm in preaching at Catherine Small's, though the congregation seemed dull. The two following days I had communion with God; but not in such a degree as I wish to experience. I long "to comprehend the length, and breadth, and depth, and height; and to know the love of Christ, which passeth knowledge, that I may be filled with all the fullness of God"; to

> Live the life of heaven above,
> All the glorious life of love.

Thursday, 18. At Mr. W.'s I met with brother Samuel Spraggs, who informed me that the preachers in Virginia intended to abide there awhile longer. Brother Spraggs preached twice, and there were some small moving amongst the people.

Lord's day, 21. There was nothing remarkable under the word at Mr. Taylor's; but there was a large company and some melting of heart at Mr. Perigau's.

Monday, 22. I met with brother George Shadford, who informed me that my brethren, Mr. Rankin and Mr. Rodda, had left the continent. So we are left alone. But I leave myself in the hand of God; relying on his good providence to direct and protect us; persuaded that nothing will befall me, but what shall conduce to his glory and my benefit. There was both attention and concern in the congregation, which was pretty large, at Capt. Stansbury's.

Lord's day, 28. Brother George Shadford was unwell with an ague. At Reisterstown I urged the necessity of family duty, and showed them how they should train up their children in the ways of the Lord.

Monday, 29. My soul was stayed upon God, and resigned to his unerring wisdom. I wish to be so subject to my Redeemer, as to move in conformity to his divine will; and in all my ways to acknowledge him as my God and my guide. I spent part of my time the next day in reading Mr. Baxter's *Gildas Salvianus,*[2] and esteem it as a most excellent book for a Gospel preacher.

Saturday, October 4. I rode thirty miles to G. B.'s to meet brother Pedicord. My mind was spiritually employed in reading, meditation, and communion with God.

Lord's day, 5. The congregation at G. B.'s were dull; but at B. G.'s there was a melting.

Tuesday, 7. The word seemed to be made a peculiar blessing to the believers at John Hagerty's; and the next day at Mr. John Evans' the power of God was present, while I feelingly urged the people from Heb. 4:16: "Let us therefore come boldly to the throne of grace, that we may obtain mercy, and find grace to help in time of need." My spirit was also divinely animated in preaching afterwards at Richard Owings', though I rode twenty miles between the two sermons. Several old professors felt the reviving influences of the grace of God; and I was in hopes they would press on their way with renewed vigor. Such is the languid disposition of the human soul, that even pure minds require a constant stimulation to keep them in the way of duty. This is one reason why God permits our minds to be tempted by Satan, and our bodies to be afflicted with diseases.

Saturday, 11. I attended and spoke at the half-yearly meeting of the Germans. And on the *Lord's day,* after preaching at Mrs. D.'s, I returned to the meeting of the Germans, where brother George Shadford and myself both spoke.

Monday, 13. Commotions and troubles surrounded me without, but the peace of God filled my soul within. We seemed to be in a strait; but my heart trusted in the Lord. These distressing times have lately induced many people to pay a more diligent attention to the things of God. So I have hopes that these temporal troubles will prepare the way for spiritual blessings.

Wednesday, 15. A heavy gloominess hung on my mind. Brother George Shadford and I rode to Mr. H.'s; and after I had enforced these words, "Therefore, my beloved brethren, be ye steadfast, unmovable, always abounding in the work of the Lord, forasmuch as ye know that your labor is not in vain in the Lord," then brother Shadford exhorted, and the hearts of the people melted under the power of the word. We likewise saw the merciful hand of God displayed the next day, at Mr. Willson's, on the bank of the Potomac.

Lord's day, 19. As I was unwell, brother Shadford preached in the morning on, "Thy kingdom come"; and there was a moving in the congregation. He also preached in the afternoon at Mr. B.'s, but it was to a large company of stupid souls.

Monday, 20. After I had preached brother Shadford met the class; and it was a very powerful season: he also met a class afterward at Mr. Sinclair's, and we were favored with a similar blessing. This has been a day of spiritual and peaceful exercises to my soul. At Mr. Hunt's on *Tuesday,* we were blessed with an extraordinary visitation of grace.

Thursday, 30. We have been detained by heavy rains at W. S.'s, for three days. The times still wear a gloomy aspect; but our trust is in the providence of a superintending God. We have been greatly blessed, and seen great displays of the divine goodness since we have been together. And we have been made a blessing to each other. We now left Mr. S.'s and rode to Rocky Creek.

Lord's day, November 2. I cried in the morning to a large congregation at Mr. Benjamin Johnson's, "We pray you in Christ's stead, be ye reconciled to God"; and in the afternoon at the Sugar Loaf, "Why will ye die?" And my soul was enlarged and blessed both times. I then rode to G. G.'s, which made about twenty miles in the day.

Monday, 3. Our quarterly meeting began, and brother Shadford preached on the subject of the barren fig tree. On *Tuesday* we held our love feast at nine, and I preached at twelve. Our brethren Owing, Samuel Spraggs, and Shadford, all spoke. There were many friends from

Virginia, and the congregation was very large. It was a powerful, melting time, and concluded in the spirit of love,

Wednesday, 5. After riding thirty-seven miles I came to Baltimore, but was very weary; though my mind was calmly stayed on God.

Friday, 7. Went to Mr. Gough's; and on Saturday preached on 3 John 4: "I have no greater joy than to hear that my children walk in truth."

Lord's day, 9. After preaching with freedom of spirit and speech at the Forks, I returned to Mr. Gough's and declared, "Ye are the salt of the earth." My soul has been kept by the grace of God; and

Calm on tumult's wheels I sit.

A FIRSTHAND REPORT OF A CAMP MEETING

A number of eyewitness descriptions of camp meetings have come down, from the very negative one of Anthony Trollope's traveling mother, Frances, to some that were very supportive. (For a discussion of camp meetings, **see Vol. 1, pp. 504-7.***) There are also some excellent drawings that make it possible to visualize these dramatic occasions. The selection following was chosen because it gives a succinct account of the physical setting and the daily schedule, as well as a record of the results of the effort. It is taken from a letter that Henry Smith, one of the clergy involved, wrote to Benjamin Lakin, and it is printed as an appendix to Charles A. Johnson,* The Frontier Camp Meeting: Religion's Harvest Time *(Dallas: Southern Methodist University Press, 1955, as reprinted in 1985 with new intro. by Ferenc M. Szasz), 258-59.*

A Report of a Long-Calm Camp Meeting,
Baltimore Circuit, Maryland, October 8–14, 1806
In a Letter from Circuit Rider Henry Smith to Benjamin Lakin

I was at a happy campmeeting in the first of October, the greatest I ever was at. Such an one I never saw before. Our Tents were pitched in form round the Stand—behind the stand were the coulered peoples tents—Three rows of tents faceing the stand—All the camp ground hedged in by a brush fence—Two gates for the Waggons to come in at—Plank seats, to seat three or four thousand people, or perhaps five thousand—Our stand was covered with a good shingle roof, and nicely plained—before it there was another stand for the Ministers and

Majestrates to sit in—Round the stand we had a pen post and rail, with three gates, or gaps, and benches inside to bring the Mourners in after preaching. We had three guards, 1. the outer guard, 2. the iner guard, 3. the official guard. The outer guard was to guard the gates, and prevent disorder in the extremities of the Camp—The iner guard were to stand in the Iles and seat the people and prevent disorder there—The official guard were to bring forward the Mourners and admit them into the pen—where active persons ready to receive them and help them on to Jesus. And then we had what we called runners—Composed of lads and Boys who whipped away dogs and hogs &c—The order of every day was as follows—At day break the Trumpets were blown round the Camp for the people to rise 20 minutes afterwards for family prayer at the dore of every tent—if fair weather—at sunrise they blew at the stand for public prayer, and then brakefasted. At 10 ocloc they blew for preaching—by 2 ocl. Dinner was to be over in every tent. At 3 ocl. preaching again, and again at night—on the left side of the stand the preachers had a large tent consisting of two rooms, a dineing room, and a bed room—in our dineing room we had a large table (where for the preachers).

The Lord owned our labours and smiled upon us in a wonderfull manner 579 professed converting grace and 118 Sanctification—The glorious flame is spreading—Now I will tell you how we parted—On the last day after brakefast the tents were struck and the people made ready to move on towards home—They were requested to stand in a circular form at the doors of the first row of tents, and when the preachers fell upon their knees at the stand to give thanks to God in silent prayer they were to do likewise. Oh! what a power while hundreds were prostrate upon the earth before the Lord. The preachers then went round the Camp ground singing a parting Hymn, the people standing in form almost drowned in tears when we got round the stand 5 or 6. Trumpets were blown at or from the stand which made a tremendious roar, and the people invited to come round the stand—Oh! Solemn seen! will I ever see anything more like the day of Judgment on this side of eternity—To see the people runing, yes runing, from every direction to the stand weeping, Shouting, and shouting for joy pray was then made—and every Brother fell upon the neck of his brother and wept and the Sisters did likewise & then we parted. O! Glorious day they went home singing and Shouting—

Baltimore Ct. November 11, 1806—H.S.

CHARLES G. FINNEY: "THE WAGES OF SIN"

*The leader of the northern expression of the Second Great Awakening was Charles Grandison Finney, who adapted the techniques of the rural southern expression to an urban and prosperous audience (***see Vol. 1, pp. 511-20***). An attorney at the time of his conversion, there was always something legalistic about Finney's thinking, as is clear in the sermon to follow. Ordained as a Presbyterian, he served as an evangelist until he was forty. Then he accepted a pastorate in New York City, in which he stayed for only a few years before becoming president of Oberlin College. He remained on the faculty the rest of his life.*

"The Wages of Sin" comes from a collection of sermons Finney preached at Oberlin that were taken down by Henry Cowles, a member of the faculty, in what he describes as "a species of shorthand." Of his method, he says that he "aimed to give the heads of the sermons and all the important statements verbatim, to retain always the substance of the thought, and especially to seize upon the illustrations and present their essential points." These transcripts were afterward read to the preacher, who corrected and then approved them. The sermon is from Charles G. Finney, Sermons on Gospel Themes *(Oberlin: E. J. Goodrich; New York: Dodd, Mead & Co., 1876), 37-56.*

The Wages of Sin

"'The wages of sin is death." Romans 6:23.

The death here spoken of is that which is due as the penal sanction of God's law.

In presenting the subject of our text, I must—

I. Illustrate the nature of sin;

II. Specify some of the attributes of the penal sanctions of God's law;

III. Show what this penalty must be.

I. An illustration will give us the best practical view of the nature of sin. You have only to suppose a government established to secure the highest well being of the governed, and of the ruling authorities also. Suppose the head of this government to embark all his attributes in the enterprise—all his wealth, all his time, all his energies—to compass the high end of the highest general good. For this purpose he enacts the best possible laws—laws which, if obeyed, will secure the highest good of both subject and Prince. He then takes care to affix adequate penalties; else all his care and wisdom must come to naught. He devotes to the interests of his government all he is and all he has, without reserve or abatement.

But some of his subjects refuse to sympathize with this movement. They say, "Charity begins at home," and they are for taking care of themselves in the first place; in short, they are thoroughly selfish.

It is easy to see what this would be in a human government. The man who does this becomes the common enemy of the government and of all its subjects. *This is Sin.* This illustrates precisely the case of the sinner. Sin is selfishness. It sets up a selfish end; and to gain it, uses selfish means; so that in respect to both its end and its means, it is precisely opposed to God and to all the ends of general happiness which he seeks to secure, it denies God's rights; it discards God's interests. Each sinner maintains that his own will shall be the law. The interest he sets himself to secure is entirely opposed to that proposed by God in his government.

All law must have sanctions. Without sanctions it would be only advice. It is therefore essential to the distinctive and inherent nature of law that it have sanctions.

These are either remuneratory or vindicatory. They promise reward for obedience, and they also threaten penalty for disobedience. They are vindicatory, inasmuch as they vindicate the honor of the violated law.

Again, sanction may be either natural or governmental. Often both forms exist in other governments than the divine.

Natural penalties are those evil consequences which naturally result without any direct interference of government to punish. Thus in all governments the disrespect of its friends falls as a natural penalty on transgressors. They are the natural enemies of all good subjects.

In the divine government, compunctions of conscience and remorse fall into this class, and indeed many other things which naturally result to obedience on the one hand and to disobedience on the other.

There should also be governmental sanctions. Every governor should manifest his displeasure against the violation of his laws. To leave the whole question of obedience to mere natural consequences is obviously unjust to society. Inasmuch as governments are established to sustain law and secure obedience, they are bound to put forth their utmost energies in this work.

Another incidental agency of government under some circumstances is that which we call discipline. One object of discipline is to go before the infliction of penalty, and force open unwilling eyes, to see that use law has a government to back it up and the sinner a fearful penalty to fear. Coming upon men during their probation, while as yet they have not seen or felt the fearfulness of penalty, it is designed to admonish them—to make them think and consider. Thus its special object is the good of the subject on whom it falls and of those who may witness its administration. It does not propose to sustain the dignity of law by exemplary inflictions. This belongs exclusively to the province of penalty. Discipline, therefore, is not penal in the sense of visiting crime with deserved punishment, but aims to dissuade the subject of law from violating its precepts.

Disciplinary agency could scarcely exist under a government of pure law, for the reason that such a government cannot defer the infliction of penalty. Discipline presupposes a state of suspended penalty. Hence penal inflictions must be broadly distinguished from disciplinary.

We are sinners, and therefore have little occasion to dwell on the remuneratory features of God's government. We can have no claim to remuneration under law, being precluded utterly by our sin. But with the penal features we have every thing to do. I therefore proceed to inquire.

II. What are the attributes of the penal sanctions of God's law?

God has given us reason. This affirms intuitively and irresistibly all the great truths of moral government. There are certain attributes which we know must belong to the moral law, e.g. one is, *intrinsic justice*. Penalty should threaten no more and no less than is just.—Justice must be an attribute of God's law; else the whole universe must inevitably condemn it.

Intrinsic justice means and implies that the penalty be equal to the obligation violated. The guilt of sin consists in its being a violation of obligation. Hence the guilt must be in proportion to the magnitude of the obligation violated, and consequently the penalty must be measured by this obligation.

Governmental justice is another attribute. This feature of law seeks to afford security against transgression. Law is not governmentally just unless its penalty be so graduated as to afford the highest security against sin which the nature of the case admits. Suppose under any government the sanctions of law are trifling, not at all proportioned to the end to be secured. Such a government is unjust to itself, and to the interests it is committed to maintain. Hence a good government must be governmentally just, affording in the severity of its penalties and the certainty of their just infliction, the highest security that its law shall be obeyed.

Again, penal sanctions should be worthy of the end aimed at by the law and by its author. Government is only a means to an end,—this proposed end being universal obedience and its consequent happiness. If law is indispensable for obtaining this end, its penalty should be graduated accordingly.

Hence the penalty should be graduated by the importance of the precept. If the precept be of fundamental importance—of such importance that disobedience to it saps the very existence of all government—then it should be guarded by the greatest and most solemn sanctions. The penalties attached to its violation should be of the highest order.

Penalty should make an adequate expression of the lawgiver's views of the value of the end he proposes to secure by law; also of his views of the sacredness of his law; also of the intrinsic guilt of disobedience. Penalty aims to bring forth the *heart* of the lawgiver—to show the earnestness of his desire to maintain the right, and to secure that order and well-being which depend on obedience. In the greatness of the penalty the lawgiver brings forth his heart and pours the whole influence of his character upon his subjects.

The object of executing penalty is precisely the same; not to gratify revenge, as some seem to suppose, but to act on the subjects of government with influences toward obedience. It has the same general object as the law itself has.

Penal sanctions should be an adequate expression of the lawgiver's regard for the public good and of his interest in it. In the precept he gave some expression; in the penalty, he gives yet more. In the precept we see the object in view and a manifestation of regard for the public interests; in the penalty, we have a *measure* of this regard, showing us how *great* it is. For example, suppose a human law were to punish murder with only a trifling penalty. Under the pretense of being very tender-hearted, the lawgiver amerces this crime of murder with a fine of fifty cents! Would this show that he greatly loved his subjects and highly valued their life and interests? Far from it. You cannot feel that a legislator has done his duty unless he shows how much he values human life, and unless he attaches a penalty commensurate in some good degree with the end to be secured.

One word as to the infliction of capital punishment in human governments. There is a difference of opinion as to which is most effective, solitary punishment for life, or death. Leaving this question without remark I have it to say that no man ever doubted that *the murderer deserves to die*. If some other punishment than death is to be preferred, it is not by any means because the murderer does not deserve death. No man can doubt this for a moment. It is one of the unalterable principles of righteousness, that if a man sacrifices the interest of another, he sacrifices his own; an eye for an eye; life for life.

We cannot but affirm that no government lays sufficient stress on the protection of human life unless it guards this trust with its highest penalties. Where life and all its vital interests are at stake, there the penalty should be great and solemn as is possible.

Moral agents have two sides to their sensibility; hope and fear;—to which you may address the prospect of good and the dread of evil. I am now speaking of penalty. This is addressed only to fear.

I have said in substance that penalty should adequately assert and vindicate the rightful authority of the lawgiver; should afford if possible an adequate rebuke of sin and should be based on a just appreciation of its nature. God's moral government embraces the whole intelligent universe, and stretches with its vast results onward through eternity. Hence the sweep and breadth of its interests are absolutely unlimited, and consequently the penalties of its law, being set to vindicate the authority of this government and to sustain these immeasurable interests, should be beyond measure dreadful. If anything beyond and more dreadful than the threatened penalty could be conceived, all minds would say: "This is not enough." With any just views of the relations and the guilt of sin, they could not be satisfied unless the penalty is the greatest that is conceivable. Sin is so vile, so mischievous, so terribly destructive and so far-sweeping in its ruin, moral agents could not feel that enough is done so long as more can be.

III. What is the penalty of God's moral law?

Our text answers, "*death.*" This certainly is not *animal death,* for saints die and animals also, neither of whom can be receiving the wages of sin. Besides, this would be no penalty if, after its infliction, men went at once to heaven. Such a penalty, considered as the wages of sin, would only be an insult to God's government.

Again, it cannot be *spiritual death,* for this is nothing else than a state of entire disobedience to the law. You cannot well conceive anything more absurd than to punish a man for disobedience by subjecting him to perpetual disobedience—an effort to sustain the law by dooming such offenders to its perpetual violation—and nothing more.

But this death *is* endless misery, corresponding to the death penalty in human governments. Everybody knows what this is. It separates the criminal from society forever; debars him at once and utterly from all the privileges of the government and consigns him over to hopeless ruin. Nothing more dreadful can be inflicted. It is the extreme penalty, fearful beyond any other that is possible for man to inflict.

There can be no doubt that death as spoken of in our text is intended to correspond to the death penalty in human governments.

You will also observe that in our text the "gift of God" which is "eternal life through Jesus Christ our Lord," is directly contrasted with death, the wages of sin. This fact may throw light on the question respecting the nature of this death. We must look for the antithesis of *"eternal life."*

Now this eternal life is not merely an eternal existence. Eternal life never means merely an eternal existence, in any case where it is used in Scripture; but it does mean a state of eternal blessedness, implying eternal holiness as its foundation. The use of the term "life" in Scripture in the sense of *real life*—a life worth living—*i.e.,* real and rich enjoyment, is so common as to supersede the necessity of special proof.

The penalty of death is therefore the opposite of this—viz., eternal misery.

I must here say a few words upon the *objections* raised against this doctrine of eternal punishment

All the objections I have ever heard amount only to this, *that it is unjust*. They may be expressed in somewhat various phraseology, but this is the only idea which they involve, of any moment at all.

(1). It is claimed to be unjust because "life is so short."

How strangely men talk! Life so short, men have not time to sin enough to deserve eternal death! Do men forget that *one sin* incurs the penalty due for sinning? How many sins ought it to take to make one transgression of the law of God? Men often talk as if they supposed it must require a great many. As if a man must commit a great many murders before he has made up the crime of murder enough to fall under the sentence of the court! What? Shall a man come before the court and plead that although he has broken the law to be sure, yet he has not lived long enough, and has not broken the law times enough, to incur its penalty? What court on earth ever recognized such a plea as proving any other than the folly and guilt of him who made it?

(2). It is also urged that "man is so small, so very insignificant a being that he cannot possibly commit an infinite sin." What does this objection mean? Does it mean that sin is an act of creation, and to be measured therefore by the magnitude of that *something* which it creates? This would be an exceedingly wild idea of the nature of sin. Does the objection mean that man cannot violate an obligation of infinite strength? Then his meaning is simply *false,* as everybody must know. Does he imply that the guilt of sin is not to be measured by the obligation violated? Then he knows not what he says, or wickedly denies known truth. What? Man so little that he cannot commit much sin! Is this the way we reason in analogous cases? Suppose your child disobeys you. He is very much smaller than you are! But do you therefore exonerate him from blame? Is this a reason which nullifies his guilt? Can no sin be committed by inferiors against their superior? Have sensible men always been mistaken in supposing that the younger and smaller are sometimes under obligations to obey the older and the greater? Suppose you smite down the magistrate; suppose you insult, or attempt to assassinate the king; is this a very small crime, almost too excusable to be deemed no crime all, because forsooth you are in a lower position and he in a higher? You say, "I am so little, so very insignificant! How can I deserve so great a punishment?" Do you reason so in any other case except your own sins against God? Never.

(3). Again, some men say, "Sin is not an infinite evil." This language is ambiguous. Does it mean that sin would not work infinite mischief if suffered to run on indefinitely? This is false, for if only one soul were ruined by it, the mischief accruing from it would be infinite. Does it mean that it is not an infinite evil, as seen in its present results and relations? Suppose this admitted; it proves nothing to our purpose for it may be true that the sum total of evil results from each single sin will not all be brought out in any duration less than eternity. How then can you measure the evil of sin by what you see today?

But there are still other considerations to show that the penalty of the law must be infinite. Sin is an infinite *natural* evil. It is so in this sense, that there are no bounds to the natural evil it would introduce not governmentally restrained.

If sin were to ruin but one soul, there could be no limit set to the evil it would thus occasion.

Again, sin involves infinite guilt, for it is a violation of infinite obligation. Here it is important to notice a common mistake growing out of confusion of ideas about the ground of obligation. From this, result mistakes in regard to what constitutes the guilt of sin. Here I might show that when you misapprehend the ground of obligation, you will almost of necessity misconceive the nature and extent of sin and guilt. Let us recur to our former illustration. Here is a government, wisely framed to secure the highest good of the governed and of all concerned. Whence arises the obligation to obey? Certainly from the intrinsic value of the end sought to be secured. But how broad is this obligation to obey; or, in other words, what is its true measure? I answer, it exactly equals the value of the end which the government seeks to secure, and which obedience will secure, but which sin will destroy. By this measure of God the penalty must be graduated. By this the lawgiver must determine how much sanction, remuneratory and vindicatory, he must attach to his law in order to meet the demands of justice and benevolence.

Now God's law aims to secure the highest universal good. Its chief and ultimate end is not, strictly speaking, to secure supreme homage to God, but rather to secure the highest good of all intelligent moral beings—God, and all his creatures. So viewed, you will see that the intrinsic value of the end to be sought is the real ground of obligation to obey the precept. The value of this end being estimated, you have the value and strength of the obligation.

This is plainly infinite in the sense of being unlimited. In this sense we affirm obligation to be without limit. The very reason why we affirm any obligation at all is that the law is good and is the necessary means of the highest good of the universe. Hence the reason why we affirm any penalty at all compels us to affirm the justice and necessity of an infinite penalty. We see that intrinsic justice must demand an infinite penalty for the same reason that it demands any penalty whatever. If *any* penalty be just, it is just because law secures a certain good. If this good aimed at by the law be unlimited in extent, so must be the penalty. Governmental justice thus requires endless punishment; else it provides no sufficient guaranty for the public good.

Again, the law not only *designs* but *tends to secure* infinite good. Its tendencies are direct to this end.—Hence its penalty should be infinite. The law is not just to the interests it both aims and tends to secure unless it arms itself with infinite sanctions.

Nothing less than infinite penalty can be an adequate expression of God's view of the value of the great end on which his heart is set. When men talk about eternal death being too great a penalty for sin, what do they think of efforts to restrain sin all over the moral universe? What do they think of the death of his well-beloved Son? Do they suppose it possible that God could give an adequate or a corresponding expression to his hatred of sin by any penalty less than endless?

Nothing less could give an adequate expression to his regard for the authority of law. O, how fearful the results and how shocking the very idea, if God should fail to make an adequate expression of his regard for the sacredness of that law which underlies the entire weal of all his vast kingdom?

You would insist that he shall regard the violation of his law as Universalists do. How surely he would bring down an avalanche of ruin on all his intelligent creatures if he were to yield to your demands! Were he to affix anything less than endless penalty to his law, what holy being could trust the administration of his government!

His regard to the public good forbids his attaching a light or finite penalty to his law. He loves his subjects too well. Some people have strange notions of the way in which a ruler should express his regard for his subjects. They would have him so tenderhearted toward the guilty that they should absorb his entire sympathy and regard. They would allow him perhaps to fix a penalty of sixpence fine for the crime of murder, but not much if anything more. The poor murderer's wife and children are so precious you must not take away much of his money, and as to touching his liberty or his life—neither of these is to be thought of. What! Do you not know that human nature is very frail and temptable, and therefore you ought to deal very sparingly with penalties for murder? Perhaps they would say, you may punish the murderer by keeping him awake one night—just one, no more; and God may let a guilty man's conscience disturb him about to this extent for the crime of murder! The Universalists do tell us that they will allow the most High God to give a man conscience that shall trouble him a little if he commits murder—a little, say for the first and perhaps the second offense; but they are not wont to notice the fact that under this penalty of a troubling conscience, the more a man sins, the less he has to suffer. Under the operation of this descending scale, it will soon come to this that a murderer would not get so much penalty as the loss of one night's sleep. But such are the notions that men reach when they swing clear of the affirmations of an upright reason and of God's revealing Word.

Speaking now to those who have a moral sense to affirm the right as well as eyes to see the operation of law, I know you cannot deny the logical necessity of the death penalty for the moral law of God. There is a logical clinch to every one of these propositions which you cannot escape.

No penalty less than infinite and endless can be an adequate expression of God's displeasure against sin and of his determination to resist and punish it. The penalty should run on as long as there are subjects to be affected by it—as long as there is need of any demonstration of God's feelings and governmental course toward sin.

Nothing less is the greatest God can inflict, for he certainly can inflict an endless and infinite punishment. If therefore the exigency demands the greatest penalty he can inflict, this must be the penalty: *banishment from God and endless death.*

But I must pass to remark that the Gospel everywhere assumes the same. It holds that by the deeds of the law no flesh can be justified before

God. Indeed, it not only affirms this, but builds its entire system of atonement and grace upon this foundation. It constantly assumes that there is no such thing as paying the debt and canceling obligation; and therefore that the sinner's only relief is forgiveness through redeeming blood.

Yet again, if the penalty be not endless death, *what is it?* Is it temporary suffering? Then how long does it last? When does it end? Has any sinner ever got through, served out his time and been taken to heaven? We have no testimony to prove such a case, not the first one; but we have the solemn testimony of Jesus Christ to prove that there never can be such a case. He tells us there can be no passing from hell to heaven or from heaven to hell. A great gulf is fixed between, over which none shall ever pass. You may pass from earth to heaven, or from earth to hell; but these two states of the future world are wide extremes, and no man or angel shall pass the gulf that divides them.

But you answer my question, "What is the penalty?" by the reply, "It is only the natural consequences of sin as developed in a troubled conscience." Then it follows that the more a man sins, the less he is punished, until it amounts to an infinitesimal quantity of punishment, for which the sinner cares just nothing at all. Who can believe this? Under this system, if a man fears punishment, he has only to pitch into sinning with the more will and energy; he will have the comfort of feeling that he can very soon get over all his compunctions, and get beyond any penalty whatever! And do you believe this is God's only punishment for sin? You cannot believe it.

Universalists always confound discipline with penal sanctions. They overlook this fundamental distinction and regard all that men suffer here in this world as only penal. Whereas it is scarcely penal at all, but is chiefly disciplinary. They ask, What good will it do a sinner to send him to an endless hell? Is not God perfectly benevolent; and if so, how can he have any other object than to do the sinner all the good he can?

I reply, Punishment is not designed to do good to that sinner who is punished. It looks to other, remoter, and far greater good. Discipline, while he was on earth, sought mainly *his* personal good; penalty looks to other results. If you ask, Does not God aim to do good to the universal public by penalty? I answer, Even so; that is precisely what He aims to do.

Under human governments, the penalty may aim in part to reclaim. So far, it is discipline. But the death penalty—after all suspension is past and the fatal blow comes, aims not to reclaim, and is not discipline, but is only penalty. The guilty man is laid on the great public altar and made a sacrifice for the public good. The object is to make a fearful, terrible impression on the public mind of the evil of transgression and the fearfulness of its consequences. Discipline looks not so much to the support of law as to the recovery of the offender. But the Day of Judgment has nothing to do with reclaiming the lost sinner. That and all its issues are purely penal. It is strange that these obvious facts should be overlooked.

There is yet another consideration often disregarded, viz., that, underlying any safe dispensation of discipline, there must be a moral law, sustained by ample and fearful sanctions, to preserve the law-giver's authority and sustain the majesty and honor of his government. It would not be safe to trust a system of discipline, and indeed it could not be expected to take hold of the ruined with much force, if it were not sustained by a system of law and penalty. This penal visitation on the unreclaimed sinner must stand forever, an appalling fact, to show that justice is realized, law vindicated, God honored; and to make an enduring and awful impression of the evil of sin and of God's eternal hostility against it.

Remarks

We hear a great many cavils against future punishment. At these we should not so much wonder, but for the fact that the gospel assumes this truth, and then proposes a remedy. One would naturally suppose the mind would shrink from those fearful conclusions to which it is pressed when the relations of mere law are contemplated; but when the gospel interposes to save, then it becomes passing strange that men should admit the reality of the Gospel, and yet reject the law and its penalties. They talk of *grace;* but what do they mean by grace? When men deny the fact of sin, there is no room and no occasion for grace in the Gospel. Admitting nominally the fact of sin, but virtually denying its guilt, grace is only a name. Repudiating the sanctions of the law of God and laboring to disprove their reality, what right have men to claim that they respect the Gospel? They make it only a farce—or at least a system of *amends* for unreasonably severe legislation under the legal economy. Let not men who so traduce the law assume that they honor God by applauding his gospel!

The representations of the Bible with regard to the final doom of the wicked are exceedingly striking. Spiritual truths are revealed by natural objects: e.g., the gates and walls of the New Jerusalem, to present the splendors and glories of the heavenly state. A spiritual telescope is put into our hands; we are permitted to point it towards the glorious city "whose builder and maker is God"; we may survey its inner sanctuary, where the worshiping hosts praise God without ceasing. We see their flowing robes of white—the palms of victory in their hands—the beaming joy of their faces—the manifestations of ineffable bliss in their souls. This is heaven portrayed in symbol. Who supposes that this is intended as hyperbole? Who arraigns these representations as extravagant in speech, as if designed to overrate the case, or raise unwarrantable expectations? No man believes this. No man ever brings this charge against what the Bible says of heaven. What is the object in adopting this figurative mode of representation? Beyond question, the object is to give the best possible conception of the facts.

Then we have the other side. The veil is lifted and you come to the very verge of hell to see what is there. Whereas on the one hand all was glorious, on the other all is fearful and full of horrors.

There is a bottomless pit. A deathless soul is cast therein; it sinks and sinks and sinks, going down that awful pit which knows no bottom, weeping and wailing as it descends, and you hear its groans as they echo and re-echo from the sides of that dread cavern of woe!

Here is another image. You have a "lake of fire and brimstone," and you see lost sinners thrown into its waves of rolling fire; and they lash its burning shore and gnaw their tongues for pain. There the worm dieth not, and their fire is not quenched, and "not one drop of water" can reach them to "cool their tongues"—"tormented in that flame."

What think you? Has God said these things to frighten our poor souls? Did he mean to play on our fears for his own amusement? Can you think so? Nay, does it not rather grieve his heart that he must build such a hell, and *must* plunge therein the sinners who will not honor his law—will not embrace salvation from sinning, through his grace? Ah, the waves of death roll darkly under the eye of the holy and compassionate One! He has no pleasure in the death of the sinner! But he must sustain his throne and save his loyal subjects if he can.

Turn to another scene. Here is a deathbed. Did you ever see a sinner die? Can you describe the scene? Was it a friend, a relative, dear, very dear to your heart? How long was he dying? Did it seem to you the death-agony would never end? When my last child died, the struggle was long; O, it was fearfully protracted and agonizing! Twenty-four hours in the agonies of dissolving nature! It made me sick; I could not see it! But suppose it had continued till this time I should long since have died myself under the anguish and nervous exhaustion of witnessing such a scene. So would all our friends. Who could survive to the final termination of such an awful death? Who would not cry out: "My God, cut it short, cut it short in mercy!" When my wife died, her death struggles were long and heart-rending. If you had been there, you would have cried mightily to God: ""Cut it short! O, cut it short and relieve this dreadful agony!" But suppose it had continued, on and on, by day and by night—day after day, through its slow moving hours, and night after night—*long* nights, as if there could be no morning. The figure of our text supposes an eternal dying. Let us conceive such a case. Suppose it should actually occur, in some dear circle of sympathizing friends. A poor man cannot die! He lingers in the death-agony a month, a year, five years, ten years—till all his friends are broken down, and fall into their graves under the insupportable horror of the scene: but still the poor man cannot die! He outlives one generation—then another and another; one hundred years he is dying in mortal agony and yet he comes no nearer to the end! What would you think of such a scene? It would be an illustration—that is all—a feeble illustration of the awful *"second death!"*

God would have us understand what an awful thing sin is and what fearful punishment it deserves. He would fain show us by such figures how terrible must be the doom of the determined sinner. Did you ever see a sinner die? And did you not cry out—Surely the curse of God has fallen heavily on this world! Ah, this is only a faint emblem of that heavier curse that comes in the *"second death!"*

The text affirms that death is the "wages of sin." It is just what sin deserves. Labor earns wages and creates a rightful claim to such remuneration. So men are conceived as earning wages when they sin. They become entitled to their pay. God deems himself holden to give them their well-deserved wages.

As I have often said, I would not say one word in this direction to distress your souls, if there were no hope and no mercy possible. Would I torment you before the time? God forbid! Would I hold out the awful penalty before you and tell you there is no hope. No. I say these things to make you feel the need of escaping for your life.

Think of this: "the wages of sin is death!" God is aiming to erect a monument that shall proclaim to all the universe: "Stand in awe and sin not!" So that whenever they shall look on this awful expression, they shall say: What an awful thing sin is! People are wont to exclaim: O, how horrible is the *penalty*! They are but too apt to overlook the horrible *guilt* and *ill desert* of sin! When God lays a sinner on his deathbed before our eyes, he invites us to look at the *penalty of sin.* There he lies, agonizing, groaning, quivering, racked with pain, yet he lives, and lives on. Suppose he lives on in this dying state a day, a week, a month, a year, a score of years, a century, a thousand years, a thousand ages, and still he lives on, "dying perpetually, yet never dead:[3] finally the universe passes away; the heavens are rolled together as a scroll—and what then? There lies that sufferer yet! He looks up and cries out, "*How long,* O HOW LONG?" Like the knell of eternal death, the answer comes down to him, "*Eternally,* ETERNALLY!" O how this fearful answer comes down thundering through all the realms of agony and despair!

We are informed that in the final consummation of earthly scenes, "the judgment shall sit and the books shall be opened." We shall be there, and what is more, *there* to close up our account with our Lord and receive our allotment. Which will you have on that final settlement day? The wages of sin? Do you say, "Give me my wages—give me my wages; I will not be indebted to Christ"? Sinner, you shall have them. God will pay you without fail or stint. He has made all the necessary arrangements, and has your wages ready. But take care what you do! Look again before you take your final leap. Soon the curtain will fall, probation close, and all hope will have perished. Where then shall I be? And you, *where?* On the right hand or the left?

The Bible locates hell in the sight of heaven. The smoke of their torment as it rises up forever and ever, is in full view from the heights of the Heavenly City. There, you adore and worship; but as you cast your eye afar off toward where the rich man lay, you see what it costs to sin. There, not one drop of water can go to cool their burning tongues. Thence the smoke of their torment rises and rises for evermore! Take care what you do today!

Suppose you are looking into a vast crater, where the surges of molten lava boil and roll up, and roll and swell, and ever and anon belch forth huge masses to deluge the plains below. Once in my life, I stood in sight of Etna, and dropped my eye down into its awful mouth. I could not forbear to cry out, "*tremendous,* TREMENDOUS!" There, said I, is an image of hell! O Sinner, think of *hell,* and of yourself thrust into it. It pours forth its volumes of smoke and flame forever, never ceasing, never exhausted. Upon that spectacle the universe can look and read: "The wages of sin is death! O sin not, since such is the doom of the unpardoned sinner!" Think what a demonstration this is of the government of God! What an exhibition of his holy justice, of his inflexible purpose to sustain the interests of holiness and happiness in all his vast dominions! Is not this worthy of God, and of the sacredness of his great scheme of moral government?

Sinner, you may now escape this fearful doom. This is the reason why God has revealed hell in his faithful Word. And now shall this revelation, to you, be in vain and worse than in vain?

What would you think if this whole congregation were pressed by some resistless force close up to the very brink of hell: but just as it seemed that we are all to be pushed over the awful brink, an angel rushes in, shouting as with seraphic trump, "*Salvation is possible—Glory to God,* GLORY TO GOD, GLORY TO GOD!"

You cry aloud: Is it possible? Yes, yes, he cries, let me take you up in my broad, loving arms and bear you to the feet of Jesus, for he is mighty and willing to save!

Is all this mere talk? Oh, if I could wet my lips with the dews of heaven, and bathe my tongue in its founts of eloquence, even then I could not describe the realities.

Christian people, are you figuring round and round to get a little property, yet neglecting souls? Beware, lest you ruin souls that can never live again! Do you say: I thought they knew it all? They reply to you: "I did not suppose you believed a word of it yourselves. You did not act as if you did. Are you going to heaven? Well, I am going down to hell? There is no help for me now. You will sometimes think of me then, as you shall see the smoke of my woe rising up darkly athwart the glorious heavens. After I have been there a long, long time, you will sometimes think that I, who once lived by your side, am there. O remember, you cannot pray for me then; but you will remember that once you might have warned and might have saved me."

O methinks, if there can be bitterness in heaven, it must enter through such an avenue and spoil your happiness there.

Notes

1. An Anglican chapel.
2. *The Reformed Pastor.*
3. This quotation is not closed in the text.

CHAPTER 20

"THE FRUITS OF FERVOR" (A)

THE SOCIAL IMPLICATIONS OF GOSPEL PREACHING

CHARLES ALBERT TINDLEY: "HEAVEN'S CHRISTMAS TREE"

Tindley spent the first eight to thirteen years of his life in slavery,[1] *but he was later ordained in the Methodist Episcopal Church and built a small congregation in Philadelphia into a church with seven to ten thousand members. Although he had little formal education, he studied privately, was able to complete an institute's program in theology, and even learned Greek and Hebrew by correspondence. This enabled him to function as a leader in the elite tradition of the black church, even though he had detractors all his life who looked down on him for his lack of formal credentials. His sermons tended to be topical in form and to be organized around a list—as the following is* (**see Vol. 1, pp. 535-38**)*. This sermon in most ways is not unlike much white preaching of the same period, reflecting as it does the Romanticism, not to say the sentimentality, characteristic of the Victorian period. Yet his* *sensitive awareness of the problems faced by members of his flock puts it in the empowering tradition of good black preaching through the ages. The sermon is taken from Ralph H. Jones,* Charles Albert Tindley: Prince of Preachers *(Nashville: Abingdon, 1982), 145-56.*

Heaven's Christmas Tree

"And on this side of the river and that was the tree of life" (Rev. 22:2).

I suppose there are many in this audience who have heard me more than once tell the story that suggested the subject that we are to emphasize tonight. If it were not for two reasons, namely, there are those in this presence who have never heard the story, and that the truths which we wish to emphasize upon your minds are most effective in connection therewith, I would not relate it again.

The story is as follows:

Some years ago, when I was serving as pastor in Wilmington, Delaware, I had an occasion to visit this city on Christmas Day. For some reason I came early in the morning. While passing along a certain street, I saw a large church with front doors open and many people, young and old, moving in and out. Out of curiosity, I crossed over so as to find out what the occasion was. When I reached the point where I could see, behold, in the lecture room of the church was a large tree, beautifully trimmed and laden with many packages. A young man was standing upon a step-ladder and by means of a rod was lifting the packages from the limbs of the tree and calling out the names that were written on them. As he would call a name some hand would go up, indicating the person it belonged to. These happy recipients were passing in groups from the church, smiling and congratulating each other upon the favors received. I stood there until the tree was stripped of packages and all the people, except a very few, had passed out into the street. I noticed a little boy, who sauntered from the building almost, if not quite, the last, with scanty clothing and pinched features. He wore a sickly mechanical smile, as though it was an unavoidable reflection from the numerous faces that surrounded him. His eyes were filled with tears, his lips moved as though his little soul was forcing audible expressions of its sad disappointment, He moved off down the street, kicking the bits of paper here and there to satisfy his empty feelings. I followed him until he turned into a little court and stood on the doorstep of one of the little dwellings.

After glancing this way and that for a minute, as though he dreaded to leave the street empty-handed and cheerless he turned the doorknob and entered what I imagined was a poor, cheerless home. Until then, I was unconscious of a tear that was rolling down my face and dropping on my bosom. With a sigh I turned away with the question: "Will there ever be a time when the spirit of Christ shall so fill and control the lives of people that everybody, young and old, rich and poor, will receive some token of love on Christmas Day?" My query was directed more heavenward than earthward.

I seemed to be asking the Christ of the Christmas rather than anyone else. The answer must have come directly from him, for it was in the very language of my text. It was a happy thought and I felt like saying thank God right out loudly. Then my mind began to reflect and search for some good reasons for this happy thought. "Is Christ really a tree? Is he a Christmas Tree?" And, if so, are there any packages on this tree? And for whom? And, yes! He is the Tree of Life. He was brought to this world and set up in Bethlehem Judea's manger more than nineteen hundred years ago. He bears a package of rare blessing, for every human being in all this world. That Christ is called a tree in the Bible is proven by such sayings as these: "If they do these things in the green tree, what shall be done in the dry?" St. Luke 23:31; "I will give to eat of the tree of life," Rev. 2:7. "The leaves of the tree were for the healing of the nation," (Revelation 22:2).

These passages of Scripture furnish good reasons for calling Christ Jesus a tree. When I read that this Tree of life yields its fruit every month and that its leaves were good for the healing of the nations, I have a right to think that there are packages on it for human beings. I call it a Christmas tree because it came to earth on Christmas Eve night. You are to imagine now that I am speaking of Christ Jesus in the light of a great Christmas tree set up in this world, bearing a package for every single creature that he has made. This means the poorest of you who have not loving friends to make your hearts glad with presents, can turn to Jesus and find in him a present just for you. Yes, a package with your name on it is hanging on the limb of heaven's great Christmas Tree. Some of you here this evening are bringing back in memory happier moments than you will ever see again on this earth. A time when your mother and father lived; when you and your brothers and sisters raced downstairs in the early dawn of Christmas morning to find out what was in your stocking or on the table. It wasn't much, but the toy horse and drum brought more joy than you have ever experienced since. In many of your lives those sweet moments have gone never to return. Those dear parents have crept behind the curtains of time and have entered the solemn realms of perpetual silence. Some of you had homes of your own just a little while ago, which memory brings fresh to your minds. You that are widows can hear the footfalls of loving husbands climbing the steps of your homes, bringing from the markets the joy of Yuletide,

The fire burned brightly; the table, fairly groaned with viands of the season. The home wore a real smile; pictures tossed compliments to pictures; bric-a-brac to bric-a-brac; furniture seemed to speak to furniture in tones of hallelujah and strains of glory. Since that sweet and rare oasis in your life's desert, crape has been on your door. That strong man has been captured by the monster death, and you have followed him to the house of cold clay in some cemetery. Need I say that no Christmas has seemed so happy since? There are fathers here who are at a loss to know what to do for their motherless children. The home is broken up, the children are at one place and they at another. The bells of Christmas simply bring fresh to their minds the joy that they once had, and which they have not now. There are those here whose sad misfortunes have made their Christmas a gloomy one. It may be that sickness has blighted and eclipsed the joy that they expected; it may be that the father is out of work and can't explain to the children why they are to have no nice presents this year.

O, there are many blighted hopes, broken prospects and saddened hearts because of circumstances so unfavorable and so crushing; but amidst it all and despite all, I am going to have you see by faith Heaven's Christmas tree, whose top reaches the ceiling and whose limbs touch all the walls of this building. It is sagging with packages fixed by fingers of light. On one of them is your name. I am going to call them off and the Holy Spirit is going to take them to everyone that is in this building, for there is one for each of you. Here is

1. HOPE FOR THE HOPELESS. This package hangs on a limb that almost touches the ground. It is the lowest limb on the Tree, and is the easiest package to reach. It shines with the light and glitter of all the promises of God to sinners and to those who are discouraged and hopeless amid life's conflicts. It is for the struggling youth who is striving for an education with little or no help; who has had to leave school because of the want of funds to pay the bills, or because of those who are depending upon his or her care. It may be aged parents, younger brothers or sisters, or relatives. It may be that I am speaking to someone tonight who is at the point of despair as touching the accomplishment of their aim in life. You have experienced the loss of courage and ambition to further try to become anything like you hoped to be. I say to you tonight that there

is a package on Heaven's Christmas Tree that holds a fit remedy for your case. It is set to the music of a beautiful song, a verse of which reads:

> Courage, brother, do not stumble,
> Tho' your path be dark as night,
> There's a star that guides the humble;
> Trust in God, and do the right.

I may be speaking to some parents who have come here hopeless of ever making anything worth while out of their son or daughter, or ever having their children become what they had hoped and prayed that they might be. I have a song for you:

> Tho' the cloud may hide your sun,
> Ere your battle has been won,
> If you still will watch and pray,
> Soon will come a brighter day.

I may be speaking to someone who has tried to live a good life, but has failed. The devil has told you that you are one of those who are doomed by your Creator to misery here and hell hereafter. You may have almost decided to quit and give up trying. I am going to beg of you a favor tonight, and that is reach up with all the strength you have left and take from Heaven's Christmas Tree this low-limbed package, HOPE. It is so low that you can reach it from the gutter; from the gambling den; from the barroom and from the lowest places on earth. I beseech you, in God's name, take this package, Hope, and try again. I point to another package on another limb a little higher up. It is marked

2. "FORGIVENESS FOR THE GUILTY." It shines with the brightness of the Redeemer's face and is stained with the blood of Calvary. It is set in a frame carved out of love of God and is dazzling with a chandelier of a thousand promises, whose jets glow with the breath of the Man of Sorrow and of many stripes. It is the most costly package on this tree. Those finger-marks you see on it were left there by the nail-pierced hand of the Man of Galilee. He tied it there in the darkness and earthquakes of that Friday afternoon when the dead woke up before the morning of the resurrection and the rocks broke their silence. There are many of you in this building tonight, who, as I do, need this package. Nobody can say that they have never sinned against God; nobody has had their sins

canceled by their own deeds or deserving. Everybody, therefore who is not now guilty of sin has been forgiven through the merits of Jesus Christ. It was the gift of God, for the sake of Jesus. Just as others have been forgiven, so everyone present and everybody in this whole world can, and may be, forgiven of all their sins. It can be done now, this very night. You who gamble can be forgiven before you leave this building if you put down your cards and all other means of gambling and give yourself to God. Every drunkard may go from this building saved, if he will accept this package and resolve in his heart to be a drunkard no more. Every sinner of every description, no matter how old, how great or how hard, may be forgiven and leave this building free from sin and happy in the Lord. You know when God forgives you he remembers your sins against you no more forever. I like that word "forever" when it is on the side of Heaven and happiness; I am afraid of it when on the side of misery and hell. But I want you to know that "forever" means just as long a time in hell as it does in heaven and just as long a time in heaven as it does in hell.

How many of you [who] are guilty of sin will take this package tonight? I see another package on another limb a little higher up still; on it is written the words

3. "HELP FOR THE WEAK." I have always thanked God for the numerous promises of help in the Bible. I don't know what Adam's strength was before the fall, but I do know that since that time human nature has not been equal in strength to the force of evil in this world. The lust of the flesh, the lust of the eye, and the pride of life are mighty armies under the management of the devil for the downfall of everything that is good in the human being. I have never known but one man on this whole earth who, from his birth to his death, could stand against the forces of this world. I need not tell you that man is Jesus Christ. He not only conquered the world, the flesh, and the devil for himself, but for every believer throughout all time.

It is this man, Christ Jesus, who promises help to everyone who wants to live for God. My belief is that there are hundreds who are in sin and on the way to hell who don't want to be there. They wish that in some way they could change their lives, but are too weak to do so. I want you to see the mighty arm that reaches down over this package of which I am speaking, out to every helpless soul who wants to leave the devil. It is that mighty strong arm which upholds the world, weighs the hills and measures the waters. It is that great arm that destroyed Egypt; leveled the walls of Jericho; flung Babylon's glory in the dust; and plucked the

Caesars from their thrones. He says, as he looks over the sea of faces tonight, I will help thee. Yes, He will help husbands to go home sober; help wives to take care of their homes and be good mothers; help children to respect and obey their parents; help everybody to be whole-hearted and true-hearted for God and fellow man. I see another package on a limb higher. It is marked:

4. FRIENDSHIP FOR THE FRIENDLESS. Do you know the value of friendship? If not, it is because you have never been friendless in this world. No matter how strong you are physically, mentally, or financially, you need a friend. Perhaps the most unhappy people in this building are not those who are poor in the things of this world, but who are friendless. Nothing can get on very well alone. I have seen cattle on my father's little farm run and call pitifully for the other cattle. I have seen a goose distressed because she was lost from the other geese. The herding of cattle and of beasts in general, as well as of birds and other creatures of the lower kingdom, are indicative of this need of friendship. Someone has said that lamps may burn, stars may shine and sun may blaze, yet dark indeed is the life that has no friendship. The cold friendship of the world is so uncertain, so ephemeral and so fleeting that no one can quite know whether tomorrow holds for them the same blessings that they enjoy today. The slender pedestals on which earth's friendship sits are so easily knocked over that one is afraid to move. If you have got money, fine clothes, beautiful home, popular relations, or great ability, you may have friends and admirers; but when these are gone your brightest day may fade into a dark and dismal night. I am reminded of an old gentleman who owned a little farm in Maryland. He had nice horses and other livestock about him and was in at least, easy circumstances. His two boys were sent away to school, one to study medicine and the other agriculture and business. About the time they graduated, their mother died, which left their father a widower. He proposed to the farmer son that he should take the farm, and all he asked of him was that he be cared for in his own home until he died. When his will was made and the property all turned over to the two boys, the wife of the son who had charge of the farm began to complain of the old gentleman. She said his language wasn't learned and therefore she didn't want him in the parlor when her learned associates were about. She complained of his style of dress and of his habits of life in general; his hands were palsied and he would shake the coffee from his cup on the clean tablecloth; his teeth were gone and he couldn't eat the hard bread which she gave him. She wanted him to sleep in the attic and he couldn't climb the stairs well because of rheumatism.

Oh, many things she complained of, until the son suggested that the old man be taken to the poorhouse. The old saint agreed to go rather than remain in the way and to the discomfort of his son and daughter-in-law. He begged for the old chair in which his lifelong friend, the mother of his children, had sat many a winter night knitting socks for the boys, before the big, open fire-place; also for his old hickory cane and the family Bible, which was covered with a piece of his own mother's dress by the hand of his departed wife. The old Bible was marked from Genesis to Revelation to indicate the chapters and verses of his choice. These were all placed in the ox-cart and himself sat in the shuck-bottomed chair. When the cart had passed through the road-gate and turned in the direction of the poorhouse, the old man turned his dimmed eyes toward the fields which he had cleared before his children were born, the ditches he had dug, the fences he had made and the buildings he had erected. After swallowing lumps that came up in his throat and wiping with his old red handkerchief the tears that were falling on his gray beard, he said to his son: "The people of my class are dead; your mother, my bosom friend, sleeps beneath yon cedar tree. Stripped and alone and without friends I go as a load of dirt to the poorhouse, and were it not for one friend whom I came to know when I was eleven years old, I would be most miserable today. That friend is the Lord Jesus Christ, who is as tenderly near me today as when I first found Him. He is going to the poorhouse with me and will remain with me until it pleases him to take my spirit, to his beautiful home on high. I fear, son," said he, "that you and your wife will occupy a house more fit to be called a poorhouse than the one you are taking me to, for where parents are not honored there is poverty indeed." The young man stopped his oxen and with face covered with his hands for a moment said: "Father, I am going to take you back home to stay there until you die, or I will stay in the poorhouse with you." I cite this narrative to show who is the true friend and what the friendship is that knows no change.

I see another package higher still; it is marked

5. "PEACE FOR THE TROUBLED SOUL." When I mention this I know I start the spring of joy and the earnest longings up from a thousand souls within this building. Only God knows the number of troubled and unhappy souls in this world. Some will tell you that the grace of God in your soul will do away with all trouble and anxiety concerning things of this earth; I don't believe it, neither do you. This is like a good many other sayings that have been put into the category of Christian expressions which have never been sustained by a single experience. I have only

to quote the words of Jesus Christ to prove that Christianity was never intended to take all the briars out of the fields and the thorns from the thorn hedges of the world. Nor was it intended to make it so that a briar or a thorn cannot pierce a believer's hand or foot as easily as it can the feet and hands of other folks. Jesus said: "IN THIS WORLD YE SHALL HAVE TRIBULATIONS." There are many kindred terms, but this one word "tribulation" is a pouch big enough to hold all the kinds of troubles and trials that one can ever have in this world. It is foolishness as well as precarious to plan to go through this world without trouble. There is one rule and one law that governs all of the physical conditions of this world. All is based upon the condition of cause and effect. Anyone who would have good effects must put in operation good causes. Christianity includes all of these good causes and therefore all of the good effects. While I do not wish to take from the Christian life any of the mysterious and supernatural elements, and there are many of them, I do wish to say that it includes also a whole lot of good common sense and real plain philosophy. A lazy and non-provident church member is bound to be in want no matter how many prayers he makes a day or how high or loud he shouts. The best saint in the world will miss a train if he is behind time. I need not go further to prove that in material things, at least one law applies to all. To say that mishaps and wrongdoings about us do not disturb us in any way is to bespeak a situation that neither Jesus Christ nor any of His disciples occupied in this world. Jesus said at one time "My soul is exceedingly sorrowful, even unto death."

The Apostles all suffered great afflictions and most of them martyrdom. Paul complained of the thorn in the flesh. Oh, no, my friends, I am not trying to make you believe that because you have religion that you are going to heaven on flowery beds of ease, but I am happy to tell you that there is promise of sweet peace to all the children of God. What peace we have in this world is not INSTEAD OF THINGS, but, IN SPITE OF THINGS. Just the thought of an unbroken and undisturbed quiet in the City of God where none can disturb or molest, where no shifting winds ever come to change the temperature, no night hides the beauty of the flowers of the new Eden, no winter time to beat the leaves from the Tree of Life, no change of government to make uncertain the social condition, and no death to break up families—such promises as these are calculated to make one bear with patience all the much conditions of poverty, afflictions, and even death in this life. Oh, ye tired mother, you who have not had a night's rest for a long time because of your sick baby or because of wayward children who would not come home until the small hours of morning; Oh you heart-broken wives, whose brutal husbands have made your lives miserable; and you fathers who have struggled against great odds and who have carried aching hearts almost from the day you stood before the minister holding the hand of that girl in solemn pledge to be her husband; I say to all of you who are troubled, there is coming a day of absolute and glorious peace, a peace that will take all the gray hairs from your head, all the wrinkles from your face, all the tears from your eyes, and all the pangs of sorrow from your heart.

When these heavy burdens and tight straps shall have been taken off your heart and from your soul you will shout in the vigor of the new morning and with life and joy of happy childhood in that land that knows no sorrow. There is just one more package that I wish to mention tonight.

It hangs on the top limb of Heaven's Christmas Tree. So bright is the light which shines upon it one cannot see it with physical eyesight. It is too far away from this world and is lighted by a sunlight too bright for the endurance of the natural sight. You will have to see it with the eyes of faith, for it is spiritually discerned. I am going to get the Holy Spirit to read the name, for every time I look that way I hear someone saying "eye has not seen, ear has not heard, neither has it entered into the heart the things that God has for them that love him." But, thank God, the Spirit has revealed them. On this top-limbed package are the words

6. "HOME FOR THE HOMELESS." I know you orphan children, you widowed women and you widower fathers are scarcely able to remain quiet under the sound of such happy news as this. As I speak to you, you are thinking of your own sweet homes of just a little while ago; sweet music and prattle of happy children come to you tonight like an echo. The joy of those days seems like a dream whose glories fade with the waking and die at the opening day. That dreaded monster death has carried your loved ones to the grave; your homes are broken up and yourselves are homeless wanderers. Some of you mothers are stopping with your children. This is a sweet and gracious providence, if these children are good to you; it is an earthly torment if they are not. Some of you are living with strangers whose treatment of you is according to the money you pay. Some of you have scarcely a home in this world. I want you to fix your eyes toward the top limb of this Heaven's Christmas Tree and reading the title of the package which is near enough to the homeland of the soul to catch the light of that eternal sun, sing with me

My Heavenly home is bright and fair;

Nor pain nor death shall enter there;
Its glittering towers the sun out-shine,
That heavenly mansion shall be mine.

I rejoice with you in the prospect of that great homecoming in the sweet by and by, where no children will mourn the loss of mothers, no funeral dirges are sung, no farewell tears are shed, and nobody will ever say goodbye.

I bid you in God's name and in the light of yon Heavenly dome and within hearing distance of the songs of the Redeemed and the hallelujahs of the Ransomed, bear your crosses and endure your pains a little longer, for

Beyond the smiling and weeping we shall be soon;
Beyond the waking and the sleeping we shall be soon.

JOHN JASPER: "THE STONE CUT OUT OF THE MOUNTAIN"

*John Jasper spent almost the first half-century of his life as a slave, and he was a preacher for half that time (***see Vol. 1, pp. 546-53***). His ministry up until his release from bondage was subject to the willingness of his master to give him time off for it. He acquired a considerable reputation for his sermons at the funeral services owners permitted for their slaves, and for a while he was permitted to go two Sundays a month to a church in Petersburg of which he was pastor. When he was freed, he set about building a church in Richmond that eventually had a handsome building and a congregation of two thousand members. As a slave, he had barely received enough education to be able to spell out words in the Bible laboriously, but he came to have an encyclopedic knowledge of the Bible and to be able to express himself eloquently in standard English. His preaching was always in the folk tradition.*

His deep faith and oratorical genius made him one of the tourist attractions of Richmond. Many of the white members of the power structure who went to hear him came away deeply moved and blessed by his words. Yet his major message was always to his own people and was intended to give them a theological perspective that would allow them to function in a white world. Thus in the sermon that follows, he identifies Daniel and the Israelites, the oppressed people of God, with his people, and Nebuchadnezzar and the Babylonians with the whites, but he does so in the encoded way that made what he said clear to his people but unnoticeable to the visitors.

This sermon is taken from William E. Hatcher, John Jasper: The Unmatched Negro Philosopher and Preacher *(New York: Fleming H. Revell, 1908; reprint, New York: Negro Universities Press, 1969), 108-20. The spelling has been standardized, but the grammar has been left as it was.*

The Stone Cut Out of the Mountain

(Text, Daniel 2:45)

I stand before you today on legs of iron and none can stay me from preaching the gospel of the Lord God. I know well enough that the old devil is mad as a tempest about my being here; he knows that my call to preach comes from God, and that's what makes him so mad when he sees Jasper ascend the pulpit, for he knows that the people is going to hear a message straight from heaven. I don't get my sermons out of grammars and rhetorics, but the Spirit of the Lord puts them in my mind and makes them burn in my soul.

It have always been one of the ways of God to set up men as rulers of the people. You know that God ordains kings and rulers and—what kind of bothers some of us—he don't always make it a point to put up good men. You know that our Lord give Judas a place among the twelve, and he turned out to be one of the grandest rascals under the sun.

Just so Nebuchadnezzar was appointed of the Lord to be king of Babylon—that same robber that took the vessels out of the temple at Jerusalem and lugged them away to his own country. That man had one of the powerfulest kingdoms ever known on this flat earth. He ruled over many countries and many smaller kingdoms, and even had under his hands the servants on the plantation and the beasts of the field. He was one of these unlimited monarchs. He asked nobody no odds, and did just what he wanted to do, and I cannot stop to tell you with what a strong hand and outstretched arm he ruled the people with an iron rod.

It come to pass that one time this king that did not fear God (though God had set him up), had a dream. Dreams is awfully curious things. They used to frighten folks out of their senses and I tell you they sometimes frighten folks now. I've had many dreams in my day that got mighty close to me. They graveled into the very cords of my soul, and made me feel like the ground under my feet was liable to give way any time, and I don't doubt that hundreds of you that hear me now have been frightened and could not eat nor sleep nor work with any peace because you done have strange dreams. You better watch them dreams. In the ancient days the Lord spoke to folks in dreams. He warned them, and I don't doubt that he does that way sometimes now.

Nebuchadnezzar's dream stirred him powerful. He rolled all night and did not sleep a wink. So he sent out and got the magicians and the astrologers and the sorcerers and the Chaldeans, and they was brought unto him. He tell them that he had dreamed a dream that had troubled his spirit. And the Chaldeans asked him what the dream was. The king say that the dream done gone clear out of him, and he can't catch the straight of it to save his soul. He tell them, moreover, that they got to dig up the dream and work up the meaning, too, and that if they don't that he going to have them cut all to pieces and turn their houses into a dunghill, and then he tell them that if they will get the dream back for him and give the explanation he going to give them nice gifts and put great honors on them. It was too much for the Chaldeans. They couldn't dream the king's dream for him, and they come square out and tell Nebuchadnezzar that no man on the earth could show such a matter to the king, and that in their opinion there is no king on the earth that would ask for such a thing from prophet or magician.

Then Nebuchadnezzar got high. He went on a tear and you know when a king gets mad you better get out of his way. He is got the power; and so he up and sent out a decree through all the regions of the kingdom that all the wise men everywhere should be slain. Just see what a mad man will do when he get furious mad. They got no more sense than a mad tiger or a roaring lion.

Just before the slaughter of the wise men come on, Daniel hear about it, and he asked the king's captain what it was all about and why the king was so hasty, and the captain told Daniel all about it. Daniel brushed himself up quick and struck out to see the king and ask him to hold up the execution of his bloody prophecy, and he'd promise to explain his dream to him.

Then Daniel goes off and gets all his godly friends together and ask them to pray to the God of heaven that he and his friends should not perish in the slaughter of the tricksters of that country. One thing the Lord can't do: he can't refuse to answer the cries of his people; and when all that praying was going on God appeared to Daniel in the night and revealed to him the secret of the king. And what you reckon? When the Lord give Daniel that dream and the interpretation thereof, Daniel raised a great shout and give thanks to God for what the Lord had done for him.

But he didn't shout long, for he had important business to attend to; and very soon he went to the king and carried with him the secret that the king had demanded at the hands of the astrologers and magicians. He told the king right to his face the thing that he had dreamed and what God meant by it. Truly Daniel did behave himself before the king in a very pretty and becoming manner. He tell the king he did not have no more sense than other people, and that he was not prepared to do things that other men could do, but that it was by the power of God that all this matter had been made known to him.

He told the king that what he saw was a great image; that the image was bright and splendid and the form of it was terrible; that the head was of fine gold, his breast and arms of silver, his belly and thighs of brass, and his legs of iron and his feet part of iron and part of clay. And he tell the king further that he saw a stone that was cut without hands out of the mountain and that the stone smote the image upon his feet and broke them in pieces, and that the stone that broke the image became a great mountain and filled all the world.

Then Daniel—that brave and fearless brother, that never quailed before the mightiest ruler of the earth—faced the king and tell him an awful and a warning truth. He say to him, "You is a great king now. You have a mighty country and all power, and thy glory covers the ground. Man and beast and fowl obey you. You is the head of gold, but after you will come another kingdom that shall not be like your'n, but still it shall be big and there shall come another kingdom and there shall be a fourth kingdom strong as iron, and this kingdom shall bruise and smash all the other kingdoms."

And then Daniel gets to the big point. He tells the king that the Lord is going to set up a kingdom and that in the times to come that kingdom shall crush and consume all the other kingdoms. That shall be the kingdom of God on the earth, and that kingdom shall stand forever and ever. You knows how you saw the stone that was cut out of the mountain and how that broke in pieces the iron, the brass, the clay, the silver, and the gold, and my God have made known to you, O king, what shall take place in the great hereafter, and this is the dream and the interpretation thereof.

That was a mighty sermon that Daniel preached to Nebuchadnezzar. It ought to have saved him, but it look like it made him worse. The devil got him for that time and he turn right against the Lord God and set at naught his statutes and counted his ways unholy.

You know about that image. It was made of gold, and was threescore cubits high and six cubits wide, and 'twas set up in the plain of Dura, not for from Babylon. You know a cubit is about eighteen inches, and if you multiply that by threescore cubits you get 1080 inches, which mean that the image was ninety foot high and nine feet broad. So you see Nebuchadnezzar got to be a Godmaker, and when he got this great image built he sent out to get all the princes and governors and all the rest of the swell folks to come and bow down and worship that great image that he had set up. Now this was the great folly and shame of the king. By that deed he defied the Lord God and the wrath of the Lord was stirred against him.

And now, my brethren, you remember Daniel told the king that the image that he saw in his dream was himself ruling over all the other kingdoms. He told him also that that stone that was cut out of the mountain and come rolling down the craggy sides and broke in pieces the iron, the brass, and the clay, that that was the kingdom of the Lord Jesus Christ. And he tell him, furthermore that the coming of the stone to be a great mountain means the growth of the kingdom of our Lord till it shall fill this world and shall triumph over all the other kingdoms. Daniel tell the king that his kingdom was going to be taken from him, because he had not feared the God of heaven, and in his folly and crimes he turned away from that God that rules in the heaven and holds the nations of the earth in the palms of his hands. He told him that the kingdom of Satan, that archenemy of God, was going to tumble flat, because that stone cut out of the mountain would roll over Satan's dominions and crush it into flinders.

Glory to God in the highest; that stone cut out of the mountain is a mighty roller. Nothing can stay its terrible progress! They that fight against Jehovah had better look out! That stone is still rolling and the first thing they know it will crush down upon them and they will sink to rise no more. Our God is a consuming fire, and he will overturn and overturn till the foundations of sin is broken up. You just wait a little. The time is fast rolling on. Even now I hear my Savior saying to his Father, "Father, I can stay here no longer; I must get up this morning; I am going out to call my people from the field; they have been abused and laughed at and been made a scoffing long enough for my name's sake. I can stay no longer. My soul cries for my children. Gabriel, get down you trumpet this morning; I want you to do some blowing. Blow gently and easy at first, but let my people hear your golden notes. They will come when I call."

Ah, my brethren, you and I will be there when that trumpet sounds. I don't think I shall be alarmed, because I shall know it is my king marshaling his people home. It won't frighten you, my sisters; it will have the sweetness of Jesus' voice to you; and, oh, how it will ring out that happy morning when our king shall come to gather the ransomed of the Lord to himself. Then you shall have a new and holy body, and with it your glorified spirit shall be united, and on that day we shall go in to see the Father and he shall smile and say: "These is my children; they have washed their robes and made them white in the blood of the Lamb; they have come out of great tribulation and they shall be with me forever and ever." I expect to be there.

"Well, Jasper," you say, "why you expect to be there. How you know?" You read the fourteenth chapter of John, will you? "I go to prepare a place for you," and that word is to rule; and so you will see old John Jasper right there, and King Jesus shall come out to meet us and take us in and show us the mansions that he have prepared for us.

"O Lucifer, how thou have fallen! You proud ones will find then that your days is over, and ye that have despised the children of my God will sink down into hell, just as low as it is possible to get. You needn't tell him that you have preached in his name, and in his name done many wonderful works. You can't fool him! He'll frown down at you and say, "I don't know you, and I don't want to know you, and I don't want to see you. Get out of my sight forever, and go to your place among the lost."

Ah, truly, it is a mighty stone, been rolling all these centuries, rolling today. May it roll through the kingdom of darkness and crush the enemies of God. That stone done got so big that it is higher than heaven, broader than the earth, and deeper than hell itself. But don't be deceived. Don't think that I don't let you off. I got something more for you yet.

You remember Daniel and Shadrach, Meshach, and Abednego. They all stubbornly refused to bow down to Nebuchadnezzar's golden image. They stood straight up. They wouldn't bend a knee nor crook a toe, and them Chaldeans was watching them. That's the way it always is; the devil's folks is always a' watching us and trying to get something on us and to get us into trouble and with too many of us they succeed. They saw that Daniel and his friends would not get down like they done, and up they jumped and away they cut and come to the king.

"Oh, king, live forever," they say. "You know, O king, what you said, that decree that you made, that at the sound of the cornet, the flute, the harp, the sackbut, the psaltery and the dulcimer and all kinds of music, that everybody should fall down and worship the golden image, and that those that does not fall down and worship should be put in the furnace; and now, oh, king, they say that a lot of those men done refuse. They don't regard you. They hate your gods and despise the image that you set up."

[Of] course the old king got mad again and in his fury they brought these three before him. He asked them if what he had heard about them was so, about their not worshiping the golden image. "Maybe you made a mistake," the king say, "but we going to have it over again, and, if when the band strikes up next time you will get down and worship, it'll go easy with you, and if you don't the fires in the furnace will be started quick as lightning and into it every one of you shall go."

These was young men, but, ah, I tell you, they was of the loyal stock. They was just as calm as sunrise in the morning. They said: "Oh, king, we ain't careful to answer about this matter. If you like to cast us into the furnace, our God that we serve is able to get us out. We ain't going to bow, and we never will bow to your God, and you just as well understand."

Right then the men went to heat up the furnace. They was told to heat it up seven times hotter than was the general rule and they had some giants to tie Shadrach, Meshach, and Abednego, and they took the young men away into the furnace. The heat was so terrible that the flames shot out and set fire to the men that had put the Hebrew children in and the poor wretches was burned up, but not a hair of the three young men was singed, and they come out a' smiling and not a blister on them from head to foot. They did not even have any smell of fire about their persons, and they look just like they just come out of dressing rooms.

Nebuchadnezzar was there, and he say: "Look in that furnace there. We didn't put but three persons in there, did we?" And they told him that was so. Then he turn pale and look scared like he going to die and he say: "Look there; I see four men inside and walking through the fire, and the form of the fourth is like the Son of God," and it look like the king got converted that day, for he lift up his voice and shout the praise of the God of Shadrach, Meshach and Abednego.

Ah, great is this story; they that trust in God shall never be put to confusion. The righteous always comes out conquerors and more than conquerors. Kings may hate you, friends despise you, and cowards backbite you, but God is your deliverer.

But I done forget. This old time religion is not good enough for some folks in these last days. Some call this kind of talk foolishness, but if that be true then the Bible, and heaven, and these Christians' hearts, is full of that kind of foolishness. If this be old fogy religion, then I want my church crowded with old fogies.

What did John see over there in Patmos? He say he saw the four-and-twenty elders seated around the throne of God and casting their glittering crowns of gold at the feet of King Jesus, and he say that out of the throne come lightning and thunders and voices and the seven lamps burning before the throne of God. And there before the throne was the sea of glass, and round about the throne was the four living creatures full of eyes before and behind, and they never cease crying: "Holy, Holy, Holy, is the Lord God almighty that died to take away the sins of the world!"

You call that old fogy? Just look away over yonder in the future. Does you see that sea of glass and the saints of God that was all bruised and mangled by the fiery darts of the wicked. I hear them singing! What is their song? Oh, how it rolls! And the chorus is: "Redeemed, redeemed, washed in the blood of the Lamb." Call them old fogies, do you? Well you may, for they is been doing that way from the time that Abel, the first man, a saved soul told the news of salvation to the angels.

"Well, Jasper, have you got any religion to give way?"

"I is free to say that I ain't got as much as I want. For forty-five years I been begging for more, and I ask for more in this trying hour. But, bless God, I is got religion to give away. The Lord have filled my hands with the Gospel, and I stand here to offer free salvation to any that will come. If in this big crowd there is one lost sinner that have not felt the cleansing touch of my Savior's blood, I ask him to come today and he shall never die."

Notes

1. Different documents give different years for his birth.

CHAPTER 21

"THE FRUITS OF FERVOR" (B)

"YOUR DAUGHTERS SHALL PROPHESY"

LUCRETIA MOTT: "LIKENESS TO CHRIST"

*From their beginning, Quakers allowed women to preach equally with men. In the seventeenth century their characteristic message was apocalyptic and sought to draw members of other churches into their fellowship. When they came to be tolerated in the next century, their preaching focused on the inner light and was aimed at keeping their own members faithful to their traditions. In the nineteenth century, slavery and other social issues came to occupy more of their attention. It is little surprise that a prominent minister like Lucretia Mott should also be well known in American history as a social reformer (**see Vol. 1, pp. 562-63**). As the following sermon shows, she also represented a trend within sections of the Society of Friends toward a theological position close to Unitarianism. This sermon is taken from* Lucretia Mott: Her Complete Speeches and Sermons, *vol. 4 of* Studies in Women and Religion, *ed. Dana Greene (Lewiston, N.Y.: Edwin Mellen, 1980). It is preserved in*

Sermons manuscript 6355 in the Friends Historical Library of Swarthmore College. Since Mott followed the Quaker tradition of speaking in meetings for worship only as she felt moved by the Spirit, her sermons owe their preservation to shorthand transcripts. Thus they are among the few Quaker sermons for which there is a full text.

Likeness to Christ

Sermon, Delivered at Cherry Street Meeting

Philadelphia, September 30, 1849

It is time that Christians were judged more by their likeness to Christ than their notions of Christ. Were this sentiment generally admitted we should not see such tenacious adherence to what men deem the opinions and doctrines of Christ while at the same time in everyday practice is exhibited anything but a likeness to Christ. My reflections in this meeting have been upon the origin, parentage, and character of Jesus. I have thought we might profitably dwell upon the facts connected with his life, his precepts, and his practice in his walks among men. Humble as was his birth, obscure as was his parentage, little known as he seemed to be in his neighborhood and country, he has astonished the world and brought a response from all mankind by the purity of his precepts, the excellence of his example. Wherever that inimitable Sermon on the Mount is read, let it be translated into any language and spread before the people, there is an acknowledgement of its truth. When we come to judge the sectarian professors of his name by the true test, how widely do their lives differ from his!

Instead of going about doing good as was his wont, instead of being constantly in the exercise of benevolence and love as was his practice, we find the disposition too generally to measure the Christian by his assent to a creed which had not its sign with him nor indeed in his day. Instead of engaging in the exercise of peace, justice and mercy, how many of the professors are arrayed against him in opposition to those great principles even as were his opposers in his day. Instead of being the bold nonconformist (if I may so speak) that he was, they are adhering to old church usages, and worn-out forms and exhibiting little of a Christlike disposition and character. Instead of uttering the earnest protests against wickedness in high places, against the spirit of proselytism and sectarianism as did the blessed Jesus—the divine, the holy, the born of God, there is the servile accommodation to this sectarian spirit and an observance of those forms even long after there is any claim of virtue in them; a disposition to use language which shall convey belief that in the inmost heart of many they reject.

Is this honest, is this Christlike? Should Jesus again appear and preach as he did round about Judea and Jerusalem and Galilee, these high professors would be among the first to set him at naught, if not to resort to the extremes which were resorted to in his day. There is no danger of this now, however, because the customs of the age will not bear the bigot out in it, but the spirit is manifest, which led martyrs to the stake, Jesus to the cross, Mary Dyer to the gallows. This spirit is now showing itself in casting out the name one of another as evil, in brother delivering up brother unto sectarian death. We say if Jesus should again appear—He is here; he has appeared from generation to generation and his spirit is now as manifest in the humble, the meek, the bold reformers, even among some of obscure parentage.

His spirit is now going up and down among men seeking their good, and endeavoring to promote the benign and holy principles of peace, justice, and love. And blessing to the merciful, to the peace maker, to the pure in heart, and the poor in spirit, to the just, the upright, to those who desire righteousness is earnestly proclaimed, by these messengers of the Highest who are now in our midst. These the preachers of righteousness are no more acknowledged by the same class of people than was the messiah to the Jews. They are the anointed of God, the inspired preachers and writers and believers of the present time. In the pure example which they exhibit to the nations, they are emphatically the beloved sons of God.

It is, my friends, my mission to declare these things among you at the hazard of shocking many prejudices. The testimony of the chosen servants of the Highest in our day is equally divine inspiration with the inspired teaching of those in former times. It is evidence of the superstition of our age, that we can adhere to, yea, that we can bow with profound veneration to the records of an Abraham, the sensualist Solomon, and the war-like David, inspired though they may have been, and I am not disposed to doubt it, more than to the equal inspiration of the writers of the present age.

Why not acknowledge the inspiration of many of the poets of succeeding ages, as well as of Deborah and Miriam in their songs of victory, of Job and David in their beautiful poetry and psalms, or of Isaiah and Jeremiah in their scorching rebukes and mournful lamentations? These are beautifully instructive but ought they to command our veneration more than the divine poetic language of many, very many, since their day, who have uttered truth equally precious?

Truth speaks the same language in every age of the world and is equally valuable to us. Are we so blindly superstitious as to reject the one and adhere to the other? How much does this society lose by this undue veneration to ancient authorities, a want of equal respect to the living inspired testimonies of latter time? Christianity requires that we bring into view the apostles of succeeding generations, that we acknowledge their apostleship and give the right hand of fellowship to those who have been and who are sent forth of God with great truths to declare before the people; and also to practice lives of righteousness, exceeding the righteousness of the scribes and Pharisees, and even of many of the chosen ones of former times.

The people in their childish and dark state, just emerging out of barbarism, were not prepared to exhibit all those great principles in the near approach to fullness, to the perfection that is called for at our hands. There is this continued advance toward perfection from age to age. The records of our predecessors give evidence of such progress. When I quote the language of William Penn, "It is time for Christians to be judged more by their likeness to Christ than their notions of Christ," I offer the sentiment of one who is justly held in great regard if not veneration by this people, and whose writings may be referred to with as much profit as those of the servants of God in former ages; and we may well respect the memory of him and his contemporaries as well as of many not limited to our religious society who have borne testimony to the truth.

It is of importance to us also, to speak of those whom we know, those whose characters we have [fuller] acquaintance with, than we can have with such as lived in past, that we should bring into view the lives of the faithful in our generation.

Jesus bore his testimony—doing always the things which pleased his Father. He lived his meek, his humble and useful life—drawing his disciples around him, and declaring great truths to the people who gathered to hear him.

His apostles and their successors were faithful in their day—going out into the world, and shaking the nations around them. Reformers since their time have done their work in exposing error and wrong, and calling for priests of righteousness in place of vain forms.

The bold utterance of Elias Hicks and his contemporaries aroused the sectarian theological world in our day. Their demand for a higher righteousness was not in vain. Their examples of self-denials and faithfulness to duty should be held up for imitation. We overestimate those who have lived and labored in days long past, while we value not sufficiently the labors of those around us, who may have as high a commission as do their predecessors.

Let us not hesitate to regard the utterance of truth in our age as of equal value with that which is recorded in the scriptures. None can revere more than I do the truths of the Bible. I have read it perhaps as much as any present, and, I trust, with profit. It has at times been more to me than my daily food. When an attempt was made some twenty years ago to engraft some church dogmas upon this society, claiming this book for authority, it led me examine, and compare text with the content. In so doing I became so much interested that I scarcely noted the passage of time. Even to this day, when I open this volume, so familiar is almost every chapter that I can sometimes scarcely lay it aside from the interest I feel in its beautiful pages.

But I should be recreant to principle did I not say the great error in Christendom is in regarding these scriptures taken as a whole as the plenary inspiration of God and their authority as supreme. I consider this as Elias Hicks did one of the greatest drawbacks, one of the greatest barriers to human progress, that there is in the religious world, for while this volume is held as it is, and, by a resort to it, war, and slavery, wine drinking, and other cruel, oppressive and degrading evils are sustained, pleading the example of the ancients as authority, it serves as a check to human progress, as an obstacle in way of these great and glorious reformers that are now in the field.

Well did that servant of God, Elias Hicks, warn the people against an undue veneration of the Bible, or of any human authority, any written record or outward testimony. The tendency of his ministry was to lead the mind to the divine teacher, the sublime ruler, that all would find within themselves [that] which was above men's teaching, human records, or outward authorities. Highly as he valued these ancient testimonies, they were not to take the place of the higher law inwardly revealed, which was and should be, the governing principle of our lives.

One of our early Friends, Richard Davies, attended a meeting of the independents, and heard the preacher express the sentiment that the time would come when Christians would have no more need of the Bible than of any other book. He remarked on this saying of the preacher, "Hast thou not experienced that time already come?" Does not this imply, or may we not infer from this, that our worthy Friend has experienced the time already come; was it a greater heresy than that uttered by the apostle Paul when he declared that those who had known a birth into the gospel had no more need of the law, that they were under a higher dispensation than were they who were bound by their statutes and ceremonies?

Let us also not hesitate to declare it, and to speak the truth plainly as it is in Jesus, that we believe the time is come when this undue adherence to outward authorities, or to any forms of baptism or of communion of church or Sabbath worship, should give place to more practical goodness among men, more love manifested one unto another in our everyday life, doing good and ministering to the wants and interests of our fellow beings the world over.

If we fully believe this, should we be most honest, did we so far seek to please men more than to please God as to fail to utter in our meetings, and whenever we feel called upon to do so in our conversation, in our writings, and to exhibit by example, by a life of non-conformity, in accordance with these views that we have faith and confidence in our convictions? It needs, my friends, in this day that one should go forth saying neither baptism profiteth anything nor non-baptism, but faith which worketh by love, neither the ordinance of the communion table profiteth anything, nor the absence from the same, but faith which worketh by love. These things should never be regarded as the test of the worshiper. Neither your Sabbath observance profiteth any thing, nor the non-observance of the day, but faith which worketh love.

Let all these subjects be held up in their true light. Let them be plainly spoken of—and let our lives be in accordance with our convictions of right, each striving to carry out our principles. Then obscure though we may be, lost sight of almost in the great and pompous religious associations of the day, we yet shall have our influence and it will be felt. Why do we wish it to be felt? Because we believe it is the testimony of truth, and our duty to spread it far and wide. Because the healthful growth of the people requires that they should come away from their vain oblations and settle upon the ground of obedience to the requirings of truth.

I desire to speak so as to be understood and trust there are among you ears blessed that they hear, and that these principles will be received as the gospel of the blessed son of God. Happy shall they be, who by observing these, shall come to be divested of the traditions and superstitions which have been clinging to them, leading them to erect an altar "to the unknown God."

In the place of this shall an altar be raised whereon may be oblations of God's own preparing. Thus may these approach our Father in Heaven and hold communion with him—entering his courts with thanksgiving, and his gates with praise, even though there may be no oral expression.

He may unite in prayer and in praise, which will ascend as sweet incense, and the blessing will come which we can scarcely contain.

JULIA A. J. FOOTE: "LOVE NOT THE WORLD"

*In the early nineteenth century, the African Methodist Episcopal Church produced a number of women exhorters and evangelists with varying degrees of official status who felt called to preach as a result of their experience of sanctification—in the Wesleyan tradition, a second work of grace after conversion. Several of these women wrote autobiographies in which they included samples of their preaching (***see Vol. 1, pp. 564-67***). The following sermon by Julia A. J. Foote may be considered typical. Foote, who was born in Schenectady, New York, in 1823 to parents who had bought their freedom from slavery, was converted when she was fifteen and later had the experience of sanctification. When she began to preach in the early 1840s, she was "read out" of her African Methodist Episcopal congregation, but she was welcomed into the pulpits of many churches of her own and other Methodist denominations. Eventually she became an official missionary of the A.M.E. Zion Church and, before her death, was actually ordained as an elder, the second woman to be so in her church. Her autobiography, from which this sermon is taken, is* A Brand Plucked from the Fire: an Autobiographical Sketch *(Cleveland: printed for the author by W. F. Schneiber, 1879). It is reprinted in* Sisters of the Spirit: Three Black Women's Autobiographies of the Nineteenth Century, *ed. with intro. William L. Andrews (Bloomington: Indiana University Press, 1986). It contains several sermons that show her gifts and the fruits of her study. Her story serves as a heartening reminder of the education, culture, and influence that could be attained by an African American woman who began preaching when many of her people were still in slavery.*

Love Not the World

"If any man love the world, the love of the Father is not in him." 1 John 2:15. The spirit which is in the world is widely different from the Spirit which is of God; yet many vainly imagine they can unite the two. But as we read in Luke 10:26, so it is between the spirit of the world and the Spirit which is of God. There is a great gulf fixed between them—a gulf which cuts off all union and intercourse, and this gulf will eternally prevent the least degree of fellowship in spirit.

If we be of God and have the love of the Father in our hearts, we are not of the world, because whatsoever is of the world is not of God. We must be one or the other. We cannot unite heaven and hell—light and darkness. Worldly honor, worldly pleasure, worldly grandeur, worldly designs, and worldly pursuits are all incompatible with the love of the Father and with that kingdom of righteousness, peace, and joy in the Holy Ghost, which is not of the world but of God. Therefore, God says: "Be not conformed to the world, but be ye transformed by the renewing of your mind, that ye may prove what is that good, and acceptable and perfect will of God" Rom. 12:2.

As we look at the professing Christians of today, the question arises, are they not all conformed to the maxims and fashions of this world, even many of those who profess to have been sanctified? But they say the transforming and renewing here spoken of means, as it says, the mind, not the clothing. But, if the mind be renewed, it must affect the clothing. It is by the Word of God we are to be judged, not by our opinion of the Word; hence, to the law and the testimony. In a like manner the Word also says: "That women adorn themselves in modest apparel, with shamefacedness and sobriety, not with broidered hair, or gold, or pearls, or costly array, but which becometh a woman professing godliness, with good works." 1 Tim. 2:9,10; 1 Pet. 3:3-5. I might quote many passages to the same effect, if I had time or room. Will you not hunt them up, and read carefully and prayerfully for yourselves?

Dear Christians, is not the low state of pure religion among all the churches the result of this worldly-mindedness? There is much outward show; and doth not this outward show portend the sore judgments of God to be executed upon the ministers and members? Mal. 2:7 says: "The priest's lips should keep knowledge," etc. But it is a lamentable fact that too many priests' lips speak vanity. Many profess to teach, but few are able to feed the lambs, while the sheep are dying for lack of nourishment and the true knowledge of salvation.

The priests' office being to stand between God and the people, they ought to know the mind of God toward his people—what the acceptable and perfect will of God is. Under the law, it was required that the priests should be without blemish—having the whole of the inward and outward man as complete, uniform, and consistent as it was possible to be under that dispensation—thereby showing the great purity that is required by God in all those who approach near unto him. "Speak unto Aaron and his sons that they separate themselves" [Lev. 22:2], etc. The Lord here gives a charge to the priests, under a severe penalty, that in all their approaches they shall sanctify themselves. Thus God would teach his ministers and people that he is a holy God, and will be worshiped in the beauty of holiness by all those who come into his presence.

Many may fill his office in the church outwardly, and God may in much mercy draw nigh to the people when devoutly assembled to worship him, but, if the minister has not had previous recourse to the fountain which is opened for sin and uncleanness and felt the sanctifying and renewing influences of the Holy Ghost, he will feel himself shut out from these divine communications. Oh, that God may baptize the ministry and church with the Holy Ghost and with fire.

By the baptism of fire the church must be purged from its dead forms and notions respecting the inbeing of sin in all believers till death. The Master said, "Now ye are clean through the word which I have spoken unto you; abide in me," etc. [Jn. 15:3-4]. Oh blessed union! Christian, God wants to establish your heart unblamable in holiness. 1 Thess. 1:13; 4:7; Heb. 12:14; Rom. 6:19. Will you let him do it, by putting away all filthiness of the flesh as well as of the spirit? "Know ye not that ye are the temple of God?" etc. 1 Cor. 3:16,17; 2 Cor. 6:16,17. Thus we will continue to search and find what the will of God is concerning his children. 1 Thess. 4:3,4. Bless God! We may all have that inward, instantaneous sanctification, whereby the root, the inbeing of sin, is destroyed.

Do not misunderstand me. I am not teaching absolute perfection, for that belongs to God alone. Nor do I mean a state of angelic or Adamic perfection, but Christian perfection—an extinction of every temper contrary to love.

"Now, the God of peace sanctify you wholly—your whole spirit, soul and body." 2 Thess. 5:23.[1] Glory to the blood! "Faithful is he that calleth you, who also will do it." Paul says, "He is able to do exceeding abundantly, above all that we ask or think." Eph. 3:20.

Beloved reader, remember that you cannot commit sin and be a Christian, for "He that committeth sin is of the devil" [1 John 3:8]. If you are regenerated, sin does not reign in your mortal body; but if you are sanctified, sin does not exist in you. The sole ground of our perfect peace from all the carnal mind is by the blood of Jesus, for he is our peace, whom God hath set forth to be a propitiation, through faith in his blood. "By whom also we have access by faith into this grace wherein we stand" [Rom. 5:2]—having entered into the holiest by the blood of Jesus.

Let the blood be the sentinel, keeping the tempter without, that you may have constant peace within; for Satan cannot swim waters. Isa. 30:7.

PHOEBE PALMER: FROM *PROMISE OF THE FATHER* (CHAPTER 4)

The high tide of Holiness influence on mainline American Protestantism is represented in and, in many ways, a result of the ministry of

*Phoebe Palmer (***see Vol. 1, pp. 567-69***). The wife of a Manhattan physician, she was led to seek the experience of sanctification by a sister who had already begun to hold in her home the Tuesday Meeting for the Promotion of Holiness. Palmer quickly became the leader of this group, in which not only women but also men came to gather to testify to or to seek the experience of holiness. Those who came or were influenced by it included many prominent clergy, including bishops and theologians. Its influence spread throughout the country and abroad. At first Palmer's role was simply presiding at the Tuesday testimony meetings, but she came to be invited around as a speaker. By the late 1850s she and her husband began to travel as evangelists in the United States, Canada, and England. The number of those converted by her preaching is reckoned to be twenty-five thousand. She wrote several influential books, including one that was a justification of the preaching of women—although she distinguished what she advocated from "technical preaching." That book, from which the following chapter is taken, is* Promise of the Father, Or, A Neglected Speciality of the Last Days. Addressed to the Clergy and Laity of All Christian Communities *(Boston: Henry V. Degen, 1859).*

Chapter 4

In What Does the Gift of Prophesy Consist?

"The Savior and his apostles bear such ample witness to the worth of woman's services in the true church, it would seem a marvel that men who profess to be Christians should ever have degraded her from the rank of visible helper, which Christ gave her." Mrs. Hale

In what does the gift of prophecy consist? We have remarked that it was not our aim in this volume to set forth the expediency of woman's preaching, technically so called. But the scriptural idea of the terms preach and prophesy stands so inseparably connected as one and the same thing, that we should find it difficult to get aside from the fact that women did preach, or, in other words, prophesy, in the early ages of Christianity, and have continued to do so down to the present time, to just the degree that the spirit of the Christian dispensation has been recognized.

And it is also a significant fact, that to the degree denominations, who have once favored the practice, lose the freshness of their zeal, and as a consequence their primitive simplicity, and, as ancient Israel, yield to a desire to be like surrounding communities, in a corresponding ratio are the labors of females discountenanced. This is a most suggestive consideration, and if anyone reading these pages is disposed to doubt the statement, let him take pains to inquire into the facts in the case. We might specify more than one denomination to which this is particularly applicable.

We do not doubt but spiritual religion is now mainly on the rise in the Church of England. The Church of Rome has made her insidious approaches in the form of Puseyism,[2] and not a few have been deluded by her sophistries, and proportionately as the deceptive principles of this fallen church prevail, will nunneries be multiplied. Yes, nunneries, which, though not confining their sad and worse than useless victims within walls,

"By vows and grates confined,"

will debar them, by church dogmas from yielding to the dictates of the Spirit, and engaging in the holy activities which Scriptural Christianity inculcates. But within the precincts of the Established Church of England, as with many other churches of the present day, as the pure flame of evangelical piety begins to revive, and the corruptions of the Church of Rome are being discountenanced, again we witness the recognition of the spirit of prophecy as poured forth in primitive days on the daughters of the Lord Almighty.

We took up a periodical a short time since, where we were pleased to see recordings by a Churchman in England, who states, as an indication, that the revival flame which had been spreading with such glorious rapidity through America, was now beginning to burst forth in Europe; and among the most prominent of his recordings corroborative of the fact, he mentions the labors of a highly esteemed Christian lady.

The item reads thus:

> A special work of grace has been going forward at Beckenham, in connection with the readings and expositions of scripture, by a lady who has for years emphatically been a female missionary. A Christian friend who was present not long since at one of these readings was intensely interested in what he heard as well as in the crowded attendance of working men and their families. Miss Marsh, the daughter of the venerable Dr. Marsh, one of the oldest teetotalers of Britain, is the lady in question. She is well known as the authoress of the 'Life of Captain Hedley Vicars,' 'English Hearts and Hands,' and a touching narrative just published entitled 'A Light for the Line,' detailing the life and conversion, useful and dying experience of a navvy.

But, in fact, the word *preach*, taken in connection with its attendant paraphernalia, oratorical display, onerous titles, and pulpits of pedestal eminence, means so much more than we infer was signified by the word *preach* when used in connection with the ministrations of Christ and his apostles, that we were disposed to withhold our unreserved assent to women's preaching in the technical sense. But our desire is to stand up fairly with truth on this point, and, fearful that we may be misunderstood, we wish to state unequivocally, that in a scriptural sense we believe all Christ's disciples, whether male or female, should covet to be endued with the gift of prophecy; then will they proclaim, or, in other words, *preach* Christ crucified, as far as in them lies, under all possible circumstances; and it is thus only that the command of the Head of the church can be obeyed, "Preach the gospel to every creature."

Says the learned Dr. Wayland, "I think the generic idea of preaching the gospel in the New Testament is the proclamation to every creature of the love of God to men through Christ Jesus. This is the main idea. To this our Lord adds, according to the other evangelists "teaching them to observe all things whatsoever I have commanded you." A discourse is not preaching because it is delivered by a minister or spoken from the pulpit or appended to a text. Nothing is, I think, properly preaching, except explaining the teachings or enforcing the commands of Christ and his apostles. The command was, Go abroad everywhere; proclaim to every creature the news of redemption; tell them of the love of God in Christ Jesus. All things are now ready; bid them come and welcome to the marriage supper of the Lamb.

"When the Israelites were bitten by the fiery flying serpents and the bite was inevitably fatal, Moses was directed to set up a brazen serpent with the assurance that whosoever that had been bitten looked upon it, should be healed. You can imagine how the first man who felt its saving efficacy flew to communicate the news to his brethren, and urge them to avail themselves of the remedy which had delivered him from death. Every man who was healed became immediately a herald of the glad tidings to others. Every one who was saved became a publisher of the salvation, or, in other words, a preacher until, in a few minutes, the news spread throughout the encampment, and, in this sense, every tribe was evangelized."

Now, imagine a female, with all the sympathies of her loving nature, to have been among these bitten and newly restored ones. Think you that she would have been less tardy than her newly recovered brethren, or less energetic, or less persuasive in her efforts in inducing other wounded ones to look and be healed?

The excellent author from whom we have just quoted again says, "Allow me to illustrate the meaning of the term *preach* as used by our Lord, by an occurrence of which I was an eyewitness. It so chanced that at the close of the last war with Great Britain, I was temporarily a resident of the city of New York. The prospects of the nation were shrouded in gloom. We had been for two or three years at war with the mightiest nation on earth, and, as she had now concluded a peace with the continent of Europe, we were obliged to cope with her single-handed. Our harbors were blockaded. Communication coastwise, between our ports, was cut off. Our ships were rotting in every creek and cove where they could find a place of security. Our immense annual products were molding in our warehouses. The sources of profitable labor were dried up. Our currency was reduced to irredeemable paper. The extreme portions of our country were becoming hostile to each other, and the differences of political opinion were embittering the peace of every household. The credit of the government was exhausted. No one could predict when the contest would terminate or discover the means by which it could much longer be protracted.

"It happened that on Saturday afternoon, in February a ship was discovered in the offing which was supposed to be a cartel, bringing home our Commissioners at Ghent from their unsuccessful mission. The sun had set gloomily before any intelligence from the vessel had reached the city. Expectation became painfully intense, as the hours of darkness drew on. At length a boat reached the wharf, announcing the fact that a treaty of peace had been signed, and was waiting for nothing but the action of our government to become a law. The men on whose ears these words first fell, rushed in breathless haste into the city, to repeat them to their friends, shouting, as they ran through the streets, Peace! Peace! Peace! Every one who heard the sound repeated it. From house to house, from street to street the news spread with electric rapidity. The whole city was in commotion. Men bearing lighted torches were flying to and fro, shouting, like madmen, Peace! Peace! Peace! When the rapture had partially subsided, one idea occupied every mind. But few men slept that night. In groups they were gathered in the streets and by the fireside, beguiling the hours of midnight by reminding each other that the agony of war was over, and that a worn-out and distracted country was about to enter again upon its wonted career of prosperity.

Thus, every one becoming a herald, the news soon reached every man, woman, and child in the city, and, in this sense, the city was evangelized. All this, you see, was reasonable and proper. But when Jehovah has offered to our world a treaty of peace, when men doomed to hell may be raised to seats at the right hand of God, why is not a similar zeal displayed in proclaiming the good news? Why are men perishing all around us, and no one has ever personally offered to them salvation through a crucified Redeemer?"

We have been informed that the ladies were in no wise less earnest in their activities on that memorable night, than their more hardy friends of the other sex in heralding the news of peace.

One of the most eminent Bible expositors who has adorned this or any other age, in his comment on Joel 2:26, says, "'Your sons and daughters shall prophesy—shall preach, exhort, pray, and instruct, so as to benefit the church.' If the reader object to this interpretation, we will present the definition given by the Holy Spirit through the apostle Paul (1 Cor. 14:3): 'He that prophesieth speaketh unto men to edification, exhortation, and comfort.' That prophecy means, in the New Testament, the gift of exhorting, preaching, or expounding the Scriptures, is evident from many places in the Gospels, Acts, and Paul's Epistles."

Rev. J. Benson, the commentator, says, "The gift of prophecy was bestowed upon some women under the Old Testament, as upon Miriam (Exod. 15:20), upon Deborah (Judg. 4:14), and Huldah (2 Kings 22:14)."

But this gift was more frequently conferred on the female sex in the times of the New Testament. Thus we read of the four daughters of Philip the evangelist who prophesied (Acts 21:9). Rev. Dr. A. Clarke says, "If Philip's daughters were prophetesses, why not teachers?" Says Barnes, in his Notes (1 Cor. 11:15), "But every woman that prayeth or prophesieth." In the Old Testament prophetesses are not unfrequently mentioned. So also in the New Testament Anna is mentioned as a prophetess (Lu. 2:36). That there were females in the early Christian church who corresponded to those known among the Jews, in some measure as endowed with the inspiration of the Holy Ghost, cannot be doubted. That they prayed is clear; and that they publicly expounded the will of God is apparent. Also see note on Acts 2:17. It would seem, however, that females shared in the remarkable influences of the Holy Spirit. Philip the evangelist had four daughters which did prophesy (Acts 21). It is probable also that the females of the church of Corinth partook of this gift.

Says the author of a work entitled "Scripture Doctrine," &c. (1 Cor. 11:5), "But every woman that prayeth or prophesieth with her head uncovered," &c. The apostle has joined praying and prophesying together; and as praying in a public assembly—for of such he was treating—is universally allowed to be a part, and, indeed, a very prominent part, of the ministerial office, and women did exercise this part of the ministerial function in being the mouth of the people to God, here we have a presumptive proof that prophesying means preaching, and, we think, a demonstration that the speaking in the church which the apostle reproves in women must be wholly confined to asking questions (whispering or chattering); otherwise it would be a prohibition against their praying as well as preaching.

For, how could women pray in public if it was a shame for them to speak in the church in the sense wherein it is frequently understood? The apostle, when he uses the word "prophecy," precisely fixes its meaning (1 Cor. 14:8-25): "He that prophesieth speaketh unto men to edification, exhortation, and comfort" (ver. 4); "He that prophesieth edifieth the church" (ver. 31); "For ye may all prophesy, one by one, (that is, all who were qualified for and called to the ministry) that all may learn, and all may be comforted." All may learn from those who prophesied; and women did prophesy; therefore women were teachers by whom the church was exhorted, edified, and comforted.

In this common acceptation we frequently find the word prophesy in the Old and New Testament. Thus (Nehemiah 6:7) it is said, "Thou hast appointed prophets to preach." Hence prophets were preachers and to prophesy is to preach. Gen. 20:7, where the Lord saith of Abraham to Abimelech, "He is a prophet, and will pray for you." Here it seems to signify a man well acquainted with the Supreme Being, capable of teaching others in divine things, and especially a man of prayer. Exod. 7:1,2, "Aaron thy brother shall be thy prophet; that is, shall speak unto Pharaoh." Acts 15:32, "Judas and Silas, being prophets, exhorted the brethren with many words." Lu. 2:38, "Anna, the prophetess, coming into the temple, gave thanks unto the Lord, and spake of him [Christ] to all them who looked for redemption in Israel." Lu. 1:67, "Zacharias prophesied, saying, Blessed be the Lord God of Israel, who hath visited and redeemed his people." Our blessed Lord styles John the Baptist a prophet (Lu. 7:26); and Zacharias, the father of John speaking of him by the Spirit of the Lord, calls him a prophet of the highest (Lu. 1:76), that is, a teacher, commissioned by the Lord himself, to instruct the inhabitants of Judea in the things which related to the manifestation of the Messiah and his kingdom (also 1 Cor. 14:25). In most of these places prophesying has no other meaning than preaching; and among the preachers we have a female.

Besides, should it be granted that prophesying means foretelling things to come, an insurmountable difficulty yet remains; for if it was unlawful for women who had that gift to speak in the church, how were they to communicate what was revealed to them? The simple fact seems to be that, though prophesying sometimes means predicting or foretelling future events, it means preaching in the common acceptation of the word; and whenever it is used in the former sense, it includes the publishing these predictions to those concerned. Hence under the law such persons were styled *nabi* (prophets), from *ba,* which signifies to come and to go, because of their coming and going between God and the people. So under the gospel dispensation they are called prophets, from *pro* and *phemi, dico,* I speak or utter forth, because ministers are the Lord's messengers, to publish his word of reconciliation to the people.

But, whatever be the meaning of praying and prophesying as it respects the man, it has precisely the same meaning as it respects the woman. Therefore some women, as well as some men, might speak to others to edification, exhortation, and comfort. This kind of prophesying or teaching was predicted by Joel 2:28 and referred to by Peter, Acts 2:17. Had there not been such gifts bestowed on women, the prophecy could not have been fulfilled. The only difference marked by the apostle was the man had his head uncovered because he was the representative of Christ; the woman had hers covered because she was placed by the order of God in a state of subjection to the man.

It was also customary amongst the Greeks and Romans, but amongst the Jews it was an express law that no woman should be seen abroad without a veil. This was and is a common custom through all the East. A modest woman never appeared in public without a veil. Should she do so, she would dishonor her head, that is, her husband; for all who did not thus recognize the custom of the time were regarded as disposed to be faithless in the marriage covenant.

Says Rev. Joseph Sutcliff, in a letter to Miss Drury, "I am fully persuaded that St. Paul's arguments against the praying and prophesying of women in public are founded on the custom of the Oriental nations not to admit mixed companies of men and women on any occasion excepting only among their own kindred; consequently, so far as European manners deviate from the Oriental, the force of these arguments are inapplicable to us." What would be thought of a Christian minister of the present day who would strenuously enforce as a scriptural requisition that every female member of his charge should adhere to the custom of coming to the house of the Lord veiled or muffled, as enjoined by the apostle Paul, 1 Cor. 11:4-16? Yet there would be far more consistency in enforcing a scrupulous adherence to this custom, which has become obsolete except in Eastern heathen countries, than in enforcing the doctrine that women shall not pray or prophesy in religious assemblies.

"Judge ye yourselves, is it comely that a woman pray unto God uncovered"?—that is, unveiled.

But it seems not to have entered into the apostle's conceptions that the daughters of the Lord would not obey the impellings of their Spirit-baptized souls and pray and speak as the Spirit gave utterance. That they would do so he anticipates as a matter of course, and therefore suggests the manner in which they shall be attired in the performance of the duty.

But why do not ministers of the present day enforce as a scriptural doctrine this ancient practice of covering the head in public assemblies, as now practiced in Eastern heathen countries? Because the dictates of common sense tell them that it was merely an enjoinment of temporary expediency suggested by the then prevailing custom, and can have no bearing on the present day. But, while justly no account whatever is made of the apostle's admonition in regard to the veiling of the head, another subject, standing in vital connection with the spiritual interest of thousands, is overlooked. Overlooked, did we say? Nay, far worse than this: by the identical passages where Paul so evidently infers that Christian women were expected to obey the constrainings of the divinity within them, and pray or prophesy as the Spirit gave utterance—by these same passages those who would restrain the Spirit's utterances justify their resistance.

Hundreds of ministers in the present day are standing in an attitude of open resistance to the use of the gift of prophecy in women. Let a female member of their charge attempt to open her lips in prayer or in speaking of the revelations of infinite grace to her soul, though all the former indices of her Christian life may have been as marked for pious consistency and eminent devotedness as that of the late Mrs. President Edwards, or the most eminent for piety of this or any other age, her character for religious propriety would be sacrificed. She would at once be branded as a fanatic and regarded as a subject of public animadversion and church discipline.

Acts 18:26. "Whom when Aquila and Priscilla had heard (Apollos), they took him unto them and expounded unto him the way of God more perfectly." "This eloquent man, and mighty in the Scriptures, who was a public teacher, was not ashamed to be indebted to the instructions of a Christian woman in matters that not only concerned his own salvation, but also the work of the ministry in which he was engaged." So says Dr. Adam Clarke.

1 Cor. 14:34. "Let your women keep silence" &c. The apostle had been treating of the gift of tongues and of persons prophesying one after another. It is evident in these public assemblies there were people of different nations, as on the day of Pentecost, and that one minister had the

gift of one tongue, and a second of another in the same diversity as they had the other miraculous gifts. That they all had not a universal knowledge of all languages is clear from the apostle Paul's words (1 Cor. 14:18), "I speak with tongues more than ye all." How reasonable it is, then, to conclude that there were a few inquisitive women in the assembly, who, not understanding what was said, but prompted by curiosity, perhaps by a better motive, might ask questions, to the interruption of the speaker and the auditory! Therefore the apostle gives this admonition: "Let your women *[that is, wives]* keep silence, and, if they will learn any thing, let them ask their husbands at home," which clearly shows that the prohibition was not a general one and that it must be confined to asking questions; at least, the silence here enjoined was never intended to prohibit those pious females from instructing and comforting the Corinthian Church to whom he had before given directions respecting their adorning while thus employed; for what has women prophesying to do with asking questions, wanting information, and asking husbands at home? There were at Corinth, it appears, some married women who were frequently asking bold, impertinent questions, occasioning debates, contention, and confusion. Let such women keep silence, and ask their husbands at home; for it is a shame for such women to speak in church.

1 Tim. 2:12. "But I suffer not a woman to teach" &c. Rev. Dr. Taft says, "I think the passage ought to be read thus: 'I suffer not a woman to teach by usurping authority over the man.' Most persons opposed to the praying or prophesying of females understand from this passage that no woman is to teach, and that all teaching by women is usurping authority over the man. But this grants too much inasmuch as it involves the following difficulties: No woman is to keep a school. No woman is to teach her children to sew, or cook, or read, or write, &c. No woman is to write books, for this is one excellent method of teaching. No woman is to pray in public, for praying is one method of conveying instruction upon doctrinal, experimental, and practical religion. No woman is to prophesy, even supposing the term applies only to foretelling future events. While that knowledge lies hid in their own mind, there is no teaching, but if God commands them to prophesy aloud, and they obey him, by this they teach to others that knowledge which before lay hid in their own breasts." If it be objected to this that the teaching here forbidden means only that they are not to teach the science of religion, still all the difficulties remain, except the two first; for the things belonging to religion may be taught by the pen as well as by the mouth, on our knees as well as in any other position.

"But the teaching here forbidden only means face to face,"—but I ask,

Is not this taking too great liberties with the text?—St. Paul does not say that this is the only kind of teaching which he forbids; but supposing it was, then the apostle contradicts himself. That he admits and encourages this kind of teaching is plain from 1 Cor. 11:4; for, in whatever sense we understand prophecy, it must of necessity imply teaching. Again, the sense of the text, as objected, is contradicted in Acts 18:26. Priscilla, a female, expounded the word to Apollos. The doctor says, "I defy any man to split that hair, and prove that expounding is not teaching. But all these difficulties will be removed by understanding the passage thus: 'I suffer not a woman to teach by usurping authority over the man.' And pray, who does? I have not heard of any such usurpation in the church."

What serious errors in faith and practice have resulted from taking isolated passages dissevered from their proper connections to sustain a favorite theory! It is thus that the Universalist would have all men unconditionally saved, inasmuch as the Bible says, "Christ is the Savior of all men," disconnected with the fact that Christ is only the special Savior of them that believe. The Antinomian may gather his faith from the Bible, inasmuch as the Bible says that "men are saved by faith, and not by works." And the evil doer may take the Bible as a plea for his evil doings, inasmuch as it is said in the Bible, "Let us do evil that good may come." And on the same principle has the passage, "Let your women keep silence in the churches," been wrested from its explanatory connections, and made subservient to the egregious and most harmful error of withstanding the utterances of the Holy Spirit from the lips of women, and thereby averting the attention of the Christian world from an endowment of power ordained by God as a speciality of the last days. And permit us here to say that we are constrained to believe that this is one among the more prominent innovations of the "man of sin "—yes, a relic of Popery, which, before the brightness of Christ's appearing, must be openly abrogated.

The scriptural way of arriving at right Bible conclusions is by comparing scripture with scripture. And had this scriptural mode of interpretation been observed in regard to this subject, a distinguishing characteristic of the last days had not been disregarded, and an endowment of power withheld from the church which might have resulted in the salvation of thousands. Yet that serious errors might occur from the misapprehension of the Scriptures, the apostle Peter foresaw, and of this he forewarned the brethren in his General Epistle to the churches. Some had even in that infant state of the church wrested the writings of Paul to the destruction of right principles, and doubtless made his doctrines contradictory, as many have done in regard to the subject before us. It was therefore Peter, in referring to the writings of Paul, said to his brethren, "Even as our beloved brother Paul also, according to the wisdom given to him, hath written unto you, as also in all his Epistles, speaking in them of these things, in which are some things hard to be understood, which they that are unlearned and unstable wrest, as they do the other scriptures, to their own destruction" (see 2 Peter 3:15, 16).

God has, in all ages of the church, called a few of his handmaids to eminent publicity and usefulness and, when the residue of the Spirit is poured out and the millennium glory ushered in, the prophecy of Joel 2:28, 29 being fully accomplished in all its glory, then probably there will be such a sweet blending into one spirit the spirit of faith, of love, and of a sound mind, such a willingness to receive profit by any instrument, such a spirit of humility, in honor preferring one another, that the wonder will then be that the exertions of pious females to bring souls to Christ should ever have been opposed or obstructed. May the Lord hasten the time!

> But what is truth? 'Twas Pilate's question, put
> To Truth itself, that deigned him no reply.
> And wherefore! Will not God impart his light
> To them who ask it? Freely;—'tis his joy,
> His glory, and his nature, to impart.
> But to the proud, uncandid, insincere,
> Or negligent inquirer, not a spark.

AIMEE SEMPLE MCPHERSON: A CHART SERMON

*A remarkable Pentecostal preacher of the first half of the twentieth century, Aimee Semple McPherson settled down from traveling evangelism to build Angelus Temple in Los Angeles and filled its five thousand–plus seats three times every Sunday (***see Vol. 1, pp. 574-78***). She became such a celebrity in the capital of the film industry that her returns from trips were greeted with tickertape parades. She founded a denomination, the International Church of the Foursquare Gospel, and a Bible institute (L.I.F.E.). A pioneer broadcaster, she also started her own radio station. While an itinerant evangelist, she often used a technique that became common, placing the outline of her sermon on an illustrated chart. The following sermon is an example of that type. Later at the*

Angelus Temple, she used more dramatic techniques to emphasize her points. This sermon is taken from Aimee Semple McPherson, This Is That: Personal Experiences, Sermons, and Writings *(Los Angeles: Bridal Call Publishing House, 1923).*

A Certain Man Went Down

Luke 10:30-35

The message which the Lord has laid upon my heart to bring to you, whilst directed to all sinners, is intended more especially for the backslider.

Oh, there are so many backsliders in the world, so many who once walked with the Lord, but have someway or other let go of His hand and have wandered far away. There is not a man or woman on the face of this earth more miserable than a poor backslider, who, once having walked in the presence and joy of the Lord, feasting upon the dainties from His bountiful hand, goes down into sin and seeks to drown the achings of his longing heart in the swirl of this world's gaudy, tinseled pleasure.

It would be impossible for one who had never been a backslider to fully understand or sympathize with the mute agony, shame, and longing in the backslider's heart. I was a poor, discouraged backslider just once since my conversion, and I know the miserable yearning and crying of the heart to be back in the sunlight of his dear smile——the leaking out—the trying to cover up our backslidden condition from those round about us——the plunge into the world to try to stifle and satisfy the restless longing that *nothing but Himself can satisfy.*

How desperately I longed for someone who could enter in and sympathize with and help me, and had there been someone to make a real effort to reach out and help me back to victory and the security of his love, I would have escaped much suffering and buffeting at the hand of the enemy.

And so tonight my whole heart goes out to the backslider, and I long to reach your hand and help you back to Jesus and the city of Jerusalem.

The first step toward getting back to Jesus is made by realizing and frankly admitting that you are a backslider.

We are going to read tonight about a certain man who went down, and I want each of you to watch, as we follow him in his journey, and see whether his case is not very similar in every respect to your own. First of all let us refresh our memory by reading the whole story. It is found in the tenth chapter of Luke, beginning at the thirtieth verse:

> And Jesus said, A certain man went down from Jerusalem to Jericho and fell among thieves, which stripped him of his raiment, and wounded him, and departed, leaving him half dead.
>
> And by chance there came down a certain priest that way; and when he saw him, he passed by on the other side.
>
> And likewise a Levite, when he was at the place, came and looked on him, and passed by on the other side.
>
> But a certain Samaritan, as he journeyed, came where he was; and set him on his own beast, and brought him to an inn, and took care of him.
>
> And on the morrow when he departed, he took out two pence, and gave them to the host, and said unto him, "Take care of him; and whatsoever thou spendest more, when I come again, I will repay thee."

Now as we go through it word by word, and follow the picture on the chart, let every backslider and sinner put themselves in the place of the "certain man" and find their location in this picture. There are many of the certain men—and women—who have been "going down," here in this room tonight, but let each forget the other—forget that there is another "certain man" in the room, and narrow the words down to his own individual case.

A certain man went down

Oh, "certain man" here tonight, you who have been wandering away from God, how easy it is to *go down.* The road to destruction and eternal sorrow of hell is just one long, swift toboggan slide. There is nothing to boast about in being a sinner or a backslider. Anybody could go down, any coward could become a sinner, but it takes the real courage and grace of God, and every spark of manhood and womanhood there is in you to go up the steep incline to heaven. A dead fish can *float down* the stream, but it takes a live one to *swim up* against the current. Any poor, spiritually dead soul can float down to destruction; it does not require any swimming or resistance. Nothing but the divine life and power of the Lord, however, can take him up again.

Went down! Oh, the depths of the precipices and pits of sin that are conveyed by that one word d-o-w-n.

From Jerusalem to Jericho

Let *Jerusalem,* on the chart, stand for all that is holy and pure and Christlike, for all that is embodied in the New Jerusalem that is soon coming down from God out of Heaven, and *Jericho* for all that is sinful and profane and ungodly.

How you, dear certain man, ever came to pass out through the gate of Jerusalem and start on your long downward Journey, I do not know. Perhaps it was lack of prayer—it may have been a failure to read God's Word (you can not dwell in the presence of the Lord without prayer and the Word any more than you could live without breathing. When you pray you are talking to God—when you read the Word He is talking to you)—it may have been that you allowed the cares of this life to press heavily upon you.

With me it was the taking away of the dear one who had led me to Jesus, and upon whose strength I had ever leaned instead of allowing the Lord to teach me to grow in him and be able to stand the storms. When my earthly support was suddenly transplanted to heaven's garden, I was left like an ivy, stripped from the oak to which it had clung. Oh, what a poor little, fallen, tumbled heap I was! But now, bless his dear name, I have learned to cling to and lean upon Jesus—a support that will never die nor leave me alone.

Be the primary cause what it may, the fact remains that the certain man went down from Jerusalem to Jericho—

And Fell

Oh, you cannot walk one single step without Jesus, no matter how strong you are, or how many years you have been a Christian; the moment you let go of His dear hand, that moment you will cease to stand, and you will fall

Among Thieves

It is not long after the backslider has begun his downward journey that he discovers that he, too, has fallen among thieves.

These thieves that we are reading about did two things to the certain man before they left him:

I. They Stripped Him of His Raiment.

II. They Wounded Him and Departed Leaving Him Half Dead.

and that is exactly what the thieves have been doing to you.

Did you ever stop to realize just what constituted the raiment which used to clothe you in Jerusalem (the city of salvation)—this priceless raiment and attire of which the enemy has stripped you?

Let us look at the chart and see what sort of raiment the holy life in Jerusalem stands for, and what you have lost.

Those who walk and live in the presence of the pure and holy Son of God must be attired in the raiment clean and white—which is the righteousness of the saints.

Each individual that goes into the marriage supper of the Lamb must have on the wedding robe Jesus has prepared—worldly garments and the cloak of self-righteousness and immorality will not suffice but will vanish before His gaze.

J stands for JESUS: When we walk with Him, he clothes us with Himself, and the garments of His righteousness (Rev. 3:18).

E stands for ENJOYMENT: His presence is fullness of joy (Ps. 16:11). He has poured the oil of everlasting joy upon the heads of His people (Isa. 37:10).

R stands for REST: In the presence of Him who said, "Come unto Me and I will give you rest" (Matt. 11:28). "The weary find rest for their souls" (Jer. 6:16).

U stands for USEFULNESS:Those who walk with the Savior, who said, "Work while yet 'tis day, for the night cometh when no man can work," will long to be soul-winners and wear the cloak of service.

S stands for SALVATION: Ah, dear backslider, do you not remember how you used to go forth, glad in the beautiful garments of salvation, which had been put upon you by Him who was *"your light and your salvation"?* (Ps. 27:1).

A stands for ADORATION: Where is there a soul that could behold his glorious Redeemer without bowing at His feet in adoration and praise? Did you not feel a great loss when the thieves stripped from you the garments of adoration and worship?

L stands for LOVE: When we dwell with the GOD who IS LOVE (1 Jn. 4:8), and He *"hath set His love upon us"* (Ps. 91:14), we will imbibe and partake of His nature until the first fruit of the Spirit, LOVE (Gal. 5:22), shall spring forth from our lives.

E stands for ENRICHMENT: No mortal tongue can tell the great, inexhaustible store of riches to be found in the Christ who became poor that we by His poverty might be made rich.

M stands for MERCY: The child of God who abides beneath the blood is covered with the MERCY (as a garment) that is "great above the heavens" (Ps. 108:4), and TRUTH (the girdle which fastens the garment about him) of Ps. 85:10, these meeting together to form His raiment.

What a dreadful loss it was when the thieves stripped YOU of YOUR raiment. It was impossible to go without the secure walls of the city of His love and to begin your downward journey toward Jericho without losing those beautiful garments. It was indeed a sad day when you were stripped of your robes of Christlikeness. Gone was your Jesus; gone your Enjoyment, your Rest. Taken away was your Usefulness, your robes of Salvation, your Adoration, Love, Enrichment, and Mercy.

The first stroke of the enemy which left you denuded of such garments was bad enough, but, Oh, the second thing that happened to the "certain man" was far, far more sad, if that were possible, for

T-H-E-Y W-O-U-N-D-E-D HIM, and departed, leaving him half dead.

What wounds the devil and his imps (the thieves who rob you of salvation, rest, and happiness in this world and the world to come) can inflict upon the backslider and the sinner! When the garments which Jesus purchased for him by his blood are taken away there is nothing left to protect the sinner from the blows rained upon him by the enemy.

The backslider, wandering far from God, who has been thus stripped and wounded, is in a critical condition indeed. The wicked old thieves nod and wink to one another as they pick up their booty and DEPART, LEAVING HIM HALF DEAD.

The mile-posts by the way, now point toward JERICHO, and each mile post the certain man reaches on his downward way means just another wound to burn and sear its way into his very soul.

Let us look again at the chart and see what these mileposts that lead to Jericho stand for—

First:

J stands for JOLLIFICATION. "Not a serious wound" you say, "just a little amusement, no serious harm in that, a little gossip, an idle jest, the theatre, novel, or a game of pool." "Young folks must have entertainment," says the enemy. Who hearkens will find that jollification has left a wound and hastened him to the second milepost—

E which stands for EVIL. I have seen the serious wound reflected in the sinner's eyes, in the lines of his face, and have heard the words of profanity rise from his heart—but O, the eyes of God look right down into the depths of that soul, and from Him there is nothing hid.

> **R** stands for RESTLESSNESS. Instead of rest which was once his, when he loved the quiet hour of prayer "alone with God," there is now a driving, irritating restlessness that goads him day and night. Anything to get away from his own thoughts is a welcome diversion.
>
> **I** stands for INDIFFERENCE. The heart that once responded to His every leading and sprang to obey his call is now indifferent to His voice.
>
> **C** stands for CALLOUSNESS. The indifferent heart soon becomes calloused and hard. Once so tender that he melted in contrition before the Lord, he now listens to the tender story of the Crucifixion, the warning thunder of coming wrath unmoved.
>
> **H** stands for HATRED. When the devil has gotten his victim into the place where he hates the Spirit who endeavors to rouse him into sense of his peril, hates good and loves evil (Mic. 3:2), he rubs his evil hands and a smile of demonic joy twists his countenance as the poor, duped soul draws near the city of eternal Woe.
>
> **O** stands for OBSTINACY. When one receives this wound he obstinately refuses to be warned of his danger or flee from the wrath to come. He walks out of the meeting, goes home and to bed, hard, unyielding, obstinate.

What a deceitful old traitor the devil is! He smiles and tricks and fools the soul along while it has life and strength and means, but when it is down and out, helpless, dying, and alone, the devil does not even take the trouble to pretend that he is his friend.

Half dead—thank God he is not altogether dead, for whilst there is life there is hope! Helpless, unable to drag himself one painful step toward the city of salvation, the sin-sick soul is left lying in the road. "*The whole head is sick and the whole heart faint; from the sole of the foot even unto to the head there is no soundness in it, but wounds and bruises and putrefying sores; they have not been closed, neither bound up, neither mollified with ointment.*" Isa. 1:5, 6.

What a picture, not only of the individual, but of the whole human race, that wandered from God.—

There Came Down a Certain Priest That Way

Surely this priest, who typifies the L-A-W, will be able to lift, heal and restore the sin-sick soul. But no, there is nothing to hope for from him, for,

He Passed by on the Other Side

And Paul explains to us that *"The law made nothing perfect"* Heb. 7:19. Moreover the law entered that offenses might abound.

"And likewise a Levite, when he was at the place, came and looked on him." Surely one would be justified in expecting help from the Levite who is filled with his good works and self-righteousness, but no, the Word tells us that all our righteousness is but *"filthy rags"* (Isa. 64:6), and that *"a man is not justified by the works of the law"* (Gal. 2:16). Turning over a new leaf or signing your name to a pledge can never lift you nor heal the wounds of your sinful soul, and thus we read of the Levite: "And he passed by on the other side."

In what a deplorable, perilous condition humanity found itself. Is it any wonder that the helpless soul should cry aloud:

"Oh, wretched man that I am, who shall deliver me from the body of this death?" Rom. 7:24. Is there no arm to save? Is there no eye to pity? Ah, yes, glory to Jesus, there is one who sees and approaches from the distance.

But a Certain Samaritan—

Who could it be but Jesus—this good Samaritan—filled with compassion and tender love for lost, wretched humanity, groveling in the dust of humiliation and despair?

As He Journeyed—

Oh, what a journey Jesus took in order to reach poor, fallen souls who lie bruised and bleeding on the road to destruction. What a journey! All the way from heaven to earth He came; all the way from the manger to the cross He went, and from the tomb to His Father's throne.

"As he journeyed"—no distance was too great to go, no soul too far out of the way for Jesus to reach him with His love and proffered help—

Came Where He Was—

Yes, this good Samaritan who was none other than the King of Glory, never rested, once He had seen the fallen condition of the world, until He had laid aside His crown, divested Himself of his Kingly raiment, taken upon Him the form of man—was not contented even with standing by the sinner's side, but must come where he was, taking his place, and, hanging upon his cross, paying his penalty, and dying his death.

"For what the law could not do, in that it was weak through the flesh,

God, sending His own Son in the likeness of sinful flesh, and for sin, condemned sin in the flesh: that the righteousness of the law might be fulfilled in us, who walk not after the flesh but after the Spirit" Rom. 8:3, 4.

Was ever such love, such mercy as this known in this universe of ours? *"Came where he was."* Why, dear sinner, dear backslider, there is not one of you who has wandered so far away, whose wounds are so obnoxious and horrible but Jesus has come where you are.

Was humanity poor? Jesus became poorer than they all.

Were any despised? He was more despised than they.

Was there any friendless and alone? He prayed on the mountainside, sweat great drops of blood in the garden alone, and groaned upon the tree.

Was any filled with sin and laden with iniquity? He bore their sins and their sickness in His own body on the tree.

Oh, how I love those words, love to repeat them over and over:

"As He journeyed, He came where he was." Why, sinner, look! Can you not see Him just now? He is standing right beside you. If you put out your hand you can touch Him and feel His nearness. *"They should seek the Lord, if haply they might feel after Him, and find Him, though He be not far from every one of us."* Acts 17:27.

Just the faintest little cry for help, uttered or unexpressed, and He will reach down His great arms and place them about you. Praise His name!

"And it shall come to pass, that whosoever shall call on the name of the Lord shall be delivered: for in Mount Zion and in Jerusalem shall be deliverance, as the Lord hath said, and in the remnant whom the Lord shall call." Joel 2:32.

"Call unto me, and I will answer thee, and show thee great and mighty things which thou knowest not." Jer. 33:3.

And When He Saw Him—

What an awful and yet what a wonderful thing it is to know that Jesus sees right down into the depths of the heart, and the intents of the human mind—that nothing is concealed from Him—that everything is laid bare and open in His sight.

Oh, what will this good Samaritan do when He looks down into your heart? Will He shake His head and walk away when you confess your awful sins? Why no, the Word tells us that when He saw him

He Had Compassion on Him—

No matter what your mistakes, your failures; no matter how vile your sins have been; if you will but truly repent and obey the Word of the Lord

He will have compassion upon you. If man were your judge there would be very little to hope for or to expect but punishment, but His heart is filled with compassion. He knows the many times that you have wept upon your pillow; He knows the heartaches and the longing; He remembers the weakness of your frame, and pities you as a Father pitieth His children. It was that great heart full of compassion that caused Him to weep over Jerusalem and cry upon the cross.

"Father, forgive them; they know not what they do."

And Went to Him—

Jesus has come to meet you, not half way, not three-quarters of the way, but all the way. He has come to you just now with pleadings and tender mercy. Just one word and He is right at your side with hope and succor.

And Bound Up His Wounds

Yes, those painful, cankerous wounds are the first thing that demand His attention. All infection must be cut away and sin destroyed. He can bind every heart-bruise so gently, pouring in oil and wine.

"But, oh!" you say, "I don't seem to have the feeling and the tender desire for the Savior which I should have. My heart seems hard, and my conscience dulled." Yes, I know; that is because of those dreadful wounds—indifference, callousness, and obstinacy, but do not let this discourage you from calling upon the Lord, for when He comes He will bring with Him his cruse of oil and will soften every hardened wound, making your heart tender, and flooding your soul with the old-time love.

"Oh, but I do not seem to have any strength. My spiritual energy seems to be so faint and at such a low ebb." Well, praise the Lord! He brings His wine with Him also. He will revive and bring back life and strength by the quickening of his Spirit.

And Set Him on His Own Beast

How many poor, timid souls, halting between two opinions, trembling at the sight of the yawning pit before them, and yet fearful to trust themselves to the Lord's tender hands say:

"Oh, I do so long to be a Christian, but I am afraid I could not hold out. I am afraid I could not hang on to my profession." Why, Hallelujah! I have such good news to tell you. This is a salvation you do not need to hang on to—it will hang on to you. This is a Savior that you do not have to uphold and keep from falling; He will uphold and keep you if you will but put your trust in Him.

"They that trust in the Lord shall be as Mount Zion, which cannot be removed, but abideth forever." Ps. 125:1.

What would you have thought of this good Samaritan had He turned to the wounded man and said:

"Now come, my man; I have bound up your wounds. I have poured in oil and wine. Here beside you stands the little beast (salvation), the sure-footed little animal that can climb the most rugged mountain without slipping or making a misstep. I want you to pick up this beast, put it on your poor, bruised back, walk back all the many weary miles to Jerusalem with this burden upon your shoulders, and mind you do not let it fall."

Was this what He said? NO, Never! He did not ask the man to carry the beast, but He brought the beast to carry the man. Therefore He set him on His own beast—

And Brought Him to an Inn—

The inn is the place of shelter and security where his wounds shall be ministered unto—in other words, the church of God. It was the good Samaritan Himself who brought him to the inn: not by his own struggles and weak efforts, was he carried thither. Put your case in the hands of Jesus and He will bring you forth by His own hand and lead you in a way you know not of. Mountains that seemed impassable in your own strength will be surmounted, and you will be borne upon wings as of an eagle over every difficulty.

And Took Care of Him

Have you ever sang that chorus:

"God will take care of you,
Through all the day, o'er all the way,
He will take care of you.
Be not dismayed, whate'er betide;
God will take care of you;
Within His arms of love abide;
God will take care of you"?

The tender, loving solicitude and care of the good Shepherd over His little lambs—of the good Samaritan over the wounded soul, can never be described. His patience and His love are boundless. He will supply every need of body, soul and spirit.

On the Morrow When He Departed

Yes, there came the day when, after Jesus had journeyed all the way from heaven to earth, and from the manger to the cross; after He had fed the multitudes and healed the sick, and comforted the broken-hearted, and taken the sinner's place, and shed every drop of His blood for the redemption of a lost world, conquered death and the grave, He fulfilled the word which He had spoken to His disciples, saying:

"Ye have heard how I said unto you, I go away and come again unto you. If ye loved me ye would rejoice because I said. I go unto the Father, for my Father is greater than I." Jn. 14:28.

"It is expedient for you that I go away; for if go not away, the Comforter will not come unto you; but if I 'DEPART' I will send Him unto you." John 16:7. And thus it was that on the morrow, *"while they beheld, He was taken up and a cloud received Him out of their sight."* But before He departed the thoughtful Saviour, who was ever providing for our good,

Took Out Two Pence—

(Salvation and the Baptism of the Holy Ghost). Two pence was a day's wages at that time; so He has left enough to supply the need for this entire day. Praise His name.

And Gave Them to the Host:

Has the host of your inn, the preacher of your church, been faithfully spending and preaching these two pence, dispensing all that they provide for your comfort? Many hosts hold back one penny and feel that when they have preached salvation and repentance they have given the man all that he has need of, and is for his good. If this is what your preacher has been doing you should go up to him and ask him what he has done with that other penny, why he is not preaching the baptism of the Holy Ghost according to Acts 2:4.

Peter, who acted as host to the three thousand on the day of Pentecost, dispensed the two pennies freely as he said:

"Repent, and be baptized, every one of you, in the name of Jesus Christ, for the remission of sins"—penny number one;
"And you shall receive the gift of the Holy Ghost"—penny number two. Acts 2:38.

And Said, Take Care of Him

Stewards, hosts, and pastors, you are responsible to God for the way you preach the Word. There is power enough, encouragement and grace enough in the Word of God to take care of and support all them who come beneath your teaching, if you preach the Word in its entirety, and they will but obey.

Whatsoever Thou Spendest More:

These words open to us such a vista of glories, such unlimited acres of promised land, with the fruits of the Spirit, the luscious grapes, and the land that flows with milk and honey, such a boundless and fathomless ocean of blessing, such heights and depths, such lengths and breadths in the great unsearchable love of God, that we cry out—

"The half has never yet been told."

"*Whatsoever thou spendest more*"; why, dear heart, salvation and the baptism of the Holy Spirit are just the beginning—just the first few toddling steps of the new-born child into the realm of the Spirit—just the a, b, c's of the gospel. To live without salvation through the blood of Jesus and the baptism of the Holy Spirit according to Acts 2:4, is to live in an abnormal condition nowhere recorded in the Word of God. Ahead of you are the gifts and the fruits and the graces of the Spirit, and a life that He longs to change from glory into glory until He has brought us unto perfection and can present us to the Father faultless, without spot or wrinkle.

When I Come Again

Why, beloved! He is coming again!! Did not He whose promises are known never to fail say:

"*If I go, I will come again, and receive you unto Myself*"? Jn. 14:3. And when the disciples had watched Him until the clouds had received Him out of their sight, did not the two men who stood beside Him, clothed in white apparel, say:

"*Ye men of Galilee, why stand ye gazing up into heaven? This same Jesus, which is taken up from you into heaven, shall so come in like manner as ye have seen Him go into heaven.*" Acts 1:11.

Did not the apostle Paul declare that

"*The Lord himself shall descend from heaven with a shout, with the voice of the archangel, and with the trump of God: and the dead in Christ shall rise first:*

"*Then we which are alive and remain shall be caught up together with them in the clouds, to meet the Lord in the air: and so shall we ever be with the Lord."* 1 Thess. 4:16,17. Did He not tell us to comfort one another with these words? Did not the Lord, speaking through John on the isle of Patmos, say:

"Surely, I come quickly." And is not the Spirit speaking today throughout the whole world, through yielded vessels:

"Behold, Jesus is coming soon; get ready to meet Him"?

"When I come again"—Oh, what a glorious day that will be when we shall gaze with open face upon the beauty of the good Samaritan, our Redeemer and Savior divine. *"And when I come again—*

I Will Repay Thee:

Why! Just one glimpse of His beautiful face—fairer than the lilies, brighter than the sun—just one smile from His tender eyes—just one "well done," and we would be a million times repaid for any little labor of love that is naught but our reasonable service when all is said and done.

Oh, dear backslider, and Oh, dear sinner, will you not speak the word just now:

"Lord, save me." He is standing right beside you. He will hear the faintest cry; His glorious salvation is ready to carry you to the safe refuge of the inn. He is waiting to care for and watch over you, and at last, when He comes again, to take you to dwell with Him forever.

Come, weary soul, by sin oppressed,
There's mercy with the Lord;
And He will surely give you rest,
By trusting in His Word.

Only trust him; only trust Him;
Only trust Him now.
He will save you; He will save you:
He will save you now.

A SERMON BY A UNITARIAN WOMAN MINISTER IN IOWA AT THE TURN OF THE CENTURY

While the majority of early women preachers were from newly founded evangelistic bodies, there was an outstanding group of Unitarian women ministers that began in Iowa in the late nineteenth century and exercised influence on the denomination until their retirement **(see Vol. 1, pp. 580-84)**. *While male resistance at the denominational headquarters prevented there being a second generation, the first generation was as impressive as it was impermanent. The sermon below is by Eleanor Gordon, one of the two founders of the group. It is an early example of a sermon form that was to become popular, the use of a current work of fiction to raise the issue the preacher wished to consider. This sermon is taken from the issue of an Iowa Unitarian periodical* Old and New *for February 14, 1906.*[3]

THE HOUSE OF MIRTH

A Sermon with Mrs. Wharton's Last Book as a Text

Eleanor Gordon, Des Moines, Iowa

I take this last book of Mrs. Wharton's for my text this morning, but if I chose to condense its many pages into one text from the Bible, I would have no difficulty in finding a suitable one.

I might take the words of the prophet Hosea: "They that sow the wind shall reap the whirlwind."

Or, the conclusion of the pessimistic author of Ecclesiastes would be fitting: "Vanity of vanities, saith the preacher, all is vanity."

But perhaps most fitting would be the words from the hand-writing on the wall: "God hath numbered thy kingdom and brought it to an end. Thou are [*sic*] weighed in the balance and found wanting."

An artist, whether he uses pen, brush, or chisel must decide whether he portrays human life as he sees it, or as it ought to be. Mrs. Wharton belongs clearly to the first class mentioned, and if Tolstoy's definition be a true one—that an artist is one who can make others see what he sees—she is an artist of high rank.

We are reminded as we consider this definition that there are many ways of seeing, that what we see depends upon what we are, upon the mind back of the seeing eye. George Eliot, no less than Mrs. Wharton, pictured men and women as she saw them, but hers was the sympathetic vision and hence finer and more nearly true.

The story is most difficult to tell in a few words, for its value depends on a subtle analysis of motive and it is almost impossible to portray this except as we watch the men and women in the drama, and follow word by word the author as with pitiless accuracy she lays bare their secrets, their plots and counter-plots.

It is a picture of society where the one essential is money and the frankly expressed rule is that if a man has not money he must marry a woman who has; if a woman has not money, she must marry a man who has.

There are two exceptions. A lawyer, Lawrence Seldon, is in this set, but not of it. He has certain fastidious tastes and honorable instincts that lead him to loathe the vulgar revels of feasting, gambling, and drinking he sees all about him. But he utters no word of criticism. He looks on with a feeling, half cynical, half amused. We cannot but believe that to a certain extent he represents Mrs. Wharton's feelings toward these people.

The other exception is a cousin of his, a Gertrude Farish, a woman interested in philanthropy. She is simple hearted, pure minded, but she fails utterly to appreciate or understand what she sees and hears.

Mrs. Wharton is probably true to life when she introduces into the story "such a negative," flavorless philanthropist as Gertrude Farish. A woman who really did represent the modern settlement worker would not have been tolerated in "The House of Mirth," but it is not fair to modern philanthropy. There is no plot in the story. The interest centers around the character of Lily Bart. She is a woman of twenty-nine, beautiful in face, with a charm of manner and voice that makes her a person of importance, although she is without fortune, and it is understood that she is in the market waiting for the highest bidder.

But for some reason when this applicant appears, Miss Bart manages to escape. At the last moment, something within, a motive she seems not to understand herself, keeps her from making the sacrifice.

She is too good to do the wrong thing but she is not strong enough to cut loose from the whole wretched business and start out to earn her own living. Her danger lay, as she herself admitted, in her own incurable dread of discomfort and poverty. She is vain, foolish in many ways, but she has a sense of honor which keeps her from being ignoble.

A woman who has called her friend, to save her own reputation, makes false statements in regard to Miss Bart's conduct. As a consequence her aunt is alienated and practically disinherits her.

And so the one who has been the petted darling of society finds herself an outcast. She has in her possession letters which would ruin her false friend if their contents were known. She knows if she should threaten to make known these letters her enemy would take means to restore her to favor. Again and again she decides to do it, for she does not dare to face the future alone. But when the test moment comes she cannot do the unworthy deed. Worn with worry and unusual work she is troubled with sleepless nights. She resorts to chloral as a remedy and one night takes an overdose and for her the struggle of life is ended.

Does anyone here this morning say: "What a strange subject for a sermon? No one here belongs to the fast set. We believe in the sacredness of love and marriage. Why should we be called upon to listen to a discussion of such disagreeable themes?"

If it were possible to draw a hard and fast line between the good and bad, the pure and the impure, the selfish and the generous, the earnest and the flippant, the high-minded and the low-minded, it were indeed foolish to bring to you this morning the message of this book. But if some supernaturally endowed messenger could come from heaven this morning and draw a line that would separate the good from the bad, the worthy from the unworthy, this line would not pass between any two of us. It would divide each and every one into two parts and some of us might be surprised to find the proportion of our real selves on the wrong side. It is for this reason that I find in the "House of Mirth" a lesson to everyone. If we are to learn from this book, we must find the cause for the weakness and wickedness it portrays. We must go back to the roots of the matter and find if we can what makes possible a Lily Bart, a Gus Trenor, a Bertha Dorset.

To do this we must try to discover their theory of life.

The reading of a half dozen pages reveals this to be love of luxury, avoidance of work of any kind, a desire for a constant intoxication of pleasure of the material and sensuous kind. In a word the end and aim of life for them is pleasure in the most material sense of the word. The pleasures they crave are the finest clothes, the richest food, the most expensive wine and tobacco. When life has but one aim and that is pleasure, simple pleasures soon pall upon the taste and all sorts of excitement must be added to save the hours from growing dull. The weekend functions are simply gambling parties, "for cards without betting would be too stupid to think of," says a favorite hostess. Before we condemn this too strongly let us ask ourselves if we do not make the same plea for certain forms of objectionable athletics when we say that the boys will not go to school if they cannot have the stimulus of football, and other rough games.

The most revolting part of this book are [*sic*] the women in it. A pretense of business gives even to the worst men a suggestion of dignity, but the women have the vices of the men plus the financial dependence. If any father, mother, or friend of girls can read of Lily Bart's attempt to earn an honest living and of her failure because she had never been trained to work, and not resolve that all girls in their care shall be educated to think work the greatest blessing of life, and trained to do a work that the world needs to have done, they must read with little appreciation. If anyone who believes that women should not be educated to be self-dependent financially reads this book then let him not throw stones at Bertha Dorset, Judy Trenor, or Lily Bart, for they are the logical result of such teaching.

When a woman says to me: "I do not have to earn my living," I want to ask her from whom came the release of obligation? If she should say, from my father, mother, or some far away ancestor, I would answer, no one, no matter how much he may care for you, can pay your debt to the world. You are nourished, clothed, and warmed, by the bounty of God. You cannot escape the debt unless you are willing to be a shirk. If you do not need to earn dollars and cents to pay for food and lodging, there is other work to do by means of which you may pay your way.

There are the ignorant to be taught, the helpless and old to be waited upon, those who have failed in the battle of life to be comforted. Children need your wise guidance. Freedom from financial worry only increases your obligation to be useful. If at night we cannot say we have tried to give value received for the good we have had through the day, we are parasites and deserve the fate of parasites.

We are shocked at the display of selfishness in the story, and yet in the homes of average means, are the children being taught today that life should mean service? Are the children being taught that that a life lived for self is a life lived in vain? The saddest sentence in the book is the one where Lily Bart acknowledges to herself that she dare not face the future alone because of her dread of poverty and discomfort. Are the children nurtured in an atmosphere that will give them the moral stamina that will lead them to rejoice in doing the hard if it be the right thing? Let us be honest with ourselves and answer these questions before we censure the men and women introduced to us by Mrs. Wharton.

Does someone object, and say, "It is not possible that the licentiousness and flagrant violation of the moral law, pictured in this book, can be caused by such small defects as love of luxury and a desire to take things easy." I reply, it is the easiest thing in the world for just this thing to happen. Easy, for all human living goes back to human motive. What is it we want? Ease, pleasure, the good things of life? These can be had only by paying a great deal of money for them. It is not an easy thing to earn, honestly, a great deal of money—but the good time I must have, therefore I must have the money, honestly, if I can get it—but I must have it.

When we have gone this far in the pathetic story the rest is not difficult to read. But is it not true that the one really essential thing in this world is personal honor? Books, music, a refined home, travel, may bring their influence of joy and beauty if they come in the line of honor, truth, and loyalty, otherwise each and every one can be dispensed with, not grudgingly, but bravely—joyfully.

This book is but a new wording of the question asked so long ago by Jesus: "What shall it profit a man if he gain the whole world and lose his own soul?"

Notes

1. Actually Ephesians 3:20-21.

2. The Oxford movement, Tractarian movement, or Catholic Revival in the Church of England, called Puseyism after Edward Bouverie Pusey, who, along with John Keble and John Henry Newman, founded the Movement. See below, pp. 476-85.

3. I am grateful to Cynthia Grant Tucker, author of *Prophetic Sisterhood: Liberal Women Ministers of the Frontier, 1880–1930* (Boston: Beacon, 1990), for a copy of this sermon.

CHAPTER 22

THE PREACHING OF ROMANTICISM IN BRITAIN

JOHN HENRY NEWMAN: A SERMON TO OXFORD UNDERGRADUATES

Few preachers have ever paid as close attention as John Henry Newman to the different needs and capacities of different congregations (**see Vol. 1, pp. 601-8**). *In his Roman Catholic days, he preached one way to the working-class congregation at the Birmingham Oratory and another way to fellow priests. While still an Anglican at Oxford and vicar of St. Mary's, the University Church, he demonstrated his amazing capacity for constructive theology in formal University Sermons, on the one hand, while speaking very directly to the needs of the late-adolescent males who made up the student congregation at St. Mary's week after week, on the other. So popular were these sermons that heads of colleges who feared his influence on their charges changed the time for Sunday dinner to make it coincide with Evensong at the University Church. Newman was later to diagnose a congregation of undergraduates as "an assemblage of the young, the inexperienced, the lay and the secular," which meant that no Christian doctrine was too basic or simple. Beyond* *that, however, in his time, the university congregation would consist of "men, not women; of the young rather than the old; and of persons either highly educated or under education." In preaching to them, in the words of a Scottish visitor, "he laid his finger—how gently, yet how powerfully!—on some inner place in the hearer's heart, and told him things about himself he had never known till then." The following sermon, taken from his* Parochial and Plain Sermons, *new ed. (London: Rivingtons, 1875), 1:41-56, shows the way he went about that.*

Sermon 4: Secret Faults

> "Who can understand his errors? Cleanse thou me from secret faults."
> Ps. 19:12

Strange as it may seem, multitudes called Christians go through life with no effort to obtain a correct knowledge of themselves. They are contented with general and vague impressions concerning their real state; and, if they have more than this, it is merely such accidental information about themselves as the events of life force upon them. But exact systematic knowledge they have none, and do not aim at it.

When I say this is *strange,* I do not mean to imply that to know ourselves is *easy;* it is very difficult to know ourselves even in part, and so far ignorance of ourselves is not a strange thing. But its strangeness consists in this, viz., that men should profess to receive and act upon the great Christian doctrines, while they are thus ignorant of themselves, considering that self-knowledge is a necessary condition for understanding them. Thus it is not too much to say that all those who neglect the duty of habitual self-examination are using words without meaning. The doctrines of the *forgiveness* of sins, and of a *new birth* from sin, cannot be understood without some right knowledge of the *nature* of sin, that is, of our own heart. We may, indeed, assent to a form of words which declares those doctrines; but if such a mere assent, however sincere, is the same as a real *holding of* them, and belief in them, then it is equally possible to believe in a proposition the terms of which belong to some foreign language, which is obviously absurd. Yet nothing is more common than for men to think that because they are familiar with words, they understand the ideas they stand for. Educated persons despise this fault in illiterate men who use hard words as if they comprehended them. Yet they themselves, as well as others, fall into the same error in a more subtle form, when they think they understand terms used in morals and religion, because such are common words, and have been used by them all their lives.

Now (I repeat) unless we have some just idea of our hearts and of sin, we can have no right idea of a Moral Governor, a Savior or a Sanctifier, that is, in professing to believe in them, we shall be using words without attaching distinct meaning to them. Thus self-knowledge is at the root of all real religious knowledge; and it is in vain,—worse than vain,—it is a deceit and a mischief, to think to understand the Christian doctrines as a matter of course, merely by being taught by books, or by attending sermons, or by any outward means, however excellent, taken by themselves. For it is in proportion as we search our hearts and understand our own nature, that we understand what is meant by an Infinite Governor and Judge; in proportion as we comprehend the nature of disobedience and our actual sinfulness, that we feel what is the blessing of the removal of sin, redemption, pardon, sanctification, which otherwise are mere words. God speaks to us primarily in our hearts. Self-knowledge is the key to the precepts and doctrines of scripture. The very utmost any outward notices of religion can do, is to startle us and make us turn inward and search our hearts; and then, when we have experienced what it is to read ourselves, we shall profit by the doctrines of the Church and the Bible.

Of course self-knowledge admits of degrees. No one perhaps, is *entirely* ignorant of himself; and even the most advanced Christian knows himself only "in part." However, most men are contented with a slight acquaintance with their hearts, and therefore a superficial faith. This is the point which it is my purpose to insist upon. Men are satisfied to have numberless secret faults. They do not think about them, either as sins or as obstacles to strength of faith, and live on as if they had nothing to learn.

Now let us consider attentively the strong presumption that exists, that we all have serious secret faults; a fact which, I believe, all are ready to confess in general terms, though few like calmly and practically to dwell upon it; as I now wish to do.

1. Now the most ready method of convincing ourselves of the existence in us of faults unknown to ourselves, is to consider how plainly we see the secret faults of others. At first sight there is of course no reason for supposing that we differ materially from those around us; and if we see sins in them which *they* do not see, it is a presumption that they have their own discoveries about ourselves, which it would surprise us to hear. For instance: How apt is an angry man to fancy that he has the

command of himself! The very charge of being angry, if brought against him, will anger him more; and, in the height of his discomposure, he will profess himself able to reason and judge with clearness and impartiality.

Now, it may be his turn another day, for what we know, to witness the same failing in us; or, if we are not naturally inclined to violent passion, still at least we may be subject to other sins, equally unknown to ourselves, and equally known to him as his anger was to us. For example: There are persons who act mainly from self-interest at times when they conceive they are doing generous or virtuous actions; they give freely, or put themselves to trouble, and are praised by the world, and by themselves, as if acting on high principle; whereas close observers can detect desire of gain, love of applause, shame, or the mere satisfaction of being busy and active, as the principal cause of their good deeds. This may be our condition as well as that of others; or, if it be not, still a parallel infirmity, the bondage of some other sin or sins, which others see, and we do not.

But, say there is no human being sees sin in us, of which we are not aware ourselves (though this is a bold supposition to make), yet why should man's accidental knowledge of us limit the extent of our imperfections? Should all the world speak well of us, and good men hail us as brothers, after all there is a Judge who trieth the hearts and the reins. He knows our real state; have we earnestly besought him to teach us the knowledge of our own hearts? If we have not, that very omission is a presumption against us. Though our praise were throughout the Church, we may be sure He sees sins without number in us, sins deep and heinous, of which we have no idea. If man sees so much evil in human nature, what must God see? "If our heart condemn us, God is greater than our heart, and knoweth all things." Not *acts* alone of sin does He set down against us daily, of which we know nothing, but the thoughts of the heart too. The stirrings of pride, vanity, covetousness, impurity, discontent, resentment, these succeed each other through the day in momentary emotions, and are known to Him. We know them not; but how much does it concern us to know them!

2. This consideration is suggested by the first view of the subject. Now reflect upon the *actual disclosures* of our hidden weakness, which accidents occasion. Peter followed Christ boldly, and suspected not his own heart, till it betrayed him in the hour of temptation, and led him to deny his Lord. David lived years of happy obedience while he was in private life. What calm, clear-sighted faith is manifested in his answer to Saul about Goliath: "The Lord that delivered me out of the paw of the lion,

and out of the paw of the bear, he will deliver me out of the hand of this Philistine" (1 Sam. 17:37). Nay, not only in retired life, in severe trial, under ill usage from Saul, he continued faithful to his God; years and years did he go on, fortifying his heart, and learning the fear of the Lord; yet power and wealth weakened his faith, and for a season overcame him. There was a time when a prophet could retort upon him, "Thou art the man" (2 Sam. 12:7) whom thou condemnest. He had kept his principles in words, but lost them in his heart. Hezekiah is another instance of a religious man bearing *trouble* well, but for a season falling back under the temptation of prosperity; and that, after extraordinary mercies had been vouchsafed to him (2 Kings 20:12-19). And if these things be so in the case of the favored saints of God, what (may we suppose) is our own real spiritual state in his sight? It is a serious thought. The warning to be deduced from it is this: Never to think we have a due knowledge of ourselves till we have been exposed to various kinds of temptations, and tried on every side. Integrity on one side of our character is no voucher for integrity on another. We cannot tell how we should act if brought under temptations different from those which we have hitherto experienced. This thought should keep us humble. We are sinners, but we do not know how great. He alone knows who died for our sins.

3. Thus much we cannot but allow; that we do not know ourselves in those respects in which we have not been tried. But farther than this: What if we do not know ourselves even where we *have* been tried, and found faithful? It is a remarkable circumstance which has been often observed, that if we look to some of the most eminent saints of scripture, we shall find their recorded errors to have occurred in those parts of their duty in which each had had most trial, and generally showed obedience most perfect. *Faithful* Abraham through want of faith denied his wife. Moses, the *meekest* of men, was excluded from the land of promise for a passionate word. The *wisdom* of Solomon was seduced to bow down to idols. Barnabas again, the *son of consolation,* had a sharp contention with St. Paul. If then men, who knew themselves better than we doubtless know ourselves, had so much of hidden infirmity about them, even in those parts of their character which were most free from blame, what are we to think of ourselves? And if our very virtues be so defiled with imperfection, what must be the unknown multiplied circumstances of evil which aggravate the guilt of our sins? This is a third presumption against us.

4. Think of this too. No one begins to examine himself, and to pray to know himself (with David in the text), but he finds within him an

abundance of faults which before were either entirely or almost entirely unknown to him. That this is so, we learn from the written lives of good men, and our own experience of others. And hence it is that the best men are ever the most humble; for, having a higher standard of excellence in their minds than others have, and knowing themselves better, they see somewhat of the breadth and depth of their own sinful nature, and are shocked and frightened at themselves. The generality of men cannot understand this; and if at times the habitual self-condemnation of religious men breaks out into words, they think it arises from affectation, or from a strange distempered state of mind, or from accidental melancholy and disquiet. Whereas the confession of a good man against himself, is really a witness against all thoughtless persons who hear it, and a call on them to examine their own hearts. Doubtless the more we examine ourselves, the more imperfect and ignorant we shall find ourselves to be.

5. But let a man persevere in prayer and watchfulness to the day of his death, yet he will never get to the bottom of his heart. Though he know more and more of himself as he becomes more conscientious and earnest, still the full manifestation of the secrets there lodged, is reserved for another world. And at the last day who can tell the affright and horror of a man who lived to himself on earth, indulging his own evil will, following his own chance notions of truth and falsehood, shunning the cross and the reproach of Christ, when his eyes are at length opened before the throne of God, and all his innumerable sins, his habitual neglect of God, his abuse of his talents, his misapplication and waste of time, and the original unexplored sinfulness of his nature, are brought clearly and fully to his view?

Nay, even to the true servants of Christ, the prospect is awful. "The righteous," we are told, "will scarcely be saved" (1 Pet. 4:18). Then will the good man undergo the full sight of his sins, which on earth he was laboring to obtain, and partly succeeded in obtaining, though life was not long enough to learn and subdue them all. Doubtless we must all endure that fierce and terrifying vision of our real selves, that last fiery trial of the soul (1 Cor. 3:13) before its acceptance, a spiritual agony and second death to all who are not then supported by the strength of him who died to bring them safe through it, and in whom on earth they have believed.

My brethren, I appeal to your reason whether these presumptions are not in their substance fair and just. And if so, next I appeal to your consciences, whether they are *new* to you; for if you have not even thought about your real state, nor even know how little you know of yourselves, how can you in good earnest be purifying yourselves for the next world, or be walking in the narrow way?

And yet how many are the chances that a number of those who now hear me have no sufficient knowledge of themselves, or sense of their ignorance, and are in peril of their souls! Christ's ministers cannot tell who are, and who are not, the true elect: but when the difficulties in the way of knowing yourselves aright are considered, it becomes a most serious and immediate question for each of you to entertain, whether or not he is living a life of self-deceit, and thinking far more comfortably of his spiritual state than he has any right to do. For call to mind the impediments that are in the way of your knowing yourselves, or feeling your ignorance, and then judge.

1. First of all, self-knowledge does not come as a matter of course; it implies an effort and a work. As well may we suppose that the knowledge of the languages comes by nature, as that acquaintance with our own heart is natural. Now the very effort of steadily reflecting is itself painful to many men; not to speak of the difficulty of reflecting correctly. To ask ourselves *why* we do this or that, to take account of the principles which govern us, and see whether we act for conscience' sake or from some lower inducement, is painful. We are busy in the world, and what leisure time we have we readily devote to a less severe and wearisome employment.

2. And then comes in our self-love. We *hope* the best; this saves us the trouble of examining. Self-love answers for our safety. We think it sufficient caution to allow for certain possible unknown faults at the utmost, and to take them *into* the reckoning when we balance our account with our conscience: whereas, if the truth were known to us, we should find we had nothing but debts, and those greater than we can conceive, and ever increasing.

3. And this favorable judgment of ourselves will especially prevail, if we have the misfortune to have uninterrupted health and high spirits, and domestic comfort. Health of body and mind is a great blessing, if we can bear it; but unless chastened by watchings and fastings (2 Cor. 11:27), it will commonly seduce a man into the notion that he is much better than he really is. Resistance to our acting rightly, whether it proceed from within or without, tries our principle; but when things go smoothly, and we have but to wish, and we can perform, we cannot tell how far we do or do not act from a sense of duty. When a man's spirits are high, he is pleased with every thing; and with himself especially. He

can act with vigor and promptness, and he mistakes this mere constitutional energy for strength of faith. He is cheerful and contented; and he mistakes this for Christian peace. And, if happy in his family, he mistakes mere natural affection for Christian benevolence, and the confirmed temper of Christian love. In short, he is in a dream, from which nothing could have saved him except deep humility, and nothing will ordinarily rescue him except sharp affliction.

Other accidental circumstances are frequently causes of a similar self-deceit. While we remain in retirement from the world, we do not know ourselves; or after any great mercy or trial, which has affected us much, and given a temporary strong impulse to our obedience; or when we are in keen pursuit of some good object, which excites the mind, and for a time deadens it to temptation. Under such circumstances we are ready to think far too well of ourselves. The world is away; or, at least, we are insensible to its seductions; and we mistake our merely temporary tranquillity, or our over-wrought fervor of mind, on the one hand for Christian peace, on the other for Christian zeal.

4. Next we must consider the force of habit. Conscience at first warns us against sin; but if we disregard it, it soon ceases to upbraid us; and thus sins, once known, in time become secret sins. It seems then (and it is a startling reflection), that the more guilty we are, the less we know it; for the oftener we sin, the less we are distressed at it. I think many of us may, on reflection, recollect instances, in our experience of ourselves, of our gradually forgetting things to be wrong which once shocked us. Such is the force of habit. By it (for instance) men contrive to allow themselves in various kinds of dishonesty. They bring themselves to affirm what is untrue, or what they are not sure is true, in the course of business. They overreach and cheat; and still more are they likely to fall into low and selfish ways without their observing it, and all the while to continue careful in their attendance on the Christian Ordinances, and bear about them a form of religion.

Or, again, they will live in self-indulgent habits; eat and drink more than is right; display a needless pomp and splendor in their domestic arrangements, without any misgiving; much less do they think of simplicity of manners and abstinence as Christian duties. Now we cannot suppose they *always* thought their present mode of living to be justifiable, for *others* are still struck with its impropriety; and what others now feel, doubtless they once felt themselves. But such is the force of habit. So again, to take as a third instance, the duty of stated private prayer; at first it is omitted with compunction, but soon with indifference. But it is not the less a sin because we do not feel it to be such. Habit has made it a secret sin.

5. To the force of habit must be added that of custom. Every age has its own wrong ways; and these have such influence, that even good men, from living in the world, are unconsciously misled by them. At time a fierce persecuting hatred of those who erred in Christian doctrine has prevailed; at another, an odious over-estimation of wealth and means of wealth; at another an irreligious veneration of the mere intellectual powers; at another, a laxity of morals; at another, disregard of forms and discipline of the Church. The most religious men, unless they are especially watchful, will feel the sway of the fashion of their age; suffer from it, as Lot in wicked Sodom, though unconsciously. Yet ignorance of the mischief does not change the nature of their sin; sin it still is, only custom makes it *secret* sin.

6. Now what is our chief guide amid the evil and seducing customs of the world? Obviously, the Bible. "The world passeth away, but word of the Lord endureth forever" (Isa. 40:8; 1 Pet. 1:24, 25; 1 Jn. 2:17). How much extended, then, and strengthened, necessarily must be this secret dominion of sin over us, when we consider how little we read Scripture! Our conscience gets corrupted. True, but the words of truth though effaced from our minds, remain in scripture, bright in their eternal youth and purity. Yet, we do not study scripture to stir up and refresh our minds. Ask yourselves, my brethren, what do you know of the Bible? Is there any one part of it you have read carefully, and as a whole? One of the gospels, for instance? Do you know very much more of your Savior's works and words than you have heard read in church? Have you compared his precepts, or St. Paul's, or any other apostle's, with your own daily conduct, and prayed and endeavored to act upon them? If you have, so far is well; go on to do so. If you have not, it is plain you do not possess, for you have not sought to possess, an adequate notion of that perfect Christian character which it is your duty to aim at, nor an adequate notion of your actual sinful state; you are in the number of those who "come not to the light, lest their deeds should be reproved."

These remarks may serve to impress upon us the difficulty of knowing ourselves aright, and the consequent danger to which we are exposed, of speaking peace to our souls, when there is no peace.

Many things are against us; this is plain. Yet is not our future prize worth a struggle? Is it not worth present discomfort and pain to accomplish an escape from the fire that never shall be quenched? Can we endure the thought of going down to the grave with a load of sins on our head unknown and unrepented of? Can we content ourselves with such an unreal faith in Christ, as in no sufficient measure includes self-abasement, or thankfulness, or the desire or effort to be holy? For how can we feel our need of his help, or our dependence on him, or our debt to him, or the nature of his gift to us, unless we know ourselves? How can we in any sense be said to have that "mind of Christ," to which the apostle exhorts us, if we cannot follow him to the height above, or the depth beneath; if we do not in some measure discern the cause and meaning of his sorrows, but regard the world, and man, and the system of providence, in a light different from that which his words and acts supply?

If you receive revealed truth merely through the eyes and ears, believe words, not things; you deceive yourselves. You may conceive yourselves sound in faith, but you know nothing in any true way. Obedience to God's commandments, which implies knowledge of sin and of holiness, and the desire and endeavor to please him, this is the only practical interpreter of scripture doctrine. Without self-knowledge you have no root in yourselves personally; you may endure for a time, but under affliction or persecution your faith will not last. This is why many in this age (and in every age) become infidels, heretics, schismatics, disloyal despisers of the Church. They cast off the form of truth, because it never has been to them more than a form. They endure not, because they never have tasted that the Lord is gracious; and they never have had experience of his power and love, because they have never known their own weakness and need. This *may* be the future condition of some of us, if we harden our hearts today: *apostasy*. Someday, even in this world, we may be found openly among the enemies of God and of his Church.

But, even should we be spared this present shame, what will it ultimately profit a man to profess without understanding? To *say* he has faith, when he has not works (Jas. 2:14)? In that case we shall remain in the heavenly vineyard, stunted plants, without the principle of growth in us, barren; and, in the end, we shall be put to shame before Christ and the holy Angels, "as trees of withering fruits, twice dead, plucked up by the roots," even though we die in outward communion with the Church.

To think of these things, and to be alarmed, is the first step towards obedience; to be at ease, is to be unsafe. We must know what the evil of sin is hereafter, if we do not learn it here. God give us all grace to choose the pain of present repentance before the wrath to come!

FREDERICK W. ROBERTSON: A SERMON ON BIBLICAL INSPIRATION

Some critics of Romanticism call it a flight from reality, but the Romantic preaching of Frederick W. Robertson was anything but that **(see Vol. 1, pp. 608-17)**. *Although most of his short ministry was spent in a proprietary chapel in a fashionable watering place, his sermons were aimed at helping people face and deal with personal problems, become aware of and respond to social problems, and recognize and meet challenges to faith that arose in the nineteenth century. Thus ten years before Darwin published* The Origin of the Species *and long before most British clergy were aware of the new biblical criticism that was arising in Germany, Robertson lectured to his people on weeknights and preached to them on Sundays to help them recognize that these new insights were more of an aid to faith than a threat. This sermon, delivered in 1850, appears in his* Sermons Preached at Brighton, *new ed. (New York: Harper & Brothers, 1905), 825-31.*

Inspiration

We then that are strong ought to bear the infirmities of the weak, and not to please ourselves. Let every one of us please his neighbor for his good to edification. For even Christ pleased not himself; but, as it is written, The reproaches of them that reproached thee fell on me. For whatsoever things were written aforetime were written for our learning, that we through patience and comfort of the Scriptures might have hope (Rom. 15:1-4).

We will endeavor, brethren, to search the connection between the different parts of these verses.

First, the apostle lays down a Christian's duty: "Let every one of us please his neighbor for his good to edification." After that he brings forward as the sanction of that duty, the spirit of the life of Christ: "For even Christ pleased not himself." Next, he adds an illustration of that principle by a quotation from Psalm 69: "It is written, The reproaches of them that reproached thee fell on me." Lastly, he explains and defends that application of the psalm, as if he had said, "I am perfectly justified in applying that passage to Christ, for 'whatsoever things were written aforetime were written for our learning.'"

So that in this quotation, and the defense of it as contained in these verses, we have the principle of apostolical interpretation; we have the principle upon which the apostles used the Old Testament scriptures, and we are enabled to understand their view of inspiration. This is one of the most important considerations upon which we can be at this moment engaged. It is the deepest question of our day: the one which lies beneath all others, and in comparison of which the questions just now agitating the popular mind—whether of papal jurisdiction or varieties of church doctrine in our own communion—are but superficial: it is this grand question of inspiration which is given to this age to solve.

Our subject will break itself up into questions such as these: What the Bible is, and what the Bible is not? What is meant by inspiration? Whether inspiration is the same thing as infallibility? When God inspired the minds, did he dictate the words? Does the inspiration of men mean the infallibility of their words? Is inspiration the same as dictation? Whether, granting that we have the Word of God, we have also the words of God? Are the operations of the Holy Spirit, inspiring men, compatible with partial error, as his operations in sanctifying them are compatible with partial evil? How are we to interpret and apply the scriptures? Is scripture, as the Romanists say, so unintelligible and obscure that we can not understand it without having the guidance of an infallible church? Or is it, as some fanciful Protestants will tell us, a book upon which all ingenuity may be used to find Christ in every sentence? Upon these things there are many views, some of them false, some superstitious; but it is not our business now to deal with these; our way is rather to teach positively than negatively: we will try to set up the truth, and error may fall before it.

The collect for this day leads us to the special consideration of holy scripture;[1] We shall therefore take this for our subject, and endeavor to understand what was the apostolical principle of interpretation.

In the text we find two principles: first, that scripture is of universal application;

And second, that all the lines of scripture converge towards Jesus Christ.

First, then, there is here a universal application of scripture. This passage quoted by the apostle is from the sixty-ninth Psalm. That was evidently spoken by David of himself. From first to last, no unprejudiced mind can detect a conception in the writer's mind of an application to Christ, or to any other person after him; the psalmist is there full of himself and his own sorrows. It is a natural and touching exposition of human grief and a good man's trust. Nevertheless, you will observe that St. Paul extends the use of these words, and applies them to Jesus Christ.

Nay, more than that, he uses them as belonging to all Christians; for, he says, "Whatsoever things were written aforetime, were written for our learning." Now this principle will be more evident if we state it in the words of scripture, "Knowing that no prophecy of scripture is of any private interpretation": those holy men spake not their own limited individual feelings, but as feeling that they were inspired by the Spirit of God. Their words belonged to the whole of our common humanity. No prophecy of the scriptures is of any private interpretation.

Bear in mind that the word prophecy does not mean what we now understand by it—merely prediction of future events—in the scriptures it signifies inspired teaching. The teaching of the prophets was by no means always prediction. Bearing this in mind, let us remember that the apostle says it is of no private interpretation. Had the Psalm applied only to David, then it would have been of private interpretation—it would have been special, limited, particular; it would have belonged to an individual; instead of which, it belongs to humanity.

Take again the subject of which we spoke last Sunday—the prophecy of the destruction of Jerusalem. Manifestly that was spoken originally at Jerusalem; in a manner it seemed limited to Jerusalem, for its very name was mentioned; and besides, as we read this morning, our Savior says, "This generation shall not pass until all be fulfilled."

But had the prophecy ended there, then you would still have had prophecy, but it would have been of private—that is, peculiar, limited—interpretation; whereas our Redeemer's principle was this: that this doom pronounced on Jerusalem was universally applicable, that it was but a style and specimen of God's judgments. The judgment-coming of the Son of Man takes place wherever there is evil grown ripe, whenever corruption is complete. And the gathering of the Roman eagles is but a specimen of the way in which judgment at last overtakes every city, every country, and every man in whom evil has reached the point where there is no possibility of cure.

So that the prophecy belongs to all ages, from the destruction of Jerusalem to the end of the world. The words of St. Matthew are universally applicable. For Scripture deals with principles; not with individuals, but rather with states of humanity. Promises and threatenings are made to individuals, because they are in a particular state of character; but they belong to all who are in that state, for "God is no respecter of persons."

First, we will take an instance of the state of blessing. There was blessing pronounced to Abraham, in which it will be seen how large a grasp on humanity this view of scripture gave to St. Paul. The whole argument in the Epistle to the Romans is, that the promises made to Abraham were not to his person, but to his faith; and thus the apostle says, "They who are of faith, are blessed with faithful Abraham."

We will now take the case of curse or threatening. Jonah, by divine command, went through Nineveh, proclaiming its destruction; but that prophecy belonged to the state in which Nineveh was; it was true only while it remained in that state; and therefore, as they repented, and their state was thus changed, the prophecy was left unfulfilled. From this we perceive the largeness and grandeur of scripture interpretation.

In the Epistle to the Corinthians, we find the apostle telling of the state of the Jews in their passage towards the promised land, their state of idolatry and gluttony, and then he proceeds to pronounce the judgments that fell upon them, adding that he tells us this not merely as a matter of history, but rather as an illustration of a principle. They are specimens of eternal, unalterable law, So that whosoever shall be in the state of these Jews, whosoever shall imitate them, the same judgments must fall upon them, the same satiety and weariness, the same creeping of the inward serpent polluting all their feelings; and therefore he says, "All these things happened unto them for ensamples." Again, he uses the same principle, not as a private, but a general application; for he says, "There hath no temptation overtaken you but such is common to man."

We will take now another case, applied not to nations, but to individuals. In Hebrews 13 we find these words from the Old Testament, "I will never leave thee nor forsake thee"; and there the apostle's inference is that we may boldly say, "The Lord is my helper, I will not fear what men shall do unto me." Now, when we refer to Scripture, we shall find that this was a promise originally made to Jacob. The apostle does not hesitate to take that promise and appropriate it to all Christians; for it was made, not to Jacob as a person, but to the state in which Jacob was; it was made to all who, like Jacob, are wanderers and pilgrims in the world; it was made to all whom sin has rendered outcasts and who are longing to return. The promises made to the meek belong to meekness; the promises made to the humble belong to humility.

And this it is which makes this Bible, not only a blessed book, but *our* book. It is this universal applicability of scripture which has made the influence of the Bible universal: this book has held spell-bound the hearts of nations, in a way in which no single book has ever held men before. Remember, too, in order to enhance the marvelousness of this, that the nation from which it emanated was a despised people. For the last eighteen hundred years the Jews have been proverbially a by-word and a reproach. But that contempt for Israel is nothing new to the world, for before even the Roman despised them, the Assyrian and Egyptian regarded them with scorn. Yet the words which came from Israel's prophets have been the life-blood of the world's devotions. And the teachers, the psalmists, the prophets, and the lawgivers of this despised nation spoke out truths that have struck the key-note of the heart of man; and this, not because they were of Jewish, but just because they were of universal application.

This collection of books has been to the world what no other book has ever been to a nation. States have been founded on its principles. Kings rule by a compact based on it. Men hold the Bible in their hands when they prepare to give solemn evidence affecting life, death, or property; the sick man is almost afraid to die unless the book be within reach of his hands; the battleship goes into action with one on board whose office is to expound it; its prayers, its psalms are the language which we use when we speak to God; eighteen centuries have found no holier, no diviner language. If ever there has been a prayer or a hymn enshrined in the heart of a nation, you are sure to find its basis in the Bible. There is no new religious idea given to the world, but it is merely the development of something given in the Bible.

The very translation of it has fixed language and settled the idioms of speech. Germany and England speak as they speak because the Bible was translated. It has made the most illiterate peasant more familiar with the history, customs, and geography of ancient Palestine than with the localities of his own country. Men who know nothing of the Grampians, of Snowdon, or of Skiddaw,[2] are at home in Zion, the Lake of Gennesareth, or among the rills of Carmel. People who know little about London, know by heart the places in Jerusalem where those blessed feet trod which were nailed to the cross. Men who know nothing of the architecture of a Christian cathedral, can yet tell you all about the pattern of the holy temple. Even this shows us the influence of the Bible. The orator holds a thousand men for half an hour—breathless—a thousand men as one, listening to his single word. But this Word of God has held a thousand nations for thrice a thousand years spellbound; held them by an abiding power, even the universality of its truth; and we feel it to be no more a collection of books, but *the* book.

We pass on now to consider the second principle contained in these words, which is, that all Scripture bears towards Jesus Christ. St. Paul quotes these Jewish words as fulfilled in Christ. Jesus of Nazareth is the central point in which all the converging lines of Scripture meet. Again we state this principle in scripture language: in the book of Revelation we find it written, "The testimony of Jesus is the spirit of prophecy," that is, the sum and substance of prophecy, the very spirit of scripture is to bear testimony to Jesus Christ. We must often have been surprised and perplexed at the way in which the apostles quote passages in reference to Christ which originally had no reference to him. In our text, for instance, David speaks only of himself, and yet St. Paul refers it to Christ. Let us understand this. We have already said that Scripture deals not with individuals, but with states and principles. Promises belong to persons only so far as they are what they are taken to be; and consequently all unlimited promises made to individuals, so far as they are referred merely to those individuals, are necessarily exaggerated and hyperbolical. They can only be true of one in whom that is fulfilled which was unfulfilled in them.

We will take an instance. We are all familiar with the well-known prophecy of Balaam. We all remember the magnificent destinies he promised to the people whom he was called to curse. Those promises have never been fulfilled, neither from the whole appearance of things does it seem likely that they ever will be fulfilled in their literal sense. To whom, then, are they made? To Israel? Yes; so far as they developed God's own conception. Balaam says, "God hath not beheld iniquity in Jacob, neither hath he seen perverseness in Israel." Is this the character of Israel, an idolatrous and rebellious nation? Spoken of the literal Israel, this prophecy is false; but it was not false of that spotlessness and purity of which Israel was the temporal and imperfect type. If one can be found of whom that description is true, of whom we can say, the Lord hath not beheld iniquity in him, to him then that prophecy belongs.

Brethren, Jesus of Nazareth is that pure and spotless one, Christ is perfectly, all that every saint was partially. To him belongs all: all that description of a perfect character which would be exaggeration if spoken of others, and to this character the blessing belongs; hence it is that all the fragmentary representations of character collect and center in him alone. Therefore, the apostle says, "It was added until the seed should come to whom the promise was made." Consequently St. Paul would not read the Psalm as spoken only of David. Were the lofty aspirations, the purity and humbleness expressed in the text, true of him, poor, sinful, erring David? These were the expressions of the Christ within his heart—the longing of the Spirit of God within him; but they were no proper representation of the spirit of his life, for there is a marvelous difference between a man's ideal and his actual—between the man and the book he writes—a difference between the aspirations within the man and the character which is realized by his daily life. The promises are to the Christ within David; therefore they are applied to the Christ when he comes. Now, let us extract from that this application.

Brethren, scripture is full of Christ. From Genesis to Revelation every thing breathes of him, not every letter of every sentence, but the spirit of every chapter. It is full of Christ, but not in the way that some suppose; for there is nothing more miserable, as specimens of perverted ingenuity, than the attempts of certain commentators and preachers to find remote, and recondite, and intended allusions to Christ everywhere.

For example, they chance to find in the construction of the temple the fusion of two metals, and this they conceive is meant to show the union of divinity with humanity in Christ. If they read of coverings to the tabernacle, they find implied the doctrine of imputed righteousness. If it chance that one of the curtains of the tabernacle be red, they see in that the prophecy of the blood of Christ. If they are told that the kingdom of heaven is a pearl of great price, they will see it in the allusion—that, as a pearl is the production of animal suffering, so the kingdom of heaven is produced by the sufferings of the Redeemer.

I mention this perverted mode of comment, because it is not merely harmless, idle, amid useless; it is positively dangerous. This is to make the Holy Spirit speak riddles and conundrums, and the interpretation of scripture but clever riddle guessing. Putting aside all this childishness, we say that the Bible is full of Christ. Every unfulfilled aspiration of humanity in the past; all partial representation of perfect character; all sacrifices, nay even those of idolatry, point to the fulfillment of what we want, the answer to every longing—the type of perfect humanity, the Lord Jesus Christ.

Get the habit—a glorious one—of referring all to Christ. How did he feel? Think? Act? So then must I feel, and think, and act. Observe how Christ was a living reality in St. Paul's mind. "Should I please myself?" "For even Christ pleased not himself"; "It is more blessed to give than to receive."

Notes

1. The sermon was preached on December 8, 1850, the Second Sunday of Advent that year. The collect (the short prayer that summarizes the theme of that day in the church calendar) for that Sunday in the 1662 Book of Common Prayer reads: "Blessed Lord, who hast caused all holy Scriptures to be written for our learning; grant that we may in such wise hear them, read, mark, learn, and inwardly digest them, that by patience and comfort of thy holy Word, we may embrace, and ever hold fast the blessed hope of everlasting life, which thou hast given us in our Savior Jesus Christ. Amen."

2. Mountains in Scotland, Wales, and England, respectively.

CHAPTER 23

TRANSATLANTIC ROMANTICISM

RALPH WALDO EMERSON: A CHRISTMAS SERMON

No American exemplified the spirit of Romanticism more than Ralph Waldo Emerson (1803–82) **(see Vol. 1, pp. 626-29)**. *While he is better known for his contribution as a transcendentalist essayist and poet, his first ambition was to follow his father into the pulpit, where, because of his love of "the strains of eloquence," he could "put on eloquence as a robe." His parish ministry as a Unitarian pastor, however, lasted only three years; his conviction that matter could not convey spirit made him unwilling to administer Holy Communion. Yet he produced in that short period four volumes of sermons. This sermon, written the year before his ordination, was preached four times. The third time was in Second Church, Boston, just before he became its junior pastor. It was rare in the history of New England preaching because the Puritans had disapproved of the celebration of Christmas, while he advocated it. In this sermon he shows the wideness of his sympathies, recognizing that something could be said for Roman Catholic devotion to the Blessed Virgin Mary, and that Greco-Roman paganism seemed to anticipate the birth of Christ. His Unitarianism is still very much in the*

Christian tradition. His Christology is Arian, and he expects Christ to return at the end of the world in judgment, opening the way to everlasting life for those who have truly followed his teaching.

This sermon appears in The Complete Sermons of Ralph Waldo Emerson, *vol. I, ed. Albert J. von Frank, intro. David M. Robinson (Columbia: University of Missouri Press, 1989), 141-48.*

Sermon XIII

Unto you is born this day in the city of David a Savior who is Christ the Lord. Luke 2:11

We are met, my friends, on the anniversary of that day which for many ages has been set apart by the great majority of Christians to celebrate the nativity of the Founder of our faith. It is hardly necessary to urge upon you the propriety of giving some extraordinary notice to the day. Our own ancestors did indeed account it superstitious and were averse to give the sanction of their countenance to the multiplication of the holidays of the church. But we who know how bitter were their feelings of dislike to the Church of England out of which they came, and how harsh and cruel a stepmother she had been to the Puritans, can easily understand how their aversion to its abuses should sometimes betray them into unjust prejudices against its best institutions.

But with us there exists no reason for similar apprehensions. Two centuries have strangely changed the aspect of affairs. The day has long gone by since men in this country learned to look with terror at the forms and rites or at the ambition of that ancient church. Our civil freedom or our freedom of conscience cannot now be endangered by the surplice or the miter so offensive to our fathers and we may copy whatever is favorable to devotion in her solemnities without peril from the usurping influence of bishops. Moreover we have the authority of the apostolic command: *Whatsoever things are true, just, honest, lovely, and of good report, wherein there is virtue and wherein there is praise, these things think upon and practice* (Phil. 4:8).

And do we think it just and becoming to celebrate with all the forms of honor and congratulation the jubilee of our Independence? Do we delight to repair to the rock of Plymouth to indulge our sympathies of joy in the unexampled prosperity of New England, and shall we not feel and admit the far higher and holier claim upon our gratitude that comes to us out of mourning and desolate Judah, from the little town of Bethlehem where the Son of Man was born who brought life and immortality to light? Were it not absurd to be overjoyed at events that affect our worldly prosperity, our freedom and civil privileges during the few years we live in the world, and at the same time to turn coldly away from contemplating an event that revealed to us all that we live for, all that we hope, our relations to God, to the universe of moral beings, and to Eternity?

Through the darkness and sin of two thousand years I see the light of the shepherds' star and am refreshed. Over that vast and dreary space of time I hear distinct above the jargon of sects, above the fearful noise of human passions, I hear the song of the angels. I hear and must listen to the sound. I should accuse myself if I could repress my joy. Yes, my friends, apart from all consideration of the propriety of these recollections, apart from all comparison between this and other seasons of general joy, this occasion has in itself a beautiful solemnity and is necessarily agreeable to the human mind.

It will not harm us to give ourselves up to the feelings it has so powerful a tendency to excite. It will not encroach upon our time. Can we not watch with our master in his cradle an hour? There is no lack among us of worldly prudence and care, there is quite an abundance of common festivity and common griefs. It cannot be said they have not their share of our attention and our time. But come, let us break away from them all; they can spare us one hour of inviolate joy. The voice that spake peace and good will to men let it speak peace to our minds and let us proclaim therein a solemn festival; a little breathing space; the sabbath of an hour to thoughts of God, of his holy child Jesus, and of our own connection with him, which outlives our connection with this perishing world.

In all other occasions of gladness, such is the imperfection of our condition, there is generally something to lament. When we exult in the successful achievement of our independence we glory in what was once an occasion of bereavement to ten thousand families. The gain of the whole is purchased by the grief of the many. In order to a triumph there must be victims. But we signalize a jubilee which is single in the Universe. Ours is a joy without reproach or deduction, a spotless, a holy commemoration, a conquest of good over evil: a conquest of souls to God: a blessed revelation to man of unheard of happiness: of pardon to sin: and of infinite progress in knowledge and enjoyment through the never-ending ages of the future.

Suffer me then, my friends, to call your serious attention to some considerations upon the peculiar circumstances and the value of that event this season commemorates. You all know the remarkable fact that there appears to have been about the time of the Advent, a general expectation, a looking for in the world of some manifestation of the will of Heaven beyond the ordinary course of Providence.

Among the Jews it arose very naturally from the strong and fervent predictions of their ancient prophets, which continually returned from their denunciation of retribution on the crimes of their own generation, to the bright and beautiful vision of the Conqueror to come, of the child to be born, of the dayspring from on high that was to illuminate the world, that should scatter the darkness that had gathered about the Divine perfections, that should reveal him to men not as their Law had revealed him, a stern and jealous Deity encompassed in darkness and thunder, with the ministers of vengeance by the side of his throne, but should declare his true and eternal character, should declare to men that God is Love, that he is our Father, who sends us a message of mercy from on high, to show us the way to heaven.

But not among the Jews alone, it would appear, this hope existed. As sometimes the occurrence of great events in the world has been preceded by unaccountable rumors which have been justified by what followed, so it would seem that the communication from God to man was waited for in expectant silence by the nations of the earth. There is a singular passage in one of the Dialogues of Plato, which, it must be remembered, were written 400 years before the birth of Christ, in which Alcibiades converses with Socrates on the proper objects of prayer, and Socrates asks him if it does not seem likely that God would send into the world some teacher who should inform us what we ought to pray for and they agree that it will be wise to wait for the instructions of that messenger.

If such expectations were entertained by the wisest in Greece it would appear also that in Rome the ancient books which were kept in their temples and called the Sibylline prophecies, had intimated also the approach of a better and clearer dispensation. The famous pastoral of Virgil inscribed to Pollio has been often compared to the prophecies of Isaiah, so similar is the language in which he foretells the coming of a more virtuous and peaceful age. The shutting also of the doors of the temple of Janus for the first time for some hundred years, which were never closed but in time of universal peace, had prepared men to expect some auspicious and unknown events.

To all this St. Paul evidently alludes when he writes to the Romans, *For the earnest expectation of the whole creation is waiting for the manifestation of the sons of God*—and afterward—*that the Creation should be delivered from the bondage of corruption into the glorious liberty of the Sons of God* (8:19, 21). This was the state of human feeling. Man wondered in the world why he that had framed this stupendous Creation had left himself without witness therein.

Man felt, whilst God was not clearly made known, what all men now feel when they live without acknowledgment of God,—a strange disproportion between his desires and his condition, between what he is and what he seems made for: so noble in his powers and so lowly in his necessities that there needed another world to explain the difficulties of this. My brethren, this feeling must have arisen in your own minds in every hour of uncertainty. I have before had occasion to allude to it more at large. You will forgive me for dwelling upon it a moment in this connection.

Though the Earth we inhabit is nobly furnished, though the heavens are arched gloriously over our heads, yet when morning breaks in the east and the sun rises, man steps forth from his little dwelling into this swelling scene to labor, to eat, to drink, to laugh, to talk, to sin, and to sleep again. He heeds it not, this wondrous majesty wherewith the great house of nature is adorned. Let the sun go up the sky and the moon shine, and innumerable stars move before him in orbits so vast that centuries shall not fulfill them, though the seasons roll and the winter cover his fields with coat of dazzling snow and the summer pour out upon them her horn of plenty, he does not care, he does not know; he is creeping in a little path of his own; he is following a few appetites; is peering round for a little bread; is devising some minute arts to get an atom from his neighbor's heap and add it to his own; he is laying stratagems in petty things for the admiration of his fellows; he is bewailing small inconveniences; he is pouting at the cold or the heat; he is absorbed in the apprehension or the suffering of his diseases.

Man felt the *absurd,* if I may so call it, of his condition. He lifted up to the heavens an eye of despair and asked to what purpose was all this prodigal magnificence if the only fact that could aid and establish him, namely the Being of God to whom he stood in relations of dependence, had no support from all. He walked on earth but there was no voice of God. He explored the stars but they were silent in their courses. He waited in Rome, in Greece, in Egypt, impatient for light to break that should show him why he was made and what was to become of him in the immense future before him.

He waited not in vain. In the sky of the East a star arose. On the midnight heaven the silver accents were heard of the heavenly host praising God and saying, Glory to God in the highest. On Earth peace, goodwill to men. This day is born in the city of David a Savior who is Christ the Lord.

I cannot but regard the manner in which it pleased God that his chosen messenger should appear in the world as peculiarly consistent with his character and office. I rejoice also in the fact as a strong incidental evidence to the authenticity of the evangelists, that they have not made any attempt to color or conceal the humble place and circumstances of his birth, which to men of their expectations and prejudices as Jews must have appeared strangely unsuitable to the character of the Messiah which he claimed. We rejoice that he was not born in the lap of majesty and ostentation. We feel the sublimity of his houseless and unfriended lot. We feel how the artificial distinctions of life, the poverty and riches, rank and lowliness, sink into dust before the greatness of him that sent him and the dignity of the office he was appointed to bear.

And now, my friends, I would invite your meditations to the excellence of the divine gift. I would not affix a superstitious regard to what has real claim enough of its own upon our gratitude and love. I would not take—I dare not take—from that awful reverence which is due to God alone and bestow it on his son who so often and so expressly denied his title to be more than the servant and messenger of the Most High, who delighted, in his humility, to represent himself as nothing;—that the words that he spoke were not his; that the works which he did were not his, brought no glory to him, but to his father in whose name and by whose power they were said and done.

But I would seriously consider the genuine divinity of the gift to ignorant and sinful men. My friends, when you have gone into your closets and shut your door, when you have knelt in secret before God and felt that you were in the immediate presence of the majesty of Heaven and Earth and have attempted strongly to conceive of the Being you addressed, have you not sometimes found it a difficult and bewildering effort? In the weakness and ignorance of our nature the human mind must often struggle ineffectually to compass the great idea of an infinite Being everywhere present in whom we live, move, and have our being.

Unless the thoughts are very powerfully concentrated they are prone to wander. The heart must be wound up to devotion. It must be warmed by the sense of some signal mercy, or, which is the great injunction of Christianity, the feelings must be trained by long use of habitual reference to the divine Presence or the affections will grow cold toward God. If this difficulty disturb our acts of devotion, and the best and wisest men have often complained of it, how much more hard was it for those who lived before the Christian Revelation to acquire and preserve in their daily life just conceptions of the character of God and of their duties to him?

The idea of Deity oppresses the imagination. It is very easy for us to understand how men were led into idol worship. They had within them, as all men have, a religious feeling, a notion of God, of some being or beings greater in nature than man, and who made and governed men. The idea of God—it encumbered them. It struggled to find expression. It tempered their joy. It authorized their hope. It added horror to fear. It armed their sorrow for sin with a scorpion sting. In obedience to this strong feeling they strove to express it and to do it honor by building idols and temples and paying it a visible and costly service, and devised a thousand ceremonies to keep alive their sense of this presence of the gods among men and this gave the mind a temporary consolation and ease.

But God by outward revelation to the Jews and by inward revelation to the minds of the wisest of the heathens taught them their error. But the rude mind of the people still found doubt and fatigue in a spiritual service. It might do for cherubim, for the stupendous intellects that waited with sleepless eye about his throne to see him unveiled. But not so with dust and ashes. Man must put something between God and his own nothingness.

They worshiped therefore in Greece and Rome imaginary gods who were personifications of the divine perfections. Minerva was his wisdom; Apollo was his light and eternal youth. The Fates were his eternal decrees. And in the Dark Ages, as we emphatically call them, when the Christian religion, grossly misunderstood, was confounded with these ancient superstitions, nations knelt before the shrines of the Virgin.

Even this superstition was a wonderful improvement on the pagan worship. There is something in a high degree religious and beautiful in the affection with which the Catholic regards the Holy Virgin, which is every way preferable to the pagan conception of Diana, of Venus and Juno, and which may serve to show that a corrupted form of Christianity is better than the finish of paganism. Her votary calls her the stainless benevolent; he supplicates with that confidence he would feel towards a mother her intercession for his sake, and the countenance which the genius of the Italian painters has delineated for the virgin has an angelic sweetness far different from, and far more attractive than, the stern beauty of the ancient goddesses.

But this was the continual tendency of human weakness feeling the necessity of supernatural protection and of some bright example by which life might be guided to run into the worship of false gods; to tremble before the true. But it pleased God in his infinite mercy to reveal his character distinctly to men. The great internal distinction, I believe you will agree with me, of this revelation we receive is, that it is the only account that has disclosed a character of God agreeable to the human mind. All former theologies, by whatever genius developed, by whatever sublimity elevated, distorted the deity with monstrous features. Something wild and prodigious for which the soul saw no reason was always added to the power and knowledge of the infinite mind.

But in the Christian Religion, God is made known to us as the God of Man. It is made clear to us that we are made in his moral image, and that to find out him we must explore ourselves, that these high faculties of ours, the Reason and the Affections of man, of which the elements exist in the humblest outcast that wears the form—when carried out to their perfection do compose a mind that fills and quickens and governs the Universe.

We are not simply told that there is a God, but God is really revealed to our minds.

We learn to regard this as the most interesting relation of man, that in the lowest cabin of the squalid savage, in the unwholesome caverns of the mine, wherever man appears, there goes one capable of seeing and loving God, capable of the most towering thought and uncompromising virtue.

We are made to enter into a sublime sympathy with our maker; to speak to him day by day; to watch his eye as it always rests on us; to perform or to forbear actions in obedience to it; to act from him, and with him; and finally we are sent forward on a great and never-ending progress to greatness in the effort to bring ourselves into his majestic likeness.

There is still one more view kindred to this which I wish to take of the subject. To show himself not the severe abstraction of justice and power, he sent a being among men to teach and in a manner to exemplify his character, one that could sympathize with men, could, like men, pursue knowledge and glory, glory in its highest forms, that of sufferance, one to be born at Bethlehem; to be hungry and tempted in the wilderness; to weep at Bethany; to be oppressed during life by the awful consciousness of his fate; to be insulted with hideous aggravation; to die on Calvary the death of a malefactor.

For these reasons we rejoice and are glad because he not only taught us that we are heirs of eternal life but because he taught us the paternal character of God; because he exhibited in his life a model for ours; taught us how a man in scrupulous obedience to the commandments of God might resist temptation and keep himself unspotted from the world; and exhibited in this way an image of the divine nature reduced within the compass of our understanding and love.

Therefore we delight to remember his nativity. Beautiful is the name of Bethlehem through all ages. Dear to human nature is the name and venerable idea of its blessed and glorified instructor. A healthful example, a cheering encouragement, a bright beacon lit up in the darkness of the old world and sending out its pure and hospitable light into all the future history of man.

My brethren, when I consider the consequences of that joyful night, when I attempt to measure the good that has accrued to the world from the Christian dispensation, the commanding check it has for ages kept upon the dangerous passions of men, how it has riveted the social bonds and brought forward so many noble spirits to the help of suffering humanity: when I look at the early history of an institution, these great and blessed mysteries which have hoarded comfort from age to age for human suffering—the august Founder, the twelve self-denying heroes of a pious renown, distancing in moral sublimity all those primeval benefactors which ancient gratitude deified; the apostles whose desiring eyes saw little luster on earth and no consolation but in extending the victories, the moral victories, of the cross; the martyrs who had found after so many sensual ages in a faith for things unseen, in a moral intellection, more than a compensation for the lust of the world and the pride of life; and after all these and better even than all these, the boundless aggregate of hearts and deeds which the genius of Christianity touched and inspired, the violence of fiery natures to which it has whispered peace, the antidote it has administered to remorse and despair, the Samaritan oil it has poured into wounded hearts, the costly sacrifices and unpurchasable devotion to the cause of God and man it has now for eighteen centuries inspired. When I consider all this, the sum of what is most precious on earth, and trace it back in its long progress to the humble manger of a Jewish inn, I am overawed by the manifest interposition of the hand of God in behalf of his sinful children, and I echo the solemn anthem that announces glad tidings of great joy to us and to all men. Glory to God, peace and goodwill to men.

Finally, my friends, let us deeply consider each of us in the silence of our own hearts what is our share in the joy of this day. True it is that everlasting life has been made known to men, that Jesus Christ the Savior who was born this day did exhibit amid the extremes of sorrow and poverty and ingratitude and persecution a radiant, a perfect, a godlike character, and taught us how we might obtain the favor of God by an obedience like his own. And have we complied with the condition? Has our daily life been led, like his, in an uniform progress from duty to duty, from faith to faith, from trial to trial, never surprised into sin by temptation, never cast down from our integrity by difficulty or opposition?

If it be so, rejoice and be glad for by the word of him that this day was born, great is your reward in heaven. But if the exceeding great and precious promises which he brought, have been slighted by you, if your days have been made dark by sin, if the immortal faculties that slumber in your breast have been neglected or abused, alas! my brother, alas! What is it to you that squadrons of angels announced his birth, what matters it though the Almighty clothed him in power to bear witness to the truth of his mighty commission, what is it to you that death could not destroy him, that the tomb rendered back its trust, that he forsook it and arose, or yet that he ascended to his Father and ever liveth to make intercession for his faithful disciples? What is it to you but another weight of sin which will be laid to your charge, inasmuch as you have sinned against this marvelous light?

You have seen what prophets and kings desired but were not able, and have averted your eyes. The prevailing eloquence of his life, the wonders of his hand, have failed to move you. The great tragedy of his death and the interposition of the Almighty for his resurrection have failed to move you; then is this day an occasion of sorrow and danger, for the light of this day shall be remembered against you as an opportunity which you have slighted, as a warning which you defied. But no, I trust in God it shall not be so with us. Let us remember that life is short, and neglected opportunities will never return; that Christ will not again appear, till he comes to sit in judgment. Let him that in body was born in Bethlehem, in spirit be born in our hearts. Let us celebrate his nativity there. Let his temper grow up in our souls. Let his laws control our actions; and govern our minds; and when he shall come to judge the earth in righteousness, we shall appear with him in glory.

PHILLIPS BROOKS: THE LAST OF HIS *LECTURES ON PREACHING*

*There is no more prestigious body of homiletical literature than the series of lectures that a parishioner of Henry Ward Beecher endowed at Yale in honor of his pastor's father, Lyman Beecher. And no set of those lectures has been referred to as often as that given by Phillips Brooks in 1877 (***see Vol. 1, pp. 637-41***). Few definitions of preaching have been* *quoted so often as Brooks's statement that "preaching is the bringing of truth through personality"* (Lectures, *5). Brooks (1835–93) is probably best known as the author of "O Little Town of Bethlehem," and indeed he did little in his whole life that was spectacular beyond preaching extraordinarily well. An Episcopal priest, his preaching attracted attention from the very beginning, and he was called as rector of one of the largest parishes in the country, Holy Trinity Church in Philadelphia, while he was still in his mid-twenties. Seven years later he went to Trinity Church, Boston, where he remained until he accepted election as bishop of his diocese shortly before his death.*

The fidelity of his pulpit ministry is reflected in the way his Beecher Lectures are much more a spirituality of preaching than they are helpful hints on how to preach. The eighth and last of the lectures sees the motivation of all good preaching to lie in a recognition of the value of the souls of one's parishioners. It appears in Phillips Brooks, Lectures on Preaching Delivered Before the Divinity School of Yale College in January and February 1877 *(New York: E. P. Dutton, 1877), 255-81.*

The Value of the Human Soul

There is a power which lies at the center of all success in preaching, and whose influence reaches out to the circumference, and is essential everywhere. Without its presence we cannot imagine the most brilliant talents making a preacher of the gospel in the fullest sense. Where it is largely present, it is wonderful how many deficiencies count for nothing. It has the characteristics which belong to all the most essential powers. It is able to influence the whole life as one general and pervading motive; and it can also press on each particular action with peculiar force. Under its compulsion a man first becomes a preacher, and every sermon that he preaches is more or less consciously shaped by its pressure; as the whole round world and each round atom are shaped and held in shape by the same laws. Without this power, preaching is almost sure to become either a struggle of ambition or a burden of routine. With it, preaching is an ever-fresh delight. The power is the value of the human soul, felt by the preacher, and inspiring all his work.

The power of that motive has been assumed in all that I have said to you. But it seems to me to be so supremely important; the ministry which is full of it is so rich; the ministry which lacks it is so poor, that I determined, when I undertook the duty which I complete today, that this last lecture should be given to a serious consideration of the importance and value of this mainspring, which lies coiled up within all the complicated machinery of the ministry, the realized value of the human soul.

As to its importance, we get our clearest impression if we look at the earthly ministry of Jesus. There are many accounts to be given of his wondrous work. People may say many ingenious things about it, and many of them are true. But we are sure that he has put his hand most certainly upon the central power of Christ's ministry, who holds up before us the intense value which the Savior always set upon the souls for which he lived and died. It shines in everything he says and does. It looks out from his eyes when they are happiest and when they are saddest. It trembles in the most loving consolations, and thunders in the most passionate rebukes which come from his lips. It is the inspiration at once of his pity and his indignation. And it has made the few persons on whom it chanced to fall, and in whose histories it found its illustrations, the men and women who represented humanity about him in Palestine—Nicodemus, Peter, John, the Pharisees, the Magdalen, the woman of Samaria, and all the rest—luminous forever with its light.

That power still continues wherever the same value of the human soul is present. If we could see how precious the human soul is as Christ saw it, our ministry would approach the effectiveness of Christ's. "I am not convinced by what you say. I am not sure that I cannot answer every one of your arguments," said a man with whom a preacher had been pleading, "but one thing which I confess I cannot understand. It puzzles me, and makes me feel a power in what you say. It is why you should care enough for me to take all this trouble, and to labor with me as if you cared for my soul." It is a power which every man must feel. It inspires the preacher; and his hearers, catching its influence, become soft and ready to receive the truth. It is strength in the arm which strikes, and tenderness in the rock which receives the blow.

The other motives of the minister's work seem to me to stand around this great central motive as the staff officers stand around a general. He needs them. They execute his commands. He could not do his work without them. But he is not dependent upon them as they are upon him; any one of them might fall away and he could still fight the battle. The power of the battle is in him. If he falls, the cause is ruined.

So stand the subordinate motives of the ministry around the commanding motive, the realized value of the human soul. They are the motives which I have had occasion to dwell on one by one in the course of these lectures. They are the pleasure of work, the mere delight in the exercise of powers which is natural to any man who is healthy both in body and mind; the love of influence, that gratification in feeling our life touch another life for some good result, which is also natural and healthy; the perception of order, that love of regulated movement, of the rhythm of righteousness in the lives and ways of men, which in its higher forms is noble, though in the lower it degenerates into routine; and lastly the pure concern for truth, the pleasure in seeing right ideas take the place of wrong ideas, which may be quite separate from any regard for the interest of the person in whom the change takes place.

These are the nobler members of the staff of the great general. There are more ignoble ones who volunteer their services and wear something like his uniform and cannot always be distinguished from his true servants; such as emulation, and the love of fame, and the pride of opinion, and the enjoyment of congenial society. I will not dwell on those. These others are the real staff of the general.

But when we look at their group, how the commanding motive whom they serve towers up far above them all. They get their highest dignity from serving him. For in his service each of them, which is abstract in itself, comes into actual contact with man; and no abstract principle has shown its full power or given its full pleasure until it has opened the essential relations which exist between it and human nature. It is the great privilege of the ministry that it is kept in constant necessary contact with mankind. Therein lies its healthiness. Man in his mystery and wonderfulness is more full of the suggestion of God than either abstract truth or physical nature.

And so the true preacher, in spite of his imperfect opportunities for study, in spite of his separation from the beauty of the natural world, has the chance to know more of God than the profoundest speculative philosophy or the most exquisite scenery of earth could reveal to him.

Let me try then to point out to you what some of the effects will be in a man's preaching from a true sense of the value of the human soul, by which I mean a high estimate of the capacity of the spiritual nature, a keen and constant appreciation of the attainments to which it may be brought. And first of all it helps to rescue the gospel which we preach from a sort of unnaturalness and incongruity which is very apt to cling to it. This is, I think, very important.

Consider what it is that you are to declare week after week, to the men and women who come to hear you. The mighty truths of Incarnation and Atonement are your themes. You tell them of the birth and life and death of Jesus Christ. You picture the adorable love and the mysterious sacrifice of the Savior. And you bind all this to their lives. You tell them that in a true sense all this was certainly for them.

I do not know what you are made of, if sometimes, as you preach, there does not come into your mind a thought of incongruity. What are you, you and these people to whom you preach, that for you the central affection of the universe should have been stirred? You know your own life. You know something of the lives they live. You look into their faces as you preach to them. Where is the end worthy of all this ministry of almighty grace which you have been describing? Is it possible that all this once took place and, by the operation of the Holy Spirit, is a perpetual power in the world, merely that these machine-lives might run a little truer, or that a series of rules might be established by which the current workings of society might move more smoothly?

That, which men sometimes make the purpose of it all, is too unworthy. The engine is too coarse to have so fine a fire under it. You must see something deeper. You must discern in all these men and women some inherent preciousness for which even the marvel of the Incarnation and the agony of Calvary was not too great, or it is impossible that you should keep your faith in those stupendous truths which Bethlehem and Calvary offer to us.

Some source of fire from which these dimmed sparks come, some possible renewal of the fire which is in them still, some sight of the education through which each soul is passing, and some suggestion of the special personal perfectness to which each may attain, all this must brighten before you, as you look at them; and then the truths of your theology shall not be thrown into confusion nor faded into unreality by your ministry to men.

The best thing in a minister's life is the action of his works and his faith on one another; his experience of the deeper value of the human soul making the wonders of his faith more credible, and the truths of his faith always revealing to him a deeper and deeper value in the soul.

I think that nobody can preach with the best power who is not possessed with a sense of the mysteriousness of the human life which he preaches to. It must seem to him capable of indefinite enlargement and refinement. He must see it in each new person as something original and new. This must be something which belongs to his whole conception of man as the child of God. It must not be the mere inspiration of his whim, attributed in great richness to some lives which chance to take his fancy but ignored in others. He must see it in all men simply as men.

When he undertakes to lead them he must feel the mystery and spontaneity of the lives that he takes under his teaching. He must be a careful student of the characters he trains, he cannot carry people over the route of his ministry as a ferryman carries passengers across the river, always running his boat in the same line and never even asking the names of the people whom he carries. He must count himself rather like the tutor of a family of princes, who, with careful study of their several dispositions, trains the royal nature of each for the special kingdom over which he is to rule.

Here is where the preacher and the poet touch. Every true preacher must be a poet, at least in so far as to see behind all the imperfections of men a certain ideal manhood from which they have never separated, which underlies the life and lends its value to the blurred and broken character of every one. A belief in the Incarnation, in the divine Son of Man makes such poets of us all. It is interesting to see in how many ministers the hopefulness of this ideal poetic view of human life overcomes the tendencies of natural temperament, the discouragement of poverty and disease and the disenchanting influence of intercourse with men, and keeps ministers the most hopeful class of men. They are always standing where, if they will, they may listen for the bells that shall "ring in the Christ that is to be."

I have seen ministers try to crush back this noble tendency of their vocation and to assume a cynicism and a hopelessness which they did not feel, so that other men might not call them childish. And I have seen men of the world disappointed when they came to such ministers and did not find in them the childlike hope and trust that they expected, but only false and despairing thoughts of human nature like their own; as if the ice came up to the fire to warm itself, and found the fire ashamed of being warm and trying hard to make itself as cold as ice.

I might dwell, also, on this value of the human soul for its own sake, as constituting the constant reserve of pleasure in the ministry. There are other pleasures in our work, as I have recounted to you already; but they are all, to a certain extent, dependent upon circumstances. A parish uproar which reveals the bad reality of life, may scatter some of them. Poverty, which deprives you of the means of culture, and takes away the power of carrying out your plans, may rob you of others. But the new pleasure of dealing with man as man, as a being valuable in himself, for this no peculiar happiness of circumstances is needed. Wherever men are, you may have it. Nobody but Robinson Crusoe is shut out from it, and even to him the Man Friday is sure to come.

And herein lies the real fellowship of the ministry. There are no fellow-workers who come so close together as fellow-workers in the ministry of the gospel; and their companionship is closest when they most deeply know this truth of the essential value of the human soul. A preacher comes to me from Africa, or from some church of another denomination in the next street, which often seems farther off than Africa. It depends upon what the power of our preaching is, how near we come together. If we are both given to machineries, each of us valuing only what a certain sort of people may become under the peculiar culture of the denomination which he represents, then we talk together, however pleasantly, only over our fences, and shake hands, however cordially, only through the slats.

If we both really value the soul of man, we understand each other; the different methods of our work do not keep us apart but bring us together, for they are the means by which we manifest to one another the deep motive which is the power of both our lives. The fences are turned into bridges. Certainly, Christian union, whenever it comes, must come thus, not by compromise and the adjustment of various forms of government and worship, but by the development in all preachers of all kinds of that value for man in Christ which burrows far beneath the differences of forms and flies far above them.

It may be given to some people in these days to take direct steps toward organic Christian union. I bid them God speed. But if that is not our task let us know, and let us rejoice in knowing, that we are doing, perhaps, as much as they for the millennium, if, in ourselves and those who hear us, by whatever partial name we and they may be called, we are doing what we can to make strong that sense of the value of the human soul which, by its very nature, is universal, and cannot be partial.

Here is where the zealous partisan, who is at the same time an earnest Christian, is often working better than he knows. He is like a jealous farmer who prays for rain to water his field that it may be richer than his neighbor's; but the heaven is too broad for him, and will not limit its bounty by the intention of his prayer. It will rain, but it cannot rain between fences; and so his selfish prayer brings refreshment for the alien acres for which he does not pray.

And as this power in the ministry lies deepest, so it lasts longest. The veteran preacher, I think, keeps the enjoyment and tries to keep the practice of his work later in life than the veteran in almost any other occupation. That always seems to me a touching and convincing proof of the excellence of our calling. It shows better and better as it grows older. The delightful French artist, Millet, used to say to his pupils, "The end of the day is the proof of a picture." *La fin du jour, c'est l'épreuve d'un tableau.* He meant that the twilight hour, when there is not light enough to distinguish details is the most favorable time to judge of a picture as a whole.

And so it is with the ministry. When the cross-lights of jealous emulation and the glare of constant notoriety are softening toward the darkness in which lies the pure judgment of God and the peace of being forgotten by mankind, then that which has been lying behind them all the time comes out; and the old preacher who has ceased to care whether men praise or blame him, who has attained or missed all that there is for him of success or failure here, preaches on still out of the pure sense of how precious the soul of man is, and the pure desire to serve a little more that which is so worthy of his service, before he goes.

Let me follow still farther the enumeration of the qualities which grow up in the preacher from his value for the human soul. Courage is one of its most necessary results. The truest way not to be afraid of the worse part of a man is to value and try to serve his better part. The patriot who really appreciates the valuable principles of his nation's life, is he who most intrepidly rebukes the nation's faults. And Christ was all the more independent of men's whims because of his profound love for them and complete consecration to their needs.

There come three stages in this matter; the first, a flippant superiority which despises the people and thinks of them as only made to take what the preacher chooses to give to them, and to minister to his support; the second, a servile sycophancy which watches all their fancies, and tries to blow whichever way their vane points; and the third, a deep respect which cares too earnestly for what the people are capable of being to let them anywhere fall short of it without a strong remonstrance. You have seen all three in the way in which parents treat their children. I could show you each of the three today in the relation of different preachers to their parishes.

Believe me, the last is the only true independence, the only one that it is worth while to seek, or indeed that a man has any right to seek. An actor may encourage himself by despising or forgetting his audience, but a preacher must go elsewhere for courage. The more you prize the spiritual nature of your people, the more able you will be to oppose their whims. There must be the fountain of your independence.

And here too is the power of simplicity and absolute reality. All turgid rhetoric, all false ornament, all doctrinal fantasticalness must disappear in the presence of a supreme absorbing value for the souls of men. The conscience and the taste, when both are pure, will coincide. Every divorce which separates them is a parting of what God has joined together. The two are most essentially united in the functions of our sacred office.

The man whose eye is set upon the souls of men, and whose heart burns with the desire to save them, chooses with an almost unerring instinct what figure will set the truth most clearly before their minds, what form of appeal will bring it most strongly to their sluggish wills. He takes those and rejects every other. The mere unwarlike-citizen goes lounging through the Tower of London, and among the old armor there he praises that which he calls beautiful. The soldier walks through the same halls and, with a soldier's instinct, thinks no armor beautiful which will not kill the enemy or protect the man who wears it.

That is the final principle of all right choice, the touchstone of good taste. The sermon is to be sacrificed to the soul, the system of work to the purpose of work always. It strikes at the root of all clerical fastidiousness and the tyranny of order. It is wonderful how the character of all ornament in a sermon declares itself. That which really belongs to the purpose of the sermon is always good. That which is there for its own sake every pure taste, however untrained, instantly feels to be bad. The one is like the sculpture on an old cathedral which, however rude, was meant to tell a story. The other is like the carving on our house-fronts which is meant merely to look pretty, and so fails of even that. There are some men born to positions of such dignity that they are doomed to be either illustrious or ridiculous. And so ornament when it is applied to a sermon must either do the lofty work of making truth plain and glorious or it fails of everything. It cannot be allowed simply to amuse or please as may the ornament of an essay or a poem.

But our principle goes deeper than this. This controlling value for the human soul must save a preacher also from a narrow treatment of the souls under his care. If he values them more than any theory of his own about how souls generally are to be treated, he will be broad and try only to lead each into that entire obedience to God which results in such different experiences for us all. The ascetic theorist values self-sacrifice for its own sake and would enforce it indiscriminately. The theorist of self-indulgence says, "No, pain is a curse. Pleasure is good. Shun pain. Do what is pleasant." The teacher who values the souls which he teaches more than any theory says something different from either. He says, "Not enjoyment and not sorrow, but the meeting of your will with the will of God, whatever it may bring, is the purpose of all discipline. Be ready for any way which God shall choose to bring your will to his." But to this large wisdom no teacher can be brought except by a true sense of the preciousness of the soul of man.

It cannot be denied, and it must not be forgotten, that this absorbing conviction of the value of the human soul has its besetting danger. That danger is not slight nor casual. It is important and essential. The danger is lest, in our eagerness to help the spiritual nature which we so highly value, we should be led to judge of the truth of any idea by what we think might be its influences on the soul for which we are so anxious. The tendency to estimate and treat ideas according to what appear their probable effects on human character has been, no doubt, a great besetting sin of spiritual teachers always.

I suppose that it cannot be wholly separated from any vocation which is bound at once to seek for truth and to educate character. This is the way in which a great deal of half-believed doctrine comes to be clinging to and cumbering the church. Men insist on believing and on having other people believe certain doctrines, not because they are reasonably demonstrated to be true, but because, in the present state of things, it would be dangerous to give them up. This is the way in which one man clings to his idea of verbal inspiration, and another to his special theory of the divine justice, and another to his material notion of the resurrection, and yet another to his notion of the Church's authority and the minister's commission. It is a very dangerous danger because it wears the cloak of such a good motive; but it is big with all the evil fruits of superstition. It starts with a lack of faith in the people and in truth and in God. Jesus bids us not to cast pearls before swine, but he does not bid us to feed even swine on pebbles.

"God forbid," says Bishop Watson, "that the search after truth should be discouraged for fear of its consequences. The consequences of truth may be subversive of systems of superstition, but they can never be injurious to the rights or well-founded expectations of the human race." There is nothing that one would wish to say more earnestly to our young and ardent ministers than this. Never sacrifice your reverence for truth to your desire for usefulness. Say nothing which you do not believe to be true because you think it may be helpful. Keep back nothing which you know to be true because you think it may be harmful.

Who are you that you should stint the children's drinking from the cup which their Father bids you to carry to them, or mix it with error because you think they cannot bear it in its purity. We must learn in the first place to form our own judgments of what teachings are true by other tests than the consequences which we think those teachings will produce; and then, when we have formed our judgments, we must trust the truth that we believe and the God from whom it comes, and tell it freely to the people. He is saved from one of the great temptations of the ministry who goes out to his work with a clear and constant certainty that truth is always strong, no matter how weak it looks, and falsehood is always weak, no matter how strong it looks.

But if we bear this danger in our minds and are upon our guard against it, then the value for our brethren's souls will help us to avoid many false standards. It will give interest to many people whom otherwise we should find very uninteresting. There is much in the minister's training to make him value purely intellectual companionships. There is a tendency in many ministers, whose disposition leads them to value truth more than men, to let themselves be drawn almost exclusively into the society of those whose ways of thought are like their own.

I think it is a wonder to many people who are not ministers, how one man who is the pastor of a great parish can be genuinely interested in so many people of such various characters and lives. A good many people and even some clergymen take it for granted that it is not possible, and treat the appearance of such universal interest as a pretence, necessary in order to keep up the parish feeling, and so a very valuable accomplishment in a minister. But it is not so. No man ever did it successfully, year after year, as a pretence.

The secret of it all is simply the great sense of the value of the human soul brought home and individualized upon these human souls committed to our care, as a magistrate sees all the dignity of the law represented in the settlement of the petty quarrel that is brought before his court. The large conception of the value of humanity must go before the special value of one's own parishioners; otherwise the pastoral relation softens into mere personal fondness, or else hardens into a rigid and formal treatment of the people according to arbitrary classifications which lose alike their general humanity and their personal distinctness.

There is a ministry which is all the more personal because of its broad humanness; a ministry which, beginning with the sacredness of man, counts all men sacred, and touches, with its own peculiar pressure upon each, the lives of strong men and little children, of women and boys and girls, of working people and people of idle lives, of saints and sinners, as the rain and dew of God which water the earth feed both the oak tree and the violet; a ministry which makes its care for every soul dearer and more sacred to that soul because it is evidently no mere personal fondness, but one utterance of that Christliness which deeply feels the preciousness of the souls of all God's children.

I have not time to dwell upon the help which a perpetual value for the souls of men must render to our own spiritual life, and so to our efficiency as preachers. Indeed, it is the great power by which our souls must grow. This is the ministry of the people to the preacher, which is often greater than any ministry that the preacher can render to the people. I assure you that the relation between the pastor and his parish is not right if the pastor thinks the obligation to be all upon one side, if while he lives with them and when he leaves them he is not always full of gratitude for what they have done for him.

A pastor who is insensible to this cannot do the best good to his people. And the sort of help which a minister gets from his congregation whose souls he values, is a direct complement of the good which he gets from his study. He needs them both. His study furnishes him with ideas, with intellectual conceptions, and his congregation furnishes him with an atmosphere in which these ideas ripen to their best result.

The minister as he grows older changes some of the opinions which he used to hold. The new opinions, it is to be hoped, are truer than the old ones were. But greater than all such changes are the deepening convictions about all spiritual things which come from the long years of dealing with men's souls and which color every opinion whether new or old. The conviction that truth and destiny are essential and not arbitrary, that Christianity is the personal love and service of Christ, and that salvation is positive, not negative,—convictions such as these they are that fill and richen the preacher's maturer years; and they are convictions whose clearness and strength he owes to that occupation which has both demanded and cultivated a value for the souls of men.

As to the nature of this value for the human soul, notice, I beg you, that it is something more than the mere sense of the soul's danger. It is a deliberate estimate set upon man's spiritual nature in view of its possibilities. The danger in which that nature stands by sin intensifies and emphasizes the value which we set upon it, but it does not create that value. I think that this is important. I think that we are sometimes apt to let our anxiety for the salvation of souls degenerate into a mere pity for the misery into which they may be brought by sin; and the result of such a low thought is that when we have been brought to believe that a soul is, as we say, "safe," that it has been forgiven and will not be punished, we are satisfied.

The thought of rescue has monopolized our religion and often crowded out the thought of culture. I think that the tone of the New Testament is different from this. I know how eminently there the truths of danger and rescue always appear. I know that Christ "came not to call the righteous but sinners to repentance," and that he was called Jesus because he should "save his people from their sins"; but all the time behind the danger lies the value of that spiritual nature which is thus in peril. It is not solely or principally the suffering which the soul must undergo; it is the loss of the soul itself, its failure to be the bright and wonderful thing which, as the soul of God's child, it ought to be.

That is the reason why the process of salvation cannot stop with the removal of penalties and the forgiveness of sins. It must include all the gradual perfection of the soul by faith and love and obedience and patience. This is the reason, too, why those who have taken only a half view of the complete salvation are apt to be severe on those who have seen only the other half. Half a truth is often more jealous of the other half than of an error.

This larger and deeper value for the human soul, I think, is seen in all the sermons of the greatest preachers. It is not mere pity for danger that inspires them to plead with men. That might move them to a sort of supercilious exertion, no matter how intrinsically worthless was the thing in peril, as one might start up to pluck even an insect from the candle's flame. But it is a glowing vision of how great and beautiful the soul of man might be, of what great things it might do if it were thoroughly purified and possessed by the love of God and so opened free channels to his power.

There are special causes which make this great power of which I have been speaking, the sense of the value of the soul, more difficult to win and keep in this age of ours than it has been in many other times. There are two characteristics of our time which have their influence upon it. One is the tendency of philosophy to divert itself from man and turn towards other nature, and in its study of man to busy itself least with his spiritual nature, most with his physical history. The other is the strong philanthropic disposition which prevails about us, the desire to relieve human suffering and to promote human comfort and intelligence. The first of these tendencies would certainly make it more than usually hard to realize the spiritual value of humanity; and the second, while it makes much of man, cares mainly for his material well-being and is always disposed to treat the individual as subservient to the interests of the mass.

The general result is one of which I think that there can be no doubt, a difficulty in the real, vivid, perpetual sense of the worth of man's spiritual nature such as has very rarely beset those in other ages who have tried to serve their fellow-men. At such a time we need to hold very strongly to the constant facts of human life which lie below all such temporary changes, and to be very sure of their reappearance. We need a keen, quick-sighted faith which shall discover the first signs of what must surely come, a reaction from the partial tendencies of the time. We need a generous fairness to discover thought and feeling which is really spiritual but which has cloaked itself, even to its own confusion, in the forms and phrases of the time.

But, more than all of these, we who are preaching in such days as these need to understand these methods by which in any time we must acquire and preserve the sense of the preciousness of the human soul. What are these methods? First of all, before a man can value the souls of other men, he must have learnt to value his own soul. And a man learns to value his own soul only as he is conscious of the solemn touches of the Spirit of the Lord upon it.

Ah, my friends, here is the real reason why he who preaches to the inner life of others must himself have had an inner life. Not that he may take his own experience and narrowly make it the type to which all other experiences must conform; but that, having learnt how God loves him, having felt in many a silent limit and many a tumultuous crisis the pressure of God's hands full of care and wisdom, he may know, as he looks from his pulpit, that behind every one of those faces into which he looks there is a soul for which God cares with the same thoughtfulness. In his closet he has first seen the light which from his closet he carries forth to illuminate the humanity of his congregation and bring out all its colors. The personal desire to be pure and holy, the personal consciousness of power to be pure and holy through Christ, reveals the possibility of other men.

Again, a preacher's view of all theology ought to be colored with the preciousness of the human soul. It is possible for two men to hold the same doctrine and yet to differ very widely in this respect. To one of them the Christian truths reveal much of the glory and mercy of God; to the other they shine also with the value of the spiritual manhood. To this last the Incarnation reveals the essential dignity of that nature into union with which the Deity could so marvelously enter. The Redemption bears witness of the unspeakable love of God, but also of the value underneath the sin of man, which made the jewel worth cleaning. And all the methods of Sanctification, all the disciplines of the Spirit open before the watchful minister new insight into the possibilities of that being upon whom such bounty of grace is lavished.

I think that we ought to distrust at least the form in which we are holding any theological idea, if it is not helping to deepen in us the sense of the preciousness of the human soul, first impressing it as a conviction and then firing it unto a passion. There is not one truth which man may know of God which does not legitimately bear this fruit. I beg you more and more to test the way in which you hold the truth of God by the power which it has to fill you with honor for the spiritual life of man.

It is evident as we look at the ministry of Jesus that he was full of reverence for the nature of the men and women whom he met. There was nothing which he knew of God which did not make his Father's children precious to him. We see it even in his lofty and tender courtesy. How often I have seen a minister's manners either proudly distant and conscious of his own importance, or fulsome and fawning with a feeble affectionateness that was unworthy of a man, and have thought that what he needed was that noble union of dignity and gentleness which came to Jesus from his divine insight into the value of the human soul.

One other source from which the knowledge of this value comes let me mention in a single word. It is by working for the soul that we best learn what the soul is worth. If ever in your ministry the souls of those committed to your care grow dull before you, and you doubt whether they have any such value that you should give your life for them, go out and work for them; and as you work their value shall grow clear to you. Go and try to save a soul and you will see how well it is worth saving, how capable it is of the most complete salvation. Not by pondering upon it, nor by talking of it, but by serving it you learn its preciousness. So the father learns the value of his child, and the teacher of his scholar, and the patriot of his native land. And so the Christian, living and dying for his brethren's souls, learns the value of those souls for which Christ lived and died.

And if you ask me whether this whose theory I have been stating is indeed true in fact, whether in daily work for souls year after year a man does see in those souls glimpses of such a value as not merely justifies the little work which he does, but even makes credible the work of Christ, I answer, surely, yes. All other interest and satisfaction of the ministry completes itself in this, that year by year the minister sees more deeply how well worthy of infinitely more than he can do for it is the human soul for which he works.

I do not know how I can better close my lectures to you than with that testimony. May you find it true in your experience. May the souls of men be always more precious to you as you come always nearer to Christ, and see them more perfectly as he does. I can ask no better blessing on your ministry than that.

And so may God our Father guide and keep you always.

CHAPTER 24

THE TRIUMPH OF ROMANTICISM

WASHINGTON GLADDEN: "THY KINGDOM COME"

*The Social Gospel movement exhibited many characteristics of Romanticism (***see Vol. 1, pp. 649-54***). While its great theologian was Walter Rauschenbusch,*[1] *its "father" was Washington Gladden. The sermon that follows shows the typical understanding of the kingdom of God as a perfect social order. Gladden's interest is not confined to the problems of working people in an industrial society, but extends as well to those of women, prisoners, the mentally ill, and slaves. Something of Gladden's rhetorical skill can be seen in his use of anaphora when he begins five successive paragraphs with the phrase "Thy Kingdom come!" The sermon is taken from his volume* The Lord's Prayer: Seven Homilies *(Boston: Houghton, Mifflin, & Co., 1881), 59-81.*

The Eternal Kingdom

Thy Kingdom come (Mt. 6:10).

What is the Kingdom of God for whose coming we are taught to pray in this second petition of the Lord's Prayer? The phrase is used with a variety of meanings in the New Testament, sometimes in a narrow sense as signifying phases of individual experience, sometimes in a large sense as including all that the world has known or can know of the power and the love of God. We must suppose that the phrase is used here in its largest sense. It is not likely that in so brief a prayer as this any partial meaning would be given to the words employed.

The orthodox Jews had a very narrow idea of what the Kingdom of God was to be. They thought that it was simply a political machine to be set up at Jerusalem—a monarchy, with a king designated by divine power, under which the autonomy of the Jewish nation would be restored, the Romans banished from the Holy Land, and the territorial inheritance promised to Abraham occupied by his descendants. This was what they were looking for; this was the Messiah's Kingdom as they conceived and expected it.

Certain Pharisees with this thought in their minds came to our Lord one day, and demanded of him when the Kingdom of God should come. He answered them and said, "The Kingdom of God cometh not with observation." "Comes not," as Robinson explains this phrase, "so that its progress may be watched with the eyes." "Neither shall they say 'Lo here! or, lo there!'" "None shall be able," says Alford, "to point here or there for a proof of its coming." It is not a matter of locality. Palestine is not the territory of its dominion; Jerusalem is not the seat of its power. "Behold the Kingdom of God is within you!" "The Savior," says Olshausen, "withdraws the Kingdom of God wholly from the local and phenomenal world and transfers it to the world of spirit."

This, then, is our Lord's answer to the Pharisees; and it may be instructive to many in this day whose faith clings to a material kingdom, who are waiting to hear some one say "Lo here! or, lo there!"

"The Kingdom of God," says Paul in his letter to the Romans, "is not meat and drink." No; and it is nothing that subsists on meat and drink. Flesh and blood do not inherit it, neither in this world nor in the world to come. The throne of its empire, the weapons of its warfare, are not carnal. What is it, then? "It is righteousness and peace and joy in the Holy Ghost." That is Paul's definition of the Kingdom of God. The Savior tells us where it is. It is not in Jerusalem; it is not visible anywhere to mortal eyes; it is unseen and spiritual. It is within you. Paul tells us what it is. It is not meat and drink,—it is not any material or earthly organization with a visible head; it is righteousness and peace and joy in the Holy Ghost.

The Kingdom of God is then in its essence a spiritual Kingdom; the seat of his dominion is in the thoughts and affections of men; the tokens of its sway are a deepening purity, and a growing love among the children of men. Of course it takes hold on things outward, also, and shapes them by its law, as we shall see by and by; it changes the manners and the fashions and the laws and the social relations of men; it is not in its essence meat and drink, but it rules the lives of men who are its loyal subjects whether they eat or drink or whatever they do.

Still it affects the forms and fashions of life only as it transforms the thoughts and the desires of men; it works from within outward; its forces are all spiritual, though its manifestations are visible in all the realms of life. And it includes everything that is true, everything that is pure, everything that is lovely, everything that is honest and brave and sound and sweet in the universe. Whatsoever is good is of God, and is a sign of the rule of his Kingdom in the world. Whatever shows improvement—whether it is from good to better, or from worse to better—is a token of the progress of God's Kingdom in the world. Wherever morality and purity are gaining, wherever the vile are becoming less vile, and the cruel less cruel, and the covetous less covetous, there the Kingdom of God is advancing.

"There is none good but one, that is God," said our Lord himself; and there is no good in any man, from the feeblest virtue in the worst man to the grandest integrity in the best man,—there is no good in any beneficent institution or in any kindly custom or in any refinement of social life,—that is not a divine inspiration; that is not the result of obedience to the divine law; that is not, therefore, a token of the presence and the prevalence in some degree of God's Kingdom.

When we intelligently offer this petition, then, we are asking for nothing less than this—that the light and love and power of God may increase and abound everywhere in the world.

I do not think we have the right to give the words any narrower meaning than this.

"God's Kingdom is here already, then," some one may say; "why should we be taught to pray for the coming of it? To say 'Thy Kingdom come' is to imply that it is not here."

To this question various answers are given. To one of the most common of these we have referred already. When we pray, "Thy Kingdom come," some say we are praying for the Second Coming of Christ. But they who thus distinguish between the Father and the Son must remember that this is a prayer which the Son bids us address to the Father. If there is any difference between the Father's Kingdom and the Son's Kingdom, it is the Father's Kingdom and not the Son's whose coming we here supplicate. Besides, as it has been intimated, we can hardly suppose that this special sense would be given to a petition meant to be as comprehensive as this one. It is far more natural to give it a broader meaning.

Others say that this is a prayer for the organization of Christianity. The Kingdom here intended, says one learned commentator, is "the Messiah's Kingdom, which in organized form had not yet come, but was proclaimed by the Lord himself as at hand." But I do not think that our Lord ever cared so much for organization as to make the fashioning of a form of church government one of the main things to be prayed for in so short a prayer as this. No doubt organization is important; but it is altogether secondary, and secondary things are not provided for in this prayer.

Besides, the church was organized in Jerusalem after the Pentecost, and it has always had an organization since. Whatever other defects may have been charged upon it, it has not often been deficient in organization since that day. It has generally had machinery enough, far too much. So that this petition must have been practically obsolete ever since the days when the first seven deacons were chosen. If, when we say "Thy Kingdom come," we mean only "Let thy church possess an organized form," we are praying an utterly superfluous prayer. For there are few of us who could honestly ask that the church have any more of organized form than it has today. One great trouble with it is that it has so much more machinery than power.

To suppose, then, that the petition only asks for the return of Jesus Christ in a bodily form to earth, or for the organization of his church, is to give it a meaning altogether inadequate. It must have that larger and more spiritual meaning which we have already found in it.

"But why then," the questioner persists, "should we say 'Thy Kingdom come'?" If God's Kingdom is the sum of all beneficent forces, of all holy influences, of all truth and all love and all righteousness, why should we pray that it may come? It is here already. The world has never been wholly destitute of righteousness. God has never been without a witness on the earth. Purity, truth, and love have always had a place on this planet. If they belong to the foundations of God's Kingdom, then God's Kingdom has always been here since the morning-stars first sang together and all the sons of God shouted for joy. Why then do we pray "Thy Kingdom come"?

Why do we wish or ask in these days of March that summer may come? That would surely be a proper wish and might be a fitting prayer. Yet all the elements of the summer are here today. The earth, from whose fruitful breast the summer springs, lies waiting here; in her veins a myriad lives are throbbing; the mighty prince of light whose kiss is to waken all this life is shining down on us every day; air and light and moisture and warmth, all the forces that make the summer, are here; every day the sun is wheeling his chariot a little higher into the sky; every day the empire of the light enlarges, and the realm of night is narrowed; yet, though the elements and forces out of which the summer comes are here, we might wish to have them here in greater fullness and in greater power.

If we should make our illustration more specific it would not be any less pertinent. Take the sunlight itself, the great source of physical life upon this planet. It is here, it has been here, who knows how many ages? The tribes of earth have been rejoicing in its beauty and nourishing themselves upon its vital heat since the mists of the world's early morning first broke above its watery wastes; yet we do not cease to desire that the sunlight may continue to come. We have it, but we still have need of it; there will never be a season when we can dispense with its life-giving influence.

Now the analogy between these two relations—that of the kingdom of life on earth to the sun, and that of the Kingdom of righteousness on earth to God—is very close. And if it is lawful and rational to pray to the Father in heaven that he will continue to send his sun upon the evil and the good, then it is lawful and rational to pray "Thy Kingdom come!" If the first prayer does not necessarily deny that the kingdoms of life are already established on the earth, the other does not necessarily deny that the spiritual Kingdom of God is already established on the earth.

The petition asks, then, not that righteousness and peace and joy in the Holy Ghost may begin on the earth, for they begun to be long ago; but that they may continue, and that they may increase. Probably it is the increase of this Kingdom that is more specifically intended. It is a fuller, a broader, a more glorious manifestation of these great principles and forces. It is a prayer that the lives which are not now under their sway may be brought into subjection to them; that the institutions that now are ruled by selfishness and strife may be pervaded by them; that the homes in which vice and greed and worldliness now reign may be cleansed and hallowed by the spirit of purity and love; that the societies in which frivolity and vanity now rule may be ruled by soberness and modesty and quietness; that many lands which are now habitations of cruelty may hear and obey the gospel of good-will.

It is not a prayer that the leaven may be brought and placed in the measures of meal, but that its subtle, transforming influence may extend until it shall pervade the whole lump. It is not a prayer that the mustard seed may be planted, but that its growth may be hastened by the gentle dews of God's grace and the sunlight of his truth until it shall become a great tree whose branches shall be vocal with the songs of Paradise, and in whose shade all the weary of the world may rest.

This is, then, the most comprehensive petition of the Lord's prayer. Indeed it is the most comprehensive petition that it is possible for man to utter; there is hardly anything that we ask for that is not summed up in this prayer. It is a prayer that the whole world may grow better and brighter; that all the people in the world may grow gentler and stronger and truer and kinder and happier year by year. And it is a recognition of the fact that this can come to pass only as the world is filled with the knowledge of God and ruled by his law; only as the people in the world come to know him better and to obey him more perfectly.

It is a prayer that has been answered too, how many times, and how abundantly! People sometimes question whether prayer is ever answered; but here is a prayer that Christians have been offering now for eighteen hundred years, and if you want to know whether it has been answered read the whole of history since Christ ascended.

"Thy Kingdom come!" the disciples prayed; and presently a bloody persecution fell upon them in Jerusalem, and drove them forth from the Holy City and made them homeless wanderers. That was a strange way of answering the prayer. But "they that were scattered abroad went everywhere preaching the word." Up and down the rugged roads of Palestine they went proclaiming the glad tidings of great joy. It was not long before the messengers found their way over the heights of Mount Taurus, and here and there a center of light was kindled in the dark provinces of Asia Minor; then the voice came to Paul summoning him to Macedonia, and Europe was invaded by the intrepid apostle, who planted the standard of the Gospel on the classic field of Philippi and on the heights of the Areopagus. From these small beginnings the leaven of Christianity has spread, until now nearly a third part of the human race acknowledge Jesus Christ as Lord.

This is simply putting into three sentences the story of the outward progress in the world of that specialized and organized manifestation of God's truth which we call the Christian religion. And while we freely admit that these peoples that are now called Christian are far from comprehending Christianity in its highest excellence and beauty, we may safely say that there is not one among them to which Christianity has not proved a blessing; not one whose darkness it has not enlightened, whose life it has not lifted up; not one in which there is not more of righteousness and peace and heavenly hope and joy than there would have been if the people had not heard of the coming of the Son of man.

But the progress of God's Kingdom in the world has not been confined to Christian lands, nor even to the Christian era. It is a prayer that devout men have always been offering and that God has always been answering. When Gautama Siddhartha, in the Indian city of Kapilavastu, four or five hundred years before the coming of our Lord, learned and taught the great renunciation, the Kingdom of God drew near to all those Eastern lands.

For though the doctrines of Buddhism are but a partial revelation of God's truth and love, and though the rays of light that were mingled with its darkness have been greatly blurred by the perversions and corruptions of later days, yet there was truth in it, and the truth in it was God's truth; and there was love in it, and it was God's love shed abroad in the heart of Gautama; and it lifted millions of people up to a higher and purer life, and there was more of righteousness and more of peace and more of holy joy in their hearts and in their homes because of it; and therefore we know that it was not wholly the kingdom of the evil one, but the Kingdom of God that Gautama Siddhartha, in some blind and imperfect way, was building.

God had some better thing for us than he had for either Jews or Buddhists; but he had some good thing for them too; and the light that they saw, though it shone through many mists of superstition, was a beam from the Eternal Sun of righteousness. And so in other lands, Christian and Pagan, God has been preparing the ways by which his Kingdom may come into the world, by which it may enter and take possession of the lives of men and work from within outward in their languages and their laws and their arts and their social customs.

"Thy Kingdom come!" good Christians prayed. And he who hears the cry of his children came down to earth and stretched forth his hand to woman, so long the slave of man's power, and the drudge of his indolence, and the victim of his passions, and lifted her up, and clothed her motherhood with dignity, and her womanhood with divinity, and gave us by her hand the blessing of home, the best of all earth's precious things.

"Thy Kingdom come!" the strong of faith were crying; and a Presence unseen by men stood among the prisoners in the dungeons that were festering dens of disease and vileness, and laid its gentle hand upon these hapless children of the evil, and lifted the weight of hate and scorn that made their lot so desperate, and sought to lead them forth to ways of purity.

"Thy Kingdom come!" God's children cried; and the victims of insanity saw a beam of hope through the mental darkness in which they were walking, and found themselves no longer chained and scourged like criminals, but gently led and kindly treated.

"Thy Kingdom come!" was the voice of millions who groaned in slavery, and of millions more who remembered their brethren in bonds as bound with them; and one by one the fetters have snapped asunder,—the strong shackles of the Roman law, the wounding cords of feudal villenage, the degrading toils of British slavery, the prescriptive manacles of Russian serfdom,—until even in our own land, and in our own day—

Our eyes have seen the glory of the coming of the Lord,

as he comes proclaiming liberty throughout the land to all the inhabitants thereof.

"Thy Kingdom come!" the children of the light were pleading; and the hierarchies that sought to confine the thought of men were baffled and paralyzed, and the Bible was unchained, and the ways that lead to the mercy-seat were opened to the feet of all penitent believers.

Thus it is by these mighty changes which have liberated and elevated and enlightened the children of men that God's Kingdom has been coming through all the ages, with increasing glory and enlarging power. Sometimes we hear the voice of his herald crying, "Who is this that cometh from Edom, with dyed garments from Bozrah, glorious in his apparel, traveling in the greatness of his strength? He who hath trodden down the people in his wrath and trampled upon them in his fury." Sometimes the voice cries, "how beautiful upon the mountains are the feet of him that bringeth salvation, that publisheth peace!" But whether he come in his might with confused noise and garments rolled in blood, or whether he come in his gentleness, stealing in by all sweet influences to men's hearts, and kindling in them better wishes and kindlier feelings,—he is always coming; and the prayer that his children night and day are lifting to his throne is answered speedily,—yea with the light of every sunrising and the smile of every watching star.

And now, we come to ask whether there is anything we can do toward the answering of this prayer. Truly we can do much and in many ways. "Though the greatest," says Mr. Ruskin, "it is that everlasting Kingdom which the poorest of us can advance. We cannot hasten Christ's coming. 'Of the day and the hour knoweth none.' But the Kingdom of God is as a grain of mustard seed; we can sow of it: it is as a foam-globe of leaven; we can mingle it: and its glory and its joy are that even the birds of the air can lodge in the branches of it."

Even the children can help to bring, in many places, this Kingdom of God for which they daily pray. I heard a mother telling the other day of her children who had quarreled sometimes, as many children do, I fear, but who had both been made so thoroughly sorry and ashamed on account of one of their quarrels that they were careful for many days after that not to say a bitter word, or to do a hateful deed. So peace came to that home through the prayer and the watching of these two Christian children; and peace, you know, is one of the signs of the Kingdom of God in the world. And I hope that when the children offer this prayer they will remember that this is one of the ways in which it is answered, and in which they may help in answering it.

And wherever we help one another to the living of better lives,—to be more truthful or upright or honorable or kind, to be more faithful in our duties to God or to men,—there we are helping to answer our prayer, and to hasten the coming of God's Kingdom.

You offer this prayer sometimes, many of you, most of you, I trust. Do you always stop to think what it means? For it has a personal bearing. I have said that it is a very comprehensive petition, and so it is but it has a very direct application to the life of every individual who utters it. It is like the "whosoever" of the Gospel; what makes it such a momentous word to me is the fact that it means *me*.

You pray that the Kingdom of God may come? Do you want it to come to Massachusetts? Do you desire that it should come to Springfield? Do you wish to have it come to your store, your office, your shop, your study, your table, your toilet, your closet, your heart?

How near to you do you desire that the Kingdom of God should come?

JOHN A. BROADUS: "IMAGINATION IN PREACHING"

The Romantic perspective on preaching became institutionalized with the publication in 1870 of what was to remain the standard textbook on homiletics for almost a century, John A. Broadus's A Treatise on the Preparation and Delivery of Sermons *(see* ***Vol. 1, pp. 654-57****). The author, a figure of Romance himself, spent most of his life on the faculty of the Southern Baptist Theological Seminary, first in Greenville, South Carolina, and later in Louisville, Kentucky. Best known as a New Testament scholar, he developed his famous textbook in the seminary's first session after the Civil War when he had only one student in homiletics (and that one blind). The thoroughness with which he prepared for any responsibility is seen in the lectures he prepared for that student. Broadus drew heavily upon the rhetorical theory of the British school of Blair, Campbell, and Whately. The section on imagination below is taken* *from* Preparation and Delivery, *new (37th) ed., ed. Edwin Charles Dargan (New York: Hodder & Stoughton; George H. Doran, 1898), 420-30.*

Chapter V

Imagination in Preaching

Imagination, as we have already seen, is among the leading characteristics of eloquence. It plays a highly important part in the construction of discourse and in style, and it has much to do even with the invention of materials. Though repeatedly referred to, under these several heads, it is thought to require at this point some more particular discussion, as to its office in oratory, and the means of its cultivation.

I. Uses of Imagination to the Orator

The popular conception of imagination still is, that it assists the orator only in the way of producing high-wrought imagery, in letting off such fire-works of fancy as sophomores affect, and half-educated people admire. But modern psychology tends more and more to assign imagination a high position and a wide and varied domain. It is coming to be recognized as giving indispensable aid in scientific research and philosophical abstraction, in the formation of geometrical and ethical, as well as of artistic ideals, in the varied tasks of practical invention, and even in the comprehension and conduct of practical life. When entering some strange country, or when brought by great social convulsions into a new state of things, most men are unable, through deficiency of imagination, fully to realize the new situation, and promptly to seize upon the central and controlling forces. Accordingly Napoleon said, "The men of imagination rule the world."

This noble faculty is possessed in a high degree by every true orator. Without it, a man may be instructive and convincing, may influence others by his practical energy, his resolution and determination, but he can never exert the peculiar power of eloquence. A preacher without imagination may be respected for his sound sense, may be loved for his homely goodness, but he will not move a congregation, he will not be a power in the community. If on the other hand he have a perverted or an undisciplined imagination, it may ruin his usefulness. It is a matter on which preachers seldom bestow any thoughtful attention; and yet few things are so important to their real success, as the possession, the culture, the control, of imagination.

The terms imagination and fancy were once practically equivalent. The latter, as shown by the old spelling phantsy, is a corruption of the Greek term *phantasia,* which was afterwards reintroduced in its longer form phantasy, and assigned by usage to special senses. Addison said that he used the words imagination and fancy indiscriminately. Some writers, particularly Ruskin, are disposed to claim that there are two distinct faculties of the mind, which they would denote by these two terms. The more common, and apparently the more correct opinion is, that what we call imagination and fancy are but different forms and modes of exercise of the same faculty. We call it fancy when playing on the mere surface of things, imagination when penetrating to the heart, the essence; fancy when sportive or cold, imagination when passionate, or at least serious. Imagination "cannot but be serious; she sees too far, too darkly, too solemnly, too earnestly, ever to smile. There is something in the heart of everything, if we can reach it, that we shall not be inclined to laugh at. The 'innumerable laughter' of the sea is on its surface, not in the deep."[2]

(1) Imagination is employed by the orator in the construction of discourse. To give familiar materials any fresh interest, they must be brought into new combinations; and to form a *discourse* at all, the materials must be made into a complete and symmetrical structure. Piles of bricks and lumber and sand are as much a house, as the mere piling up of thoughts will constitute a discourse. The builder, of palace or of cabin, works by constructive imagination; and it is the same faculty that builds a speech. In fact imagination, the wonder-worker, does much more than this. It is only a lower imagination that takes fragments of material, and builds them, each fragment preserving its individuality, into a new structure; high, intense imagination fuses the materials, reduces them to their natural elements, and forms of them a structure possessing complete unity. The one process is a new composition of fragments; the other a new organization of elements. The one cements the materials together, or at best welds them together; the other makes them *grow* together, by furnishing a principle of vitality which takes up the analyzed material and organizes it according to new laws. Imagination does not create thought; but it organizes thought into forms as new as the equestrian statue of bronze is unlike the metallic ores when they lay in the mine. This constructing, fashioning, organizing function of the imagination is exercised in forming a poem, or a story, but still more in forming a discourse,

where there is far greater need of unity, symmetry, and adaptation to a specific design.

And not only is it needed in constructing discourses, but every paragraph, yea every sentence, is properly a work of imagination, a work of art. The painter, sculptor, architect, does not fashion merely the general outline of his work, and leave the details to chance. The whole is but the parts taken together. Each part must have a certain completeness in itself, and yet must be in itself incomplete, being but a fragment of one whole. So must it be in the construction of discourse.

(2) If, as Porter says, "to invent or discover, is always to recombine, to adjust in new positions objects or parts of objects which have never been so connected before,"[3] then imagination has no little to do with the invention of thought. What are its precise functions in this respect, students of psychology have not yet settled. There can be no doubt that it does somehow aid us in penetrating to the heart of a subject, and developing it from within; that it thus assists the work of original analysis, as well as that of exposition; though Ruskin's theory of "the penetrative imagination" is, as he virtually confesses, uncertain and obscure.

(3) The orator uses imagination in the production of images. Often the idea he wishes to present can itself be converted into an image. Imagination thus gives the masses of thought a definite shape, a clear-cut outline, and sometimes makes them stand out as in a stereoscopic picture. This excites the imagination of another, and thus affects his feelings. Objects of sense affect the feelings most powerfully, and images more closely resemble objects of sense than do mere ideas. Thus if, instead of dwelling upon the idea of benevolence, we bring forward the image of a benevolent man or a benevolent action, it is much more affecting.

And whether the particular idea can or cannot be converted into an image, we may associate with it, may group around it, by resemblance or analogy, or by contrast, some other idea or ideas which *can* be formed into images, and which will reflect their light and splendor upon the thought in hand. This is Illustration, with all its power not only to gratify the taste, but to assist comprehension, to carry conviction, and to awaken emotion.

It is thus mainly through imagination that we touch the feelings, and thereby bring truth powerfully to bear upon the will, which is the end and the very essence of eloquence. And on the other hand passion kindles imagination. Love, for instance, will cause the dullest mind to give forth some sparks of imagination. Anger, overwhelming grief, passionate supplication, will often struggle to express itself by means of the boldest images. Thus imagination and passion continually act and react, causing the one to glow more brightly and the other to grow fiercer in its blaze.

(4) Another use of imagination, though not wholly distinct from the last, is in realizing and depicting what the Scriptures reveal. We have already noticed how much of the Bible consists of narrative, and how important it is that the preacher should be able vividly to describe its scenes and events. "Historical imagination," in reproducing the past, is one of the favorite ideas of our day. In the exercise of it great care must be taken that it shall be directed and controlled by thorough knowledge of the times reproduced, and true sympathy with their spirit, or we shall carry back our own experiences and our modern conceptions, and make, as historical description often has done, an utterly erroneous representation. But with this caution, historical imagination may be declared indispensable, not only to description of scripture history, but to the just comprehension of the whole system of doctrine and duty, for all rests upon a basis of fact. Controversialists, for example, often greatly err, from failing to realize the circumstances of the primitive age, and thus misconceiving the precise aim of many a lesson or observance; and likewise from failing to understand the real views and sentiments of those whom they oppose.

And not only as to the past is imagination needed; it is requisite if we are justly to conceive and vividly to realize the scripture revelations concerning the unseen world and the eternal future. Faith believes these revelations, and imagination, aroused by faith and called into its service, makes the things unseen and eternal a definite reality to the mind, so that they affect the feelings almost like objects of sense, and become a power in our earthly life. It may also to some extent fill out the Bible pictures of the unseen world, by following the analogies of this world; but there is here demanded a moderation and reserve, a care in distinguishing between the revealed and the supposed, which in some books and many sermons are sadly wanting.

2. Means of Cultivating the Imagination

If this faculty has so much to do with the construction and style, and even with inventing the materials of discourse, it becomes a matter of very high importance that preachers should employ the best means of giving it thorough cultivation, and bringing it under complete control.

(1) Imagination is awakened and invigorated by communion with *nature*. A certain indefinable sympathy exists, by a law of our being, between external nature and ourselves. Its forms and hues have a meaning for us more subtle than language conveys, and excite in us strange longings and kindlings of soul, till we idealize all we behold.

And our thoughtful observation of nature may be quickened and exalted by science. The systematic study of minerals, vegetables, animals, reveals to us new and wonderful things, teaches us to read, where we had not seen it before, the handwriting of our God. Geology acquaints us with earth's mighty past, Astronomy introduces us to the ever widening and brightening glories of the wonder-crowded universe, till the "music of the spheres" attains for us a sublime, orchestral grandeur, an unearthly sweetness, a wealth of precious meaning, which the wise Greek never knew.

We need not now to people all natural objects with unseen, half-human creatures, nor need we lose ourselves in the vagueness of pantheism; our personality may everywhere indulge its longing for communion with a person, we may find in all nature the personal God.—But words are here vain. If we wish for power of imagination, let us observe, contemplate, commune with nature.

(2) *Art* and *Literature* may greatly aid us. Nature is by most of us very imperfectly understood and appreciated till interpreted to us by the poet or the artist. Perhaps we grew up amid glorious mountains, or beside the many-sounding sea, and yet little knew their meaning, little felt their inspiration, till some high priest of nature had taught us, by the pen or the pencil, how to behold and comprehend and sympathize.

Sculpture, painting, architecture, music, have a strange power to develop the imagination in general, and sometimes to stimulate it for particular efforts, and they can be devoid of interest to none who possess this faculty in even a moderate degree. When Andrew Fuller stopped suddenly amid the architectural glories of Cambridge, and proposed to his guide to go home and discuss with him the doctrine of justification, he betrayed that deficiency of imagination which is conspicuous in the structure and the style of his otherwise admirable sermons. There is many a preacher who could tell how some picture, perhaps casually looked at, has helped him in making a sermon; there is many a one utterly unable to tell how much the general study of works of art has contributed to develop his imagination.

In our country few have any considerable opportunity for beholding the most inspiring works of art. But the *poets* are accessible to all, and they are here our chief teachers. They see the analogies of external nature to moral and religious truth as most of us cannot; and they open up to us unknown depths in our own nature. From them we may learn how to observe and compare, how to depict and interpret; though we must not forget that they aim mainly to please, while we must subordinate everything to spiritual profit, and that such difference of aim should lead to great difference of method.

And it is not of necessity those poets who seem to the general reader to show most imagination, but those who most kindle *our* imagination, that will in this respect be most useful. Thus the poems of Wordsworth and the Brownings are much more profitable than those of Moore and Scott. We must seek by effort of our own imagination to conceive the poet's image, if we are to have not mere entertainment but improvement; and he is for us the best poet who awakens our imagination, gives it general direction, stimulates it by some of the most suggestive details, and leaves it to do all the rest for itself. That is to say, in order to [gain?] the benefit here proposed, we must *study* poetry.

There is much highly imaginative prose which has a similar value. Novel-reading, while well known to injure many, would if properly managed be to some preachers exceedingly profitable, in respect to imagination and literary taste. As a rule, one should read only the very best works of the very best novelists; and he should never read two novels in succession, but always put between them several works of a very different kind. And there is often more to be *learned* from a novel, if at an early period we turn over and find out how the story will end, or if we deliberately examine one previously read.

Goethe, Edgar Poe, and many others, have given us imaginative writings not properly called tales, which may in like manner be profitable. Some of the historians powerfully appeal to and exercise the imagination of their readers; for example, Macaulay and Motley. And the great orators and preachers present to us imagination operating in precisely those methods with which we are most concerned. If one wishes to stimulate in himself the desire for affluence of imaginative thought and diction, let him read Plato, Cicero, Chrysostom, Jeremy Taylor, Milton, Burke, Chalmers; if he wishes to chasten himself into a more sober and regulated use of imagination, so that it shall be duly subordinated to other faculties, let him read Demosthenes, Tacitus, Daniel Webster, Robert Hall. In general it must be remembered that here, as elsewhere, appetite is not always a sure guide.

(3) After all, the great means of cultivating imagination, as is the case with all our faculties, is actual *exercise*. The excessive display of second-rate

imagination which some men make so offensive, drives other men to the opposite extreme, so that they shrink from illustration and imagery where they are really needful, and never stop to consider how numerous and varied and surpassingly important are the functions of this much-abused faculty. Let a man freely exercise imagination, in constructing and inventing, in picturing and illustrating, in reproducing the past and giving vivid reality to the unseen world; but let him everywhere exercise it under the control of sound judgment and good taste, and above all of devout feeling and a solemn sense of responsibility to God.

There is also another, an ethical, sense in which we must learn to control the imagination. "Religion is the art of disciplining the imagination."[4] The imaginative reproduction of scenes witnessed, read, or heard of; and the imaginative construction of new scenes, may be helpful or harmful to the moral nature according as these scenes are good or bad, elevating or degrading. It is impossible to estimate what a profound influence a man's imagination has upon his moral and spiritual life; and thus through these channels, as well as more directly, it has for the preacher a momentous importance in his preaching.

Notes

1. Clyde E. Fant Jr. has translated Rauschenbusch's sermon notes from German with the aid of Robert Payne's shorthand transcription in *20 Centuries of Great Preaching: An Encyclopedia of Preaching* (Waco, Tex.: Word, 1971), 7:144-69. The speeches range from lectures representing early conceptual developments of "A Theology for the Social Gospel" to relatively traditional sermons to his working-class German Baptist congregation in Hell's Kitchen on such subjects as heaven, salvation, and total abstinence.
2. Ruskin, *Modern Painters,* 2:166. (The only footnotes of Broadus that are included here are citations of words quoted in the text. No effort will be made to trace bibliographical information about the works he cited.)
3. *On the Human Intellect,* § 364.
4. Abraham Tucker, quoted by Hervey, 68.

PART V

THE CENTURY OF CHANGE

CHAPTER 25

PASTORAL COUNSELING THROUGH PREACHING

HARRY EMERSON FOSDICK: THE PROJECT METHOD OF PREACHING

*The first great innovation in homiletical theory in the twentieth century was made by Harry Emerson Fosdick, the Baptist preacher for whom John D. Rockefeller was to build Riverside Church in New York City (**see Vol. 1, pp. 665-69**). That innovation was made, however, in an article Fosdick published in a popular magazine while still in his first pastorate. It was his assumption that to be effective, a sermon needs to begin with a real problem or issue in the lives of the people who hear it and offer them a way of dealing with it victoriously. While he thought of this as pastoral counseling on a group scale, his understanding of such counseling did not have the psychotherapeutic implications that it was later to acquire.*

A pacifist and a leading advocate of historical-critical biblical interpretation in the fundamentalist-modernist controversy, Fosdick was also one of the first preachers to have his sermons aired on a national radio network. In the period between the two World Wars, his was one of the most familiar voices in America.

The article was not originally written for a professional journal, but for a secular periodical, Harper's Magazine; *it appeared in the July 1928 issue. It was reprinted in* Harry Emerson Fosdick's Art of Preaching: An Anthology, *ed. Lionel Crocker (Springfield, Ill.: Charles C. Thomas, 1971).*

What Is the Matter with Preaching?

One might think that such a subject would presuppose preachers as an audience and that an article on it should appear in a magazine devoted to their special interests. On the contrary, there are only about 200 thousand preachers in the United States, but there are millions who more or less regularly enjoy or endure their ministrations. Whatever, therefore, is the matter with preaching is quantitatively far more a concern of laymen than of clergymen. Moreover, if laymen had a clear idea as to the reasons for the futility, dullness, and general ineptitude of so much preaching, they might do something about it. Customers usually have something to say about the quality of goods supplied to them.

Of course, there is no process by which wise and useful discourses can be distilled from unwise and useless personalities, and the ultimate necessity in the ministry, as everywhere else, is sound and intelligent character. "You cannot carve rotten wood," says a Chinese proverb. Every teacher of preaching sometimes feels its truth when he tries to train his students. Whether the grade of intelligence now represented in candidates for the ministry is lower than it used to be cannot easily be determined. As we grow older, we tend to idealize the state of things in our youth and to suspect the progressive deterioration of the human race. One theological professor, aged seventy, obviously did this when he told his classes that each new generation of students had known less than their predecessors and that he was curiously hoping to live to see the next, which he was certain would know nothing.

The best brains today are naturally drawn into occupations other than art, literature, music, education, and religion. These spiritual interests are not the crucial and distinctive concerns of our era. We are magnificent in scientific and commercial exploits but mediocre in affairs of the spirit, and one result is the draining of most of our virile minds into scientific invention and moneymaking. The ministry of religion suffers along with other kindred callings which serve the souls of men with goodness, truth, and beauty. This relative and, I think, temporary inferiority of spiritual callings, however, does not necessarily mean an absolute decline in the intellectual quality of religious leadership, and there is no reason why we should not have much better preaching than we ordinarily get.

One obvious trouble with the mediocre sermon, even when harmless, is that it is uninteresting. It does not matter. It could as well be left unsaid. It produces this effect of emptiness and futility largely because it establishes no connection with the real interests of the congregation. It takes for granted in the minds of the people ways of thinking which are not there, misses the vital concerns which are there, and in consequence uses a method of approach which does not function. It is pathetic to observe the number of preachers who commonly on Sunday speak religious pieces in the pulpit, utterly failing to establish real contact with the thinking or practical interests of their auditors.

Even in the case of a preacher poorly endowed, this state of affairs is unnecessary. No one who has any business to preach at all need preach uninteresting sermons. The fault generally lies not in the essential quality of the man's mind or character but in his mistaken methods. He has been wrongly trained, or he has blundered into a faulty technic, or he never has clearly seen what he should be trying to do in a sermon and so, having no aim, hits the target only by accident.

No bag of tricks can make a preacher, but if I were to pick out one simple matter of method that would come nearer to making a preacher than any other, it would be the one to which this paper is devoted.

II

Every sermon should have for its main business the solving of some problem—a vital, important problem, puzzling minds, burdening consciences, distracting lives—and any sermon which thus does tackle a real problem, throw even a little light on it, and help some individuals practically to find their way through it cannot be altogether uninteresting.

This endeavor to help people to solve their spiritual problems is a sermon's only justifiable aim. The point of departure and of constant reference, the reason for preaching the sermon in the first place, and the inspiration for its method of approach and the organization of its material should not be something outside the congregation but inside. Within a paragraph or two after a sermon has started, wide areas of any congregation ought to begin recognizing that the preacher is tackling something of vital concern to them. He is handling a subject they are puzzled about, or a way of living they have dangerously experimented with, or an experience that has bewildered them, or an ideal they have been trying to make real, or a need they have not known how to meet. One way or another they should see that he is engaged in a serious and practical endeavor to state fairly a problem which actually exists in their lives and then to throw what light on it he can.

Any preacher who even with moderate skill is thus helping folk to solve their real problems is functioning. He never will lack an audience. He may have neither eloquence nor learning, but he is doing the one thing that is a preacher's business. He is delivering the goods that the community has a right to expect from the pulpit as much as it has a right to expect shoes from a cobbler. And if any preacher is not doing this, even though he have at his disposal both erudition and oratory, he is not functioning at all.

Many preachers, for example, indulge habitually in what they call expository sermons. They take a passage from scripture, and proceeding on the assumption that the people attending church that morning are deeply concerned about what the passage means, they spend their half hour or more on historical exposition of the verse or chapter, ending with some appended practical application to the auditors. Could any procedure be more surely predestined to dullness and futility? Who seriously supposes that as a matter of fact, one in a hundred of the congregation cares, to start with, what Moses, Isaiah, Paul, or John meant in those special verses or came to church deeply concerned about it?

Nobody else who talks to the public so assumes that the vital interests of the people are located in the meaning of words spoken two thousand years ago. The advertisers of any goods, from a five-foot shelf of classic books to the latest life insurance policy, plunge as directly as possible after contemporary wants, felt needs, actual interests, and concerns. Even moving picture producers, if they present an ancient tale, like Tristan and Isolde, are likely to begin with a modern girl reading the story. Somehow or other, every other agency dealing with the public recognizes that contact with the actual life of the auditor is the one place to begin. Only the preacher proceeds still upon the idea that folk come to church desperately anxious to discover what happened to the Jebusites. The result is that folk less and less come to church at all.

This does not mean that the Bible has either lost or lessened its value to the preacher. It means that preachers who pick out texts from the Bible and then proceed to give their historic setting, their logical meaning in the context, their place in the theology of the writer, with a few practical reflections appended, are grossly misusing the Bible. The scripture is an amazing compendium of experiments in human life under all sorts of conditions, from the desert to cosmopolitan Rome, and with all sorts of theories, from the skepticism of Ecclesiastes to the faith of John. It is incalculably rich in insight and illumination. It has light to shed on all sorts of human problems now and always, and as for the personality of Jesus, if Rodin, the modern sculptor, could feel that Phidias, the Greek sculptor, could never be equaled—"No artist will ever surpass Phidias—for progress exists in the world but not in art. The greatest of sculptors . . . will remain forever without an equal"—it is surely open to even the most radical of Christians to adore Christ as Master and Lord.

What all the great writers of scripture, however, were interested in was human living, and the modern preacher who honors them should start with that, should clearly visualize some real need, perplexity, sin, or desire in his auditors, and then should throw on the problem all the light he can find in the scripture or anywhere else. No matter what one's theory about the Bible is, this is the searchlight, not so much intended to be looked at as to be thrown upon a shadowed spot.

That much insight into contemporary human problems which almost all preachers use in thinking about the practical applications at the end of their sermons might do some good if it were used, instead, at the beginning of their sermons. Let them not end but start with thinking of the auditors' vital needs, and then let the whole sermon be organized around their constructive endeavors to meet those needs.

III

An increasing number of preachers, too modern by far to use the old, authoritative, textual method which we have just described, do not on that account light on a better one. They turn to what is called topical preaching. They search contemporary life in general and the newspapers in particular for subjects. They discover that in comparison with dry, textual analysis there is such attractive vividness in handling present-day themes, such as divorce, Bolshevism, America's foreign policy, the new aviation, or the latest book, that they enjoy their own preaching better, and more people come to hear it. It is at least a matter of contemporary and not archeological interest.

The nemesis of such a method, however, is not far off. Most preachers who try it fall ultimately into their own trap. Watch the records of any considerable number of them and see how large a proportion peter out and leave the ministry altogether. Instead of starting with a text, they start with their own ideas on some subject of their choice, but their ideas on that subject may be much farther away from a vital interest of the people than a great text from the Bible. Indeed, the fact that history has thought it worth while to preserve the text for so many centuries would cause a gambling man to venture largely on the text's superior vitality.

Week after week one sees these topical preachers who turn their pulpits into platforms and their sermons into lectures, straining after some new, intriguing subject, and one knows that in private they are straining after some new, intriguing ideas about it. One knows also that no living man can weekly produce first-hand, independent, and valuable judgments on such an array of diverse themes covering the whole range of human life.

And deeper yet, one who listens to such preaching or reads it knows that the preacher is starting at the wrong end. He is thinking first of his ideas, original or acquired, when he should think first of his people. He is organizing his sermon around the elucidation of his theme, whereas he should organize it around the endeavor to meet his people's need. He is starting with a subject, whereas he should start with an object. His one business is with the real problems of these individual people in his congregation. Nothing that he says on any subject, however wise and important, matters much unless it makes at the beginning vital contact with the practical life and daily thinking of the audience.

This idea that we are applying to preaching is simply the project method, which is recognized as the basis of all good modern teaching. The old pedagogy saw on one side the child as a passive receptacle and on the other side a subject, like mathematics or geography, waiting to be learned and so seeing the situation, proceeded to pour the subject, willy-nilly, into the child. If he resisted, he was punished; if he failed to assimilate it, he was accounted stupid. No good teacher today could tolerate such an idea or method. The question now is why the child should wish to know geography and what practical interest in the child's life can be appealed to in the endeavor to have him desire to know geography. Modern pedagogy starts not with the subject but with the child. It adapts what is to be learned to the learner rather than vice versa. Even the food which the child eats for breakfast, coming from the ends of the earth, is used to fascinate his interest in other lands, and we find our children getting at their mathematics by measuring the cubic space of the front parlor or estimating the distance per second which they have walked in an hour.

All this is good sense and good psychology. Everybody else is using it, from first-class teachers to first-class advertisers. Why should so many preachers continue in such belated fashion to neglect it? The people often blindly know that there is something the matter with the sermon although they cannot define it. The text was good and the truth was undeniable. The subject was well chosen and well developed, but for all that, nothing happened. The effect was flat. So far as the sermon was concerned, the congregation might as well have stayed home. It may have been a "beautiful effort," as some kindly woman doubtless told the preacher, but it did no business in human lives. The reason for this can commonly be traced to one cause: the preacher started his sermon at the wrong end. He made it the exposition of a text or the elucidation of a subject instead of a well-planned endeavor to help solve some concrete problems in the individual lives before him. He need not have used any other text or any different materials in his sermon, but if he had defined his object rightly, he would have arranged and massed the material differently. He would have gone into his sermon via real interest in his congregation and would have found the whole procedure kindling to himself and to them.

IV

The meaning of this method can best be seen in some of its corollaries. For one thing, it makes a sermon a cooperative enterprise between the preacher and his congregation. When a man has got hold of a real difficulty in the life and thinking of his people and is trying to meet it, he finds himself not so much dogmatically thinking for them as cooperatively thinking with them. His sermon is an endeavor to put himself in their places and help them to think their way through.

The difference in tone and quality which this makes in a sermon is incalculable. Anyone accustomed to hearing preaching must be aware of two diverse effects commonly produced. One type of minister plays "Sir Oracle." He is dogmatic assertive, uncompromising. He flings out his dicta as though to say to all hearers, Take it or leave it. He has settled the matter concerning which he is speaking and is not asking our opinion; he is telling us. This homiletical dogmatism has its own kind of influence on credulous and impressionable minds. Such minds are numerous, so that such preaching can go on for years ahead. As Jesus said about the Pharisees, such preachers have their reward.

Their method, however, has long since lost its influence over intelligent people, and the future does not belong to it. The future, I think, belongs to a type of sermon which can best be described as an adventure in cooperative thinking between the preacher and his congregation. The impression made by such preaching easily is felt by anyone who runs into it. The preacher takes hold of a real problem in our lives and stating it better than we could state it, goes on to deal with it fairly, frankly, helpfully. The result is inevitable: he makes us think. We may agree with him or disagree with something vital to us, and so he makes us think with him even though we may have planned a far more somnolent use of sermon time.

Here, too, we are dealing with preaching in terms of good pedagogy. The lecture method of instruction is no longer in the ascendant. To be sure, there are subjects which must be handled by the positive setting forth of information in a lecture, but more and more good teaching is discussional, cooperative. The instructor does not so much think for the students as think with them. From the desire to use some such method in religious instruction has come the forum in modern churches and the questionnaire group after the sermon, where those who wish can put objections and inquiries to the preacher, and discussion groups of all sorts where religious questions are threshed out in mutual conference. The principle behind such methods is psychologically right. We never really get an idea until we have thought it for ourselves.

A good sermon should take this into account. A wise preacher can so build his sermon that it will be not a dogmatic monologue but a cooperative dialogue in which all sorts of things in the minds of the congregation—objections, questions, doubts, and confirmations—will be brought to the front and fairly dealt with. This requires clairvoyance on the preacher's part as to what the people are thinking, but any man who lacks that has no business to preach anyway.

Recently, in a school chapel, so I am told, the headmaster was only well started on his sermon when a professor mounted the pulpit beside him and offered a criticism of what he was saying. Great excitement reigned. The headmaster answered the objection, but the professor remained in the pulpit, and the sermon that day was a running discussion between the two on a great theme in religion. To say that the boys were interested is to put it mildly. They never had been so worked up over anything religious before. It turned out afterward that the whole affair had been prearranged. It was an experiment in a new kind of preaching, where one man does not produce a monologue but where diverse and competing points of view are frankly dealt with.

Any preacher without introducing another personality outwardly in the pulpit can utilize the principle involved in this method. If he is to handle helpfully real problems in his congregation, he must utilize it. He must see clearly and state fairly what people other than himself are thinking on the matter in hand. He may often make this so explicit as to begin paragraphs with such phrases as, "But some of you will say," or "Let us consider a few questions that inevitably arise," or, "Some of you have had experiences that seem to contradict what we are saying." Of course, this method, like any other, can be exaggerated and become a mannerism. But something like it is naturally involved in any preaching which tries to help people to think through and live through their problems.

Such preaching when it is well done always possesses an important quality. It is not militant and pugnacious but irenic, kindly, and constructively helpful. How much the churches need such discourses! We have endless sermons of sheer propaganda where preachers set out by hook or crook to put something over on the congregation. We have pugnacious sermons where preachers wage campaigns, attack enemies, assail the citadels of those who disagree, and in general do anything warlike and vehement. But sermons that try to face the people's real problems with them, meet their difficulties, answer their questions, interpret their experiences in sympathetic, wise, and understanding cooperation—what a dearth of them there is!

Yet not only is such preaching the most useful, it is the most interesting. This is the only way I know to achieve excitement without sensationalism. Constructively to state the problem of meeting trouble victoriously or of living above the mediocre moral level of a modern city, or of believing in God in the face of the world's evil, or of making Christ's principles triumphant against the present international and interracial prejudice is surely not sensationalism, but it is vitally interesting. A breathless auditor came up after one such sermon saying, "I nearly passed out with excitement, for I did not see how you possibly could answer that objection which you raised against your own thought. I supposed you would do it somehow but I could not see how until you did it." There is nothing that people are so interested in as themselves, their own problems, and the way to solve them. That fact is basic. No preaching that neglects it can raise a ripple on a congregation. It is the primary starting point of all successful public speaking, and for once the requirements of practical success and ideal helpfulness coincide. He who really helps folks to understand their own lives and see their way through their spiritual problems is performing one of the most important functions in the modern world.

V

No method of preaching is without its dangers and of course this one which I am espousing has perils in plenty. I presented it once to a group of experienced ministers and collected a galaxy of warnings as to its possible perversions. They thought of times when they had tried it with disappointing results. They had endeavored so precisely to deal with a real problem that Mr. Smith had vexatiously waked up to the fact that they were talking about objections to their thought, that they had overstated the opposing side and then had neither time nor ability to answer it, or they had been so practical in thinking about some definite problem that they had become trivial and had forgotten to bring the wide sweep of the Gospel's truth to bear in an elevating way on the point at issue, or they had been so anxious to deal with felt needs in the congregation that they forgot to arouse the consciousness of need unfelt but real.

All these dangers are present in the method which we are suggesting. It can be offensively personal, argumentatively unconvincing, practically trivial, and narrowed to the conscious needs of mediocre people. But these perversions are the fault of just such unskilled handling as would wreck any method whatsoever.

The best antidote to making a wrong use of the project method in the pulpit is to be discovered in the ideal of creative preaching. The danger involved in starting a sermon with a problem is that the very word *problem* suggests something to be merely debated and its solution may suggest nothing more than the presentation of a helpful idea to the mind. But we all want something else in a sermon than a discussion even about one of our vital problems, no matter how wise the discussion or how suggestive the conclusion. The best sermons, I still maintain, are preached on the project method, but after all, in the preacher's hands it means something more than the same method in a classroom. It is the project method plus.

What this plus is can easily be seen. When a preacher deals with joy, let us say, he ought to start not with joy in the fifth century B.C. nor with joy as a subject to be lectured on but with the concrete difficulties in living joyfully that his people actually experience, he should have in mind from the start their mistaken ideas of joy, their false attempts to get it, the causes of their joylessness, and their general problem of victorious and happy living in the face of life's puzzling and sometimes terrific experiences. This is a real problem for everybody, and the sermon that throws light on it is a real sermon. But that real sermon must do more than discuss joy—it must produce it. All powerful preaching is creative. It actually brings to pass in the lives of the congregation the thing it talks about. So, to tackle the problem of joy so that the whole congregation goes out more joyful than it came in—that is the mark of a genuine sermon.

Here lies a basic distinction between a sermon and an essay. The outstanding criticism popularly and properly launched against a great deal of our modern, liberal preaching is that though it consists of neat, analytical discourses, pertinent to real problems and often well conceived and well phrased, it does nothing to anybody. Such sermons are not sermons but essays. It is lamentably easy to preach feebly about repentance without making anybody feel like repenting or to deliver an accomplished discourse on peace without producing any of the valuable article in the auditors. On the other hand, a true preacher is creative. He does more than discuss a subject; be produces the thing itself in the people who hear it. As an English bishop said about Phillips Brooks: "He makes one feel so strong."

Obviously, personal quality is the major factor in producing spiritual power. There is a real reason for the halos which the painters have put about the heads of the saints. They are symbols of something intangible but real—an effluence that ordinary men do not possess, a radiance that is not the less powerful because it is ineffable.

Nevertheless, even a moderately endowed preacher, who never would suggest a halo to anybody, may have some of this power to create what he discusses. Whether he does or not depends a great deal upon whether he sees the objective clearly enough to head for it with precision. If he thinks of his sermon merely as a discussion of somebody's problem, he will play with a series of ideas, but if he thinks of his sermon as an endeavor to create something in his congregation, he will play on motives. There is where much of our modern preaching fails. The old preachers at their best did know where the major motives were. Fear, love, gratitude, self-preservation, altruism—such springs of human action the old sermons often used with consummate power. To be sure, they sometimes outraged the personalities of both adults and children by the way they did it, but for all that, they often showed an uncanny insight into the springs of human action. I often think that we modern preachers talk about psychology a great deal more than our predecessors did but use it a great deal less.

One often reads modern sermons with amazement. How do the preachers expect to get anything done in human life with such discourses? They do not come within reaching distance of any powerful motives in a man's conduct. They are keyed to argumentation rather than creation. They produce essays, which means that they are chiefly concerned with the elucidation of a theme. If they were producing sermons, they would be chiefly concerned with the transformation of personality.

This, however, brings us back to our major issue. If a preacher is to use the project method, as a preacher should, not simply to discuss the real problems of real people but to create in the people the thing that is discussed, his chief interest must be in the individuals in his congregation. He must know them through and through, not only their problems but their motives, not only what they are thinking but why they are acting as they do. Preaching becomes thrilling business when it successfully achieves this definite direction and aim. A sermon, then, is an engineering operation by which a chasm is spanned so that spiritual goods on one side are actually transported into personal lives upon the other.

VI

Throughout this paper we have held up the ideal of preaching as an interesting operation. That is a most important matter, not only to the audience but to the man in the pulpit. The number of fed-up, fatigued, bored preachers is appalling. Preaching has become to them a chore. They have to "get up" a sermon, perhaps two sermons, weekly. They struggle at it. The juice goes out of them as the years pass. They return repeatedly to old subjects and try to whip up enthusiasm over weather-beaten texts and themes. Their discourses sink into formality. They build conventional sermon outlines, fill them in with conventional thoughts, and let it go at that. Where is the zest and thrill with which in their chivalrous youth they started out to be ministers of Christ to the spiritual life of their generation?

Of course, nothing can make preaching easy. At best it means drenching a congregation with one's lifeblood. But while, like all high work, it involves severe concentration, toil, and self-expenditure, it can be so exhilarating as to recreate in the preacher the strength it takes from him, as good agriculture replaces the soil it uses. Whenever that phenomenon happens, one is sure to find a man predominantly interested in personalities and what goes on inside of them. He has understood people, their problems, troubles, motives, failures, and desires, and in his sermons he has known how to handle their lives so vitally that week after week he has produced real changes. People have habitually come up after the sermon, not to offer some bland compliment but to say: "How did you know I was facing that problem only this week?" or "We were discussing that very matter at dinner last night," or, best of all, "I think you would understand my case—may I have a personal interview with you?"

This, I take it, is the final test of a sermon's worth: how many individuals wish to see the preacher alone?

I should despair, therefore, of any man's sustained enthusiasm and efficiency in the pulpit if he were not in constant, confidential relationship with individuals. Personal work and preaching are twins. As I watch some preachers swept off their feet by the demands of their own various organizations, falling under the spell of bigness, and rushing from one committee to another to put over some new scheme to enlarge the work or save the world, I do not wonder at the futility which so often besets them. They are doing everything except their chief business, for that lies inside individuals.

If someone utterly "sold" to our American worship of size and our grandiose schemes for saving the world should protest that this means individualistic preaching, he would only reveal his own obtuseness. In one sense, all good preaching and all good public speaking of any kind must be individualistic—it must establish vital contact with individuals. Even if one were speaking on the rings of Saturn, one might as well not begin unless one could cook up some reason why the audience should wish to hear about them. The failure to recognize this fact explains why so much of our so-called social preaching falls flat or rouses resentment. A man who on Sunday morning starts in to solve the economic question or the international question as though his people must have come that day of a purpose to hear him do it deserves almost any unpleasant thing that can happen to him. He may be a Ph.D. in psychology, but I doubt whether he knows enough about the way men's minds do actually act to be a successful grocer's assistant.

His special business as a Christian preacher with economic and international questions is profound and vital, but insofar as he sticks to his last, his interest as a minister is distinct from anyone else's, and it calls for an approach of his own. The world's economic and international situation is not alien to our personal problems. It invades them, shapes them in multitudinous ways; it undoes in us and around us much that the Christian should wish done, and it does much that the Christian most should fight against. Let a preacher, therefore, start at the end of the problem where he belongs. Let him begin with the people in front of him, with what goes on inside of them, because social conditions are as they are, with the economic and international reasons for many of their un-Christian moods, tempers, ideas, and ideals, with their responsibilities and obligations in the matter, and in general with the tremendous stake which personal Christianity has in those powerful social forces which create the climate in which it must either live or die. Such preaching on social questions starts, as it should start, with the individuals immediately concerned, establishes contact with their lives, and has at least some faint chance of doing a real business on Sunday.

Every problem that the preacher faces thus leads back to one basic question: how well does he understand the thoughts and lives of his people? That he should know his gospel goes without saying, but he may know it ever so well and yet fail to get it within reaching distance of anybody unless he intimately understands people and cares more than he cares for anything else what is happening inside of them. Preaching is wrestling with individuals over questions of life and death, and until that idea of it commands a preacher's mind and method, eloquence will avail him little and theology not at all.

CHAPTER 26

THE RESURGENCE OF ORTHODOXY

NORMAN H. SNAITH: A SERMON FOR BIBLE SUNDAY

The Second Sunday in Advent was called Bible Sunday because the collect for that date in the Book of Common Prayer since its first edition in 1549 had been as follows:

> *Blessed Lord, who hast caused all holy Scriptures to be written for our learning; Grant that we may in such wise hear them, read, mark, learn, and inwardly digest them, that by patience, and comfort of thy holy Word, we may embrace, and ever hold fast the blessed hope of everlasting life, which thou hast given us in our Savior Jesus Christ. Amen.*[1]

The occasion was observed in Great Britain by Protestants as well as Anglicans.

In the sermon that follows, Professor Norman H. Snaith uses the occasion to set forth a theology of the Scripture that was consistent with the emphases of the biblical theology movement (see Vol. 1, pp. 677-87)*. Snaith, who served as principal of Headingley College, Leeds, was himself a leading scholar of the movement. His book on* The Distinctive Ideas of the Old Testament *was a classic statement of its thought.*

The sermon appeared in The Expository Times *63 (1951–52): 58-59.*

Second Sunday in Advent—Bible Sunday

Thy word is a lamp unto my feet, and a light unto my path.
Ps. 119:105.

For how many of us is it really true that the Bible is uniquely "a lamp unto our feet and a light unto our path"? One lamp among many lamps perhaps, and one light in a giant candelabra, but is it for us, in any sense, the One Lamp that shines out in a darkling world, the One Light that beckons and guides the wanderer home?

I have often heard it maintained, though not so much latterly as in days gone by, that solely as literature the Bible is the equal of any other book. In deed there are some who claim that even on that ground it surpasses every other book. Rabbi Solomon ben Isaac the Levite (sixteenth century) wrote:

> In the Bible, without doubt, are history and tale: proverb and enigma: correction and wisdom: knowledge and discretion: poetry and word play: conviction and counsel: dirge, entreaty, prayer, and every kind of supplication: and all this in a Divine way superior to the prolix benedictions of human books.

The good Rabbi goes on to point out the super-excellence of the Bible in that it contains the names of the Holy One, and so forth, but I doubt whether any one could write down that first sentence if he were not definitely partisan.

There are certainly passages in the Bible which merit a place in any collection of literature. The skill of the writer of the story of David's earlier troubles (whether that writer is Ahimaaz or another) is superb, and the title "The Father of History" certainly belongs to him and not to Herodotus, whom he preceded by some five hundred years. There are passages from the Prophets, in the Psalms, and in Job which cannot be excelled anywhere. The dirge for the expected fall of Tyre in Ezekiel 27 is one of the treasures of literature—the picture of her as a stately ship sailing out to meet her doom on the high seas which had brought her such wealth and treasure.

The plays on words which are so common in First Isaiah and the long flowing sentences of Second Isaiah—these and many other passages in the Old Testament are truly pearls of great price from the literary point of view. In the New Testament, the plain straightforward story of Mark has a charm of its own, and no one can read the Gospel according to St.

Luke without having his heart made as warm as that of the beloved physician himself.

And yet, at the same time, it has to be admitted frankly that there are passages in the Old Testament which would never find a place in good literature on their own literary merit alone. They are obscure beyond measure, and this is the case apart from the accidents of transmission during a period which, so far as the Old Testament is concerned, is far longer than the earliest times of Greek and Roman literature. Amos, for instance, was preaching before the first sod was turned in the building of ancient Rome. There are parts of the New Testament epistles which, in both Authorized and Revised Versions, are by no means easily intelligible, and their literary style on occasion leaves much to be desired. The most that can be claimed for the Bible along literary lines is that it is one lamp among many, albeit, here and there, shining with a brilliance that has not often been equaled. Even the sun has spots on its surface, and so has the Bible from a literary point of view.

No. If the Bible is the One Lamp above all others unto our feet, it is not because of its literary and artistic virtues. When the Bible has brought hope to the hopeless and life to the dying, it has been because of something else, something other than its literary and artistic value. We are beginning once more to realize what some of us had forgotten—this is a book in which a man may find God. What the pillar of fire was to the Israelites by night on the long journey to the Promised Land, so this book is the light of God whereby he can guide us to a land that is beyond.

It is generally agreed, though falsely, that when the Reformers broke with the Roman Church, they replaced a belief in the infallibility of the Church with a belief in the infallibility of the Bible. This is not true of the Reformers, by which term I mean the men who first broke away from the Roman tyranny. They certainly gave the Bible pride of place, but they took care to distinguish clearly between the scriptures as a whole and the Word of God which they contain. Hans Denck, who died in 1527, wrote, for instance "I esteem Holy Scripture above all human treasures, but not so highly as the Word of God."

This distinction between the scriptures and the Word of God is characteristic of the Reformers. Luther once said that a boy of nine with the Bible knew more about divine truth than the Pope without it, but this does not mean that Luther believed every part of Scriptures to be equally the Word of God. He distinguished clearly between what was of local and temporal significance and what is still relevant for the believer. This latter is centered around the blessed message of salvation by grace through faith. The Bible is here before us for every man to read, and the

Holy Spirit can bear witness with our spirit that in it, here and here and here, is Christ, the Word of God. The scriptures are essentially a witness to Christ, and wherever we find Christ in the scriptures there we find the Word—always the Christ who saves us by his grace.

There was a day when the Risen Lord walked with two wayfarers. Their hearts burned within them as he opened to them the scriptures, and showed them what and where they spake of him. Later, towards eventide, in the breaking of bread, they recognized him. What the Risen Lord was to Cleopas and his companion, he can be now in the Bible to the believer. Just as the Lord Jesus came up and walked between those two men, so between the two covers of the Scriptures we can see him now. For us, as for them, his name is Jesus, "for it is he that shall save his people from their sins."

This book contains no treatise on the nature of God; it contains no argument concerning his existence. In it we meet God himself, and, by the Holy Spirit, he speaks to our hearts. We find no particular appreciation of the beauty of nature. What beauty we find is the beauty of the Lord who comes to save his people, and it is then that all the natural world rejoices, the trees of the field clap their hands, and the valleys laugh and sing. This book is concerned with the activity of the Savior God, and anything else it contains is incidental. It is not because of these incidental things, however splendid and praiseworthy many of them are, that this book has survived the trials and accidents and deliberate onslaughts of the centuries, but because of this one thing, that herein there is told for all who have ears to hear the story of the God who came to seek and to save that which was lost.

In these days we are seeing a revival of the recognition of the Bible as the Word of God, after a period when liberal thought had largely failed to interpret it as such. The successors of the Reformers did not maintain that distinction which was vital to the Reformation, namely, the distinction between the scriptures and the Word of God.

It was hard for those who lived in a world of authority to rely on an authority which could be neither seen nor touched. It is therefore understandable that in their struggle against the authority of the Roman Church, they should turn to an infallible book.

It is no easy matter to maintain a doctrine of salvation by grace through faith alone, and to keep a balance between the inner witness of the Holy Spirit and the reasonings of the human mind. Further, it is a great temptation to trust in a book that can be handled and seen as against that inner witness of the Holy Spirit which can be maintained only by much prayer and communion both with God himself and with the brethren of the faith.

When the Word of God came to be identified with the scriptures, every verse came to be regarded as being equally authoritative with every other verse. This did no great harm so far as the Bible was concerned till the rise of the modern critical study of the Bible. The results were then serious. Those who paid heed to the new approach tended to lose the sense of the uniqueness of both the scriptures and the Word of God, whilst those who paid no heed to the new approach tended to ascribe (to quote Denck again) "to the dead letter what belongs to the Spirit," an attitude not clearly to be distinguished from the legalism against which both our Lord himself and later St. Paul fought so hard.

Now that we are learning once more to make the distinction which the Reformers made, biblical criticism is enabling us to sift as never before what is local and temporary from what is universal and eternal. The Bible once again is being restored to its true and unique position. The Light of the World shines clearly above the half-lights of man, and Christ speaks to us out of Scripture in tones that are clear and loud. We see with opened eyes the Word of God, and that is why we praise God today. There is clear before us today, as in the time of the Reformers, a "lamp unto our feet and a light unto our path."

Note

1. In the 1979 American edition of the Prayer Book, this collect is used for Proper 28, the Sunday closest to November 16.

CHAPTER 27

PREACHING AS AN ELEMENT OF WORSHIP

REGINALD FULLER: PREFACE TO *PREACHING THE LECTIONARY*

The liturgical movement has caused Roman Catholics to have much more interest in the Bible and preaching and has caused Protestants to show greater interest in the church year and the lectionary **(see Vol. 1, pp. 688-702)***. This startling convergence is manifested in the work that follows. In the preface to his commentary on all the readings for the three-year lectionary cycle, Reginald H. Fuller tells how to do lectionary preaching.*

Fuller, an Englishman and an Anglican, was trained at Cambridge—under a great pioneer of the biblical theology movement, Sir Edwyn Hoskyns—and at Tübingen in Germany. He married an Austrian woman, Ilse Barda, and the two of them have helped keep English-speaking New Testament scholarship aware of what is going on in Germany through their many translations. Most of Fuller's teaching has been in the United States, at Seabury-Western, Union, and Virginia Theological Seminaries.

The author of many books, Fuller originally wrote his lectionary commentary as a series of articles for Worship*, a Roman Catholic journal with an ecumenical readership, to help clergy prepare for their upcoming* *homilies. These were then collected by The Liturgical Press and published as a single volume. Because of his closeness to Roman Catholicism and Lutheranism as well as his own Anglicanism, he was able to write with ecumenical sensitivity as well as New Testament scholarship that was state-of-the-art at the time of publication. Since he had written one of the first books to appear on liturgical preaching, he was singularly well equipped to write this preface on homiletical method. It is taken from* Preaching the Lectionary: The Word of God for the Church Today, *rev. ed. (Collegeville, Minn.: Liturgical Press, 1984), xvii-xxxi.*

Preparing the Homily

Introductory Considerations

Since the Second Vatican Council, it has become increasingly accepted that the ministry of the word is an essential part of the liturgy. It is my understanding—and my observation of current practice bears this out—that in the Roman Catholic communion a homily is expected at every celebration of the liturgy. The same is undoubtedly true, and probably always has been, among Lutherans, though for them this would normally mean only on Sundays. I must confess to a sense of shame when I attend Holy Communion in my own Anglican tradition and observe that Anglican priests of all complexions, evangelical as well as High Church, are content to celebrate the Eucharist without preaching. They ought to have a strong sense of guilt at their dereliction of duty.

This requirement, or at least this desirability, that there should be proclamation of the word undoubtedly makes many demands upon the preacher, and very little help has been given in the procedure to be followed in the preparation of a homily. It was to fill this gap that, as an emergency measure, I undertook to write the commentaries that appeared in *Worship* over a space of three years and have since been reissued in book form. In what follows I shall try to analyze the procedures that I followed. Here I must confess that I did not start out with any clear-cut methods or prior understanding. True, I had certain ideas about the function of liturgical preaching, for I had written on the subject some fifteen years previously. I had a general idea, gathered from my German Lutheran contacts, that there were basically three stages of sermon preparation, the third being the actual composition of the sermon.

First, it should begin with exegesis. Exegesis, as I understand it, poses the question: What did the text mean in its original situation? The disciples of Bultmann, following Karl Barth, insist that exegesis itself already poses the question: What does the text mean today? and that until one has heard it speak to the contemporary situation, one has not heard the text. But I agree with such different scholars as Dean Krister Stendahl and Bishop Stephen Neill in assigning this concern to a later stage—the stage of exposition. Users of the *Interpreter's Bible* will remember the two divisions exegesis and exposition. I follow the arrangements of this commentary and distinguish between exegesis, which asks: What did the text mean? and exposition, which asks: What does it mean today?

The homilist who understands his/her own task in these terms will be concerned with two poles: the word of God as it is attested in Scripture, and the concrete situation in which the congregation finds itself today. The homilist's task is to take what Scripture said and make it say the same thing, but in such a way that it can address the congregation today.

The first part of the homilist's task is, in theory, always the same. What Scripture said remains said in that situation for all time. What Scripture says is in principle variable, because the new situation always slants, though it does not determine, what was once said. Here we stumble upon Bultmann's hermeneutical principle of the *Fragestellung,* the question we bring to the text. Our questions to some extent condition what Scripture says to us. Of course, we should try to be as objective as possible in exegesis, recognizing that complete objectivity is never wholly possible. But at any rate we should not make a virtue of our lack of objectivity, as the Bultmannians seem to do.

The second part of the homilist's task is that for which he or she is uniquely and properly equipped—an intimate knowledge of the congregation, of their concerns, their joys, sorrows, temptations, and sins. Parish calls, counseling sessions, and the hearing of confessions should equip the preacher for this. It is not here but in the preliminary work of exegesis that the pastor and homilist is likely to find real difficulty. Exegesis demands certain academically acquired skills, and the homilist may well fight shy of this. The commentaries in this book were designed to help particularly at this point. They were motivated by the conviction that I had developed in Germany when I studied at Tübingen in 1938–39, that a true proclamation of the word of God depends upon a correct exegesis of the text. I will now try to lay bare some of the presuppositions of my method and the procedures that in large part developed as I went along month by month producing the commentaries.

Exegesis—Some General Considerations

To do exegesis, every method of biblical criticism must be brought into play where appropriate, for the first task of exegesis is to reconstruct the situation for which the text was originally written. Especially important here is the question of the audience or addressee(s). As Willi Marxsen has observed, this is really more important than the question—so beloved of students who have just made their acquaintance with biblical criticism—of authorship. Yet authorship is also important, precisely in this connection. It makes a difference to the situation envisaged whether one thinks, for example, that the letter to the Colossians was written by Paul or by an unknown Paulinist in the subapostolic age.

Here it is important not to be afraid of critical positions. It is useful, for instance, to divide the Pauline letters into the homologoumena (those letters about whose Pauline authorship there is no reasonable doubt) and the antilegomena (those about whose Pauline authorship there are varying degrees of doubt). The antilegomena, if post-Pauline, are to be understood as witnesses to early Catholicism—that is, to the institutional consolidation of Christianity after the deaths of the original witnesses and the non-arrival of the parousia.

We need not, of course, dismiss early Catholicism as an aberration or degeneration, like Käsemann, who discovered or rediscovered its importance. We may regard it, as I do personally, as a natural, inevitable, and justifiable development. But we cannot ignore it in our exegesis; otherwise we will make the antilegomena more Pauline than they actually are. Texts that witness to the institutionalization of the Church in this way should not be harmonized with the genuine Paul or explained away but should be allowed first to speak in their own right. But neither should their difference from the authentic Paul be so exaggerated that the texts concerned are dismissed as valueless for preaching. It has been said, for instance, that in Tübingen today the view is held that one cannot preach from a text in Acts because Acts is early Catholic and un-Pauline, and therefore is not gospel!

Turning to the gospels, the modern view, a view that has become widely accepted since the fifties, is that these documents consist of three strata. On the top level we have the theology of the evangelist, which is commonly known as the evangelist's redaction. Below this lies the tradition, the Jesus material as it was constantly put to use in the oral period between A.D. 30 and 65/70. At the bottom is the stratum of the authentic Jesus material—authentic sayings and parables spoken by him, authentic memories of his career from his baptism to his crucifixion. As has frequently been observed, Catholics especially should feel no discomfort at this modern understanding of the gospels as largely the product of the Church, for their high doctrine of the Church should help them to accept this view.

The arrangement of a three-year cycle of readings from Matthew, Mark–John, and Luke successively has made the topmost level of the Gospel tradition—the respective evangelist's redaction—particularly important to the homilist. I once heard a parish priest complain that the same incident came up more than once in three years in the different evangelists. He suggested, therefore, that the lectionary needed revision. But the fact of the duplication of a pericope directs the homilist to what is distinctive in that particular evangelist.

Above all, the homilist must avoid the temptation of harmonizing. A conspicuous instance of this occurred when the Marcan form of the temptation narrative was read for the first time on the first Sunday of Lent. I heard a homilist start by saying that Mark had obviously abbreviated the story, and proceed to preach about the three temptations as recorded in Q (Matthew and Luke), which he treated on a purely historical level! He thus missed the challenge of facing up to the temptation as presented by the Marcan redaction. *Why,* if he knew the Q tradition, did Mark omit the three temptations? Where did his real interest lie? Those are the questions the homilist should have asked.

A study of the Lectionary shows that most of these duplications occur on the major feasts and holy days of the year. Not only the temptation story but particularly the passion account is taken each year from a different Gospel on Passion (Palm) Sunday. The homilist should concentrate upon what is distinctive in the particular evangelist's presentation.

It is clearly important to acquaint oneself with the methods and principles of redaction criticism. The redaction is discernible in such factors as the arrangement and order of individual pericopes in any given gospel, in touches that the evangelist has clearly added with his own hand. Where we possess the evangelist's source, this is relatively easy, for we need only compare the evangelist with that source. Thus, if we accept the two-document hypothesis (the priority of Mark and the common source of Matthew and Luke, commonly called Q), we can see where Matthew and Luke have altered Mark and where Matthew and Luke diverge in their presentation of the Q material. In the latter case, of course, it is more difficult to decide which of the two reproduces the original and which has made the alteration, but a knowledge of the stylistic peculiarities and theological interests of the two evangelists helps us to answer this question.

Where we do not possess the source of the evangelist's material, namely, in the case of Mark and in the case of the special material of Matthew and Luke, source criticism is of no use. Here only form and tradition criticism can help. Thus we can distinguish between the pure form of a pericope and the disturbance of this form by later comment or application. Even here we cannot be sure whether the accretion is due to the evangelist himself or had already taken place earlier in the tradition. But as we become more familiar with the style and concerns of any given evangelist, we learn to discern the sort of thing which that evangelist is likely to have added himself. The third type of material that allows us to pinpoint the evangelist's redaction is that composed as fresh material. A good example of this is the Marcan summaries, such as Mark 6:53-56.

This distinction between the three different levels of the tradition can be very helpful for the preacher, for it offers three possibilities of treating a particular pericope. A good instance of this is the parable of the sower. At the Jesus level, this consists of the pure parable itself (Mk. 4:3-8). At a later stage in the tradition, the Hellenistic missionary Church added the allegorical interpretation (Mark 4:14-20). Finally, the evangelist Mark added from another tradition the passage on the interpretation of parables (Mark 4:10-13). The homilist will have to decide which of these three levels speaks most directly to the situation of the congregation and treat the parable at that level. It would be a mistake to reject the later levels of the tradition as valueless because they do not go back to the historical Jesus. The later levels represent successive expositions of the Jesus tradition in a new situation. Tradition is a living and growing thing. In fact, the homiletical use of a text is itself part of the history of its tradition.

Many of the Sunday pericopes consist of miracle stories. Here again there are, at least in principle, three levels of tradition. First, there is the miracle as it actually occurred in our Lord's ministry. Authentic sayings of Jesus show that for him exorcisms and healings were signs of the inbreaking of the eschatological reign or kingdom of God. Next comes the shaping of these miracle stories in the post-Easter community. Usually this is in the interests of a particular Christology. Thus they may present Jesus as the eschatological prophet or the divine man.

A good example of this is the feeding of the multitude that occurs several times in the Gospels and is read more than once in the three-year cycle. Personally, I do not doubt that Jesus celebrated an eschatological meal with his disciples in a tense atmosphere of crisis at the turning point of his ministry. But later, in the post-Easter community, this authentic memory was taken up and shaped by two different interests. The eschatological meal became a model for the church's eucharistic meal, while the interest in Jesus as an eschatological prophet led to the development of an emphasis on the miraculous multiplication of the loaves, a greater feat than that of Elisha (2 Kgs. 4:42-44).

Finally, there is the evangelist's redaction of the miracle tradition. Mark clearly wished to reduce the emphasis on the miraculous. The reason for this was that the Christians in his church were being tempted by false teachers (Mark 13:6, 22) to think of Jesus as a divine man who displayed his divine powers solely through his miracles. Mark did not altogether reject the picture of Jesus as a miracle-worker, for he accepted and preserved a relatively large number of such stories. But he toned them down by the device known as the "messianic secret." Demons that confessed Jesus as the Son of God (apparently a title that the false teachers used in association with their Christology) were silenced. People who were healed were likewise silenced. And above all, the disciples were silenced after the transfiguration—until after the resurrection!

Mark's point seems to be that Jesus can only be rightly confessed as Son of God in the light of his crucifixion and resurrection. We must recognize that we are dealing here, not with history as such, but with Mark's interpretation of history. The "divine man" Christology was allowed into the canon of Scripture only after it had received this Marcan correction. This would seem to forbid the homilist from exploiting the miracles of Jesus for their own sake. They can be safely treated only as prefigurations (to use Austin Farrer's word) of the supreme messianic miracle, which is the death and resurrection of Jesus. Thus, redaction criticism helps the homilist to use the miracle stories as a real proclamation of the gospel.

We see something similar happening in the great Johannine signs that occur in the Lenten series of readings. Here the "divine man" tradition is corrected, but in a different way. The miracle stories are frequently used as a launching point for typically Johannine dialogues and discourses. The best examples are the miracles of the feeding of the multitude, the blind man of Siloam, and the raising of Lazarus in chapters 6, 9, and 11 respectively. The feeding of the multitude is explained in the ensuing discourse as a sign that Jesus is the bread that came down from heaven and gives life to the world. The healing of the blind man is a sign that he is the light of the world, and the raising of Lazarus a sign that he is the resurrection and the life. Here again the homilist would not want to treat the miracle stories as they are found in the pre-Johannine tradition—simply as signs that Jesus is a great wonder-worker, perhaps the greatest of wonder-workers. Rather, to preach the gospel, the homilist will use the miracle stories as signs of what the Johannine discourse reveals Jesus to be.

The passion narratives, which are read in Holy Week, benefit the homilist if critically treated. Quite early on, the form critics saw that these narratives differ from the rest of the gospel material in that they are more or less continuous, not a string of pericopes. Basic to them is genuine historical reminiscence of the end of Jesus—his arrest; the preliminary investigation before the Sanhedrin; the trial proper before Pilate, which established that Jesus could without too much difficulty be disposed of as a messianic pretender; and finally his actual crucifixion and death. These bare facts, however, do not themselves contain the gospel. The gospel comes from the way these bare facts were interpreted by the post-Easter Church. We know from 1 Cor. 15 that from the very early days the death of Jesus received a threefold interpretation.

First, Jesus' death took place *in fulfillment of the scriptures*. The cross was a scandal not only for the Jews but even for the believers themselves. They had to come to terms with it in their own minds, and the only way they could do so was to discover predictions of the passion in the scriptures—what we now call the Old Testament. This led them first to those psalms that speak about the righteous sufferer and his vindication, notably Ps. 118:22, which speaks of the rejected stone that became the chief cornerstone. Then there were the great passion psalms—Psalms 22 and 69. Details from these psalms have undoubtedly colored the passion narratives, and it is always a moot point whether the facts led to the prophecies or the prophecies suggested the facts. Probably it was a bit of both. The basic facts of the passion (like Judas' betrayal of Jesus, Simon's denial, and the disciples' forsaking Jesus) were so scandalous that they drove the early Christians to the scriptures, whereas peripheral details, like the casting of lots for Jesus garments, could well have been added to fulfill the prophecy of Psalm 22.

Second, the early community asserted that Jesus died *for our sins*. This atonement theology probably entered at a slightly later stage, perhaps after the community had hit upon Isa. 53, and possibly in connection with its Passover celebration. Anyhow, it is clear that this motif has had little effect on the passion narrative itself, only upon the institution at the Lord's Supper, which was probably a separate pericope on its own (see 1 Cor. 11:23-25).

The third motif was that Jesus died *as Messiah*. This is strongly attested by the title on the cross, whose historicity is beyond all doubt, though in the intention of those who perpetrated it the title meant a political pretender. But this motif has colored the Marcan form of the trial scene before the Sanhedrin (note its absence in John's Gospel), while the king motif is particularly stressed in the trial before Pilate.

Then comes each evangelist's own treatment of the passion. Mark was probably the first to combine the passion narrative with pericopes about the words and deeds of the earthly Jesus. This, too, was part of his attempt to tone down the "divine man" motif. Mark emphasizes the *theologia crucis* in his own distinctive way, which is different from that of Paul. Jesus is forsaken by all, finally even by God, for he dies with the words "My God, my God, why hast thou forsaken me?" on his lips. This must not be harmonized with the words from the cross in the other Gospels.

Matthew basically followed Mark but played down Jesus' isolation, stressing the paradox of his royalty in the midst of humiliation and the motif of scripture fulfillment. Luke probably had an independent passion narrative that he touched up with additions from Mark. It has been said that Luke transposed the passion story from the key of tragedy to the key of pathos. John, lastly, emphasizes the majesty of Jesus in his suffering. Jesus remains master of the situation throughout. The passion is the manifestation of his glory. He dies with the triumphant cry *Tetelestai,* which the Revised Standard Version, following the King James Version, weakly renders: "It is finished." The Vulgate was better: *Consummatum est.*

In the Easter season the preacher has to handle, among other things, the resurrection narratives. We have to remember that the New Testament nowhere narrates the resurrection as such. The event in which God raised Jesus from the dead is shrouded in the mystery proper to an eschatological event, occurring at the precise point where observable history comes to an end. The two this-worldly events that are narrated are the discovery of the empty tomb and the appearances of the risen Lord to his disciples. Here the basic facts belong to the earliest tradition (1 Cor. 15:3-8), but the *stories* of the empty tomb and the appearances are the product of later development. Surprisingly, it was the pericope of the empty tomb that first took shape (Mark 16:1-8). It was used as the vehicle for the Easter proclamation. This is uttered by an angel—*angelus interpres,* a frequent scriptural device: "He is not here, he is risen."

As 1 Cor. 15:3-8 indicates, the appearances were first listed, not narrated. The appearance stories apparently had not yet taken shape by the time Mark's Gospel was written, unless we are to suppose that episodes like the walking on the water and the transfiguration are post-resurrection stories retrojected into the earthly ministry. The appearance stories as found in the later gospels are used as vehicles for the Church's post-Easter theology, which springs from its faith in the resurrection.

The Easter event is the foundation of the Church as the eschatological community and the inauguration of the Church's mission. The kerygma and the two sacraments of baptism and the eucharist are grounded importantly upon the Easter event, but even they have some roots in the historical Jesus. The apostolate is similarly grounded. The emphasis on the material reality of the Lord's risen body in Luke 24 and John 20, which is at variance with the more "spiritual" presentation of the earlier appearance story (Matt. 28; John 21), guards against the interpretation of the encounters as purely subjective experiences rather than as revelatory disclosures of eschatological reality.

The Church Year

The context in which the homilist operates is that of the Church year. This provides a kind of hermeneutical framework in which the liturgical use of Scripture is set. It is therefore important for the homilist to understand something of the rationale of the Church year.

The Church year is centered upon the reality of salvation history, focused in the Christ-event. In the earliest Church there were two main celebrations: the Lord's Day, or Sunday, and the period of the *Pentecosté*. The first weekly observance of the Lord's Day was not so much a historical commemoration of the resurrection as the fulfillment of the Sabbath, the proleptic participation in the rest that remains for the people of God (see Heb. 4:9; Epistle of Barnabas 15.8). The second celebration was the *Pentecosté,* the period of fifty days that began with the (Christianized) Passover and concluded with the day of Pentecost.

It could be argued that we ought to have returned to this simple calendar, with its exclusively eschatological emphasis. But for pedagogic and other reasons, it was deemed advisable to retain the articulated church year as it developed in the main after the Age of Constantine. All the same, it is important that we learn to understand the articulated church year in the light of the simpler eschatological scheme—an understanding as important for the preacher as for all participants in the liturgy. The articulated Church year breaks down the total complex of the Christ-event into its constitutive parts, yet it does so not merely for historical commemoration but to expound a particular aspect of the total eschatological event. Each separate "mystery," to use the language current in Roman Catholic theology, must always be seen as part of the total mystery of the Christ-event.

The church year starts with the first Sunday of Advent, whose theme is the culmination of the future eschatology taken over from the end of the previous year. Thus, one year dovetails into another. It is this prominence of future eschatology that has led in part to the dropping of the old pericope for the day, namely, the entry into Jerusalem, which however is still retained as an option by the Lutherans. Today's theme is not the first coming of Christ in humility but his coming again in glory. It is only on the second Sunday of Advent that the thought of the first coming begins to take over in preparation for the celebration of Christ's birth.

On the second and third Sundays of Advent the figure of John the Baptist moves to the center of the stage. This is significant. At first sight John the Baptist would seem to postdate the coming of Christ, if by that coming we have in mind his birth at Bethlehem. But the appearance of the Baptist at this point calls our attention to the fact that when we speak of the first coming of Christ, we are referring not merely to Bethlehem but to his first coming in its totality, which includes the whole ministry capped by death. It is for this total coming that John serves as the forerunner.

On the fourth Sunday of Advent the Blessed Virgin Mary takes over the stage, thus serving as the immediate preparation for the birth of Christ.

Although Christ's first coming in humility is the primary focus during the second, third, and fourth weeks of Advent, the theme of the second coming is not dropped altogether. The two comings must always be considered together. The first is an anticipation of the second, and the second is the completion and fulfillment of the first. Thus, the theme of the second coming is carried through to Christmas itself, especially in the propers for the midnight Mass. The word *epiphania* is used in the Christmas readings from Titus to signify *both* comings.

When they come to deal with the incarnation itself, the propers of the Christmas Masses are clear about the place of the nativity story in the mystery of Christ. The birth is emphatically only *Vorgeschichte,* a prelude to the Christ-event proper, which really begins with the baptism of Jesus and continues through his crucifixion and subsequent vindication. In this prelude God is inserting into human history the One through whom the act of redemption will be wrought. This is the biblical way of looking at the birth stories. They are not concerned with the combination of humanity and divinity in a single person, as though humanity and divinity were abstract qualities. Thus, the affirmation of the Johannine prologue that the Word became flesh is not merely an interpretation of Christmas but declares the inauguration of a history in which the Word will be dynamically enfleshed in the career of Jesus from Jordan to Calvary. For the flesh of Jesus, in Hoskyns' words, is his whole observable history, not abstract humanity.

Although the arrangements of the revised Roman calendar at Epiphany did not go as far in the right direction as they might have, the tendency of the reform is clearly to play down the story of the Magi and to upgrade the baptism of Jesus, which was the original emphasis of this festival and which, though obscured in the West, has always remained preeminent in the East. It is in the baptism that the process of the revelation of God in the human history of Jesus properly begins; the baptism is therefore, rightly understood, the first of the epiphanies. The visit of the Magi, like the rest of the infancy stories, is only a prefigurement of the revelatory event proper.

Even though the Roman calendar has introduced the rather colorless designation of Sundays "in ordinary time" for the period between Epiphany and Lent, the propers themselves, notably the gospels and the accompanying Old Testament readings, maintain the Epiphany themes. In the stories of the early ministry, Jesus is manifested as the Messiah in word and deed. In the Episcopal and Lutheran adaptations of the Roman calendar, these epiphanies are fittingly climaxed on the last Sunday before Ash Wednesday in the reading of the transfiguration story, which the Roman Lectionary, following its ancient but purely adventitious tradition, designates for the second Sunday of Lent.

In recent times Lent has come to be thought of almost exclusively as a season of personal penitence (the Lutheran tradition has been an exception; as a glance at the Lutheran hymnals will show, even the earlier part of Lent is devoted to the passion). It is not surprising that voices continue to be raised in favor of a shorter Lent. Of course, there is a place for personal penitence, but to keep it up for forty days and forty nights tends to pall.

Wisely, the revised calendar makes a shift in emphasis that people have not yet understood. Ash Wednesday becomes the great day of penitence in the Church, a sort of Christian Yom Kippur. The readings of the Sundays in Lent now focus upon the baptismal mystery, a theme that is now reinforced by the rites of the catechumenate. Together, catechumens and faithful prepare to participate, or to renew their participation, in the baptismal mystery at the paschal feast. Thus, the emphasis of the readings is the new life to which the baptized are called and its ethical demands.

Of course, this still involves the note of penitence, but it is penitence placed in a proper evangelical perspective rather than a pious work. The second readings are drawn largely from the Pauline exhortations, or parenesis, which are based upon Hellenistic catechetical formulas, while the gospels in year A (which form the best series and are recommended for invariable use when the rites of the catechumenate are celebrated) comprise the great Johannine signs, long viewed as symbols of the Christian experience of baptism.

Holy Week speaks for itself. On Passion Sunday the theme of the triumphal entry (except in the Presbyterian/United Church of Christ adaptation of the calendar) is clearly relegated to the subordinate position it has always really had. The homily should be based upon the passion, and if it deals with the entry into Jerusalem at all, it should treat it only as the curtain-raiser to the passion.

The ancient unitary paschal feast has been split up into a group of three celebrations—Holy Thursday, Good Friday, and the Easter Vigil. Each of these three days has its own distinctive color, expressed by the different ways in which the Eucharist is celebrated on it. Holy Thursday is a brief outburst of joy. When the service concludes with the stripping of the altar and the darkening of the church, the brevity of this outburst is dramatically emphasized. The Good Friday communion—whether it be from the reserved Sacrament, as in the Roman and Episcopal provisions, or whether the eucharist itself is celebrated, as in the Lutheran tradition and in an increasing number of Anglican churches—is celebrated in the bare church in an atmosphere of extreme austerity. At the Easter Vigil, the great point about the Eucharist is that it marks a transition from darkness to light, from sorrow to joy, from bondage to freedom, from death to life.

It is a pity that in modern parish life the fifty days of Easter count for so little compared with the forty days of Lent. The rites of the catechumenate provide some hope that a more constructive use may be made of this period. It is a time when the church should be especially conscious of both the presence of the risen Lord in its midst and the presence of the newly baptized. The liturgical gospels reflect these two themes. We first read the appearance stories and later the farewell discourses of the Fourth Gospel. The newly baptized are, with the rest of the faithful, now enjoying the foretaste of eternal life in the Spirit-filled community.

Ascension Day emphasizes one aspect of the Easter season. This season is the celebration not only of the victory of Christ over death but preeminently of his exaltation as Lord, or *Kyrios,* of the Church and the world. Ascension Day does not inaugurate a new period but is merely an incident within the fifty days of Easter. Finally, although Pentecost celebrates the gift of the Spirit, it too merely highlights a theme that is present to some extent throughout the great fifty days. Note, for instance, the use of John 20:19-23 as the gospel on Pentecost. This has caused some perplexity. Why read on Pentecost what happened on Easter Sunday? Such objections indicate a naive historical way of thinking. The gift of the Spirit is the outcome of the total Easter event. Probably the risen Lord conveyed his Spirit in every one of his appearances, and it was not confined to a single day in the way the Lucan schematization suggests.

If Pentecost marks a single event at all, that event is the inauguration of the kerygma. And in the church year it also marks the conclusion of the Easter season. The post-Pentecost season begins at once, and the Pentecost observance is, very rightly, no longer extended into an octave, which unduly prolonged the fifty days and obscured their unique significance.

The post-Pentecost season is bounded at each end by a solemnity—the feast of the Holy Trinity at one end and the feast of Christ the King at the other. In the post-Pentecost season the systematic reading of scripture, begun in the post-Epiphany season, is resumed. After the excitement of Christmas-Epiphany and Lent–Holy Week–Easter, it is sound to relax somewhat. Now scripture is read in course, and the reading of it is less colored by the season of the year. Here is the chance for broad themes of theology and ethics to be broached. It is important, however, to note that at the tail end of the Sundays of the year, or the post-Pentecost period, a futurist-eschatological note comes. So we end where we began—with the theology of Christian hope.

From Exegesis to Preaching

In the first part of this introduction we offered some general considerations about exegesis, laying considerable stress on the value for the preacher or homilist of the critical approach to the Bible. We will now briefly summarize the main steps in exegesis and then consider how one might move from exegesis to sermon composition.

Ideally, exegesis should start with a translation of the passage from the Greek (or Hebrew, in the case of the Old Testament). Very few, however, will be able to attempt this, so we must be realistic and suggest that where this is not possible, the best alternative would be to compare at least two different modern translations. Any marked variations will call attention to a disputed point of exegesis and send the homilist to commentaries for closer investigation. In the light of findings there, the homilist must weigh the pros and cons and decide which interpretations to accept.

Second, the homilist should then look in the margins of the various versions to see if there are any disputed readings (text criticism). These too can be checked in commentaries, so that a decision can be reached as to which text to accept.

Third, the homilist should turn to points of literary criticism. What is the literary genre of this passage (e.g., miracle story, parable, sayings collection)? Having ascertained this, the homilist should look for signs of redaction that are visible, for example through the disturbance of the original genre by additional material or through changes made in a known source. What light is thrown on the evangelist's understanding of the passage by the place in which he locates it? In other words, the homilist must study the context of the passage. Introductory questions are also relevant here (date, authorship, addressees), for they determine the situation to which the text was addressed.

Fourth, the homilist should look for any significant theological words in the passage and make a study of those words with the help of a concordance or theological dictionary. The context of other passages should be considered; words should not be looked at simply in isolation.

Fifth and last, in the light of the information gathered, the homilist should write out a paraphrase of the passage, stating in his or her own words what the biblical writer was saying to those addressed.

The next stage forms a bridge between the exegesis and the sermon. It is what the Germans call the *Predigtmeditation,* or sermon meditation. The preacher has to be concerned with two poles—the original message of the pericope, as distilled from the exegesis, and the current situation of the audience or congregation when gathered for the liturgy. Here the homilist will have to draw upon personal knowledge of their concerns as disclosed through parish visits, counseling, and the confessional, or through the media or current literature. Then it must be decided how the text speaks in judgment and mercy, in wrath and grace, to this situation. The homilist must ask: What is the law and what is the gospel contained in the text? Finally, the homilist should envisage the result sought for from the hearers: repentance, renewed faith, some act of devotion, or some concrete act of obedience.

These are the considerations that I had in view and developed as I wrote my commentaries on the readings, and it is my hope that these observations may be of help to the homilist as he or she continues the responsible task of declaring the word of God to the people of God.

CHAPTER 28

A HOMILETICAL EPIPHANY: THE EMERGENCE OF AFRICAN AMERICAN PREACHING IN MAJORITY CONSCIOUSNESS

MARTIN LUTHER KING JR.: A VERSION OF "THE THREE DIMENSIONS OF A COMPLETE LIFE"

Many preachers through the ages have used the same sermon a number of times, but the conditions under which Dr. King preached meant that he was constantly adapting an old outline to a new situation (**see Vol. 1, pp. 703-10**)*. He always spoke very directly to the situation at hand, but to do so, he called upon frameworks and set pieces from his memory. In this way he was able to devote the limited time he had for preparation to the unique character of that moment. The basic idea for this sermon was borrowed from Phillips Brooks, but King developed his form of it during his student days, and he preached variations of it throughout his ministry. This was his trial sermon at Dexter*

Avenue Baptist Church in 1955, and he preached it at St. Paul's Cathedral in London on his way to receive the Nobel Prize in 1964. The version below was preached during the 1967 Chicago campaign.

Since most of King's published sermons were edited to appeal to a wider audience, it is fortunate that this version is taken verbatim from a tape recording. It even has congregational responses included parenthetically in the transcription. Thus we are given the authentic voice of Dr. King himself, in so far as it can be transmitted as type on paper. This sermon comes from A Knock At Midnight: Inspiration from the Great Sermons of Reverend Martin Luther King, Jr., *ed. Clayborne Carson and Peter Holloran (New York: Warner, 1998), 121-40. It was delivered at New Covenant Baptist Church, Chicago, Illinois, on April 9, 1967.*

The Three Dimensions of a Complete Life

I want to use as the subject from which to preach: "The Three Dimensions of a Complete Life." (*All right*) You know, they used to tell us in Hollywood that in order for a movie to be complete, it had to be three-dimensional. Well, this morning I want to seek to get over to each of us that if life itself is to be complete, (*Yes*) it must be three-dimensional.

Many, many centuries ago, there was a man by the name of John who found himself in prison out on a lonely, obscure island called Patmos. (*Right, right*) And I've been in prison just enough to know that it's a lonely experience. (*That's right*) And when you are incarcerated in such a situation, you are deprived of almost every freedom, but the freedom to think, the freedom to pray, the freedom to reflect and to meditate. And while John was out on this lonely island in prison, (*That's right*) he lifted his vision to high heaven (*All right, he did*) and he saw, descending out of heaven, a new heaven (*All right*) and a new earth. (*That's right*) Over in the twenty-first chapter of the Book of Revelation, it opens by saying, "And I saw a new heaven and a new earth. (*All right*) And I John saw the holy city, the new Jerusalem, (*All right*) coming down from God out of heaven." (*Oh yeah*)

And one of the greatest glories of this new city of God that John saw was its completeness. (*That's right*) It was not up on one side and down on the other, (*All right*) but it was complete in all three of its dimensions. (*Yes*) And so in this same chapter as we looked down to the sixteenth verse, John says, "The length and the breadth (*He did, he did*) and the height of it are equal." (*Yes, sir*) In other words, this new city of God, this new city of ideal humanity, is not an unbalanced entity (*No*) but is complete on all sides. (*Yes*) Now, I think John is saying something here in all of the symbolism of this text and the symbolism of this chapter. He's saying at bottom that life as it should be and life at its best (*Yeah*) is a life that is complete on all sides. (*That's right*)

And there are three dimensions of any complete life to which we can fitly give the words of this text: length, breadth, and height. (*Yes*) Now, the length of life as we shall use it here is the inward concern for one's own welfare. (*Yes*) In other words, it is that inward concern that causes one to push forward, to achieve his own goals and ambitions. (*All right*) The breadth of life as we shall use it here is the outward concern for the welfare of others. (*All right*) And the height of life is the upward reach for God. (*All right*) Now, you got to have all three of these to have a complete life.

Now, let's turn for the moment to the length of life. I said that this is the dimension of life where we are concerned with developing our inner powers. (*Yeah*) In a sense this is the selfish dimension of life. There is such a thing as rational and healthy self-interest. (*Yeah*) A great Jewish rabbi, the late Joshua Leibman, wrote a book some years ago entitled *Peace of Mind*. And he has a chapter in that book entitled "Love Thyself Properly." And what he says in that chapter, in substance, is that before you can love other selves adequately, you've got to love your own self properly. (*All right*) You know, a lot of people don't love themselves. (*That's right*) And they go through life with deep and haunting emotional conflicts. So the length of life means that you must love yourself.

And you know what loving yourself also means? It means that you've got to accept yourself. (*All right*) So many people are busy trying to be somebody else. (*That's right*) God gave all of us something significant. And we must pray every day, asking God to help us to accept ourselves. (*Yeah*) That means everything. (*Yeah*) Too many Negroes are ashamed of themselves, ashamed of being black. (*Yes, sir*) A Negro got to rise up and say from the bottom of his soul, "I am somebody. (*Yes*) I have a rich, noble, and proud heritage. However exploited and however painful my history has been, I'm black, but I'm black and beautiful." (*Yeah*) This is what we've got to say. We've got to accept ourselves. (*Yeah*) And we must pray, "Lord, help me to accept myself every day; help me to accept my tools." (*Yeah*)

I remember when I was in college, I majored in sociology, and all sociology majors had to take a course that was required called statistics. And statistics can be very complicated. You've got to have a mathematical mind, a real knowledge of geometry, and you've got to know how to find the mean, the mode, and the median. I never will forget. I took this course and I had a fellow classmate who could just work that stuff out, you know. And he could do his homework in about an hour. We would often go to the lab or the workshop, and he would just work it out in about an hour, and it was over for him. And I was trying to do what he was doing; I was trying to do mine in an hour. And the more I tried to do it in an hour, the more I was flunking out in the course. And I had to come to a very hard conclusion. I had to sit down and say, "Now, Martin Luther King, Leif Cane has a better mind than you." (*That's right*) Sometimes you have to acknowledge that. (*That's right*) And I had to say to myself, "Now, he may be able to do it in an hour, but it takes me two or three hours to do it." I was not willing to accept myself. I was not willing to accept my tools and my limitations. (*Yeah*)

But you know, in life we're called upon to do this. A Ford car trying to be a Cadillac is absurd, but if a Ford will accept itself as a Ford, (*All right*) it can do many things that a Cadillac could never do: It can get in parking spaces that a Cadillac can never get in. [*Laughter*] And in life some of us are Fords and some of us are Cadillacs. (*Yes*) Moses says in "Green Pastures," "Lord, I ain't much, but I is all I got." [*Laughter*] The principle of self-acceptance is a basic principle in life.

Now, the other thing about the length of life: After accepting ourselves and our tools, we must discover what we are called to do. (*Oh yeah*) And once we discover it we should set out to do it with all of the strength and all of the power that we have in our systems. (*Yeah*) And after we've discovered what God called us to do, after we've discovered our life's work, we should set out to do that work so well that the living, the dead, or the unborn couldn't do it any better. (*Oh yeah*) Now, this does not mean that everybody will do the so-called big, recognized things of life. Very few people will rise to the heights of genius in the arts and the sciences, very few collectively will rise to certain professions. Most of us will have to be content to work in the fields and in the factories and on the streets. But we must see the dignity of all labor. (*That's right*)

When I was in Montgomery, Alabama, I went to a shoe shop quite often, known as the Gordon Shoe Shop. And there was a fellow in there that used to shine my shoes, and it was just an experience to witness this fellow shining my shoes. He would get that rag, you know, and he could bring music out of it. And I said to myself, "This fellow has a Ph.D. in shoe shining." (*That's right*)

What I'm saying to you this morning, my friends, even if it falls your lot to be a street sweeper, go on out and sweep streets like Michelangelo painted pictures; sweep streets like Handel and Beethoven composed music; sweep streets like Shakespeare wrote poetry; (*Go ahead*) sweep streets so well that all the hosts of heaven and earth will have to pause and say, "Here lived a great street sweeper who swept his job well."

If you can't be a pine on the top of a hill
Be a scrub in the valley—but be
The best little scrub on the side of the hill,
Be a bush if you can't be a tree.
If you can't be a highway just be a trail
If you can't be the sun be a star;
It isn't by size that you win or fail—
Be the best of whatever you are.

And when you do this, when you do this, you've mastered the length of life. (*Yes*)

This onward push to the end of self-fulfillment is the end of a person's life. Now, don't stop here, though. You know, a lot of people get no further in life than the length. They develop their inner powers; they do their jobs well. But do you know, they try to live as if nobody else lives in the world but themselves? (*Yes*) And they use everybody as mere tools to get where they're going. (*Yes*) They don't love anybody but themselves. And the only kind of love that they really have for other people is utilitarian love. You know, they just love people that they can use. (*Well*)

A lot of people never get beyond the first dimension of life. They use other people as mere steps by which they can climb to their goals and their ambitions. These people don't work out well in life. They may go for a while, they may think they're making it all right, but there is a law. (*Oh yeah*) They call it the law of gravitation in the physical universe, and it works, it's final, it's inexorable: Whatever goes up can come down. You shall reap what you sow. (*Yeah*) God has structured the universe that way. (*Yeah*) And he who gets through life not concerned about others will be a subject, victim of this law.

So I move on and say that it is necessary to add breadth to length. Now, the breadth of life is the outward concern for the welfare of others, as I said. (*Yeah*) And a man has not begun to live until he can rise above the narrow confines of his own individual concerns to the broader concerns of all humanity. (*All right*)

One day Jesus told a parable. You will remember that parable. He had a man that came to him to talk with him about some very profound concerns. And they finally got around to the question, "Who is my neighbor?" (*All right*) And this man wanted to debate with Jesus. This question could have very easily ended up in thin air as a theological or philosophical debate. But you remember, Jesus immediately pulled that question out of thin air and placed it on a dangerous curve between Jerusalem and Jericho. (*He did, he did*) He talked about a certain man who fell among thieves. (*Right*) Two men came by and they just kept going. And then finally another man came, a member of another race, who stopped and helped him. (*Oh yeah*) And that parable ends up saying that this good Samaritan was a great man; he was a good man because he was concerned about more than himself. (*Oh yeah*)

Now you know, there are many ideas about why the priest and the Levite passed and didn't stop to help that man. A lot of ideas about it. Some say that they were going to a church service, and they were running a little late, you know, and couldn't be late for church, so they kept going because they had to get down to the synagogue. And then there are others who would say that they were involved in the priesthood and consequently there was a priestly law which said that if you were going to administer the sacrament or what have you, you couldn't touch a human body twenty-four hours before worship. Now, there's another possibility. It is possible that they were going down to Jericho to organize a Jericho Road Improvement Association. That's another possibility. And they may have passed by because they felt that it was better to deal with the problem from the causal source rather than one individual victim. That's a possibility.

But you know, when I think about this parable, I think of another possibility as I use my imagination. It's possible that these men passed by on the other side because they were afraid. You know, the Jericho Road is a dangerous road. (*That's right*) I've been on it and I know. And I never will forget, Mrs. King and I were in the Holy Land some time ago. We rented a car and we drove from Jerusalem down to Jericho, a distance of about sixteen miles. You get on that Jericho road—I'm telling you it's a winding, curving, meandering road, very conducive for robbery. And I said to my wife, "Now I can see why Jesus used this road as the occasion for his parable." (*Yes*) Here you are when you start out in Jerusalem: You are twenty-two hundred feet above sea level, and when you get down to Jericho sixteen miles later—I mean, you have sixteen miles from Jerusalem—you're twelve hundred feet below sea level. During the days of Jesus that road came to the point of being known as the "Bloody Path." So when I think about the priest and the Levite, I think those brothers were afraid. (*All right*)

They were just like me. I was going out to my father's house in Atlanta the other day. He lives about three or four miles from me, and you go out there by going down Simpson Road. And then when I came back later that night—and brother, I can tell you, Simpson Road is a winding road. And a fellow was standing out there trying to flag me down. And I felt that he needed some help; I knew he needed help. [*Laughter*] But I didn't know it. I'll be honest with you, I kept going. [*Laughter*] I wasn't really willing to take the risk. (*That's right*)

I say to you this morning that the first question that the priest asked was the first question that I asked on that Jericho Road of Atlanta known as Simpson Road. The first question that the Levite asked was "If I stop to help this man, what will happen to me?" (*That's right*) But the good Samaritan came by and he reversed the question. Not "What will happen to me if I stop to help this man?" but "What will happen to this man if I do not stop to help him?" This was why that man was good and great. He was great because he was willing to take a risk for humanity; he was willing to ask "What will happen to this man?" not "What will happen to me?" (*All right*)

This is what God needs today: (*Yes*) men and women who will ask "What will happen to humanity if I don't help? (*Oh yeah*) What will happen to the civil rights movement if I don't participate? (*Yes*) What will happen to my city if I don't vote? (*Oh yeah*) What will happen to the sick if I don't visit them?" This is how God judges people in the final analysis. (*Oh yeah*)

Oh, there will be a day, the question won't be "How many awards did you get in life?" Not that day. (*Yeah*) It won't be "How popular were you in your social setting?" That won't be the question that day. (*Yeah*) It will not ask how many degrees you've been able to get. (*All right*) The question that day will not be concerned with whether you are a "Ph.D." or a "no D." (*That's right*) It will not be concerned with whether you went to Morehouse or whether you went to "No House." (*Yes*) The question that day will not be "How beautiful is your house?" (*That's right*) The question that day will not be "How much money did you accumulate? How much did you have in stocks and bonds?" The question that day will not be "What kind of automobile did you have?" On that day the question will be "What did you do for others?" (*That's right*)

Now, I can hear somebody saying, "Lord, I did a lot of things in life. I did my job well; the world honored me for doing my job. (*Oh yeah*) I did a lot of things, Lord; I went to school and studied hard. I accumulated a lot of money, Lord; that's what I did." It seems as if I can hear the Lord of Life saying, "But I was hungry, and ye fed me not. (*That's right*) I was sick, and ye visited me not. I was naked, and ye clothed me not. I was in prison, and you weren't concerned about me. So get out of my face. What did you do for others?" (*That's right*) This is the breadth of life. (*Oh yeah*)

Somewhere along the way, we must learn that there is nothing greater than to do something for others. And this is the way I've decided to go the rest of my days. That's what I'm concerned about. John, if you and Bernard happen to be around when I come to the latter days and that moment to cross the Jordan, I want you to tell them that I made a request: I don't want a long funeral. In fact, I don't even need a eulogy (*No*) more than one or two minutes. (*All right*) I hope that I will live so well the rest of the days—I don't know how long I'll live, and I'm not concerned about that—but I hope I can live so well that the preacher can get up and say "He was faithful." (*Yes*) That's all, that's enough. (*That's right*) That's the sermon I'd like to hear: "Well done, my good and faithful servant. You've been faithful; you've been concerned about others." (*That's right*) That's where I want to go from this point on the rest of my days. (*Oh yeah*) "He who is greatest among you shall be your servant." I want to be a servant. (*Yes*) I want to be a witness for my Lord, to do something for others.

And don't forget in doing something for others that you have what you have because of others. (*Yes, sir*) Don't forget that. We are tied together in life and in the world. (*Preach, preach*) And you may think you got all you got by yourself. (*Not all of it*) But you know, before you got out here to church this morning, you were dependent on more than half of the world. (*That's right*) You get up in the morning and go to the bathroom, and you reach over for a bar of soap, and that's handed to you by a Frenchman. You reach over for a sponge, and that's given to you by a Turk. You reach over for a towel, and that comes to your hand from the hands of a Pacific Islander. And then you go on to the kitchen to get your breakfast. You reach on over to get a little coffee, and that's poured in your cup by a South American. (*That's right*) Or maybe you decide that you want a little tea this morning, only to discover that that's poured in your cup by a Chinese. (*Yes*) Or maybe you want a little cocoa; that's poured in your cup by a West African. (*Yes*) Then you want a little bread and you reach over to get it, and that's given to you by the hands of an English-speaking farmer, not to mention the baker. (*That's right*) Before you get through eating breakfast in the morning, you're dependent on more than half the world. (*That's right*) That's the way God structured it; that's the way God structured this world. So let us be concerned about others because we are dependent on others. (*Oh yeah*)

But don't stop here either. (*No, sir*) You know, a lot of people master the length of life, and they master the breadth of life, but they stop right there. Now, if life is to be complete, we must move beyond our self-interest. We must move beyond humanity and reach up, way up for the God of the universe, whose purpose changeth not. (*Right*)

Now, a lot of people have neglected this third dimension. And you know, the interesting thing is a lot of people neglect it and don't even know they are neglecting it. They just get involved in other things. And you know; there are two kinds of atheism. Atheism is the theory that there is no God. Now, one kind is a theoretical kind, where somebody just sits down and starts thinking about it, and they come to a conclusion that there is no God. The other kind is a practical atheism, and that kind goes out of living as if there is no God. And you know there are a lot of people who affirm the existence of God with their lips, and they deny his existence with their lives. (*That's right*) You've seen these people who have a high blood pressure of creeds and an anemia of deeds. They deny the existence of God with their lives and they just become so involved in other things. They become so involved in getting a big bank account. (*Yeah*) They become so involved in getting a beautiful house, which we all should have. They become so involved in getting a beautiful car that they unconsciously just forget about God. (*Oh yeah*)

There are those who become so involved in looking at the manmade lights of the city that they unconsciously forget to rise up and look at that great cosmic light and think about it—that gets up in the eastern horizon every morning and moves across the sky with a kind of symphony of motion and paints its technicolor across the blue—a light that man can never make. (*All right*) They become so involved in looking at the skyscraping buildings of the Loop of Chicago or Empire State Building of New York that they unconsciously forget to think about the gigantic mountains that kiss the skies as if to bathe their peaks in the lofty blue—something that man could never make. They become so busy thinking about radar and their television that they unconsciously forget to think about the stars that bedeck the heavens like swinging lanterns of eternity, those stars that appear to be shiny, silvery pins sticking in the magnificent blue pincushion. They become so involved in thinking about man's progress that they forget to think about the need for God's power in history. They end up going days and days not knowing that God is not with them. (*Go ahead*)

And I'm here to tell you today that we need God. (*Yes*) Modern man may know a great deal, but his knowledge does not eliminate God. (*Right*) And I tell you this morning that God is here to stay. A few theologians are trying to say that God is dead. And I've been asking them about it because it disturbs me to know that God died and I didn't have a chance to attend the funeral. They haven't been able to tell me yet the date of his death. They haven't been able to tell me yet who the coroner was that pronounced him dead. (*Preach, preach*) They haven't been able to tell me yet where he's buried.

You see, when I think about God, I know his name. He said somewhere, back in the Old Testament, "I want you to go out, Moses, and tell them 'I Am' sent you." (*That's right*) He said, just to make it clear, let them know that "my last name is the same as my first, 'I Am that I Am.' Make that clear. 'I Am.'" And God is the only being in the universe that can say "I Am" and put a period behind it. Each of us sitting here has to say "I am because of my parents; I am because of certain environmental conditions; I am because of certain hereditary circumstances; I am because of God." But God is the only being that can just say "I Am" and stop right there. "I Am that I Am." And he's here to stay. Let nobody make us feel that we don't need God.

As I come to my conclusion this morning, I want to say that we should search for him. We were made for God, and we will be restless until we find rest in him. (*Oh yeah*) And I say to you this morning that this is the personal faith that has kept me going. (*Yes*) I'm not worried about the future. You know, even on this race question, I'm not worried. I was down in Alabama the other day, and I started thinking about the state of Alabama where we worked so hard and may continue to elect the Wallaces. And down in my home state of Georgia, we have another sick governor by the name of Lester Maddox. (*Yes*) And all of these things can get you confused, but they don't worry me. (*All right*) Because the God that I worship is a God that has a way of saying even to kings and even to governors, "Be still, and know that I am God." And God has not yet turned over this universe to Lester Maddox and Lurleen Wallace. Somewhere I read, "The earth is the Lord's and the fullness thereof," and I'm going on because I have faith in him. (*Oh yeah*) I do not know what the future holds, but I do know who holds the future. (*Yes*) And if he'll guide us and hold our hand, we'll go on in.

I remember down in Montgomery, Alabama, an experience that I'd like to share with you. When we were in the midst of the bus boycott, we had a marvelous old lady that we affectionately called Sister Pollard. She was a wonderful lady about seventy-two years old and she was still working at that age. (*Yes*) During the boycott she would walk every day to and from work. She was one that somebody stopped one day and said, "Wouldn't you like to ride?" And she said, "No." And then the driver moved on and stopped and thought, and backed up a little and said, "Well, aren't you tired?" She said, "Yes, my feets is tired, but my soul is rested." (*All right*)

She was a marvelous lady. And one week I can remember that I had gone through a very difficult week. (*Yes*) Threatening calls had come in all day and all night the night before, and I was beginning to falter and to get weak within and to lose my courage. (*All right*) And I never will forget that I went to the mass meeting that Monday night very discouraged and a little afraid, and wondering whether we were going to win the struggle. (*Oh yeah*) And I got up to make my talk that night, but it didn't come out with strength and power. Sister Pollard came up to me after the meeting and said, "Son, what's wrong with you?" Said, "You didn't talk strong enough tonight."

And I said, "Nothing is wrong, Sister Pollard, I'm all right."

She said, "You can't fool me." Said, "Something wrong with you." And then she went on to say these words: "Is the white folks doing something to you that you don't like?"

I said, "Everything is going to be all right, Sister Pollard."

And then she finally said, "Now, come close to me and let me tell you something one more time, and I want you to hear it this time." She said, "Now, I done told you we is with you." She said, "Now, even if we ain't with you, the Lord is with you." (*Yes*) And she concluded by saying, "The Lord's going to take care of you."

And I've seen many things since that day. I've gone through many experiences since that night in Montgomery, Alabama. Since that time Sister Pollard has died. Since that time I've been in more than eighteen jail cells. Since that time I've come perilously close to death at the hands of a demented Negro woman. Since that time I've seen my home bombed three times. Since that time I've had to live every day under the threat of death. Since that time I've had many frustrating and bewildering nights. But over and over again I can still hear Sister Pollard's words: "God's going to take care of you." So today I can face any man and any woman with my feet solidly placed on the ground and my head in the air because I know that when you are right, God will fight your battle.

"Darker yet may be the night, harder yet may be the fight. Just stand up for that which is right." It seems that I can hear a voice speaking even this morning, saying to all of us, "Stand up for what is right. Stand up for what is just. Lo, I will be with you even until the end of the world." Yes, I've seen the lightning flash. I've heard the thunder roll. I've felt sin-breakers dashing, trying to conquer my soul. But I heard the voice of Jesus saying still to fight on. He promised never to leave me, never to leave me alone. No, never alone. No, never alone. He promised never to leave me, never to leave me alone. And I go on in believing that. Reach out and find the breadth of life.

You may not be able to define God in philosophical terms. Men through the ages have tried to talk about him. (*Yes*) Plato said that he was the Architectonic Good. Aristotle called him the Unmoved Mover.

Hegel called him the Absolute Whole. Then there was a man named Paul Tillich, who called him Being-Itself. We don't need to know all of these high-sounding terms. (*Yes*) Maybe we have to know him and discover him another way. (*Oh yeah*) One day you ought to rise up and say, "I know him because he's a lily of the valley." (*Yes*) He's a bright and morning star. (*Yes*) He's a rose of Sharon. He's a battle-ax in the time of Babylon. (*Yes*) And then somewhere you ought to just reach out and say, "He's my everything. He's my mother and my father. He's my sister and my brother. He's a friend to the friendless." This is the God of the universe. And if you believe in him and worship him, something will happen in your life. You will smile when others around you are crying. This is the power of God.

Go out this morning. Love yourself, and that means rational and healthy self-interest. You are commanded to do that. That's the length of life. Then follow that: Love your neighbor as you love yourself. You are commanded to do that. That's the breadth of life. And I'm going to take my seat now by letting you know that there's a first and even greater commandment: "Love the Lord thy God with all thy heart, (*Yeah*) with all thy soul, with all thy strength." I think the psychologist would just say "with all thy personality." And when you do that, you've got the breadth of life.

And when you get all three of these together, you can walk and never get weary. You can look up and see the morning stars singing together, and the sons of God shouting for joy. When you get all of these working together in your very life, judgment will roll down like waters, and righteousness like a mighty stream.

When you get all the three of these together, the lamb will lie down with the lion.

When you get all three of these together, you look up and every valley will be exalted, and every hill and mountain will be made low; the rough places will be made plain, and the crooked places straight; and the glory of the Lord shall be revealed and all flesh will see it together.

When you get all three of these working together, you will do unto others as you'd have them do unto you.

When you get all three of these together, you will recognize that out of one blood God made all men to dwell upon the face of the earth. . . .[1]

Note

1. Recording interrupted.

CHAPTER 29

MAINSTREAM PROPHECY

WILLIAM SLOANE COFFIN JR.: "HOMOSEXUALITY"

No white person epitomizes the social protest preaching of the 1960s and 1970s so well as Coffin, who spent those years first as chaplain of Yale University and then as senior minister of Riverside Church in New York City **(see Vol. 1, pp. 731-41)***. Although he came from a background of affluence and social position and is a person of many talents, he came to oppose any form of elitism.*

There are a number of qualities that make his preaching on social issues more effective than that of many others who turned pulpits into barricades during this time. First, he did not harp on such issues, but preached on them only as occasion demanded. Then he made sure that he was well prepared and knew what he was talking about when he did. Even then, however, he tried to challenge people in a kindly way—which is not at all to say that he soft-pedaled issues out of a desire to be liked. The position he took was always grounded in theology, which gave it a right to be heard in church. And he made himself available for discussion afterwards.

In preaching this way, he sought to fulfill Augustine's statement of the duty of a preacher: "to teach what is right and refute what is wrong, and in the performance of the task to conciliate the hostile [and] to rouse the careless."

The sermon that follows is taken from his book The Courage to Love *(San Francisco: Harper & Row, 1982), 39-46.*

Homosexuality

Aside from their extraordinary contributions to human progress and happiness, what did the following have in common: Erasmus, Leonardo da Vinci, Michelangelo, Christopher Marlowe, King James I of England, Sir Francis Bacon, Thomas Gray, Frederick the Great of Germany, Margaret Fuller, Tchaikovsky, Nijinsky, Proust, A. E. Housman, T. E. Lawrence, Walt Whitman, Henry James, Edith Hamilton, W. H. Auden, Willa Cather, and Bill Tilden, the greatest tennis player of his time?

Some of you, no doubt, have the answer: they were all homosexual. And why do I bring up this subject, probably the most divisive issue since slavery split the church? Because the once unmentionable has become unavoidable. Christian ministers are claiming divine authority for the judgment that gay men and women are not only different, but sinfully different; gay men and women are being physically and psychologically abused; they are being excluded from their families, frozen out of churches, and discriminated against in a variety of painful legal ways. We have no choice but to bring up the issue. Straight and gay American citizens, and especially American Christians, can remain neither indifferent nor indecisive.

What is hard, of course—and hard for many gays too—is to approach the subject with open minds rather than fixed certainties, with hearts full of compassion rather than repugnance. That is why I suggest you read the biblical account of Saint Peter's struggle to abandon his own fixed certainties, to overcome his own repugnance. In Acts 10:1-20 he protests three times when in his trance he hears the Lord order him to rise and kill and eat birds and reptiles and pigs. Hardly surprising, when you remember that ever since he was a tot he has had it drilled into him: "Every swarming thing that swarms upon the earth is an abomination; it shall not be eaten. Whatever goes on its belly, and whatever goes on all fours, or whatever has many feet, all the swarming things that swarm upon the earth, you shall not eat; for they are an abomination." That is Holy Writ, part of the holy Levitical Code, the Word of God as Jews understood it. And now God suddenly is telling Peter just the opposite: "Kill and eat. . . . What God has cleansed, you must not call common."

Moreover, all his life Peter has been instructed not to associate with Gentiles. But when the emissaries of Cornelius arrive, Peter accompanies them to the latter's house, where Peter confesses, "Truly I perceive that God shows no partiality, but in every nation any one who fears him and does what is right is acceptable to him."

So the question is whether those of us who were drilled, as was Peter, to think a certain way are as willing as he to risk reexamining what we were taught. Moral judgment has a progressive character, criticizing the present in terms of the future. Perhaps the Holy Spirit in our time is leading each of us to a new conviction, a new confession: "Truly I perceive that God shows no partiality, but in every sexual orientation any one who fears him and does what is right is acceptable to him."

Several years ago James B. Nelson, a professor of Christian ethics, suggested that there were four primary theological stances toward homosexuality. The first was a rejecting-punitive position; the second a rejecting-nonpunitive position; the third a conditional acceptance; and the fourth an unconditional acceptance. I think these four positions reflect the differing attitudes of most church members today.

The Jerry Falwells of the land obviously take the rejecting-punitive position. To them homosexual acts are perverse, repugnant, and sinful. Like Peter's argument with God, theirs too is based on Levitical law—in this case, "You shall not lie with a male as with a woman; it is an abomination."

What they never point out is that "abomination" (*toevah* in Hebrew)—the word used in reference to homosexual acts—is also used in reference to eating pork, to misuse of incense, and to intercourse during menstruation. Generally it does not signify something intrinsically evil (like rape or theft, which are also dealt with in the Levitical Code), but something that is ritually unclean. So, like Peter, we may be called to recognize the distinction between intrinsic wrong and ritual impurity.

There are some other things never mentioned by the Jerry Falwells. To avoid idolatry, the Israelites went to great lengths to separate their worship of God from the fertility cults of their neighbors, whose rituals involved male as well as female prostitutes. But their primary concern was with idolatry, not homosexuality. Likewise they rejected the practice widespread in the Middle East at the time of humiliating captured foes by forcing them to submit to anal rape in a fashion similar to what goes on in prisons today. Again, the emphasis was not on prohibiting homosexuality; it was on not dishonoring a fellow human being. It was also widely believed—and by the Israelites as well in this case—that the male seed alone carried life; women provided only the incubating space. Hence any ejaculation outside of a woman's body was a form of abortion, and procreation was mighty important to a very small nation in a sea of hostile ones.

Most of all, what we need to remember is that nowhere does Scripture address a specifically homosexual orientation. Biblical writers assume that homosexual acts are being committed by people whose basic orientation is heterosexual. The problem they are addressing is, in modern terms, perversion rather than inversion. The Bible says nothing directly one way or another about the loving, lasting relationships known by so many of the people I listed at the outset, the loving, lasting relationships that patently exist today between so many gay people in this country, in every city, and in so many churches.

As for Sodom and Gomorrah, scholars are far less clear about what happened there than are most contemporary evangelists. If, however, we allow the Bible to illumine its own cloudy passages, we find that the destruction of Sodom and Gomorrah had little if anything to do with homosexuality. In Ezekiel we read, "This was the guilt of your sister Sodom: she and her daughters had pride, surfeit of food, and prosperous ease, but did not aid the poor and needy." In the first chapter of Isaiah, where Judah is rebuked through a comparison with Sodom, homosexuality is never mentioned among the specific sins, which again include a failure to pursue justice and to champion the oppressed. The most likely other sin of Sodom was a failure to show hospitality to strangers—a possibility indicated by Jesus' words to his disciples: "Whenever you enter a town and they do not receive you . . . I tell you it shall be more tolerable on that day for Sodom than for that town." How ironic that because of a mistaken understanding of the crime of Sodom and Gomorrah, Christians should be repeating the real crime every day against homosexuals!

Clearly, it is not Scripture that creates hostility to homosexuality, but rather hostility to homosexuality that prompts certain Christians to retain a few passages from an otherwise discarded law code. The problem is not how to reconcile homosexuality with scriptural passages that appear to condemn it, but rather how to reconcile the rejection and punishment of homosexuals with the love of Christ. I do not think it can be done. I do not see how Christians can define and then exclude people on the basis of sexual orientation alone—not if the law of love is more important than the laws of biology.

The rejecting but nonpunitive stance, while condemning homosexual acts, strives not to condemn the homosexual person. According to this second view, homosexuals are not criminals or sinners so much as victims of arrested development or some other form of psychic disorder, because fundamentally homosexuality is "unnatural." The problem with this position is that most gay people assert that they did not choose their orientation, they discovered it; and scientific research supports the assertion. Psychology professor John Money, a leading authority on character development, claims that it is not possible to force a change from homosexual to heterosexual "any more than it is possible to change a heterosexual into a homosexual." If that is the case, the offer to "cure" gays of their "sickness" carries the danger of raising false expectations, and then guilt when the cure does not work.

Besides, how sick are gays? I was impressed when in 1973 the American Psychiatric Association voted to remove homosexuality from its list of mental disorders. The association did not deny that many homosexuals are disturbed, it only acknowledged that many are not. And what is the meaning of "natural" and "unnatural"? I come back to the law of love and the laws of biology. If we as Christians judge what is natural according to the law of love, and if we can affirm that gays can be as loving as straights, then why is homosexual love contrary to human nature? Should a relationship not be judged by its inner worth rather than by its outer appearance?

That brings us to the stance of conditional acceptance. Many sensitive straight Christians have struggled to reach this position. They now believe that all rights should be accorded gay people. They believe in the ordination of avowed gays, if only because they see the hypocrisy involved in supporting job opportunities outside the church only to deny these same opportunities within. But they cannot picture a gay spouse in the parsonage; they are uncomfortable with public displays of gay affection. In their heart of hearts they feel that homosexuality is not really on a par with heterosexuality.

I have tended to lean toward that position, but I think it is untenable. Consider Jewish-Christian relations. Most Christians will insist that Jews should enjoy the same rights as Christians because they are as good or as bad as we are; we are all equal. Nevertheless in their heart of hearts they think Judaism is inferior to Christianity. But can you champion equality while nourishing the theological roots that make for inequality? Finally, does not Judaism have to be not inferior, not superior, just different? There are dilemmas, major ones, particularly for Christians who feel that Jews never recognized God's love in person on earth. But dilemmas we can live with and even find creative; the worst thing we can do with a dilemma is to resolve it prematurely because we lack the courage to live with uncertainty.

I think straight Christians have to reach the same position vis-à-vis gays. They are different—that's all. What I have come to recognize is that just as "the black problem" turned out to be a problem of white racism, just as "the woman problem" turned out to be a problem of male sexism, so "the homosexual problem" is really the homophobia of many heterosexuals. I know gays have hang-ups; so do straights, and I leave these hang-ups to the psychologists. I am appalled at the promiscuity of some gays, but no more appalled than are many other gays. Promiscuity is cruel and degrading in any sexual orientation, but straights bear a special responsibility for the promiscuity of gays. Just as blacks used to be labeled shiftless by whites who made sure there would be no reward for their diligence, so straights call gays promiscuous while denying support for overtly gay stable relationships—the spouse in the parsonage.

So enough of these fixed certainties. If what we think is right and wrong divides still further the human family, there must be something wrong with what we think is right. Enough of this cruelty and hatred, this punitive legislation toward gay people on the part of straight Christians. Claiming to be full of principles, these Christians are proving to be full of prejudice. Peter widened his horizons; let's not narrow ours. It has been said that a mind once stretched by a new idea can never return to its former shape. Let's listen, learn, let's read and pray—none of this is easy—until with Peter's conviction we can make a similar confession: "Truly I perceive that God shows no partiality, but in every sexual orientation any one who fears him and does what is right is acceptable to him."

What Saint Augustine called the duty of the preacher is the obligation of all: "to teach what is right and to refute what is wrong, and in the performance of this task to conciliate the hostile [and] to rouse the careless."

A GROUP REFLECTION ON THE GOSPEL IN SOLENTINAME

An effective form of social preaching was used from the mid-1970s to the early 1980s in a Roman Catholic community formed on a Lake Nicaragua archipelago by a priest, Ernesto Cardenal, and a few other outsiders in addition to the local campesinos *(**see Vol. 1, pp. 743-46**). Either during the Sunday Mass or just after it, copies of the gospel for the day were passed out to those who could read and then the passage was read aloud, a few verses at a time. Then the faithful who were gathered said what the passage meant to them.*

The priest reconstructed what was said from memory at first, but later began transcribing it from a recording. Cardenal published four volumes of these group sermons, and they have been very influential in a number of places. The sermon here came from Ernesto Cardenal, The Gospel in Solentiname, *vol. 2, trans. Donald D. Walsh (Maryknoll, N.Y.: Orbis, 1978), 51-62.*

The Mustard Seed and the Yeast

Matthew 13:31-35

The kingdom of heaven is like a mustard seed
that a man sowed in his field.
It is certainly the smallest of all seeds,
but when it grows
it becomes the largest of plants
and gets to be a tree,
so big that the flying birds
come to make nests in its branches

MANUEL: "It seems to me that the word of God is a very delicate thing, very tiny. At first it seems insignificant and therefore many people despise it, but afterwards it grows like a mustard tree. And so at first Jesus spoke his word to twelve people, and that was very insignificant, but it spread to others and was scattered throughout the world. And it has spread so far it has reached even us in Solentiname. It also seems to me that the word of God is tiny and insignificant because it sprouts in our hearts and you almost can't see it. But then I tell it to someone else, and so it grows and spreads like a great tree, and this tree is the transformation of the world."

DOÑA ADELA, a little old lady, said: "We who are here have seen that little seed growing." I asked what that "kingdom of heaven" was that Jesus compared with the mustard seed.

NATALIA answered energetically: "It seems to me that the kingdom of heaven is unity. When all of us join together and all of us love each other, that will be the kingdom of God."

I said it was strange that for so long people believed that the kingdom of heaven was in heaven. And even today many educated Christians continue to believe this. The fact is that it was easier to think of the kingdom in the other world so as not to have to change this one. We know that Matthew used the word "heaven" because of the Jewish custom of not saying the word "God." If the kingdom of God were heaven, there would be no sense to all those parables about the kingdom: that the kingdom of heaven is like a net that catches good and bad fish, that it's like a field in which there is wheat mixed with weeds, that it's like a buried treasure, that it's like a seed, that it's like yeast.

And there would be no sense to another parable, found in one of the apocryphal gospels but apparently an authentic one: The kingdom of heaven is like a woman who carries a bowl of flour home without noticing that the bowl is broken, and when she gets home she finds that all the flour is gone. I said also that this last parable is like an image of the church, compromised by power and money, preferring to think of the kingdom only in the other life and not in this one. And therefore now that humanity is on the point of making bread (transforming the world), the church has lost all the flour. Jesus told Pilate that his kingdom was not of this world, but by this he meant that it was in contrast to all the other political kingdoms, because it was not a kingdom of power. This kingdom, as Natalia has said very well, is union, love.

WILLIAM said: "That's why he compares it with a mustard seed. Because instead of a kingdom of worldwide power, which the Jews were waiting for (which was a reactionary idea), the kingdom of Jesus is shown as a very humble little group, which goes unnoticed at the beginning: a carpenter with a few poor people. Among his disciples he didn't have one important person. Later it will also be a political kingdom that will control the earth, and that's why he says it will be greater than all the trees. But at the beginning it was an invisible kingdom."

And TERESITA, William's wife, with her son Juan in her arms, said: "The truth is that the kingdom belongs to the poor, and that's why it's unnoticed at first. But the poor will control the world and will possess the earth."

LAUREANO: "And you can say the same about the revolution: at the beginning nobody notices it. It's little groups, cells."

The poet CORONEL URTECHO, who was visiting us, said: "Like this little group now that's telling us these things in Solentiname." And he added, after a pause: "On the other hand, there are ostentatious works of the church, created with great pride, that give promise of being great things, and end up in nothing. They are the opposite of the kingdom of God, like the Jesuit Central-American University."

LAUREANO: "And the guerrilla groups are small, insignificant, poor.

And they're often wiped out. But they're going to change society. Can't we apply also to them the parable of the mustard seed?"

MARCELINO, with his calm voice, said: "I don't know about the mustard seed, but I do know about the *guasima* seed, which is tiny. I'm looking at that *guasima* tree over there. It's very large, and the birds come to it too. I say to myself: that's what we are, this little community, a *guasima* seed. It doesn't seem there's any connection between a thing that's round and tiny, like a pebble, and that great big tree. It doesn't seem either that there's any connection between some poor *campesinos* and a just and well-developed society, where there is abundance and everything is shared. And we are the seed of that society. When the tree will develop we don't know. But we know that we are a seed and not a pebble."

I said: "The great tree with all its branches and its leaves is already present in the seed, even though in a hidden form. In the same way the kingdom of heaven, which is a cosmic kingdom, is already present in us, but in a hidden way. A tree is the product of the evolution of a seed, and in nature everything is produced by a process of evolution. And it seems to me that with this parable of the seed Christ is also telling us here that the kingdom of heaven is the product of the same process of evolution that formed stars, plants, animals, people. And it grows in us impelled by the same forces of nature that impelled the evolution of the whole cosmos, which is to say that the kingdom of heaven is evolution itself."

ELVIS: "The birds that make their nests in the branches, it seems to me, are humanity now free: people who can go freely everywhere without borders of any kind and who will feel safe in the universe, without any of them ever being in need."

TERESITA: "This parable also teaches us that we must be patient, because a tree isn't created in a single day, and all the processes of nature take their time."

OLIVIA: "The kingdom of heaven or the kingdom of love begins with a tiny bit. When we work on it, that seed grows and grows."

"I've seen that seed growing here, blessed be God," said DOÑA ADELITA in her faint voice.

OLIVIA continued: "The kingdom of heaven is also taking shape in our homes with the growing children that we are shaping. They are growing up, and the kingdom of love is taking shape, which is the kingdom of heaven. It has to take shape in a child. And then it goes on developing, and if the children develop well they are going to extend that kingdom of love also. Yes, you can notice also how the kingdom of heaven is growing inside the child."

He also gave them this other example:
The kingdom of heaven is like the yeast that a woman puts into three measures of flour,
to make all the dough ferment.

MANUEL: "It's the same thing. Because the yeast is also small and makes all the dough grow."

I asked what the dough was, and he answered very emphatically: "Everybody!"

I said: "So the yeast is the love that there is in humanity. At the beginning it may have seemed small, insignificant. We still see it quite small inside ourselves, but it grows and develops, and it is going to unite us all."

LAUREANO: "In the book we're reading now in the Youth Club we've seen how revolutionary groups have acted as catalysts for the people. That's like being the yeast of the people."

DOÑA ADELITA: "Faith is the yeast."

ELVIS: "The yeast comes out of the people themselves. But at the beginning it's a little group and it makes the dough grow. Without the yeast the dough doesn't grow and there's no bread."

CESAR: "The kingdom of heaven is love, and therefore Jesus says it's like a seed that a man sows on his land and like yeast that a woman puts in the dough. Because it's the love that God has put in us, so that it will grow."

ELVIS: "It almost comes to the same thing. The two things are tiny at first and afterwards they grow."

I said: "And this is also so that we won't be discouraged. Here we see that our group is tiny. Many people are afraid to come. But Jesus tells us that the kingdom of heaven begins with something very tiny. You have to remember that this little group is also a ferment inside its dough."

DONALD: "In many places there is yeast that breaks things apart."

I: "What Donald says is quite true, and Christ also somewhere else tells us to be wary of 'the yeast of the Pharisees and the yeast of Herod,' because evil is also a little group, an elite that corrupts all the dough. The yeast of the Pharisees seems to be the corruption of the religious elites, and the yeast of Herod the corruption of the power elites. He spoke that warning after the multiplication of the loaves. . . ."

FELIPE interrupted me: "And here too he's talking about bread. Why does Jesus give bread as an example? It seems to me that it's because bread is a material reality (although it's not only material), because we have to fulfill love in a material way: by means of food, drink, clothing, housing, and all the other things produced by nature and the work of people. That's why Jesus uses that materialistic parable."

I said that in fact the kingdom of heaven is to satisfy hunger, all of our hunger, naturally including all the material necessities. And that's why Jesus compares it with a loaf that is going to be baked; and the yeast that will make it grow is love. I also said that on the eve of the French Revolution, when the first signs of popular uprising were beginning to be seen, the revolutionaries in Paris were saying: "The bread is rising." They were referring to the mass of the people who were rising up, but they also saw it as a mass of flour. And the revolution was the great loaf of bread. We can still say that the bread is rising wherever the people are rising. It's the whole universe that is rising impelled by evolution and revolution, until it reaches its perfection, which is the kingdom of heaven, as Saint Matthew says, or the kingdom of God, as the other evangelists say, or the kingdom of love. And this is also the same eucharistic bread that we raise up at the altar, "Which earth has given and human hands have made," as we say in the Offertory. We offer it to God as a representation of all the fruits of earth and of work.

ALEJANDRO: "And this bread is to be shared by everyone. That's why the miracle of the multiplication of the loaves was also another teaching: to teach us to share the bread."

CESAR: "The flying birds go all over the place, right? They don't have any nests. Those birds who didn't have any place to live reach the tree and find a place to be. They have a nest. Now we're told one more thing about the kingdom of heaven: that it's like a loaf of bread that takes away your hunger."

DOÑA ADELITA: "When I begin to bake a loaf of bread, it's God who makes it grow for me. I say to myself: 'Oh, what am I going to do to make it grow!' And would you believe? It grows. And it's the same way with my love for God every day: Will it grow? And it grows more and more."

LAUREANO: "The only thing I would say is that we've got to play the part assigned to us, as a seed that's going to grow and not a seed that produces nothing. And as a good yeast that makes the bread rise."

WILLIAM: "There are two little words here that we must notice: The woman put the yeast in three measures of flour, and so she made all the dough ferment. This means, in the first place, that we have to mix in with all the dough, get inside it and make ourselves one with it. In the second place, it means that it's the total mass that is called on to ferment, it's with all people that the loaf is going to be formed. And this is what 'Catholic' means: universal. This church has this name because it's not one more religion, separated from the other religions. Its goal is the unity of the totality of people, the creation of the Universal Person."

The poet CORONEL said: "And why three measures of grain? Why not two—or four?"

Some of us smiled. We didn't answer. And he repeated: "Surely that was the quantity that the women of that time were accustomed to mix, three measures. Like saying now an arroba of flour. But I think that maybe there is something more than that."

I told him to tell us.

CORONEL: "The Trinity. The Trinity, which is the mystery of the love of God, of the community of God: the Father, the Son, and the Holy Spirit. And also the love of the family: William and Teresita with Juan, who has been born to them and who is the son. The three measures, then, must be the love of two people who produce a third. The fruitfulness of love that always engenders love."

LAUREANO said: "In Cuba the Communist Party is considered to be a vanguard that makes the whole mass advance. And it really is an elite of the most sacrificing and most revolutionary people, and in that sense you can say that it also is a yeast."

PANCHO: "We're talking about the gospel, not about Communism. . . ."

I said that in Cuba Christianity had turned out the opposite of the way Christ had wanted. It had been a Christianity of dough and not of yeast. Whereas the yeast there had been Communism.

CORONEL, turning to me: "With regard to Christianity and Communism, some thoughts on the subject occurred to me recently and I intended to tell them to you, and I'll tell them now to the whole community. Here they are: Communism cannot absorb Christianity without ceasing to be completely Communist and changing into Christianity, whereas Christianity can absorb Communism (Marxism-Leninism) and continue to be Christianity and even be more Christian. To put it another way, the Communist cannot become a convert to Christianity without ceasing to be exclusively Communist and becoming a Christian, whereas the Christian can become a Communist (Marxist-Leninist) and be even more of a Christian."

We went on to the last verses, in which it is said that Jesus spoke only in parables, in order to fulfill what the prophet had said:

I shall speak by means of examples;
I shall say things that have been secret
since God made the world.

Nobody made any other commentary and I said: "The kingdom of heaven has been gradually taking shape since the beginning of the world. First it has been slowly developing with the very slow evolution of the universe and afterwards, more swiftly, with the revolutions of human society. But neither nature nor human beings knew where all this was leading, until Christ came to reveal it. The secret of evolution and of revolution (of the universe and of people) it seems to me is that secret that was hidden from the beginning of the world. Christians are not necessarily more revolutionary or more loving than non-Christians. But the Christians, as one of the Latin American theologians of liberation has said, are the ones who know. They know, through the gospel, where the revolution is going, and what the goal of love is. And Christ is now revealing that secret hidden from the beginning of the world here to this little group in Solentiname."

And I said afterwards that Christians and Communists had always believed that Christianity and Communism were opposed to each other, but recently the gospel itself has revealed to us what the poet Coronel has just said: that the Christian can become a Communist and be even more of a Christian. And this is also a truth that up to now had been hidden.

CARDINAL ARNS: A SERMON FOR THE FUNERAL OF A WORKER

An example of the prophetic liberation preaching **(see Vol. 1, pp. 741-43)** *that can be done by a member of the hierarchy is this sermon by the Archbishop of São Paulo in Brazil, the largest Roman Catholic diocese in the world. Paulo Evaristo, Cardinal Arns, did not hesitate to speak out against a corrupt military dictatorship, voicing the needs of the poor to whom he had devoted most of his ministry. A case in point is this sermon that he preached at the Requiem for Santo Dias de Silva, a metallurgical worker killed by the police while trying to shield others with his own body in a labor dispute. The sermon was published in* Proclaiming the Acceptable Year, *ed. Justo L. Gonzalez (Valley Forge, Pa.: Judson, 1982), 22-24.*

It Is Not True! Not True!

Paulo Evaristo, Cardinal Arns

(A homily at the funeral mass of laborer Santo Dias de Silva in the Metropolitan Cathedral, October 31, 1979)

Ana, the wife of our brother felled by violence,
repeatedly told me, even last night:
"It's not true! It's not true!"

It is not true that the father of two children is dead,
the husband, at the very time when he was building his own life with so much sacrifice and love,
and yet kept
the best of himself
to lend courage and support to those who suffer more.
It is not true that love is dead.

It is not true that the laborer is dead,
in the struggle for justice.
Throughout his life, laborer Santo
looked upon the lives of his fellow workers,
and read the Gospel,
and knew the love of Christ for the laborers.
He shared in the discussion of the church and the state
seeking only one goal:
that the workers would have more justice.
It is not true that justice must die.

Also, *it is not true* that the nonviolent
is killed by violence:
That the laborer, who set the example of resisting
without ever injuring,
of being courageous
without wounding,
of offering his life
without taking another's
must be murdered.
The violence arms the hand of another poor man,

who should benefit from the same struggle,
but who, in spite of it, because he is a policeman,
takes the life of a brother
and a possible friend.

It is not true.
Hardly anything is true, in this time and place.
That they go with firearms,
who go to meet the people,
the people whose arms are crossed in peace.

Hardly anything is true
when the very millions who build the wealth of a city
are considered scandalously bold
because they wish to give bread to their children.
Bread.
Simply bread and peace.

Hardly anything is true, in this city,
inasmuch as there are two weights and two measures:
one for the master, and the other for the laborer.

My friends:
Although *it is not true,* although *hardly anything is true,*
today begins anew
the trek of our Hope.
When worker Santo shielded with his body
the life of his brothers,
he did like Christ:
He restored life and hope to us.

Because of the hour when Santo, laborer Santo, died like a grain of wheat,

many laborers will be able
to give new bread
to their fellows and their children.
Every age, and even sometimes every event,
must have its Christ,
because only thus
will the fellow workers remain united
and will not lose hope.

Before faith and before history
we can say, with absolute certainty:
The life and death of worker Santo
had the greatest significance.
We hope that, on the basis of his life
and of his commitment to his fellow workers,
there will begin a birth
of understanding
and of justice
for the entire working world.

May God keep us in our faith on the meaning of life
and on its continuation for the good of others.

We shall meet again, Santo, our worker-brother!

CHAPTER 30

A GREAT COMPANY OF WOMEN

TAMSEN WHISTLER: "A WOMAN'S FAITH"

Elaine J. Lawless, an ethnographer who teaches at the University of Missouri, has made a specialty of studying women clergy. In Women Preaching Revolution,[1] *she devoted her attention to the way women preach* (**see Vol. 1, pp. 762-64**)*. She found the way ordained women she studied used storytelling in their sermons to be innovative. She considered the women's fresh approach to biblical stories, in which they often called attention to aspects previous sermons had ignored. This was especially true of the way the women sought the perspective of persons marginalized in their societies. These characteristics and most of the others noted by Lawless are exemplified in one sermon she included in her book, that by the Reverend Tamsen Whistler, who was associate rector of Calvary Episcopal Church in Columbia, Missouri, at the time it was preached (June 26, 1988). Lawless describes it as "a powerful sermon on the hemorrhaging woman story she reinserted into the lectionary readings and used as her sermon text" (p. 91). The text of the sermon is taken from pp. xxiii-xxviii of Lawless's book.*[2]

A WOMAN'S FAITH

The lesson for this Sunday comes to us
from the Gospel of Mark:
"And one of the leaders of the synagogue named Jairus came
and when he saw him, fell at his feet and begged him repeatedly,
'My little daughter is at the point of death.
Come and lay your hands on her,
so that she may be made well, and live.'
So he went with him.
. . .
—Some people came from the leader's house to say,
'Your daughter is dead. Why trouble the teacher any further?'
But overhearing what they said,
Jesus said to the leader of the synagogue,
'Do not fear, only believe.'
He allowed no one to follow him except Peter, James, and John, the brother of James.
When they came to the house of the leader of the synagogue,
he saw a commotion, people weeping and wailing loudly.
When he had entered, he said to them,
'Why do you make a commotion and weep?
The child is not dead but sleeping.'
And they laughed at him.
Then he put them all outside,
and took the child's father and mother and those who were with him,
and went in where the child was.
He took her by the hand and said to her,
'Talitha cum,'
which means, 'Little girl, get up!'
And immediately the girl got up and began to walk about
(she was twelve years of age).
At this they were overcome with amazement.
He strictly ordered them that no one should know this,
and told them to give her something to eat." [Mark 5:22-24, 35b-43, NRSV]

The Gospel passage this morning
is a fairly straightforward miracle story,
particularly dramatic
because beyond healing,
Jesus raises someone from the dead.
A twelve-year-old is restored to life,
because of her parents' faith.
There's a pattern to miracle stories in the Bible,
and what we have heard this morning
follows the pattern pretty well.
Human resources are exhausted.
Jairus in desperation approaches Jesus.
Jesus encounters opposition in the pressing crowd
and the jeering mourners.
The miracle itself is private—
only parents and three disciples
witness Jesus' raising the girl.
Jesus both touches and speaks to the child.
Everyone is astonished
when she gets up and walks.
After requesting silence about the miracle
and making sure that the child eats,
Jesus leaves.

At issue here for us
in the twentieth century
is often the question,
"Is this really a miracle?
Did it really happen?"
But we can trap ourselves
so effectively
in the "Is it real" question
that we may not move beyond it
to the real issue,
the issue of faith.
Do we believe that God
can intervene in our lives?
Can we recognize God's action?

And there's another issue also,
which lies in the fact

that what the lectionary provides for us
this morning
in the healing of Jairus' daughter
is only *part* of the story.
You may have noticed in your bulletins
that what we heard a short while ago
were verses 22-24 and 35-43
of the fifth chapter of Mark.
Verses 25-34, which we did not read,
contain another story,
another healing miracle,
which interrupts the story of Jairus' daughter,
while providing an explanation
of Jesus' delay in reaching Jairus' house.
Let me read this passage.

"And a large crowd followed him and pressed in on him.
Now there was a woman who had been suffering from hemorrhages for twelve years.
She had endured much under many physicians,
and had spent all that she had; and she was no better, but rather grew worse.
She had heard about Jesus, and came up behind him in the crowd
and touched his cloak,
for she said, 'If I but touch his clothes, I will be made well.'
Immediately her hemorrhage stopped;
and she felt in her body that she was healed of her disease.
Immediately aware that power had gone forth from him,
Jesus turned about in the crowd and said,
'Who touched my clothes?'
And his disciples said to him,
'You see the crowd pressing in on you; how can you say, "Who touched me?" '
He looked all around to see who had done it.
But the woman, knowing what had happened to her,
came in fear and trembling, fell down before him,
and told him the whole truth.
He said to her, 'Daughter, your faith has made you well;
go in peace, and be healed of your disease.'" [Mark 5:25-34]

An obvious question here,
of course,
is why did the designers of our lectionary
leave the woman with the twelve-year issue of blood
out of the story of Jairus' daughter?
We could get caught for a long time
in speculation about this,
and probably the explanation
is something simple like,
"The story of Jairus' daughter
stands on its own" or
"one healing makes the point as well as two"
or "the hemorrhaging woman is less tasteful
than the little girl."
It's apparently fairly clear
in the oldest Greek manuscripts of Mark
that the healing of the hemorrhaging woman
is written in better Greek
than the healing of Jairus' daughter.
So the writer of Mark
probably inserted the story to begn with.
Perhaps our lectionary designers left it out
because it began as an insertion.
Whatever the reason,
it's been left out.
But I think it's important that we consider it;
first, because the use of the "story within a story"

is fairly typical of the gospel of Mark,
but primarily because
the two stories together
offer us more about the nature of Jesus
and faith
than either story does on its own.
Without the story
of the hemorrhaging woman,
the healing of Jairus' daughter
invites us to concentrate
on the beautiful vision of a child lost,
now restored to her parents.
It is possible for us to talk about
the great spiritual meaning
of the child's return to life
without giving much thought
to the physical—
beyond the touch of Jesus' hand
and his command
that she be given something to eat.
We can be thrilled
that Jesus has acted
in such a dramatic way,
and we can recognize that children,
as well as adults,
are recipients of God's grace.
But we can stand outside the story
and watch.
And we can speculate
about the reality of miracles.
We can sidetrack ourselves,
while we admire the great spiritual revelation
of the child's return to life.
If we consider the healing
of the hemorrhaging woman
in the context of the healing of Jairus' daughter,
we find powerful contrasts.
The hemorrhaging woman
is not somebody we'd want to be around.
She's drained and desperate.
She's spent all her savings
seeking a cure,
and she's only grown worse.
For twelve years—
as long as Jairus' daughter has been alive—
the hemorrhaging woman
has been denied access
to the practice of her religion,
because she's unclean.
Close contact
with another human by her
renders that other person unclean, also.
The woman is an outcast,
one to be avoided,
one for whom life
within the structure of a supportive community
is impossible.
She is unclean;
and no decent person
should have anything to do with her.
In her desperation,
the woman forces herself through the crowd
toward Jesus,
seeking only to touch his clothing
to heal herself.
But the healing comes from Jesus.
She touches his garment
and feels within her body
that she is cured.
And he feels within his body
that someone has touched him.
His disciples think he is silly
to seek a particular person
in a pressing crowd,
but he recognizes
that a particular individual
has encountered him,
and he looks for her.
Overwhelmed by the fact of her new wholeness,
the woman is frightened.
Nevertheless,
she goes to Jesus as he seeks her,
and she tells him her whole story.
His response to her?
"Daughter, go in peace.

Your faith has healed you."
Another miracle, to be sure,
but the two stories together
help bring home to us
that an encounter with Jesus Christ
on any level
involves both the physical,
concrete, world
and dialogue with Jesus Christ.
The reality of experience
is imperative,
in our relationship with God.
We don't simply encounter Jesus Christ
on some esoteric plane
separate from our daily lives.
Instead, we encounter God in Christ
in our physical being,
our life in the world,
and our death.
The encounter involves both touch
and conversation.
Without the dialogue,
between Jesus and the woman,
Jesus and the child
and the child's parents,
the miracles have little meaning.
Without the dialogue,
what happens simply happens
and there's nothing to allay
the resulting fear.
When the woman is healed,
she is frightened.
Jesus gives peace
by acknowledging her faith,
and that's a miracle
beyond the physical healing.
We are like the hemorrhaging woman
and the little girl
because we are embodied beings.
We will undergo physical and emotional
pain;
and we will die.
We are like them also
in that we know the world
through our physical presence,
through our senses as well as our
thoughts,
and we need both
for wholeness in our daily lives.
The physical aspect of our lives
is not somehow separate
from our spiritual development.
We have to live that development out
in our bodies,
in the world,
in the here and now,
in the decisions we make,
in our connections with those around
us.
How do we participate
in God's healing action?
We touch each other;
we talk to each other.
We love.
These stories are given to us
that we might learn something about
faith,
not that we get sidetracked
on the issue of whether they really
happened,
whether they're really miracles,
but that we might focus on the issue
of how it is that we encounter God.
Do we believe in the resurrection?
How do we live that belief,
act it out in our physical lives?
Can we recognize that concrete action—
touch and dialogue—
are the way we know each other
and the Christ within us?
Body and blood,
word and action—
the miracle of faith
lies in the concrete,
the particular,
the physical,
our daily lives.
We eat and drink together
that we might more fully know
our connection with each other,
with the hemorrhaging woman,
the dead and living child,
the crucified and risen Christ.
Amen.

BARBARA BROWN TAYLOR: "LIFE GIVING FEAR"

There is probably no woman whose preaching has received as much attention as that of Barbara Brown Taylor (**see Vol. 1, pp. 766-69**)*; almost anyone who wishes to compile a list of the most effective preachers active today will include her among the top ten or twelve. She is the only woman Beecher lecturer to speak about the preaching task as it looks to one who practices it. An Episcopal priest, Taylor has served as assistant at a large parish in Atlanta and rector of what was a small parish in north Georgia when she went there; now she holds an endowed chair at Piedmont College in Demorest, Georgia, and is heard frequently as a guest lecturer or preacher. The sermon below is documentation for the thesis that nothing has done so much recently to improve the quality of preaching as the admission of large numbers of women into the ranks of those who do it. It is taken from* Home by Another Way *(Cambridge, Mass.: Cowley, 1997), 69-72. It also appeared in* The Christian Century *(March 4, 1998).*

Life Giving Fear

At that very time there were some present who told Jesus about the Galileans whose blood Pilate had mingled with their sacrifices. He asked them, "Do you think that because these Galileans suffered in this way they were worse sinners than all other Galileans? No, I tell you; but unless you repent, you will all perish as they did." Luke 13:1-9.

When I was a hospital chaplain, the calls I dreaded most did not come from the emergency room, the psychiatric ward, or even the morgue. They came from the pediatric floor, where little babies lay in cribs with bandages covering half their heads and sweet-faced children pushed IV poles down the hall. One day I received a call to come sit with a mother while her five-year-old daughter was in surgery. Earlier in the week, the girl had been playing with a friend when her head began to hurt. By the time she found her mother, she could no longer see. At the hospital, a CAT scan confirmed that a large tumor was pressing on the girl's optic nerve and she was scheduled for surgery as soon as possible.

On the day of the operation, I found her mother sitting under the fluorescent lights in the waiting room beside an ashtray full of cigarette butts. She smelled as if she had puffed every one of them, although she was not smoking when I got there. She was staring at a patch of carpet in front of her, with her eyebrows raised in that half-hypnotized look that warned me to move slowly. I sat down beside her. She came to, and after some small talk she told me just how awful it was. She even told me why it had happened.

"It's my punishment," she said, "for smoking these damned cigarettes. God couldn't get my attention any other way, so he made my baby sick." Then she started crying so hard that what she said next came out like a siren: "Now I'm supposed to stop, but I can't stop. I'm going to kill my own child!"

This was hard for me to hear. I decided to forego reflective listening and concentrate on remedial theology instead. "I don't believe in a God like that," I said. "The God I know wouldn't do something like that." The only problem with my response was that it messed with the mother's worldview at the very moment she needed it most. However miserable it made her, she preferred a punishing God to an absent or capricious one. I may have been able to reconcile a loving God with her daughter's brain tumor, but at the moment she could not. If there was something wrong with her daughter, then there had to be a reason. She was even willing to be the reason. At least that way she could get a grip on the catastrophe.

Even those of us who claim to know better react the same way. Calamity strikes and we wonder what we did wrong. We scrutinize our behavior, our relationships, our diets, our beliefs. We hunt for some cause to explain the effect, in hopes that we can stop causing it. What this tells us is that we are less interested in truth than consequences. What we crave, above all, is control over the chaos of our lives.

Luke does not divulge the motive of those who told Jesus about the Galileans whose blood Pilate mingled with their sacrifices. The implication is that those who died deserved what they got, or at least that is the question Jesus intuited. "Do you think that because these Galileans suffered in this way they were worse sinners than all other Galileans?"

It is a tempting equation that solves a lot of problems. (1) It answers the riddle of why bad things happen to good people: they don't. Bad things only happen to bad people. (2) It punishes sinners right out in the open as a warning to everyone. (3) It gives us a God who obeys the laws of physics. For every action, there is an opposite and equal reaction. Any questions?

It is a tempting equation, but Jesus won't go there. "No," he tells the crowd, "but unless you repent, you will all perish as they did." In the south, this is what we call giving with one hand and taking away with the other. *No,* Jesus says, *there is no connection between the suffering and the sin.* Whew. *But unless you repent, you are going to lose some blood too.* Oh.

There is no sense spending too much time trying to decipher this piece of the good news. As far as I can tell, it is not meant to aid reason but to disarm it. In an intervention aimed below his listeners' heads, Jesus touches the panic they have inside of them about all the awful things that are happening around them. They are terrified by those things, for good reason. They have searched their hearts for any bait that might bring disaster sniffing their way. They have lain awake at night making lists of their mistakes.

While Jesus does not honor their illusion that they can protect themselves in this way, he does seem to honor the vulnerability that their fright has opened up in them. It is not a bad thing for them to feel the full fragility of their lives. It is not a bad thing for them to count their breaths in the dark, not if it makes them turn toward the light.

It is that turning he wants for them, which is why he tweaks their fear. *Don't worry about Pilate and all the other things that can come crashing down on your heads,* he tells them. *Terrible things happen, and you are not always to blame. But don't let that stop you from doing what you are doing. That torn place your fear has opened up inside of you is a holy place. Look around while you are there. Pay attention to what you feel. It may hurt you to stay there and it may hurt you to see, but it is not the kind of hurt that leads to death. It is the kind that leads to life.*

Depending on what you want from God, this may not sound like good news to you. I doubt that it would have sounded like good news to the mother in the waiting room. But for those of us who have discovered that we cannot make life safe nor God tame, it is gospel enough. What we can do is turn our faces to the light. That way, whatever befalls us, we will fall the right way.

Notes

1. *Calling for Connections in a Disconnected Time* (Philadelphia: University of Pennsylvania Press, 1996).

2. Lawless also discusses the sermon at length and includes its text in "The Issue of Blood: Reinstating Women into the Tradition," the introductory chapter to

Women Preachers and Prophets, ed. Kienzle and Walker, (Los Angeles and Berkeley: The University of California Press, 1998), 1-18. The Reverend Ms. Whistler, who is now rector of Trinity Episcopal Church in St. Charles, Missouri, is a former student of mine. While I cannot claim credit for her accomplishment, I do take great pleasure in it.

CHAPTER 31

EVANGELISM IN AN ELECTRONIC AGE

BILL HYBELS: "NOBODY STANDS ALONE" (PART ONE)

Evangelism in a megachurch is conducted at the same weekend times as other churches conduct their regular worship (**see Vol. 1, pp. 785-93**)*. The difference is that the event at the megachurch is designed to attract those who are not church members, those who are called "seekers." Bill Hybels, founding leader of the prototypical megachurch, Willow Creek, located in a suburb of Chicago, has stated what it takes to make a good seeker service: "a regularly scheduled, high-quality, Spirit-empowered outreach service where irreligious people can come and discover that they matter to [God] and that Christ died for them."*

In practice, that amounts to holding services in a building that looks more like a theater than a church, one in which there are no traditional religious symbols, one in which there is a stage rather than a sanctuary. High on the walls of the stage are two enormous TV screens that show close-ups of what is happening. A band plays music that has the sound of current popular music; words keyed to the sermon are sung by a chorus dressed like entertainers rather than robed as a choir. After their opening number, a dramatic presentation introduces the issue to be addressed by the sermon, and the point is reinforced by a personal testimony from someone. After another song, the "lesson," as it is called, is given. Its purpose is to prompt the seekers to inquire more closely, in hope that they will be converted and integrated into the life of the community. The sermon that follows is well designed to serve that purpose. Bill Hybels preached it at Willow Creek on September 26 and 27, 1999.

Nobody Stands Alone (Part One)

Let's see if great minds think alike tonight. That would be your mind and mine. The news of the shootings in the Baptist church in Texas comes across the airwaves a couple of weeks ago. Your heart is filled with compassion for the victims and the families. You shake your head, and you wonder how much more random violence our country can take. Then, the newscaster says, "We know very little about the gunman. But as facts come in, we'll fill you in on his identity."

Now, if you're like me in those moments, you start predicting what the life circumstances of the shooter are going to turn out to be. There's one word that turns up in almost every description of a violent criminal. As they're giving his background and living situation, a newscaster will say, somewhere in the description of the person, "He or she was a loner."

As you learned last week, the Texas gunman certainly was a loner. That didn't surprise you, and it didn't surprise me. A few years ago, was anybody shocked when the Unibomber was finally apprehended in a mountain shack, no utilities, in the middle of nowhere? He was a loner, too. I've just come to expect that general background description when someone does some awful thing.

Well, let's check our thinking along another set of lines. The parents of a six-year-old go to the kid's teacher for a normal teacher-conference deal. The teacher says, "Your son/your daughter doesn't mix with the other students very well. He or she has no friends. They rarely engage with anybody—not during recess, before or after school. They keep to themselves. It's like they're in their own little world."

Question: Should those parents be concerned? How concerned? If right now you're thinking, "Pretty darned concerned," then you're thinking right. They ought to be very concerned. Let's try one more. You're dating Mr. or Ms. Right. Hints of tying the knot slip into the conversation every once in a while. Then you learn that your heartthrob has no friends.

They've never really been interested in friendship—not in grade school, high school or college. Your heartthrob has mainly been dreaming of the day that they could finally be married. How much of an "uh-oh" is that little discovery? Is it a small "uh-oh," a medium "uh-oh," or a very large "uh-oh"? It ought to be a very large "uh-oh."

If you know much about life and relationships, or better yet, if you know much about theology, you would know that friendship issues are huge in the overall scheme of things—huge for you, huge for me, huge for our world, huge for God. There are not many issues God is more concerned about than the condition of our relational world, especially moving people from aloneness into rich, caring, Christ-honoring community—from standing alone, to standing together.

That objective has been near the top of his "to do" list since he created human beings in the garden and told them to love and serve one another. Now, because God created human beings to function best in the context of a loving relationship, the Bible is full of warnings regarding the dangers of isolation. It's also full of exhortations for people to take responsibility for moving toward the formation of strong friendships.

Ecclesiastes 4:8-10 is a classic text in this regard. I'll paraphrase it a little bit and put it in modern day language. The Bible says, "Don't stand alone. Someday trouble or heartbreak is going to come your way. In your hour of greatest need, you'll be so glad that you have a friend or two, and that you didn't have to bear the trial or the tragedy all by yourself."

We heard that first-hand from Russ and Lynn's life in their recent trial and tragedy. "Don't stand alone," the text continues. Life's greatest accomplishments rarely come from solo performers. Teams of like-minded people working together and multiplying each other's effectiveness always produce the best long-term results. So team up with some brothers and sisters, and see what happens when mutual effort is multiplied, whatever the objective.

From cover to cover, there are exhortations for people to leave their isolation and move toward community—for all kinds of reasons. And there are sobering warnings in the Bible about the dangers of doing life alone. Several proverbs remind us that the quality of our decision-making is tied directly to the quality of the people around us who will give us wise counsel. "Woe be to the one who stands all alone and attempts to make huge, personal, vocational or financial decisions without input from others," the Bible says.

They just stand exposed to their own blind spots. Their individual wisdom cannot possibly compete with the collective wisdom of a high-quality team. The Bible goes on. "Woe to the one who stands alone—they're going to have to find their way through this difficult life without the encouragement of other people; without the affirmation of other people; without the creative ideas of others; without the prayers of others; without the accountability; without the spiritual stimulation of others."

The Bible reminds all of us that we're created in the image of a relational God. We were created to function best when we leave isolation and move into little communities of friendship, where we learn how to love and how to support, how to receive grace, and how to give grace to those who desperately need it.

So the question that we need to ask at this point of the game is, "How does a person who is currently standing alone move from that condition to one of standing together—as the vocalist led us at the beginning part of this service—standing together, hand in hand, heart to heart, arm in arm?" As Russ said, "I know that many of you are currently engaged in small groups. You have some friends. You have close, growing relationships."

If that's true in your life as it's true in mine, we need to be reminded tonight that that really is one of the greatest blessings we can receive from God. We need to celebrate it and thank God for it. We're reminded too that several thousand of us, in this church, are still standing alone for whatever set of reasons. We've never moved into a little community where we share our lives with other people.

Some of us are between groups right now. There was a time when we were closely connected with some other folks, and that's just not true now. Well, all I want to do tonight is set the tone—set the context—for what life could be like if you were living it the way that God designed it. God hoped you would live it in little communities. I'm going to give you some painstakingly practical kinds of wisdom to move you from isolation into relationship.

So indulge me for just a little while as I review the ABCs of relationship building. Let me begin by making sure we have the right idea about the nature of relationships to begin with. What does it really mean to be in a healthy, God-honoring friendship or relationship or community experience with other people? Let's start on the negative side—talking about what friendship is not.

Friendship is not trying to get someone else to take care of you. If you want to wreck the possibility of being in a real great relationship, go into it with the idea that there is someone out there just sitting on a park bench waiting to nurture you, fawn all over you, soothe you, comfort you, and listen endlessly to your travails and troubles.

Do you want to wreck a friendship? Go into it expecting that there's someone, somewhere, just pining to affirm and encourage you, sitting on pins and needles waiting to develop you spiritually, aching to envelop you with around-the-clock care, and all you have to do is show up with your 150 pounds of need.

If that's the expectation that you have—if that's the orientation that you have—about friendship, it's not a good one, and it will wreck every single attempt that you make to form and build and sustain loving, honoring relationships. When friendship candidates catch the sniff of that kind of orientation coming from you, they will make themselves curiously scarce and you will stand alone—all alone—probably for the rest of your life.

Friendship is not just trying to get someone to take care of you. Further, friendship is not latching on to someone who has a life, because you haven't gotten around to having one yourself yet. Further still, friendship is not hitching your life to a rising star so that you can progress professionally or academically, financially or politically. Almost every time I go to Washington D.C., I am made aware, again, of how shamelessly people use and discard other people in that city for the purpose of self-advancement.

It makes me think of what Harry Truman said one time. "If you want a true friend in Washington, D.C., buy yourself a dog," because people are just using each other to get where they're going. Friendship is not hitching our lives to rising stars for self-advancement purposes. Friendship is not pretending to care about somebody so that they'll join your cause or buy your product.

You see, you just can't build lasting, loving friendships with all that junk going on. Some of us might be halfway through our lives and still standing alone because we're trying to do friendship in a bogus way—in a way that does not contribute to the kind of community that the Bible describes.

We've got to have the right idea about the true nature of friendships if we're going to build some that work and last. Fortunately, the Bible speaks clearly to this issue. In summary form, the Bible teaches that true friendship is a commitment among individuals to genuinely seek the well being of the other. And this, friends, is a radical idea if you really think about it.

I like what the Apostle Paul says in Philippians 2. "Do nothing out of selfish ambition or vain conceit, but in humility consider others more valuable than yourself; each of you should look not to your own interests only, but more to the interests of others."

I'll give you some other Biblical descriptions of friendship. It's the intentional decision to do life with a few other people whose hearts have grown intertwined with yours. It's the decision to leave the shadows of hiddenness to disclose yourself—to disclose your heart, to entrust your heart—to a few people whom you've built a trusting relationship with. It's the joyful sublimation of your own agenda, quite often, for the sheer pleasure of meeting a need or bringing a smile to the face of the befriended.

It's the consistent effort to help the other person reach their fullest potential spiritually, relationally, vocationally—it doesn't matter. But, it's seeking the well being—the full potential—of the other. It's resisting the urge to be independent and self-preoccupied or narcissistic. It's agreeing with God's internal wiring pattern, which urges you to live in loving, openhearted ways with a few people.

But I'll say it again. We'll never build the kind of friendships most of us yearn for until we get the right idea about the true nature of friendship. We've got to get that straight. It's a covenant among individuals to seek the well being of the other. One time Jesus said, "Give, and then it will be given unto you. Serve, and then in due time, others will serve back. Disclose, open yourself up, and in due time, others will. It'll come back to you. Believe in others, and in due time, others will believe in you."

Do you have this idea clearly? I fear our culture has such a warped concept of relationship. It's, "What's in it for me?" It's, "Where can I go where someone can fix me, help me, serve me," and so on. The Bible says, "You'll never do a very good job of building covenant relationships if you go about it that way." So we've got to get it straight—straight from God whose design of our relational world is the right one, and the true one.

Once we have it straight, what the true nature of relationships is all about—giving ourselves to some folks—then there's a second, sobering reality about the friendship-building process. It is that selecting and building significant friendships is an inexact, often lengthy and frustrating endeavor—one that requires energy and risk, quite possibly hurt and disappointment, quite often a lot of patience in the process. That's just truth. Don't let anybody tell you otherwise.

The Bible often refers to quality friendships as being like silver or gold. It's underscoring the fact that not only are friendships precious and valuable, but I think it's also underscoring the fact that friendship selection involves a certain amount of excavating, searching, trial and error, experimentation, and sometimes having exciting discoveries that turn out not to be the real thing.

The Bible is saying that there's a price to be paid up front for the possible discovery of the mother lode—of silver and gold kinds of friendships—later on down the road. In today's world, we don't want to pay that price. We prefer a drive-up window where we come and we place our order, "I'll take two great friends one with, one without"—whatever that one with or one without is—"and change back for my dollar. I'd like it very quickly, please."

A while back, I met a guy who relocated his entire family here mainly to be around Willow. A group of us got together to ask that individual how we could pray for him. He said, "One thing I'd like to ask you to pray for is that God would bring some new friends, some close friends, into my life," friends with whom he could form deep community. That was a wonderful desire, and several of us agreed to pray for him about that exact issue.

As we were leaving his house that night, I felt a prompting by God to pull this guy aside. I said, "Our church is a fantastic place to form and build friendships. But it may take a little longer than you think." "How long?" he said. "How long is long?" I said, "Well, don't be surprised if it takes a couple of years." I could just see his face fall. He said, "Oh, okay."

A couple days later he called me, and he said, "Boy, you took the wind out of my sails in that deal." He said, "I had no idea that it might take me that long." Well, it's been a couple years now, and it's proven to have been a fairly accurate statement in his case. He has some wonderful friendships now. But it took a whole lot longer than he would have liked.

There are exceptions to this rule of thumb. Sometimes we hook up with somebody, we meet someone, and there's an eerie connection that forms almost overnight. The friendship grows and it develops and it lasts. But in my experience, that's quite a rare occurrence. Most of the time, the formation of solid friendships is an arduous process. It begins very awkwardly.

You know what this is like. You're in a social setting, you're standing at the sidelines of a soccer game, you're at a church function, whatever. You dabble in some surface conversation. You process hundreds of verbal and non-verbal pieces of data that's going on while you're pretending to be interested in what they're saying.

The whole time you're wondering in the back of your mind, "Could this be a person with whom I could become deeply connected someday?" "Would I want to?" "Would this person want to?" "Would a friendship with this person work?" "Would it fizzle out?" "Is it worth a try?"

You're doing a whole cost-benefit analysis while you're going through this conversation thing. You're asking if you think it might be worth the risk. You say, "I wonder what would happen next? What would I need to do next?" because this phase of friendship building is so awkward and uncomfortable and sometimes painful and disappointing. Tons of people refuse to engage in it after a time. They sit home, night after night, and they hold pity parties for themselves.

They say, "Oh, I'm lonely. I'm not connected. I don't have close friends." Or sometimes people take the other approach and they just exhaust themselves in superficial relationships that don't really satisfy.

Still other people, especially Willow folks, corner some of us leaders here at Willow once in awhile. They tell us to place them in a loving, nurturing small group, with four or five other people with whom they'll experience instantaneous affinity and community, preferably on Monday nights, in Crystal Lake.

Then, sometimes, they get mad at me or Russ or other leaders in the church. They get mad when we say, "It's not quite that simple. Friendship building isn't that easy." Very seldom can relationships just be arranged for somebody like a Far Eastern marriage. There are no shortcuts to the relationship-building process. There are no shortcuts to body building—staying in shape. There are no shortcuts to knowledge building. There are no shortcuts to faith building.

You slug it out. You put one foot in front of the other, and you just do the hard work of it all day by day. Then, over the long haul, the harvest comes. Well, friendship-building requires an internal "want to" factor that's strong enough to sustain people through these awkward early stages of starts and false starts that are just part of the friendship formation process.

In relationship formation, there has to be enough "want to" to push through the hurts and the disappointments when it doesn't work out right. You've got to just keep reaching out and risking and trying until someday you sense some progress is being made, and you sense some connections are forming heart to heart. Pretty soon the payoff comes, when you stand with a few people, hand in hand, heart to heart, and you know that you're going to come through for them, and they're going to come through for you.

You're going to understand and accept them, and they're going to understand and accept you. Pretty soon, you feel what the Bible talks about as that silver and gold. You feel the preciousness of a relationship. But you've got to pay that rent up front. You've got to pay the price first.

So if you're clear about what friendships really are, and if you have the "want to" sufficient to propel you into motion, I have a couple of practical suggestions that I can give you about this friendship building process. First, if you're looking for places or environments in which to build some friendships, head into the environments that are made up of the kind of people you would most like to befriend.

This summer, after one of our sailboat races, one of the members of my crew dragged me to the post race party tent to listen to a live band that was playing. I've been racing for seven or eight years now, and I know what goes on in these party tents. I just don't go there. But he dragged me there after one of the races this summer. There I saw about a thousand inebriated sailors drinking, dancing, and lying about the races that they had participated in that day.

Do you know what I thought to myself as I was looking around at all these folks? I thought, "I'm really glad that I already have several circles of close friends who are kind of straight about what they really want to see happen with their lives. I'm glad I'm connected with some people who really want to grow spiritually and intellectually and vocationally, because I think it's slim pickings in this tent for high caliber friendships."

I'd never send my young son or daughter into a tent like that and say, "Look for some real great friendships in this tent. This is where you want to hang out to form the relationships that will be like silver and gold for you for the rest of your life." When you're friendship building, be wise as serpents; gentle as doves. Go into the environments that most attract the caliber of people that you like to build friendships with.

Obviously, for many of us, a significant reason why we're so devoted to this church is that in addition to building our faith here and growing spiritually here, it is here that many of us have found and developed our most significant relationships. It's here that we have stumbled our way through the awkward phases of friendship development, and we've been rewarded with some relationships that touch us to our core. We're building friendships that are enhanced by a common faith, by shared values, by similar life goals.

You know, it's Saturday, and already this week I've been to two parties—two parties with Willow folks—celebrations of kinds. Both nights I was at these parties this week, I looked around the rooms—the two rooms that I was in—and I saw people that I love so much, that I feel so much connection and affinity with. I realized that I have benefited in an overwhelming way from being a part of this church.

Not only has my spiritual life been formed and built here, not only have I found my spiritual gifts and I'm able to serve people with those gifts here, but I have found some people who are like family to me right out of this church. The church is an ideal place to move toward folks and to take those awkward risks of reaching out. I want to challenge those of you, right now, who are not very well connected to other people around this church to take a risk.

Sooner or later, you're going to have to put your hand out and invite someone that you meet here a little bit. Invite them to a cup of coffee in the Atrium after a service. You're going to have to say, "Why don't you come over to our house?" Next week, as Russ told you, we're going to have some large tents. We're going to invite everybody after services to come out and hang out.

It's going to be much easier for some of you who are standing alone to beeline toward your car. Don't do it. Go into those environments. Get to know some people. Another tremendous way to build some friendships around here is to volunteer to serve in some way. When you're working shoulder to shoulder with some folks, you're going to get to know some people pretty well.

A lot of times it's in serving opportunities that the strongest friendships are formed. Or try one of our Sports and Fitness ministries. You'll play volleyball with each other. You'll play basketball with each other. You'll get to know some people. Go into the inner city—take an inner city plunge—serve the poor with some other folks from this church. You'll find some high caliber people with whom you can form friendships. But it's your move, and you've got to do it.

In a couple of weeks we're going to celebrate the twenty-fourth anniversary of this church. I always get a little nostalgic around anniversary time. I think there was a time when I walked out of a college classroom and I could have gone left down the hall and gone to my car. I was a commuting student at Trinity College.

Or I could have gone right down the hallway and knocked on Dr. Bilezekian's door and said, "Dr. B., would you be willing to talk to me? I know you don't know me and all that but what you're talking about in class, about the potential and the beauty of a church, interests me. Could we get to know each other a little bit?" Every year around this time, I think of that day when I turned right and went to his office, and extended a hand of relationship to him and he extended one back to me.

It was out of that friendship that Willow Creek eventually formed. If I hadn't taken that risk—if I hadn't knocked on that door and reached out my hand—I don't know what my life would be like. You don't know what your life could be like if you reached out a hand to somebody. You don't know what's on the other side of that door you're going to knock on. A whole new kind of life could open up to you if you would take the kinds of relational risks necessary to form and build friendships that can really last.

One final thing I just want to talk to you briefly about as we talk about the formation of significant community. All of us, probably, have a hope somewhere in our heart that someday we're going to be able to move beyond the level of superficiality in our relational world to a deeper kind of friendship that could really impact our life and our hearts. All new relationships start at a safe and shallow level. That's just natural.

Trust has to be built; a knowledge base has to develop. But most of you know how empty it is to sit in a setting and hear superficial babble hour after hour after hour about the weather and the stock market and pro sports and politics and so on. You just get an emptiness in your spirit at some point, and you say, "There must be more."

I like what happened in John 4. One time Jesus was walking with his disciples, and they came to a well. The disciples went into town for something to eat, and Jesus was alone at this well—alone with a Samaritan woman. He could have just drawn water himself and gone his way, stood alone. She could have just done the same. A very interesting thing happens. Jesus takes a relational risk, and he asks the woman a question. He said, "Would you mind drawing some water for me?"

He was just testing the relational waters, if you will. He's seeing if there's any openness on the part of this woman for friendship. She gives him some water, and then she takes a risk. She asks him a question. She says, "Why would you, a Jewish man, have anything to do with me, a Samaritan woman? What's this all about?"

The asking of a significant question, by each of them, eventually opened the door for conversation that developed. Pretty soon they were talking about spiritual issues and moral issues, marital issues, eternal issues. It changed the whole course of that woman's life. Do you know what I've found has changed the course of my relational life?

Do you know what I have found that has moved many of my relationships from just being that superficial babble that bored me to death to the kind of deep, heart to heart relating patterns that I've enjoyed with some of my friends? It's the asking of a significant question. They don't have to be like rocket science questions. Most of the time, when we're with friends, we say, "How are you doing?" "I'm doing fine. How are you doing?" "Fine."

Sometimes, I just take it one step further. I say, "How are you doing, really? Because I'll listen if you want to tell me. How are you doing really?" Then, sometimes, I'll push it one step further, "How are you doing, really, in the marriage?" if they're married. "How are you doing, really, at work?" "How are you doing, really, with your parents because I know that they're aging and sickly—how's that going, really? Really?"

Just by asking the question, "How are you doing, really?" opens the door for people to say, "You want to know?" Say, "Yes, I do." I've told you before that the management team of our church—the senior leaders of our church—meet in my office every Tuesday: Russ and Nancy Beach, Lori Peterson, Dick Anderson, Greg Hawkins and others.

The first hour-and-a-half all we do is just sit around in a circle in my office. We have food brought in. We say, "So how are we all doing, really?" We spend an hour-and-a-half opening up our lives to each other. You'd be amazed at what would happen if you would—in your marriage, with your kids, with your friends—just say, "How are you doing, really?"

I have another question that I ask people when they tell me what's going on in their life. Someone will say, "I lost a huge account at work today." I say, "Well, how'd that make you feel? How do you feel about that?"

People will stop and they'll go, "What do you mean, how do I feel about that?" "Tell me how you feel about it." "Well, I feel scared about it. I don't know if I can replace that account." "What do you do when you get scared?" "Well, I drink." "How does that work?" Now, we're off and running. Now, we're talking about important things.

Someone says, "My boss yelled at me." It's so easy to say, "Rage happens—who are the Bears playing?" Now, wait a minute, stop. "Your boss yelled at you. How'd that make you feel?" "It made me feel small. It made me feel stupid. It made me feel worthless." "Oh. What happens inside of you when you feel those kinds of feelings?" Well, now we're off to the races. Now, we're talking about something really important.

I don't know if it's true with you. It sure is with me. Whenever I have a moment of relational warmth with somebody, when there's a tender moment of self-disclosure, something inside of me says, "I was created for moments like this. I was designed by God for these moments of heart connection—these life giving, little segments of time, when material stuff, achievement stuff, work stuff, fades into the background, and I sense an internal richness of spirit welling up inside of me."

I find myself saying, "It's these moments that I'm going to most remember when I'm near the end of my life, and I'm reviewing what meant most to me in life." I've had several friends who have faced life-threatening medical procedures—the kind where you have to get your house in order and say your "good-byes" before you're wheeled into the operating room because it could go one way or the other.

When I've had conversations with these folks about the very real possibility that they might die, almost every person has remarked to me, that facing death dramatically clarifies what's most important in life. To a person—folks have told me that when the chips are down—it's relationships. It's friendships. It's loving community amongst family and friends that matters most, and everything else fades.

I say, friends, let's not wait until we're staring at the ceiling from a hospital bed to reach that conclusion. Let's get that one straight, right here and right now, so we have time to do something about it; so we have time to move from isolation to community. In closing, I want to tell you that yesterday I attended one of the most extraordinary funeral services in the history of Willow.

It was held right here in the main auditorium. It had to be. There wasn't room in the chapel. In fact, the night before—Thursday night—over 700 people came and stood in a very long line for a visitation service. You're probably wondering what kind of a high-powered, high profile person would receive such an outpouring of sympathy and love.

It wasn't the cover person of a magazine, a media personality, a corporate czar or a senior staff member at this church.

It was Larry Clark, a volunteer here at Willow, who died. He spent the last 20 years of his life trying to help people who were standing alone leave their aloneness, find God, and find community. That was his life's mission—to find people who were standing alone and help them find God and find community.

He spent 20 years of his life doing that until he was killed in a traffic accident last Saturday. Lynne and I were sitting three-quarters of the way back, in the auditorium here, just looking at the hundreds and hundreds of people's lives that Larry Clark had touched. All we could do was fight back the tears and ponder the power of a single life that was devoted to honorable purposes. Larry's life was just devoted to people. I doubt that any person who was at that funeral will ever forget it.

I'll also bet that most of us who were there will do our best to carry on Larry's legacy of helping people who are standing alone find God through Jesus Christ, and then find a place in community. We will do our best to find some brothers and sisters to link arms and link hearts with—until it can be said of this church and our whole community that nobody stands alone—nobody. We will not let it happen.

You know, with God's help, with my investment in that objective and yours as well, that dream can become a reality in this church and in our community—nobody standing alone. Now, let us stand for closing prayer.

CHAPTER 32

A CRISIS IN COMMUNICATION

FRED CRADDOCK: AN "INDUCTIVE" SERMON

The "New Homiletic" is characterized chiefly by an agreement that the earlier model of preaching (often called "deductive") does not speak to the needs of contemporary people. Each theoretician of the movement has proffered a different prescription for what should be done instead. A pioneer and leading member of the movement is Fred B. Craddock, who taught first at Phillips Theological Seminary and then at the Candler Divinity School of Emory University **(see Vol. 1, pp. 800-806)**.

Craddock called his alternative to deductive preaching "inductive preaching." While he defined that in his As One Without Authority, *a recommendation he makes in his textbook,* Preaching, *sounds very much like inductive preaching, although he does not apply that term to the pattern in the later book.*

> *Beginning at that intersection of message and hearer, the sermon begins to unfold, moving from where they are, through the text, using analogies, examples, images, perhaps even pleasant interruptions in the form of asides or hints of roads not now to be taken, until preacher and congregation know the message has been said (p. 188).*

No one preaches that way better than Craddock himself, as the following sermon shows. It is taken from The Twentieth-Century Pulpit, *ed. James W. Cox (Nashville: Abingdon, 1981), 2:47-52.*

Praying through Clenched Teeth

For I would have you know, brethren, that the gospel which was preached by me is not man's gospel. For I did not receive it from man, nor was I taught it, but it came through a revelation of Jesus Christ. For you have heard of my former life in Judaism, how I persecuted the church of God violently and tried to destroy it; and I advanced in Judaism beyond many of my own age among my people, so extremely zealous was I for the traditions of my fathers. But when he who had set me apart before I was born, and had called me through his grace, was pleased to reveal his Son to me, in order that I might preach him among the Gentiles, I did not confer with flesh and blood, nor did I go up to Jerusalem to those who were apostles before me, but I went away into Arabia; and again I returned to Damascus. Then after three years I went up to Jerusalem to visit Cephas, and remained with him fifteen days. But I saw none of the other apostles except James the Lord's brother. (In what I am writing to you, before God, I do not lie!) Then I went into the regions of Syria and Cilicia. And I was still not known by sight to the churches of Christ in Judea; they only heard it said, "He who once persecuted us is now preaching the faith he once tried to destroy." And they glorified God because of me. Gal. 1:11-24.

I am going to say a word, and the moment I say the word I want you to see a face, to recall a face and a name, someone who comes to your mind when I say the word. Are you ready? The word is "bitter." Bitter.

Do you see a face? I see a face. I see the face of a farmer in western Oklahoma, riding a mortgaged tractor, burning gasoline purchased on credit, moving across rented land, rearranging the dust. Bitter.

Do you see a face? I see the face of a woman forty-seven years old. She sits out on a hillside, drawn and confused under a green canopy furnished by the mortuary. She is banked on all sides by flowers sprinkled with cards: "You have our condolences." Bitter.

Do you see a face? I see the face of a man who runs a small grocery store. His father ran the store in that neighborhood for twenty years, and he is now in his twelfth year there. The grocery doesn't make much profit, but it keeps the family together. It's a business. There are no customers in the store now, and the grocer stands in the doorway with his apron rolled up around his waist, looking across the street where workmen are completing a supermarket. Bitter.

I see the face of a young couple. They seem to be about nineteen. They are standing in the airport terminal, holding hands so tight their knuckles are white. She's pregnant; he's dressed in military green. They are not talking, just standing and looking at each other. The loudspeaker comes on: "Flight 392 now loading at Gate 22, yellow concourse, all aboard for San Francisco." He slowly moves toward the gate; she stands there alone. Bitter.

Do you see a face? A young minister in a small town, in a cracker box of a house they call a parsonage. He lives there with his wife and small child. It's Saturday morning. There is a knock at the door. He answers, and there standing before him on the porch is the chairman of his church board, who is also the president of the local bank, and also the owner of most of the land round about. The man has in his hands a small television. It is an old television, small screen, black and white. It's badly scarred and one of the knobs is off. He says: "My wife and I got one of those new twenty-five-inch color sets, but they didn't want to take this one on a trade, so I just said to myself, 'Well, we'll just give it to the minister. That's probably the reason our ministers don't stay any longer than they do, we don't do enough nice things for them.'" The young minister looks up, tries to smile and say thanks. But I want you to see his face. Bitter.

Will you look at one other face? His name is Saul, Saul of Tarsus. We call him Paul. He was young and intelligent, committed to the traditions of his fathers, strong and zealous for his nation and for his religion, outstripping, he says, all of his classmates in his zeal for his people. While he pursues his own convictions, there develops within the bosom of Judaism a new group called Nazarenes, followers of Jesus. They seemed at first to pose no threat; after all, Judaism had long been broadly liberal and had tolerated within her house of faith a number of groups such as Pharisees and Sadducees and Essenes and Zealots, so why not Nazarenes? As long as they continue in the temple and in the synagogue, there's no problem.

But before long, among these new Christians a different sound is heard. Some of the young radicals are beginning to say that Christianity is not just for the Jews but for anyone who believes in Jesus Christ. Such was the preaching of Stephen and Philip and others: it doesn't really matter if your background is Jewish as long as you trust in God and believe in Jesus Christ. This startling word strikes the ear of young Saul. "What do they mean, it doesn't matter? It does matter! It is the most important matter. No young preacher can stand up and say that thousands of years of mistreatment and exile and burden, of trying to be true to God, of struggling to be his people and keep the candle of faith burning in a dark and pagan world mean nothing. What does he mean, it doesn't matter to have your gabardine spat upon, and to be made fun of because you are different? Of course, it matters!"

Imagine yourself the only child of your parents, but when you are seventeen years old, they adopt a seventeen-year-old brother for you. When you are both eighteen, your father says at breakfast one morning: "I have just had the lawyer draw up the papers. I am leaving the family business to our *two* sons." How do you feel? "This other fellow just got here. He's not really a true son. Where was he when I was mowing the lawn, cleaning the room, trying to pass the ninth grade, and being refused the family car on Friday nights? And now that I'm eighteen, I suddenly have this brother out of nowhere, and he is to share equally?" How would you feel? Would you be saying, "Isn't my father generous?" Not likely.

Then imagine how the young Saul feels. Generations and generations and generations of being the people of God, and now someone in the name of Jesus of Nazareth gets this strange opinion that it doesn't matter anymore, that Jews and Gentiles are alike. You must sense how Saul feels. All your family and national traditions, all that you have ever known and believed, now erased completely from the board? Every moment in school, every belief held dear, every job toward which your life is pointed, now meaningless? Everything that grandfather and father and now you believed, gone? Of course, he resolves to stop it. The dark cloud of his brooding bitterness forms a tornado funnel over that small church, and he strikes it, seeking to end it. In the name of his fathers, in the name of his country, in the name of God, yes.

Now, why does he do this? Why is he so bitter at this announcement of the universal embrace of all people in the name of God? Do you know what I believe? I believe he is bitter and disturbed because he is at war with himself over this very matter. And anyone at war with himself will make casualties even out of friends and loved ones. He is himself uncertain, and it is the uncertain person who becomes a persecutor, until like a wounded animal he lies in the sand near Damascus, waiting for the uplifted stroke of a God whom he thinks he serves.

But Paul knows his is a God who loves all creation. He knows; surely he knows. Saul has read his Bible. He has read that marvelous book of Ruth, in which the ancestress of David is shamelessly presented as a Moabite woman. Certainly, God loves other peoples. He has read the book of Jonah and the expressed love of God for people that Jonah himself does not love. Paul has read the book of Isaiah and the marvelous vision of the house of God into which all nations flow. It is in his Bible. Then what's his problem? His problem is the same problem you and I have had sometimes. It's one thing to know something; it's another thing to *know it*. He knows it and he does not know it, and the battle that is fought between knowing and really knowing is fierce. It is sometimes called the struggle from head to heart. I know that the longest trip we ever make is the trip from head to heart, from knowing to knowing, and until that trip is complete, we are in great pain. We might even lash out at others.

Do you know anyone bitter like this; bitter that what they are fighting is what they know is right? Trapped in that impossible battle of trying to stop the inevitable triumph of the truth? Do you know anyone lashing out in criticism and hatred and violence against a person or against a group that represents the humane and caring and Christian way? If you do, how do you respond? Hopefully you do not react to bitterness with bitterness. We certainly have learned that such is a futile and fruitless endeavor, just as I hope we have learned we do not fight prejudice with prejudice. A few years ago, many of us found ourselves more prejudiced against prejudiced people than the prejudiced people were prejudiced. Then how do we respond?

Let me tell you a story. A family is out for a drive on a Sunday afternoon. It is a pleasant afternoon, and they relax at a leisurely pace down the highway. Suddenly the two children begin to beat their father in the back: "Daddy, Daddy, stop the car! Stop the car! There's a kitten back there on the side of the road!" The father says, "So there's a kitten on the side of the road. We're having a drive." "But Daddy you must stop and pick it up." "I don't have to stop and pick it up." "But Daddy, if you don't, it will die." "Well, then it will have to die. We don't have room for another animal. We have a zoo already at the house. No more animals." "But Daddy, are you going to just let it die?" "Be quiet, children; we're trying to have a pleasant drive." "We never thought our Daddy would be so mean and cruel as to let a kitten die." Finally the mother turns to her husband and says, "Dear, you'll have to stop." He turns the car around, returns to the spot and pulls off to the side of the road. "You kids stay in the car. I'll see about it." He goes out to pick up the little kitten. The poor creature is just skin and bones, sore-eyed, and full of fleas; but when he reaches down to pick it up, with its last bit of energy the kitten bristles, baring tooth and claw. Sssst! He picks up the kitten by the loose skin at the neck, brings it over to the car and says, "Don't touch it; it's probably got leprosy." Back home they go. When they get to the house the children give the kitten several baths, about a gallon of warm milk, and intercede: "Can we let it stay in the house just tonight? Tomorrow we'll fix a place in the garage." The father says, "Sure, take my bedroom; the whole house is already a zoo." They fix a comfortable bed, fit for a pharaoh. Several weeks pass. Then one day the father walks in, feels something rub against his leg, looks down, and there is a cat. He reaches down toward the cat, carefully checking to see that no one is watching. When the cat sees his hand, it does not bare its claws and hiss; instead it arches its back to receive a caress. Is that the same cat? Is that the same cat? No. It's not the same as that frightened, hurt, hissing kitten on the side of the road. Of course not. And you know as well as I what makes the difference.

Not too long ago God reached out his hand to bless me and my family. When he did, I looked at his hand; it was covered with scratches. Such is the hand of love, extended to those who are bitter.

EDMUND STEIMLE: PREACHING THE STORY

Edmund Steimle, a retired homiletician from Union Seminary, and two of his former graduate students, Morris Niedenthal and Charles Rice, seemed to intuit the drift of consciousness in the culture when they published Preaching the Story *(Philadelphia: Fortress, 1980;* ***see Vol. 1, pp. 811-12****). They anticipated a time that would soon come when sermons organized by image, narrative, or metaphor would be more appealing than those with a strictly logical organization.*

The three writers did not distinguish sharply between the three categories, lumping them together generally as "story." They did, however, include in their book examples of the kind of sermons they had in mind. The one below, written by Steimle, is unified by the image of the eye of a storm, which communicates something of what the birth of Jesus and the situation in the world of his congregation was like. The use of the image made it possible for Steimle to cut through the sentimentality of a Christmas Eve service to the reality of the Incarnation.

The Eye of the Storm

In those days a decree went out from Caesar Augustus that all the world should be enrolled. This was the first enrollment, when Quirinius was governor of Syria. And all went to be enrolled, each to his own city. And Joseph also went up from Galilee, from the city of Nazareth, to Judea, to the city of David, which is called Bethlehem, because he was of the house and lineage of David, to be enrolled with Mary, his betrothed, who was with child. And while they were there, the time came for her to be delivered. And she gave birth to her firstborn son and wrapped him in swaddling cloths, and laid him in a manger, because there was no place for them in the inn.

And in that region there were shepherds out in the field, keeping watch over their flock by night. And an angel of the Lord appeared to them, and the glory of the Lord shone around them, and they were filled with fear. And the angel said to them, "Be not afraid; for behold, I bring you good news of a great joy which will come to all the people; for to you is born this day in the city of David a Savior, who is Christ the Lord. And this will be a sign for you: you will find a babe wrapped in swaddling cloths and lying in a manger." And suddenly there was with the angel a multitude of the heavenly host praising God and saying,

> *"Glory to God in the highest,*
> *and on earth peace among men with whom he is pleased!"*

When the angels went away from them into heaven, the shepherds said to one another, "Let us go over to Bethlehem and see this thing that has happened, which the Lord has made known to us." And they went with haste, and found Mary and Joseph, and the babe lying in a manger. And when they saw it they made known the saying which had been told them concerning this child; and all who heard it wondered at what the shepherds told them. But Mary kept all these things, pondering them in her heart. And the shepherds returned, glorifying and praising God for all they had heard and seen, as it had been told them. Luke 2:1-20

I think I shall never forget the time when hurricane Hazel, back in the fifties, was sweeping through eastern Pennsylvania and hit Philadelphia, where we were living at the time, head on. Unlike most hurricanes, which lose much of their force when they turn inland, this one hit with all the fury of a hurricane at sea: drenching rains, screaming winds, trees uprooted, branches flying through the air, broken power lines crackling on the pavements. It was frightening. Then suddenly there was a letup, a lull. Shortly all was still. Not a leaf quivered. The sun even broke through briefly. It was the eye of the storm. "All was calm, all was bright." And then all hell broke loose again: branches and trees crashing down, the screaming winds, the torrential rain, the power lines throwing out sparks on the pavement. But that was a breathless moment—when we experienced the eye of the storm.

Christmas Eve is something like that, like the experience of the eye of the storm. At least the first Christmas night. So Luke reports: "And she gave birth to her first-born son and wrapped him in swaddling cloths, and laid him in a manger, because there was no place for them in the inn." The Christmas crèche and the Christmas pageantry picture it so today: "All was calm, all was bright."

Mary . . . resting now, after the pain of the contractions and the delivery without benefit of anesthetic.

The child . . . sleeping peacefully in the swaddling cloths and the straw. At least we like to think him so. "Silent night, holy night." Of course, maybe his face was all contorted reds and purples with the frantic bleating of a newborn child, fists clenched, striking out at this new and strange environment after nine months in the warmth and security of the womb. But no. Let's picture him sleeping, exhausted perhaps from his frantic protests. "All is calm, all is bright. . . . Silent night, holy night." The eye of the storm.

For make no mistake, he comes at the center of a storm—both before and after the birth. The storm before: From devastation of a flood expressing the anger of God with a people whose every thought and imagination was evil, to his anger at the golden calf, to the destruction of Jerusalem and the Exile in Babylon, to Jonah desperately trying to run away from this God, to the narrow legalism of the Pharisees, to the oppression of the Roman occupation. He comes at the eye of the storm before.

And what followed this "silent night, holy night"? The storm after: The massacre of the innocent male children two years old and under by Herod in his frantic effort to deal with the threat of this child sleeping in the manger. And as he grew up, his family thought him a little bit nuts, his hometown neighbors threw him out of the synagogue when first he tried to preach. Then the sinister plots to do away with him, the angry mob crying for his blood on that first Good Friday, and the end? Death to the child.

What we tend to forget on Christmas is that these lovely stories of the birth—the manger, the shepherds, the angel chorus in the night sky, the wise men following the star and presenting their rare and expensive gifts—are not children's stories. If you think it takes children to make a Christmas, then you don't belong in church tonight. These are adult stories for adult Christians. Oh, let the children delight in them of course—and get out of them what they may. But they were written down by adult members of the early Christian community for other adult members of the Christian community.

Moreover, they are postresurrection stories, that is, they grew up in the tradition after the resurrection. Who knows where they came from? They came into being in the years following the resurrection as Negro spirituals came into being, as mature Christians pondered the mystery of the beginnings of this life whom they had seen die and rise again from the dead. They knew about the storm which preceded the birth. And they knew even more—first hand—about the storm that followed. They were not carried away by "the romantic fantasies of infancy." Like one standing in the eye of a hurricane, they were aware of the storm that went before and that followed.

And so tonight you and I come here, not wanting, I hope, to block out or forget the storms around us. Because if we do, we miss the whole point. We too are aware tonight of the storms which surround this "silent night, holy night."

We are aware of the confusion and destruction around us in the world. The violence in the Middle East, southern Africa, and Northern Ireland, the hunger in the Third World. Or closer to home, the muggings on the streets, the unemployment (a grim and passive kind of violence), the ghettos, the injustice to the blacks, the inner cities gutted by poverty and inflation and the massive indifference—sloth is the old-fashioned word for it—on the part of so many of us who do not live in the gutted inner cities. Moreover, we are aware of the precarious future which haunts all of us. People are dying this Christmas night as people die on every night. As one day, one night, you will die and I will die. And before that the inner loneliness which no one of us can entirely shake, and the specter of hopelessness which haunts us—for peace in the world, for the end of inflation, for families breaking up, for our nations as they drift along often so aimlessly, and for ourselves and our future.

The point is, we don't forget all this on Christmas Eve—or block it out. Like a person standing in the eye of a hurricane, we are aware of it all. If you want to forget it all tonight—OK! Go home and listen to Bing Crosby dreaming of a white Christmas. And there's a place for that—but not here!

For what other message on Christmas Eve is worth listening to? What peace? What hope? If it is simply a forgetting—when we can't forget, really—then we're reducing the Christmas story to a bit of nostalgia and indulging ourselves in the sentimental orgy which Christmas has become for so many, or we are reduced to the deep depression which grips so many others on Christmas Eve.

No. The Bible—praise God—tells it like it is. They saw the birth of the child as the eye of the storm—a peace which passes all understanding because it is not a peace apart from conflict, pain, suffering, violence, and confusion; that's the kind of peace we can understand all too well. But it's a peace like the peace in the eye of a hurricane, a peace smack in the middle of it all, a peace which indeed passes all understanding.

So in this hour, this night, worshiping at the manger of the child when "all is calm, all is bright," we rejoice in the hope born of the conviction that the storm, the destruction, the violence, the hopelessness, does not have the last word. But God—who gives us this "silent night" in the middle of the storm—he has the last word.

So rejoice . . . and sing the carols . . . and listen to the lovely ancient story and light the candles . . . and be glad—with your families, your friends, with the God who is above all and through all and in you all, who comes to us miraculously in this child, this night, when "all is calm, all is bright."

DONALD CHATFIELD: A STORY SERMON

While "narrative preaching" has been a watchword of the New Homiletic, few of the principle's advocates have been so consistent as to preach sermons that never leave the narrative mode, sermons that are nothing but a story **(see Vol. 1, pp. 814-15)**. *One who does is Donald F. Chatfield. His* Dinner with Jesus and Other Left-handed Story-sermons: Meeting God Through the Imagination *(Minister's Resources Library. Grand Rapids, Mich.: Zondervan, 1988) is a collection of such sermons; the one below appears on pp. 17-25.*

Dinner with Jesus

And as he passed on, he saw Levi the son of Alphaeus sitting at the tax office, and he said to him, "Follow me." And he rose and followed him. Mark 2:14

Memo

TO: Chief Collector, Capernaum Tollhouse, Interior Receiving Section
FROM: Levi ben Alphaeus, former collector
SUBJECT: Resignation

Dear Howie:

I know I should have gotten this memo to you two weeks ago, when I actually did this crazy thing, but there just hasn't been time. I know,

I know, you probably figure what with me gallivanting around the countryside, eating and drinking and listening to the Boss teach, I should have had plenty of time to drop you a little note. Edgar saw me Monday and said you were really steamed that I didn't let you know whether I was coming back. Boy, that gave me a real guilt trip! To think you've been saving me a place all this time. . . .

But I did want to write you more than just a few lines: "I quit. Your Friend, Levi." I mean, you might think I didn't *like* working in the Interior Receiving Section. But the IRS has been good to me, and you've been a great boss, and a real friend as well. So I figured you deserve more of an explanation.

Thing is, Howie, I couldn't figure out how to explain this whole thing so you could understand it. I mean, this guy comes barging into the office that Wednesday morning, walks right over to my station—where I'm arguing with Joseph ben Jacob about the valuation I'd just put on the four jars of spices Joseph was bringing in from Damascus—and the guy says to me, he says, "Follow me"!

Well, this I don't need, because Joseph is giving me a real hard time. (So what if I valued them a little high; Joe and I both knew what he was carrying in the false bottoms of those jars, and it certainly wasn't his dirty socks!) So I said, "Just hold your horses, Mac." That was when I noticed these four other guys with him, giving each other looks when I said that—looks like, "Who does he think he is *talking* to like that?" But you know how it is, Howie, when you sit at the custom desk, you're king, and folks just got to wait until you're good and ready.

Oh, I forgot to tell you about these four guys. They were fishermen. I knew *that* much as soon as they blew in the door! But the main guy, I couldn't figure; looked like a worker, though. (Turns out he'd been a carpenter over in Nazareth with his old man.) Anyway, these four guys were Simon and Andrew, and James and John. I recognized them. Now, this wasn't the Sabbath, it was a workday; so what were the owners of the two largest fisheries on the north coast doing, wandering around like four guys on welfare? Started me wondering: Who *was* this bozo, anyway?

(Howie, I'm afraid that kind of distracted me, and I quit listening so good, and when I came out of it I realized Joseph had really beat me down. You'll find the paperwork on my desk. But don't hassle him about it. Next time you see him, tell him Levi says, "God bless." That'll blow his sandals off!)

So Joseph goes off, and I turn back to this guy, and as I do, I hear

James ben Zebedee say something to him and end up calling him "Rabbi." Well, naturally, I get up; I would've in the first place, if I'd have known he was a teacher of God's Law. I mean, I may not have time to study it or keep much of it, but you gotta show a little respect! So there I am face to face with this guy, and he's just waiting patiently for me, and I get a really good look at him. People who've never seen him think he must really look different, but he doesn't. Just an ordinary-looking guy; the difference I guess is mostly in the way he talks. Like, when I suddenly remember that he said something to me a couple of minutes before, and I say, "What did you say?" And he just says it again: "Follow me."

Now this is the part I can't explain, Howie. I mean, is this crazy, or what? Guy wanders in and wants me to drop everything and go with him. I shoulda asked him a thousand questions, like, "Where are we going? How long? Can it wait until I can arrange a leave of absence? What's the salary? Fringes? (How's he gonna beat 30 thou a year plus all the bribes and skim-offs you can manage?) Do I get paid vacations? Who's gonna take care of my widowed mother?" (My ma just laughed when she read this part . . . I'm typing it at home. . . . "Who's going to take care of *you* is more like it," she said.) But I didn't say *any* of that to him. I just pushed my chair back and followed him out into the street. Me, four fishermen, and a wandering rabbi! What the heck did I think I was doing?

Edgar calls out to me, "Hey, Levi? It's too early for your lunch break." I let it go. He owes me plenty of lunch breaks. Funny, isn't it, Howie? One part of me was thinking, I'll be back this afternoon. But my feet knew they'd never be parked under that desk again.

Well, as we walked along, it rose on up from my feet and dawned on the rest of me: This is a whole new life! This is really something big! Here I am, Levi the publican, the tax collector, not exactly the most popular man in town, and now I'm a rabbi's disciple. Wouldn't Simeon the Pharisee be surprised, I thought. He hates it that I even live in his neighborhood, me with my unreligious friends and our all-night parties. He hates all us people who don't keep Moses' law to the letter, figures it's because of us that Israel is under the lousy Romans; it's God's punishment 'cause I didn't tithe my pomegranates. And he hates us tax collectors worst of all, because we work for the Tetrarch, who cooperates with Rome. Wouldn't this give Simeon fits, I'm thinking, if he could see me hobnobbing with a real live rabbi. Here's one rabbi that sure doesn't pick his disciples for social class! Course, I think, as I look at Simon and Andrew, he doesn't pick 'em for bouquet, either. Whew!

Anyway, I guess it was thinking about old Simeon's eyes bugging out that makes me forget myself and go up to the Rabbi and say, "How's about dropping by my place for dinner tonight?" He just stops dead and looks at me, and I hear the four Mackerel Brothers stop behind me and suck wind through their teeth. And then I realize, Oh boy, have I put him on the spot! A real live rabbi asks me (me!) to be one of his bunch, and I embarrass him by asking him to eat with me. Not just come to my house, which would be tough enough, but to actually sit down at the same table and dip in the same dish with me, a publican. He probably eats kosher, prays every day, and goes to synagogue on the Sabbath. It's like asking him to eat with a Gentile, or worse, a Samaritan.

So I'm getting ready to say something like, "Of course, I know you're busy, got lots of teaching to do, busy schedule, no sense hiking out to the suburbs, why don't I just reserve a table at Rachel's Religious Restaurant and Seafood Emporium over there, save you a lot of . . . But he just turns to the others and says, "Well, boys, what do you think of that?" And they kind of look at each other for a second, searching for something to say, and then big Simon (the Rabbi calls him "Petros"—the Rock), he bursts out, "Master, I think the shepherd who left the ninety-nine safe sheep has found one who was lost." And so the Rabbi throws back his head and roars with laughter, and all the others do too, and Rocky blushes bright red ("Tell you the story later," he mumbles to me). And the Rabbi throws his arm around my shoulders and says, "I'm going to call you "Matthew" (Imagine! He calls *me,* a tax collector, the "Gift of God"!). "And Matthew," he says, "it will be a joy to come to your house for dinner tonight."

And that's when I remember, Howie—it's Wednesday! The weekly gathering of the poker club is at my house tonight. They'll be expecting a quiet evening away from the wife and kids, with pizza, beer, cigars, and dealer's choice; and what'll they get? A rabbi! It'll be a contest who'll walk out the door first, them, or the Rabbi when he gets a look at my collection of no-good friends.

I'm real itchy all afternoon, because I want to get back and see what magazines I have to hide. I even think of asking Simeon if I can borrow his house and servants for the evening, that's how crazy my head is getting! Suddenly the Rabbi looks at me, and he says, "Matthew Levi, a man once gave a banquet and invited many people; but when the food was ready, they all made excuses to his servant, who returned with no dinner guests. The man was angry, so he sent his servant to drag people to the feast from bus stops, doorways and alleys, greasy-spoon diners—and tollhouses." I musta looked blank, 'cause then he says "Matthew Levi, it's time to go to your house for dinner." I'm thinking about what he said all the way to my place. A bunch of down-and-outs got a nice meal because some fat cats didn't feel like showing up. Did the Boss call *me* because somebody else, a Pharisee, maybe, turned him down? I decided that would be okay. This was about the biggest thing that ever happened to me: if I found it because someone else dropped it, well, finders keepers losers weepers I always say.

As we came up the road, I saw Simeon studying the Law in the neat little courtyard in front of his house. When he saw us coming, he looked for a long time, and then it was like he recognized the Rabbi, because he suddenly jumped up and ran in the house. I guess he had a few phone calls to make. We trooped into my place, and that's when it all really came to a head. Fast Eddie was already there, practicing his one-handed triple cut. Sam had already popped a beer and was working his way through *Playboy.* (He wasn't always there; this week he had Wednesday night off from tending bar at the Capernaum House.) Jocko was making some entries in his little black notebook that we all knew not to ask him about. They all kind of looked up when we waltzed in the door, and Fast Eddie fanned the air away from his nose when he got acquainted with the aura of the Four Friendly Fisher Folk.

"Guys," I said—I had to say it twice before I got the word out from where it was stuck in the back of my throat—"I'd like you to meet some new, uh, friends of mine, maybe you know these guys from the fish market? Simon ('Call me Rocky,' he said with a broad smile, as he stuck out one big paw) and his brother Andrew; and these here are James and John, the sons of Zebedee. And this," I said, taking a deep breath, "is . . . our, uh, rabbi, you know, our teacher, um, uh . . ."

"Jesus," he said. And then he went to each of them, got their names, started talking with them. Boy, the looks I got! In the middle of this I heard the air horn as Jimmy and his partner the Jericho Kid pushed their eighteen-wheeler up in front of the house. Well, I just couldn't take any more, Howie, so I ran into the kitchen and worked off some uglies by hollering at the servants for a while, got 'em rustling up extra food and stuff. When I came back in with the dip and chips, I stopped dead in the doorway. All the guys were sitting on the floor, and the Boss was sitting on the sofa in front of them, making like a rabbi. Only, he didn't talk a lot of religion like the scribes and teachers of the Pharisees usually do. Like, when I came in, he was telling them this story; I never will forget it.

"A Pharisee and a tax collector," he said (glancing at me), "went up to the temple to pray. The Pharisee went right up front, confident in his own virtue. The tax collector was on his knees, way back by a pillar. The Pharisee was glad in his heart, and prayed like this: 'Dear God, I thank you that I am a good man, keeping the law, keeping myself pure and holy for you, praying for your holy people and for Jerusalem, tithing to your temple from all that you have given me; thank you for giving me the light of your law to guide my steps, so that I am not unrighteous, or an adulterer, or a Sabbath-breaker, or an idol-worshiping Gentile, groping in deep darkness; I thank you that I am not an extorter of money and oppressor of the poor of my people, like that tax collector back there, never lifting a finger to keep your holy law. Who does he think he is, even coming in here to your sacred temple?'"

Jesus looked up at me as he said these words, Howie, and it felt like he was looking right into the heart of my shame. Who *did* I think I was, pretending to be a rabbi's disciple? I had never paid the slightest attention to God! A couple of the guys were looking at me, and that's when I realized that there were tears on my face. I just let 'em be, stood there holding the dip and chips.

The Boss went on: "But the tax collector didn't even lift up his eyes to heaven, but beat on his chest, calling softly, 'God, have mercy on me, a sinner.'" Then Jesus' voice got a tone in it that made us all hold our breath: "Amen, amen," he said, "I tell you the truth: *this* man went home at rights with God, *and not the first*!"

See, Howie, that's when it happened. With a handful of words this guy opened a door to God for a bunch of rum-dums and fast operators like us. It was like he made us all his brothers. That's when I decided, I'm going with this guy wherever he goes. This is my Boss from now on. Maybe it seems crazy to some people; but when you've had heaven handed to you on a platter, and a new name, and a new family, and self-respect . . . well, you just gotta go with it.

Oh, I forgot to tell you, Howie, that just then I noticed Simeon the Pharisee and some of his cronies standing at the door, probably came over to holler about Jimmy and Jericho's rig standing out front. But I knew from the look on their faces that they had heard the last bit about the Pharisee who didn't get right with God. Boy, were they mad! But for some reason they stayed there, as if the Boss's teaching had a hold on them, too. So they listened to all he said (one of them was even taking notes), and they were there when the whole motley crew of us bellied up to the table. I saw Simeon turn green at the unrighteous assortment of food I'd scrounged up, but Jesus never blinked an eye. They watched as he sat down in front of that strange mess of food and folks, took the bread, lifted his eyes to heaven, and blessed God who had brought us the bread out of the ground. Then he broke it and passed it to each of us, and I tell you, that bread tasted better than any I'd had in years!

I can't describe the meal, Howie, too much happened. (It always does, when Jesus is around.) But once, when I got up to refill the glasses, Simeon waved me over to the door. You know, I felt so good, I said, "How's about you and your friends coming in and having a bite with us. I know the Rabbi will be glad to have you." But Simeon just looked at me and kept his toes firmly on the other side of my threshold, and I felt unclean and sinful next to all his purity, just the way I always did. But somehow I suddenly understood the look on his face. He was jealous! He wanted Jesus to he at *his* house. Here he was, the best man in the neighborhood (I gotta admit it; he really is!), and when a real live rabbi comes around, he comes to the house of a ripe old sinner like me!

So I saw the longing and the hurt in his eyes as he said, watching the Boss with his hand on Andrew's arm, "Why does your . . . your Master . . . eat with tax collectors and sinners? *We* are the God-fearing people. I don't understand!"

Jesus must have heard him from across the room, because he called out to him, "Simeon, people who are well don't need a doctor; sick people do." Then he said something that haunts me, I don't know why. "I didn't come to call virtuous people, but sinners." And he kept his eyes on Simeon's face, until Simeon turned on his heel and went back over to his place, him and his friends. You know, I think that made the Boss a little sad.

Well, that's about it, Howie. This guy has really turned me around, and I'm with him from now on. I feel like I'd follow him to death, if I had to.

We're going off for a while, hit some of the other places around Galilee, pick up a few disciples, who knows? Just give Edgar my back pay, he can bring it by my ma. You know, I thought she'd throw a fit, me quitting and running off with some guru, but it turns out she and her bridge club had been driving over to Nazareth on the quiet to hear him for a couple of weeks, so she knew all about him before he shows up in Capernaum, thinks he's terrific, gives me her blessing and all. Rosie's really hot, though; says how are we going to get married now, me having no future anymore. She even cried. I felt like a heel, but I told her, you gotta hear him for yourself. She wasn't buying any. Well, someday, maybe.

So take care of yourself, Howie. Give my regards to the staff. I'll give you a ring when we get back to town. Have you out for dinner with Jesus.

THOMAS TROEGER: AN IMAGINATIVE SERMON

A poet, hymn writer, and musician, Thomas Troeger is one of the most creative members of the homiletical community (**see Vol. 1, pp. 815-17**)*. He suggests that sermons can be bound together by something other than logical connectivity: an image, story, phrase, or vision. The selection below is a book chapter in which he has included a sermon. Since the book is about how to preach, it is natural that the sermon is too. Indeed, it was written for members of the Academy of Homiletics and preached at their annual meeting nearest the three-hundredth anniversary of the birth of Johann Sebastian Bach. Bach takes over as preacher of the sermon, and urges that preachers go about their task in the way that he set sacred texts to music. The chapter is from Thomas H. Troeger,* Imagining a Sermon, *Abingdon Preacher's Library (Nashville: Abingdon, 1990), 135-39.*

Return to the Source

I am suffering a malady that is common to all preachers: overdosing on words. This illness is not commonly discussed in the city of homiletical wisdom, but it ought to be. The best cure is an activity that is nonverbal. So I have turned to my flute and after a few scales begin to practice the solo treble accompaniment of a Bach aria that I am going to perform in a worship service.

The principles of the homiletical imagination are like the warm-up exercises on my flute. Just as scales and arpeggios prepare the way for inspired playing, so also the practice of being attentive with eye, body, and ear helps to sustain our creative preaching. Nevertheless, homiletical principles are never ends in themselves, and their mere application does not guarantee inspired preaching.

I continue practicing my flute, but my mind is not fully on the music. I am reflecting on the difference between the sermon that is perfectly crafted, but dead, and the sermon that is alive. Is there a homiletical principle that moves us beyond technique to the vital nerve of preaching?

Beyond Technique to the Vital Nerve

I put down my flute to catch my breath and gaze up through the skylight. The crown of the great silver maple tree that stands in my backyard is wreathed in fog this morning. It appears as if the mist were coming down from heaven instead of rising from the earth. I cannot tell whether I am looking upward to a great height or downward to a great depth.

Suddenly I hear a voice: "You better keep practicing if you are going to perform my music next week."

I pick up my flute and start playing the obbligato to Bach's aria. The notes spill into the air, and the mist of sound that rises from the silver pipe in my hands blends with the cloud that approached from heaven. For as long as I play, Bach and I talk with each other.

He announces to me: "I have the homiletical principle you are looking for, and as a member of the great cloud of witnesses that Hebrews describes, I am going to preach the final sermon to you and to all the preachers who are reading this book. You have been talking about 'overdosing on words' and the need for preachers to take a rest from speaking. I can tell you from all my years in the organ loft, preachers do have a tendency to go on."

"I know they do, Bach. But tell me: how are you going to deliver a sermon?"

"You will play the flute, and I will preach through my music."

I explain to Bach: "Guest preachers are always introduced. What should I say about you?—'We are honored today to have as our preacher Johann Sebastian Bach, choir director and organist of St. Thomas's Church, Leipzig, composer of The St. Matthew Passion, The Mass in B Minor, The Art of the Fugue, The Brandenburg Concerti. . . .'"

"No, no, that will not do at all. Where I am now, no one impresses anyone with his or her credentials."

"Wait a minute, Johann. Did I hear you say 'his or her'? Are you using inclusive language?"

"Of course, I am. We would not use anything else in the cloud. Don't you read your Bible? 'There is neither Jew nor Greek, there is neither slave nor free, there is neither male nor female; for you are all one in Christ Jesus.' In the cloud we live these words completely. You can tell them that in introducing my sermon."

I promise Bach that I will and then ask him: "What else do you want me to tell them?"

"I want you to explain my sermon outline to them, how carefully the music follows the poetic text:

And though with muted, feeble voices
the glory of the Lord be praised,
If [the] Spirit send the word on high,
then does it seem the loudest cry
that yet to heaven has been raised.[1]

Bach continued: "The verse answers your question about the difference between dead and living sermons. Preaching depends on the Spirit, and I make that point clear in my sermon. I am telling people with my music what I learned from a lifetime of composition: You may have perfected every method and technique, but without the Spirit the music is dead. And that is true for preachers as well. Their outline, their biblical interpretation, their use of language, their mastery of every homiletical rule and norm may all be polished, but only 'If [the] Spirit send the word on high' will the sermon sing and soar. I say this to all preachers: Follow the pull of the Spirit to return to the Source, to God who made you and Christ who redeemed you. Understand all of your imaginative work as an effort to return to the Source."

"With Sighs Too Deep for Words"

I ask Bach, "Where did you get this idea for your sermon?"

"From Paul the apostle, who wrote: 'We do not know how to pray as we ought, but the Spirit's own self intercedes for us with sighs too deep for words.' All of us are familiar with these sighs, but not all of us listen to them. Yet, it is those sighs too deep for words that have lifted up the greatest music from my soul."

But Paul's words do not only apply to composers! Whatever our talent, if we listen in faith and in prayer, we can hear the Spirit sounding in our lives.

When someone we love more than we love ourselves is with us
we can hear the sigh . . . oooooo . . .
When we listen to the Emille bell tolling out the cries of the oppressed women
we can hear the sigh . . . oooooo . . .

When our souls grow deep like the rivers which are "older than the flow of human blood in human veins"

and we realize our racism,

we can hear the sigh . . . oooooo . . .

When the sleepy couple in the stable moves us to act for the rights of others

we can hear the sigh . . . oooooo . . .

When we cringe at the injustice of our government

and a holy anger possesses us

we can hear the sigh . . . oooooo . . .

When we go to our study to prepare our sermons

and the brutality of this world weighs our hearts

we can hear the sigh . . . oooooo . . .

"All of these are the sighs of the Spirit," Bach stated, "and if we listen to them, we will hear God calling us—calling us to love, calling us to compassion, calling us to justice. This is why it is foolish to contrast the life of action with the life of prayer, silence, imagination, art, and music. In listening to the sighs of the Spirit, we receive power to do what is good and just and right. And when preachers attend to the sighs of the Spirit, their words take on the quality of heaven's voice and their speaking awakens in the listeners an awareness of the Spirit sighing within them."

All the time that Bach has been speaking I have been playing my flute. I come to the end of the aria and put down my instrument. There is an empty quiet to the room. I look out to the city beyond my dormer, then to the city of homiletical wisdom, and finally up through my skylight. The clouds have lifted now, and everything I gaze at is bathed in a single stream of pure and primal light. For a brief moment, heaven and earth shine with splendor upon splendor, and from my heart there arises a great long deep sigh . . . oooooo. . . . In that sigh I hear a prayer, asking that all of us who preach may renew our imaginations by returning to the Source, that with heart and soul and mind and strength we may listen to the One who is praying for us in sighs too deep for words . . . oooooo. . . .

PATRICIA WILSON-KASTNER: A SERMON CONNECTED BY AN IMAGE

While Troeger suggests a number of possibilities, Wilson-Kastner concentrates on the one of joining a sermon by a single image (**see Vol. 1, pp. 817-18**)*. Her image in the sermon included here is the Rich Man and Lazarus in the parable of Jesus. Instead of retelling their story, she sets up the contrast between these two vivid figures "who see but do not encounter one another" (p. 87). She sees a modern parallel to that contrast in the one between a luxury hotel in Dallas, where she attended a meeting of a scholarly society, and the run-down neighborhood where she grew up in the same city, which she visited after the meeting. She then asks why the contrast is allowed to continue. While the sermon is based on a story, the way the story is used in it is as a static image. The sermon is from her book* Imagery for Preaching, *Fortress Resources for Preaching (Minneapolis: Fortress, 1989), 90-94.*

Dives in Dallas

"There was a rich man, who was clothed in purple and fine linen." He was an honest, upstanding member of the community, enjoying his diligently earned wealth. He dressed and ate according to his station in life, and lived in the palatial home appropriate to his wealth. In the tradition of the Latin church he has come to be called Dives, "the rich one," as his proper name. He was the very model of a productive citizen.

If we had been able to interview him as he strode purposefully from his home to the marketplace, he probably would have identified himself as happy, satisfied with his life and the way the world had treated him. He worked hard and played hard. He fulfilled his social obligations, paid his temple tax, was obedient to his civil rulers, and was hospitable to his friends.

But as we walked to find Dives to interview him, we might only have noticed a bundle of rags near Dives's gate. The pile was called Lazarus. He did not even have enough energy to be a street person. He lay at the gate of the rich man's house, wishing for any small help—the scraps from the rich man's table. But Dives, being a responsible member of society ("waste not, want not"), appears not to have allowed leftovers to be randomly distributed to the undeserving poor. So Lazarus waited in vain.

Not even having the energy to care for himself, Lazarus was infected by sores festering on his body. The only members of Dives's household who found Lazarus interesting were the dogs, who came and licked the open sores as he lay there. Lazarus does not even seem to have known how best to exhibit his pain and distress to excite the sympathy of passers-by, who might generously have consoled him for the blow God had given him. He just lay listlessly there by the gate of Dives's clean and spacious home.

The Law of Moses is clear. The rich are obligated to aid the poor from their own abundance. According to the Law, Dives ought to have helped Lazarus. He should, if nothing else, have given aid to all the beggars who sat by his gate. But he didn't. Lazarus continued to squat silently in his poverty. The Law's judgment on Dives was deferred. Nothing happened. Or so it appeared.

Now a few years ago I went home to Dallas, on a dual-purpose journey. There I attended a conference of the American Academy of Religion, duly delivering a paper. I also went home to visit with my parents in the house in which I grew up.

The conference itself was in one of Dallas's magnificent new hotels, with large open courtyard spaces, flamboyant banners, and sleek glass and aluminum elevators. Nothing was spared to make this hotel an expression of the power of Texas oil and commercial money. The architectural lines were straight and powerful; the space was almost overwhelming. The chairs, the shops, the plants, and the escalators were new, sturdy, and overtly expensive.

The ordinary clientele of this luxuriant hotel bustled busily to and fro. They were the wheelers and dealers in high finance, oil brokers, managers and owners of new industries who have come to the Sun Belt to escape the unions and build factories with cheap labor. All wore silk, finely woven cottons, or thin woolen suits. The women's gold and silver jewelry was of the best contemporary design, and the men were discretely and elegantly clothed.

When my father picked me up at the hotel and we drove home, our old neighborhood was much as I remembered it from childhood. Some houses had been repainted and refinished. Others had declined further, with paint peeling, doors coming off hinges, and ever-expanding holes knocked in the walls. The alley was still full of ruts, the neighbor's trash still overflowed the cans, and the front lawn next door still looked like a perpetual garage sale.

A couple of blocks from our house stood the same row of rooming houses I remembered from my childhood. On the porches and the balconies still sat rank upon rank of mothers with hopeless faces, most without spouses or supportive family, watching their children, for whom they sometimes can find clothes. As always, the dull welfare diet nourishes vacant faces and limited horizons for both young and old.

So the cycle repeats itself. A few miles from the affluent hotel live households of people who are unsure if they will be able to have shoes when the ones they are wearing disintegrate, who cannot obtain a physician's help, and who cannot send their children to school without fearing that they will be gunned down in the hallway. It appeared to me that Lazarus lives in East Dallas near the fairgrounds, and Dives still eats at Antoine's, shops at Neiman-Marcus, and drives home to Highland Park.

Why is Lazarus still at the gate? Why is Dives still free to ignore Lazarus and care only for himself? Will justice be deferred until the last judgment, perhaps so that the poor can suffer more and warm the fires more intensely for the oppressive rich? Are Dives and Lazarus doomed to eternally destructive alienation from each other?

In Georges Bernanos's *The Diary of a Country Priest* the Cure de Torcy speaks to the young priest about the mystery of poverty. Out of his own experience as an activist who worked with his congregation of Flemish miners to improve their conditions, and who is now laboring as a pastor in a small French town, he struggles to express the pain of his effort to aid his own people, and of his realization that there will always be rich and poor.

"The poor you will always have with you because there will always be hard and grasping people who want power even more than possessions." The poverty of those who do not have possessions, the Cure de Torcy suggests, is simply the physical image of a fundamental human illusion, to which rich and poor can be prey. Poverty is the emptiness in our hearts and in our heads. All of us share in this illusion. Some are forced to live out in their everyday lives the physical manifestation of this emptiness; others let poverty overcome their souls, so that they grab possessions for themselves and push others into a poverty that enchains the body and sometimes the soul as well.

For this reason the poor—who are more truly called those whom our society has made poor—enrage us who have power and possessions. If we truly see them, we behold the emptiness in ourselves and in all we make. We recognize that we have made the poor to feed our emptiness. Our comfortable souls wax prosperous if we behold them trapped in despair or pinching their money to aim for a comfort they can never attain. Because we can never accept them, or the emptiness in ourselves that causes them, we make the poor, asserts the Cure de Torcy, into "a dead weight which our proud civilizations will pass on to each other with fear and loathing."

But Jesus' parable suggests another ending is possible. If Dives had looked into Lazarus's face he would have been compelled to see the emptiness in his own soul, the vulnerability of his own suffering and death, the thin margin of luck keeping him in the mansion and not crippled by the gate. If Dives had gazed into Lazarus's eyes, he could no longer have continued to dress in fine linen while Lazarus suffered in dirty rags. If Dives had spoken and heard Lazarus, then he could not have continued to feast while Lazarus starved.

On the other hand, if Lazarus had looked up to Dives and spoken to him as one human being to another who had been luckier than he, then could Lazarus have fallen back into the same helplessness, the passivity that sapped from him the energy even to clean his sores? If Dives and Lazarus had ever known each other, spoken to each other, seen each other's vulnerability and emptiness, or had given to each other, then what might have resulted? But such an encounter never occurred.

Today Dives and Lazarus, rich and poor, haves and have-nots, those who have a little but need more, still live—in Dallas, New York, and in all our cities and parishes and homes. What emptiness, what bitterness, what hostility between us, what refusal to meet each other, to acknowledge the need of each to find ourselves in the other! If we remain apart, Jesus warns, judgment will come inevitably—judgment by God in the afterlife and, we add, through social dissolution and revolution in this life. Such a fate may be postponed for a time, but inevitably God's judgment expressed in violent social revolt will pull down nations and peoples.

God calls the church to declare the coming of this inexorable judgment to Dives and Lazarus today, just as Jesus did in his own time. But as Jesus did, we proclaim hope also. Through Christ's death and resurrection we are given the commission to begin to establish in this world God's reconciling love. We are invited to share together at one eucharistic table, in which God strengthens and nourishes us with one food and drink, his own life offered to us. We anticipate on earth the heavenly banquet, in which there will be neither rich nor poor, but where we will all share together in one communion with God. Lazarus, Dives, and all of us sit as equals at one table of the Lord. Here Dives and Lazarus meet and help each other. Here they are joined in Christ's communion.

Fed in hope by God, we are empowered by God's grace to share together here and now the earthly food belonging to all of us as God's children, and as sisters and brothers of one another. The good news summons us to envision a world in which rich and poor live together with each person receiving by right enough for a genuinely human life. In our homes, our parishes, and our governments, God calls us to work in every way we can to make that vision real here and now. This very day God puts judgment and hope before us. In the power of the Holy Spirit, let us go forth into the world to struggle to bring God's reign of love and justice to every part of our waiting world.

DON WARDLAW: A SERMON THAT FOLLOWS THE FORM OF THE TEXT

Most of the New Homileticians agree that sermons should be shaped in accordance with the form of the text on which they are based **(see Vol. 1, pp. 819-21)***. As editor of a book that concentrates on that aspect of sermon design, Don M. Wardlaw illustrates his principles in a sermon based on the context of the story of Peter's vision in Acts 10. In the book, the sermon is discussed in advance and has indications of its strategic development interspersed throughout its text, but here the sermon stands alone as an adequate interpretation of its own purpose and method. It is taken from* Preaching Biblically, *ed. Don M. Wardlaw (Philadelphia: Westminster, 1983), 75-80.*

Inviting Others to Our Table

The scene: the bustling Gentile seaport of Joppa. Peter sits on the rooftop porch of Simon the tanner. It is noon, and he stares at the tall sails of fishing boats nearby. He tries to pray, as is his noonday custom, but he is restless and preoccupied. The smell of cooking food downstairs reminds him of his hunger.

But the other smell, of those freshly tanned animal hides drying in the sun, tells him that he is surrounded by uncleanness. When he goes downstairs to eat, he, the scrupulous Jewish Christian, will go down to an unclean table and the sight of his host, Simon the tanner. Simon will eat with hands permanently stained with tanning acid. And behind Simon, those animal hides will hang there, beasts Peter would hardly touch, much less eat.

Peter puts back his head and closes his eyes. He wonders why the Lord wants him in Joppa anyway. Here he is surrounded by all this Gentile uncleanness, trying to start a new colony of Christians. But the unclean table these days revives the old revulsion of Gentiles that he learned long ago at a separate, clean table when he was a child.

He wonders: "Why should I have to bother with these common people in spreading the gospel? Better to be like Jonah, who caught a ship here in Joppa to escape a mission to the Gentiles, than to have to offer Christ to these *others.*" The noontide heat intensifies; Peter slips into a dream.

Peter can't believe what he sees. Coming down from the sky, wrapped in a huge sailcloth, a great bundle of all kinds of beasts, reptiles, and fowl. And the voice of Christ: "Rise, kill, eat!" But Peter's soul is too tied to that childhood table. "No, Lord; for I have never eaten anything common or unclean." Christ answers, "What God has cleansed, you must not call common."

Again, the insistent Christ: "Rise, kill, eat!" Again the stubborn, prejudiced Peter: "No, no, no, Lord, I can't eat that kind of meat!" Again, Christ answers, "What God has cleansed, you must not call common." A third time the demanding Christ: "Rise, kill, eat!" Now, fully frustrated, Peter cries, "No, no, no, Lord, I can't do it, I can't do it!" Echoes of other threefold litanies with Christ, such as, "Peter, I go to Jerusalem to die." "NO, NO, NO, LORD!" "Peter, this night you will deny me three times." "NO, NO, NO, LORD!" And now, "Peter, rise, kill, eat! Rise, kill, eat!" "NO, NO, NO, LORD!" The cries seem the last wretched convulsion of the demon of prejudice that has to come out. The denials seem to drive the strange, flying menagerie back up into the sky to end the dream

But what a difference between the rebellious Peter in the dream and the cooperative Peter after the dream. The same Peter who shouts, "NO, NO, NO," in the dream becomes genial host to Cornelius' servants, and probably sat down to eat with them. The same Peter who railed at Christ in the dream hikes thirty miles the next day to admit to Cornelius that he will never call anyone common or unclean again. This same Peter readily baptizes Cornelius and his people and is content to stay there some days, probably sitting down to eat with them. Those whom God cleansed Peter no longer calls common. How do we explain the difference? The resistance in the dream seems the final frenzy of the powers of death as they loosen their grip on Peter's prejudice. The NO, NO, NO! sounds like the birth pangs of a new openness. Peter did some heavy and necessary work in his dreams.

Another scene: the bustling Joppa of your life, with its commerce of frustrations, false barriers, and dreams.

You, a latter-day Simon Peter, in your noontide heat of restlessness and preoccupation. You keep finding yourself at table with people who seem unclean. In Joppa it's not like it used to be. People don't look like they ought to look in Joppa. They don't wear Jordache jeans and Gant shirts like they ought to. Instead, they make the scene in yellow tank shirts and purple socks. Some wear grossly upswept hair, and wobble by on long, thin spiked heels. Some don't care if their hair is swept up or down. It's frizzy, unwashed, unparted . . . ungodly. They're unclean nowadays in Joppa.

They don't act like they ought to act here in Joppa. They're not smooth enough for our table. They snort when they laugh at parties. They talk too loud, swig their beer, belch in front of their neighbors. Some give a redneck "10-4, good buddy" on their two-way radios, a sound not too pleasant in Joppa.

Some in Joppa are unsettled sexually. Some are having babies without husbands, and choose to raise them alone in spite of our frowns. Some have come out of their closet to say they are gay and we in Joppa don't know what to say. Some say sex belongs more to a relationship than to the institution of marriage, and we don't know how to respond with much that makes sense . . . here in Joppa.

They're so unclean here in Joppa. They don't value what's important to us. Some don't value work the way we do in Joppa. Some don't want to get ahead, and even want us to tell them where "ahead" is when we get there. Some don't want our 7:18 train in the morning, and don't care for the 5:18 evening express either. They're not awed by our steeple or by our pastor, nor are they moved by the organ and the stained glass. They're not even sure what sin is anymore. They live together without commitment and then sue for palimony. It's so unclean here nowadays in Joppa.

O to hop ship and clear out of Joppa! To leave those aliens who should have been Anglos. To leave those crude folk for the smooth folk. To leave those unstable people for together people. And to cry with Peter, "Why should I have to bother with these people, Lord?"

Yes, Peter, we can hear the anger in your voice. But even more, we can sense the fear that underlies it all.

The noonday heat intensifies, and you, Peter, slip into a dream. Out of the sky comes a great picnic cloth holding a weird assortment of 150 people. You see whiners, demanders, seducers, cheaters. You see blacks, yellows, browns, reds, whites. You see the supercool and the very uptight. You see experimental dudes and revolutionary cats.

Then, the voice says, "Set your table for these." You respond, "No, Lord, I don't eat with these." But Christ rejoins: "What God has cleansed, you must not call common. Set your table for these!" Now you're stubborn: "No, no, Lord, I can't get with these." "What God has cleansed, you must not call common," Christ keeps insisting. A third time the demand, "Set your table for these." Now you're boiling: "NO! NO! NO! LORD, I CAN'T, I CAN'T."

The last convulsion of a defeated demon: "I can't change the fact that mainline Christianity seems to be for the privileged only; I can't change the fact that most of us go to church to get rather than to give; I can't change the fact that most of us work with an antiseptic Christianity that is attracted only to the clean; I can't change the fact that many of us are so preoccupied with bazaars, banquets, and Bible study that we have little time to worry about refugee families, suicide centers, drug abuse, and unfair employment; I can't change the fact that those unclean ones don't seem to care, don't want to be decent. Lord, these unclean don't deserve our effort!" Listen to you, Peter. That fear is boiling up out of you. You're doing some heavy and necessary work in your dreams.

And look again, Peter. Your heavy dreamwork seems to be paying off. How else do we explain the difference between your resistant self in the dream and your cooperative self after the dream?

This same you who shouts, "NO! NO! NO!" in the dream, who shouted "NO" in 1964 with the civil rights legislation, who shouted "NO" in 1968 when your child marched on the Pentagon, now finds yourself at the bargaining table on Tuesday with people you once swore you'd never talk to. This same you we see on Wednesday night at Village Hall with types you turned your back on five years ago. This same you we see at the breakfast table this morning with your daughter's husband whom you once said you'd never speak to again. This same you who rails at Christ in the dream goes thirty miles out of the way to say to a woman that you apologize for your sexist jokes, that you are not only unsure about what to do with her sexuality, but also you are not that certain about what to do with your own. This same you that habitually fences off your table, now finds yourself no longer that comfortable only with Norman Rockwell faces around the table. What God has cleansed, Peter, you are no longer content to call common!

What's going on in you, Peter? You're breaking bread with a different breed of people today. What God has cleansed, you no longer call common. Something has come out of you, kicking and screaming. You seem more at ease now.

It didn't come easily, did it, Peter? It rarely does come easily, such basic change. You always did resent those unclean folk, mainly because you never felt you were that clean. At bottom the real issue has been your uncleanness, hasn't it, Peter? How much easier to see others' shortcomings than your own! That's the way it is with all of us.

But then the Christ who pushed you in your dream kept setting his own table with a name place for you, Peter. Frequently, he kept inviting you to his bread and cup. He knows all about you, Peter, your wiles, your betrayal, your fear, your uncleanness. Even so he wants you at his table, Peter. And then he speaks: "What God has cleansed, you must not call common." Peter, he's talking about you! He's insisting you are clean.

No wonder, Peter, your table is beginning to look more and more like his.

Note

1. "And though with Muted, Feeble Voices," Cantata 36, *Schwingt frendig euch empor (Soar Joyfully on High)*.

Scripture Index

SUBJECT INDEX

www.ingramcontent.com/pod-product-compliance
Lightning Source LLC
Chambersburg PA
CBHW070930150426
42814CB00029B/347
9781501833786